ROONEY

ROONEY

A Sporting Life

Rob Ruck,
Maggie Jones Patterson,
and Michael P. Weber

University of Nebraska Press
Lincoln and London

Library of Congress Cataloging-
in-Publication Data

Ruck, Rob, 1950–
Rooney: a sporting life / Rob Ruck,
Maggie Jones Patterson, and Michael
P. Weber.
p. cm.
Includes bibliographical references and
index.
ISBN 978-0-8032-2283-0 (hardcover:
alk. paper)
1. Rooney, Art, 1901–1988.
2. Football coaches—United States—
Biography. 3. Pittsburgh Steelers
(Football team) I. Patterson, Margaret
Jones. II. Weber, Michael P. III. Title.
GV939.R689R84 2009
796.332'092—dc22
[B]
2009031103

Set in Sabon by Kim Essman.

For Alex Ruck and Pittsburgh's next generation

Contents

Illustrations

Preface

ROB RUCK

This biography has been ten years in the making, but its genesis goes back further, to the late 1970s when I met Michael Weber. I was a graduate student at the University of Pittsburgh writing a dissertation on sport in black Pittsburgh. Mike, then a historian at Carnegie Mellon University, was one of a handful of scholars whose work helped me understand the history of Pittsburgh in its ethnic and racial complexity. Mike had a quick smile and an incisive mind, and he carried himself with the agility of the college wrestler he had been. He became the dean of the Graduate School of Liberal Arts and Sciences at Duquesne University in 1986 and its provost and vice president for academic affairs in 1987.

In 1981, while writing his superb biography of David Lawrence, *Don't Call Me Boss: David Lawrence, Pittsburgh's Renaissance Mayor*, Mike interviewed Lawrence's close friend, Art Rooney. I had talked with Rooney a year before, about Gus Greenlee, the numbers baron who owned the Pittsburgh Crawfords, a team in the Negro National League.

Greenlee had been a patron of sport in black Pittsburgh. Several of the older sandlot and Negro League players I had interviewed about him responded by telling me stories about Art Rooney instead. They spoke warmly about how Rooney had befriended them. One called him a Robin Hood for black athletes; another added that he had never tolerated racial nonsense on the sandlots. I had never heard African Americans in Pittsburgh discuss a white person in such adulatory terms.

I spoke with Rooney in his office at Three Rivers Stadium, which was built on the site of Exposition Park, where he had played as a young man. Rooney, then seventy-nine, turned in his chair and gestured toward the photographs of former players and old buddies that surrounded him. As he spoke of his friendships with Gus Greenlee and Cumberland "Cum" Posey, the owner of the Homestead Grays, I better understood why he was held in high regard by the black community. Rooney had quietly helped Posey and Greenlee make Pittsburgh the crossroads of black baseball during the 1930s and 40s. I had known of Art Rooney mostly as the owner of the Pittsburgh Steelers; I began to realize that he was much more than that. Rooney's life tracked the evolution of sport from the sandlots in the early twentieth century to its emergence as a corporate juggernaut in the 1980s.

"How come nobody's ever written your biography?" I asked near the end of the interview. Rooney shrugged off the question: "It's been written a hundred times." When I pressed him, he suggested that I read a recently published biography of his friend, Chicago Bears owner George Halas. Halas was the one worthy of such attention, he said.

A few days later, I left for Cuba to research Caribbean connections to the Negro Leagues. I returned with some cigars that I sent to Rooney, who responded as if they were his favorite smokes in the world.

Several years later, I asked Joe Gordon, the Steelers' extraordinary public relations director, if he thought Rooney would be amenable to a biography. He doubted it; "Mr. Rooney" did not relish being the center of attention. Art Rooney died not long afterward, in 1988. I let the idea of a Rooney biography slip until I was asked to put together a session about him for the American Studies Association meetings held in Pittsburgh in 1994. Mike Weber and I were talking with Dan Rooney following the session when I mentioned that I had long thought that his father's life would make a worthwhile biography. Mike seconded that notion. Dan, who knew Mike because he was on the board of trustees at Duquesne University, replied that he would think it over.

He thought about it for a long while. Five years later, Dan gave Mike the green light for the two of us to write a biography of his father. Dan, a man with a passion for history, promised us access to Steeler materials and his full cooperation, with the understanding that he would have no editorial say in the final product. Dan's brother Art Jr. also readily agreed to help.

Mike and I began working on the book in 1999 and conducted

interviews over the next year and a half. Mike was poised to retire from Duquesne in the summer of 2001 and work full-time on the book when an illness he thought he had beaten recurred. He died in July 2001. This book would not have been written without Mike's involvement; his thinking about Pittsburgh has guided how we approached it. If Mike had lived, he would have made it a better book.

At Mike's funeral Mass, Father Sean Hogan, Duquesne's vice president for student life, stopped as he led the procession from the University Chapel. Taking one of my hands in both of his own, Father Hogan said, "You're going to finish the book, aren't you?" I did not think he meant it as a question. I told him that I would. Art Rooney Jr., who had sat behind Maggie Patterson and me during the Mass, then tapped me on the shoulder and said, "You should get Maggie to work on this with you; you're not going to get the Irish Catholic part of the story." Art Jr.'s advice made sense. Maggie Patterson, Mike's Duquesne University colleague and my wife, had played a substantial editorial role in almost everything I had ever written. When she offered to write this book with me, I gladly accepted.

We soon discovered that many Pittsburghers, as well as folks from New York to Northern Ireland, had a story or two about Art Rooney. Most were respectful, but some hinted at racketeering and skullduggery. Our backgrounds in journalism and history had prepared us to become cynical and disillusioned about Art Rooney as we dug into the less savory aspects of his life. We looked for evidence that would confirm Rooney's involvement in illicit activities. But we found no direct evidence of Rooney engaging in illegal activities. The circumstantial evidence amounted to little more than guilt by association and uncorroborated hearsay. Art Rooney was a friend to bootleggers, gamblers, and ward heelers, and he was a gambler himself. But scant evidence indicates that he was more than peripherally engaged. Art Rooney was no angel. But we heard much more about his generous actions, known only to their recipients, than about any perfidy. Surprisingly, the more we researched his life, the more respect and affection we felt for him.

A son of the sandlots, Rooney took his team from Pittsburgh's Northside into the National Football League. He helped that league survive the

Depression and World War II and championed the one-for-all, all-for-one ethos that made it the most successful venture in American sport.

It is largely forgotten today, but Rooney might have been the best all-around athlete in Pittsburgh during the 1920s. Yet, he left more of a mark off the field. A product of Pittsburgh sport and the city's hard-working people, he was also their paladin. The city and its football team struggled for much of the century, but both of them persevered and ultimately triumphed. As success dawned, Pittsburghers placed sport and Rooney's Steelers at the core of their collective identity. More than any other individual, he shaped Pittsburgh into the City of Champions.

Rooney is more than a Pittsburgh story. It is the saga of American sport and its century-long journey from the sandlots to corporate boardrooms. *Rooney* recalls a time when sport emerged more from the nation's communities than from its commerce. In those bygone years, sport helped people craft a sense of identity. It was the one arena where immigrants, native-born Americans, and black migrants challenged each other on relatively level footing. Art Rooney's story reminds us of a different era, when a saloonkeeper's son could ditch his image as sport's all-time loser and become Pittsburgh's favorite son, the nice guy who finished on top.

Acknowledgments

Writing this book depended on people willing to think about the past and share their recollections with us. We interviewed over one hundred individuals, several on multiple occasions. Many of them searched family records and dug through scrapbooks and memories. Their participation was an invaluable contribution to our efforts to recreate Art Rooney's life, and we are deeply obliged to each of them. Their names are listed below.

Many Rooneys, McGinleys, and Laughlins helped us along the way, answering questions and expediting our investigations. Dan Rooney, Art's oldest son, was especially gracious and engaged. His encouragement and friendship mean much to us. His brother Art Jr. was also an encouraging ally in our endeavors and ever ready to help. Both Dan and Art Jr. published their own memoirs during the time it took us to finish this book; we hope our conversations aided them in their own writing. Dan's wife, Patricia Regan Rooney, was another source of help, as were Art's other three sons, Tim, John, and Pat; his nephew Jamie Rooney and Jamie's wife, Susan; his niece Kathy Rooney; his brother-in-law Jack McGinley; and his sister Margaret Laughlin Rooney, who reached back into childhood memories and who died with an early draft of chapter one beside her reading chair. Kathy Rooney helped us gather the photos that illustrate this book. Joseph A. Rooney at Lynn University provided information about the Rooneys as saloonkeepers. Mary Ellen Davisson shared some early Rooney history, and Paul Greenaway, who read the manuscript, Anne Jackson, and Father Ray Utz gave us insight into the Murray side of the family.

The staff of the Pittsburgh Steelers was enormously supportive and friendly, confirming what football writers around the country know about the competence and affability of that organization. Dave Lockett, Jan Rusnack, Vicki Uni, Ty Ryan, Monica Shields, Stacie Lawrence, Geraldine Glenn, Ron Wahl, and Mike Fabus were a delight to work with in researching this book. So were Art Rooney Jr.'s very able assistant, Dee Herrod, and Kathleen Klotz at the Palm Beach Kennel Club.

Our investigations relied heavily on the staffs of the following libraries and institutions: Duquesne University, the University of Pittsburgh, Carnegie Library of Pittsburgh, The Senator John Heinz History Center, Georgetown University, Indiana University of Pennsylvania, and the Pro Football Hall of Fame; The National Library of Wales (Llyfrgell Genedlaethol Cymru) in Aberystwyth; the National Library of Ireland in Dublin; the Newry and Mourne Museum and the Arts Centre and Museum in Newry, Northern Ireland; the Montreal Central Library; the Ebbw Vale and Tredegar, Wales, town libraries; and the Gwent County Council records in Ebbw Vale. A special thanks to Eugene Sawa of the university library system at the University of Pittsburgh, Lauren Uhl at the Heinz History Center, Gemma Reid and Noreen Cunningham at the Newry Museum, Paul Demilio in the Duquesne Archives, Marilyn Holt of the Pennsylvania Room of Carnegie Library, the Whitegates Community Centre in Newry, and the researcher at the Tredegar town library who gave up the best microfilm reader and guided us through the oddly organized 1871 and 1881 British censuses.

Roy McHugh, the dean of Pittsburgh sportswriters, was a source of much insight and a terrific sounding board. Anne Madarasz, the chief curator of the Western Pennsylvania Sport History Museum at the Heinz History Center, shared her intimate knowledge and contacts in Pittsburgh sport. Joel Tarr, James Barrett, and Marcus Rediker wrote in support of the project. Anne Knowles of Middlebury College helped us understand Wales and Welsh émigrés. Gerry McCauley, a Pittsburgh native, Pitt grad, and exemplary agent, led us to Bob Diforio, our agent, who found our manuscript a good home at the University of Nebraska Press and a good editor in Rob Taylor.

In investigating the Rooneys and Murrays, several area residents went out of their way to help us track down genealogical information and recreate a sense of what Coultersville, Monaca, Wireton, and the Northside were like when the Rooney and Murray families were there. They include Ray, Jim, and Estelle Shepherd in Coulter; John Canning on the Northside; Dolores Morrison in Wireton; Bob Bauder in Beaver County; and William Irions and colleagues at the Beaver Falls Carnegie Library.

In researching Shamrock Farm and Art Rooney's career in racing, we are indebted to Jim and Chrissie Steele, Cindy Deubler of the Maryland Horse Breeders Association, Phyllis Rogers at the Keeneland Library, and Bob Curran of The Jockey Club. Jeanne Schmedlen and Troy De-Frank helped us track Jim Rooney's legislative career.

The following individuals and institutions located church and company records: Mrs. Nancy Yuhasz, chancellor, Diocese of Youngstown; the National Library of Ireland, Dublin; Father Michael Hagerty, Ebbw Vale, Wales; and Pat Jaynes at Corus Steel in Ebbw Vale.

Our families have retained their Pittsburgh connections even though they no longer reside in the city. Several of them read drafts of the manuscript, including Rob's parents, Elaine and Mort Weissman (who also researched Florida racing); his sister and brother-in-law, Linda and Bruce Mittleman; and Maggie's brothers Ken Jones and Dave Jones. Ken suggested we include a map while Dave, a metallurgical engineer, researched the particulars of nineteenth-century iron production. Maggie's other brother, Bob Jones, kept us laughing.

We received financial support from the National Endowment for the Humanities through the McAnulty College of Liberal Arts at Duquesne University and the Central Research Fund at the University of Pittsburgh that allowed us to travel to Ireland, Northern Ireland, and Wales to investigate the Rooneys' Old Country antecedents. Support from Alec Stewart, dean of the Honors College at the University of Pittsburgh, made it possible for Gordon Burk and Bill Schlacter to do yeoman's work for us in the archives. Pitt students Jimmy Jones, Pete Jones (Maggie's nephew), and Michael Cunningham, as well as Ryan Hardesty and Gabriel Celli as part of the First Research Experience Program, tracked down dozens of leads and pored over microfilm.

At Duquesne University, Mary McIntrye was Mike Weber's assistant in the provost's office. She was of immense help and transcribed many of the early interviews. Jen Pearson spent hours and hours in the Steelers' archives; Kelley Crowley helped with family records; registrar Pat Jakub found old student records; and administrative assistants Jane Gardner and Sally Richie and graduate student Jamey Stewart performed many acts of kindness that made this work easier.

Members of the history department at Pitt have long known that its staff—Molly Dennis-Estes, Kathy Gibson, Patty Landon, and Grace Tomcho—is a precious group of personable and highly competent women. Their contributions to this project are too great to enumerate.

Many colleagues and friends helped us with this project. The Rooneys are bound by history and values to Duquesne University, which gave frequent and generous support to this project. Father Hogan never lost his concern for Mike Weber's legacy. Maggie's colleagues in the journalism and multimedia arts departments have been loyal and cooperative while she spent years researching and writing. In addition to their moral support, colleagues gave their expertise: John Shepherd on technology and sports; Mike Dillon on biography; and Joe Sora and Rob Bellamy about publishers. They and other faculty and administrators shared their excitement and enthusiasm for this endeavor while helping to make the work easier.

In Rob's peripatetic academic career he has never known a finer department or a better group of colleagues than those in the history department at the University of Pittsburgh. It is, as Alejandro de la Fuente calls it, *mi patria pequeña.* The department has molded Rob as a historian and influenced his approach to sport. As chair of the department, Bill Chase navigated university minefields to create the time and space for Rob to finish a draft of the manuscript; good friend Reid Andrews has been a longtime source of wisdom and laughs over dinner and on the bike trails. Ted Muller is a Pittsburgh native who returned and became the city's foremost historian. His insights, shared over coffee most weekday mornings, have shaped a vision of Pittsburgh. Bernie Hagerty gave this manuscript a penetrating read-through and conveyed his thoughts and bonhomie many an early morning. Loyalty defined Art Rooney as much as anything. It's the same for Marcus Rediker, with whom Rob has run the gamut, including some of the sweetest evenings at the Petersen Center (the House that Brandin Knight Built) and Madison Square Garden.

Our good buddy David Bear was the first to read anything we had written. He sits beside us during Steeler games and pushes Rob's limits along the Youghiogheny River and their journeys into the backcountry. Jay Reifer read the manuscript, as did his father, Irwin Peewee Reifer. Jay and Ken Boas contributed their thoughts during runs in Schenley Park. Mark Cohen has had Rob's back in travel and on trial since 1970. He's been a counsel on this project and the best of coconspirators along the way.

Maggie's dear friend Liane Norman read early drafts of the manuscript and wisely advised us to keep the language and organization simple and straightforward, as befits the subject. Patty Weber encouraged us to continue after Mike's death and became our most faithful advocate. She and John Brungo read drafts of the book and cheered for us at every step. Our son, Alex, not only put up with his parents' preoccupation with this project but spurred us on with his interest in history and intense love of Pittsburgh and its football team.

Introduction

American Football Conference Playoff

Three Rivers Stadium, December 23, 1972

As writers in the press box composed their epitaphs for the Pittsburgh Steelers, Art Rooney stood and headed to the elevator. Pittsburgh had won its first division title in forty years that season, but Rooney's Steelers were losing 7–6, and only 22 seconds remained in their playoff game against the Oakland Raiders. Facing fourth-and-ten from their own 40-yard line, they needed to gain 25 yards to get within field goal range. Pirates announcer Bob Prince held the elevator door for Art, two priests, and a friend. Art said nothing as the elevator slowly descended. "I figured we had lost," he later explained, "and I wanted to get to the locker room early so I could personally thank the players for the fine job they'd done all season."

On the field, quarterback Terry Bradshaw had one last chance. Coach Chuck Noll called a play designed to hit rookie receiver Barry Pearson down the middle and put Pittsburgh in field goal range. Bradshaw dropped back to pass under a heavy rush. A Raider grabbed him around his shoulders, but he twisted free. Steeler halfback Frenchy Fuqua curled into the center of the field, deep enough to give Roy Gerela a shot at a field goal if the pass could be completed, and the game clock stopped by quickly downing the football. But another Raider lurched toward Bradshaw and he was forced to unload the ball. "I saw Frenchy and I didn't see anyone around. Then I don't know what happened," Bradshaw said. "I got knocked down."

The football, Frenchy Fuqua, and defensive back Jack Tatum converged at Oakland's 35-yard line. The ball bounced off Fuqua or Tatum or both and ricocheted backward. Fuqua, who had not seen Tatum coming, fell to the turf, dazed. "He gave me a good lick. Everything was dizzy." But then Fuqua looked downfield in disbelief. "I saw this dude at the 5-yard line and I couldn't figure out why." The dude—teammate Franco Harris—had caught the deflected football at his shoe tops and was crossing the goal line.

By midnight the play had a name: the Immaculate Reception.

Art saw none of it. He was inside the elevator grappling with what he would tell his players when the stadium reverberated. "We heard a wild scream from the crowd," Art said. "It could only mean one thing but no one in the elevator dared believe it." He had waited a long time for this moment, only to miss it.

Sandlots to Pros

The Pittsburgh Steelers wandered sport's wastelands for nearly half a century before winning the hearts and minds of the people of Western Pennsylvania. As they blossomed into football's best team ever, the hardboiled man who had created the team from a group of scrappy sandlotters on the city's Northside became the region's icon.

Art Rooney was once described as a cross between Charles Bronson, the rough-hewn actor from Cambria County's coalfields, and Jiggs, the comic strip character. Rooney personified the evolution of sport as it grew from the sandlots to corporate money-ball. Yet throughout his eighty-seven years he remained close to his roots and as much a part of Pittsburgh as its shot-and-a-beer taverns. Pittsburghers called him The Chief, a nickname his twin sons had given him for his resemblance to Perry White, Clark Kent's editor in the *Superman* television series.

Art's heart always belonged more to the sandlot than the bottom line, and his life tells a story America likes to hear about itself. Fans across the country, many with no connection to Pittsburgh, see something of America's smokestack spirit in Rooney and his Steelers.

Rooney was shaped by his Irish Catholic immigrant family, by Pittsburgh, and by sport. His people came to Pittsburgh from Ireland via Canada, Wales, and Youngstown, Ohio, arriving at the dawn of the steel age. Their descendants saw that epoch end. The men on the Rooney side of the family worked in iron and steel for three generations; those on his mother's side, in coal. There was nothing lace curtain about either.

In more recent times, sport—even more than iron and steel—has broadcast an indelible image of Pittsburgh to the world. It has offered Pittsburghers a way to tell their story of sacrifice and commitment, loss and triumph. Art Rooney was both a product of that heritage and its paladin.

No other city of comparable size experienced such singular success in twentieth-century American sport, especially at the professional level. The Pirates, Crawfords, Grays, Penguins, and Rooney's Steelers won more than a score of championships while creating some of sport's most unforgettable icons and moments: Honus Wagner scooping up dirt and pebbles along with the ball from his position at shortstop; Josh Gibson swatting a ball into the heavens; Bill Mazeroski rounding third, leaping into the air, and heading for home to end the 1960 World Series; Roberto Clemente unleashing a throw from right field; and Franco Harris catching a football before it touched the turf in the 1972 playoffs. Rumpled and unfazed, puffing on a cigar, Art Rooney was there for each of these moments.

But Art was more than a bystander, and his persona as homegrown sports mogul is only part of the story. An extraordinary athlete, Art grew up in a Runyonesque setting, a neighborhood called the Ward on the Northside in Pittsburgh where his father owned Dan Rooney's Cafe and Bar, known for its nickel beers, free lunches, and the sportsmen and politicians who congregated there.

The family lived atop the saloon, near honky-tonks, gambling parlors, and Exposition Park, home to the Pirates until 1909. Art loved the neighborhood, where the Irish and their descendants set the tone, with Gaelic spoken in many homes and wakes lasting for days. After moving there as a boy in 1913, Art never really left. He and his wife, Kass, bought a large Victorian house on the Northside in 1939 and stayed in it for the rest of their lives while the area's racial and class balance shifted. After they died their son Dan and his wife, Patricia, moved in.

Art came of age on the Phipps Playgrounds, a short walk from home.

At Phipps, Exposition Park, and the St. Peter's Lyceum, Rooney's mantra was to think ahead of the play, and he did that on and off the field all his life. He was a prodigy, combining speed, agility, and strength—if not much size—with a keen comprehension of the game and competitive zeal. His body control and hand-eye coordination allowed him to excel in baseball and football. Few could best him in a footrace or a fight, and when he took up golf in middle age he became a scratch player.

By the 1920s Art Rooney had become Pittsburgh's best all-around athlete. He was in full stride, playing for college and semipro teams. On the diamond he battled future Hall of Famers Cum Posey, Martin Dihigo, Joe Cronin, Oscar Charleston, and Smokey Joe Williams. On the gridiron he held his own against Jim Thorpe and the Canton Bulldogs. Knute Rockne tried to lure Art to Notre Dame, while the Red Sox and Cubs offered him the chance to play professional baseball. In the ring he beat 1920 Olympic gold medalist Sammy Mosberg.

Although Art boxed professionally and starred in the minor leagues, he put away his gloves and his spikes for good by the 1930s. He recognized that his real talent was promoting sport, not playing it. In 1933 he transformed the Hope Harveys, a sandlot club he had formed on the Northside, into an NFL franchise. As a boxing promoter he helped make Pittsburgh a fight town second only to New York. His career intertwined with those of Billy Conn, Fritzie Zivic, Ezzard Charles, and Ray Robinson. Rooney's greatest notoriety as a player came at the racetrack. In 1937, the year Seabiscuit became the people's choice on the track, Art was heralded as America's greatest horse player.

His football teams, however, remained perennial losers. After more than a decade as NFL doormats, Rooney's Steelers finally enjoyed success after World War II. Jock Sutherland coached them into the playoffs, only to die of a brain tumor following the 1947 season. Pittsburgh returned to mediocrity, but Art began putting his stamp on the NFL. He helped to make it the best-run league and most popular ticket in American pro sport.

While his team could not beat George Halas's Chicago Bears for the longest time, when the league decided whether to recognize the players' union, Rooney—not Halas—prevailed. George Preston Marshall talked louder and longer about how television revenues belonged to each team, but Rooney waited until the Washington Redskins' flamboyant owner talked himself out. In the end the owners adopted Rooney's position to share and share alike.

Rooney's influence within the NFL was cloaked to the public, but he was a consummate inside politician. He knew how to get people to compromise, to sacrifice immediate and personal interests for the long-term collective good. Rooney was patient and affable, but he could be tough and skilled at creating win-win deals. His political mentors, Pennsylvania governor David L. Lawrence and state senator James J. Coyne, had prepared him well.

Art held the NFL together when arguments between Halas and the Giants' Tim Mara or George Marshall's histrionics threatened to pull it apart. His fingerprints were on every decision that defined the league. Art convinced the NFL not only to recognize the players' association but to accept it as a partner. He persuaded his colleagues to share television revenues, a decision that every small-market team has come to view as the cornerstone of its existence. And when the other NFL teams balked about joining the less-attractive American Football Conference, Rooney moved the Steelers to ensure the merger. A seeming sacrifice at the time proved to be a pivotal moment in turning the Steelers into winners. Art had a knack for turning virtue into success. Sometimes it just took awhile.

Loyalty was his chief virtue. In 1970 when Art was still regarded as professional football's champion loser, sportswriter Myron Cope asked why he had never sold the club. "Money has never been my god—never," Rooney replied. "Back in the early 1950s, I could have moved to Baltimore, and then later, to Buffalo, Atlanta, New Orleans, Cincinnati. The propositions they made were fantastic." Other owners might have leaped at the chance, but not Rooney. "If you didn't have ties," Rooney reasoned, "if you didn't care for your city and its people, if you were just looking for wealth, you could have picked up and gone. But that's not you, not if you care for your city . . . I believe if we win, we'll do as good as we would in probably any of those other towns." Art's Steelers would win, but only after his sons assumed bigger roles.

By 1980 Pittsburgh reigned as the City of Champions. Sport had become its persona: tough, hardworking, and resilient. In other words: Rooney. People came to identify Pittsburgh sport with its professional teams. But the city's sporting excellence was rooted in the sandlots that dotted western Pennsylvania. These sandlots had always been Rooney's domain. There, boys and men created a sporting life that did more than lay the foundation for the city's emergence as a citadel of sport. That sporting life helped generations of men cope with their lives in mills and mines at a time when Pittsburgh still was referred to as "Hell with the lid off." Though Rooney moved on to Madison Square Garden, the Saratoga racetrack, and the Los Angeles Coliseum, he never turned his back on the sandlots of his youth, the values he formed there, or the players who embodied them.

Despite his celebrity, Rooney remained an unpretentious man, loyal to the city where he lived all but a few of his eighty-seven years. A bit of a rogue and a poker-playing raconteur who rarely missed morning Mass, Rooney displayed the constancy and loyalty that characterize Pittsburgh—and sport—at their best. This is his story.

Arthur J. Rooney's Family Tree

Daniel Rooney and Maggie Murray's children

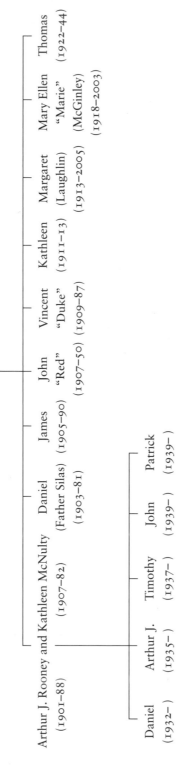

Daniel
(Father Silas)
(1903–81)

James
(1905–90)

John
"Red"
(1907–50)

Vincent
"Duke"
(1909–87)

Kathleen
(1911–13)

Margaret
(Laughlin)
(1913–2005)

Mary Ellen
"Marie"
(McGinley)
(1918–2003)

Thomas
(1922–44)

Arthur J. Rooney and Kathleen McNulty
(1901–88)   (1907–82)

Daniel
(1932–)

Arthur J.
(1935–)

Timothy
(1937–)

John
(1939–)

Patrick
(1939–)

ROONEY

1

Coming to Pittsburgh

Coal Dust and Iron Shavings

Like steel, Art Rooney came from iron and coal. His father's family was forged in the iron furnaces of Ireland, Montreal, Wales, Youngstown, and Pittsburgh. His mother's people, the Murrays, worked in the gritty coal mines of Ireland and Pennsylvania's Allegheny Mountains. By the twentieth century, the union of these natural resources—iron and coal—made Pittsburgh the steelmaking capital of the world. A child of this union himself, Art Rooney rode an arc of success in sport that paralleled Pittsburgh's steelmaking and ultimately surpassed it.

Art's great-grandfather, James Rooney, was a skilled ironworker and labor aristocrat. He was born around 1826 in County Down, Ireland, and probably came from a clan of farmers and herders associated with Rooney's Meadow in Newry, a town that straddles Counties Armagh and Down in what is now Northern Ireland. Rooney is a Newry name, and word passed down through the family that Newry was their ancestral home.

Jonathan Swift had once urged his fellow Irishmen "to burn everything English except their coal." Newry grew rich fulfilling that wish. Barges of Irish coal from the shores of Lough Neagh threaded down the Bann River and through a canal to Newry, where they pushed into the Irish Sea to coal-hungry Dublin. The canal, the first major man-made waterway in the British Isles, made Newry an international trading center that surpassed Belfast. Traders from Europe and the West Indies brought exotic tongues and cosmopolitan sophistication to the port.

While James trained at a small ironworks near the canal in the 1840s, he forged the family's fortunes that would bring his descendants to Pittsburgh. Although it was a mere toy compared to the mammoth industrial furnaces being built in England and Wales, the primitive, charcoal-fired shop allowed James to turn iron into tools and soak up knowledge of metallurgy.

Newry's prosperity did not last long. In the 1840s, an airborne spore— *Phytophthora infestans*—that probably traveled to Europe on manure boats from America spread over Ireland's potato crop. It destroyed the potato's leaves, then the stalk, and finally the tuber before nearly destroying Ireland itself. Without potatoes, the staple of their diet, hungry people fled the countryside. In the Great Famine's winter of 1846–47, thousands staggered into Newry seeking food and a chance to emigrate. Many businesses closed, including the forge where James worked.

James found passage to Montreal on a ship that had unloaded timber and turpentine at a British shipyard. The desperate Irish took whatever meager belongings and scraps of food they had on the six-week passage and also served as ballast for the ship's return to Canada. They crowded below deck where typhus spread quickly. Thousands slipped past Quebec's ineffective quarantine and sailed into Montreal. Ships' crews dumped passengers onto the wharves, where many died without ever setting foot in their new country. Others filled "fever sheds," warehouses along the docks that served as emergency hospitals.

Like many Irish who survived, James Rooney settled in Montreal's St. Ann's parish near the Lachine Canal, itself largely constructed by earlier Irish immigrants. He landed work as a millwright at one of the foundries that edged the canal. The plants produced steam engines and boilers and were far more sophisticated than his ironmonger's shop in Newry. James seized this chance to apprentice himself. As a millwright, he assembled, set up, and repaired machinery, lifting himself into labor's aristocracy.

In 1851, James's wife, Mary, gave birth to their only child, a son they named Arthur, who would become grandfather and namesake of the Steelers' founder. The three Rooneys sailed back across the Atlantic, perhaps to Ireland for a time. In 1871, twenty years after Arthur's birth, the British census shows that James was working as an iron rougher in the Ebbw (pronounced "ebb-a") Vale Iron and Steel Works in Wales. His son Arthur was his apprentice.

2

The Ebbw Vale Works was one of the most technologically advanced mills in the world. Its puddling furnaces made iron; its Bessemer furnaces mass-produced steel. The Works shipped rails and merchant bars around the world.

Its paternalistic Quaker masters built company houses and paid their workers in scrip that could be redeemed only at company stores. Since the Quakers prohibited alcohol on their property and fined any workers found drinking, the Rooney men walked up Briery Hill, where twenty-eight taverns crowded onto the only patch of independent land. For men working twelve-hour shifts six days a week, pub socializing was a favorite pastime. Bartenders accepted sacks of sugar from the company store in exchange for brews and provided back rooms where the men could throw down bets on boxing matches and cockfights. When production slowed, men played rugby on the town's only playing field.

James, Mary, and Arthur lived along Forge Row, where Ebbw Vale's skilled workers enjoyed better housing than the poorer, unskilled Irish laborers in the shabby rows of Newtown across the valley. Most of their neighbors were Anglicans or Welsh "Non-conformists," so the Rooneys prayed with the other Irish at the All Saints Roman Catholic missionary parish. When Arthur came of age, he looked among these pews for a wife. His fancy settled on a brown-haired, Irish-born lass whose father labored in the Works. Pretty Catherine Regan, with wide-set eyes, high cheekbones, and sturdy optimism, captured Arthur's eye and then his heart.

They married at All Saints Church on September 14, 1872, when they were both twenty-two, and moved in with James and Mary on Forge Row. The Rooneys shared the house with an Irish puddler and a Welshman who worked in the Works laboratory and boarded in the "back house," a room behind the kitchen with its own entrance. The Rooney women cooked these men's meals and washed their clothes.

Arthur and Catherine's children came fast and healthy, a blessing at a time when one in five infants died. Bridget was born within a year of their marriage, and Daniel followed in September 1874. All Saints Church had just begun keeping official records and wrote his baptism on page one.

No one had much privacy in the Rooneys' home, which contained a living room, kitchen, and the boarders' room on the first floor. Steep, narrow stone stairs spiraled up and around the heavy masonry fireplace to the second floor, where three small rooms were aligned like railroad cars. Occupants passed through one room to get to the next.

In the winter when snow piled up to the roofline, fireplace coal spit black soot onto clothes drying on wires strung between the ceiling beams. In the summer, open windows and the upper portion of the split front door admitted a festival of bedbugs, fleas, and cockroaches that fell from the ceiling, crawled out from the walls, bit sleeping children, and burrowed into the pockets of clothes hung on hooks for the night. When the summer sun dried up the mountain springs, Bridget and Daniel listened for the company's horse-drawn water trucks and rushed out with Catherine to fill the family's jugs. Animals wandered down from the common grazing land and poked their heads through the front doors, foraging for a handout and frightening children.

Each working day, James and Arthur trekked down from the Forge Rows into the Works with their singing Welsh coworkers. Inside the mill, while the rollers and roughers waited for the molten metal they would shape, mill managers led them in Welsh part-songs or choruses by Handel or Mendelssohn. To James and Arthur, who learned to speak some Welsh, the lilting Celtic refrains, full of joy and longing, came familiar to their Irish ears. Except for Sunday worship, the Irish were part of this Welsh and English community.

While the Rooneys enjoyed a camaraderie with Welsh and English skilled workers, they needed no reminders that they were Irish. Their neighbors and coworkers, mostly Protestant dissenters, also resented the British Anglicans, who lorded money and political power over them. Ebbw Vale's ironmaster, Abraham Darby, who had converted to Anglicanism, tithed his workers to build the stately Christ Church on the hill above the Forge Rows. But their Welsh and British coworkers periodically bashed Irish heads, branding them as foreign papists who betrayed other workers by accepting lower wages. In 1853, rioters had stoned Irish workmen out of the Ebbw Vale Iron Works, shutting the rolling mills down for a week. James Rooney would witness another flare-up in 1882, when Irish nationalist movements provoked rioting in Ebbw Vale.

In the 1870s, steel, strong and malleable, began chasing iron from the marketplace and with it the jobs that had given skilled workers like the Rooneys a measure of autonomy and dignity. As the Ebbw Vale Iron and Steel Works shifted to steel, seventy years of benevolent paternalism faded away. The company's new owners were absentee financiers who imposed authoritarian discipline from afar, and the labor aristocrats who had once been at the heart of ironmaking found themselves obsolete.

Many South Wales workers escaped to the United States. James Rooney, who had already moved from Ireland to Canada to Wales, stayed put. He lost his job as a rougher during Ebbw Vale's conversion to steel and was demoted to common labor. After his wife Mary died in the 1870s, James left Forge Row to board with a laborer's family in Irish Newtown. He died in Ebbw Vale in 1886, having made it into his early sixties and outliving most laboring men.

Coming to America

James's son Arthur and daughter-in-law Catherine left Ebbw Vale to chase the iron industry to the New World, joining the torrent of Europeans flooding North America. During the Great Famine of the 1840s, James had spent six miserable weeks on his way to Montreal aboard a ship plagued by sickness and death. In the 1870s, Arthur and Catherine's passage took less than half as long.

Arthur Rooney initially settled in Youngstown, Ohio, where he rolled iron bars for fabrication into nails and spikes at Brown, Bonnell and Company. A wiry, red-bearded Irishman with coal dust and iron shavings embedded in his skin, Arthur brought home a decent wage, befitting a second-generation craftsman who belonged to the upper echelon of industrial workers. But after five years, an economic depression blew into Youngstown, and Arthur felt the chill of impending layoffs. His father James had taught him the arts of puddling, roughing, and rolling iron in South Wales, as well as the commensurate skill of moving ahead of threatening economic and technological changes.

As a nationwide downturn doused many factory furnaces, itinerant workers passed the word, one to the next. Arthur cocked an ear to this network and what he heard proved fortuitous: Pittsburgh promised a viable place to ply his trade. The city was part of a labor circuit stretching across North America's industrial heartland and over the sea to the British Isles. Working men went wherever mills fired up. This time the Rooney family's move was mercifully short, just sixty miles.

Arthur was thirty-three years old and in his prime when he moved to Pittsburgh early in 1884. Catherine, pregnant with their fifth child, relied on Bridget, eleven, Daniel, ten, and John, eight, to help pack their belongings and keep a watchful eye on three-year-old Mary Ellen, their first American-born child. The family must have felt anxiety as they approached Pittsburgh. The Rooneys had never seen manufacturing unleashed on such a scale; nevertheless, this clanging, smoke-belching metropolis was now their best hope.

They rented rooms on Bingham Street along the flood plain of the Monongahela River. Pittsburgh's Southside flats, known then as old Birmingham, sat in the shadow of the grand, growling American Iron Works, commonly referred to as the Jones and Laughlin plant. Downtown Pittsburgh rose up across the river, as did the Carnegie Steel plant. Smaller mills and forges lined the shores of the Monongahela, Allegheny, and Ohio Rivers. Clattering trains carried coal, and tugboats pushed barges of it to feed the mills and homes of the nation's industrial workshop.

It was winter, and the soft bituminous coal burning in homes and factories spewed clouds of fine gray grit that darkened the city. Downtown executives changed dirtied shirt collars by midday, and housewives draped tea towels over pies set out to cool on windowsills. But few complained; this sooty air meant prosperity.

Arthur and Catherine found much that was familiar. Pittsburgh was, in many ways, Ebbw Vale writ large. Pittsburgh's surging population of 200,000 dwarfed Ebbw Vale's shrinking 13,000. But like Ebbw Vale, Pittsburgh had hills that rose steeply above a smoky, industrial river. South Wales' grassy green hills had long since been denuded of trees; Pittsburgh's slopes were still blanketed with maples, oaks, and sycamores. A majority of its people were immigrants, the Southside its fastest growing and most working-class section. Many came from the British Isles, and almost half were Irish Catholics, who gave parishes, saloons, and fraternal groups a strong Irish American flavor.

Arthur Rooney fit into Pittsburgh in the 1880s like molten iron into a mold. The city was the center of the nation's iron and steel industry. Its craftsmen's empire allowed skilled workers to govern much in the workplace and surrounding neighborhoods. But by the time Arthur entered the city's labor force in the winter of 1884, that empire had begun to crack. The two changes that had undermined the craftsmen's world in South Wales—steel replacing iron and absentee financiers ousting local owners—were already threatening Pittsburgh.

Arthur started in the Southside mills as a laborer. Most immigrant men offered only their strong backs and eager hands to potential employers. Arthur, however, could hope that his craftsman's skills would be needed sooner rather than later.

As the days grew warmer and Catherine approached her confinement, she and Arthur settled into their respective routines. Catherine saw to the children's religious and secular education, managed family finances, cooked, and cleaned. Arthur came home from ten- or twelve-hour workdays with just enough energy to wash up, eat, and fall into bed.

Pittsburgh was not a woman's town, the *Pittsburgh Survey* observed in 1909, and levels of women's employment outside the home lagged well behind most other urban areas. But Catherine Rooney worked, and worked hard, her entire life. The mill's demands cut deeply into domestic life. Shift and Sunday work meant that the household revolved around Arthur's schedule. If he worked nights, Catherine kept the crowded apartment quiet during the day and fixed meals for him when he arrived home. At first light, she gathered up the children and set out to fetch water. The ritual was familiar to her. In Ebbw Vale, she had headed up the hill to a spring near Christ Church, the village's Anglican edifice, whose steeple cast a shadow over the Forge Rows. During the dry months of summer, the Ebbw Vale women had sometimes waited all night. Catherine had queued up there—as she did now in Pittsburgh—chatting and waiting her turn.

Mills upstream sucked in so much from the sluggish and sludgy

Monongahela River that by late summer, most of the Southside lacked water from early morning until the day-turns ended in the evening. The Monongahela carried sewage from homes along with contaminated spill from the mills and acid drainage from mines. But this rank, polluted water was all the Rooneys had for drinking and washing.

In Ebbw Vale, the Rooneys had witnessed outbreaks of cholera, smallpox, typhoid, and scarlet fever caused by poor sanitation. Ebbw Vale lacked piped water, sewage lines, and even latrines. When the Rooneys lived there, families dug latrine holes in the garden and screened them with sheets of iron. During rainstorms, a mud blackened by coal dust and human waste ran down the hillsides until the dirt roads between the rows of homes became ankle deep in it.

Similar conditions sickened Pittsburghers. At the turn of the century, the city led the nation in deaths due to typhoid. Diphtheria and pneumonia were particularly bad on the Southside. Arthur replenished his sweat-drenched body at work with ladles taken directly from the Monongahela, compromising his health. His children were even more vulnerable.

On May 16, 1884, as the leaves unfolded on the trees that lined Bingham Street and dotted the Southside slopes, Catherine delivered the Rooneys' third daughter. Her parents gave the child her mother's name. Nine days later, they took little Catherine Cecilia to be baptized at St. John the Evangelist Church, their largely Irish parish. Catherine gave this baby daughter the same loving care with which she had nurtured her siblings, but Catherine Cecilia died before her second birthday. Infants, without the benefit of pasteurization and vaccines, often succumbed to diarrhea, smallpox, whooping cough, or typhoid.

Soon, however, a little good fortune brightened their lives. Arthur moved up from common labor to a job as a puddler, one of the mill's most physically demanding and highly skilled positions. Puddlers performed the first of several highly skilled tasks required for iron production by stirring molten iron as if they were keeping a pudding from scorching. Arthur now had a status akin to that of an independent contractor.

Arthur cleaned and refueled his furnace with a crew he hired himself. The men loaded the furnace with a six-hundred-pound charge of pig iron. When it was molten, Arthur wrapped his hand with heavy rags to protect against the heat, then pushed his ten-foot "rabble" pole through the furnace's door. He stirred the metal to a "boil," when it sent up gaseous spurts and dancing blue flames. His trained "batting eye" discerned slight color differences while his hands felt subtle changes within the molten mass, so that he could separate the iron from its impurities. A wrong judgment here could result in "cobbles," or burnt iron, which would cost him a fine or even his job. Arthur plied apart hundreds of pounds of the hot, spongy metal into puddled balls, using only his eyes and arms to measure out the weight required. A two-wheeled buggy then took the molten mass to the rolling machines. As soon as one heat was finished, the men reloaded the furnace and began the next. Iron-making was still more of an art than a science, and skilled men like Arthur were indispensable to it.

In 1886 after the Rooneys had been in Pittsburgh two years, Arthur moved along the production line to become a rougher and then a roller. He had apprenticed for these jobs in Ebbw Vale, and now directed a crew of a dozen men and boys to squeeze the puddler's molten iron balls through a series of rolling machines. Rollers were the mill's highest paid tradesmen, and Rooney brought home more than $10 a day while a laborer made only $1.40.

The Rooneys moved to a nicer home on the Southside. Now they could eat better and stash away some savings. Skilled workers appointed their homes with lace curtains, wallpaper, and carpeting. Catherine was pregnant again, and she gave birth to another girl on February 8, 1886. Arthur, who had been an only child, delighted in such a big family. With bittersweet memories, they also baptized this infant as Catherine Cecilia. She, too, did not survive.

Putting Down Roots

Welshmen who had trained in towns like Ebbw Vale were at the heart of Pittsburgh's iron and steel industry in the 1880s. Arthur, even though he was of Irish heritage, belonged to their brotherhood. American plants lagged behind the innovative Ebbw Vale Works, and skilled Welsh workers came to reclaim their badge of honor where iron survived. Skilled

laborers controlled their lives in Pittsburgh more than they ever had under Ebbw Vale's Old World paternalism. Few lived in company houses;
men received cash instead of company scrip and patronized independent
merchants. These workers and their neighbors—shopkeepers, tradesmen, and tavern owners—were central to a blue-collar network that
elected candidates who were sympathetic to their needs. They, not the
elites, shaped popular culture and sport.

Sport was moving from the back rooms of taverns into the mainstream of working-class life, and Arthur's children and grandchildren
would eagerly jump into this sporting life. Although Arthur had little chance to partake, many young men with leisure and inclination
played as hard as they worked. The Southside fielded scores of ballclubs, and its ironworkers and glassblowers led the city's emergence
as a national center for rowing. Two Pittsburgh scullers—glassblower
James Hamill and puddler's helper Eph Morris—had reputations that
crossed the Atlantic.

The city's brotherhood of craftsmen reached out to help the newest
immigrants find jobs and housing in America just as they had in Welsh
and English beneficial societies. Welshman James Davis, who left a memoir of his life as a Pittsburgh iron puddler, described them as men with
"muscled arms as big as a bookkeeper's legs" and a self-confidence borne
from their knowledge of "the secrets of the trade."

By sticking together and leveraging the power that their knowledge
of production gave them, Arthur and his fellow craftsmen gained a
mastery over their labor that few workers in later years could imagine.
Grandson Art believed that Arthur had been an activist in the Amalgamated Association of Iron, Steel, and Tin Workers. The union negotiated favorable wages and working conditions and made Pittsburgh a
craftsmen's fiefdom over which ironmasters held dominion—but not
control—into the 1890s.

Arthur Rooney was at home in this world. Family legends sketch a
portrait of a staunchly independent and militant man. His great-great
grandchildren grew up with stories of him leading the St. Patrick's Day
parade on a white horse. Arthur had lived in three countries in less than
forty years, but after he and Catherine settled in Pittsburgh in 1884,

they put down roots that would bind the family to the region into the twenty-first century.

Precarious Fortunes

In 1887, Catherine gave birth to another daughter, Agnes, who grew into a strong, healthy girl. Catherine now had five children to mind, diapers to wash, and meals to fix. This determined daughter of one of Ebbw Vale's poor Irish laborers could squeeze a dollar. The children doubled up to make room for boarders, single Irishmen and Welshmen, who like Arthur, came home from the mill dirty, hungry, and tired. Catherine cooked their meals, packed their lunch buckets, and scrubbed sweat and soot from their heavy work clothes by hand—without running water—rubbing her fair Irish hands and arms red and raw.

By the time Agnes turned two in May 1889, Catherine was pregnant again. A son, Arthur, was born in August, but like the two Catherine Cecilias before him, this baby was unable to withstand the disease-ridden environment that threatened so many newborns on Pittsburgh's Southside. Catherine and Arthur had now lost three children in their five years in Pittsburgh.

Arthur's skills and Catherine's careful money management allowed them to make a stab at upward mobility. In 1890, the family purchased its first property and then quickly another. For the first time since their families had left Ireland, a Rooney and a Regan owned a piece of land. In January, they bought a $1,260 plot on Main Street in the borough of Mansfield, which became part of the industrial suburb of Carnegie, west of Pittsburgh. In April, they paid $7,000 for a house on East Carson Street, the Southside's main thoroughfare. The former appears to have been an investment property, the latter their home.

But the family's modest prosperity, like the nation's, was precarious. Hard times hit Pittsburgh in the 1890s, and the city's ironworkers searched desperately for employment. "Those who had jobs divided their time with needy comrades," reported puddler James Davis. "A man with hungry children would be given a furnace for a few days to earn enough to ward off starvation." Those who could, moved on.

Arthur was less mobile. He had ridden out several industrial depressions, but this one portended the same conversion to steel that had changed Ebbw Vale. In 1892, Catherine gave birth to a healthy boy, Miles Patrick, the Rooneys' sixth surviving child and their last. The family was living on Carson Street and Arthur was working as a roller. But that same year, his attention—and much of the nation's—turned to Andrew Carnegie's Homestead Steel Works, a few miles upriver from the Southside.

The Amalgamated Association, the successor to the Sons of Vulcan, was one of the nation's most powerful unions, but Andrew Carnegie and his associate Henry Clay Frick were determined to break it. When Frick locked the Homestead Steel Works' gates, the union surrounded the mill with pickets. On July 6, 1892, the company brought a barge of armed Pinkerton guards up the Monongahela River to escort strikebreakers into the mill. But the workers, too, were armed. In the ensuing fight, seven workers and nine Pinkertons died before the latter surrendered. At Frick's behest, the governor sent eight thousand state militia to break the strike, which dragged on for months before the workers conceded. Their defeat set back organized labor in steel for decades, and Carnegie made the shift from iron to steel in his plants without unionism.

According to family lore, Arthur wielded a shotgun against the Pinkertons and was forced to leave town afterward. There was no doubt where his loyalties lay. "You better believe I grew up as a union guy," his grandson Art would say decades later. "I used to listen to all the stories about my grandfather fighting the Pinkertons." But after Arthur saw his union defeated, he abandoned his profession. No occupation is listed for him in the 1893 City Directory. By 1894, the family had sold its Mansfield property, and Arthur had been bumped back to a lowly laborer.

Arthur may have been the victim of a backlash against union activists after the Homestead clash or of the economic downturn of the 1890s when millions lost their savings and property. It is also possible that his health was failing.

His name did not appear in the 1895 and 1896 city directories, and he apparently slid into serious debt. In August 1895, the Rooneys sold their Southside home to their oldest daughter, Bridget, and Michael Concannon, the Irishman she had married in 1891. Both Arthur and Catherine signed the agreement with an "X," implying that neither could write.

The Concannons immediately transferred the deed back to Catherine. Both transactions were for $7,000, the price the Rooneys had paid for the property five years earlier. These same-day sales could have been a maneuver to put the house in Catherine's name alone as protection against Arthur's creditors.

The transition from iron to steel hit the men who made metal in Pittsburgh hard, just as it had in Wales. New technologies rendered craftsmen's skills irrelevant and marginalized puddlers, roughers, and rollers like Arthur. Steel production needed far more unskilled labor, jobs filled by immigrants from southern, central, and eastern Europe. The workday lengthened, as twelve-hour shifts returned, and accidents increased. Powerful corporations consolidated their grip on manufacturing. Capital, not labor, soon exerted control at work with repercussions in politics and culture.

The age of the artisan was passing. Rather than accept the lowered status of laborer, Arthur left the industry. At forty-six, he was too old to take much more of what the mills demanded of a man anyway. He could give up mill life—the only work he and his father had ever known—but he hung on to the fierce independence and dignity that work had given him.

A New Way of Life

Arthur took the poor man's route to the middle class, opening a saloon on the Southside's Carson Street. The saloon required little capital up front, and the family lived upstairs. His son Daniel, twenty-three, quit the mill to tend bar. In Pittsburgh—as in Ireland and Ebbw Vale—the tavern was the nexus of news and gossip, an informal hiring hall, card parlor, boxing ring, stage for storytellers, and diversion from family squabbles. Pittsburgh workingmen began a tradition of chasing a shot of whisky with a mug of beer, probably because beer was cheaper and the men believed it replaced fluids lost at work. The practice branded Pittsburgh "a shot and a beer" town. Behind the bar, Arthur, once a leader among these men in the mill, became arbiter of their disputes, a confidant in troubled times, and their informal banker, holding pay and cutting them off before they drank away the rent money.

The household above the bar was crowded with children, relatives, and any others needing a place to stay. With the older children out on their own, Catherine took in more boarders. Bridget and husband Michael had four children by 1900 and lived a few doors away. In February 1899, Daniel moved out. Since they had arrived in Pittsburgh sixteen years earlier, Arthur and Catherine had resided at six different addresses on the vibrant, noisy, and filthy Southside. In 1900, they, their youngest four children, and five boarders resided above the Carson Street saloon.

But the Rooneys disappeared again from Pittsburgh's city directory in 1901. In February of that year, Catherine paid $300 for two lots along the Pennsylvania and Lake Erie railroad tracks just up from the Anderson Road Station in Crescent Township (later called Wireton). The workingman's circuit had carried the news that blue-collar jobs were plentiful there. In this tiny town, twenty-three miles down the Ohio River from the Southside, Catherine opened Rooney's Hotel. She rented twenty rooms to unattached men flooding the area for jobs in nearby river towns.

In 1903, Arthur died at the age of fifty-two. Pneumonia and related ailments took the lives of many ironworkers, who breathed a fine particulate matter that floated in the mills and went out into winter's chill wearing sweat-drenched work clothes. Arthur was buried in St. Mary's Cemetery in Lawrenceville, a neighborhood along the southern shores of the Allegheny River. A half-century of life was about all a man who worked in the mills could expect, and Arthur had used his up.

Daniel would inherit his parents' spirit of independence and their warm generosity that welcomed itinerant workers and young people who needed a place to stay. He would carry these traits into the next generation.

Coultersville: Arthur J. Rooney Is Born

After working in his father's saloon, Daniel became the proprietor of a small saloon and boarding house in Coultersville, Pennsylvania. His parents put up $4,000 to buy the building in 1898. The coal mining villages of Alpsville, Coultersville, and Osceola, with a combined population of nine hundred, nestled between the foothills of the Allegheny Mountains and the Youghiogheny River. They lined up along a horseshoe river bend, eight miles upstream from where the Youghiogheny spilled into the Monongahela at McKeesport. Trains and barges carried coal north toward Pittsburgh.

On January 9, 1899, in the tiny St. Patrick's church that local mine owner Nicholas Bigley had built, Daniel married eighteen-year-old Margaret Murray, whom he declared to be "the prettiest girl in Alpsville." They were a handsome pair. Daniel was now twenty-four and had fair skin, blond hair, and large, rather sad, blue eyes. His nose was straight, his jaw square, and his lips full. Maggie had a rich mass of dark auburn hair swept up into a Gibson girl bun. Her dainty features were centered and compact, with small eyes that conveyed sensitivity and serenity.

On January 27, 1901, Maggie Murray Rooney gave birth to Arthur Joseph Rooney. He was baptized at St. Patrick's and named for his paternal grandfather, the Montreal-born ironworker who would die before his grandson got a chance to know him. The baby's young mother looked at the infant's halo of red-blond fuzz and thanked God for placing a beautiful golden boy in her arms.

Maggie Murray and Daniel Rooney brought a common background to their marriage. Like the Rooneys, the Murrays were poor but upwardly mobile Irish immigrants. Like old Arthur Rooney, Maggie's father was a fiercely independent man. Michael Murray had been born in 1849 in County Roscommon, Ireland. He held a skilled job as the coal mine's fire boss, a leadership role comparable to Arthur's as a crew leader in Pittsburgh's ironworks. Murray entered the mine three hours before the morning shift. Lifting his safety lamp to the air currents, he read their flows and checked for gases. His chalk mark guaranteed the safety of each working area and allowed the foreman to open the mine each day. During shifts, he supervised repair of regulators and timbering.

In the 1880s, when his daughter Maggie was born, Michael was making $3 per day. Although much less than Arthur Rooney's $10 per day wage, it placed him among the highest-paid men in the mine. The family was proud of its status and home, a step above the company-owned shanties.

Murray's work, like Arthur's, left him limp with exhaustion at the end of each dirty and demanding ten-hour shift. Like all coal miners, he faced the constant risk of explosion, cave-in, and gas poisoning. Even if miners were spared disaster, coal dust snatched away their stamina and left them gasping for breath in the middle of the night. Many miners, like ironworkers, died young, leaving wives to raise their young children.

At home, "Pap" Murray, who chewed tobacco and ruled over his family with a fiery temper, was as beloved as he was feared. When he died in 1925 after achieving the rare age of seventy-six, his widow Mary Ann wrapped his threadbare sweater around her shoulders as a comforting shawl. His oval-framed portrait hung in the living room above his favorite chair where, even a decade after his death, no one dared sit. He bequeathed his bright blue eyes and thick mass of reddish-brown hair to most of his five daughters and four sons and almost all of his grandchildren. A number of them also inherited his temper.

In both the Rooney and Murray households, deeply religious and heartily loving women smoothed their husband's rough edges. Maggie Murray, everyone said, was a lot like her mother, Mary Ann Summers, who had worked as a maid and nanny in coal merchant Nicholas Bigley's home to help support the family after her father died. Her younger sisters and brothers followed her into Bigley's service in his home or his mines.

Mary Ann and her siblings held a deep religious faith infused with spirits and miracles. Family stories were filled with angels, saints, and unholy, restless spirits that moved among them.

In her autobiography, Art Rooney's cousin, actress Anne Jackson, remembered her grandmother Mary Ann's magisterial calm. "Grandma had a way of commanding respect without ever having to ask for it," Jackson wrote. "Any gossip and backbiting that went on around her was soon quelled by the force of her silence." Her daughter Maggie Murray Rooney, Jackson recalled, "was the dearest and calmest woman in the entire Murray clan, and she had Ma'am's gentleness and beautiful manners."

Following Their Fortunes

Monday through Saturday at Rooney's Hotel in Coultersville moved in tandem with miners' shifts. Hundreds of men hopped off ferries or slow-moving freight trains and joined local residents tramping to the coal slopes that opened into the hills. When the shift ended, Maggie Rooney was ready with ham sandwiches and pies. Daniel poured drinks while the men joked and gambled.

But Coultersville's fortunes faded when the mines petered out. In August 1902, Daniel and Maggie left for Monaca, a new development along the Pennsylvania and Lake Erie Railroad. Their property was just three miles down the Ohio River from Crescent, where Catherine Rooney managed her new boarding house.

The move proved fortuitous. Paying $1,050 for a plot of land, Daniel and Maggie built the Colonial Hotel and saloon across from the Colonial Steel Works, which fired its first heat of crucible steel on St. Patrick's Day 1902. Monaca was an industrial boomtown, and the young couple added an adjacent land parcel for $300. Their second son, named Daniel* for his father, was born there in January 1903. Suddenly, in July 1904, Daniel and Maggie sold their Colonial Hotel for $16,000, a sizable gain on their initial $1,350 investment. But they bought no new property with their windfall. Instead, Daniel disappeared.

Art was three years old, and Maggie, pregnant, was left with her two sons. She moved in with her mother-in-law at Rooney's Hotel in Crescent Township. Catherine adored the winsome Maggie, so much so that her own daughters, Mary Ellen and Agnes, complained that she favored Maggie over them. These Rooney women—the recently widowed Catherine, her daughters and daughter-in-law—supported themselves and helped Maggie through the birth of her third son, James, in 1905. The women cooked and cleaned for the boarders and doted on the three Rooney boys—Art, Dan, and Jim.

According to family legend, Daniel headed west to dodge gambling debts. Years later, Art Rooney would say that his earliest memories were of a trip to the 1904 World's Fair in St. Louis with his mother and brother Dan for a reunion with his father. If Art remembered the trip, he probably also had some recollection of his family's unraveling fortunes. Although Daniel and Maggie's Colonial Hotel had brought a handsome

*We call this baby, Art's brother, "Dan," and continue to call their father "Daniel."

profit, they were unable to buy new property for almost a decade. There is evidence that Daniel continued to be plagued by creditors. Years later, Art would become an enormously successful gambler himself. But, unlike his father, he never lost control of his betting.

When Daniel finally returned home, he and Maggie rented a house in Pittsburgh's Homewood section. Two more sons were born there, John in 1908 and Vincent in 1910, as the Rooneys struggled to win back lost prosperity. Daniel worked as a salesman in a paint store, and Maggie squirreled away pennies until Daniel could finally go back into business on his own.

2

The Young Athlete

The Northside

In a crinkled and tattered photograph, Daniel Rooney's Café and Bar is draped with flags, pennants, and bunting for the Fourth of July, 1918. The Great War in Europe would soon end in victory for the Allied Powers. Although the conflict had brought carnage to Europe and upheaval at home, these were the best of times for the Rooneys. Art had been too young to enlist when the United States entered the war and his father Daniel too old, but the war fueled Pittsburgh's economy, and workers patronizing the Northside saloon brought the family a wartime bonanza. The establishment on General Robinson Street gave the Rooney patriarch a position of respect in the Ward and allowed his sons the freedom to play and study instead of work.

Three boys in knickers pose in front of the bar alongside six somber workmen, jackets open and caps or fedoras tilted back on their heads. Though Daniel, forty-four with thinning blond hair, shares the solemn miens of the men leaning on the brass rail that runs across the tavern's front windows, he is prospering. Daniel and Maggie have seven healthy children, and thanks to the saloon, a steadily growing bank account. Eight year-old Vinnie leans back against Daniel, whose arms envelop his chest. John, ten, stands alongside, his elbows hooked behind the rail.

An older boy can be seen in an upstairs window. But Art, Dan, and Jim, now in their teens, are too old to be encircled in Daniel's protective arms. They have already begun exploring their own way in the world, using sport as their compass.

Though Daniel occasionally used his boxing skills to keep order in the saloon, his youngest brother, Miles, was the only Rooney of their generation to develop his athletic prowess. While in the Air Corps during the war, Miles sparred in Europe with heavyweight champ Jack Johnson, then a fugitive from a trumped-up conviction for transporting a woman across state lines for immoral purposes.

Art, seventeen, would play that afternoon for the Phipps Athletic Association team in a July Fourth doubleheader with the Homestead Steel Works team. He would be the youngest player on the field, a baseball prodigy already drawing attention on Northside sandlots. As sport entered its "Golden Age," Art Rooney was embarking on the athletic career that would define his life.

Moving In

Though Daniel had knocked about after he and Maggie sold their hotel in Monaca in 1904, he never returned to the mills. The Rooneys were unwilling to surrender their future to the vagaries of steelmaking. By August 1913 they had enough capital to buy another property, the saloon on General Robinson Street. Daniel, the five boys, and Maggie's sister Stella Murray moved their belongings into the apartment above the bar, while Maggie, thirty-three years old and pregnant, arranged their new nest.

Although Maggie Murray Rooney was good-natured and generous, she had taken lessons from her mother-in-law Catherine about how to guard her family. Michael and Mary Ann Murray—Maggie's parents—put their names on the deed for the saloon. But it seems unlikely that they actually paid for it. By all appearances, the Murrays, who had lost several properties to sheriff sales, were close to bankruptcy. Four months after the initial sale, Maggie bought the building back for the same $6,000 price. What seems likely is that Maggie had been finding ways to duck Daniel's creditors. If the Rooney men had a penchant for gambling, their wives knew how to hedge their bets.

The saloon anchored a three-story yellow brick building with brown trim. Its windows were partially whitewashed, and Daniel had painted "Dan Rooney Café and Bar" on them. Every day but Sunday, he sold drinks along the deep mahogany bar. Tables lined the fifty-foot room, brightened in the daytime by its big windows. In the back room, men played cards and caucused over union or ward politics. A cook baked hams and simmered cauldrons of soup, sending savory helpings upstairs on a dumbwaiter that opened into the family's dining room.

Each night, Daniel locked the bar and climbed the stairs to the family's quarters. Dumping change into his bureau drawer, he turned over the day's cash to Maggie, who took it to the bank in the morning.

Shortly before the couple moved to the Northside, their daughter, Catherine, had died of the whooping cough. But another daughter, Margaret, was born in December 1913, followed by Marie in 1918, and their last child, Tommy, in 1922. Despite their large brood, Daniel and Maggie always opened their doors. "Just put another nail in the wall, Ma," Daniel sang out when one of the children's friends needed a place to hang up a jacket and stay for a meal or a few months.

The children internalized their parents' expectations. One summer, young Margaret followed friends to the nearby Clark Candy factory, intending to earn $1 a day plucking stems from strawberries. Her mother, who had seen child labor in the mines, tracked her down and frog-marched her back home. Maggie also forbade foul language. "I never did curse," Art said later. His strongest epithet was "Phoo," which became his nickname. While Maggie disciplined the children, Daniel usually laughed at their antics.

In these halcyon days before Prohibition, the Rooneys were clambering out of the working class. Life was secure, if not luxurious. In winter, icy winds from the Allegheny River leaked through cracks around dormers and loose tiles on the roof. The boys shivered awake on the third floor to find their blankets coated with snow. Scampering downstairs, the children dressed around a stove that served as the only source of heat.

Spring brought floods. "If you spit in the Allegheny River, the flood came up," Art remembered. Until locks and dams upstream regulated the Allegheny's erratic waters, the river swelled over the Northside's banks. "It wasn't anything unusual for us to leave for school by going out a second-floor window in a skiff," Art said. He, Dan, and Squawker Mullen almost drowned that way. "We were paddling that canoe right through Expo Park, right through the outfield." That is, until Squawker stood and upended it. "We started swimming for the third-base grandstand. Squawker and Dan weren't wearing boots, so they made it easy enough. But I had on boots and an overcoat. That was the last gasp I had when I got hold of that grandstand."

The Pittsburgh Pirates had played down the block from the saloon at Exposition Park until 1909, when Barney Dreyfuss moved them across town to Forbes Field. Flooding had hurt attendance and rotted Expo Park's wooden bleachers. More distressing to Dreyfuss, the German immigrant who bought the franchise in 1900, was the Ward's rough reputation. "The better class of citizens," he complained, "especially when accompanied by their womenfolk, were loath to go there." Expo Park still hosted carnivals and fairs, and the boys watched the Pittsburgh Rebels play there. The Rebels belonged to the Federal League, a short-lived rival to the major leagues. While lacking the Pirates' élan, the Rebels battled for the 1915 pennant until season's end, and ball games infused the saloon with game-day energy. "All the baseball players loafed in my father's saloon," Art recounted. "I knew 'em all."

Maggie tried to keep her boys out of the saloon, but Daniel was less protective. Ballplayers, politicians, and carnies befriended his gregarious lads and were sources of wonder for them. Barely in his teens, Art watched carefree ballplayers plunk down their beer money and tucked away the notion that a career in sport might be an attractive option.

The Northside

The Northside was an exciting new world for Art. Born in the quiet coal-mining town of Coultersville, he had taken his early steps in two small Ohio River towns and spent his middle childhood in the sleepy, tree-lined Homewood section of Pittsburgh. For Art and his brothers, the door at the bottom of their apartment's stairway opened onto an urban clamor that exerted a powerful pull to both good and evil.

Until Pittsburgh annexed the Northside in 1907, it had been the separate city of Allegheny. The Rooneys' neighborhood was known as the Ward. Its first settlers were English and Scottish Presbyterians, including Andrew Carnegie, whose family emigrated from Dunfermline, Scotland, in 1848. Parts of Allegheny became posh, but in its shadowy reaches, less-licit entrepreneurs plied the region's vice trade. By 1900, Allegheny was called "Little Canada," a place beyond the reach of the law, where police were on the take and fugitives assured of haven. By the time the Rooneys arrived, Allegheny's elites had departed. Although crime had diminished, corruption lay semidormant, waiting until 1920, when Prohibition's rain of illegal booze would reawaken it. Maggie sensed the threat to her sons.

In September 1913, shortly after moving in, she enrolled them at St. Peter's, the parish school. She conveyed her concerns to its nuns. Art and his brothers Dan and Jim often pummeled each other to settle their disputes. Art and Dan displayed worrisome tempers. Jim was more easygoing, but he joined their battles, which spilled onto the streets.

Maggie had witnessed her father's red-faced tantrums and plenty of barroom brawls. On paydays, the workingmen who packed Rooney's saloon often topped off the evening by arguing over the merits of County Galway versus those of County Cork. When fisticuffs erupted, a disapproving Maggie leaned out of an upstairs window to watch the horse-drawn paddy wagon (named for the Irish passengers it frequently carried) back up to the saloon's double doors.

At the wagon's clarion call, wives and mothers tumbled out of homes to rush to Rooney's and rescue their men. While police ushered the rowdies into the wagon, the women grabbed their collars, shouting, "No, that's my Michael" or "me Paddy." The revelers sometimes shook off the women, figuring the night would go easier in jail than at home. The cops often sat up with their prisoners, playing cards, singing ballads, and swapping tales from the old country.

Maggie Rooney worried about her sons' proximity to this world. The nuns and priests at St. Peter's nurtured their religious faith as an antidote to their anger and the depravity of the street. But catechism alone would not stave the boys' boundless energy. For that, St. Peter's had an athletic program. The Rooneys were ready recruits; for them, the classroom was little more than an interlude between matches on the playing fields.

The Sporting Life

Art Rooney might not have hit a home run the first time he picked up a bat nor broken free for a touchdown the first time he carried the ball, but it would not have surprised sporting aficionados if he had. Few bested him on the field, in a race, or with their fists. Art and his brothers had inherited "the batting eye," musculature, and stamina that their great-grandfather and grandfather had put to work separating molten iron from its impurities. Three generations removed from Ireland's famines, they enjoyed the luxury of putting their gifts to work in the batter's box instead of the iron forge.

Art began exploring the Northside's archipelago of fields and gymnasiums and its one large island, Exposition Park. The scruffy mix of blue-collar Irish and Germans who had replaced the wealthy Scots Irish on the Northside had inherited a rich athletic history and infrastructure. Old Allegheny's river plains of flat land—a scarce commodity in hilly Pittsburgh—hosted the area's earliest cricket matches and sheltered boat clubs after the Civil War. The Alleghenies started playing baseball there in 1882, joined the National League in 1887, renamed themselves the Pirates in 1891, and staged the first World Series at Expo Park in 1903. Prophetically, Expo Park hosted what the National Football League regards as the nation's first professional football match when the Allegheny Athletic Association paid former Yale star Pudge Heffelfinger $500 to play football there in 1892.

The Northside had all the elements for a culture of sporting excellence—facilities, intense rivalries, solid coaching, and strong role models. This sport-suffused environment nurtured the boys' athletic talents. "My father and his brothers spent every day in the summer, the whole day, on Phipps playground," Art's son Dan explained. Art developed athletic confidence on Phipps' dirt fields, which were oiled down for games, and at the Saltworks on Beaver Avenue, where long balls to right field went through the National Casket Company windows.

Art moved rapidly from playing with the boys at school to competing with men on the sandlots. As he fetched water and stray balls for semi-pro teams, his talent and affability impressed older players, who let him into their world. Art's first and favorite club was Phipps. "That's when he found out he could play," concluded his son Dan. "It wasn't anything for me when I was fifteen years old—when I weighed 135, maybe 140 pounds—to be playing baseball against the famous colored teams, the Homestead Grays and the Kansas City Monarchs," Art recounted. "All of those barnstorming teams—the House of David, for example— they all came to the Ward."

Art and his contemporaries learned how to become men, not just athletes, on the ball field. Sport was a manhood rite, where Art's abilities won him extraordinary standing at a young age. Sport also began shaping the other qualities Art had inherited. He commanded authority on the ball field in the same way his grandfathers had at work. At the same time, he exhibited the faith and charm of his maternal grandmother, Mary Ann Summers, and the tough and sunny determination with which his other grandmother, Catherine Regan Rooney, had withstood hardship. A little of the Murray temper and the Rooney love of gambling added spice to his character.

From the time he stepped onto these Runyonesque streets at the age of twelve, Art was a child of the Ward. He explored its overlapping spheres of business, crime, politics, and sport and found mentors on the street, in Daniel's saloon, and on the ball field. Men gravitated to this talented, warm-hearted boy in whom they saw something of their own youthful promise and that of their growing city.

Art's decision to fashion a career in sport was easy. The harder choice was deciding which sport. An ants-in-his-pants kid who generally avoided sitting still or being alone, he played them all. "Seasons didn't overlap each other so much," Art recalled. "Football season was football season and baseball season was baseball season, so you just went from one season to the other."

Art combined speed, agility, and strength. Although small in stature, his body control and eye-hand coordination allowed him to excel. He developed an ability to scope out plays and anticipate opponents' moves. His mantra was to "think ahead of the play," and he practiced it on and off the field.

For all of his ability, Art was fortunate to come of age just as American sport entered its postwar golden age. It provided him a field on which to play out his life story. How he played became who he was. Sport—along with the saints, politicians, and scallywags who hung around it—shaped him and let him express himself through action. He believed that a man revealed his nature by what he did, not what he said. Like Pittsburgh, Rooney came out of a heritage of coal and iron. Now the city, like Art, increasingly saw sport as the grand metaphor for its character.

The Sporting Life at Duquesne

Art's sporting baptism came in the Ward, but he first gained a reputation as a fifteen-year-old freshman at Duquesne University's prep school in 1916. Duquesne had opened its doors in 1878 as the Pittsburgh Catholic College of the Holy Ghost, a project of the Spiritans to educate immigrant children. Although the order had roots in eighteenth-century France, Duquesne reflected, above all, the influence of its Irish-born fathers.

Art's paternal grandparents, Arthur and Catherine, might have been illiterate, but Daniel and Maggie Rooney were determined that their sons would complete high school and attend college. Duquesne offered Art a chance to hone his athletic skills, but also imposed rigorous academic standards. Duquesne expanded Art's Northside cohort to a city-wide network of upwardly mobile Catholics. It strengthened his attachments to Catholicism, Irish Americanism, and Ireland, but also to an ecumenical ethos transcending religion, nationality, and race.

Duquesne, which formed in reaction to the city's Scots-Irish Presbyterian elites, helped working-class youth climb to positions in business and the professions. Students attended Mass and read about "Self-Determination in Ireland," but Duquesne was far from parochial.

Art met all kinds of boys on the Bluff overlooking the Monongahela River where the campus perched. Irish or not, they were outsiders in a Protestant-dominated city. Each came rightly to see himself as Art Rooney's good and loyal friend. Among Art's schoolmates were Samuel Weiss, later a judge and NFL referee; Patrick O'Malley, a teammate and ward leader; John Holahan, who became business manager for Rooney's football team; Brew Jackson, who worked as its trainer; and Moon Klinzing, who played for it. At Duquesne, Rooney also befriended Cumberland Posey, who became his mentor in sport. That the man Art emulated was African American might have been unusual in business or politics, but less so in sport, the most democratic arena of Pittsburgh life.

Duquesne's coaches quickly saw what Art's sandlot coaches already knew. Art gave his all to play, and he had much to give. His first scholastic competition came in his fourth-best sport, basketball, where he was among the leading scorers. But baseball was his passion.

In the spring of 1917, military drills and enlistment fever hampered Duquesne's college ballclub, but the preps were undeterred. Art patrolled the outfield and routinely carried off batting honors for the high school team. In June, military drills preempted use of the ball field and cut short the season. The *Pittsburgh Post* published a photo of the prep ballclub with Art sitting solemnly in the middle, his hair trimmed and slicked back.

His first year at Duquesne, Art scraped through Latin, algebra, and geometry and performed capably in history, geography, and physiology. Taking the academic curriculum, he read *The Last of the Mohicans*, *The Rime of the Ancient Mariner*, Boswell's *Life of Johnson*, and Washington's "Farewell Address." Art would always read, but his taste would lean more toward newspapers and racing forms than the classics.

The Sandlots

When classes ended, Art jumped back to the sandlots. His neighbor Bill Pickels, who managed Phipps, needed no persuading to put Art in the lineup. "Rooney's fielding at third was sensational," the *Pittsburgh Post* noted after a game with Pleasant Valley. The paper regularly applauded his play. Unlike his brother Dan, who was becoming a power hitter, Art relied on speed and strategy. Whether he stole a base, bunted a runner up, or got in the path of a pitch, Art usually factored in the scoring.

While he had played with boys at Duquesne prep, sandlot baseball featured older men. Art's talent astonished observers. "Only once in a blue moon would a teenager be able to come up and play at that level," sandlotter John Kennedy observed. At sixteen, Art played under that blue moon. To hold his own, he had to shed boyish ways and observe the rules of manly behavior. He had to respond to coaching and learn his strengths and weaknesses. Back in the world of boys, these qualities stood out.

"When I was younger, I used to see Art play all over the Northside," said Kennedy, who grew up in Pleasant Valley near the Ward. Pleasant Valley had its share of Irish, Germans, and African Americans, including Kennedy's neighbor, Negro League slugger Josh Gibson. While Rooney never rivaled Gibson as a ballplayer, Kennedy testified to Art's skill. "There wasn't any better talent playing on the sandlots. He could cover the outfield just like he was made of grass. And God, was he fast," Kennedy recalled. "There was none faster. When he got on first base, it was automatic he was on second base. I never saw him thrown out in my life."

Back to Duquesne

By the fall of 1917, more than two hundred Duquesne students had enlisted in the military. Only sixteen, Art stayed in school and joined the prep football team. Dan, newly enrolled, made Duquesne's junior squad, which had done so well in years past that it played older, bigger, and more experienced teams considered out of its class.

Students were dejected that October when Duquesne's former star, "Greenfield" Jimmy Smith, now a New York Giant, did not play in the World Series. But Art's gridiron debut eased their disappointment. The prep team won seven of nine games, tied one, and lost another by 3 points. "In measuring ability," the *Duquesne Monthly* wrote, "Halfback Rooney stands head and shoulders above his companions." Art was an elusive broken-field runner, devilishly difficult to bring down. He accounted for over half the team's touchdowns. In the biggest game of the season, against archrival Homestead, he dropkicked two field goals for the game's only points.

"Art Rooney has proven himself to be one of the greatest halfbacks in High School circles," the *Duquesne Monthly* declared. "This is all the more remarkable when we consider that it is his first year on the team." Meanwhile, with brother Dan at halfback, the Juniors forgot the Catholic virtue of mercy as they thrashed Leetsdale High School 111–0. Holding opponents scoreless, the Juniors completed their third consecutive undefeated season. While Art's team was declared the region's high school champs, Dan's squad grabbed junior high honors.

As soon as football ended, Art returned to basketball, where he was a tough defender but not the player he was in football. Practice brought him into contact with varsity star Charles Cumbert. Most fans knew that Charles Cumbert was Cumberland Posey using an alias because he also played semipro ball. Ten years Art's senior, Posey became his athletic model. Cum's father, Captain Cumberland Willis Posey Sr., was black Pittsburgh's foremost citizen. A successful entrepreneur, the Captain presided over the Loendi Social Club, the Warren A. M. E. Church, and the *Pittsburgh Courier*. Cum would surpass his father and become one of the most remarkable sportsmen in black America. His Homestead Grays baseball team and Loendi and Monticello basketball squads would rank among the nation's best. Art idolized him.

Midway through the 1918 baseball season, Duquesne suspended collegiate competition because of the war and the flu epidemic. High school baseball staggered on; Art's season was marred by cancellations but only one defeat. He was among a trio of hard-hitting outfielders dubbed the "wrecking crew," and Dan's junior varsity team went undefeated.

Summer Sandlots

On the sandlots, Art established himself as more than a boy wonder. He played more games that summer with Phipps than he had for Duquesne that spring. Because few homes had telephones, managers used newspapers to contact players. Grabbing the late-night bulldog edition, Art looked for his name on the sports pages, along with marching orders about where to report the next day.

Phipps was one of several hundred local clubs. The top teams, sponsored by steel mills and factories, paid their players and hired ex-major and minor leaguers. Other clubs fielded younger players and offered only the chance to play. While the war was damaging major league and college baseball, sandlot teams benefited. Professional players facing the Secretary of War's "work or fight" edict took defense industry jobs and played on workplace teams. As a result, Art faced top opponents.

Pittsburgh papers covered sandlot ball more extensively than major league baseball (excepting the Pirates), and Northsiders keenly antici- pated local match-ups. When Phipps played the Merkles from nearby Troy Hill, ropes were stretched to keep spectators from spilling onto the outfield. After defeating the Northside Board of Trade, Pleasant Valley, the Merkles, and the Allegheny Independents, Phipps was hailed as the Northside's amateur champion. The team's 32-4 record equaled its best since its founding in 1905.

Art played in all but four games, batting .311, stealing 10 bases, and scoring 31 runs. His athleticism brought him increasing notoriety, but if ever his head began to swell, Art could count on his brothers and bud- dies to pound him down to size. Keeping inflated egos in check was an Irish and a Rooney tradition.

Football and Boxing

In the fall of 1918, "Death Calls Local Star" captioned photos of ath- letes killed overseas or by the "Spanish Floo." Thousands perished in Pittsburgh, and many more, including Maggie Rooney, were stricken. Art prayed all day at St. Peter's while his mother successfully battled the devastating influenza.

High school sport, unlike college athletics, played on during the ep- idemic. Duquesne recognized Art's play by awarding him one of ten prep athletic letters granted at commencement. Northside fans recog- nized him, too. Sandlot football pitted neighborhood against neighbor- hood to the accompaniment of brass bands and parades. Art had begun playing for two lightweight squads, the Hope A. C. and the Harvey A. A., when he was sixteen. By 1918, the two teams had combined into the Hope Harvey Football Club, which played at Expo Park. Art could not have imagined that Hope Harvey would eventually evolve into the Pittsburgh Steelers and make its home grounds on the same site.

The team's name came from two deeply rooted Ward institutions. The Hope Number 1 Engine House on Martindale Street, which had served the Ward since 1862, sponsored neighborhood sport. A stately brick structure with a tower overlooking the Northside, the firehouse was Hope Harvey's locker room. Dr. Walter Harvey, who had played col- lege football at Indiana University and studied medicine at Penn before opening his practice on Western Avenue, enjoyed backing the boys with a few dollars and his medical skills. He took care of boys who got hurt. "Nothing cost us a cent," Art recounted.

Art preferred baseball but was leaving a mark on the gridiron, where his managerial skills were emerging. Other teams contacted him to arrange contests, and on game days, teammates deferred as he set the lineup and called plays.

Boxing 1919

Art, who had not yet graduated from high school, shrugged off classes in January 1919 and turned to boxing. Those boyish jousts that had troubled Maggie Rooney had become second nature to Art and boys in the Ward. Ray Downey, who grew up nearby, put it simply: "If you couldn't fight on the Northside, you couldn't exist for long. It was a tough neighborhood, tough enough that you had to protect yourself." Boys replicated their fathers' brawls from the Old World. Although the Rooneys were three generations removed from that history, the Galway boys called them "yellow bellies." "We were from Northern Ireland," Art explained. "Even tho' we went to the same parochial school, we had plenty of fights with those other Irishmen." However, the Irish boys could set aside their intramural squabbles for a good knockdown against the Germans, the Northside's second-largest nationality.

Daniel Rooney understood that his sons had to defend themselves, just as he had while growing up on the Southside. He got them a punching bag and boxing gloves one Christmas.

"Old Dan was tough, and so were his sons," George Quinlan, a raconteur and Jim Rooney's friend, recalled. Daniel showed them how to throw a punch, as well as how to dodge one. "Boy, could they fight!" Quinlan recalled. "I took Duke [Vincent] to a hospital one day after a fight with Jim. They couldn't bring him to." Art and Dan became two of the Ward's toughest scrappers, often turning on each other.

Art battered Dan until, Quinlan said, Dan outgrew him and "started 'lathering' Art. So one day Art said, 'Dan, this is disgraceful, two brothers fighting. We've got to stop this.' And Dan said, 'I'm just now beginning to enjoy it.'" Dan, a light-heavyweight, towered over his welterweight brother and outweighed him by forty pounds. Younger brothers Jim and John boxed as amateurs, while Vincent would fight professionally as 'Duke York.'

Games often ended in scraps, with the Rooneys' fists swinging in the middle of them. Given his size, Art battled to establish his bona fides. He had mellowed by the time Ray Downey managed one of Art's teams. "He didn't look for a fight then," Downey said, recalling one donnybrook. "Art was in the middle of the field with his arms folded. Someone said, 'Art, why aren't you in there?' He said, 'They're doing all right without me.'"

The brothers refined their boxing skills at St. Peter's Lyceum. "In those days," Art explained, "each neighborhood had a boxing team." The *Pittsburgh Post* called St. Peter's the city's best, and Art considered it the equal of any in the world. Boys "would come over in a parade and fight under St. Peter's," he remembered. Boxers shared a limited supply of skin-tight sweat suits that covered their arms and legs. Art always volunteered to box first because "after a couple of fights," his son Tim explained, those sweats "were soaking wet and smelled to high heaven."

Even while boxing as amateurs, Art and Dan picked up a few bucks in the ring. "Some years," Art reminisced, "my brother Dan and I would leave town in the summer with a semipro [ballclub], and we'd travel through Ohio, West Virginia, Pennsylvania, and New York, playing for $10 or $20 a game. We'd play in chautauquas," week-long carnivals that visited small towns. The carnivals often had athletic troupes with fighters who would take on anybody in the house. "You'd get three dollars a round for as long as you could stay," Art said. "Well, that was made to order for Dan and me because we could lick all those carnival guys . . . They could handle a farmer all right, but they were very ordinary fighters." The brothers were anything but ordinary. Their biggest challenge was making the fight last the maximum three rounds before putting their opponents away. After awhile, the carnival managers asked the Rooneys to stay away. "It was a reasonable request," Art recalled, "so we did—but that was easy money while it lasted."

The Rooneys also fought at carnivals at Exposition Park. One of the most popular, the Johnny J. Jones carnival, featured a boxer from the Ward. The man had "done the buck"—that is, worked as a strike-breaker—on the railroad, and was driven out of the ferociously pro-union neighborhood. "As soon as we heard about him coming back," Rooney remembered, "we got ahold of Squawker Mullen. Squawker was a national amateur champion—just a little fellow, maybe 110 pounds, but boy, could Squawker fight." Squawker, however, was out of shape and struggled. Between rounds, Dan Rooney instructed Squawker to navigate the carnival fighter into a corner. When he did, Art explained, "our Dan, who was a heavyweight, just reached up over the ropes and hit the fellow—he nailed him like you would nail a bird in midair. Right away, someone hollered, 'Hey Rube!' That was the way carnival workers alerted each other to trouble." What the carnies didn't know was that boys in the Ward also used "Hey Rube" to muster support. Chaos ensued. "Every tent in the carnival went down that night," Art smiled.

In 1918, Art debuted in the ring at the Americus Republican Club downtown. Fighting at 130 pounds, the seventeen-year-old defeated Johnny Farrell from the Polish Lyceum and won a gold watch. Amateur fighters often received a watch or a merchandise certificate, which they exchanged for a few dollars from the promoter, a ruse that preserved amateur eligibility.

"Rooney is a high-class lad, who has been showing well in recent bouts," the *Pittsburgh Post* reported after Art beat a Philadelphia fighter at the Pittsburgh Athletic Association (PAA) in Oakland. "Anyone he meets will have to step some to win." St. Peter's "clever all-around athlete" was ascending the amateur ranks.

Boxing took Art on the road. In January 1919, he defeated the best amateur in his class at the New York City Athletic Club. In Pittsburgh, he was featured during intercity tournaments that climaxed the season. In March, Art won the 135-pound regional American Athletic Union championship. A few days later, he boxed at the Allegheny Social Club in a benefit for soldiers back from the war.

The next week, Art traveled to Toronto for Canada's amateur championships. One of two American winners, he waded into opponent Charley Tossell "like a whippet tank going for one of Jerry's pill boxes." Rooney peppered away with both hands, the *Toronto Daily Star* wrote. "It was only a matter of time until one of the 'good night Kates' connected." After Art's first-round knockout left Tossell unconscious for a minute, the press hailed him as the championships' best fighter. "He is a good, two-handed boxer and will take a lot of beating," one writer observed.

Two weeks later, Art went to Boston for the 1919 AAU championships. "You'd have to fight four and five times in a day against guys from all over the country," he recalled. "It was great." Before a partisan crowd at Mechanics Hall, he defeated hometown hero Tansey Norton in the quarterfinals. "Rooney knew too much, packed a stiff punch in either hand, and never allowed Norton a chance to get going," the *Boston Herald* reported. But Frank Cassidy decisioned Art in the finals. The victory entitled Cassidy to represent the United States in a tournament in Scandinavia. Rooney's consolation was befriending Norton, his quarter-final opponent. Norton introduced him to Tip O'Neill, the future Speaker of the House.

Art got a rematch with Cassidy in May at the PAA. "There will be no dull moments while Rooney and Cassidy are in the ring," the *Post* reported. Art, one reporter disclosed, felt that he "didn't get the best sort of a deal [in Boston] and is out to show his friends at home that he can beat Cassidy. The press made no mention of who won the fight, only that Art caught a train to Clarksburg, West Virginia, afterward so he could join the barnstorming Pittsburgh Collegians baseball team.

Back home, Rooney fought on a St. Peter's card benefiting the Irish Freedom fund. Middleweight contender Harry Greb headlined the bouts. For a young man, Art traveled in fast company.

Art segued smoothly to baseball in the summer of 1919, gracing the lineups of Phipps, Damascus Bronze, and the Pittsburgh Collegians, who barnstormed the tri-state region for weeks at a time. He often played for two teams on the same day. Phipps had another tremendous season, finishing 32-8-2. By season's end, Art knew baseball was his game.

Indiana Normal School, 1919

Art returned to school that fall, but not to Duquesne. Instead, he headed fifty-five miles northeast to Indiana Normal School and enrolled in the college preparatory program. Art could finish his high school degree there, but mostly, he wanted to advance his athletic career. Indiana, he figured, offered the best chance to explore his options, even if that meant bypassing an opportunity at Notre Dame. That September, *Pittsburgh Leader's* sports editor Richard Guy wrote Notre Dame's Knute Rockne about "Art Rooney, A.A.U. champion lightweight boxer, who is also a splendid prospect in football . . . The purpose of this letter is to learn if you can handle him at Notre Dame, either in the varsity or one of the prep teams. He would require his expenses." There is no record of Rockne's reply, but Art confirmed that the legendary coach invited him to Notre Dame, and Vince Rooney remembered Rockne coming to their home to recruit his brother.

Perhaps turning down Notre Dame was the naïve choice of an unsophisticated eighteen-year-old, but Art had already calculated that baseball offered greater promise. While professional football scarcely existed in 1919, baseball players could make a good living. With the exception of a few boxers, they were sport's best-paid performers. Art was already earning money by playing baseball, his size was better suited for the game, and he liked it more. Finally, Art was so rooted in Pittsburgh that he rejected several promising offers in order to stay close to home.

Indiana State Normal School's primary mission was to train teachers, but it also enrolled seventy "College Preps," students readying themselves for college. More than a fourth of the preps were female, as were a majority of the college students, a much higher percentage than at Duquesne.

The preps were eligible to compete on college teams, and Art took full advantage of the opportunity, playing football, basketball, and baseball and running track during his three semesters. Athletics left little time for academics, and it showed. Art registered for sixteen courses. He withdrew from two, failed to complete three, and received Ds or Fs in six more. Art's two highest grades—eighty-two in plane geometry and eighty in botany—came in classes taught by football coach Don Beeler. Art's recollection of his academic record improved with age. Years later, he claimed, "I always went to class, even though a lot of athletes didn't. In fact I may have set a record at Indiana for going to class all the time."

One teacher, he said, held class despite a heavy snowstorm "because she knew I'd be there no matter how much snow there was."

Indiana played other teachers' schools and freshmen teams from Pitt, Syracuse, Penn State, and Carnegie Tech. Although usually the smallest man on the football field, Art made an immediate impact. In November, Indiana ended California State Normal's eleven-game winning streak after Art scored touchdowns on a dazzling run and an interception. After defeating Mansfield 14–0, Indiana was crowned the 1919 state normal school champion.

Meanwhile, Dan Rooney took over at Duquesne prep. The *Pittsburgh Post* welcomed him as "the brother of Art Rooney, the boxer, who won fame on the Bluff as a left halfback on last year's eleven." Dan led the team in running, passing, and kicking, and played with characteristic Rooney toughness. The big news, however, was not the prep team's showing but the announcement that Duquesne would resume college football in 1920. When word leaked out, students exploded in celebration, ignoring the bells summoning them to class.

Back in Indiana, Art boxed and played basketball that winter, and ran track and played centerfield in the spring. He posed for the yearbook with the track team, a wiry, unsmiling but invigorated group. Rooney's arms were heavily muscled; his reddish-blond hair parted in the middle.

Boxing 1920

His love of baseball notwithstanding, Art's greatest success came in the ring. Polishing his techniques under St. Peter's coach Red Buckley, he picked up pointers from older fighters, watching how they fought and how they lived. Art sparred with Patsy Scanlon from the Point and future champ Harry Greb from Garfield, tough fighters who knew all the tricks and were willing to use them. Scanlon was too much for Art, numbers banker Woogie Harris recalled. "I saw Patsy and Art work out, and Art was a bulldog. He fought like Henry Armstrong." That was high praise from Harris, who rarely missed the chance to watch Armstrong, the first man to win championships in three weight classes. "But Patsy batted the hell out of [Rooney]," Harris laughed. "He hasn't hit Patsy yet."

Irish Americans dominated local boxing, and some fighters adopted

Irish names to boost their popularity. Pittsburgh's Ancient Order of Hibernians objected that Izzy Grabowsky fought as Patsy O'Brien, Sammy Schultz as Jimmy Kelly, and Tony Caruso passed himself off as Tommy Murphy. Those "who hide their real nationality under a moniker that might stamp the wearer as being from the Emerald Isle," the fraternal group warned, "had best look for other business names." Meanwhile, the true sons of Eire fought to raise funds to support Irish independence from England and assist the Fund for Destitute Women and Children in Ireland.

Harry Greb, seven years older than Art, won America's light heavyweight title in 1922 by becoming the only man to beat Gene Tunney. When Greb fought, Pittsburghers of all stripes traveled to his bouts in train coaches called "Greb Specials." Art started riding on them while he was in high school. Alcohol flowed freely, and the police were waiting when the train arrived. Greb taught Art how to fight and gave him a realistic glimpse of the toll exacted by prizefighting and the lush life accompanying it.

In the style of many champs, Greb "lived large," drinking heavily and engaging in liaisons with more than one woman at a time—sometimes in his dressing room before a fight. Greb fought 299 pro bouts. During the last hundred of them, he was blind in one eye and losing vision in the other. In 1926, he died of complications from surgery; he was thirty-two.

In 1920, Art and New Yorkers Sammy Mosberg and Frank Cassidy were the elite of America's 135-pound amateur class. In February, Art, the regional AAU champion, defeated Mosberg in Pittsburgh. An angry Mosberg refused to shake hands afterward. They fought again, two weeks later, in New York City.

Art skipped classes to travel to New York. He had an advantage in height and reach over his older opponent and forced the three-round fight from start to finish. Under Olympic rules, two judges decided who won. If they disagreed, the referee invariably ordered another round before casting the determining vote. Rooney and Mosberg exchanged flurries of hard shots, and when the judges ruled it even after three rounds, another round was ordered. Afterward, Mosberg won a controversial decision. When they met a third time in April, Mosberg again triumphed by referee's decision.

In July 1920, Pittsburgh hosted Olympic boxing regionals. The finals to select the U.S. team were held a few days later in New York City. This should have been Art's moment of triumph. But he skipped the regionals, even though he was the odds-on favorite to make the squad.

Four American fighters in the 135-pound class boarded ship for the Olympics in Antwerp—including Cassidy, who won the qualifiers, and Mosberg. By beating the other alternates on the voyage over, Mosberg become the second American lightweight in the Olympic tournament. In Antwerp, he won the gold medal.

Mosberg, a tough Jew from Brooklyn five years older than Art, was more physically mature and experienced. Spike Webb called him the greatest Olympian he ever coached. But Art had held his own with Mosberg.

Several accounts indicate that Art made the Olympic team but didn't go. The truth is that Art never tried out. Tim Rooney thinks he knows why. His father had been playing semipro baseball for money. At a game in McKeesport, he saw the head of the AAU in the stands. Tim believes that his father feared that if he fought in the Olympic trials, the AAU official would challenge his amateur status.

In 1912, Jim Thorpe had won both the pentathlon and the decathlon at the Stockholm Olympics in one of the most impressive athletic displays ever. But Thorpe was stripped of his medals when a story broke that he had played minor league baseball. The incident was a cautionary tale.

After the Olympics, Rooney had another go at gold medalist Mosberg at the PAA. The PAA's director was the same AAU official who had seen Art play semipro ball. "He knew that if he fought there," Tim Rooney explained, "this guy sure wasn't going to blow the whistle on him about playing baseball, seeing as he was asking my father to fight at his place." Before the fight, Rooney laid down one condition to the PAA: His Northside buddies would be welcome at the ritzy club. The boys, who crowded into a coal truck and arrived at the fight covered with soot, cheered wildly as Art beat Mosberg. Art's amateur status might have been secure that night, but the PAA's safe was not. It was cracked. "To this day," Art chuckled half a century later, "I think those guys feel my buddies did it."

Baseball 1920—Pathway to the Pros

Instead of traveling to Belgium for the Olympics, Rooney returned to Indiana. The dean of men, Walter Whitmyre, coached Indiana's baseball team. Art admired Whitmyre and babysat his children. The affection was mutual. "Arthur was one of my favorite students," Whitmyre remembered. He was on hand to celebrate one of Art's boxing triumphs.

Art was returning victorious from a boxing tournament. He took a train from Pittsburgh to Blairsville, where he was put in a caboose on a coal train to Indiana. When the train backed into town that night, the entire student body was out to greet him. Art was overwhelmed. He was especially surprised that the coeds' curfew had been lifted so that they could welcome him. Art had fought several bouts and it showed. "I had two big, black eyes, so big you couldn't hardly look through them," Art recalled. "In those days, we used to put leeches on our eyes to cut the swelling . . , I looked like somebody . . . from outer space." Whitmyre took one look at him and said, "Arthur, I thought you won the fight."

As the 1920 sandlot season began, politics kissed the hand of sport. Baseball's prospects hinged on whether Pennsylvania would reauthorize daylight savings time, a wartime measure designed to add daylight to the workday. Because few fields were lit, sandlotters needed daylight savings to play after work. Around Pittsburgh, sportswriter F. P. Alger wrote, baseball was the sole "enjoyment of thousands of workmen in the evenings after their hard labors." To hinder twilight ball was to thwart Americanism, the *Pittsburgh Post* declared. Baseball "brings the foreigner of the steel mill in direct touch with native born Americans, teaches him the language and the customs." Without it, the newspaper warned, "Pittsburgh will suffer."

Daylight savings was reauthorized and scores of leagues formed in Pittsburgh, many with factory backing. Company sport was a national phenomenon as industrialists experimented with ways to combat the absenteeism, turnover, and labor unrest that had plagued them during the war. Industrial managers provided English instruction, clean rest-rooms, and athletics to win employees' hearts and minds. While factory teams rarely achieved that goal, they energized local sandlots.

Highly sought after, Art played for several clubs that season. In the spring, he went back and forth between Phipps and Indiana Normal. During the summer, he played outfield for the Damascus Bronze Company and the Pittsburgh Collegians. Some days, Rooney had to remember which uniform to put on. About the most consistent aspect of Art's season was that he batted first. So did his friend, Cum Posey, who was taking the Homestead Grays to the top of Pittsburgh sandlots.

Dan, following in Art's athletic footsteps, caught for Phipps. Whether it was baseball, football, or boxing, Art left a daunting record for Dan to match. Dan, who was bigger and just as tough, invariably met the challenge.

At the end of a strong sandlot season, many local players signed pro contracts. "Nearly every kid you meet these days is slated to go to the minors next season," the *Pittsburgh Post* noted. Hugh Duffy, scouting Art for the Boston Red Sox, liked what he saw. In August, the *Post* reported that "Arthur Rooney of the Northside, left fielder of the Pittsburgh Collegians, yesterday signed a contract to report to the Boston American League club next spring. Rooney, who is a former A.A.U. lightweight champion, will do no more boxing, neither will he play football." Art's professional career was poised to take off.

Fall 1920—Double Duty

But Art changed his mind. Struck by the football fever sweeping post-war America and the sport's restoration at Duquesne, he returned home to play, if not necessarily to study. Art registered for courses in accounting, business, and law, but there is little evidence that he attended any of them.

Accustomed to playing for several sandlot teams simultaneously, Art agreed to play football for Indiana State Normal as well as Duquesne that season. Playing for two colleges at the same time was unprecedented, even for Art. Neither the press nor the colleges mentioned his double duty although it is hard to believe that it went unnoticed. Eligibility rules were often ignored. Cum Posey, for example, had routinely flouted amateur rules at Duquesne. Besides, Art was enrolled in Indiana's preparatory program, not its college, which might have allowed him to skirt the conflict.

Duquesne fielded several "tramp athletes" who floated from school to school, playing football but rarely attending class or even enrolling. Years later, at a reunion of Duquesne's 1920 team, the toastmaster provoked guffaws by recounting the days when the school enlisted ringers for tough out-of-town games. Pat O'Malley was on that squad. "My dad played on the Bluff," his son, the Reverend Jack O'Malley, confirmed. "I have pictures of him in his uniform, but I don't know how often he went to school." Pat and his brothers hired themselves out on weekends. "They'd go everywhere."

Duquesne's football comeback started poorly; Art's strong play at quarterback could not avert a 20–0 loss to Marietta. Two days later, Indiana overwhelmed the Punxsutawney Independents 39–0. Rooney "uses his head at the proper time and calls signals well," the *Indiana Evening Gazette* wrote. Art played back-to-back games in different cities throughout the season.

On October 15, he was on the Bluff for Duquesne's first home game, a 35–0 victory over Muskingum. "Stellar plays predominated," the *Duquesne Monthly* wrote, "but none of the spectacular flashes counted for more efficiency than the all-round work of Art Rooney, the resourceful little athlete who played quarterback for the victorious eleven. Art was almost a will-o'-the-wisp for the sturdy Muskingum tacklers." A week later, he played in a scoreless tie against St. Mary's of Emmitsburg, Maryland, then hurried back to Indiana to play Penn State's frosh later that day. He should have stayed home; Penn State crushed Indiana 54–0.

Indiana repeated as normal school champions. Art showed "unusual stuff," according to the yearbook, running 50 yards to score against Syracuse on the first play of the game and skirting right end for a 50-yard touchdown to upset Pitt 7–0. Duquesne, meanwhile, won two of its last three games, finishing 3-3-1. In all, Rooney played in 16 games that season. "Notwithstanding the fact that Art was in love throughout the entire football season," the Indiana senior class yearbook noted, "he was the individual star of the team." How Art had time for "love" remains unanswered.

Georgetown University

After the season, Art finally grabbed an opportunity that took him away from home. He was twenty when he headed to Washington, DC, in January 1921 and enrolled at Georgetown University. Not everyone believed Rooney would stay the course. "There is a rumor," wrote "Biff-Bang" in his *Pittsburgh Post* boxing column, "that Art Rooney will enter State College [Penn State]. Art is one of the best 135-pound boys that the amateurs ever turned out in this city." According to Art Rooney Jr., his father was offered part of the program concession to attend Penn State, a common arrangement at the time. But Art, intent on playing baseball, bet that Georgetown offered his best shot at the majors.

Georgetown was a baseball powerhouse. When tryouts began, Art was among 28 rookies on a 50-member squad. He registered to study law, but sport, not academics, propelled him. The *Hoya*, Georgetown's student paper, noted his arrival: "Rooney was wanted by the Red Sox, but at present is cavorting on the Varsity Field and looks like a real outfielder."

But when the season began, Art was glued to the bench. He never budged during the first four games, finally playing in an eleven-inning 5–4 victory over Fordham. Art walked his first time up but failed to get on base in his next two at-bats. The following day, Art walked and got his only hit of the season before returning to the bench.

Art chafed at watching others play in his stead. His roommate, who ran track, showed him around campus, pointing out different athletic venues. "And everything he's mentioning," Art's son Tim recalled, "my father says: 'Oh, I can do this.'" When they got to the gym, the roommate mentioned to physical director John O'Reilly, who also coached baseball, that Art boxed. O'Reilly immediately put him in the ring against Georgetown's fighters. "These kids were just college boxers, and before he was finished he had boxed the whole team," Tim said. "And he beat them all, one after another."

O'Reilly hired Art to give boxing lessons at Georgetown's prep school and gave him the chance in the ring that he denied him on the ball field. In April, while the Hoyas were playing baseball in Richmond, Art traveled to Boston for the national AAU championships as Washington's welterweight representative. "Pittsburgh," Art remembered, "put up an awful beef about it. They said that I was a Pittsburgher." His first two opponents at Boston's Mechanics Hall were Pittsburghers. "One was a black guy named Willie Murphy," Art recalled. "I always remember his name because Boston was predominantly Irish. He was black as the ace of spades." Art beat Murphy handily. His other foe was Jack Revesto, a top Pittsburgh amateur. Art beat him, too, but lost the championship. Dan, representing Pittsburgh, won the light-heavyweight silver medal.

Back at Georgetown, Art played a few more innings but his patience had worn thin. He concluded that he never had a chance at Georgetown; its team was already set. Confronting John O'Reilly, Rooney declared he was leaving. The physical director demanded, "Where are you going?" Art told him he was trying out for the major leagues. "You can't even make this team!" O'Reilly scoffed. "What do you think you're doing?" Art knew the answer to that. His interest in school and college athletics waning, he was going pro.

No Place Like Home

Art signed with Boston, who sent him to their Flint, Michigan, club. But he soon returned to Pittsburgh. Money had become more pressing since Prohibition had put his dad out of work. "I signed with the Red Sox for $250 a month, but I could make $500 a month barnstorming," Art later explained. "With all the coal miners and millers having their money on the line, an outstanding pitcher, for instance, could come in and get $100 a game."

But the 1921 sandlot season in Pittsburgh was a letdown, undercut by an abrupt, if brief, recession. Unemployment, virtually unknown during the war, soared afterward, and Pittsburgh endured a tough stretch. Factories curtailed sponsorship and spectators threw less into the passing hat. Sandlot baseball as a participant sport was gaining in popularity, but the money to pay players was drying up.

Art and Dan played for Phipps and the Pittsburgh Collegians that summer, with Dan joining Art in the outfield. The brothers were on the road for weeks at a stretch, as the Collegians made their way through the region. The club was one of the few that could survive by barnstorming. As he did for the rest of his life, Art relished traveling in the company of men. Life that summer consisted of ball games, rides through the mountains, and evenings spent in small hotels and bars.

Injured

Art would play his last college football game in 1921, for Duquesne. He registered to study law as he had at Georgetown, but as usual his energy went into playing ball. At training camp, he and Dan competed at quarterback. Dan got the nod, while Art moved to halfback.

Days before Duquesne's first game, the Rooneys led Hope Harvey to a 14–0 win over Monaca, with Dan scoring on a long run. Duquesne then held heavily favored Marietta to a 7–7 tie. The draw was costly; Art badly injured his shoulder. Perhaps he had played too much at too many different sports over the past five years. For Art, there was no off-season. He had been doing double duty during football and baseball seasons, combining college and independent play. In between, he had boxed, leaving scant time for his body to recuperate. But now, injury forced the issue. He was out for the season, and his shoulder would plague him for years. It limited his arm strength and probably cost him a shot in the majors. Athleticism had largely, but not entirely, defined this young man. Rooney had never been on the sidelines. He had no intention of remaining there, but the injury was sobering. Knowing he needed to think ahead of the play, Art assessed his options.

3

On Life's Learning Fields

1922–28

Prohibition sucker-punched the Rooneys. On January 17, 1920, the nation went dry, and the Rooneys were forced to close their Northside saloon. The family stayed upstairs, slowly accepting its diminished circumstances. Daniel was forty-six years old with few prospects; Maggie was a strikingly handsome woman of forty with seven children. Marie, the youngest, was two; Art, the oldest, almost nineteen. Their household included two orphaned relatives, and one of Maggie's sisters who helped with the youngsters.

The children would remember the time when Rooney's Café and Bar bustled with business as the happiest of their childhoods. But the now-shuttered saloon that had sustained them since 1913 quickly lost its charm. So did the Ward. Prohibition cost Daniel his livelihood and his place at the center of the Ward's social politics. If he was angry, he turned it inward. Prone to melancholy, Daniel soldiered on, but he was never the same. In 1923, the family moved to a house on Perrysville Avenue, on the hill above the Northside. The three oldest sons, Art, Dan, and Jim, stayed behind. Each of them was—or soon would be—setting the course of his life.

Prohibition shaped their choices and dramatically altered the atmosphere in which they made them. The Eighteenth Amendment, part of a postwar nativist backlash, took aim at the Irish, with their upward mobility and heavy drinking. But the Irish were not easily dislodged from the positions of power they had attained, especially in sport.

For Art, Prohibition slammed the door on his youth by criminalizing his father's profession. He would now contribute to his family's survival and help chart its future. Art maintained only the pretense of being a student. He enrolled in his last courses at Duquesne in the fall of 1922 but rarely attended class. Amateurism, meanwhile, had worn thin; Art needed to be paid to play. He competed as a semipro, brought home what he made, and looked for ways to earn more. He rejected minor league offers because sandlot ball paid better. By 1923, he had recovered sufficiently from his shoulder injury to reconsider major league baseball. But while playing ball, Art also pursued his fortune in arenas where Irish Americans held sway. His alternatives, while more diverse than those his father and grandfather had enjoyed, were nevertheless constrained by the Protestant backlash.

The Rooneys, deeply rooted in working-class Pittsburgh, knew what was plain to all Pittsburghers: a Scots-Irish, Presbyterian elite tightly clasped the city's industrial wealth and political power. The Rooneys—like many successful Irish Catholic families—occupied a middle ground between the elites and the immigrants from Southern and Eastern Europe who had flooded Pittsburgh by the 1920s. The Irish had made an uneasy accommodation with the old guard. In turn, they were allowed positions of authority—but only in endeavors that the elites relinquished to them. When the three oldest Rooney boys eventually stepped off the ball fields, each pursued a career where Irish Catholics had achieved success: Art in sport, Dan in the Church, and Jim in politics.

The Rooneys saw Prohibition as an attack on their way of life, an attempt to control and limit their behavior. Prohibition transformed the Northside and reconfigured its politics. By closing the pubs, it set adrift the sportsmen, workingmen, and politicians who had congregated at Rooney's Bar and Café. But it did not discourage immigrants or their wayward drinking habits. Instead, it triggered defiance.

Federal enforcement proved futile. In Pittsburgh, where the amendment had been roundly opposed, law enforcers pocketed bribes and winked at violations. Illicit speakeasies replaced Rooney's brightly lit saloon, facilitating prostitution and gambling. The Northside soon reclaimed its sinister reputation as "Little Canada," a vice-ridden territory beyond the federal law's reach.

The three oldest Rooney boys were caught up in the social chaos swirling around them. Each knew his way around Prohibition's netherworld, but they were never fully of that underground. Faith and family exerted an equal—although not always oppositional—influence on them.

Art grew up sharing his neighborhood's tolerance for bootlegging, gambling, and prostitution. Prostitutes, whom he greeted with a tip of his hat, were simply women working to get by. The rackets created entrepreneurial opportunities in which the city's "outsiders" collaborated. "If you couldn't be in with the 'ins,' you had to pull together with the 'outs,'" Art's son John argued. Gambling burgeoned into a modest-sized industry and, like sport, was more tolerant of race and religion than mainstream society. "Back in those days, 'bookmaker' wasn't a dirty word," recalled Msgr. Charles Owen Rice, Pittsburgh's Irish-born labor priest. "It was okay to gamble as long as you paid the man. After all, we are not Prohibitionists." During the 1920s, Art made his mark in this sporting life.

On their own turf, the Irish could either provide refuge for other immigrants or block their access to American society. As historians James Barrett and David Roediger put it, "Whether they wanted to save their souls, get a drink, find a job, or just take a walk around the corner, the newcomers had to deal with the entrenched Irish." While a barkeep in the Ward, Daniel Rooney had opened gates for immigrants. His sons followed suit.

For immigrants, sport provided a near-meritocracy in a country otherwise pinched by tightening intolerance. The sandlots belonged to Pittsburgh's many tribes—Rooney's Northside Irish, Cumberland Posey's Homestead blacks, and Paul Muzzio's West View Italians. These teams battled on the playing field, with fights spilling into the stands. But their clashes created a larger social solidarity. Sandlot contests validated both sides; the better the opponent, the more satisfaction one took from the game. Despite professional sport's continuing racial divide, the sandlots were forging a sporting fraternity where black migrants from the South competed with native-born and immigrant whites.

The Irish, as sport's gatekeepers, often opened doors to others. Irish émigrés had brought a sporting heritage across the Atlantic and adapted it to America with alacrity. Sport Americanized immigrant boys who had a foot in two worlds—one of their fathers, the other of secular

America—but it served a special role for the Irish. Their sons played ball and boxed as rites of passage and dominated both sports. As Art came of age, forty percent of top boxers, half of all major leaguers, and more than two-thirds of their managers were Irish American. In sport, Art's heritage was an asset.

Art was so good at three sports that he found it hard to specialize. He relinquished boxing first, after a handful of prizefights. His style in the ring was to go right at opponents, but that meant absorbing punishment from the older, tougher foes he faced as a pro. Art was en route to Australia when the wife of Australian champ Tommy O'Brien confronted him in the dressing room after a fight in Milwaukee. "I understand you are going to Australia to fight," she said. Noting that Art's background offered alternatives to the ring, she implored him not to go. "It's a rough place. It isn't like this America." Art remained in Milwaukee for a week before coming home. "She did me the biggest favor of my life," he reflected. Besides, baseball beckoned.

Wheeling, West Virginia, May 25, 1925

Art Rooney hopped into the batter's box, took a few swings, and glanced back into the Wheeling Stogies' dugout. The day before, his club had fallen into last after dropping a doubleheader to the Johnstown Johnnies. Losing infuriated Art, but the day had dawned brightly. From inside the dugout his brother Dan was mugging back at him. Dan had arrived in the gritty Ohio River town that morning after finishing the term at Duquesne. Wheeling's coach penciled him in as catcher, batting cleanup.

Art saw Johnstown shortstop Joe Cronin cheating toward second base to hold Wheeling's base runner close to the bag and centerfielder Rip Collins creeping in for a play at the plate. Seeing Collins so shallow in the outfield, Art slipped his grip to the knob of the bat and waited for a fastball. When he got one, he drove it back over Collins' head. By the time the centerfielder chased it down, Art had circled the bases. Teammates slapped his back as he returned to the dugout. Art looked at Dan and grinned; he scored three runs that afternoon.

The Rooney brothers frustrated opposing pitchers all summer long.

Dan was unstoppable, powering the Stogies to a string of come-from-behind victories, while Art was back at the top of his game. The shoulder injury that had cut short his 1921 football season had sobered the young Rooney, but he dared to hope again for a baseball career.

Wheeling played in the Middle Atlantic League, a new, highly competitive circuit stocked with prospects. The Rooneys played with confidence, outperforming Johnstown's two future stars. Centerfielder Rip Collins, from Altoona, would play for the St. Louis Cardinals' Gashouse Gang in two World Series, but Art was his match in the outfield that season. Shortstop Joe Cronin debuted with the Pirates the following spring and averaged over .300 in a Hall-of-Fame career. But Art and Dan outhit him.

The brothers had exceptional seasons, and Art figured that they would soon be major leaguers. Art led the league in games played, runs, hits, and stolen bases (an astonishing 58) and hit .369, only .003 behind the league leader. Art also hit for power, with twenty-six doubles, five triples, and eight home runs, reminding many why Boston and Chicago had come after him. Dan did even better. At the summer solstice, he led the league with a sizzling .415 batting average. After a seventeen-game hitting streak, the younger Rooney led the league in home runs, one ahead of Art. Blessed with considerable power and some speed, Dan finished third in batting with a .359 average and led the league with 35 doubles.

But the Rooneys' batting feats failed to lift Wheeling out of last place. With Dan catching and Art in centerfield, the Stogies were strong up the middle, but woeful elsewhere. The roster got so thin that Art had to pitch. An eight-game losing streak in July blew the brothers' fuses, and fights marred games. A spat that began on the field in Frostburg, Maryland, resumed afterward in a restaurant, with the Rooneys in the thick of it. Years later, Art told two of his grandsons that he could not attend their Washington & Jefferson College team's game at Frostburg. After the fight, he explained, the police had banned the Rooneys from the town forever.

Despite the season's frustrations, Art and Dan relished the camaraderie of traveling with a team. The league's geographic footprint covered part of the Allegheny Mountains and the rivers cutting through them. To get to games, players navigated narrow roads over thickly forested mountains, sometimes getting out to push their touring cars. Away from the decorum and the comforts that women provided at home, they wolfed down meals in roadhouses, played cards, and bantered insults. Too lazy to do their own laundry, the Rooneys simply threw away dirty clothes and bought new ones.

Art, who had been born in these coal-rich foothills, understood the railroad, mining, and mill families that saw them play. There was little distance between players and fans; all were working stiffs. Although the nation as a whole was prospering, in these hardscrabble towns, workers were losing ground. Prices for coal had plunged, provoking guerilla war in the coalfields surrounding Pittsburgh. Against a backdrop of grueling work, tragic accidents, and workplace strife, baseball brought respite.

Art hit his athletic peak during the mid-1920s. Pitchers knew the odds of keeping him off base were slim and that if Art got on base, he would look to steal. On the gridiron, defenders who tried to tackle him often clutched air instead. On the diamond, he battled future Hall of Famers Martin Dihigo, Oscar Charleston, and Smokey Joe Williams; in football, he held his own against Jim Thorpe and the Canton Bulldogs.

But late that summer of 1925, somewhere along those mountain roads, Art began letting go of his major league dreams. His baseball career had crested. He had played the best baseball of his life that season, but the scouts let him know—directly or by their silence—that he was no longer in their sights. Art could hit, run, and catch—three of the five tools that baseball desires in prospects—but he lacked power and never developed the arm strength to play centerfield in the majors. He wasn't going to join the elite fraternity of four hundred major leaguers.

Art and Dan's earnings from sport had been the family's source of support since Prohibition closed the saloon. By 1925, however, Art knew that his body could take only so much more punishment. He was good enough to make a living on the field but smart enough to realize his future lay elsewhere. He played baseball and sometimes managed teams for another eight seasons, until 1933. Dan and Jim often joined Art in the lineup for the Northside Board of Trade, Bellevue, the Ottie

Cochranes, and a team that Honus Wagner managed based in Denison, Ohio. Art was always paid, but baseball was his labor of love. It would not be his life's work.

Exploring Other Roads

Art and Dan returned home at the end of the 1925 season to rattle around the apartment above the old saloon. Their uncle John ran a quiet speakeasy in the darkened bar downstairs. Art faced a turning point. He had awakened from his baseball dreams, disappointed but not unprepared. He had considered alternatives since injuring his shoulder at Duquesne. That fall, while playing for Hope Harvey, he took a steely look at his options.

While sport remained his top choice as a means to make a living, politics, gambling, and horse racing were in the mix. In everything Art tried, he sought counsel from older men. In sport, he turned to Cumberland Posey.

Art had patterned his game on Posey's since they met at Duquesne, where Posey played basketball and baseball. Like Cum, Art was a centerfielder who relied on speed, toughness, and intelligence. But Posey was even more of a model off the field as a promoter. Over the next decade, Art barnstormed against Posey's Homestead Grays. Although major league baseball was segregated, semipro teams crossed the color line. Art and Cum's friendship—like their ballclubs—could not erase segregation, but they bridged it with humor and goodwill.

"One time, we were playing in West Virginia in a coal mining town," Art reminisced. "We were just a swing ahead of [the Grays], when one of their automobiles didn't show up. Cum called me on the phone and said, 'I need a player.'" Art obliged. "I sent him a kid, a red-haired Irish fellow," he said, laughing decades later at Posey's response. "[Cum] called me on the phone and said, 'Didn't you have something darker?' He was really something."

Indeed, he was. Romeo Dougherty, black America's senior sportswriter, called Posey "America's greatest Negro basketball player." Hall of Fame journalist Wendell Smith went further, dubbing Posey the outstanding black athlete of the 1920s. But for Art, the wiry, light-skinned Posey was more than a talented and versatile athlete.

He had played as a point guard and organized two basketball teams, the Loendis and Monticellos, that won national black titles during the 1920s. At the same time, he was taking the Grays to the heights of black baseball. Art would follow Posey's path from player to player-manager and finally owner. Just as Posey encouraged growth and stability in the Negro National League, Art would become a defining force in the NFL.

Posey modeled resilience, entrepreneurial talent, and a knack for organizing. Though he faced much tougher odds than Art would ever encounter, Cum taught him how to make his way in sport.

Football: 1925

Posey's influence was apparent that fall. Art would not let defeat drag him down. After abandoning major league baseball, he worked through his disappointment by playing football. And if he was going to play football, he was going to win.

That November, Art took a snap from center and cut to his left across Phipps Field. When his Hope Harvey blockers, brother Dan and buddy Mose Kelsch, leveled a pair of Bradley Eagle defenders, Art streaked untouched into the end zone. Later in the half, Art took the snap and lateraled the football to a teammate who faked a run and pitched it back to him. Art dashed to his right, saw a wall of defenders coming up quickly, and wheeled back to his left. Skirting the end, Art scored the second touchdown of the game. His third score, a quick burst through the line for 49 yards, delivered Hope Harvey's coup de grace.

The biggest sandlot crowd in years cheered wildly as Art tossed the ball to the official and trotted away. Rooney, the *Pittsburgh Post* exclaimed, had "dashed, dodged and squired his way to three great touchdowns, putting a hit of color into the contest." The paper called it the season's best display of open field running. On the sandlots, where scoreless ties were commonplace, Art's three touchdowns invited comparisons with Illinois' Red Grange.

Art, who also managed Hope Harvey, was beginning to appreciate the magnitude of Cum Posey's accomplishments as player, manager, and promoter. Sport's economics were unforgiving. Art and Northsider Chris McCormick, who was Hope Harvey's business manager, tried to professionalize operations, but they received little cooperation. When McCormick proposed games, competitors ducked him. Teams dodged tough opponents so that they could go undefeated far into the season and attract larger crowds. Balancing the books was no easier. After Art's three-touchdown performance, enthusiastic fans dropped $800 into the collection, but even this exceptional take spread thinly across thirty players, officials, and expenses.

Managing players proved equally frustrating. Absent player contracts, McCormick and Rooney ran around like sheepdogs, trying to keep men with the team. At Thanksgiving, undefeated Hope Harvey was preparing to meet undefeated Valley Strip and at the same time trying to stop the Strip from raiding its lineup. When the teams met, Mose Kelsch, who had played for Hope Harvey that season, wore Valley Strip's uniform.

No team wanted to see Kelsch across the line of scrimmage. When opponents wrapped their arms around him, he dragged them downfield. They could only hope that enough teammates latched on to pull Kelsch down with their combined weight. But Kelsch was no match for Dan Rooney. Dan's punts pinned Valley Strip deep in its own territory, and his touchdown pass won the game. Hope Harvey lost only once, 3–0 to the Burns A. A. before 5,000 fans in New Kensington, but the defeat cost it the regional championship, which went to Brownsville, a team that had ducked McCormick's effort to schedule a game.

The *Pittsburgh Post* selected both Rooneys for its 1925 independent football All-Star team. "Art Rooney, little Northside lad, had a great campaign and his spectacular playing earned him the quarterback position," the *Post* wrote. The All-Star selectors were impressed by what struck almost everybody who watched Art play: he was tough, preternaturally quick, and saw precisely what he needed to do on any play. "He was," the *Post* wrote, "well-drilled in the art of football." The paper called Dan the best sandlot kicker in years.

Despite the high caliber of play, most sandlot clubs lost money in 1925, unable to overcome bad weather and competition from college football. Both the sandlots and the pros badly lagged college ball at the gate and in the nation's psyche. The reasons were largely socioeconomic; sandlot and pro football resonated feebly outside the working classes.

Though the NFL had struggled since its creation in 1920, Red Grange gave it cause for hope by turning pro at the end of the 1925 college season. When Grange, college's most exciting, best-known player, finished his career at the University of Illinois, he signed with the Chicago Bears. The announcement sent adrenaline surging through the sporting world. Chicago would reward Grange handsomely—at least $100,000—for a whirlwind eighteen-game tour. The gamble paid off, and not just for the Bears. Grange, who drew fans like never before, gave the NFL glamour. Even Grantland Rice and Damon Runyon, who had previously snubbed the pros, graced the press box.

But one man could not close the class divide in football, and nowhere was it more apparent than in Pittsburgh, where workingmen played on the sandlots before working-class and immigrant fans. In this city—and in much of the country—the fissure that separated immigrants from the native-born was becoming the deepest social divide of the era. In Pittsburgh's blue-collar neighborhoods, sandlot teams forged strong loyalties among the foreign-born and non-Protestants. On the other side of the class divide was the University of Pittsburgh, a private school that played big-time football and represented Protestant Pittsburgh.

Jim Rooney

In 1925, Jim Rooney crossed the breach. Big, fast, and adept at passing and kicking, he was heavily recruited. Rather than follow his brothers to Duquesne, Jim, like most of Western Pennsylvania's best players, succumbed to the allure surrounding Jock Sutherland. An All-American at Pitt during the teens, Sutherland had returned to his alma mater in 1924 to coach. A Scotsman, Sutherland was not immune to the nativism surrounding him, but his desire to win tempered his prejudices. He sent Jim to prep for a year at Bellefonte Academy, a boarding school where Pitt recruits went to mature athletically. At Bellefonte, Jim befriended teammate Albert "Luby" DiMelio. A friendly, good-looking guy, DiMelio joined Jim at Pitt in the fall of 1925 and moved in with the Rooneys on Perrysville Avenue. As Art quipped, "They never had a cold bed there."

Pitt's freshmen rolled over opponents that fall, shutting out archrival Penn State with Jim running easily on a muddy field that sent other players sprawling. He boomed a 58-yard punt, scored a touchdown, and kicked two extra points. But like Art, Jim had an easier time finding his way to practice than the classroom. He made varsity the next season, but both he and Luby flunked out in 1927, infuriating Sutherland. Regaining their eligibility, Jim and Luby propelled Pitt's rise to the top the football world in 1928. As Sutherland's single wing quarterback, the 6-foot-2 inch, 210-pound Rooney called plays, blocked, and sometimes carried or passed the ball. He became best known as a kicker, arguably the greatest ever to play in the region.

Jim, the sweetest, most easy-going of the Rooney boys, was a junior in 1928. Tradition dictated that the juniors elect Pitt's next captain. Luby DiMelio was a team favorite, but Sutherland did not consider him acceptable. Although he encouraged players from Eastern and Southern Europe to Anglicize their names when they got to Pitt, Luby had not done so. Sutherland called Jim into his office and stressed the importance of electing the "proper sort" of fellow, which Jim took to mean an Anglo-Saxon fraternity boy. Jim said he understood.

At the postseason banquet at the PAA, boosters came wearing tuxedos. At the end of the evening, with the band playing "Hail to Pitt" and boosters clapping in unison, the juniors carried in a big silver football with their next captain concealed within. Slowly, they tore off the foil. "And who's sitting there," Jim chortled whenever he told the story, "but Luby, looking like he just got off a banana boat!" Sutherland, Jim recalled, was not amused.

Pitt rolled over opponents Jim's senior year. In October 1929, President Herbert Hoover welcomed Pitt to the White House. "The President should be a good quarterback," Jim commented. "He's got the brains, anyway." Hoover was at the peak of his popularity; within the month the stock market would plummet and with it, estimates of Hoover's intelligence.

When unbeaten Pitt was invited to play in the Rose Bowl, slapdash Jim darted to the train station at the last minute with only his shaving kit. But he had learned a few tricks from his brothers. Wherever the train stopped, Jim rushed to a haberdasher and bought a change of clothes. When his clothes got dirty, he tossed them out and stopped at the next department store. Luby, who shared Jim's sleeping compartment, was more frugal than his devil-may-care friend. Retrieving Jim's castoffs, Luby came home with a new wardrobe.

usc humbled Pitt in the Rose Bowl, 47–14. On the ride home aboard the Santa Fe Limited, the team stopped at the Grand Canyon. When players came down to breakfast at Hotel El Tovar on the canyon rim, Charles Lindbergh and his bride greeted them. Before returning to Pittsburgh, the players rode down to the Colorado River, sorely testing their mules. In Pittsburgh, they were feted at the Schenley Hotel and received their letters. Still miffed over Luby's selection, Sutherland unilaterally anointed Eddie Baker as the next captain. Baker, a buddy of Jim's, also bunked at the Rooneys.

Slim Hopes for Pro Ball

Art Rooney saw some faint hope for the nfl in Pittsburgh in Jim's incredible ride at Pitt. But while Pitt drew as many as 50,000 fans to Pitt Stadium, Hope Harvey was lucky to attract 7,000. Red Grange's leap to the Bears in 1925 jump-started the pro game elsewhere, but Pennsylvania's Blue Laws blocked commercial entertainment on Sundays, the only viable day for the pros. Dating to 1794, the Blue Laws reflected the Quaker abhorrence for breaking the Sabbath. High-profile athletic events charging admission were not permitted on Sundays; the Pittsburgh Symphony could not even schedule a Sunday concert. Nor could pro teams play on Saturdays, which belonged to the colleges.

Hope Harvey often played on Sundays outside the city, where the ban was routinely ignored, and sometimes risked Sunday games at Phipps. But in 1926, after five years of tolerating occasional Sunday play, the city clamped down. Hope Harvey's opener was among the games jeopardized.

Sandlot backers mobilized. "The oppressed sandlot football teams of

Pittsburgh have risen in protest," the *Pittsburgh Post* proclaimed. Art's business manager, Chris McCormick, chaired a meeting of the hastily formed Pittsburgh Association of Football Clubs. Speakers representing fifty clubs bemoaned the hardships imposed on men who labored six days a week but were denied the chance to enjoy sport on their day off. They argued that their games were not commercial ventures, with the gate barely covering costs. When players suffered severe injuries, teams staged benefits to cover medical expenses. The association adopted a defiant resolution and circulated petitions to mobilize support, but the ban stood.

Hope Harvey was forced to play its home games in Steubenville, Ohio, that season, and few Pittsburghers saw them perform. Art was especially annoyed with the Blue Laws when he secured a Pittsburgh game against an NFL opponent, the Canton Bulldogs, led by the incomparable Jim Thorpe. Though Thorpe was well past his prime, Canton was heavily favored to trample Rooney's sandlotters. Spectators saw a better contest than expected but its weekday scheduling limited attendance. Canton eked out a 3–0 victory, only the second time Hope Harvey had lost in two years.

"The Canton Bulldogs are not what they used to be, and the Hope Harveys are evidently more than they ever were," one writer concluded. Thorpe, who had intended to play only long enough to forge an insurmountable lead, never left the field. Still a hard man to bring down, he dragged three or four would-be tacklers with him when he had the ball. Thorpe was not the only one to impress. "Art Rooney, one of the famous Rooney family of grid stars," the *Post* wrote, "acquitted himself in splendid fashion." Though defeated, the Hope Harveys continued their season-long streak of not surrendering a touchdown.

The Bulldogs had given Art more than a payday with a topnotch team. They put him on the NFL's map. Tough, skilled, and smart, Art gained the Bulldogs' respect as a player and, more importantly, as a promoter. The NFL had its eye on Pennsylvania for new franchises, and Rooney had his on the NFL. Only the Blue Laws stood between them.

With Chris McCormick's assistance, Art began shifting roles. They ran Hope Harvey as a business, scouting opponents, turning down games with insufficient guarantees, and building a loyal following of North-siders who traveled to away games. Playing less and promoting more, Art took the field only when the outcome was in question.

In October 1926, Hope Harvey beat the undefeated Johnstown Collegians 14–0 at Ideal Park. As often happened, a fight on the field spilled into the stands. Johnstown Mayor Louis Franke persuaded the police not to arrest anybody. Instead, Franke escorted the team to the station, where he pulled Art aside. "Listen Art," he said, "my wallet got stole in the fight and I want it back with everything that was in it." Art said, "You know I didn't take it.'" Franke knew that. But, he said, "Whoever took it is on that train and you can get it back." Pulling a ring out of his pocket, Franke gave it to Art. "That's your brother Jim's ring." Jim had lost it in the fight. "Get me that wallet."

Art approached several "wise guys," as he called them, who were shooting craps on the train. When they feigned ignorance, Art told them, "You know who took it or you *will* know who took it. We go to Johnstown and do well. The mayor's a friend of mine, we play them every year, and I want to continue playing them every year. I want that wallet." When the train pulled into Pittsburgh, Art called the mayor: "I got your wallet with everything in it." Franke laughed and replied that he had told his wife, "That wallet is safer than if we had it in our safe at home."

Despite Art's efforts, the Hope Harveys rode a roller coaster during the 1920s. They returned to the Northside in 1927, but many of their players went elsewhere. The press still boosted Hope Harvey, hailing Art as the "field general" and the team as "his usual classy club." But it wasn't. In 1928, Art did not even field a team. He sponsored a lightweight club called the Rooney Reds, but neither played nor coached. Art understood the limitations that the Blue Laws imposed on sandlot ball. Meanwhile, he explored his options.

Other Mentors, Other Paths

For Art, the sandlots were the hub of a sporting life connecting ward politics, his father's saloon until Prohibition, and the neighborhood, including its racketeers. Wherever he went, Art encountered the same people. The men taking part in politics played on the sandlots and sat ringside at fights. They gambled in the illegal parlors that dotted the Ward, and attended Mass at St. Peter's. "You just didn't separate those things," Art's nephew Jamie Rooney observed. "They were all part of your fiber."

The mentors Art had collected since he had begun sneaking into his father's saloon frequented these venues. They saw in Art some of what his mother had seen on the day he was born: an Irish American golden boy—now confident, gregarious, and good-looking with a touch of roguishness. He deferred to his elders and expressed himself in feats of athleticism and kindness. The men befriending him were entrepreneurs finding their way outside Scots-Irish strongholds. With access to financial and corporate power blocked, they gathered on the edges of respectability. Like Cum Posey, they adopted Art and took him into the back rooms where the city's outliers brokered the crumbs of power the exclusive Duquesne Club crowd let fall from their tables.

Art grew up knowing the players in politics, racing, and the rackets, ventures where the Irish had clout. Rooney's saloon had served as a workingmen's Duquesne Club where politicians, sportsmen, and gamblers struck deals. Prohibition redrew but did not erase these connections. In critical ways, it strengthened them.

Politics—Lawrence and Coyne

As Art shaped Hope Harvey into Pittsburgh's top sandlot team, he was embedding himself in Ward politics. A trusted lieutenant of Republican Party boss James J. Coyne, he kept close ties across party lines with his boyhood chum, David Lawrence, who led the fledgling Democratic Party.

Politics, like sport, was a man's world, and Art had loved it since he was a boy. "Coming from the Ward . . . you knew politics from the day you were able to speak," Art once declared. "In the Ward, everybody knew about politics." And every Irishman, he added, was a politician.

In most cities where the Irish gained power, they gravitated toward the Democrats. In Pittsburgh, they planted their feet in both parties. The Rooneys were Republicans, which had been the party of laboring men *and* industrialists in the nineteenth century. The GOP had represented a coalition of interests, including those of skilled workingmen like Art's grandfather, Arthur, the ironworker who emigrated from Wales to the Southside. It subsequently became the vehicle for local elites but retained a working-class base in Pittsburgh, the most Republican of cities.

Around the dining room table, the Rooneys consumed politics along with ham and potatoes. While they might chew on the struggles in Ireland or the rights of labor, more often the discussion focused on jobs, alliances, and local campaigns. "For Irish Catholics coming to Allegheny County," Jamie Rooney observed, "politics was the venue to advance." Daniel Rooney had held a center seat until Prohibition bumped him out of it. "My grandfather owned a bar," Jamie Rooney reasoned. "That's as much social politics as you can get." An Irish barkeep heard stories, witnessed deal making, and often brokered peace and power. "My father," Art explained, "was very highly thought of by the politicians."

Art's political education—at home and in the Ward—prepared him to make his signal contribution to sport: helping the NFL become the most successful pro league in American history. Ward politics taught him how to trade favors, care for constituents, broker deals, and deal with blowhards. While much of Art's influence in the league was cloaked to the public, he created the kind of win-win deals he had learned to forge on the Northside. He knew how to get people to compromise and sacrifice immediate personal interests for the long-term collective good. He was patient and affable but tough when closing a deal.

Art's two Irish political tutors, one a Democrat, the other a Republican, completed his schooling. David L. Lawrence, twelve years Art's senior, and James J. Coyne, older by seventeen years, were larger-than-life figures who shaped Pittsburgh politics for much of the twentieth century.

As a boy, Art had admired Lawrence, a future mayor and governor. When Lawrence brought his teams to the Northside, Art followed him around like a puppy. "It would have been 1913, '14, '15," Art recalled half a century later. "I was always his batboy, ballboy, and waterboy." Lawrence was never the athlete that Art became, but they shared a passion for sport. "He had some of the best semipro teams around here,"

Art said. Lawrence also managed fighters, including Patsy Scanlon, a sparring partner who mercilessly pummeled the young Rooney in the ring. Lawrence, like Cum Posey, showed Art how it was done.

Lawrence was born in 1889 in the Point, the Irish neighborhood that took shape on the triangle of land where the Monongahela and Allegheny join to form the Ohio River. The Point was a jumble of modest houses, workshops, gambling dens, and rail yards. The "Point Irishmen," from rugged County Galway, worked in the city's burgeoning industrial economy while the women labored as domestics. Their Gaelic tongue struck native-born Pittsburghers—even other Irishmen—as rough hewn and foreign.

Lawrence's mother, Catherine Conwell Lawrence, had bottled whiskey and sold some of it to Daniel Rooney for his saloon. Davey, as he was called, and his brothers often rode the wake of stern-wheelers as if they were catching waves at the beach. Because the Point had few ball fields, Lawrence crossed the river to the Northside to play.

Lawrence had a long, rectangular face but sported a broad smile that rounded his cheeks, crinkled his eyes, and brightened his countenance. The magnetism in his eyes, the self-assurance in his carriage, and his unpretentious manners attracted people. Early on, Lawrence spotted Rooney's leadership qualities. As the boy became a man and the years between them shrank in significance, Rooney and Lawrence discussed politics along with sports. Their different party affiliations meant little; Art relied on Lawrence's political savvy as he fought the Blue Laws, flirted with a political career, and campaigned for a municipal stadium.

Art's other political coach was James J. Coyne. A state legislator from Oakland, Coyne caucused at Rooney's saloon with the men who swung votes on the Northside. With his florid complexion, small gray eyes, and fondness for big cigars, Coyne looked like central casting's model of an Irish American pol. Although he he was a member of the state house, not the senate, everyone called him the Senator. Coyne's personal charisma captivated Art and a cohort of men who stuck with him during his rise to power in the 1920s and long after his decline.

Coyne became a player by aligning himself with the all-powerful Mellon family, then led by Secretary of the Treasury Andrew Mellon.

Mellon, it was said, was the only Secretary under whom three presidents served. With holdings that made them one of the richest families in the world, the Mellons ran Pittsburgh.

William Larimer Mellon, cofounder of Gulf Oil and Andrew's nephew, was the dynasty's political point man. He used Coyne to mobilize constituents in working-class wards. Coyne, in turn, relied on Art Rooney on the Northside, Gus Greenlee on the Hill, and Pat O'Malley in the Strip District. These lieutenants were sportsmen as well as politicians. They respected Coyne, who was assertive, witty, and focused. "I thought he was a great leader and a tremendous person," Art said. Coyne crafted alliances based more on personality and dependability than ideology. "He did everything he could for his people," Art maintained. But Coyne could be tough. "You only lied to Coyne once and you only double-crossed him once," Art observed. "He never gave you another chance."

Art could be just as tough. A columnist, noting that Rooney "fears no person," described an incident after thugs threatened Art's lieutenants. "Art, alone, walked into their den and said, 'I understand you propose to beat up some of my friends. Why not start with me?'" Nobody took him up on his offer. But unlike Coyne, Art could be forgiving. A good judge of character, Art chose compatriots carefully, but once he accepted someone, he was loyal for life.

Coyne's alliance with the Mellons was understood as the price of doing business. "There may have been Senator Coyne from Galway running things politically," Art's son Tim explained, "but when it got down to rug-cutting time, the Mellons ran things." The tough-minded Coyne chafed at their power but bowed to it. "Coyne was the boss," explained Ed Kiely, the Steelers' long-time PR man, "but Coyne was Mellon's man."

Art told his son Tim about a call Coyne received from a top Mellon man while they were at dinner. The caller wanted Coyne to fill a government job with "'a good, church-going, Christian man.' It was obvious that they didn't want a Catholic." The Mellons were Northern Irish Presbyterians, not Catholics. "We never thought of the Mellons as Irish," Tim Rooney sniffed, and the distinction was clear to both groups. Nonetheless, the Senator toyed with the caller. "'I have the perfect guy for you," he said. 'His name is Francis Xavier Muldowney and he goes to Mass and Communion every day.'"

Coyne earned trust in working-class Pittsburgh because he belonged there. Born in 1882 in the Galway countryside, Coyne worked in England before joining most of his fourteen siblings in Pittsburgh. He drove a team of horses, labored in the mills, and worked construction. Although he attended night school, Coyne's real education came in ward politics.

Coyne controlled a speakeasy, the Monaca Club, conveniently located across from the Oakland police station, from which police delivered confiscated liquor to the club. The personable, fun-loving Irishman became the Fourth Ward's boss by knowing how to trade favors. According to his nephew, Philip Coyne, people knew "that you just had to go to him to get a truck to deliver coal to you." Coyne dispensed aid to Irish, Jewish, and Italian constituents, who faithfully backed his slate of candidates.

Lawrence and Coyne molded Art's political sensibilities, teaching him how to be an Irish Catholic in a town run by Presbyterians. Perhaps most importantly, they and his father taught him loyalty.

When Ward leader John O'Donnell put up a candidate against an aging alderman, Abernathy, who was dying from diabetes, Art was tempted to act for the sake of expediency. If Abernathy died in office, a judge would select his replacement, and that replacement would not come from their ranks. As Art and another committeeman were heading to vote for the party's replacement, Daniel Rooney spoke up. "I will tell you," Daniel said, "he was the alderman here before most of you were born. He has been good to everybody. Just because he is not going to make it . . . well, it would be a terrible thing for all of you to put up opposition." Art decided his father was right and persuaded O'Donnell to stand by Abernathy. "If he makes it," O'Donnell concluded, "wonderful. If he doesn't, we can get along without the alderman for six years." Abernathy died two weeks later, but for Art, staying loyal mattered more than keeping power. He would regard loyalty as an absolute.

Art became the Ward's Republican chairman in the late 1920s and used the position to stitch together his far-flung connections. The job so suited Art that Ward residents came to him with their problems long after he had relinquished the office. One old lieutenant called him every night for decades to report on doings around the Ward.

Prohibition, Bootlegging, and the Rackets

In Prohibition Pittsburgh, politics and the rackets were joined at the pants pocket. Betting parlors, speakeasies, and brothels operated brazenly, stuffing police and politicians' coffers. So many gambling houses did business on the Northside that they divvied up the nights of the week to do business. Little Canada is back, the *Post* proclaimed about the Northside in 1926. "Here is all the color and lawlessness, all the vice and romance, all the sordidness and squalor of the nights when Eddie Guerin, back from his desperate escape from Devil's Isle, strutted the gas-lit streets with blond Chicago May and hobnobbed with the Albany Kid."

Northside vice turned deadly when a Chicago syndicate tried muscling in. By 1932, police were investigating a hundred gangland slayings. One fatality, Maurice Curren, was killed doors away from the Rooneys on Perrysville Avenue. Curren, who sold sugar and yeast to bootleggers, had foolishly ratted out his clients.

Despite the syndicate's bravado, Pittsburgh racketeers and police refused to surrender. Legend has it that Art threw a couple of Chicago toughs into the Allegheny. Chicago's gangsters, Ray Sprigle wrote, were not tolerated in the dripping wet Northside, especially the Ward, which sheltered a third of the city's eleven hundred speakeasies. The *Pittsburgh Press* investigative reporter estimated that the rackets generated $10 million annually in payoffs. With so much at stake, Pittsburgh politicians and police partnered with local racketeers to keep both sides flush and Chicago out.

As Coyne's lieutenant, Art was privy to much of what was going on. But was he corrupted by it? There are only a few clues to suggest how deeply the Rooneys dabbled in illegality. What Art's father Daniel did to support himself during Prohibition—from 1920 to 1933—remains shrouded. In the 1923 city directory, Daniel said he was in the soft drink business. So did Daniel's brother John. In September 1923, Daniel Rooney and Edward McKeown paid the astounding price of $100,000 for the Independent Brewing Company in Braddock, a Monongahela River mill town. Four months later, McKeown sold his share of the property for $1 to the newly incorporated Home Beverage Company, in which he was a partner with twenty-three-year-old Art and J. C. Hazelbaker. Was the Home Beverage Company bootlegging? In 1927, police raided a distillery suspiciously close to it; in 1928, John Rooney was cited for running a speakeasy in his brother Daniel's old saloon.

Certainly, the Northside was awash in Prohibition booze, and the Ward flooded with it. Art knew the geography of speakeasies, stills, and nightclubs, and he ran with bootleggers, numbers men, bookmakers, and thugs for much of his life. Nor did he repudiate any of them. "I touched all the bases," Art often said. But Art was clean enough—or smart enough—to avoid being tagged out. He wasn't the only one.

Joe Carr, a Northsider and Art's first NFL hire, also sidestepped trouble. As a youth, Carr played piano on a floating speakeasy that cruised the Ohio River. When he had enough saved to buy a car, he visited aunts who summered as domestics in Ontario and returned with carloads of booze. "The Northside was wide open," Joe's son Hugh reported. "An entrepreneurial teenager could make a buck." Art's brother Dan made similar runs, according to their sister Margaret Rooney Laughlin. Dan drove trucks full of empty barrels up north. They were full when he returned.

These few facts and secondhand memories construct a skeleton that has been dressed up with any number of Rooney legends. The truth can only be surmised. There is no doubt that on the Northside, sport, politics, Prohibition, and the rackets converged. Local politicos often met inside Nettie Gordon's well-appointed brothel.

A savvy entrepreneur who owned considerable property, Nettie donned a stylish hat and gloves every Monday for her stroll to the bank with the weekend's cash, which she had ironed and sprinkled with perfume. Nettie was also a Republican committeewoman, so influential that Northside police ignored repeated orders to close her brothel.

Nettie kept one manicured hand in politics and the other in vice, illustrating a point that the press made about Pittsburgh: "In every ward and every precinct, the man who handles the vote is the man who handles the bawdy house concessions and the gambling privileges." The ward chairman dictated racketeering in his district; nothing operated without his say-so. As a player in ward politics, Art lived in this world.

Sporadic crackdowns and newspaper exposés targeted Art's buddies. In July 1926, the *Pittsburgh Post* fingered Mose Kelsch, Art's sandlot warhorse, for running a speakeasy, slot machines, and prostitutes. Police raided Kelsch's Cosy Corners Inn after his piano player shot a woman and shut it down after they uncovered that plans for a fatal holdup had been hatched there. But Kelsch's legal entanglements never kept him off the field. Nor did the law bother Art's friend Milton Jaffe, who received top billing in the *Post's* "Roll of Shame." At Jaffe's bawdy house in the Ward, patrons could order "high test" beer injected with a shot of alcohol and rent a room upstairs with female companionship for three dollars.

Local officials did little more than skim profits from vice, federal agents even less. Secretary of the Treasury Andrew Mellon, whose portfolio included Prohibition enforcement, failed miserably in his hometown. The area's first director of Prohibition was indicted for taking payoffs. Five of his successors were indicted or quit. Bootlegging, meanwhile, scarcely missed a beat. Efforts to stop the flow of booze were episodic until June 1928.

That summer, a federal grand jury completed a nineteen-month probe that heard from twelve hundred witnesses and provoked city-wide anxiety. The jury indicted 167 Pittsburghers, charging them with a gigantic plot to defy Prohibition. Among those accused were the superintendent of police, three police inspectors, two state legislators, thirteen police lieutenants; and five ward chairmen. Four of the five, including Art's close friend John O'Donnell, ruled Northside wards.

The probe alleged a vast conspiracy of police, politicians, and bootleggers. The Northside was hit the hardest, with seventy-three indicted. No Rooneys were mentioned, but O'Donnell's arrest cut close. A widower, O'Donnell sent his daughter Edith to boarding school, but she spent her summers and holidays bunking with Margaret and Marie

Rooney on Perrysville Avenue. Art had enough friends under indictment to field a team, including the O'Malley brothers—Pat, the Strip's ward chairman, Thomas, and Mark ("Moo"). Pat and Moo had played football with Art.

When the indictments against the Northsiders meandered to trial in November 1928, the prosecution's case fizzled. After twelve days of testimony, the judge interrupted proceedings and directed the jury to acquit for lack of evidence regarding a conspiracy. Several defendants were subsequently retried and convicted, but by then Prohibition was wobbling toward its inevitable demise. When Democratic presidential nominee Franklin Roosevelt campaigned at Forbes Field in the fall of 1932, the crowd's biggest cheer came when he called for Prohibition's repeal. After FDR's election, the Eighteenth Amendment was revoked, violence ebbed, and what reporter Sprigle called "an orgy of crookedness and crime and graft" quietly ended.

Half a century later, Art remained tightlipped about the ties between politics and the rackets. "Maybe [racketeers] contributed to the campaign and all that," he said, "but they had absolutely no other connection . . . I don't say that they operated without our knowledge." His brother Jim was less circumspect. "There were all kinds of rackets: the numbers, bootlegging, speakeasies, sporting houses," Jim said. "They all paid off. If they didn't pay, they didn't open." Jim joked that when he was a legislator, he advised new members to make sure they had a transom above their office door so payoffs could be tossed in after hours.

Certainly, the Rooneys were splashed by the illegal booze that doused the Northside, but no evidence supports fables of Art's extensive involvement with bootlegging. Even if he had been, the standards at that time would not have judged him harshly. Prohibition was wildly unpopular in Pittsburgh, and few Irish Catholics regarded bootlegging as immoral. Some priests and rabbis even ordered outsized quantities of exempted sacramental wines to better serve their congregations. But if federal agents had evidence that Art or his family were major players, Art's stature would not have protected them from the 1928 federal indictment that charged 167 people, including the chief of police.

Gambling

During his twenties, Art honed his most lucrative skill: gambling. He told his sons that he had started early, standing across a craps table from revolutionary Pancho Villa in a Mexican border town when in his teens. His father Daniel introduced him to the horses at Cleveland's Maple Heights at about the same time. Daniel may also have given Art a backhanded lesson in gambling's pitfalls when he suddenly sold the family's Ohio River hotel and disappeared, apparently to dodge debts, while Art was a toddler. Daniel's gambling probably caused many of the family's ups and downs. His name was periodically scrubbed from deeds of family properties in a series of sales that ended with Maggie as the sole owner. If these maneuvers were designed to evade claims against him, they taught Art a lesson he took seriously. Art shared his father's love of gambling but not his recklessness. He learned to walk away if he was losing.

"Dago" Sam Leone, one of Art's earliest acquaintances, encouraged his fondness for the ponies. During World War I, the Army fingered Sam for the cavalry after he bragged about his knowledge of horses. But Sam was a bettor, not a rider, and he ended up mucking out stables. After the war, Leone settled back into his professional life: working dice games, dealing poker, and hustling pool with Art's brother Dan.

Sam raved about the Rooney brothers to his gambling buddy Milton Jaffe, who shared the outsider status that Art appreciated in his friends. The son of Jewish immigrants, Jaffe had grown up in the Hill District, an integrated neighborhood above downtown. His brother George ran nightclubs and burlesque joints. Milton ran on his wits.

Jaffe was living near Senator Coyne when Leone brought Art over. Jaffe was unimpressed. He later told Art's sons that their father had shown up wearing a varsity letter sweater with a bad case of the *schpilkes*—a Yiddish word that roughly translates as "ants in the pants." Jaffe razzed Leone for bringing Joe College by, but Art grew on him. Art was twenty-one when Jaffe began teaching him his craft. Jaffe, a wizard at calculating odds with a keen eye for cardsharps and scammers, found that Art caught on quickly. He sharpened Art's ability to "play face," the quick capacity to judge character and veracity so important to gamblers. "Jaffe was a partner with my dad in the gambling business," Art's son Dan confirmed. By the time the kid with *schpilkes* was in his late twenties, he and Jaffe were running the Showboat.

Docked on the Allegheny River near the Sixth Street Bridge, the classy floating nightclub featured illegal liquor, gambling, and top entertainers on layovers between New York and Chicago. Years after it closed, Art was dining in New York when Groucho Marx sat down nearby. Art stretched over and asked him, "Do you remember Milton Jaffe of Pittsburgh?" Groucho smiled and said, "Do you guys still have that river boat?"

"Milt had know-how and pizzazz," Art Rooney Jr. said. "My father had the connections." Both men had a knack for seizing opportunities, and they combined their talents. Rooney and Jaffe started taking the train to the Kentucky Derby each May. "By the time they got there," Art's son Dan said, "they would have broken the whole train playing craps." At Churchill Downs, they headed straight for the bookmakers' circles.

Art also hooked up with William "Gus" Greenlee in the 1920s. Greenlee had arrived in Pittsburgh in 1916, during the great migration of African Americans out of the South. After serving overseas during World War I and running liquor during Prohibition, Greenlee opened the Crawford Grill, a premier jazz club. Seated at the bar, "Big Red," as he was known because of his complexion, chomped on a cigar and oversaw the books for his club and the illegal numbers game he ran. Art frequently took up a stool beside him, chomping on his own cigar. Like Rooney, Greenlee had his hands in many pots. Along with the Crawford Grill, he directed one of the city's largest numbers banks and was a Coyne lieutenant.

Greenlee was known in the Hill for his philanthropy. In 1926, he bought uniforms for a youth team sponsored by the Crawford Bath House. As the Crawfords became a serious ballclub, Gus took them on. In 1930, when Greenlee sought Art's advice about taking the Crawfords professional, Art encouraged him. Soon, Greenlee's Crawfords were challenging Posey's Grays for bragging rights in black Pittsburgh.

Greenlee recruited the best black ballplayers in the nation. He lured a lanky right-hander named Satchel Paige to town and raided the Grays, taking Oscar Charleston, Judy Johnson, and twenty-year-old catcher Josh Gibson, who had gotten his start on the Crawfords when they were still a sandlot club. Paige and Gibson formed baseball's most legendary battery, and Greenlee's backing allowed the Crawfords to vie for national black baseball supremacy. The Crawfords and the Grays made Pittsburgh the center of black baseball during the 1930s and 1940s.

Bad Timing

In 1928, with the grand jury handing down indictments, Art did not play baseball. Instead, he went to Florida and tried bookmaking at Hialeah Park. But he was a better bettor than bookmaker. After a bad run at Hialeah wiped out his $20,000 stake, he borrowed $100 and built it back. It didn't last long. He was down to $250, enough for him and a friend to return to Pittsburgh. Someone tipped him to a "paddock special" and he went for $200. He lost. "Well," Art later said, "I figured we might as well be stone broke as have fifty and so I took the fifty and won a bet and then ran it up to twelve thousand." He wanted to book again, but couldn't afford the track's fee. "So I bought up the stand of another book who had gone broke," Art recalled. "It must have been an unlucky stand. We blew the twelve thousand that day and started to take the kinks our of our thumbs for the hitch-hike home." He came home broke and despondent.

The perennial optimist had been knocked down—like his father and his grandfather—by forces largely beyond his control. The sporting life seemed stacked against him. But to the surprise of many, sandlot football rebounded in 1928. Sportswriter Fred Alger declared it the greatest of all seasons and Art returned to the fray in 1929. He was ready to make a risky bet—that pro football might capitalize on the popularity of college ball. His timing could not have been worse. On October 29, 1929, the stock market crashed. The Great Depression had begun.

4

Dreams, Depression, and Commitment

1929–33

Art Rooney often recalled the morning he began working at a blast furnace. At the break, the nineteen-year-old asked his uncle, Michael Concannon, who had gotten him the job, how much he made as a foreman
after fifteen years. The answer unsettled him. "I can make more than
that playing baseball," Art replied. He left without collecting his half-
day's pay. Art liked to say he had never worked a day in his life. For him,
work was play. Sport bound his life together and set his daily agenda. He
calibrated the seasons by the shape of the ball in play. Although American sport was taking on the trappings of business in the 1920s, for Art,
it was always more about camaraderie than bottom lines.

Approaching thirty, Art's muscles remained taut, but his earnings
as an athlete were waning. He had bid farewell to the gridiron, not entered a boxing ring for years, and was nearing his final at-bat. Still, he
never seriously considered pursuing a living in any arena than sport.
In every sport he played, Art had overcome his lack of size by squeez-
ing through openings. He had inherited his grandfather's "batting eye."
That vision allowed him to slip between defenders on the gridiron and
spot a hole in his opponent's guard in the ring. Now he had to find that
opening off the field.

Generations of Rooneys had pounced on opportunity. Art's great-
grandfather James had sailed from famine-ravished Ireland to Montreal, where he honed his ironworking skills and carried them back
across the Atlantic to Ebbw Vale. His grandfather Arthur left Wales
when steel production rendered those ironworking skills irrelevant. By
coming to Pittsburgh, he bought himself another decade as a craftsman.
When Pittsburgh's iron industry succumbed to steel, Arthur opened a

saloon. His widow Catherine watched where factories opened along Pittsburgh's rivers and ran boarding houses nearby. Art's father Daniel followed suit, operating saloons and hotels. Like many immigrants, the Rooneys were blue-collar entrepreneurs, taking risks and struggling through setbacks.

In 1928, Art had flopped at making book in Florida but figured out what he did best in life—play the ponies. He began to study handicapping with more diligence than he ever exhibited in school. At the same time, Art moved to professionalize sandlot football. But even as his commitment to football deepened, Art hedged his bets, dabbling in boxing, dog racing, and hockey.

The Art of Promoting

"It looks as if Art Rooney means business with his Hope Harvey team this year," Fred Alger wrote in his *Sandlot Grid Gleanings* column before the 1929 season. Seeking to stabilize his team's finances, Art filled his lineup with well-known ex-collegians and tried to schedule NFL opponents. He also found a sponsor, convincing the Majestic Radio Company that it could win goodwill and sell radios by underwriting his team. The company furnished new leather helmets and green uniforms with white stripes down the arms and "Majestic Radio" embroidered across the chest.

Art courted the press but had no need for a public relations firm; he was his own best publicist. He befriended sportswriters, who helped him gain recognition. When Art scheduled a game with West View, a team across the river from the Northside, the press ballyhooed the impending contest between these "sturdy sons of the sandlots." By kickoff, Expo Park was packed. The press also helped Art book games. The *Post-Gazette's* Alger threw down the gauntlet, declaring that any club seeking regional honors had to best Rooney's Majestics.

But that fall, the stock market nosedived from its dizzying heights. For the moment, Pittsburghers could still afford their distractions, and football prospered despite the gloom unfolding off the field. Runners-up to the McKeesport Olympics as the 1929 champs, the Majestics were the region's top independent attraction. Art's attempts to spruce up the game were working, and the semipros enjoyed their most successful season in years.

During the off-season, Art contended with Prohibition's haphazard enforcement. In the early morning hours of May 15, 1930, federal agents raided the Showboat, the floating speakeasy and gambling parlor docked downtown. As agents rushed aboard, revelers fled, dumping hip flasks on the floor, stuffing betting rolls down their pants, and knocking over a roulette wheel. Local officials expressed "shock" at finding gambling and liquor onboard. Milton Jaffe, the club's owner, was arrested and charged with violating gambling laws, but Art, his silent partner, avoided implication.

That summer, muckraking journalist Walter Liggett targeted several Rooney associates in an exposé that called Pittsburgh the "Metropolis of Corruption." Mose Kelsch got in trouble again, this time for a stickup. Raids and arrests made headlines, but prosecutors lacked the will to follow through. The Showboat, Mose Kelsch, and the "Metropolis of Corruption" were soon back in business.

The 1930 Season

Despite the deepening depression, Art resolved to make football profitable. He spearheaded the creation of the West Penn Conference, featuring the region's best heavyweight squads, to elevate sandlot ball's profile. In order to duck Blue Law enforcement, Art begrudgingly moved the Majestics to the Bridgeville Speedway outside town. He arranged for game-day bus service from the Northside and added Bridgeville players to attract local fans. Part of the gate from each game went to relief efforts.

The Majestics received better coverage than any team except Pitt and Carnegie Tech. A half-page spread featured "Those Majestic Rough-Riders" with player headshots pasted on the shoulders of bucking bronco riders. Art, wearing his trademark Irish cap, was at the center of the layout. Writers touted their games, and stories about Rooney's "Irish" squad grew longer and more glowing, even as crowds grew smaller.

Unable to entice an NFL team to Pittsburgh, Art lined up Fritz Pollard's nationally renowned Chicago Colored All-Stars. The press reported that Art was responding to the black community's demand for such a game, but fans of all stripes boosted turnout. The Majestics won, further burnishing their image.

With Jim Rooney, flanked by the burly Mose Kelsch and the elusive Jimmy Levey (an ex-Marine who violated his baseball contract with the St. Louis Browns to play), the Majestics hardly needed Art on the field to win the West Penn Conference championship. They hoisted its Honus Wagner Trophy, named for Art's hero, the Pirate shortstop whose photo would hang in his office. The papers ran a photo of the victorious squad with their mascot, eight-year-old Tommy, seated at the feet of his brothers Jim and John Rooney.

The *Post-Gazette* named Jim Rooney the region's top player and captain of its 1930 All-Star squad. "Rooney," it crowed, "was the life of the Majestic team, running the team to perfection and outclassing all other kickers." It was no wonder that NFL clubs wanted to sign him. Art took the field just once that season—his final appearance on the gridiron—against archrival West View.

Sportswriters called the West Penn Conference's inaugural season the realization of a dream, but it had been a fiscal nightmare. The Depression was inescapable. The leading clubs paid players an average of $40 a game, a good payday at a time when a working coal miner averaged $76 per month. Still, no player quit his day job—if he had one. Discounting Art's efforts to professionalize sandlot football, sportswriter Fred Alger called the season a financial debacle. The conference, he claimed, had been a sad financial mistake with teams losing about $2,000 each. But if Art was discouraged, he was too busy to acknowledge it.

Multiple Commitments

Complicating his life further was Kathleen McNulty, a Northsider whom Art had known since she was a girl. Kathleen was now making Art turn his thoughts to a family of his own. Six years younger than Art, "Kass" was the daughter of John McNulty, who made pickle and cracker barrels for the Heinz factory on the Northside and market houses downtown. The Rooneys and McNultys had known one another for years, and some said that Art's brother Dan had bootlegged beer in McNulty's

74

barrels. When Art was still a student, darting in and out of Pittsburgh, boxing and playing ball, Kass McNulty occasionally caught sight of him. She thought he was a charming and handsome athlete, but Art hardly noticed her.

Very little outside Art's manly world of sweat and cigar smoke ever distracted him. But when Kass McNulty blossomed into a willowy young woman, Art found reasons to call at her house whenever he came home. He escorted her to the Showboat where he introduced her to Groucho Marx and Imogene Coco, with whom he allegedly had a brief flirtation. Dazzled by Art's sophistication, Kass was also impressed by the unpretentious way he greeted celebrities, politicians, gangsters, and hatcheck girls, all with the same ease and respect. In fact, Kass would later say, she liked just about everything about Art except the way he blew his nose. His jealous warnings about the "jerks" she dated while he was away tickled her. To Kass, Art Rooney was head and shoulders above the competition, and she was only waiting for him to make his move. But Art hesitated. He was at ease in a man's world, and succumbing to feminine charms felt as uncomfortable as a scratchy tweed suit in July.

Art's reluctance to settle down was as ageless as courtship itself, but its duration had a uniquely modern quality. During the 1920s, women bobbed their hair, put on pants, and bound their breasts to look more like boys. More than appearances changed. They also drove and worked more outside the home, which gave them greater independence. While their mothers would have caused a scandal by entering a saloon, younger women frequented speakeasies. And while the older generation expected a marriage proposal to follow a man's first romantic expression, the Jazz Age generation was embarking on a new institution: dating. The Rooney boys took young women to movies and clubs without contemplating immediate commitment. If that behavior puzzled their parents, young people found dating fun, even if they remained somewhat confused about its rules.

Art's faith and values survived the tumultuous 1920s, even as the generation that had brought them from Ireland passed on. Catherine Rooney, Art's grandmother, died suddenly in June 1925, a month after buying a home in Pittsburgh's West End. A widow for almost a quarter

of a century, Catherine had run the family's boarding houses. A cun
ning businesswoman, the Rooney clan matriarch had counseled her
sons on major decisions. Art's grandfather Michael Murray, the hot-
tempered coal miner, died the next year. Art saw his generation moving up a notch, poised to take over a world that had changed radically
since the Rooneys had arrived in Pittsburgh.

Brothers Rooney

By the mid-1920s, Art, Dan, and Jim no longer shared the apartment
above the saloon. Dan left first, heading to Panama in the fall of 1926
to play baseball. His career was picking up where Art's had left off. The
best North Americans played winter ball in Cuba, with Panama several
rungs below. Dan dated a girl there, and at home, he often took out Julia
Vaughan, the sister of sandlot teammates. But Dan also began talking
with Father Michael O'Shea at St. Peter's parish house about stirrings
he felt toward the priesthood. As Father O'Shea clarified his options,
Dan was drawn to the Franciscans. Modeled on the simple life of St.
Francis of Assisi, the Franciscans took the vow of poverty to mean that
they should give away everything—all worldly goods and family relationships—and die naked and alone.

In 1927, Dan enrolled at St. Bonaventure, a Franciscan school in upstate New York. He played football there as "Mike" Rooney, a ploy
to get him on the field even though he had exhausted his eligibility at
Duquesne. "Mike" cocaptained the team, played fullback, and punted.
His contemplation of the priesthood, however, had not quieted his notorious temper. It erupted one day with teammate and fellow Northsider
Dave Packard. Packard was a "tramp" athlete who boasted of playing
tackle for thirteen colleges over nine seasons. But this afternoon, he was
doing such a lousy job blocking that Dan confronted him in the huddle. Packard whined that he was doing the best he could. That was all
Dan needed to hear. When the huddle broke, Packard lay unconscious
on the field, and Dan signaled the ref that a man was down. Packard
should have known better. Dan had decked him once before when they
played at Duquesne.

Tales of Dan's temper were commonplace. In the summer of 1928, he came home to play baseball for Bellevue, a township bordering Pittsburgh. During one game, the Homestead Grays' future Hall of Famer Smokey Joe Williams beaned him. Knocked down, Dan leapt to his feet and chased Williams off the field.

Such displays did not trouble the scouts tracking him. The Cincinnati Reds had given Dan a tryout in 1927, but he was not ready to sign. After the 1928 season, both New York and Cleveland offered contracts. Dan, however, had decided on another calling. "The New York Yankees is a fine ball club, and you do me great honor with your offer," Dan wired the team. "However I cannot accept it. I am entering the priesthood." Turning his back on a $5,000 signing bonus and the chance to play with Ruth and Gehrig, Dan returned to St. Bonaventure and joined its Franciscan order.

Eighteen months later, Jim Rooney made his own career commitment. John O'Donnell, 22nd Ward chairman, accompanied Pitt on the train back from the 1930 Rose Bowl. A solemn-looking man with big, sad eyes behind round wire-rimmed glasses, O'Donnell sat down next to Jim. "He asked me if I wanted to be in the legislature," Jim later recounted. O'Donnell's backing assured the party's endorsement, and with Republicans ascendant in Pittsburgh, that was all he needed to win election. Jim nonchalantly accepted. "I didn't think much of it at the time," he recalled.

While at Pitt, Jim had earned $25 a night carrying a derringer and working as a bodyguard for his brother and Milton Jaffe. He sometimes picked up a few dollars playing semipro football on Sundays in Ohio, a fairly common practice by college players. Jim was, by nature, the sunny, less aggressive younger brother. He never took himself as seriously as did Dan, nor was he as rough. He had Art's skills with people, and, like all the Rooneys, was generous. Jim, who took a breezy attitude about money, was known on the Northside as the guy who tipped a streetcar conductor $20 to let him off between stops.

During the 1930 election campaign, Jim captained the Majestics on weekends and pressed the flesh during the week. Tall, handsome, and known from football, he outpolled his Democratic opponent six to one for the Seventh District seat in the state House of Representatives. Only twenty-five years old and still enrolled at Pitt when he took office in January 1931, Jim was the youngest legislator in Harrisburg. His political science professor, who lost his bid for office in the same election, asked Jim, "How can you, one of my students, win and I got beat?" Jim responded, "If you want to get in, you have to know the boys." He meant that you had to know the right people, especially the politicians. The Rooneys knew them all.

Depression, Booze, and the Blue Laws

Hailing him as the gridiron star destined to become a political "big shot," the press carried Jim to Harrisburg in a sedan chair. "Diplomat Rooney," one journalist raved, "has acquired the political touch early."

In keeping with his expansive personality and the Rooney approach to politics, Jim eschewed ideology in favor of practical measures that would help people. He boosted his strong support among working people by championing their right to drink beer on Saturday nights and play ball on Sundays. He introduced a resolution calling for Pennsylvania to petition Congress to amend Prohibition to permit four percent beer. Jim voted for every pro-labor measure that came before the House, including one of his own calling for the assumption of interest payments on loans to World War I veterans. Jim also attended to constituents' needs during hard times, canvassing residents armed with cash for groceries and coal. One paper called his district the best organized in Pittsburgh.

In the interest of working folks as well as his brother, Jim pushed to loosen the Blue Laws by allowing Sunday play for pay anywhere local voters approved. When the *Sun-Telegraph* ran a "postcard vote" to gauge reader sentiment, over 30,000 respondents favored ending Blue Law prohibitions on play, while fewer than 6,000 opted for the status quo. What had seemed a distant prospect in the early 1920s now loomed on the horizon.

"All in all," one journalist wrote, "Captain Rooney has been rolling up gains on the legislative gridiron at almost every try." Jim, like Dan, had escaped Art's formidable shadow. With Art working more behind the scenes and Dan in the seminary, Jim was the Rooney featured in the press—with one notorious exception.

Miles's Murder

On January 19, 1931, another Rooney stole the headlines. The night before, Art's uncle Miles, his father's youngest brother and the family's wild child, had hooked up with a Northside buddy, James Soldan, at a nightclub. They then went to Miles's apartment above a speakeasy. Soldan, the press reported, told Miles that he intended to kill his own brother. Hearing that, Miles grabbed Soldan's gun and refused to give it back. They struggled and Miles, thirty-eight, was shot dead. Family accounts, however, suggest that they fought over a woman.

Miles had recently been fired as a policeman after he was found wandering drunk in the Strip, far from his Woods Run beat. He was subsequently arrested for assault and battery and carrying a concealed weapon. Art's father, Daniel, had often given his younger brother the dickens for his recklessness. But when Miles was shot, Daniel had him laid out at the house on Perrysville Avenue.

It was quite a wake. Northside madam Nettie Gordon placed an ostentatious flower arrangement by his casket. Agnes, Miles's sister, took offense and moved the flowers into a corner. Someone moved them back, and a silent tussle sent the arrangement back and forth throughout the wake. Maggie baked hams while Art and his brother Vince carried home baskets full of bread for sandwiches. Entertainers and guests arrived after the Showboat closed, and the wake lasted until dawn. In the morning, Tommy Rooney came downstairs crying that someone had stolen his piggy bank.

Political Missteps

As the weather warmed up that spring, so did pressure on Jim in Harrisburg. Rooney's athletic reputation did not shield him from criticism when he proposed that Pittsburgh's school board, whose appointed members served without pay, become an elected and salaried body. Newspapers, chiding Jim's "outrageous impertinence," attacked his bill as a ploy to gain control of the board's budget and patronage jobs, which it was.

Editorials demanded "No Rooney-izing of the Schools!" while writers took aim. "The young lawmaker was never much for knowing his lessons it seems, and former schoolmates recall that James occupied the last seat a good deal of the time," one columnist wagged. "At Pitt practically everything except football was all Greek to him."

Realizing he was beaten, Jim let the measure die in committee. But he had sustained damage and was attacked as a mouthpiece for the Coyne machine. The press smacked him again when he opposed a bill to allow Pittsburgh to opt for a city manager form of government. Jim shrugged off the criticism, boasting, "I am not a reformer, and do not favor reform movements."

That spring, when Northside Republican ward chairmen caucused to select a candidate for a city council slate that was part of Coyne's push to consolidate power, Art persuaded them to run Jim. City council would suit Jim more than the legislature because it offered access to patronage jobs and the chance to steer city contracts.

After the slate was announced, Art Rooney and numbers baron Gus Greenlee met Coyne in a back room at the Crawford Grill to discuss the campaign. They were huddled around a table when a young woman sashayed in and whispered a plea for money in Gus's ear. Gus shooed her away. "That's not the way you talked last night, honey," she snapped. Hooking the cigar out of his mouth, Gus looked her in the eye. "Last night was last night," he said. "When I'm hard, I'm soft. When I'm soft, I'm hard. Beat it." The woman turned away, and the men returned to politics when an ashtray whizzed past Coyne's ear and crashed against the wall. After that, the Senator insisted they meet in Oakland.

Rooney and Greenlee's ballclubs boosted Coyne's candidacy and that of district attorney Andrew Parks, who had gone easy on Milton Jaffe and Mose Kelsch. Rooney's Northside Civics and Greenlee's Crawfords sported uniforms emblazoned with "Coyne for County Commissioner" and "Andrew Parks for District Attorney." But it was to no avail. The 1931 primary was unusually vicious. The twelve Republicans running for the two county commissioner spots attacked each other as common criminals and despotic bosses. Despite his party's endorsement, Coyne finished fourth.

Meanwhile, the Brotherhood of Railroad Trainmen backed Jim for council, saying he had always given labor one hundred percent support.

Jim had voted to abolish the notorious coal and iron police, repeal the Blue Laws, and allow the sale of wine and beer. Jim's ads stated that "He Has Made Good In Every Public Trust," but the public mistrusted his association with Mayor Charles Kline and Senator Coyne. In a cartoon about city hall corruption, the press caricatured Jim and his council slate as "Hear no evil, see no evil, speak no evil" monkeys. He was narrowly defeated.

The balance of power within Republican ranks was shifting, and Art Rooney and John O'Donnell found their clout waning. Their ally, Mayor Kline, was indicted on forty-six counts of malfeasance amid charges of massive electoral fraud. Some indictments struck close to home. The press reported that a thousand names from the Rooneys' ward, each written in the same hand, had been added to the voting rolls one weekend when the office was closed. Three campaign workers for the candidate who exposed the attempted fraud were assaulted.

"My father idolized Rooney," explained William Good, whose father Leo served as his committeeman. "In his mind, there was no better." But politics could be rough. "If your candidate was losing an election, you went in and burned the ballot boxes," Good recalled. "No one thought anything of it. Whatever it took, you did."

After losing the primary, Coyne—and Rooney—backed Democrat David Lawrence in the general election. Coyne, who grew up on an Irish farm, lived in Pittsburgh's Oakland district but owned a farm on Babcock Boulevard, north of the city. Lawrence owned an adjoining property. When Coyne, Lawrence, and Rooney conferred at Coyne's farmhouse, class, nationality, and religion outweighed party differences.

While Lawrence lost the election, he tallied an unprecedented number of votes for a Democrat. Lawrence sensed where things were heading. Coyne was on the defensive and the Republicans would pay dearly for holding office during a depression. Coyne, Art later reflected, had limited power. "He could never elect anyone. All he did was beat you. He was powerful that way." But his power and that of the GOP were fading. After the primary, Art played baseball and went to the Kentucky Derby. Upon his return, he made quick plans to leave town again.

Married in NYC

Art was not the only man admiring Kass McNulty and her long, lean figure and her stylish clothes worn with flair. Lush dark hair set off her fair skin, sweet smile, and a pretty face that she fretted over because an automobile accident had scarred it slightly. Demure with strangers, Kass displayed a charming wit to those who knew her. And Art had been getting to know her better and better. He began to get the jitters in the spring of 1931 about the "jerks" ringing Kass's doorbell every time he left town. If he did not act soon, he realized he would lose her. And Art hated to lose.

Kass, a clerk at the Joseph Horne Department Store, was twenty-four, old enough for marriage. However, her father was unimpressed with Art as a suitor. John McNulty considered Art a poor prospect. Instead of having a business or profession, Art played games, gambled, and ran with thugs. Miles Rooney's murder and the raid at the Showboat had done little to soften McNulty's impressions.

Kass admired her father, who had raised the family since his wife's death, but she resisted him. For years she had consumed romantic novels that took her heart and imagination to exotic locales while her real-world horizons remained restricted. By contrast, Art's blue-collar sophistication and gregarious ease impressed her. She believed his ambition and accomplishments offered possibilities far beyond her father's imagination. Although Art hid his vulnerabilities, she understood that his impatience was balanced by empathy.

Kass was crazy about Art and accepted his proposal. For his part, Art had courted Kass with a passion he usually reserved for sport. Hurried along by love and the demands of the racing season, Art and Kass caught the train to New York City, where Wall Street still lay devastated by the crash. Art's buddy George Engel—who had managed boxing champ Harry Greb—met them at the station and stood as best man at a civil ceremony on June 11, 1931. They married in defiance of John McNulty and the church they both revered. Elopements were commonplace during the Depression, and Art and Kass hated being the center of attention, as they would have been in a family wedding. Even so, a civil ceremony was highly uncharacteristic for these deeply religious

Catholics. Their impetuous behavior perplexed their families and would puzzle their children.

Two days later, the couple attended the Belmont Stakes, an event they would not miss for the rest of their lives. They watched Twenty Grand take the purse in the third leg of racing's Triple Crown. But "ten grand" was every bit as memorable. After the newlyweds checked out of their room the next morning and joined George Engel for breakfast, Art realized that he had left his $10,000 bankroll inside a hotel pillowcase. Art and George dashed upstairs but the bed had already been stripped and the linens shoved down a laundry chute. Rushing downstairs, they concocted a story about a lost object of great sentimental value, which they presented to the head of housekeeping. Although dubious, she let them search a bin of dirty laundry where they found the pillow case and the cash.

If Kass had any illusions about the man she had married, their honeymoon painted an unmistakable portrait. Belmont was, as Kass discovered, the first stage of a coast-to-coast, track-to-track honeymoon. "We stopped at every racetrack from here to Tijuana," Kass remembered. They rarely traveled alone. George Engel joined them for the first leg of the journey, and other buddies, including sandlotter Harp Vaughan, who acted as a bodyguard, met them along the way.

Harp also watched a few racehorses that Art was taking along on the train. Art found Harp in the car with the horses one day, cleaning a shotgun. "Are you crazy?" Art asked, grabbing the gun and tossing it off the moving train. Harp was furious, shouting how much the shotgun had cost. But Art stood his ground. "They'd put us in jail and we'd never get out," he said, ending the argument. "Use your brains and your fists."

In San Diego, Art and Kass stayed at the Old Grand Hotel, an elegant place to which they often returned, and visited Tijuana's frenetic Agua Caliente racetrack across the border. Kass, who had dolled up for her first trip abroad, became anxious when they stayed late. She warned Art that the border crossing would close for the night. "Don't worry," Art reassured her. Kass was unconvinced. "We're going to end up stuck in this place," she retorted, looking around as the skies darkened and the border town grew more sinister. Sure enough, the crossing was closed when they arrived.

"Come on," Art said, heading along the border fence to a place where immigrants had bent up the wire mesh. Art motioned for Kass to crawl under. She might have stamped her foot in indignation, but her choices were limited. Crawl under the fence, ruin her dress, and risk arrest, or stay the night in Tijuana. Kass scooted underneath. They returned to the hotel with a memory Kass would share with her children.

Art and Kass might have dated and married in a modern fashion, but underneath they held more traditional attitudes. Art assumed, and Kass apparently agreed, that she would adjust to his world. From the time Art had been a toddler in his grandmother's hotel on the Ohio River, his mother and aunts had taken care of his domestic needs. He took for granted that his plate would be full at dinnertime and his clothes clean on laundry day.

The Rooney and Murray women commanded the spheres that men relinquished. They derived strength from their interdependence in the family, not from the kind of independence that the 1920s "new woman" vaunted. They held their families together with faith and frugality when rough times or gambling debts took the bread from their tables. They managed homes, raised children, sent them to school, and taught them their prayers. The Murray women had instilled in Art a Catholic faith so powerful that the church's rituals marked the rhythms of his life as much as the rituals of sport. His sister Margaret often found him praying when the nuns took her class to St. Peter's Church for Mass. When his mother Maggie had fallen ill during the flu pandemic, Art prayed inside St. Peter's from the time the doors opened until the sanctuary closed that evening. Maggie recovered, and for the rest of his life, Art attended Mass daily, prayed novenas, and said the rosary.

Kass knew that Art's unconventional life would govern hers. She called him "her traveling man" and accepted from the start that he would leave her alone as often as he blew his nose. But she never doubted that his fierce fidelity would keep him faithful wherever he roamed.

When Art and Kass returned from their honeymoon, they were married again at St. Peter's Church after a stern scolding from the priest.

According to family legend, Kass did penance by kneeling at the altar rail during Sunday mass. Art's penance—if there was any—was less memorable, or at least less public.

The 1931 Season

Despite taking a financial shellacking, the West Penn Conference roared back for an encore in 1931. "Never before in the history of the game," *Press* reporter Tom Birks wrote, "has the sport got away to such an auspicious start." Cheerleading by the column inch, Birks noted that "fans and cleat wearers are all agog for the start of another season." Paul Kurtz tempered his colleague's enthusiasm, believing hard times would undercut the season.

Unfazed by its failure to break even, the Conference added the Homer Laughlins, a team sponsored by the East Liverpool, Ohio, pottery manufacturer that soon began marketing its popular Fiestaware line. They turned down another six clubs seeking admission and set up seven affiliated conferences of younger, lightweight teams. Unemployment had left many with time to play ball.

As Art had hoped, the conference stabilized independent football. Its balanced schedule allowed teams to better promote the season. He again tried to lure NFL opponents to Pittsburgh, and set his sights on the New York Giants, whose owner Tim Mara he knew from the track. The *Pittsburgh Press* reported that Art had scheduled a game at Forbes Field. "It has been his ambition to have Pittsburgh entered in the National Football League and this may be his first move in that direction." The contest would gauge Art's ability to compete with the pros. He negotiated with Mara in Manhattan, after they watched Primo Carnera defeat Jack Sharkey for the heavyweight championship. Although willing to schedule exhibitions to boost revenues, Mara decided against a midseason clash with a tough opponent like the Rooneys that could leave his team battered.

Crippled by the Depression, Majestic Radio withdrew support for the team. Art quickly renamed it the J. P. Rooneys to boost Jim's visibility. Despite Jim's city council defeat, Art banked on his brother's political fortune rebounding. In the meantime, he pinned his hopes on

Jim's football prowess. "The popular North Side sportsman is going to build his club around the educated toe of Brother Jimmy," Tom Birks wrote, echoing the consensus that Jim was the conference's top player. "His generalship left nothing to be desired, his throwing of passes and carrying the ball was not surpassed, and he always has been rated the greatest punter Pitt ever had." Nor did Jim's legislative duties ever interfere with football.

Besides Jim, Art counted on several of his brother's buddies from Pitt and on Northside sandlotters Harp Vaughan, Mose Kelsch, and John Rooney. They practiced at night outside the Clark Candy Factory in the Ward to take advantage of its lights but had nowhere to play games in the city. Unable to reach agreement with the Pirates or Duquesne University, Art moved games back to the Bridgeville Speedway.

The club got off to a fast start against the Dan Burns, drawing 9,000 fans to a match in New Kensington, which ended in a 7–0 Rooney victory when Mose Kelsch bulled across the goal line for a touchdown. After defeating McKeesport 3–0 in front of 8,000 fans on Jim's field goal, the Rooneys took on their primordial foes, West View. "The North Side Senator" accounted for all their scoring in a 9–0 win.

With Jim quarterbacking and booming 70-yard punts, the press called the Rooneys the unstoppable Big Green Machine. Sportswriters treated them as if they were an NFL squad and debated Art's use of players, especially veteran Kelsch. "Artie has not been working Kelsch much," one explained. "If you'll pardon, he's not being groomed for the junior prom, but for those home-stretch contests which the Northside's 'Mayor' is desirous of copping."

The rematch with West View presented the perfect spot to unleash Kelsch. One of the oldest and paunchiest players on the sandlots, Kelsch was a hard man to bring down. He had the body and face of an English bulldog with a soft openness about the eyes that suggested a sweet aspect to his nature—but not on the field. Pittsburgh fans loved tough running backs, especially ones willing to run into the teeth of the defense. With the crowd yelling "Let Mose carry the ball," he did, making most of the team's sixteen first downs. "Kelsch, who was never bedecked in college toggery, showed how a fullback should pick up yardage," one writer enthused. He took advantage of former Duquesne star Ray Kemp's blocking. A native of Cecil, a nearby coal mining patch, Kemp was one of the conference's few black players. The game was scoreless with time running out when Kemp addressed Kelsch in the huddle: "Come through my place, Mr. Kelsch." Mose did just that as Kemp cleared the way. The Rooneys' victory clinched their second conference championship. The "Big Green Machine" had surrendered only one touchdown all season and drew the biggest crowds of any club on the road, as thousands of Northsiders followed them and created a home-field feel wherever they played.

Hard Times

The Depression walloped Western Pennsylvania, hitting steel and mining towns especially hard. By 1933, as the downturn reached its nadir, more than one of seven white and two of five black workers in Pittsburgh were on relief. Along the rivers, where steel mills barely exhaled, the average workweek was cut in half and U.S. Steel ran at fourteen percent capacity. Young people took to the road, fathers abandoned families, and the homeless built a ramshackle "Hooverville" in the Strip District.

Witnessing this devastation, Art committed football to relief efforts. Football was a solace to people down on their luck and unable to get a drink when they needed one the most. Art lined up a benefit game with Ernie Nevers' All-Stars to end the 1931 season. Nevers was one of football's all-time greats, and his team was a solid draw. But Nevers reneged, and Art substituted a match with a conference All-Star team with proceeds helping to feed people. If the Rooney boys had internalized any lessons from the Baltimore Catechism, none was more evident in their behavior than its Corporal Works of Mercy. Art knew that whatever success he achieved promoting sport came from the threadbare pockets of working stiffs, and they were hurting.

Young women wearing sashes reading "Surplus for the Needy" circulated during the game, which was played on the winter solstice. Firemen volunteered to direct traffic, the park waived its fee, and players and the

Pittsburgh Letter Carriers' Band played for free. The scoreless outcome was less important than the show of support for the community.

Art embodied that spirit as a ward leader. A go-to guy for those in need, he rarely turned anybody away. He intervened in emergencies and got food or coal to families in difficulty. As unemployment and under-employment became more commonplace than holding work, the 22nd Ward Republican Club staged benefits at its Cremo Street clubhouse. Art conducted a neighborhood survey and supervised relief efforts.

Art marshaled pallbearers for funerals and quietly paid for funerals to ensure that even the broke and friendless had proper sendoffs. "The people were poor," Art explained, "and probably the only time a lot of them ever had a ride in an automobile was going to the cemetery when someone died." Art commandeered caravans of cars to the cemetery and back to the wake afterward. "People would hang onto the car's running boards," he recounted. "We'd arrive at the graveyard, and everybody would scatter." Many went to visit their own relatives. "Then you would hear them hollering the *caohine*, which is the old Irish cry. It was fantastic . . . You could hear them hollering the *caohine* all over the graveyard . . . Coming back, everybody stopped at least once to get a drink."

The Ward's wakes attracted revelers from all over. "Some of them were just professional moochers, but everyone would be there. It'd last for three days, and it would be like a carnival," Art remembered. "One time," he said, "the wake lasted so long, we ended up just putting the deceased outside the door, in the street." For the Irish, wakes hearkened back to the countryside and folk religion. For Art, they were part of his sense of duty to the Ward.

As the season closed, the sport pages crowned Jim Rooney the region's best all-around player. *Post-Gazette* sportswriter Harry Keck asked Jim if his team dominated because they were better trained, practiced more, and fielded former college stars. Jim laughed at the question. "We seldom practice . . . and we do very little training," he told Keck. "And the best player on the team [Mose Kelsch] never wore the spangles for a college team and doesn't know what it is to train." Kelsch by now had taken on the status of local legend. "Unstoppable," Jim said, "the best natural football player I have ever seen."

88

At Pitt, Jim had played in Jock Sutherland's punishing single wing offense and endured hard-hitting practices daily. "I realize now," he admitted, "that many times I went out on the field all tightened up physically and mentally . . . I felt so stiff when game time arrived that my uniform seemed to be too tight on my body and I felt as if I would like to rip it away." It was different now. "I get a kick out of playing the game for the game's sake." Keck painted Jim as a philosophical but down-to-earth athletic hero, happier now than when he had played at Pitt.

Other Seasons, Other Sports

Football alone never exhausted Art's energies. Politics, promoting fights, and the racing circuit were constants. But he now added something new. In July 1932, he became the father of Daniel Milton Rooney, whom he named for his father and his buddy Milton Jaffe.

Jaffe had been in the headlines. He was getting into his car outside St. John's racetrack in Jacksonville, Florida, when two men jammed guns into his ribs and said, "Not your car—this one." Pushing him into a nearby vehicle, they sped off. Milton's brother George received a ransom demand the next day.

In Pittsburgh, the press speculated that the abduction was payback for heavy losses incurred at the Showboat: "It is known that Eastern gunmen threatened him here several months ago after men well known in theatrical circles had lost heavily." George Jaffe went to Hot Springs, Arkansas, a notoriously wide-open town where ballclubs often trained, and ransomed his brother back for $30,000.

That summer of 1932, Art played baseball and searched for ways to support his family. Art and James Egan, a Boston promoter who managed the Bridgeville Speedway, announced plans to bring dog racing to the site, which sat dormant for much of the year. Though dog racing was forbidden in Pennsylvania, Art figured he could finesse the law.

A 30-day racing program was announced for August, with betting on a pari-mutuel basis. Most betting was still done with bookmakers, who set odds on a race and stuck to them. Pari-mutuel odds, however, reflected the amounts bet on each entrant in a race and kept changing until a bell cut off wagering. As a bettor, Art preferred bookmakers. But as a promoter, pari-mutuels allowed him to take his cut as a percentage of the total bet before the winners were paid.

There was one obstacle: Governor Gifford Pinchot unequivocally opposed dog racing. Art, believing he could convince local authorities to look the other way, announced that some of the proceeds would go to local relief and hired seventy-five unemployed men to prepare the track.

After three hundred greyhounds arrived, hundreds of fans attended a free racing card the night before the season was to begin. But District Attorney Andrew Parks, a Coyne ally for whom Art had campaigned, was forced to intervene. While Parks would have tolerated gambling, he could not ignore the governor. Parks told Art that he could hold races but not accept wagers. Since nobody cared about dog racing without betting, the races were cancelled.

Art knew when he was beaten. He and Egan tried instead to buy the Pittsburgh Yellow Jackets of the International Hockey League. The franchise had been in receivership after its owner, politician Roy Schooley, was incapacitated by health and legal problems. Bidding for the franchise required Art to engage in complex financial dealings. Previously, he had negotiated little more than $1,000 guarantees for sandlot games. In August 1932, the Pennsylvania Trust Company, which held the franchise's assets, approved the takeover. Art's offer included a five-year lease to play at Duquesne Gardens and the assumption of $75,000 in club debt. He arranged for loans and negotiated an agreement to operate the team pending the National Hockey League's approval.

Art went to New York to seal the deal with Bill Dwyer, who owned Pittsburgh's NHL territorial rights. He offered Dwyer a piece of the action not to exercise his veto, but Dwyer hesitated to relinquish control of his territory. Frustrated, Art retracted the offer. By then, the possibility of an NFL franchise loomed larger.

Football 1932

The J. P. Rooneys were rising to the top of the sandlots while Pittsburgh's economy was collapsing. At a preseason meeting, forty candidates in search of twenty roster spots showed up at Chris McCormick's home, spilling out on to the sidewalk. Western Pennsylvania, the most fertile source of gridiron talent in the nation, was overstocked with players.

Art turned over coaching to Jim, who had declined offers to play in the NFL that season. As the Rooneys prepared to defend their back-to-back conference championships, Art knew that financial viability required finding a home field. Although many Northsiders had traveled to the Bridgeville Speedway, the facility was too far from the Ward to attract large crowds. He entertained a bid to play in Erie, but not seriously. For Art, the closer to the Ward the better.

Pittsburgh's Oakland section, where the Pirates, Pitt, and Carnegie Tech played, had two suitable venues: Pitt Stadium and Forbes Field. Pitt Stadium was a magnificent bowl, but the university held professional football in contempt and would never rent to semipros. Forbes Field, the second-best option, could be reconfigured for football, but it had few good seats and the Pirates feared damaging their field.

So Art turned to his buddy Gus Greenlee. After assembling the Pittsburgh Crawfords, which rivaled any team in baseball, Greenlee had built a ballpark on the Hill to showcase their talents. Greenlee Field, the finest black-owned field in the nation, had opened for Negro League baseball that spring. Art met Gus at the Crawford Grill and quickly hammered out an agreement to play there.

The Rooneys dominated play, shutting out their first six opponents and capping their third championship season by defeating inmates at the Rockview State Penitentiary. Even so, attendance was down. Pittsburgh's economy had hit bottom, and for the first time in its history, U.S. Steel lost money. The average steelworker's wages provided only half of what he needed to maintain a healthy standard of living, leaving little for entertainment. The game with West View, normally a big draw, had netted $61. Afterward, Paul Muzzio pulled the plug on West View's season. So did the Dan Burns after their game with the Rooneys in New Kensington brought in $300, down from $4,000 two years earlier. Art's club had not lost a game since their opening day defeat in 1930, but success on the field was not translating into profit.

Jim Crashes

Meanwhile, Jim Rooney ran for reelection in 1932, declaring his unequivocal support for the people's right to play on Sundays and drink anytime. He easily won the Republican nomination, but that was not enough in the general election. The Depression had turned the tide, and local Democrats rode FDR's coattails to victory in November 1932. A huge Democratic turnout buried Jim and other Republicans.

At least the Democrats adopted the causes that Jim had championed. Prohibition was on its last legs and Blue Law reform inevitable. Art felt confident that soon, perhaps within the year, he would get the chance to stage the Sunday games he needed to join the NFL.

Art quietly negotiated for an NFL franchise, assuming that Jim would quarterback his squad. But sometime after midnight on March 22, 1933, Jim, boxing manager Albert "Irish" Kane, and Northsider James Toth were traveling on the Lincoln Highway (Route 30) near Bedford, Pennsylvania. Jim intended to rendezvous with Polly Lux, a Philadelphia actress, and announce their engagement. He never arrived. With snow hindering visibility, the vehicle skidded on an icy curve and slammed into a brick wall.

The three men lay unconscious until a passing motorist found them. Toth, who the press identified as Trotch, Troth, and Tost but who was known on the Northside as "Ticky Tock," escaped with a concussion. Kane, respected for how he treated fighters but not for any great success in boxing, never regained consciousness and died from a fractured skull. The local fight community held a benefit to pay for his funeral, the crowd standing silently as the timekeeper tolled ten to honor their colleague.

Jim lay in a coma for days. With a fractured skull, dislocated hip, fractured knee, and crushed chest, he was given little chance of recovery. But he eventually awakened to find his family and Polly Lux at his bedside. Jim survived but never married or played ball again. Even with a built-up shoe, he walked with a limp and endured pain from the injuries for the rest of his life.

"Jim was a tragic figure," his nephew Tim Rooney reflected, "an Irish tragic figure that Eugene O'Neill could have done a good job with. When I'm talking about tragedy, I'm talking about having ability and not succeeding. Jim was a very intelligent, extremely well-liked, man, and he should have been very successful in life." But things did not work out that way.

Two months after Jim's car wreck, Senator Coyne was charged with electoral fraud stemming from the 1932 election. Although fifty-nine local politicos were convicted on similar charges, Coyne's jury failed to reach a verdict after forty-seven hours of deliberation. In a retrial, the jury acquitted him and Pat O'Malley, Art's old teammate.

Although the press pilloried Coyne, Art argued that he had delivered jobs for his constituents and helped in hard times. Art's politics reflected similar community-oriented pragmatism. "Politics is people," Coyne said. "Don't ever think you can get it out of books."

Until the 1930s, Democrats had hardly mattered in Pittsburgh. As late as 1929, registered Republicans outnumbered Democrats in the city by 169,000 to 5,200. In fact, Republicans took turns running as Democrats for offices requiring minority representation. "I used to have to get a guy and say, 'You be the Democrat. Go and change your registration,'" Art recalled with a laugh. Sometimes the designated Democrat complained, "I was the Democrat last time."

But the depression had shifted Pittsburghers' focus from local to national policies, and FDR's victories had pulled Democrats into office. Republican rule in Pittsburgh was over. Coyne lamented that his party had not been the one to take on the New Deal's populist mantle. "Mr. Roosevelt is a very astute politician," Coyne reflected. "He has produced on a national level what most of us have been doing and trying to do on a local level all our lives. He has fed more people through the WPA [Works Progress Administration] and the PWA [Public Works Administration] than his political opponents. It's too bad our Republican presidents before him didn't have the same idea."

Art shared Coyne's sentiments about the New Deal. As a young man with a knack for seeing what was around the corner, he might have jumped parties early and joined his other mentor, David Lawrence, in the Democratic Party. But Art's ability to think ahead of the play was balanced by his sense of loyalty. He often said that there were three things a man should never change: his religion, his wife, or his party. Art held steady with each. He stuck with Coyne, whose organization evaporated. The Monaca Club closed, and Coyne was defeated for re-election in 1936. When the Senator lay dying at the age of seventy-two in July 1954, Art was at his bedside.

With his brother Jim out of politics and Senator Coyne operating from behind the lines, Art disengaged from overt politicking. He had other matters to attend to that mattered more to him and to Pittsburgh. But the lessons he had learned in Ward politics, he would use again—in the NFL.

5

Pittsburgh Joins the NFL

1933–36

At age thirty-two with a wife and son, Art needed to make a living. He had earned his last dollar as an athlete, and betting horses was too risky a foundation for family life. Despite his nearly perfect sense of athletic timing, Art's search for a livelihood could have hardly come at a worse moment, the Depression's lowest ebb. He soldiered on with faith that hard work needed just a pinch of luck to succeed.

He got it in 1933 when Franklin Delano Roosevelt's inauguration unleashed whirlwinds of change. In addition to shoring up capitalism's fragile underpinnings, the nation legalized alcohol and Pittsburgh embraced Sunday sport. The latter brought the National Football League to Pittsburgh and set the course of Art's life.

While the country celebrated Prohibition's demise, Art put his father back into business at the Braddock Brewery. Whether Daniel had been brewing beer or soda pop there during Prohibition, he was legit again. Daniel, fifty-nine, was done running saloons. He would supply them instead.

In July, after the Pennsylvania legislature relaxed the Blue Laws to permit communities to decide whether to allow professional sport on Sundays, Pittsburgh's city council quickly placed the question on the November ballot. Passage would make the NFL a viable option for Art. Because Saturdays belonged to the colleges and high school football ruled on Friday nights, Sunday was the only day for the pros to play in Pittsburgh. Confident that Pittsburgh would vote to curtail the Blue Laws, Art plunked down $2,500 in July 1933 for the rights to a franchise. It took a leap of faith.

The NFL had battled for credibility since a group of semipro owners had formed it in a Canton, Ohio, automobile showroom in 1920. Pro football was far less popular than college ball. A dozen franchises had fizzled since 1929 alone, and the depression imperiled the survivors.

A palpable sense of crisis galvanized NFL owners into action after the 1932 season. Rather than contract in the face of depression, they expanded, adding franchises in two potentially lucrative markets, Pittsburgh and Philadelphia. Pittsburgh, the birthplace of the pro game and the rare city with three strong college teams, was an intriguing addition.

Art had built a strong blue-collar following on the sandlots that would likely back an NFL club. If he could also tap the throngs who had packed Pitt Stadium when Jim played for Pitt, his franchise would prosper.

When owners convened at the Fort Pitt Hotel in the summer of 1933, they welcomed three new members. Art Rooney was a blue-collar Catholic from Pittsburgh; Eagles owner Bert Bell was a blueblood from Mainline Philadelphia; and the Cardinals' new owner, Charles Bidwill, owned Sportsman's Racetrack in Chicago. They joined Chicago's George Halas, New York's Tim Mara, and Boston's George Preston Marshall to form the core of the NFL. Halas, a league cofounder, was a shrewd, tough-minded man. Mara, who bought the New York Giants franchise for $500 in 1925, was a successful bookmaker. Marshall, the Washington, DC, laundry mogul, was a cunning promoter and marketer. Fierce competitors on the field, they searched for common ground off it.

The owners spoke frankly about what plagued them. Rules favoring the defense made for boring football and countless scoreless ties. At Marshall's urging, they divided the league into two five-team divisions whose winners would meet in a championship game. To enliven play, they allowed passing from anywhere behind the line of scrimmage and moved the hash marks in from the sidelines to give the offense more effective use of the field. They also brought the goal posts forward to make kicking field goals easier. A year later, they would make the ball skinnier and easier to throw.

Art was the youngest man at the table. Although he knew Mara, Bidwill, and Bell from the track, he mostly watched and listened, knowing he needed to earn the respect of this eclectic mix of elders before asserting himself. Art soft-pedaled his own interests and accepted the schedule he was handed. He knew he had much to learn.

The Pittsburgh Pirates Football Club

Art never worked harder than he did between securing the franchise in July and the start of the season in September. He built his team on the fly. In August, he convened the board of directors, which elected him chairman of the board. Art held 60 of the club's 180 shares of stock, as did his gambling mentor Milton Jaffe, who was indifferent to football. Two ward politicos, Patrick O'Malley and William McCole, split the remaining sixty shares. It's likely that only Art actually put up money. Although capitalized at $24,000, the team's bank account was in Art's pants pocket.

Hoping to cash in on the popularity of the city's baseball team, Art called his squad the Pittsburgh Pirates Football Club. He hired Forrest "Jap" Douds, a former All-American who coached at nearby Washington & Jefferson College, to do double duty as a coach and a player. For training camp, he secured Newell's Grove near Greensburg, an hour's drive to the east. Finding a place to play during the season was more difficult.

The University of Pittsburgh, which scorned the pros, refused to make its stadium available; Art could never fill it anyway. His buddy Gus Greenlee offered Greenlee Field on the Hill. Initial plans called for the team to play home games there on Fridays, until the November referendum allowed Sunday play. But Greenlee Field was too small, so Art approached Bill Benswanger, president of the Pittsburgh Pirates Baseball Club. Benswanger appreciated Rooney's role in lifting the Blue Laws, which had penalized his team for decades. And as a Jew, he shared Rooney's status outside Pittsburgh's clubby WASP elite. He agreed to rent Forbes Field to Art for games that fall.

Because Art had jumped into the NFL on the eve of the season, he tapped the local talent he knew best. On August 9, thirty candidates arrived in Newell's Grove. Some were former collegians: All-American tackle Jess Quatse had played alongside Jim Rooney at Pitt while tackle Ray Kemp had started at Duquesne. Marty Kottler was from Carnegie

Tech, and Jap Douds had played at Washington & Jefferson. Other men, like Mose Kelsch, who had run over opponents for over a decade, had earned their degrees on the sandlots. Sadly, Jim Rooney, whom Art had hoped would be his quarterback, was missing.

The team trained for six weeks, scrimmaging against semipros in Beaver Falls, Tarentum, and Uniontown. Coach Douds wanted to forge a cohesive squad, but his players were fighting each other for roster spots that would save them from slipping into the Depression's sinkhole. Eventually, a twenty-two-man squad emerged from Newell's Grove. It bore little resemblance to a modern pro squad; the players were fewer in number and smaller in size. Smaller rosters kept down costs and bigger men lacked the stamina to play both offense and defense, something that the limited-substitution game required.

Although he had been a hands-on owner on the sandlots, Art gave Coach Douds free rein with one proviso: "I don't care if they lose every game," he said, "just so the fans get a run for their money." Art wanted Pittsburgh fans to see their own hard-working, hard-hitting ethic played out on the field. Art stayed out of Douds' way, but he had lied about one thing: he cared deeply about losing.

The Family and the Fight Game

Art's family was his quiet joy. The unassuming Kass took care of his domestic needs, just as his mother, grandmother, and aunts had done before her. When he left home, she packed his bag without complaint. Kass's demands upon him were so few that her objection to Art's adventures as a pilot stands out. Art had learned—more or less—to fly the simple aircraft of the day. He had convinced a trickster pilot to give him lessons during which they circled the city, zooming down along the rivers and under bridges. One day, left alone in the hangar, Art decided to solo. He got the craft aloft and navigated above the Northside, buzzing a sandlot game and almost scraping a chimney. Art landed in one piece, but Kass had had enough. She clipped his wings.

They settled into a second-story apartment on Western Avenue, a few blocks from Dan Rooney's old Robinson Street saloon. Art's sister Margaret and her husband, restaurateur Johnny Laughlin, rented a flat next door. While their babies napped, the two women—both young and fun loving—stuck their heads out the windows to chat between buildings. They strung clotheslines across the flat rooftops and sunned themselves on their tarpaper beach with diapers and sheets flapping in the wind.

Art and Kass had few luxuries, but many around them were going hungry. On his walks around the Northside, Art watched sheriffs evicting families. Art hated to see people so bereft and without support. That August, while frantically putting his team together, Art staged a benefit for people in the neighborhood with one of sport's most colorful figures, heavyweight champion Primo Carnera, who had knocked out Jack Sharkey in June to win the title. Art had won more than enough on the fight to buy his NFL franchise.

A sensational-looking if suspect fighter, the 6-foot-5-inch 270-pound Carnera had taken the title under dubious circumstances. Many figured that mobster Owney Madden, who ran the Cotton Club and "owned" Carnera, had fixed the fight. When Budd Schulberg exposed the mob's grip on boxing in his 1947 novel, *The Harder They Fall*, he based his protagonist on Carnera. Art, well acquainted with sport's unseemly underbelly, was untroubled by such transgressions. When he asked Bill Duffy, Carnera's manager, to provide his fighter for a benefit, Duffy wired back, "You know it goes without saying that anything in the world I can do for you, I will." In the fight world and among racketeers, Art was regarded as a stand-up guy.

As Art escorted Carnera though Pittsburgh, the champ drew adoring crowds, especially in Italian neighborhoods. Dressed in a dark blue suit, Carnera signed autographs and posed for photographs. Art snapped a shot of the champ cradling his baby Danny in one huge hand.

At St. Anthony's Italian Orphanage in Oakmont, the children held back in awe until the gentle giant coaxed them forward. A photograph that showed Carnera exchanging fascist salutes with the boys, dressed in shorts, knee socks, and white shirts, disturbed some readers. But for most, fascism's cruelty was not yet apparent. The boys serenaded Carnera with a fascist hymn and folk songs.

A crowd of 3,000 jammed inside the St. Peter's gym, where the nuns had first sent the Rooneys to vent their tempers, for the benefit. The fight was all show and no mayhem. Sparring with local fighters, the champion pranced about the ring. Dropping his hands while his opponents flailed away, Carnera mugged: "I can take it, boy." The crowd, which included countless politicians, roared its approval. Afterward, Carnera presented the training gloves he had used before the Sharkey fight to Mayor John Herron. The mayor, in turn, praised Carnera for waiving his $1,000 appearance fee and thanked Art for giving the depressed city a lift. After taking Carnera to the train station, Art returned to football and the campaign to rescind the Blue Laws.

Opening Day

On Wednesday, September 20, 1933, the Pittsburgh Pirates football team debuted at Forbes Field. Art had prevailed upon Tim Mara to bring the Giants to town for the opener, hoping that the big-name team would launch the franchise with fanfare and a solid payday. Art got both, along with a butt-kicking on the field. "The greatest collection of ex-college football stars to ever appear here will strut their stuff in the opening encounter," one writer exclaimed, but he was writing about the Giants. Pittsburgh's talented ex-collegians and sandlot standouts were no match for New York.

Twenty-five thousand fans filed into Forbes Field. Art kept ticket prices low—from 55 cents to $1.65—and handed out a thousand free passes. But Forbes Field, built for baseball, was ill suited for football. Plopping a gridiron down inside meant that most fans lacked clear sight lines. Many fans, accustomed to watching up close on the sandlots, looked down at the field from dizzying heights. Several thousand of them infiltrated empty seats along the field.

Despite the Giants' lopsided victory, fans left with respect for the NFL. "Practically every one departed," a journalist wrote, "with praises of [Giants halfback Harry] Newman on his lips and hoping the locals will be able to buy, borrow or steal a gent who comes close to the dark haired Hebrew lad in all-around grid ability." But Art was unaccustomed to defeat. Commissioner Joe Carr cautioned him to temper his expectations. The *Post-Gazette* concurred: "It can't be done in a jiffy. Rooney has laid a very promising groundwork on which to build."

It was a tolerable financial start. Art's buddy Havey Boyle at the *Post-Gazette* estimated that hosting the Giants cost Rooney about $10,000. Most of that went to the visitors' $4,000 guarantee, salaries ($2,200, or $100 per player), and $1,000 for rent. Art had made that much and enough to cover the costs of training camp. But the opener was his biggest crowd of the season.

When Pittsburgh played the Chicago Cardinals at Forbes Field a week later, fans cheered wildly as Marty Kottler scored Pittsburgh's first-ever touchdown, intercepting a pass at the 1-yard line and running the length of the field. After a second touchdown tied the game 13–13, Mose Kelsch waddled on to the field, helmetless, his bald pate gleaming.

Most sandlot players in Pittsburgh had banged bodies with Kelsch and every fan had seen him play. They exulted when their bulldog warrior, the oldest man in the league at thirty-six, kicked the extra point that gave them a 14–13 victory. The *Post-Gazette's* Jack Sell called Kelsch the greatest sandlotter in local history. He was the man of the hour, "the fair-haired boy . . . who never trod a college campus, never cut a period or a quiz." Mose was more circumspect. "This National League must be a soft touch," he quipped, "if they make a hero out of you for kicking." On the sandlots, he said, fans would run a kicker out the park if he missed.

A telling aside was that each team fielded one black player, Chicago halfback Joe Lillard and Pittsburgh tackle Ray Kemp. They were the only African Americans in the league that season. None remained the following year. The NFL never voted to eliminate black players, nor has any owner ever confirmed an informal agreement to purge them. African Americans simply disappeared from the league, and no team seriously considered hiring one until after World War II. Whatever the cause, pro football remained segregated until 1946.

After Pittsburgh split the next two games, the press lauded Art for assembling a competitive squad. "We went into professional football," Art admitted, "not knowing whether our judgment that it would be popular here would be vindicated. Now we know." Football could make it in Pittsburgh. Meanwhile, the hastily recruited roster remained a work in progress. Next year, Art vowed, his players would be bigger and faster.

After playing its first four games at home, Pittsburgh tasted reality on the road. The Green Bay Packers, one of the league's founding franchises, stomped them 47–0. After a scoreless tie against Cincinnati in ankle-deep mud and a surprising win in Boston, the Pirates played at Brooklyn's Ebbets Field. Mose Kelsch reprised his hero's role. Pittsburgh advanced into Brooklyn territory down 3 points with time for one play. With Harp Vaughan holding the ball for Kelsch as he had so many times on Pittsburgh sandlots, Mose split the uprights for a tying field goal.

On their way home, the team bus stopped so that players could help two women whose car had swerved onto the railroad tracks after a blowout. The scene was playing out like a silent movie, with a train barreling down the track, when the linemen picked up the car and carried it to safety. The women cheered the players on their way, but these were the last cheers they would hear that season. Pittsburgh did not win again. Nonetheless, the franchise's most important victory came a few days later, at the ballot box.

Sunday Football

Support for Blue Law reform was deep in Pittsburgh. If puritanical Protestants still backed the old law, they no longer had the muscle to enforce it. The Committee in Favor of Sunday Sports mobilized eight hundred sandlot baseball and football managers, who, in turn, mustered players and families to get out the vote. The baseball Pirates, forced on the road for Sunday games that owner Bill Benswanger said added as many as three thousand miles of travel per season, also embraced the campaign.

On election day, eight games into the 1933 NFL campaign, Pittsburgh voters overwhelmingly endorsed Blue Law reform. The *Post-Gazette* trumpeted the vote as an end of hypocrisy and one of the best features of the New Deal. Working families, it noted, had been denied their sporting outlets, while no one had ever interfered with Sunday sport for the wealthy at country clubs.

Confident of the outcome, Art had scheduled a game for the Sunday following the vote. When he realized that city council needed to pass an authorizing ordinance, he visited the police superintendent, who laughed away his concerns. The police could not block the game without coming through him. "Give me a couple of tickets, and I'll go to the game," he said. "That'll be the last place they'll look for me if they want to stop it."

The fans turned out in their Sunday best on a sunny autumn afternoon to see Pittsburgh meet Brooklyn. The game featured five former college All-Americans on each team. Art, who had anticipated a crowd of 25,000, was disheartened when half that number attended. Sandlot ball offered stiff competition; games around Pittsburgh that Sunday had drawn 70,000 fans, six times what the pros drew.

Nonetheless, the press hailed the event as a breakthrough. Liberals, the *Post-Gazette* noted, had no intention of compelling anyone to attend Sunday games. "Blue law supporters were never quite so fair, for they not only wanted to be protected against temptation in this respect, but they also wanted every one else to be forbidden what will seem to many to be innocent and wholesome amusement."

The game was anticlimatic; Brooklyn trampled Pittsburgh 32–0. Losing their last three games by a collective score of 84-9, the Pirates finished 3-6-2. Art reduced his financial losses by playing an exhibition against the Reading Pros at Forbes Field. Torn by the devastation that hard times had wrought in Pittsburgh, he gave part of the gate to relief efforts.

The Off-Season

The NFL had survived the Depression's worst year and even looked a bit better off. Under its new rules, teams scored twice as many points, completed more passes, and played fewer tie games. But only a few NFL clubs were profitable. Pittsburgh, which had averaged 11,400 fans a game at home and 8,500 on the road, was not among them.

Art was shell-shocked. He had never lost so many games or so much money before. He threw a party for his players and sent them home. After a few postseason maneuvers to acquire players, Art turned to other matters. John O'Donnell, the Ward's Republican chairman and a member of the Pirates' board, had died during the season, adding to Art's political duties. And while better-off owners focused solely on football, Art needed to make a living. Florida's tracks beckoned. As winter descended along the banks of the Allegheny River, Art, Kass, Danny, and a few buddies headed to Miami. He wintered there, betting the horses to cover his football losses and support his family.

Football 1934

When Art returned, he replaced Jap Douds as coach but kept him on at tackle. "Between you and me," Jim Rooney confided, "he was no coach." Art tried to sign Greasy Neale, who had taken Washington & Jefferson College to the 1921 Rose Bowl. But Neale opted to coach running backs at Yale instead; college positions, even as an assistant, paid better than the pros. Art finally hired Luby DiMelio, Jim Rooney's pal at Pitt, who made Jim his assistant. Jim was edging back into public life after winning the Republican slot on the November ballot for his old seat in the legislature.

Most of Art's players came from the working classes. Mose Kelsch, Harp Vaughan, and Walter Heller were blue-collar buddies from the Northside, John Oehler had worked as a tipple boy in the coal mines, and Dave Ribble carried a Teamsters union card. The Depression made recruiting easier. Steady work was scarce, and football fed the family better than federal relief jobs.

Art also signed that star player he had been seeking, an eye-popping player who could bring fans out of their seats. John "Blood" McNally was a lanky free spirit with the lean cheeks, tousled hair, and bad-boy smile of Clark Gable. McNally's compass unerringly pointed toward trouble. Arrested in St. Louis for "borrowing" a taxi to escort a chorus girl and in Havana for carousing, Blood was a ne'er-do-well son of a wealthy family. A precocious student, he had finished high school before he was fifteen and enrolled at Notre Dame. After a raucous St. Patrick's Day, the school tossed him out before he ever got to play. McNally took his nickname from Rudolph Valentino's movie *Blood and Sand*, which he and a buddy had spotted on a theater marquee from the motorcycle they were riding to a semipro tryout in Minneapolis. Needing fake names to preserve their college eligibility, McNally told the coach, "My name is Blood and this guy's name is Sand." The name stuck.

Blood had starred in Green Bay but his off-the-field shenanigans persuaded the Packers to sell him to Pittsburgh. He had been traveling as a ship's purser when he was traded, and the *Sun-Telegraph* pictured him in sailor's garb doing the hornpipe. Art took "a fancy to me," Blood remembered. "He liked Irishmen. But . . . he no doubt was a little disappointed in me. He pressed me to go to confession, to make a better Roman Catholic out of me. Let's just say that I came under the heading, but spell it with an 'i', an 'n,' and an apostrophe. I was a roamin' Catholic."

Art could laugh off such apostasy but not the injury that sidelined Blood, his highest-paid player, for much of the season. Pittsburgh opened at home against Cincinnati, a team so pathetic that it folded midway through the season. Jack Dempsey, the former heavyweight champ and a buddy of Rooney and Milton Jaffe, sat with them on the bench as Pittsburgh shut out Cincinnati 13–0. Afterward, Dempsey stuck around long enough for Jaffe to take some of his money playing cards.

Pittsburgh lost its next three games, during which Mose Kelsch's heroic aura was pierced when he twice missed extra points that cost Pittsburgh ties. Fans were unforgiving, but despite torrential rains, they turned out 17,000-strong for the Giants game. "You can write it down," the *Sun-Telegraph's* Harry Keck contended. "This brand of the sport has come to Pittsburgh to stay."

The Pirates rallied to beat the Eagles in Philadelphia and returned home, where more than 19,000 fans turned out for the game with Chicago. Art could not yet hold his own with his edgy, wily elder, Bears owner George Halas, in NFL meetings nor on the field, where the Monsters of the Midway crushed his Pirates 28–0 in their first encounter.

Pittsburgh unraveled and lost its last seven games. Art fretted as the gate, his only source of revenue, dwindled. He made little from radio broadcasts of games on WWSW, and the baseball Pirates, who owned Forbes Field, pocketed all concession revenues. Nor had NFL teams developed the marketing savvy to sell jerseys, hats, and other paraphernalia.

Art scheduled nonleague exhibitions to supplement income, but that taxed his players.

Playing exhibitions in small coal and mill towns solidified the club's base among western Pennsylvania workingmen. But the travel and extra play frustrated coach DiMelio and exhausted his players. Although Luby and Art maintained a friendly relationship, losing angered both of them. One day, Luby was talking with Art in the office when he tossed an off-hand remark about football players being tougher than prize-fighters. Art, who knew well what each sport demanded, scoffed at the claim. When Luby persisted, Art sent for boxing gloves while he and Luby rearranged the office furniture. The two men squared off. Luby was younger and bigger but stood no chance against his more skilled and quicker foe. Art slapped him silly for a few rounds but refrained from hurting him. When Pittsburgh ended its second season 2-10, Coach Luby was gone.

On the bright side, home attendance jumped twenty-five percent to average 14,306 per game, and Jim Rooney won his November election. Although Art had exceeded the NFL's average attendance of 8,211, he lost $5,000 to $10,000 on the season. Amidst speculation he would quit football, one columnist reported that Art had "no idea of giving up the game and only recently turned down a sizeable offer for his franchise."

After the regular season, Pittsburgh played a college All-Star team to boost its legitimacy with potential college recruits. Art could have used the game's proceeds, but he staged it as a benefit with Dan Hamill. An entrepreneur with an eighth grade education, Hamill had built the Paper Products Company into one of the city's most successful Irish Catholic–owned businesses. Dubbed the "Midnight Bishop of Pittsburgh," the devout Hamill attended Mass twice daily. He and Art played handball at the Keystone Club, poker on Saturday nights at the Fort Pitt Hotel, and attended hundreds of sporting events together.

The All-Star game's proceeds funded a summer camp for boys and a convalescent home for indigent mothers. Hamill and Rooney persuaded benefactors to buy blocks of tickets for youngsters from Catholic orphanages, the Jewish Big Brother Society, and the county detention home. On game day, 18,531 fans filled the seats at Forbes Field.

"The only discordant note," the *Post-Gazette*'s Al Abrams commented, was sounded by jeering fans still rankled by Mose Kelsch's missed extra points in the Giants' game. "It rubs the grain to see a grand, like the bald-headed Northsider, getting the 'raspberry' instead of being cheered," Abrams lamented. It was Kelsch's last game.

Off-Season

While the Depression was inescapable, the NFL was the only pro league to increase revenues in 1934. Pittsburgh, though, had been a bust on the field and at the bank. The team's new publicist, Dick Guy, contended that its payroll was among the league's highest and its ticket prices the lowest. Rooney, he added, had scouts all over the country evaluating talent. It was a nice spin, but Art had not yet hired scouts. He was better connected at the track than in college football.

Art did find a new coach, Joe Bach, who had led Duquesne to an 8-2 season in 1934. Bach had first gained celebrity as one of the "Seven Mules" who blocked for Notre Dame's "Four Horsemen," the backfield that Grantland Rice immortalized in 1924. But Art reckoned that better players and a top coach would not be enough.

He also needed the NFL to change its inner workings. Since joining the league, Art had cultivated the other owners. He had taken them to his favorite restaurants and his Catholic guests—Mara, Halas, and Bidwill—to Mass at St. Peter's. This was his turf but he made them the center of attention. Art had studied his ambitious colleagues. New York Giants owner Tim Mara was an old friend from the track and his chief ally. The two most difficult owners were the Bears' Halas and the Redskins' Marshall, whose prickly personalities annoyed each another. Halas' large jaw and jutting chin gave him a fierce appearance that was reinforced by his attitude that "sentiment was for softies." Marshall, hot-blooded in his pursuit of women, was headstrong in negotiations. But he had a flair for promotion and marketing. He, Mara, and Halas were driven by a desire to top each other and better their own lot.

Art and Eagles owner Bert Bell, however, simply wanted to survive. Their genius lay in persuading the other men to compete *on* the field but cooperate *off* of it. Bell and Rooney were an unlikely pair to forge an enduring alliance. A fireplug of a guy, "Bert" de Benneville Bell had aristocratic roots. His grandfather was a congressman and his father served as Pennsylvania's attorney general, but Bell never acquired the airs of his Main Line background. A playboy, he had quarterbacked and coached for Penn. "Bert drank too much and gambled too much as he worked his way down from riches to rags," Arthur Daley wrote in the *New York Times*. But his sweetheart, Ziegfeld Follies girl Frances Upton, sobered him up. "If you marry me," Bell proposed, "I'll never take another drink." She did and he kept his word. Frances bankrolled Bert's purchase of an NFL franchise after his free-spending proclivities and the stock market crash left him without capital. By 1935, however, Bell was losing money so fast that Art began calling after games on Sundays to ask if he needed money, even though his own receivables were flagging.

In May 1935, when Art hosted the league meetings at the Fort Pitt Hotel, he joined forces with Bell to stop the bidding wars over college prospects. "Something has to be done about new players," Art warned. "Our club lost just a bit less than $10,000 last year, yet when we try to sign a new man from the college ranks, we find other clubs immediately jack up the price." Better players gravitated to the richest teams—the Giants, Redskins, Bears, and Packers—whose success and profitability perpetuated competitive imbalance, undermining fan interest and the league's viability.

Art challenged the league to limit the number of new players that first-division teams could sign. "That will give the others a chance, assure a more even race, and prevent an eventual collapse of the league from sheer top-heaviness." Art was concerned, one sports writer said, that the league not reach a point where "the wealthiest teams have a sinecure on the championships and the other clubs a sinecure on bankruptcy."

"Every year," Bell reminded the owners, "the rich get richer and the poor get poorer." He and Art proposed to level the playing field by creating an annual draft of college seniors in which the team with the worst record picked first, the one with the best last. If a player could not agree on a salary with the club that drafted him, the league president would arbitrate.

Art lobbied for the resolution behind the scenes, putting to work the political arts he had learned at his father's saloon. New York owner Tim Mara was the key. If Mara would put his big-market moneymaking franchise behind the proposal, other owners were likely to follow. It fell to Art to persuade his friend to place the league's long-term interest ahead of his team's short-term gain.

Mara and Halas, who owned the league's two powerhouse franchises, stood to lose the most. But when Mara backed the college draft, Halas concurred. "People come to see a competition," Mara reasoned. That, he said, required balance; one-sided games hurt business. The more teams in contention, the better for the league. Besides, as Halas acknowledged, the draft would restrain salaries.

Instituting a draft proved to be a turning point. Cooperation trumped competition as the NFL set a course that emphasized parity and competitive balance. It veered away from the trajectory taken by major league baseball in which the richer teams won disproportionately. The NFL focused instead on collective survival. Although relative newcomers, Rooney and Bell had won acceptance of principles that would stabilize the league.

1935: A Tough Season

That winter, Daniel Rooney slipped on the ice and fractured a hip. The former saloonkeeper had begun brewing Rooney's Pilsner at his General Braddock Brewery after Prohibition's repeal. Daniel took brewing seriously. When Art sent him a player to work during the off-season and Daniel caught him tossing a football around, he fired him on the spot.

Prohibition's end had ignited a beer war, with breweries fighting to get their brands into bars. Rooney's Pilsner increased sales by five hundred percent without much sales effort—the result, the brewery claimed, of its superior taste. Joe Carr, who ran the team's ticket office and drove Daniel to work each morning, told a different story. He said that any tavern that failed to carry the brew received a brick tossed through its window. The next day, Joe Carr would call on the saloonkeeper and ask him to reconsider carrying Rooney's Pilsner, "the peer of all beers."

After his fall, Daniel contracted pneumonia and hovered near death at St. John's Hospital. He survived, but his hip and his spirits were damaged afterward. Daniel's decline was sobering.

So was Art's inability to steer his franchise to success. For most of his life, he had exorcised tension by going all out on the field or in the ring. Now, he conducted much of his business over meals. Art relished eating and steadily gained weight. At thirty-four, his once wiry and lithe body was getting pudgy.

To let off steam, Art started playing baseball again. "At present," he wrote Eagles coach Lud Wray, "I'm going at full speed, leading the league in hitting and base-stealing. My club [the Rooneys] is in first place." For a man so in tune with his body, feeling good about his physical abilities was rejuvenating. His renewed energy carried over to football.

He negotiated with Allegheny County to allow his team to train at South Park in exchange for playing a free exhibition there during the county fair. Bach, who scoured the country for players, brought forty-four candidates to camp in August. Earl Harbes reported after hitch-hiking for six days from Houston, Maurice "Mule" Bray was a range rider, and tackle John Gildea had played previously for the Shenandoah Presidents in the coalfields.

While his players trained, Art took to the nearby links. Milton Jaffe, who had taken up golf, introduced Art to the game. On their first out-ing, the two gamblers haggled over the terms of play. Jaffe was no ath-lete, but he had taken lessons and felt confident enough to wager his new clubs against $100 that he could win at a sport that Art had never tried. He should have known better; Art took Jaffe's clubs home that afternoon. Art golfed mornings, and played baseball in the North Hills League in the twilight.

Bach, a master at motivating players, also excited fans, who turned out 3,500 strong for an intrasquad match at Greenlee Field. The next contest, the free county fair game, drew 85,000, a local record. Art was ecstatic. Bach built the squad around a core of Pittsburghers, including six men he had coached at Duquesne. No college sent more players to the same NFL team. Art believed in cultivating fans by using sandlot he-roes, but two familiar faces were missing when the season began.

Harp Vaughan, who had injured his knee playing baseball for the Rooneys that summer, was done with football, and on the eve of camp, Mose Kelsch died in a crash. His skull was crushed when an auto driven by a former teammate sideswiped his car minutes after Mose left his Northside café. Art hung Mose's jersey in his office, and no Pirate wore his number 37 that season. No longer a starter, Mose had been the rare specialist, performing primarily as a place kicker. As one writer put it, he could have played in a dinner jacket.

Born in 1897 in Troy Hill's German enclave, Mose Christian Kelsch had grown up in an orphanage. His schooling was limited, but his athletic resumé stretched across Western Pennsylvania's ball fields. His first team was the North Side Market Eleven, his last the Pittsburgh Pirates. In between, he played for Hope Harvey, Majestic Radio, and the J. P. Rooneys, as well as some of their opponents.

Kelsch's game-winning feats during the Pirates' first season brought national celebrity. "Mose's fame was secure after that," Chet Smith wrote in his obituary. "The metropolitan columnists seized him as a gift from the gods and wrote reams about him, not permitting the facts to interfere with their imaginations. They made him out a sinister character of the underworld." Mose, Smith protested, was no such person. "He figured in several feuds among rival gangs, especially during the days when there were rich returns for the boys who could sneak a few kegs of beer past the watchful eyes of Uncle Sam's minions, but Mose was far from being a gangster." Art had known Mose since they were kids and had told him he could play for him for as long as he wanted. Art helped to carry his casket at Mass.

Art felt like fate's punching bag after the blows he had taken: his brother's near-fatal accident, his father's fall, and now Mose's death. A religious man, he struggled not to second-guess what life was handing him. His family was his consolation; Kass was pregnant again.

In September 1935, the Pirates opened on the road and surprised the Eagles—whose squad featured four former Pitt stars—beating them 17–7. The game drew a record 20,000 fans. "It looks as if this is the big year we have been waiting for," NFL Commissioner Joe Carr (no relation to the Pirate ticket manager) told Damon Runyon. "The pro game has definitely and finally arrived."

A few days later, Art homered to lead the Rooneys to a come-from-behind victory in their last at-bat to win the North Hills League title. He had to savor that baseball victory for a long while. Misfortune struck his football team when Joe Bach's wife died. Absent Bach, the dispirited Pirates fell 42–7 to the defending league champion Giants before a record paid crowd of 23,298 at Forbes Field. The schedule did Art no favors, slating the Giants, Bears, and Packers, the league's best teams, in succession. Pittsburgh fell into last place.

When Bach returned, he rejiggered the roster. He had little of Art's sentiment about players and had released almost half his squad by mid-season. One face Bach brought back was an old one, that of scatback Jimmy Levey, who had just finished playing baseball in the Pacific Coast League. Levey was accustomed to switching from one sport to the other overnight. At 150 pounds, he was lightning fast and took most of the snaps at his position.

On October 18, 1935, Art took Kass to the hospital for the delivery of their second child. Following an Irish tradition of naming the first son for the baby's paternal grandfather and the second for his father, they named this boy Arthur J. Rooney Jr. Art was also stepping into a more fatherly role with Tommy, fourteen, while their father, Daniel, convalesced. The press hailed Tommy, "the midget brother of the famous Art," for his play at Annunciation High.

Bach boldly predicted a win at home against Chicago's "other team," the previously unbeaten Cardinals. He whipped his players into such a fury that three were ejected for fighting. With Pittsburgh protecting a lead near the end of the game, Chicago drove to the 1-yard line. The Cardinals—believing there were 28 seconds left—erupted when field judge Earl Cavanaugh fired the gun to end the game. They chased down Cavanaugh, and owner Charley Bidwill snatched the watch from his hand. Players scuffled, and Pirate Cy Casper was knocked out. Bach rushed his players off the field while Bidwill protested that Cavanaugh's watch proved his case. Art defended the embattled Cavanaugh, who owned a tavern in Pittsburgh's Garfield section. "I have implicit faith in the honesty of all the football officials who have worked our games," Art told the press, which failed to report whether he was grinning.

Art and Bach shared a laugh about the fight, recalling a game Bach had played for Hope Harvey. "Early in the first quarter," Art recalled, "we blocked a punt, and naturally that started a brawl. After a while, the crowd got into the spirit of the thing and poured onto the field. So instead of a fight, we had a riot." Bach, figuring the game was over, left. "The next day," Art said, "I sent someone to Joe's house to pay him his $75. Bach refused to take it, until my guy told him, 'Go ahead, the Hope Harveys haven't finished a game yet.'" In later years, when Art bragged about his sandlot clubs, Kass interjected that they rarely lost because anytime they trailed late in a game they instigated a game-ending altercation.

Pittsburgh improved to 3-4 and climbed into second place, a game behind New York in the East. Though they had started strongly, injuries were decimating the lineup, and Art could not afford replacements. The whiff of first place intoxicated the team, which lost four of its last five games. "They are daily getting worse," one columnist scolded. "It takes high-powered football players to stay in this big show and the Pirates, up until the present time, do not have enough of them." Another disquieting note came when the American Professional Football League announced plans to begin play in 1936 and put a team in Pittsburgh.

Pittsburgh finished with a 4-8 record, then played a fundraiser for the Vincentian Center. Afterward, Art threw a party and paid his players' train fare home. Attendance had fallen to 12,489 fans per game, marginally ahead of the league standard. "In those days," Art said later, "nobody got wealthy in sports. You got two thrills. One came Sunday, trying to win the game. The next came Monday, trying to make the payroll." Art dug into his reserves to keep the team afloat.

Hope dawned with the first NFL draft, held at Philadelphia's Ritz-Carlton Hotel in February 1936. Picking first, last-place Philadelphia took Heisman Trophy winner Jay Berwanger. The Pirates followed by selecting Notre Dame's Bill Shakespeare. But the triple-threat Shakespeare never authored a play in Pittsburgh. He declined to play pro ball, as did Berwanger. The Pirates managed to sign only two of nine picks; the Eagles signed none of theirs. The NFL was still not the place to be.

1936: Turning the Corner

With a nod to continuity, Art gave Joe Bach the chance to build on his first year coaching Pittsburgh. Bach re-signed a core of ex-Duquesne players familiar with his style and acclimated to the NFL's tougher, faster style.

During the preseason, Pittsburgh rolled over the McKeesport Olympics at Edgar Thomson Field in Braddock, won before 80,000 fans at the free county fair game, and beat the Rox Rangers in a game in which players threw punches and much of the crowd joined in the fray. To Art, it seemed like old times.

After the Pirates began the 1936 season with three wins, Art thought he had turned the corner. A week later, a record 28,777 fans piled through the turnstiles to watch the Bears score 27 unanswered points and win 27–9. After beating Philadelphia, Pittsburgh traveled to Chicago and lost again. Art had taken the game to help out Tim Mara, who wanted to avoid playing Chicago to improve New York's chances of winning its division. In return, Art would receive a bonus for playing Chicago twice.

The game gave rise to one of Art's favorite stories. When they split the gate, Art claimed that Bears owner George Halas was shortchanging him several thousand dollars. Halas, mistrustful by nature, may have been testing this young upstart, whose friendship with his rival Mara annoyed him. Halas, who had led the University of Illinois in the 1919 Rose Bowl and briefly played for the New York Yankees, had the most distinguished athletic pedigree in the NFL. After founding the Bears in 1920 as a workplace team for the A. E. Staley Starch Company, Halas played for them for a decade and would coach them for forty seasons. The two men stood toe to toe, but Halas conceded before they came to blows. Halas drew himself up proudly and expressed his relief that he was not forced to duke it out with the smaller Rooney. "George," Art shrugged, "you were no sure bet."

Ticket manager Joe Carr stuck around to collect Pittsburgh's cut. After Carr left the stadium with the cash in his valise, a man with a gun demanded his wallet. Carr pulled out his wallet and asked if he could keep his identification. The thief agreed and Carr handed him his cash. After filing a police report, Carr headed to the train station. A few days later, a Chicago policeman called to say that they had arrested a suspect. Would Joe return and identify him? "No thanks," Carr replied. "Just tell the guy there was $8,000 in the valise."

Art was determined to spend more time promoting the team. He persuaded ex-Pitt star Toby Uansa to rename the Rox Rangers the Rooneys and become his farm club. But Art never sustained his commitment to building an organization with the monomaniacal focus that Halas or Marshall displayed. He had too many other interests.

Art dabbled in politics, chairing the Republican campaign on the Northside in the fall of 1936. He also applied to the state athletic commission for a license to promote boxing and wrestling. The election was an uphill climb for Republicans, as FDR's enormous reelection victory carried New Deal Democrats to power in locales where they had never before held office. Art, who had no issue with New Deal policies because they meant greater security for working people, adapted to the changing environment, even though it swept Senator Coyne out of office. Jim Rooney, now thirty pounds over his playing weight, would serve out the remainder of his term and retire from politics for good in 1937.

In November, after Armand Niccolai kicked a pair of field goals to beat Philadelphia 6–0, the Pirates' record was 6-3. One more victory would clinch the division. This was heady stuff for a franchise that had never won more than four games in a season. "The happiest football fellow in town these days," a *Post-Gazette* columnist reported, "is none other than Art Rooney." His team was marching toward a title and making money. "When you call the Pirate headquarters these days and if Rooney answers the phone you always hear this: 'Hello, Champs' Headquarters.'" Bookies had them 7-to-5 favorites to win the division and host the NFL championship at Forbes Field.

But Pittsburgh, playing its last three games on the road, lost the first two. That put the division title on the line on November 29. With two weeks off, the team took the train to Los Angeles. Art, who had promised a buddy who owned a team there a chance to play his NFL team, needed the payday.

By the time the Pirates traveled back across the continent to play in Boston, they were exhausted, and Bach was furious. It wasn't the first time he and Art had argued about midseason exhibitions. Pittsburgh made its poorest showing of the season in the most important game in franchise history and lost 30–0 to a team it had beaten 10–0 in the season opener. Bach blamed Art and they came to blows on the train ride home. Players separated them before either was hurt.

At a farewell party in the Fort Pitt Hotel, Art paid each player his $65 share of the playoff pool for finishing second in the East. Art was disappointed; Joe Bach was disconsolate and would not return for a third season. Not holding on to Bach would become one of Art's greatest regrets.

Pittsburgh finished 6-6, its best record yet, and increased home attendance by an astonishing 50 percent, to 18,093 per game, twenty percent above the NFL average. The crowds were even more impressive given that a rival team, the Pittsburgh Americans, had started up that fall. For the first time, Art made money in pro football.

Before heading to Florida, Art convened the annual meeting of the board of directors, which placed the entire management and control of the corporation in his hands. These actions formalized what had been clear for some time: the team was Art's, and he alone bore its costs.

Art persuaded Johnny Blood to return as a player-coach, then settled into his postseason routines: a month in Miami with Kass, the boys, and the horses, and springtime in Pittsburgh. Well before the 1937 football season began, however, Art Rooney would become a national sensation.

6

Rooney's Ride

1937

Art Rooney was no stranger to the track, but he remained beneath the racing world's notice until the summer of 1937 when his anonymity vanished. After a remarkable run at the track, Art could hardly go into the men's room without tripping over someone hucking him for a tip. By the time the NFL resumed play that fall, Art had become to betting what Seabiscuit was to racing: the people's choice.

In late July, Art and former middleweight Buck Crouse left a plumbers' union function in Harrisburg and drove through the night to the Empire City Racetrack in Yonkers, New York. Seabiscuit, Art's favorite horse, was running that afternoon.

They arrived Saturday morning, July 24, the last day of the three-week Empire City meet. The weather was clear, the track fast. Art, carrying a small bankroll, wandered through the bookmaking stalls looking for Tim Mara and his wide, ready, Red Skelton smile. Tall and barrel-chested with light, wavy hair that he parted high and slicked back, Mara had begun running bets for bookmakers near Manhattan's Union Square when he was twelve. Now forty-nine, the New York Giants owner was an established legal bookmaker who favored dark suits, white shirts, and wide ties.

Mara was Rooney's talisman that racing season. In May at Belmont Park, where Mara had made book since 1921, he had vouched for the relatively unknown Rooney in the betting ring. "This fellow here is Art Rooney," he told bookmakers. "He's got the Pirates Football team. I'll okay his credit for anything he wants." Establishing Art's bona fides, Mara then touted several horses. "He picks a Hirsch Jacobs horse,

Fly Me," Art later explained. "I bet $1,000 at 7-to-1. That's how the streak all began."

Two months later, Art was back at the track. After listening to Mara that morning, Art bet $200 in the first race with a bookmaker in the grandstand ring. Winning $800, he returned to the grandstand "to give the bookie a chance to get even." Instead, the bookie got even worse. "I had three or four winners," Rooney told Red Smith, "and wound up knocking him out of the box." Mara's advice so far was unimpeachable. Art then plunked his "whole gob"—about $5,000—on a 5-to-1 shot. When his horse crossed the line first by a nose, Rooney pocketed $25,000. "Right there and then," Mara later said, "I told him to quit, go home, get away."

But Art was just getting started. Playing with the bookmakers' money now, he ignored Mara and began slapping down $10,000 a race. One of those bets was on Seabiscuit in the Yonkers Handicap, the featured race of the day.

The year before, Seabiscuit was a relative unknown with an underwhelming record, kind of like Art. His original owner, Gladys Mills Phipps, was the daughter-in-law of millionaire Henry Phipps, whose father was the Northside shoemaker who had parlayed his friendship with Andrew Carnegie into a fortune. Art knew the Phipps family; he had grown up on Phipps Field and played for the Phipps A. A. ballclub. Though the Phippses were known as the horsiest people in America, Gladys Phipps had badly underestimated Seabiscuit and sold him to Charles and Marcela Howard. Since then, trainer Tom Smith and jockey Red Pollard had turned Seabiscuit into the runaway sensation of the sporting world.

Undefeated since the Santa Anita Handicap in February, Seabiscuit had become America's darling. In the Yonkers Handicap that afternoon at Empire City, he was carrying 129 pounds, including his jockey's weight, 15 pounds more than the next horse in the field and the most he had ever carried.

Seabiscuit broke fast from the gate but was trailing in the backstretch when Pollard let him loose. At the top of the homestretch, Pollard put away his whip, "a gesture no rider dares make unless he is supremely confident that the opposition is beaten off," *New York Times* writer Bryan Field observed. Seabiscuit won by four lengths in a track-record 1 minute 44 and one-fifth seconds. Art cashed $19,000 on his $10,000 wager.

In the next race, bookies refused to take Art's action on Count Stone, who was 12-to-1. "I'll tell you what I'll do," Art proposed to one bookie. "I'll toss a coin with you—heads I bet on Count Stone and tails Jimmy Cabaniss." The coin came up tails, and Art bet $10,000 on Jimmy Cabaniss at 4-to-1. Count Stone won; if Art had gotten his wager down on Count Stone, he would have won $120,000.

Art's day caught the attention of the *Journal American*'s Bill Corum. "Here are the exact figures on 'Roll 'em High Rooney's' play," Corum claimed. "These are the honest figures. They're the kind an honest man writes down on his income tax blank, between sobs." Despite losing $20,000 to bookmaker Frank Erickson on an 8-1 long shot, Art wound up $19,000 ahead on the day. Mara reckoned it was closer to $25,000.

With Empire City's meet over, Mara grinned widely and repeated his advice: "Stick that dough in your kick and forget about the horses. I should know. I'm a bookmaker. It's my business to take money from guys like you."

Art and Buck headed into Manhattan for dinner at Joe Madden's Broadway saloon, a gathering spot in the theater district that had begun as a speakeasy in the cellar of a run-down boarding house. An ex-prizefighter and former longshoreman whose name was Joseph Augustin Penzo before he adopted an Irish moniker for the ring, Madden dabbled as an author and sported a five o'clock shadow. Like Art, he carried a cigar jammed back in his gums. Damon Runyon once described Madden as the quintessential Broadway character. According to writer John Lardner, Madden served Art and Buck a couple of steaks and listened to tales of Yonkers. "What's your next move, Artie?" he asked. When Art replied, "Back to Pittsburgh," Madden would not hear of it. He talked Art into heading instead for upstate New York where Saratoga's meet would begin on Monday.

Saratoga

"The next morning," Art told writer Red Smith, "Buck and Madden and I were driving to Saratoga in Madden's old car. It broke down three or four times and the radiator kept boiling over going over the mountains." With Crouse and Rooney pushing it over several hills while Madden steered, they reached Saratoga late Sunday evening. They stopped first at Tim Mara's cottage outside Saratoga, hoping to bunk down. He wasn't there so they grabbed a $1.50-a-night room. Art hardly noticed. He had slept in worse and planned on staying up to dope out the races anyway.

Saratoga, one of racing's crown jewels, had boomed since the repeal of New York's gambling statute three years earlier. Vanderbilts, Firestones, Whitneys, Phippses, and Guggenheims brushed elbows with high rollers, hit men, and desperate horseplayers in this upstate town known for its racetrack, healing springs, and nightlife. Many spent the morning drinking and bathing in Saratoga's therapeutic waters, then went to the track, where the women, attired in white, often outnumbered the men. During the evening, they could wager at Lucky Luciano's Chicago Club, Meyer Lanksy's Piping Rock, or the Hi-de-Ho. Although the United States was mired in the eighth year of the Great Depression, horse racing had defied the doldrums. Seabiscuit's meteoric rise and War Admiral's Triple Crown victories were captivating the nation in 1937.

While most of Saratoga was sleeping off the weekend, Art attended early Mass on Monday and arrived at the track before the sun had burned through the swirling mist. He bellied up to the rail alongside trainers, owners, and clockers to watch the horses run their morning workouts. Few activities gave him more satisfaction. Watching a horse run, chatting with trainers, and deciphering a jockey's style or attitude were as important to Art's calculations as the figures on a racing form.

After the workouts, Art asked Jimmy Owens, who timed workouts for Tim Mara, whom he liked. An African American who wintered in France and drove a Stutz-Bearcat—which he left with the Mara boys when abroad—Owens knew horses. "His opinion was highly esteemed," Tim Mara's son Wellington recalled.

Art joined Owens, trainers, and their employees for a stable break-fast of fried chicken and steak, creamed potatoes, cornbread, homemade preserves, and Saratoga melons. He listened to them talk horses. Like Seabiscuit, Art had a tremendous appetite and was taking on weight along with the information.

Art then settled down with a cigar and the racing form. His affinity for numbers allowed him to understand performance charts better than most horseplayers. He factored in what he had gleaned that morning with his own appraisals of times, weights, and post positions. He studied the entire field in each race. The more he knew about the horses, the more his confidence grew. Then, Art took one last step: he talked to Mara.

Saratoga had spent $200,000 renovating the track and building a state-of-the-art betting ring where bookmakers displayed slates with their odds. Mara, despite his advice to Rooney to go home, was not surprised to see the well-fed figure with a cigar approaching him that morning. Mara advised Art to scope out the scene for a few days before putting his money down. "It's a muddy track, a tough card, and there are a lot of strange horses here from the West. Wait until the end of the week and by then you can get a better line on them." Art let Mara finish before asking him about the day's races. "He gets me to mark his card for him," Mara told a writer later. "I said 'All right, sucker, go ahead and blow your dough. I'll be here when the races are over if you want car fare back home.'"

Before the first race, lightning zigzagged through the barns, leaving one thoroughbred dead and knocking eight others unconscious. The dazed steeds recovered. "The bolt that struck the bookies in their fancy new betting enclosure was far more destructive in its results," Bill Corum wrote. "This lightning took the form of a young man from Pittsburgh named Art Rooney."

In the first race, Art bet Taken at 5-to-1 odds. Pushing Dan Cupid, ridden by Hall-of-Fame jockey Eddie Arcaro, to the outside in the homestretch, Taken galloped home first. Little Marty made it two in a row in the second race. In the third, Art tried to get 10-to-1 odds on Dressy, but the bookmakers, afraid of Rooney, refused his bet. Instead, Art switched to Little Miracle, who had Seabiscuit's jockey, Red Pollard, atop. It was the only race Art lost all day.

"I had Tim Mara's figures," Art explained to Red Smith, "but sometimes I'd see something the charts didn't see, like a change of jockeys or post position, and I'd use my own judgment." Art was placing his wagers with Peter Blong, who was working for Frank Erickson, one of the biggest bookmakers. "If Erickson had been there I'm sure he would have kept on taking my action," Art explained, still a bit wistful years later about not being able to get some of his bets down.

In the fourth race, Maetall led post-to-post and paid Art 13-to-5, while in the fifth, Jay Jay moved up steadily after the first quarter mile and won going away. Art knew the muddy track was ideal for both horses. The payoff on Jay Jay was only 7-to-5, but Art was betting larger and larger amounts. Quick Devil paid 7-to-1 in the sixth race.

Art's pick Quel Jeu was part of a photo finish in the seventh race. "In that race," recalled Madden, "the four horses came out of the fog and hit the finish line in a heap—it looked like a dead heat for all four nags." The track's new camera system developed finish-line photos in less than a minute. "As I had a few clams on this event," Madden explained, "I nearly died waiting for the picture to come down. But Artie lit a cigar, got out of the crowd, and went to the men's room, and when I brought him the good news there, he was telling the colored groom the difference between the single wingback and Warner's double-wing."

Art remained unflappable. During the intervals between races, he wandered through the stands, peddling ten-cent raffle tickets to help his brother's church in China. By now, people were drawn to him, hoping his luck might rub off. According to Mara, Art sold a thousand dollars' worth of tickets. "He was sure making Christians out of the boys," Mara laughed.

Word about Art had spread from Frank Erickson's shop to the other bookmakers and their people in the betting ring. Before long, the yardbirds knew Rooney was picking winners and betting big. How big was a subject of conjecture.

"Rooney wasn't betting me," explained Mara, the principal source for many of the stories written about Rooney's ride. "He was betting some of the other fellows in the ring. When the races were over I asked him how he made out. 'Pretty well,' he said. 'I won $108,600. How'd you do?' I didn't tell him but I'd lost close to three grand on the day. Mara, the smart guy, too." Art never did let on just how much he had won. But it was enough to allow Art, Buck Crouse, and Joe Madden to check out of their buck-and-a-half flophouse and rent a suite of rooms at the United States Hotel.

All of Saratoga buzzed about Rooney that evening. Who was this guy wreaking havoc among the bookmakers? Some horse people already knew him; now doormen, high society folks, and newsmen did, too. "We had always wanted to know what a fellow who had won a hundred grand on the races would do with his evening," Bill Corum wrote in his *Journal American* column. "Monday night we found out. Rooney met Jack Mara [Tim's son] at a picture show in Lake Lucerne, and when the show was over, said, 'Let's go some place and have a dish of ice cream.'" Art picked up the tab. "That's what ruins these fast-gaited guys," Corum concluded. "Nibbling at ice cream at 9:30 at night, when sober, hard-working folk are in the shucks."

After attending early Mass, Art was at the rail again Tuesday morning. He saw little reason to change his routines, and when the races began, he picked up where he had left off the day before.

In the first three races Happily, Up-and-Doing, and Birdlea kept Art a winner. He piled his winnings on Caballero II in the fourth. Six lengths behind at the turn, Caballero II slid through on the rails to win by a neck. By now, bookmakers were gunshy, afraid that Art had inside information or was too hot to handle. Some lowered the odds on his bets; others turned their backs on him.

In his Tuesday morning column, "It's Art But They Don't Like It," Bill Corum teased bookmakers. Corum, who scooped other writers on Rooney's hot streak, placed his Saratoga opening day winnings at $90,000, a figure he subsequently revised upward. Corum wrote that a friend (probably Buck Crouse) had urged Art to quit after he had bet $6,500 on Jay Jay and "seen him jay-walk home . . . going away. 'There's no law against my hitting two more winners,'" Art had responded. "'Besides which, they'll be running here again tomorrow. I might as well bet these two heats on Monday while I'm hot, as two on Tuesday when I may be cold.'" As it turned out, Art was hot on both days. "When you're losing," Art told the *New York Post*'s Toney Betts, "pull up. And when you're winning, send it along."

When Corum conveyed to Art that Redskin owner George Marshall, a reformed horseplayer but incorrigible playboy, disapproved of his betting. Art replied, "When George gives up the broads, I'll give up the nags."

The People's Choice

If Corum's Tuesday morning column chiseled the broad outlines of Art as a lovable heroic figure, other sportswriters sharpened the image that summer. Like Seabiscuit, Art was portrayed as an undersized perennial loser who was bouncing back. He was Dagwood Bumstead from Smoketown, the owner of a losing football team in the fumbling NFL. As the Great Depression dragged on, Americans had developed an insatiable appetite for stories about overcoming adversity. Whether they were about a man named Rooney or a horse called Seabiscuit, people wanted to read tales of good men and women who bumbled their way from rags to riches and remained unchanged. If Art was not a perfect fit for the part of the inadvertent hero, he was close enough.

Syndicated columnist Bob Considine knew that his Depression-weary readers lived vicariously through Art's triumphs. "Mr. Rooney," Considine offered, "is the gentleman who apparently is doing what the average citizen would rather do than eat. He is, to all accounts, making a quick fortune by driving the horse park bookmakers to the poor house. If you are up on your horse racing and your legends, you will remember that young Mr. Rooney first leaped into national prominence when he emerged from the haze of Pittsburgh with a lumpy roll of coarse cash, entrained for [Empire City] and proceeded to give the boys who sit on the stools beneath the stands a merry walloping."

The racing press portrayed Art as the antithesis of a racetrack sharpie. Their Rooney was a pudgy guy with a working-class accent, a pregnant wife, and a couple of kids back in Pittsburgh. He was Jimmy Stewart at the racetrack, dumbfounded by his own luck. By Wednesday night in

Saratoga, Betts wrote: "The casinos were licking their chops in anticipation of the new plunger. But Rooney never touches the dice, cards or
wheels. It's against his principles; it's gambling. Rooney goes to church
almost every morning, never swears, puffs an occasional cigar and sips
a little beer from his own brewery . . . He also made a considerable donation to charity." Betts, one of the nation's top turf writers, got most
of it right. He knew that Art loved Seabiscuit. "He'll bet $50,000 if the
Hard Tack colt ever meets War Admiral." But he knew nothing of Art's
history as a cardsharp.

Art was not talking. His silence made it easy for Mara to step in and
give the writers what they wanted to hear. "He's got the perfect disposition for a plunger," Mara told them. "He's a good sport and he's got
ice water in his nerves. He had $12,000 bet on Seabiscuit the last time
it was out, and he was standing right over there talking football with
some guy when a fellow ran up to him and yelled that Seabiscuit won
but was disqualified. Rooney never batted an eyelash, but kept right on
talking football."

Toney Betts picked up on Rooney's calm demeanor, writing that he
wagered $10,000 as nonchalantly as flipping a coin. "And he does flip
a coin to choose a horse when in doubt," Betts claimed. While acknowl-
edging that Art had a knack for recognizing the slightest edge, Betts mistakenly wrote that Rooney was deaf to paddock information. He de-
tailed Art's bets at Empire City and Saratoga, but his info was hearsay.
Mara, who knew that Art was sharp and connected, cheerfully reported
otherwise to any writer in earshot. "I saw him flip a coin over a couple
of horses the other day," Mara proclaimed, "and bet ten grand on the
one that came out heads. It won. Another day they picked his horse out
of a photo finish, and it meant $50,000 to him. That's a lot of sugar."

Mara figured that racing gained if the average Joe believed that he
could become the beneficiary of random good fortune. "Rooney's as
plain as an old shoe," Mara told Bob Considine. "You'd never recognize
him as a big operator if he hadn't had all that publicity. The day he won
$100,000 around here he was selling ten-cent chances on some kind of
charity thing his brother, who's a priest, is behind. What do you think
of that?" Considine, who golfed with Art, thought it was great copy.

Reporters and bookies shared a common investment in this tale. In fact, bookies were some of Rooney's biggest supporters. "This might seem like a paradox on the face of it," Considine pointed out, "but the boys are shrewd enough to realize that it is good business for them for the word to get around that they are being taken for a ride by a citizen. It prompts other citizens to attempt the same, and prompts Mr. Rooney himself to try to live up to his recent reputation and make bigger and better bets." Those who knew about Art's early morning research at the stables, his careful calculations of the figures, and his expert advice kept quiet. Few reporters arose early enough to see for themselves how Art studied the field, track conditions, and jockeys. Nor did they know that he was a savant at calculating the odds on cards as well as horses.

Damon Runyon was among those who underestimated Art, maybe because of Pittsburgh's record in football. He concluded that Art knew little about racing and owed his good fortune to Tim Mara and luck. "The world loves a winner," Runyon reasoned. "The crowds now trail Mr. Rooney to find out how he is betting, but they will let him severely alone the minute he begins losing."

By Tuesday, reporters were shadowing Art. When he strolled into a nightclub, the orchestra struck up "Little Annie Rooney," the 1890 tune that inspired a Mary Pickford movie and the popular comic strip, *Little Orphan Annie*. Even Art had to chuckle at his newfound celebrity. He had been a virtual unknown the day before. "Now," Toney Betts wrote, "Art finds out that every one in Saratoga knows him."

By Wednesday morning, Art's story was splashed over the sports pages, and sportswriters were comparing his streak to racing legends. Corum of the *Journal American* was the first to call Rooney "Pittsburgh Art," an allusion to the legendary "Pittsburgh Phil," racing's star gambler of the 1890s. But Corum refused to anoint Art as Pittsburgh Phil's successor. "Somehow I don't believe it [Art's luck] will keep up. This is the sixteenth season your correspondent has come to Saratoga at least once during the meeting—and it never has kept up. Still, it sure is fun while it lasts, ain't it, Mr. Rooney?"

"Mr. Rooney," Damon Runyon speculated, "perhaps is too young to have heard of the immutable law of the turf: 'All the horse players die broke.'" But Runyon noted the coincidence that Art "should represent the same city that produced one of the few exceptions to the law—Mr. Pittsburgh Phil Smith, the greatest race track plunger of the gay nineties." Smith had left millions in his estate, and his grave in Allegheny Cemetery bears a sculpture of a man clutching a racing form. But Runyon did not expect Rooney to reprise Pittsburgh Phil's success.

Toney Betts revealed that Art's parents, Daniel and Maggie, lived just two doors away from Pittsburgh Phil Smith's old home on Perrysville Avenue. This "short, swarthy man with smiling Irish eyes," he enthused, "was having a "history-making run of wagers . . . [that] made the tall tales of Pittsburgh Phil seem like bedtime stories." Betts offered another legendary comparison. "The ghost of Bet-a-Million Gates is haunting the betting ring at Saratoga, and today bookmakers covered their frightened faces and rushed blindly into sheltered corners to avoid the new terror of the horse players."

Art's traveling companion, Buck Crouse, also provided columnists with terrific material. Crouse was a rugged-looking but easygoing man who had gone a few too many rounds with Harry Greb. He had taken a pounding in the ring, and as his punch drunk syndrome worsened, he sometimes believed that he was St. Francis of Assisi. Buck, who attended Mass daily, said he prayed for Art to win for three days. But when Art decided to return to the track for a fourth day, the ex-pug told Art he was forced to pray for him to lose. "He doesn't want Art to win too much," Betts reasoned, "because then, like the camel through the needle's eye," Art would be a million-to-one shot against making it to heaven.

A few writers, who understood Art's gambling prowess, felt compelled to reveal it. "Mr. Rooney, be it known, plays hunches," wrote Kent Hunter in the *Evening Journal and New York American*. "But Mr. Rooney picks his horses before he picks a hunch to fit it. Mr. Rooney picks up information round and about in the sporting world, and makes many friends with an infectious Irish grin. But Art Rooney doesn't play 'hunches' as most race-goers understand them, any more than 'bet-a-million' Gates, or John Drake, or 'Pittsburgh Phil,' or 'Chicago' O'Brien or Arnold Rothstein did." Hunter could see Art's exceptional discipline for a gambler.

Between two $100,000 days at Saratoga and another big day later that summer at Aqueduct, Art was reported to have made wagers of a size not seen since the days of Arnold Rothstein, ranging from $25,000 to $50,000. Rothstein, best known for his role in fixing the 1919 World Series, had frequently bet $100,000 on a race. One writer professed that Art had won so much cash at Saratoga that Pinkertons escorted him to the bank. Hunter's story, "Hunches and Some Irish Horse-Sense," concluded that Rooney had won $300,000 by the time he left Saratoga. He had defied Damon Runyon's expectation that he would crash and burn. Runyon and Rooney would become friends, and Art spent time with him when the older writer was dying from throat cancer.

Art liked reporters but shunned the spotlight. Notoriety made it harder for him to bet. Even so, Art's photo at the track regularly appeared in the press into the fall. Coming from a culture where drawing attention was disdained, he usually dragged someone else—often Tim Mara—into the picture with him. In most photos, Art wore a rumpled suit with a fedora tipped up on his forehead and held a cigar as he stared intently at a racing form. The stories were headlined, "Art Rooney Wins Again! Denies $100,000 Killing," "Rooney Prays, Then Slaughters Books," and "Bookies Cry for Help, Art Rooney's at Races." One story captured the mythic Rooney in a few lines: "Dear Boss: I'm fainting. That fellow, Rooney, has horseshoes in both hands! Can't Wait came in at 16-to-5. That's $64,000 he won on that race."

Home and Away

While in Saratoga that week, Art had ignored the home front. But after three unbelievable days, he stopped picking winners and knew it was time to go home. The gambling debts that had forced his father to temporarily abandon the family when Art was a toddler had left their mark. He got in a round of golf at Glen Falls and left for Pittsburgh the next morning. Changing trains in New York City, Art returned home on Friday, July 30.

He stopped first to see Kass and the boys, then his parents, and finally his priest. While Arthur had been at Empire City and Saratoga, Kass had been confined to the apartment on Western Avenue with four-year-old Danny and two-year-old Art Jr. during the heat of the summer. She was due to go into labor. But Art brought good news—they would never have to worry about money again, he told her. At his parents' house, a few blocks away, he dropped a bundle of cash in his mother Maggie's lap. At St. Peter's, the story goes, Art visited the Reverend Michael O'Shea. "Father," Art began, "I understand you had a collection here last Sunday for the orphanage." Father O'Shea replied, "Yes, Arthur, we did and we missed you." Reaching into his pocket and pulling out his bankroll, Art answered "Well, I want to do my bit." He counted out ten $1,000 bills and, according to one account, "lays 'em on the table and walks out."

After Saratoga, Pittsburgh was a quiet oasis where Art could be himself. Word of his luck was spreading, but he escaped the spotlight in his hometown. Art was a familiar figure there, not the projection of hard luck dreams.

By Wednesday, August 4, with Kass mollified and a suitcase of fresh clothes packed, Art took the train back to Saratoga. He hardly missed a beat. On Thursday, Frank Ortell announced in *The Telegram*: "Art Rooney, the turf's most daring plunger around today, who clipped the bookies for more than 100 grand last week, returned yesterday to belt the layers for another $50,000." After Art's horse, Time Signal, won the first race, bookmakers began cutting the odds on his bets. "To be sure," Ortell wrote, "the layers today are wrapped in gloom, for with Rooney in their midst they never know what to expect."

As Mara regaled journalists with stories about Art, they resurrected the mythic Rooney, the plunger who played hunches. "When he first invaded the Spa," Bill Farnsworth wrote in the *Evening Journal and American*, Art "didn't know the difference between a hoss and a 52nd St. cabaret singer. But the lovable Mara gave him a few tips, and before Art returned to Smoketown he had belted the layers for $120,000."

In two days upon his return, Farnsworth argued, Art hit the bookies for another $75,000. One race, Mara said, was a photo finish. "And do you know what that Rooney says afterward? He says 'The biggest kick I got all day was waiting for them to develop the pictures to see whether my horse won or not. That was real fun. It's no fun when your horse gallops home.'"

On Friday, Art called home and found out that Kass was experiencing signs of labor. Art, who had been staying at Mara's place, told him, "Tim, I'm never going to let you forget this day because I'm going to name this baby after you." He couldn't resist one more whack at the bookies before leaving. On Saturday, Mara's son Wellington stood at the rail with Art during the first race. "I don't remember whether he bet $10,000 or stood to win $10,000," Wellington recalled. "His horse won but was disqualified. He said, 'Well, my luck has changed, so I'm going home.'" In a hurry, he took a taxi 190 miles from Saratoga to New York City, then boarded the train for Pittsburgh. He stopped at St. Peter's to pray and rushed to Mercy Hospital where Kass had gone into delivery. Fifteen minutes later, Kass gave birth to their third boy, nine-and-a-half-pound Timothy, on August 8, 1937.

The next day, while Kass and baby Tim rested, Art caught the train back to New York City, then up to Saratoga. He stayed there for four days, returning on Friday, August 13. Frank Ortell wrote that Rooney had put $100,000 of his winnings into annuities by then to keep it out of the bookies' hands. "They'll never get that back," Art said. Ortell expected Art back in Saratoga for a fourth fling before the end of the meet, but with Kass and the new baby coming home from the hospital, Art stayed in Pittsburgh for a couple of weeks.

To Aqueduct

With his team training that August in Two Rivers, Wisconsin, Art left for Aqueduct. According to Frank Ortell, "The season's most spectacular plunger—they say he'd bet on a crippled yak if he had a hunch on the beast—picked three winners at the Long Island track opening yesterday and walked off with something like $100,000." Ortell catalogued Rooney's betting for the day. After winning $25,000 on Jack Be Nimble at 5-to-1 in the first race at Aqueduct, Art sat out the next three races. He lost a sizeable bet in the fifth race but recouped it when he wagered $20,000 on Undulate at even money in the sixth. In the final race, Art won $80,000 on Wrenace, a 2-to-1 favorite who came from well back in the pack to win at the wire.

Reporters trailed Art like ducklings. Several openly pulled for Art to win to keep the story alive. When Art confronted a Hearst reporter about a story that he was cleaning up when he was not, the reporter laughed: "Nobody's interested in losers. I'm going to keep you alive because I like the assignment.'" Art was miffed. "He was making such a big deal out of me in the papers that if I went to the men's room I had nine guys behind me waiting to see if I might give up a tip on a horse."

The hype only intensified. "The bookies at Aqueduct very nearly fainted in a body today," the Associated Press reported, "when the word got round that Mr. Art Rooney, the man who comes from Pittsburgh with a pocketful of cash and hunches, was coming out to the track to watch the gee-gees scampering again. He said, 'I sort of like it here.' About the time that Wrenace was winning at 2-to-1 with $40,000 down."

After cashing in at Aqueduct, Art and Mara headed into the Bronx, where they sat ringside at Yankee Stadium as Joe Louis took on Tommy Farr, the British champ from Wales who had worked in the coal mines that fueled the Ebbw Vale Iron Works, where Art's grandfather and great-grandfather had worked. Louis, who had taken the heavyweight championship from the Cinderella Man, James Braddock, only two months before, won a bitterly fought 15-rounder. Although many of the 36,000 in attendance booed the decision, both Rooney and Mara gave the nod to Louis. Art, the papers wrote, won $400 betting that Farr would go the distance. But he told reporters that they exaggerated his winnings at the track and distorted those at ringside. His only wager was on Louis to win.

It mattered less and less what Art said—which wasn't much—or even what he did. He regularly denied that he had won as much as reported, but the more he protested, the less he was believed. At Aqueduct, a writer observed, "People weren't interested in the Woodmere Claiming Stakes: the attraction was Art Rooney . . . This was one man, like his Pittsburgh predecessor Phil who had beaten the races."

Toney Betts' story that he dropped $50,000 at Aqueduct in September was one of the few to nick Art's image as the luckiest bettor in

America. "The Rooney legend has gained such credence," Betts wrote, "that it is hard for his admirers to believe he was thrown for a loss. But even at the height of his plunging at Saratoga, Rooney was differed out of $86,000 when Gosum was disqualified."

Bob Considine later wrote that Rooney also missed a chance to bet $50,000 on a 10-to-1 shot—and win $500,000—when Frank Erickson was not at his bookmaking post and his assistant, shaken by the magnitude of the wager, refused the bet. Art watched his horse scamper home the winner. "Rooney lost his chance to win a pot that would have lasted him darn near a week," Considine chuckled.

To everyone else Art was an untarnished winner. The *New York Herald Tribune* reported in September that even golfers were afraid of him: "He bounced a second shot off a shelter house, onto the green and rapped in a 15-footer for a birdie on the 396-yard fifth at Bayshore, thereby causing his companions acute pain." Stories about Art's betting reached from coast to coast. They painted him with a Norman Rockwell brush. "Rooney never curses," one reporter stated, and "one of his worst dissipations is ice cream . . . With all his surface hardness, his Pittsburgh friends will tell you that there is a heart of gold in Art Rooney, who is noted for his own style of welfare work among unfortunates in and out of his own bailiwick."

Art had clipped the bookies, but his streak was terrific for horse racing. He was Everyman, the symbol of high times returning to the track. "Not since the wild days of 1920 has there been so much money around the racetrack," Frank Ortell exclaimed in *The Telegram*. "The way the boys are laying it on the line indicates there is no such thing as a Depression any more." In Saratoga, the gaming rooms took in twice as much action as they had the year before, and money flowed in a "wild orgy" at the nightspots.

At the end of the eastern racing season, Bob Considine offered the definitive summary of Rooney's summertime ride. His source was likely Mara or Madden. Considine argued that Rooney had parlayed his winnings over five races on opening day at Saratoga into a hundred grand. "He was credited with another $100,000 day at Aqueduct," Considine added, "but it was in reality a $50,000 one." Considine said that Art recorded his daily wins and losses in a tiny red book. It included one race where he won $39,850 and another day when "he trudged away a flat $30,000 loser—which was the final day at Aqueduct. That was his worst afternoon." Considine concluded that Art had won about $400,000 at the track, half of which he gave back to the bookies. "But he is definitely $200,000 ahead," Considine claimed. His 1937 winnings of $200,000 would have added up to $3 million in 2008 dollars.

Considine reported that Art had never really made a big bet before that summer when he plunked down $5,500 on Mara's advice on a 4-to-1 shot. "Since then he has lived in the kind of daze you and I would be in if we suddenly kicked up a gold mine." Art would dispute that notion, saying that he had been betting "big money" at the track for some time. "No one paid any attention to me, though, until some newspaperman got hold of the news one day that I had won several thousand dollars. He worked it up to something big because I was on a good streak. I had won and lost as much before that, but no one ever said anything about it."

In the public's eye, Art remained the average Joe with the Midas touch. On any given day that racing season, dozens of people asked Art if they could rub his back for luck. His fan mail reached movie star volume. Some of those who sought his counsel at the track—like Al Capone and J. Edgar Hoover—were famous. Most were just hard-luck guys looking to escape the Depression. A playwright asked Art to back his play on Broadway; a single mother asked for help to go to college and care for her child. No one had the poor taste to wonder why his luck had not carried over to football.

Art's success made him a marked man. "Since his big splurge at Saratoga several weeks ago, he hasn't had a minute of peace," Les Biederman wrote in the *Pittsburgh Press*. While Rooney talked to Biederman by telephone from his hotel room in New York that September, reporters and photographers waited for him to appear in the lobby. Biederman knew Art well enough to understand that he preferred to be left alone. "Funny thing about Rooney and all that money he won," Biederman wrote. "Usually persons on hearing of such a streak discount the luck of the bettor and say, 'Well, I hope he loses it all.' But in Rooney's case, there wasn't a friend in town who hasn't said he was darn glad to hear of it and it was time Art was getting a break. A swell fellow."

While Art's story played almost universally as that of Everyman striking horse racing's mother lode, a few writers dug deeper. Several alluded to Art's earlier involvement at the track. "You know," Art told writers who cornered him at the Turf and Gridiron Club after a loss to Mara's Giants in October, "I was just fooling you bookmakers this season. You fellows thought I was green. Why, shucks, I've been playing horses for twenty years. I made my first bet at the old Wheeling racetrack when I was managing that club in the Middle Atlantic League." Art, characteristically, turned the subject to baseball. "I'm a better baseball player than a horse player," he contended.

Art was wrong. He was better at the track. The same attributes that made Art an exceptional athlete and promoter made him an outstanding horse player. He could recognize a winner, see when athletes or horses were performing at their peak, or when they were slumping. He understood how bio-rhythms and game conditions affected performance.

But Art's real edge came not so much in horse sense as in gambling sense. "I didn't necessarily know more about horses than the next guy," he confided to Red Smith, "but I might have known a little more about playing. I was never afraid to bet." When he was in his teens, his father had taken Art to Cleveland's Randall Racetrack, and Milton Jaffe had introduced him to Pittsburgh's horse rooms. Jaffe also taught him how to handle his gambling. For Art, betting was an intellectual, not an emotional, act. "He was a very warm-hearted individual," Wellington Mara explained, "but he was a cold-blooded gambler . . . He used to say 'I don't know much about horses, but I know how to bet.' I think he meant that he had control of himself at all times."

Art often said that his career as a horseplayer began during the summer of 1925 when he played baseball for the Wheeling Stogies. His biggest bet then was $200. Art's first trip to the Kentucky Derby came in 1928, when he traveled to Churchill Downs with Milton Jaffe and David Lawrence. He never missed another one until he was in his eighties.

Rooney's ride would be increasingly difficult to repeat as pari-mutuel betting pushed legitimate bookmakers from the tracks. Art adamantly preferred betting with bookmakers. Under the pari-mutuel system, the racetrack handled the bets and continuously recomputed the odds on each horse to reflect the amounts bet until the race began. This system allowed states to take a cut of the wagers. But Art hated it because he wanted the odds he bet to stick. With so many gamblers trying to get money down on any horse that Art bet, his odds worsened under a pari-mutuel system. "A horse player who bets more than a deuce around the mutuels is asking for a flop in the poorhouse," he complained.

The Winnings

Art's success did not change his lifestyle. "Rooney," Bob Considine wrote approvingly, "has a horror of ostentation. He has put none of his easy dough into display. The 16-cylinder Cadillac which he is supposed to have bought is in reality a matronly Buick." Considine reported that Art purchased $75,000 worth of annuities. Other stories said that he donated $10,000 to an orphanage and sent $50,000 to Dan for his mission in China. Art later laughed that if he had sent that much money, his brother would have owned a province or two.

Art did hand out thousands of dollars in small amounts to people who came by his office in the Fort Pitt Hotel or to his home on the Northside, as he would do all his life. And he told Kass that it was time to leave their apartment on Western Avenue and find a house for their growing family. She could buy any house she liked, just as long as it was near the Ward on the Northside. Finally, Art took some of his newfound cash and put it into his football team. He badly wanted to win at football, and he was willing to spend to achieve that goal.

7

Between the Races and the Fights

1937–38

As his team readied itself for the 1937 season, it seemed that Art's luck at the track might carry over to football. It did, for a week or two. With Kass house hunting, Art felt so good he began working out with his players at Greenlee Field. He didn't look much like a football player anymore, but he bet Wilbur Sortet, the lone holdover from the 1933 squad, that he could kick a field goal from the 30-yard line. Splitting the uprights, Art won a buck.

It got better. On opening day, John Blood, in his debut as Pittsburgh's coach, brought fans to their feet with a 92-yard kickoff return. Blood, the oldest player in the league at 33, scored twice as Pittsburgh beat Philadelphia at Forbes Field. The injuries that had washed out Blood's 1934 Pirate season were healed. When Pittsburgh shut out the Dodgers in Brooklyn the following week, Art thought that his summertime ride was continuing.

The press loved Blood. His devilish charm and wickedly wild behavior made great copy. Blood had played on three championship teams in Green Bay, and fans hailed him as the savior to make Pittsburgh a contender. "Prospects have never looked rosier," Art's brother Vince exclaimed to reporters. Pittsburgh, he said, was "entertaining serious thoughts of a National Pro Championship."

Blood still shipped out as an able-bodied seaman between seasons. Like many sailors, he read widely and held strong, often radical, opinions. In 1934, he had taken part in the bitter conflict on the San Francisco wharves that led to a citywide general strike. Despite being in the twilight of his career, he drew fans. "Cap'n Blood is without a doubt the most colorful and romantic performer in the Big Time," the *New York*

Post's Jack Murphy wrote on the eve of Pittsburgh's clash with New York. He noted that Blood's real name was "McNally, as fine an Irish name as you'd ever hope to find." Murphy claimed that when Art, "the Pittsburgh racetrack plunger who also owns the Pirates," was looking for a new coach, only "a fellow with the Blood of Auld Erin coursing through his veins" would do.

That was news to Jap Douds, Luby DiMelio, and Joe Bach, none of whom had Irish roots. Blood was simply Art's kind of guy, a hell-raiser with a sense of humor whose career would be capped by induction in the Hall of Fame's first class.

Blood was the focal point on the field. On offense, he kicked, passed, ran, and caught the ball; on defense, he played end; on special teams, he returned kicks. On top of that, Blood called the plays and made substitutions. Against Detroit, he stepped in to punt when Pittsburgh was deep in its own territory despite the fact that quarterback Johnny Gildea could kick the ball into orbit. "John's wrong," Rooney said to halfback Max Fiske on the bench. "I don't care if he kicks it out on the 1-yard line, he's wrong." But when that was exactly what Blood did, Rooney nudged Fiske and said, "You know I've never seen anything like that Johnny Blood."

But by the third game of the season, Blood was wearing down and the team suffered commensurately. The hopes that skyrocketed when the Pirates began the season with two victories fizzled as they lost their next five games. Blood cut and traded several players, including Max Fiske, whose problems were not all football-related.

After the third game, Fiske and Jean McNulty, Kass Rooney's younger sister, eloped to West Virginia. She was a stunning model, and he was an athlete in his prime. But by Monday, Fiske was no longer a Pirate. Art traded his brother-in-law to the Cardinals. Fiske's release had more to do with family than football. Art's sister-in-law Alice, the self-appointed guardian of the McNulty sisters, disapproved. Alice saw football players as predators best kept away from her sibling.

Blood might have been better served by trading himself. In game seven, after his turnovers caused Pittsburgh's defeat, he injured his shoulder and was done for the year. The season bottomed out in late November, when only 3,706 dispirited and shivering fans watched Brooklyn shut out Pittsburgh in the final game. The toast of the racing world that summer, Rooney was a loser again that fall. Pittsburgh finished a mediocre 4-7. While NFL attendance cracked the one million mark, Pittsburgh's plummeted from an average of 18,093 fans per game the year before to only 13,272. That confounded Rooney. The NFL was making it. Why not in Pittsburgh?

The *Post-Gazette*'s Havey Boyle figured Rooney was jinxed. In October, Boyle had brushed away four of the defeats by blaming inexplicable fumbles, bad officiating, and uncharacteristic rampages by otherwise lackluster opponents. A month later, he was dour. "The fans here will not support in great style a loser," Boyle warned. "Pittsburgh is used to pretty nearly the best and second division stuff with them is out." Boyle estimated that Art lost $25,000 in 1937, the fourth season of five in the red.

While the league as a whole was picking up steam, Pittsburgh, Brooklyn, Philadelphia, and Cleveland finished 1937 with losses ranging from $10,000 to $30,000. At the league meetings, Art argued that losing clubs should receive two draft picks before winning teams made their first in order to improve their rosters. His motion failed.

In the meantime, Art needed a quick fix to make his club a winner and box office success. He set his sights on Byron "Whizzer" White, a triple-threat star who could kick, pass, and run the team to victory while packing Forbes Field. "He's all set to make the young man an offer he will not be able to turn down without plenty of deliberation," sportswriter Harry Keck reported. But getting the Colorado University star to play pro football would not be easy.

Of Quarterbacks and Thoroughbreds

At this stage in Art's life, football was the interlude between racing seasons, not his raison d'être. But he launched a spirited campaign to persuade Whizzer White to play for him. The most exciting player in the college ranks, Whizzer was more than an All-American quarterback. He was the All-American boy.

Byron White had grown up in the tiny town of Wellington, a mile above sea level in northern Colorado. He began working in the beet fields when he was six and hardened his body wielding a sledgehammer on a railroad section crew during high school. In the fall of 1934, Byron followed his brother Sam, a football star and Rhodes scholar, to the University of Colorado. By the time he graduated summa cum laude in 1937, president of the senior class and the best collegiate player in the nation, Whizzer was a national sensation, a young man virtually every mother and father in America would have loved to have as a son-in-law.

White had worked his way from fourth string his freshman year to an All–Rocky Mountain Conference player as a junior. His senior year, now 6 foot-1 and 185 muscled pounds, White became the focal point of Colorado's single wing offense, where his triple-threat abilities could be maximized. White set a conference record for points scored. He could pass, run, and kick, as well as return kicks and play defense. No player in the last half-century had gained as many total yards in a season as Whizzer White did in 1937. In one game, he was good enough and tough enough to carry the ball seventeen times in a row.

The most talked about and respected player in the nation, White had curly blond hair, high cheekbones, and green eyes that gave him looks to match his physique and intellect. Yet he remained a modest, even shy bookworm who waited tables at a sorority house and hit the books as hard as he hit opponents. Hoping to study law at Oxford University in England, he entered the Rhodes Scholarship competition.

It was no surprise when months before the draft, White informed the Cleveland Rams, who held the top selection, that he did not intend to play professionally. The Depression might have made the NFL a more viable option for ex-collegians who could not find work, but White had alternatives.

Undeterred, Rooney announced that he would pursue White in the December draft. "If his name is on the league's draft board when it comes my turn," Art declared, "I think I'll make him my first choice." Unlike contemporary NFL clubs that are obsessively secretive about their intentions, Rooney staked out a public claim to White. Other owners then backed off. They doubted White would play in the NFL but realized they would all benefit if he did. That December, they applauded Art's gamble when he selected White in the draft.

The publicity alone helped the club. "I thought Rooney was trying to bring some class to the league," *Washington Post* writer Shirley Povich concluded later. "The idea of a Phi Beta Kappa All-American had family box-office appeal, and Rooney wanted to exploit it."

White, however, had been thinking only about his Rhodes Scholar interview in San Francisco, where he impressed the selection committee and won the Rhodes. White then joined his teammates in Texas for the Cotton Bowl, while Art drove to Miami. He telegraphed White an unheard of offer—$15,000—twice what Sammy Baugh, the best-paid player in the league made, and went to the track.

In Florida, Kass and her sister Alice tended to the boys while Art hung out with Dan Hamill, John Blood, Jim Rooney, Milt Jaffe, and Walt Kiesling, who were along for the ride. Ed Karpowich, who played tackle for Art, joined the traveling party to watch over Danny, Artie, and Timmy. He divided his time between protecting the boys from Miami and Miami from the boys.

An early riser, Art played a round of golf after Mass most mornings and then headed to the track, where he shared a box with Tim Mara. But his luck had run out, and America's greatest plunger was giving back some of what he had taken from the bookies in 1937.

Art and Blood made a quick trip to New York to see White play basketball at Madison Square Garden in the inaugural National Invitational Tournament on St. Patrick's Day. They cornered him in the locker room afterward, and Blood followed up by visiting White in Boulder. "No one I've ever met in the athletic realm has impressed me more," Blood declared. "I think his talents, and his makeup in general, represent the difference between a good football team and a great one." But White was unbending.

Art returned to New York for opening day at the Jamaica racetrack. Despite his reversal of fortune, his photo and picks for the day were in the papers. He was still portrayed as "the sensation of the betting firmament." One columnist said he bet $1,000 bills with "the nonchalance of a Vassar graduate getting into a box of chocolates." When Art won $3,200 at Jamaica, the press dismissed the sum as paltry. Rooney told reporters that he needed Whizzer more than a winning horse. The press countered that if Art had four more paydays like opening day at Jamaica, he could afford the $15,000 he had offered White.

Art had begun buying thoroughbreds that spring and applied to the Wheeling Downs, West Virginia, jockey club for permission to race. His jockeys and horses wore emerald green silks with a gold "R" on them. Though Art missed opening day, he was the center of attention. "Art Rooney, a fellow who won a bundle of money on eastern tracks last summer and dropped a big share of it at Miami during the winter," Claire Burcky reported in the *Pittsburgh Press*, "cashed in a sizeable chunk" on the first day of racing. Burcky said Rooney had bet $1,000 on his horse, Gray Chieftan, with Pittsburgh bookies. The stallion paid $13.20 and was part of a daily double that paid $68.80. Art frequently showed up at Wheeling Downs, usually with Blood or Karpowich, to watch Gray Chieftan and his other horse, Halo, run. On one visit, his two horses combined to win the daily double. Art also tried backing a legal bookmaker again, bankrolling Abe Meyer's operation at Belmont Park that summer. It was a losing proposition.

Art was a better bettor. He finally got the chance to bet on Seabiscuit against Samuel Riddle's Triple Crown winner War Admiral in their famous match race at Pimlico. Art had said earlier that year that he would bet $50,000 on Seabiscuit if the race took place. If he did, he cleaned up. Seabiscuit, an 11-5 underdog, won.

But it appeared that Art had lost his bet on Byron White, who announced in June that he would attend Oxford in the fall. Rooney made one last unsuccessful pitch and gave up. Then, in late July, White wavered. Before leaving Oxford, Sam White asked the Rhodes Trust if his brother could delay his arrival until January. While flatly denying requests in the past to wait a complete year, it was willing to consider a one-semester deferral. After deliberating, the Trust wired permission for White to defer for three months. White immediately cabled Art to confirm that his offer was still good. On August 1, able to sign the richest contract in NFL history and keep his scholarship, White called Art at one in the morning to accept the Pirates' offer to play the 1938 season. His first call reached a clerk at the Paramount Motion Pictures' local shipping office. His next call awakened an elated Rooney.

Whizzer arrived a week later. Art, known for his equanimity but nervous about how much he had riding on this young man, paced back and forth at the airport. The plane landed three hours behind schedule after hopscotching from Denver to Pittsburgh. Overwhelmed, Art collapsed on a bench while White, full of energy, joked with the press.

Whizzer White

Art preferred keeping a low profile, but he relished milking Whizzer's. On August 10, 1938, White signed his NFL contract during a national broadcast on KDKA radio. The contract for $15,000 plus a share of the gate for exhibition games was double what any player in the league had ever made. It was also guaranteed. White would be paid even if injured, an exception to league practices. Art distributed a thousand posters with Pittsburgh's home schedule superimposed over an action shot of White: "The World's Greatest Football Player." He was football's most hyped rookie since Red Grange. The *Press*'s Eddie Beachler called White "Greater than Grange."

The next day, White arrived at camp at St. Francis College in Loretto. "We'll have a better team, and perhaps a championship team, solely because of the Whizzer," Blood proclaimed. Art predicted that Pittsburgh would be the team to beat.

Columnists claimed that Art's financial success was assured while Art, after seeing White play, said, "I was worried for awhile, but now I'm satisfied that he's got it—and plenty. Harry Keck uttered a lone cautionary note—that White's unprecedented contract might precipitate "salary headaches" when other players compared it with what they made. His worry was lost amidst the euphoria.

At camp, Coach Blood immediately challenged White to a 100-yard footrace and won easily. Blood scrimmaged the rookies against the veterans, who gave White a working over. But over the next ten days, White led the rookies to victories over the veterans in two of three intrasquad games, including a 21–0 shutout. While respecting Whizzer's ability, some vets resented his salary and celebrity. White tried to show he was a team player, not a prima donna, but jealousy lingered.

Art was also hearing from other owners, who privately complained that he had exploded the salary scale. George Marshall demanded: "What are you trying to do?" Art told him that he was trying to bring some class to the NFL.

As successful as Art had been in wooing Whizzer and fanning the hype around him, he failed to capitalize on his coup. He could blame himself for some of that. White was tough, agile, and intelligent. Like Art, he also had that knack for thinking ahead of the play. But he was beaten up and exhausted before the regular season even began.

Art had wedged in exhibition games against local semipro clubs to make money. He also, against his better judgment, allowed White to play in the College All-Star game against the league-champion Redskins. He worried that perpetually disgruntled Redskins, who were angry with owner George Marshall over their salaries, might vent their frustrations on the highly paid player. But recognizing that White was the game's chief draw, Art let him play.

White emerged from the game with a black eye from a punch and a gashed forehead from a slip in the shower. The next day, White headed to Rhode Island for another college All-Star contest. The day after that, he squeezed in a 54–0 victory over the St. Rosalia Preps and then checked into St. John's Hospital with a bruised sacroiliac. White was released in time to rush to Detroit by plane for the league opener. "White played, but he shouldn't have," Rooney reflected. "As a matter of fact, he played throughout the season in a crippled condition because of those preseason injuries." Art would have preferred that White's NFL debut occur in Pittsburgh, but he was hostage to a dreadful schedule. Some of the problem was the baseball Pirates' fault. Poised to return to the World Series for the first time since 1927, they said that Forbes Field would be unavailable in late September and early October. That left Art with a badly unbalanced schedule. Pittsburgh would play its first three league games in three different cities in six days in early September. Worse, only three of eleven games were at home.

The scheduling chaos would be for naught. The Pirates' pennant hopes were dashed by a September collapse climaxed by Gabby Hartnett's infamous "Homer in the Gloaming." With darkness enveloping Wrigley Field and the score tied in the bottom of the ninth, Hartnett homered to beat Pittsburgh and put Chicago in the World Series.

Frustrated by Forbes Field's limitations, Art talked to Duquesne University about building a football field on campus that he would share with the school. Nothing came of the effort, and for the time being, Art was stuck at Forbes Field. Pitt Stadium was off limits, and Allegheny County did not allow admission charges at South Park.

Regular Season

Although White scored in the opener, Pittsburgh lost 16–7 before a capacity crowd of 18,000 in Detroit. Sportswriters praised White, who led all rushers, returned punts, and played well defensively. Even Detroit fans stood and applauded when he came out of the game. The Lions had given White "the business," one Buffalo reporter wrote. "But the Whizzer took his initiation with a smile." He had shown that he could "take it." Fans mobbed White as police escorted him off the field while Art told writers that White was worth every cent of his salary. "I am sold on him."

But reporters posed a troubling question. Where was White's blocking? *Pittsburgh Press* sportswriter Chet Smith's answer: "The Pirate line was busily engaged in picking violets and tying their shoelaces." The Lions "could neither quench [White's] spirit nor dim his sparkle," one reporter commented. "Yet colossal as he is, he would have had to be a Seabiscuit or a War Admiral to carry the handicap posted by his Pirate mates." White's teammates had failed to block for him.

Returning home on Saturday, players practiced at Phipps Field and were back on the field Sunday to play their second game in less than forty-eight hours. White again impressed fans with his play, gaining 175 yards running, catching, and returning nine kicks against powerful New York. But Pittsburgh tired in the second half, and New York came back to win 27–14. Art began having misgivings about the season. Only 17,340 fans had attended. Some of the luster had worn off White's Pittsburgh debut by the team's defeat two days earlier.

Beaten on Friday and Sunday, the Pirates traveled to Buffalo on Monday to ready themselves for yet another game, against Philadelphia on Wednesday. Over a thousand Pittsburgh fans, including Mayor Cornelius Scully and the city council, traveled to the game aboard a Ham and Cabbage Special. Owney McManus, a downtown restaurateur, packed train coaches with fans and served them ham and cabbage along the way. Arriving in Buffalo in a haze of cigar smoke, the Pittsburgh contingent walked out of the station into a steady rain that delayed the game for two days.

If fans were disappointed, the Pirates were relieved to have the rest. As it was, they faced the Philadelphia Eagles in Buffalo on Friday for their third game in eight days. Counting college All-Star and exhibition games, White had played six games in two weeks and spent the rest of the time in trains, planes, and hospitals.

The Eagles clobbered the exhausted Pirates, whose championship hopes were reeling. "My payroll probably is twice as large as any other club in the league," protested Art. "On paper it's a better team than last season, but there's something wrong. In all our three league games, the blocking and interference has been very poor." Sportswriters, less circumspect, accused White's teammates of dogging it. A Buffalo columnist wrote that if the Pirates were not laying down on the job, White would be better off playing with a high school squad. "The Pirates," he remarked, "presented the sad case of a $15,000 player performing with a collection of 10 cent blockers."

A few days after their third defeat, the Pirates released three players, including starting backs John Karcis and Izzy Weinstock. The press wondered whether they were let go due to poor performance, a salary dump, or discord on the squad. Karcis and Weinstock denied that White was the issue. Their problem was with Blood. The aging player-coach had played almost the entire Philadelphia game to the dismay of players who wanted a chance. But speculation that teammates were jealous of White persisted.

"If I find out there's dissension on this club I'll tear it apart and wreck it," Art vowed. "So far as I can see, the players like the Whizzer and are for him because he came in here unspoiled and a regular fellow." He also scoffed at reports that he would fire Blood. "I never change motors in the middle of the ocean," he said. "I started out this season with Blood and I'll finish with him."

For his part, White dismissed accusations that teammates were not blocking for him. "That's a lie," he said. "Everybody on the team, from Art Rooney down, has been swell to me. The players give me everything they've got. My failures are my own. I threw away that game to Philadelphia right at the start when I fumbled the ball. But there wasn't one word of criticism, or one dirty look from any of the players." His denial, however, could not stop the stories.

"The super back of '37," Gene Ward alleged in the *New York Daily News*, "is a flop in professional football. And it may not be his fault." Ward wrote that White was being "jobbed" by resentful former Pitt and Duquesne players who had given him a rough going-over from day one. "Clever observers, watching the Pirates in every game, have seen key men fall down on their jobs time after time when White lugged the leather."

In Pittsburgh's 17–3 victory over Brooklyn a few days before, White had gained just 1 yard on 17 carries. Ward accused Pittsburgh captain Armand Niccolai of "standing up and watching White trying to dent the Dodger line by his lonesome. It didn't happen just once—and Niccolai wasn't the only offender." Ward suggested that White's teammates were upset by the release of Karcis and Weinstock a few days before: "It doesn't add up to anything with a pleasant odor."

Ward's story angered and embarrassed Pirate players, who met at the hotel where they were staying between games in New York. They wired Ward: "We took this means of assuring Byron that these rumors are entirely false . . . There are no cliques on the team whatsoever." White had their total support. "All [of us] admire him and have confidence in his ability as a great player."

The blocking was noticeably better in the next game and Pittsburgh beat the Giants in New York for the first time. Coach Blood, though, was losing his players' confidence. He put himself into the game several times when Pittsburgh verged on scoring, only to have each drive fizzle. "Our captain went to the referee," Art later told Myron Cope, "and

said, 'What happens if I don't accept a player coming into the game?'"
The ref told him he had that prerogative. The next time Blood tried to
enter the game, the captain refused. "We immediately scored on a pass
and won the game," Art recalled.

White played better as the season progressed, gaining twice as many
yards per carry after the team meeting as he had before. Opposing players kept pounding White, however, and his Byronic good looks were
marred by blackened eyes, gashes, and bruises.

His teammates were exhausted. Since the end of camp in early September, the road-weary Pirates had hardly spent a day in Pittsburgh.
They had been in Detroit, Buffalo, Brooklyn, Boston, and New York and
spent more time in transit than in Pittsburgh. Meanwhile, Art was still
searching for a place to practice; Greenlee Field, which he had used since
1933, was being torn down to make way for a public housing project.

Cutting Losses

The Pirates finally came home in October, but after losing 17–7 to Brooklyn, they fell into last and stayed there. The season had become a competitive and financial disaster, compounding Art's troubles at the track.
Still, Art was smitten with White. He could see something of himself in
the young man, including an intellectual side that he had never developed as deeply.

But hiring White for $15,000 had created problems with other own-
ers, his own players, and his bottom line. In late September, Art discussed dealing White to Brooklyn and then Detroit. He could not complete either trade. Deep down, Art wanted to keep White, despite the
heavy losses. Art told the press, "If you want my honest opinion, I believe Whizzer will finish out the season in a Pirate uniform."

White did, but many of his teammates would not. In October, Rooney
began shedding players to raise cash. Injuries further hobbled his team,
and Rooney postponed his scheduled home contest with Cleveland on
October 16. He said his team was too beat up to compete, and would
play Cleveland in Chattanooga, Tennessee instead, in December. But
Art's credibility was thin. The Pirates had sold two players and cut another the day before, and they had played and lost an exhibition game

before 11,000 fans in Cincinnati on October 11. "Actually, we cancelled it because there weren't going to be any customers there," Art later acknowledged.

Incensed, Cleveland owner Thomas Lipscomb tried to oust Pittsburgh from the league. "I personally think Rooney is a swell fellow, but this postponement of the game is a terrible blow to us. Our team has been going 'hot' and we don't want them to cool off."

Art scoffed at the idea that he would be kicked out of the NFL. "Why, I'm the one that went to bat for the Rams to get them in this league," he said. Art argued that the entire league would have benefited if the season had played out as expected. A better schedule, he said, would have bathed White in limelight. Lipscomb quickly backed off, but Pittsburgh's distress was evident, both on the field and at the box office.

Rooney continued his fire sale of players, "lopping off heads with the abandon of the Soviets," one wag wrote. Art weakly protested that he was stockpiling draft picks for the 1939 campaign by trading players. The Pirates, Claire Burcky noted in the *Pittsburgh Press*, had played to their smallest crowds ever and put Rooney in his deepest hole yet. "I wanted a winner this year," Rooney shrugged, "so I paid some pretty fancy salaries. The team is the highest salaried in the league." But it had fewer and fewer players.

Perhaps Art had gambled too much on White. If good fortune at the track in 1937 had intoxicated him, he was now paying the devil his due in 1938. "Unless Art Rooney locates a fresh bankroll," one columnist warned, "Pittsburgh may not be represented in the National League next year." Speculation had the franchise heading to Boston or Los Angeles while columnists began whacking Rooney for the impact White's contract had on league salaries. Even Bert Bell complained that college players were now demanding the moon. "They think we have printing presses that turn out money."

With so many players sold, released, or hurting, Art struggled to field a team. Of the twenty-two players who traveled to Green Bay in late October, eight had never appeared in a regular season game. Two of the others were coaches—Blood and Kiesling. The outcome of the game was never in doubt. "Another sad chapter," Jack Sell lamented, "was added to the dismal story of the Pittsburgh Pirates gridiron campaign of 1938."

Nevertheless, Art sought exhibition games wherever he could to stanch the fiscal hemorrhaging, estimated at $35,000 so far for the season. Despite a depleted roster, he scheduled back-to-back exhibition games later that month, one in McKeesport, a Monongahela River steel town, the other in Warren to the north. In Warren, before a crowd of 4,000 fans in a town of only 14,000 people, White ran for 150 yards against the Red Jackets, a team of men who worked in factories or taught school during the week. The Pirates changed in the Moose Club afterward and rode the bus back to Pittsburgh.

Rooney marketed White, selling his likeness to local merchants and department stores and to advertise Chesterfield cigarettes. Though White did not receive a cut of the endorsements, he did not object. He said that he had been "exhibited like a freak" since joining the league, but, "If I paid a player $15,000 I would exploit him to the hilt, too."

Despite the Pirates' disappointing season, nobody blamed White. In fact, he won adulation. Like Pittsburgh sporting immortal Honus Wagner, White turned down a lucrative cigarette endorsement for himself. "Frankly, the Whiz stumps me," Chet Smith wrote in November. "He seems too good to be true." Few young men could have handled such hoopla with humility and grace. When White told Smith, "I'd tear up my contract and play for nothing if it meant we could win the championship," the veteran scribe believed him.

"The hard-bitten Mr. Rooney," Smith wrote, "spent the first four weeks of the league season chasing White with a check before he caught up with him." According to Smith, Rooney was to pay White $1,400 after each game, another $1,000 after the season, and extra for exhibitions. Art told Smith that White had $7,000 coming but had been reading about his troubles and wouldn't take it. "If I never get anything else out of football," Art said, "it's worth what it has cost me just to find out there are people like this in the world." After all, Art had spent much more to watch a two-minute horse race and come up with nothing to show for it.

Before the final home game, Rooney stopped by the *Sun-Telegraph* to see sports editor Harry Keck. "If the thing had worked out right, I would have been the smartest owner in the league for taking the big gamble," Art rationalized. "It didn't, so I have to take the rap." Keck blamed Rooney's woes on a crazy schedule, which had clustered three games in eight days to begin the season and four other games after two-week layoffs. Pittsburgh never found a rhythm. "And yet," Keck pointed out about Rooney, "he's the fellow everybody likes and says deserves the best." Rooney, Keck said, doesn't have as much money as people thought, "[He is] a fellow who see-saws up and down in the chips and has had rough going this year."

In the final home game, Washington shut out Pittsburgh before fewer than 13,000 fans, the smallest house to watch the Redskins in 1938. After Art paid the $5,000 visiting team guarantee, he was short $3,000. To make up for it, Pittsburgh entrained to Colorado Springs and Los Angeles to play exhibitions."

Pittsburgh had hit bottom, winless in over a month. Coach Blood stuck around Los Angeles after the exhibition to visit friends and skipped the train back. "John was known to enjoy a good time," Rooney later said, "so we didn't see him the whole week." The next Sunday, Blood stopped in Chicago to watch the Bears play on his way back to Pittsburgh. But his team was playing the Philadelphia Eagles in Charleston, West Virginia, that afternoon. Prior to the kickoff, assistant coach Walt Kiesling watched a plane circling the Charleston stadium. "If a parachute drops out of that plane, Johnny Blood will be in it," he said. "He always likes to make an entrance."

But Blood was being oblivious, not dramatic. In Chicago, a writer in the press box asked him why he wasn't with his club. "Oh, we're not playing this week," Blood replied just as the public address announcer gave the final score, Philadelphia 14, Pittsburgh 7.

Blood missed a brilliant 79-yard touchdown run by White, who averaged 11 yards per carry that day. Granted, Pittsburgh's schedule had been quirky, and Rooney and Bert Bell, trying to draw a better crowd, had moved their game to Charleston, where rain postponed it a few days. Even so, Art was miffed. "The ballplayers came to me," he later laughed, "and asked me not to fire him. And I said, 'Well, this is peculiar.

I always thought the coach worried about the ballplayers.' But in this case, the ballplayers worry about the coach." Art liked Blood and maintained that he would have been a tremendous coach if he had only paid attention to football. But he did not. As Art concluded: "You couldn't depend on John a whole lot."

Before embarking on the West Coast swing, Rooney had announced that despite Pittsburgh's brutal record, he would retain Blood for the 1939 season. Havey Boyle, as close a buddy as an owner could have on the sports pages, wrote, "Rooney, who is noted for friendships, almost to the point of fatuity, denies that his decision about the coaching job is in any way associated with friendship with Blood. It is, he insists, strictly a business proposition." Boyle knew better. Art's sense of loyalty overrode what he knew he should do—fire Blood.

The season ended with one final indignity, the postponed game with Cleveland. Art arranged to play it in New Orleans and got in touch with the city's former mayor, T. Semmes Walmsley. "Coming from the Ward, where you knew politics from the day you were able to speak, I knew who Walmsley was," Art explained. Walmsley assured Art that New Orleans' current mayor, Robert Maestri, would back the game.

Rooney, who paid Cleveland extra to travel to New Orleans, arrived early to promote the game. At the train station, Art asked two priests if they were going to the game. They knew nothing about it and apparently, neither did anyone else. Art took Whizzer with him to see Mayor Maestri, on the assumption that while the mayor might not know Rooney, he would know White. "Well, Maestri and I talked a little bit, but right then and there I knew I was dead." Maestri had never heard of Rooney or White, and he thought the Pirates were a college team there to play Tulane. He told Art, somewhat lamely, "I'll see what I can do."

On game day, Art sat with Walmsley in a deserted Sugar Bowl. Walmsley kept saying that everybody came late to events in New Orleans, but the stands never filled. Cleveland won the game, and later that evening, the police called Art to tell him they'd pinched a few players for causing a ruckus. Art asked the sergeant to hold them until they were ready to board the train home.

White had begun the game battling the Giants' Tuffy Leemans for the league lead in rushing. After carrying thirteen times for 81 yards, he won the title, undermining the persistent stories that teammates had undercut him. White, who treated the squad to a New Orleans dinner the next day, never gave the stories any credibility. He told *Sports Illustrated* in 1962, "As far as I'm concerned, that was just a figment of some people's imagination." White, who roomed with Ed Karpowich, said, "I knew he never would have put up with that sort of thing." Art agreed, recalling how Karpowich had picked Whizzer off the ground when the veterans were piling on during practice and yelled, "Don't anybody else touch him—we can't afford to lose this guy." Johnny Blood added, "Whizzer was our meal ticket. It would have been crazy to sandbag him."

White's accomplishments could not hide Pittsburgh's dismal record. "The team that looked as if it might actually put up a close fight for the pennant," Havey Boyle observed, "has proved the worst disappointment" of any Rooney squad. Boyle had never seen a year with three bigger flops than the baseball Pirates, who folded in September, Pitt football, which despite its vaunted "Dream Backfield" had lost to Duquesne and Carnegie Tech, and Rooney's football team. The only solace for Pittsburgh sport was boxing, where a cohort of young fighters was on the rise.

Art told White he wanted him back for another season but could not afford anywhere near the $15,000 White had made in 1938. "Money won't enter into it if I decide to play another year," White responded. After some New York papers claimed that White had given back $6,000 of his $15,000 salary, Art protested. "Gee, I ought to know about those things . . . It is the silliest of all the ridiculous yarns." He said he had the cancelled checks for the entire salary. "He got every penny he was guaranteed . . . and unless he's spent it all for some of those bicycles over at Oxford, he still has it as far as I know."

Before sailing on the *Europa* for England on January 3, 1939, White stopped in Pittsburgh to bid Art farewell. "It may be three years before I see you fellows again," he said, explaining that he intended to stay overseas during his breaks to catch up on his studies and travel. Art was sorry to see him go. "He's a great guy," Art told anybody who would listen. He said he would welcome him back the next season, "with a brass band."

Art, boxer Billy Conn, and Milton Jaffe drove Whizzer to the Pennsylvania Railroad Station to catch his train for New York. Jaffe, vice president of the club, had been upset when Rooney signed White for so much money. Jaffe did not feel it was fair to the Pirates' owners, who were shouldering liability (at least on paper). Art told him, "I don't think you understand football," to which Milton replied, "I don't think I do either. You can have my end of this club." Art took the shares, but it is unlikely that any money was exchanged. He had given them to Jaffe in the first place.

The Pirates had lost 9 of 11 NFL games and more money than ever before. Art wasn't ready to give up on football, but as he pulled away from the train station and looked at Billy Conn in the back seat, he saw the face of Pittsburgh's sporting future. Conn, four months younger than White, had spent as much time in the ring as the Rhodes scholar had in the classroom. Art figured he was ready to make his next move, back to boxing.

8

Returning to the Ring

1939–41

In early 1939, Art Rooney found himself saddled with a costly stable of thoroughbreds, a chronically losing football team, and a bumbling bookmaker or two he was bankrolling. The Pirates' losses of $35,000 for the 1938 season pushed Art's six-season NFL deficit over $100,000. By some accounts, he had dropped twice that much at the track in the last year. Art's bankroll and his psyche were taking a pounding. For a guy who loved to win, Art was doing nothing but lose. His persona as the most versatile athlete in Pittsburgh was long gone, his flash of fame as a bettor dimming, and his investment in Whizzer White a colossal bust. Now, he was the owner of a hapless football team in a city indifferent to its fate.

Art was thirty-eight, with three sons and a pregnant wife. Although he had bought sizable annuities with his winnings at Saratoga, he had no fallback income. Scratching around for a financial and psychological diversion, he settled on boxing.

Boxing had always been Art's best sport, where his toughness, speed, and intelligence mattered more than his size. Though he had rejected a professional career, Art remained close to the local fight scene. He knew everybody in Pittsburgh boxing and they knew him. Moreover, Pittsburgh was on the cusp of becoming a fight town again, soon able to boast that five of the eight world champions were native sons. Art became central to their careers.

If nothing else, putting on fights would get Art out of his increasingly crowded home. Art was a loving father; his brother-in-law Max Fiske's favorite memory of Art was watching him assemble an electric train for the boys on Christmas Eve. But he had little patience with toddlers clamoring for attention.

As much as he loved his family and city, Art took off for much of the year. He spent January in Miami with his buddies because Kass was too late in her pregnancy to travel. That February, he missed Valentine's Day, telegraphing her from another racing venue: "A speedy message of love to the one who is always my Valentine, Arthur." Art's absence on Valentine's Day might have been dismissed as a bit of male wanderlust, but his presence in Chicago on "football business" when Kass went into labor in March was more egregious. The twin boys, John and Patrick, were a surprise. Kass had had only the slightest inkling that she might be carrying more than one baby; her brother John's wife, a nurse, had thought she heard two heartbeats. Kass received another telegram from Art: "Congratulations. I do not know what else to say. I am sorry I was not there. With all my prayers and love, Arthur." As Kass recuperated in Mercy Hospital's maternity ward, telegrams and well wishes poured in from the Maras, Bells, boxer Fritzie Zivic, John Blood, and her congressman. She even received an offer to book her five boys with Eddie Cantor's five girls for a vaudeville tour. Kass smiled indulgently over each message and forgave Art's absence. She understood the man she had married.

With Kass and their five boys at home, Art returned to racing. In May, it was the Kentucky Derby, in June and July, Aqueduct and Empire City. Art knew every stop and porter on the train between Pittsburgh and Manhattan, and he could find his way around Madison Square Garden in the dark.

Boxing, however, gave him cause to be in Pittsburgh. Realizing that Pittsburgh was about to harvest its richest crop of fighters ever, Art and Barney McGinley had formed the Rooney-McGinley Boxing Club in 1936. Before Rooney-McGinley, boxing historian Roy McHugh observed, most promoters in Pittsburgh were "fly-by-night guys who operated out of their pants pocket." Art and Barney, however, were rooted in Pittsburgh sport.

They shared an Irish heritage, a zeal for politics and sport, and a common friend, Owney McManus. The former bantamweight ran a

restaurant on Fourth Avenue downtown that was a center for Pittsburgh's sporting life and the place where McGinley and Rooney began
their friendship.

As a boy, Barney McGinley led donkeys out of Cambria County coal
mines. During the 1920s, he left the coalfields for Braddock, a Monongahela River mill town near Pittsburgh. Anchored by the historic Edgar Thomson Steelworks, Braddock flourished during the 1920s. So
did McGinley. After Prohibition ended, McGinley opened a bar and
ran a horse parlor where bettors waited for race results from the ticker
or radio.

In March 1939, Rooney and McGinley expanded operations, announcing a series of fight cards under the lights at Forbes Field. Boxing aficionados applauded the news. Rooney-McGinley, Chet Smith
exclaimed, "is by far the happiest thing that has happened to the fight
industry in Pittsburgh in many long years."

Art was no newcomer to the business. He had fronted the money for
New York fight manager Bill Duffy to rent theaters around the country
to show films of popular matches, including the Carnera-Louis bout. He
also promoted fight cards, often as benefits. Regis Welsh, Pittsburgh's
leading boxing writer, applauded Art's entrepreneurial spirit and national
connections. "Rooney's entry is a welcome sign of high-class production. He will, at least, make an effort to bring bouts of high caliber—
and if they are not high class he will not bother with them."

Bernard McGinley had learned about boxing by subsidizing it. He
had been taken "by almost everyone who had an idea he could promote
so long as Barney would 'bankroll,'" Welsh wrote. McGinley lost "angel" investments backing fights at Hickey Park in Millvale and Motor
Square Garden in East Liberty. But he had always made good on his
obligations.

Rooney and McGinley hired Ray Foutts, a veteran fight man from
East Liverpool, Ohio, as matchmaker. Tapping into deep reservoirs
of goodwill and trust with the usually skeptical fight world, Rooney-
McGinley enjoyed impeccable timing. The local economy was pulling out of the doldrums by 1939; more important, Pittsburgh, which
once had nurtured boxers Harry Greb, Frank Klaus, and George Chip,

now had several contenders in training. In gyms scattered about the city, hundreds of boys and young men were pulling on gloves every day of the week. The better ones fought in preliminary bouts on Rooney-McGinley cards. The best headlined main events.

Boxing's constituency overlapped with professional football's. Most young boxers had climbed into the ring out of the region's hardscrabble working-class and, by now, second-and third-generation immigrant neighborhoods. They hoped for the prize money that made fighting a reasonable alternative to low-wage jobs or no work at all. In the ring, they could be somebody. Their fans came from the same milieu. Tales of Harry Greb, Pittsburgh's most famous boxer, inspired them; so did James Braddock, the Depression's Cinderella man whose fights they heard on the radio, and Joe Louis, who came out of Detroit to take Braddock's belt away.

No single nationality dominated the ring, and the old practice of taking Irish names had faded. Teddy Yarosz, son of Polish immigrants, was from Monaca, an Ohio River mill town. Sammy Angott, born Samuel Engotti, was an Italian American from Washington, PA. Ferdinand 'Fritzie' Zivcich (Zivic) was one of five fighting sons of Croatian immigrants who settled in Lawrenceville. Billy Conn, "The Pittsburgh Kid," hailed from an Irish American neighborhood in East Liberty. Charles Burley lived on the Hill, a child of the great migration of African Americans out of the South. All but Burley would win titles.

Chet Smith singled out Conn as a tremendous draw any time he entered the ring and Burley, Zivic, and Angott as candidates to fight lightweight champ Henry Armstrong. "The new club hits the deck at an opportune time," he said. "The city is starving for a taste of high-class boxing."

Art saw that hunger when he drove to Madison Square Garden with *Post-Gazette* sports editor Havey Boyle in July for the light-heavyweight title bout between Billy Conn and Melio Bettina. A thousand Pittsburghers were there, including four hundred who arrived on train coaches Owney McManus organized. Removing the rubber band from his bankroll, Art took all the action he could get on Conn. Art and Milton Jaffe had helped to guide Conn's career although neither had a direct financial interest in him.

Billy, who would become Pittsburgh's most famous fighter since Harry Greb, first showed up at Johnny Ray's gym when he was fourteen. Ray, an old stablemate of Greb's who drank heavily, told the youngster to get him some moonshine if he wanted to learn to fight. Conn returned with Ray's fee and began training. He made his inauspicious debut in 1934 when he was sixteen, losing a four-round preliminary to a 25-year-old foe in Fairmont, West Virginia. The purse was $2.50; Billy's cut was fifty cents.

Conn soon found his form. Fighting mostly in his hometown, he went undefeated from late 1935 until the summer of 1937 and held his own against seasoned opponents like Teddy Yarosz and Fritzie Zivic. Two spectacular fights with Fred Apostoli in New York City won him the title shot in the Garden against Melio Bettina. In his fifty-second professional bout, Conn beat Bettina to become the sixth Pittsburgher to win the light-heavyweight title.

The next day, Art was at the Empire City Racetrack. "No, I'm not exactly through with horses," Rooney told writer Toney Betts, who had mythologized him after Saratoga in 1937. "But I don't bet them as high as I used to. I was toying with hundred-dollar bills yesterday and wound up a two-fifty winner on the day. Beer money for the boys to toast the new world light-heavyweight champion." Turning to a bookmaker, Art admitted his luck had turned: "Sure, it was soft when I was picking winners, but you bookmakers caught up with me all right."

Betts, who had credited Tim Mara for Rooney's epic 1937 run, figured that Art had gone the way of all horseplayers. "When he became the Great Art Rooney all the trainers and touts on the turf stuffed his ears with paddock information. That was the finish." Art played along with Betts' assessment, but Betts was wrong. He had underestimated Rooney's resiliency.

Rooney-McGinley staged its first Forbes Field promotion a few nights after the Conn-Bettina bout. Fritzie Zivic and Charley Burley headlined the card, which also featured Sammy Angott and Teddy Yarosz. Arthur Donovan, boxing's most famous ref, officiated.

Zivic and Burley, who had split two brutal bouts, were popular fighters. Zivic grew up on Plum Alley in Lawrenceville, near the Black Diamond Steel Works where his father worked. He was the fifth Zivic
brother to enter the ring. Pete and Jack had made the U. S. Olympic team
in 1920, the year Art surprisingly declined to try out. "When you grew
up in Lawrenceville," Fritzie said, "your only choices were to fight or
stay in the house. The kids at school made a fighter of me the first time
they heard that my name was Ferdinand."

Over a career of more than two hundred bouts, Zivic emerged with
a flattened nose and a reputation as one of the dirtiest fighters around.
"He choked his opponents, thumbed them, spun them by the elbow,
used the laces of his gloves, and hit low," observed *Pittsburgh Press*
sports editor Roy McHugh. After fighting Zivic, Billy Conn quipped,
"My mother didn't recognize me for five days."

Charles Burley had grown up on the Hill, a couple of miles from Zivic.
After losing in the 1936 Olympic trials, he had traveled to Barcelona to
fight in the People's Games, an antifascist alternative Olympics sponsored by Spain's Republican government. When the Spanish Civil War
caused their cancellation, Burley, a southpaw who could hit hard with
either hand, turned pro. Legendary trainer Eddie Futch called him the
greatest all-around fighter he ever saw. Burley's neighbor, playwright
August Wilson, modeled Troy Maxson, the fictional protagonist of his
Pulitzer Prize winning play *Fences*, after him. Like Maxson, a former
Negro Leaguer who never got the chance to play in the majors, Burley never got the chance to fight for a championship. Like Maxson, he
wound up working as a garbage man on the Hill.

Zivic and Burley had split two matches in which Zivic was on his nas-
tiest behavior. The crowd of 20,000 figured it would be a spite match,
but they were underwhelmed. Burley decisioned Zivic, and one writer
joked, "The citizens were legging it for the exits on the theory that they
could easily rush home and pick a better fight with the little lady."

But the other bouts brought fans to their feet. Yarosz, the son of Polish immigrants, had held the middleweight throne in 1934. Though
past his prime, he stole the show, decisioning Al Gainer, a black fighter
from New Haven. Angott, who would win the lightweight title in 1940,

outboxed Pete Sarron, his battle-scarred Syrian opponent. Art was elated by the gate, which surpassed $32,000 and left Rooney-McGinley with $10,000 in profits for the evening. The fighters were pleased, too. The featured boxers made between $900 and $2,500 each, more than their usual take.

With Rooney and McGinley shepherding boxing's resurgence, Chet Smith concluded, "we won't be bothered with phony matches . . . and all the other skullduggery that has all but killed boxing . . . To anyone who wonders why Rooney-McGinley-Foutts has been able to enlist the backing of every newspaper in Pittsburgh, there's your answer."

Only one discordant note marred that evening. When announcer Joe Tucker introduced Billy Conn at ringside, Yarosz fans booed loudly. They were still upset with the new light-heavyweight champ for his ugly brawls with their hero. Yarosz and Conn had fought three epic clashes. Conn won the first, a fight that Chet Smith called a vicious hooligan brawl. He also took the second slugfest but by an unpopular split decision. The third time they fought, Conn's manager Johnny Ray was in the hospital drying out, and Billy went into a rage, throwing kidney punches and hitting below the belt. Yarosz responded in kind. The two men thumbed, gouged, and exchanged more punches between rounds than during them. Conn lost the decision and the favor of many fans and writers, who blamed him for the disgraceful conduct in the ring.

Still, Conn's hometown heckling before the Yarosz–Gainer fight shocked many. "There couldn't have been, by any stretch of imagination, a reason for anyone to howl in derision at a home boy who has elevated himself to championship heights the hard way," one columnist lamented. Johnny Ray, Conn's manager, was infuriated, and his anger had repercussions for Art and Barney.

Rooney-McGinley had been tapped to copromote Conn's title defense at Forbes Field in September. It would be the first title bout held locally in years and a huge payday for them. But Johnny Ray claimed that Rooney-McGinley matchmaker Ray Foutts, Yarosz's former manager, had orchestrated the insults directed at Conn. He demanded that Foutts withdraw from the bout. Sports editor Havey Boyle, who had just assumed the coveted Western Pennsylvania slot on the State Athletic Commission, called a meeting.

They argued through the night. Boyle told Ray that his indignation was unfounded. When Ray continued to balk at Foutts's involvement, Art interjected, "Johnny, I'll tell you something. Foutts is not to be in on the promotion, not even to being seen or heard around the fight headquarters or the fight itself. But he works for Barney and me and we will pay Foutts on the same basis for this show as we paid him for the first show he put on for us." Ray would not budge, but neither would Art. "That is the way we do business," Art maintained, "and that's the way we are going to do this business—if we get it."

Emerging from the session at dawn, a rumpled Rooney told reporters that after due consideration, he was temporarily withdrawing from boxing. He refused to bend his principles to get the lucrative bout. The *Pittsburgh Press*'s Chet Smith called Art a "stand-up guy, which is another way of saying that his word is as good as money in the pants pocket and he doesn't let down a friend." Art laughed off Foutts's offer to quit. "We'll stick together," he told the matchmaker, "and if they don't want us, the only thing we stand to lose is a headache." That September 25, when Conn successfully defended his title against Melio Bettina at Forbes Field, Rooney-McGinley had no part in it.

Art and Barney did not stay sidelined for long. For many, especially outside the city, Billy Conn was the face of Pittsburgh boxing. Rooney and McGinley were disappointed not to copromote the Conn fight—they genuinely liked Billy—but they still had Charley Burley, Fritzie Zivic, Sammy Angott, and Teddy Yarosz to offer fans.

Rooney-McGinley shared the two rooms at the Fort Pitt Hotel that Art used for football. Football was still small potatoes, and boxing kept the team afloat. "Boxing paid the rent from January until the team went to camp around the first of July," Barney McGinley's son Jack recalled.

In boxing as in football, Art insisted on shooting straight and putting people before profit. But in boxing, his stance had more of a direct payoff. Rooney-McGinley would dominate Pittsburgh boxing through the early 1950s, securing exclusive rights to host shows at Duquesne Gardens and Forbes Field in Oakland as well as summers at Hickey Park in

Millvale. Local restaurateurs served as ticket agents. Owney McManus sold tickets at his Fourth Avenue joint downtown, Johnny Laughlin peddled them at the Shamrock on the Northside, and Goldstein's Restaurant near the Pittsburgh Lyceum, where many of the city's best white fighters trained, handled uptown.

Joe Carr kept football tickets in one drawer and boxing tickets in another. He and Jack McGinley, who began working full-time for the fight club after graduating Pitt in 1941, cranked out press releases on a mimeograph machine and mailed them to one hundred papers in a market that extended north to Erie, west to Youngstown, and east to Johnstown. Carr and young McGinley took care of all arrangements except for matchmaking. That job belonged to Foutts, then Art, and finally Jake Mintz. When Mintz began managing Ezzard Charles in 1947, Jack McGinley took over matchmaking.

Art's brother-in-law Johnny Laughlin brokered a different sort of match. Jack McGinley, a tall, handsome, fair-haired man, spent part of his summers in Ligonier, a little mountain village where many better-off Pittsburghers retreated to escape the heat. Barney McGinley had taken his family there for years, and in the summer of 1939, Johnny Laughlin and his wife, Margaret Rooney, began renting a cottage near the McGinleys for $7 per week. Laughlin winked and asked Jack McGinley to give his wife's younger sister, Marie Rooney, a ride home. "That was a happy day that I'll never forget," Jack recalled. He married Marie in 1942.

Boxers fought as often as once a month, and Rooney-McGinley filled cards with local talent. The ideal fight featured two Pittsburghers or a native son versus a nationally known fighter. Fritzie Zivic, who beat Henry Armstrong to win the welterweight throne in 1940, faced Conn, Angott, Burley, and Jake LaMotta a total of seven times.

By the time the lights dimmed on a fight night and ring announcer Joe Tucker climbed through the ropes, the ring was clouded in a haze of cigar smoke. Although men in the crowd vastly outnumbered women, fights in the stands were rare. Bookies kept low profiles, with most betting taking place among the fans, who had paid between $1 and $3 for admission.

Fights drew a cross-section of Pittsburgh, with priests and politicians mixing with businessmen, workers, and thugs. "We had a standing list of ticket holders," Jack McGinley explained. "It didn't matter who was fighting, they came." David Lawrence had four seats in the front row. "He'd never miss," McGinley affirmed, "and he never took a ticket. He paid for every one." United Steelworkers of America president Phil Murray was a regular, often accompanied by David McDonald, who would succeed him at the helm of the mighty industrial union. So were Milton Jaffe, Dan Hamill, Woogie Harris, and Gus Greenlee. Harris and Greenlee had popularized the numbers game in Pittsburgh.

The fighters took home most of the gate, leaving Rooney-McGinley with about $1,500 on a good night. Unlike football games, fight cards consistently made money. The best paydays came when they sold out Duquesne Gardens or hosted fights at Forbes Field.

In many cities, black fighters were routinely denied top billing, and thought they had to knock out a white foe lest the judges steal the decision from them. Rooney-McGinley, however, consistently featured African Americans on their cards, and enjoyed an unparalleled reputation in the black community. Art was already well known among black athletes because of his friendships with Cum Posey and Gus Greenlee, who managed black light-heavyweight champ John Henry Lewis. More important, black fighters felt that Rooney-McGinley treated them fairly. "Black guys won as much as white guys," Jack McGinley affirmed. "Our judges and referees were above reproach, they really were." Nor did Rooney-McGinley's matches exploit the popularity of white versus black grudge matches. "You tried to make the best matches you could make regardless of color," Jack McGinley said, and that meant featuring black fighters.

New Home

In July 1939, Art and Kass and their five boys moved into a rambling house as big as some of the boarding houses his parents and grandparents had once owned. After winning big in Saratoga, Art had given Kass free reign to select any house she wanted, as long as it was in the Ward. She found a traditional house with a center door and a sitting room on each side of the entry hall at 940 North Lincoln, just a few blocks and a few worlds away from Daniel's old saloon on General Robinson Street. Located a block behind Ridge Avenue, which was dubbed Millionaires Row in its turn-of-the-century heyday, the house sat among other down-at-the-heels mansions where the Scots-Irish of the old social register had once entertained. William Forsyth, an oil refiner, had built the house in 1868. It had sold for $24,000 in 1887, but the Rooneys paid only $5,000 for it fifty-two years later. By then, most of the old-money Presbyterians had long ago left these smoky streets for the breezier neighborhoods of Shadyside or Sewickley, and many of their mansions were being converted into apartments.

The boys were soon bouncing off the home's walls and each other. On the eve of the team's departure for training camp in Two Rivers, Wisconsin, Danny, now seven, christened the house with its first of many sports injuries. He was charging a tackling dummy in the basement when his pal pulled it away. Danny slammed into the basement steps, breaking his wrist in two places.

Football Season 1939

Rooney-McGinley's success had made Art a winner again. Boxing, instead of the horses, was now paying the bills. But it didn't solve the problem that had plagued him since 1933: what to do about his pitiful football team. With Whizzer White bicycling around Oxford in academic regalia, Rooney searched for a new savior—Jock Sutherland.

Sutherland's fifteen-year record at Pitt of 111 wins, 20 losses, and 12 ties included four undefeated seasons and five national championships. But Sutherland had left the university in a huff after the 1938 season when the chancellor uncharacteristically placed the school's academic and financial welfare ahead of its football team. "I have felt for a long time that Dr. Sutherland is the best coach in the profession," Art stated. "If his present plan is to stay out of college football for a year, I believe it would be a good idea to work for us and keep from getting rusty."

Art wooed the living legend, but Sutherland felt qualms about staying in Pittsburgh and abandoned coaching that year. Art was crestfallen but hoped that someday he would persuade the revered coach to work for him.

He had no better luck with Whizzer White. The outbreak of war in Europe brought White home. "Don't be surprised if he is back in our lineup this season," Art said hopefully in August. "Here's a tip on how certain we feel that he'll be back." The team had just reordered 5,000 new envelopes with the picture of Whizzer on them. But White enrolled at Yale Law School rather than return to football.

That summer, Art spent most of his time in Pittsburgh. When he hosted the league meetings at the Fort Pitt Hotel in July, Bears owner George Halas came in early to play a round of golf with him and John Blood. Blood had replaced Milton Jaffe as Art's patsy on the links. "We have a friendly little bet on each hole," the coach laughed, "and if I don't soon watch out, he'll be into my 1940 salary."

Blood took the team to a remote part of Wisconsin to train, but Art stayed home. The team opened at Brooklyn in mid-September. With only three starters back, they retained an aura of the unknown. But by game's end, they were revealed as no better than the squad that had lost its last six games the year before.

Pittsburgh fans listening to the game on radio heard talk of the spirit and fight displayed by their inexperienced players, but Brooklyn's seasoned veterans trampled them. Coach Blood cut four players after the game. Art's brother-in-law Max Fiske was among them, his on-and-off career with the team off again.

Before their second game, Harry Keck wrote wistfully, "One thing about the Pirates. If the well wishers of Art Rooney, the owner, had their way, the club would win the championship every year. And, if it ever does win, it will be one of the most popular sports achievements ever recorded in this town." But Pittsburgh lost 10–0 to the Cardinals and the following week 32–0 to the Bears before a disappointing Forbes Field crowd of 10,326 fans. They had now lost nine in a row.

Green Bay had traded Chester "Swede" Johnston to Pittsburgh before the season. "That's where you wound up when you were through," Johnston later recalled. "We had a nut for a head coach—Johnny Blood. But you couldn't help liking him." Blood, full of sayings, had his players shout "Pirates never quit!" during calisthenics. But even Art realized that Blood was not committed to the fundamentals of football. "I let my coaches have a free hand," he later confessed, "but it didn't work."

After the Bears game, Johnny Blood walked the plank. He did it on his own; Art would never have pushed him. "You've got to win in this league," Blood acknowledged, "and I'm not winning, so I resigned to let somebody else try it." Karl Marx once remarked that historic events occurred "the first time as tragedy, the second time as farce." If Blood's first time as a Pirate was tragically cut short by injuries, his second time had become a farce.

Walter Kiesling took over. "Kies," once a top NFL lineman and among its biggest at 270 pounds, had played and coached in Pittsburgh for two seasons. More disciplined than Blood, he put the team through a grueling practice on his first day as head coach and led the squad to their first victory, albeit against the semipro McKeesport Olympics. Even then, the Pirates had to come from behind to eke out a 9–6 win. A few days later, they lost Kiesling's NFL coaching debut to the Giants. They beat another semipro team in Richmond, Virginia later that month, but otherwise, the Pirates lost week after week before diminishing crowds. It got so bad that Art asked the Dodgers if he could play a game scheduled in Pittsburgh in Brooklyn instead. That way, Art would be paid the visitors' guarantee instead of having to pay it.

By November, local journalists were predicting that Rooney would not be able to withstand spiraling deficits. As offers came from Louisville, Boston, and Buffalo, most felt Art would sell or move the franchise. Even Art had his doubts.

"Rooney deserves considerable credit for holding on," one sportswriter observed. "A less venturesome fellow long ago would have picked up his dishes and called it quits." Local sportswriters hoped that Art would get a break—in the weather, on the schedule, or on the field. "Rooney has been trying hard to produce a winner that will please the fans," one said in his defense. "He has suffered a lot of tough luck and dropped a bundle of money." But no breaks came.

The national press speculated more matter-of-factly. One reporter commented that Art, who two years ago could have bought the entire

NFL with his winnings at the track, was entertaining offers from Boston and Los Angeles to bail him out. No one—perhaps least of all Art—was sure of what he was doing.

Election Season 1939

If boxing was not enough of a diversion, Art was trying his hand at politics, too. The previous summer, he had agreed to run in the Republican primary for the registrar of wills of Allegheny County. He did so less out of any desire to hold office than as a favor for James Coyne. Coyne's political star had imploded, but he remained a behind-the-scenes player. In Coyne's last hurrah, he asked Art to join his slate of candidates challenging the dominant GOP faction.

Art ran a low-key campaign, so unorthodox that it attracted national notice. He spent little time or money on it and often traveled to rallies in the company of his friend David Lawrence, Pittsburgh's leading Democrat, with whom he shared political sensibilities if not party affiliation.

Art drew rave reviews for his first campaign appearance. It came in friendly territory, Coyne's Fourth Ward stronghold near Forbes Field. Those who saw Art that evening said it might have been the most honest and humble political oration ever delivered in Pittsburgh.

Art opened by warning that he knew little about speechmaking and that anyone who expected soaring oratory should leave the hall. Then he startled his audience. "I'm a candidate for register of wills," he explained, "but I don't know any more what I'm supposed to do if I am elected than any of the other fellows who are running for things know what they're supposed to do." The crowd, taken aback by the admission, was silent for a beat then rocked the hall with cheers. "In fact," Art continued, "I don't know where the register of wills office is, so I wouldn't know where to go if I won." That brought forth, one writer said, "a riotous outburst of hand-clapping." But Rooney had more to say. "People keep coming to me and asking me if I could handle the register of wills office. I tell them that offices of that kind depend on the folks who work under the boss. I guess if the register of wills spends his time in Kankakee, the business would go on just the same. That must be right because a lot of politicians stay away from home a lot."

Not done yet, Rooney appraised his own credentials. He had staged profit-making fights but never made money in the NFL. "So I guess it's a question whether or not I'm a good businessman. But I'll bet I could be as good a register of wills as anybody." Art told some stories and sat down. A candidate seated next to him whispered, "Art, that was the swellest political talk I ever heard but please don't make it again. You're going to ruin the rest of us."

The fuss made Art snort. "I only told 'em what I thought was true," he said. The *Scranton Times* applauded Art's "refreshing frankness," as did *Time* magazine. But writers ribbed him when he unwittingly scheduled a campaign appearance across county lines. Art laughed, "Those votes may come in handy when I run for governor."

With Coyne delivering the votes, Art handily won the September 12 Republican primary, including all 113 recorded votes in one district. His campaign headquarters at the Fort Pitt Hotel were the most crowded in the county on election night. Coyne also won the GOP nomination for city council, prompting the *Bulletin Index* to anoint him the top Republican in the county after four years of unwilling semi-retirement.

Conceding the legitimacy of FDR and the New Deal, Art parted with the decidedly more conservative national Republican Party in the general election. He stressed his own credentials, asking people to "Vote for the man who never broke his word." He also confronted an issue that troubled voters: his gambling. "Very truly it is said I have occasionally bet on horses. That's right. I have. I have bet where betting is as legal as selling groceries or any other legitimate enterprise." Millions of citizens bet on horses without anyone questioning their ethics, he argued.

Art's Democratic opponent, John Huston, attacked Coyne but tread more carefully with Art. The *Pittsburgh Post-Gazette* called Art a man of engaging frankness but dubious qualifications. *Pittsburgh Press* editor Edward Leech, who railed against Coyne, criticized Art for cynically campaigning for an office he knew nothing about. But because Huston had been tinged by scandal, the paper withheld endorsement and urged abstention.

Antipathy toward Catholics stung several candidates. An unidentified group distributed palm cards urging voters to deny their support for any Catholic candidate. The card read, "In short—Vote for all Republican candidates and cut Arthur Rooney and James J. Coyne on that ticket, substituting in their place John M. Huston and John Duff. Please spread this information among your Protestant friends."

Art campaigned half-heartedly. The weekend before the election, he watched Billy Conn defend his light heavyweight title against Gus Lesnevich on Friday night at Madison Square Garden. On Sunday, Pittsburgh played the Giants at the Polo Grounds. Art was more incensed over rumors in New York papers that he was "ready to toss in the sponge" and quit football than by the anti-Catholic politicking. The *New York Post* savaged the Pirates, calling them "The National League's weakest entry since the play-for-pay game became big-time," a team whose "disheartened gridders weren't even running out all plays." Another paper claimed that Pittsburgh was in such dire straits that they had arrived in town without enough helmets for everybody. "Unless Rooney locates a fresh bankroll," it concluded, "Pittsburgh may not be represented in the National League next year." Rooney's characteristically cool demeanor was slipping.

Brooklyn punched the Pirates' lights out on Sunday, and Art took it on the chin at the polls on Tuesday. In a strongly Democratic year, Art ran well ahead of other Republican candidates, but lost the election by fewer than 9,000 votes out of the 450,000 cast. If a few thousand Republicans had voted against Art because of his faith, that would have swung the election. Although he hated losing, Art was relieved. He never wanted the job. Coyne lost too, as voters ousted the last remaining Republican officials in Pittsburgh. Art's close friendship with Democratic kingpin David Lawrence would now become his source of political clout.

The team's winless streak reached 16 games in November, and McKeesport businessman Bill Sullivan reportedly offered Art $50,000 for the franchise. The rumor was fueled by a sighting of Sullivan and Jock Sutherland chatting at the last game of the season.

Art responded to rumors of the club's imminent sale or departure from Pittsburgh with ambivalence. "I'm keeping the team," he explained, "unless somebody offers me a lot of money." Despite endless speculation, Art had received only one specific offer, which came via George Marshall from a wealthy Washington family. "They wanted to buy 50 per cent and move the team to Boston. I might have been talked into selling 49 percent and keep the team here, but they had no interest in that," Art told the *New York Times*. "You can say again for me that I'm afraid I'll have the team next fall, unless somebody makes me an offer I'd be crazy to refuse."

Bruised and bewildered, their ranks thinned by injuries, Pittsburgh faced Philadelphia on November 26 to conclude a season in which they had yet to win a game. Art collaborated with the Polish Refugee Relief Fund to make the game a fundraiser to publicize the plight of Poles who had fled Germany's September 1, 1939, invasion. Two parades converged outside Forbes Field, one led by the Polish Falcons from the Southside, the other by the Conemaugh Polish Alliance band that started in Polish Hill. Over ten thousand fans turned out, far more than would have otherwise come to see two hapless teams. The Pirates won their first victory in a season and a half, ending a 1-9-1 season.

Reflections and Projections

Art, who lost $8,000, labeled it "a sad season," but added he had survived five others that cost him even more. He announced that he would retain Kiesling as coach and change his strategy. Rather than pursue expensive All-Americans, the Pirates would sign less-known and less-expensive players who would build their careers in Pittsburgh.

Art waxed philosophical with his newspaper friends before Christmas. Although he had dropped a bundle at the races and in football and lost an election, too, he stuck a plug of chew in his mouth and said that his holidays were the merriest in some time. "Those things all even up in the end. We're going to have a great team next season, we'll toss in a few good fights in the summertime, and my kids are getting bigger and better every day."

He denied he would quit. "They tell me around here I'm fighting a losing battle, that I'll never be able to make a go of it against the three college teams we have in Pittsburgh, and all of those fine high school teams. But I know different."

Art said he wanted to win for the sake of the city's workingmen. "In this workshop of the world there are many thousands of mill workers who never went to college and who don't get a chance to attend the college games because of their work. Sunday is their day of recreation and they would go for a good pro team."

After New Year's day, Art headed to Miami and went fishing off Key West with Jim Rooney, Walt Kiesling, Ed Karpowich, and Billy Conn. They headed back with a full catch, but Art's testiness after the fall's frustrations had not dissipated. The customary practice, with which Art was unfamiliar, was that the crew—locals called Conches—got to keep or sell whatever fish the party did not take. "They got into the dock," Dan Rooney explained, "and my father took one of the fish that was jumping around and threw him back in. One of these guys said to my father, 'Hey, those are our fish.'" Art didn't like his tone and fired back: "What do you mean, they're your fish?" When the crewman remained belligerent, Art said, "These are our fish" and dumped them all into the water.

The crew started swinging, but they hadn't reckoned with whom they were fighting. Conn hung back, afraid of injuring his hands, but the Rooneys, Kiesling, and Karpowich knocked the crew into the water. Other crews entered the fray and before long the police descended on the docks. They arrested the crew and told Art, "Look, these guys needed a lesson, but they don't fight fair like you do. You're liable to get shot or stabbed. Get out of here and don't come back." Art knew that he was losing his equilibrium. The year's losses had exacted their toll, and he needed some peace of mind to face the decisions that haunted him.

9

Season of Reckoning

1940–41

January 27, 1940

On the Saturday he turned thirty-nine, Art felt uncharacteristic anxiety as he knelt in prayer and meditation. Kass and the boys telegraphed their birthday greetings to him at the St. Paul of the Cross Monastery, where he had gone on retreat with Dan Hamill. The nineteenth-century monastery sat high on the Southside slopes overlooking the industrial bottomlands along the Monongahela where Art's grandparents had settled in the 1880s. The Passionist priests who trained young men here to enter their ranks provided refuge for anyone of faith seeking guidance. Art's thoughts were his own as he prayed and did penance. But it's likely he wrestled with what to do about his losing team.

At the end of prior seasons, Art had scrambled to make good on the team's financial losses and brainstormed for a solution to its competitive woes. But he never gave serious thought as to whether he would keep the franchise. Art was not a quitter, and selling or moving the Pirates would foreclose the possibility of ever becoming a winner in Pittsburgh football. He badly wanted to wipe away the stench of eight losing seasons that had cost him more than $100,000. But he had to confront his pride, one of the seven deadly sins. Was he being foolishly stubborn keeping the club?

The Passionists were available to hear his concerns during walks in the garden, where statues depicted Christ's stations of the cross, or among the burial vaults underneath the chapel. In St. Paul's hushed confines, Art considered the alternatives. That fall, a year after Jock Sutherland left Pitt, his confidant, Bill Sullivan, approached Art with a deal. Jock

would purchase controlling interest in the team and become its head
coach and general manager. Art was unwilling to surrender control, but
he badly wanted Sutherland as his coach. When they met on December 31 at the Fort Pitt Hotel, Art had offered Sutherland a contract for
$7,500 and 20 percent of any profit. Sutherland decided to coach the
Brooklyn Dodgers instead. Their millionaire owner, Dan Topping Jr.,
offered Jock twice the amount that Art could afford to pay. "I wish Art
Rooney all the luck in the world," Sutherland said, "but I do not feel
that it would be appropriate for me to coach professional football in
Pittsburgh." It was some consolation that Sutherland was joining the
league, but Pittsburgh's prospects remained bleak.

Without Sutherland to rescue his team, Art faced his season of reck-
oning with conflicting pressures. On one side, Art held a substantial
stake in the NFL, which was finally achieving success. "Maybe this is
just a pipe dream," John Keiran prophesized in the *New York Times*,
"but the notion in this corner is that professional football is going to
grow into something like professional baseball." With the war in Europe reviving America's economy and more collegians matriculating to
the pros, the NFL was gaining traction. Halas, Mara, and most of all,
Marshall, were building winning teams that were prospering at the gate.
Art felt an abiding camaraderie with these men. Few things made him
happier than being a part of the league, especially when he was getting
pounded at the track.

On the other side, winning in Pittsburgh seemed like a flight of fancy
and turning a profit delusional. Even his buddies in the press had lost
faith. Selling the team seemed inevitable. Art's patience was wearing thin,
but he had declined several offers during the season because he worried
that new ownership would move the franchise.

Out of deference to the studious seminarians, Art and Dan Hamill
whispered in the hallways. But during meals, they joked with the priests,
and at night in their simple room, they shared their concerns. Catholicism was their bedrock. Rooney and Hamill spent more time with priests
than they did playing the horses. They observed Holy Thursday each
year by making a procession to seven churches, a tradition that had
its origins in ancient Rome, where worshippers did a penitential walk
to the seven basilicas. They started at St. Mary's of the Point, crossed

the Allegheny River to St. Peter's on the Northside, came back across to the Strip, and finished in Lawrenceville, stopping at seven churches along the way.

Hamill was a shrewd man who could pick stocks, play poker, build a successful company, and—if necessary—get a call through to FBI director J. Edgar Hoover. Known as the "Cardinal without a collar," Hamill guided Art within Catholic Pittsburgh's charitable infrastructure, just as James Coyne and David Lawrence had taught him politics and Milton Jaffe instructed him in gambling. Hamill involved Art in fundraising for St. Vincent de Paul and other Catholic projects. He had initiated a monthly luncheon of one hundred men to support Father Silas, as Dan Rooney was now known, and his mission in China.

Hamill's daily devotions outdid Art's, and if Art was in need of spiritual or financial repair, Hamill could help to mend him. When Art had fallen short of money after the disastrous 1938 season, Hamill stepped forward with cash without being asked. During the 1939 season, Art made him a vice president of the team.

That weekend, Hamill advised Art to hang on to the team and see if he could make a go of it. When Art returned from the monastery on Sunday, he had decided to give himself one more season to make football a success in Pittsburgh. But if the Pirates weren't winning games and making money by season's end, he would give them up.

Rooney then announced his decision. "I'm definitely going to keep the team in Pittsburgh another season. I hope I can always keep it here, but I can't go on losing money with the team here. I'll try it once more in Pittsburgh. But if I lose for the seventh time in eight seasons I guess I'll have to take one of these offers." He mentioned one from Tansey Norton, a friend since they fought in the 1919 AAU championships, who represented Boston businessmen interested in bringing the team to their city. Art had fielded proposals from Washington, DC, Cincinnati, and the West Coast, too. "They're very good offers," he acknowledged, "not quite as much as the Detroit Lions sale price of $225,000, but not far from that. However I've refused all of them for the time being."

Instead, Rooney scoured the country for players that winter and marketed the team with renewed vigor, offering five-game season tickets for $6, a savings of $5. He judged amateur boxing matches and spoke at luncheons and banquets to promote the team. He even announced a contest to find the team a new name.

Calling his team the Pirates had been unimaginative. While piggybacking on the popularity of the baseball team had seemed pragmatic, it had not put fans in the grandstands. More than three thousand entries were submitted. Many played on geography—the Alleghenies or Golden Triangles—while others emphasized the club's Irish roots—the Shamrocks or Rooney Buccaneers. But the greatest number of suggestions came out of Pittsburgh's industrial past—the Vulcans, Tubers, Ingots, Iron Masters, Steelmen, and Puddlers. Art's journalistic buddy Havey Boyle pushed for the Puddlers. He knew that Art's grandfather Arthur had labored as one on the Southside in the 1880s.

In early March, Dan Hamill, Joe Bach, and Walt Kiesling chose the winning entrant—the Steelers. Twenty-one contest winners had their picture taken in the Fort Pitt Hotel. They included John Harris, who owned the Pittsburgh Hornets Hockey team; Arnold Goldberg, the sports editor of the *Uniontown Daily News*; John Tirek, a worker at a CCC camp outside the city; and a single woman. When Margaret O'Donnell of the Northside collected her prize—two season tickets—Steelers ticket manager Joe Carr gave her more than a passing glance. Margaret wound up with a lifetime pass when she became Mrs. Joe Carr.

Chet Smith of the *Press* was dubious about the new name. "No matter what you call a grapefruit, it still squirts in your eye." The franchise's ineptitude was deeply rooted. Nonetheless, Art stayed more focused on football than he had in previous off-seasons. In February, he and Kiesling set off for Altoona to try to persuade center Mike Basrak to play again. The team's top draft pick in 1937, Basrak had been one of their best players before retiring. After a snowstorm stranded them in the Laurel Highlands for two days, Kiesling drove on by himself. When Kiesling returned to pick up Art, he told him that Basrak would sign. The two men skidded dangerously, but happily, back over the mountains, but Basrak changed his mind and decided to coach high school football instead.

Nevertheless, Art's recruiting was on the upswing, and those trying out for the team evinced greater commitment than in past years. Some players even showed up before camp to study the offense with Kiesling.

Speculation about a buyout continued. The *Post-Gazette* reported that although Rooney was "in the football financial dumps," he had nixed an offer of $150,000 for the franchise because the team would have left Pittsburgh. But further deficits, the *Sun-Telegraph*'s Havey Boyle wrote, would force Art to sell. "He has a franchise that stands him between $150,000 and $200,000, and obviously, he will have to try to get a part of his money back by sale, if not through gate." A winning club would draw in Pittsburgh, Boyle argued, but competition from college football and major league baseball limited the Steelers' prospects. "It would be too bad," Boyle concluded, "if Pittsburgh would lose representation in a sport that is growing and has a bright future." But the veteran sports editor was resigned to that eventuality.

There were hopeful signs. According to the *Post-Gazette*, "[Damon] Runyon and [Bill] Corum told Rooney that eventually he can't miss, pointing out the great success the big laundry man, George Marshall, is enjoying in Washington." Others took heart in the 1940 schedule that had the Steelers playing four of their first five games at home. In fact, season tickets were selling better than ever.

Art was more effective resolving NFL matters that he was in addressing the Steelers' woes. In April, he caught the train to New York City to help defuse a battle between Tim Mara and George Marshall that was threatening the league's equanimity. Marshall had been fuming since a critical officiating call had gone against Washington in a key game with Mara's Giants the previous season. The two moguls were now squaring off over the selection of a new commissioner. The NFL's core—Mara, George Halas, Marshall, Bell, and Rooney—were each, in his own way, headstrong and competitive. But Art, well schooled in pragmatic politics, was able to remind them that the league's future required cooperation off the field. As mediator, he counseled all parties about their common goals.

Boxing Maneuvers

Meanwhile, Art had a business to run. After a successful first season, the Rooney-McGinley Boxing Club was ready to reprise its Forbes Field cards that summer. First, it needed to replace matchmaker Ray Foutts, who quit after helping to make Rooney-McGinley Pittsburgh's most successful fight club in decades. Foutts complained that he was spending too much on aspirin. New York boxing mogul Mike Jacobs and his Twentieth Century Club monopolized the best fighters, including Billy Conn, whose manager, Johnny Ray, refused to deal with Foutts. Praising Art and Barney, Foutts said, "Now that I'm out, they have a chance to move in and put on a big show with Conn in the summer. I'm persona non grata there, you see, and I know what that means because I just looked it up."

Art took over matchmaking and mastered the art of politicking among rival fighters, managers, and promoters. The boxing world's disputes were not so different from those that split the Republican Party or NFL, and Art's personal magnetism pulled off matches where others failed. He had little chance of promoting a Conn fight, but better luck with Fritzie Zivic, who became a Rooney-McGinley main-eventer.

When Johnny Ray rejected a proposed bout in Pittsburgh between Conn and heavyweight contender Bob Pastor, Art tried to make a match between Zivic and Sammy Angott. Sportswriters had called Zivic-Angott "the match that couldn't be made." Charley Jones, Angott's manager, hated Luke Carney, who handled Zivic. Jones swore that even if he were starving and in a breadline, he wouldn't take the match if Carney would make a buck out of it.

In August, Art bobbed and weaved between Jones and Carney, persuading them that the potential gate of a Zivic–Angott fight outweighed their mutual dislike. Jones was in Louisville, training Angott. "The story goes," one writer said, "that Art called Jones in Louisville on the hottest night of the summer and talked to him so persuasively—and so long—that Jones finally agreed to the match in order to get out of the steaming telephone booth."

The press was incredulous. Al Abrams of the *Post-Gazette* argued that no other promoter could have pulled it off. With the winner promised a shot at welterweight champ Henry Armstrong, writers anticipated that the August 26 fight would be the best local bout since the third Conn–Yarosz bloodbath.

But on the day of the fight, as Art drove back from Erie, where the

Steelers had played the Bears the night before, and McGinley motored in from Ligonier, both encountered a hard rain that postponed the bout. Back-to-back doubleheaders at Forbes Field pushed it back two more days.

When Angott and Zivic finally stepped through the ropes, Henry Armstrong and his manager, Eddie Mead, were at ringside appraising their next opponent. Zivic decisioned Angott in ten rounds. Mead had promised Rooney he could stage an Armstrong title bout with the winner in Pittsburgh, where it would bring in the biggest gate. But Mike Jacobs, whose promotional rights to Armstrong trumped Mead's, nixed the deal. He set the Armstrong–Zivic bout for Madison Square Garden on October 4.

Jacobs never hesitated to exercise his prerogatives, but he respected Art and hated to cut him off completely. Conn's manager, Johnny Ray, meanwhile, told Jacobs that "Conn wants to fight before a hometown crowd, and wants to help Rooney and McGinley and the Dapper Dan," the Pittsburgh charity that would copromote the fight. "Give us that one, and you won't find any trouble," Ray urged. After Conn knocked out Bob Pastor in the thirteenth round of a sensational bout on September 6, Jacobs gave Rooney-McGinley the nod to promote a Billy Conn–Buddy Knox fight for September 30. The fight was slated as Conn's tuneup for a title fight with heavyweight champ Joe Louis. But the match came apart when Knox lost his next bout. Knox was no longer deemed a worthy opponent, and the Forbes Field fight was cancelled.

Art had little time to feel sorry for himself. He was at Madison Square Garden in October when Fritzie Zivic, his friend from Lawrenceville, upset Armstrong and won the welterweight belt. Art also had a football team to worry about.

Favorable Winds

Art saw ample opportunity to build his fan base. Pitt football had been in free fall since Sutherland's departure, and Carnegie Tech was de-emphasizing the sport. Duquesne was on the rise, but the number of Duquesne players on the Steelers—a quarter of those in camp that summer—meant that its ascendancy would draw more, not less, attention to the Steelers. All three schools were starting play after the Steelers, temporarily allowing them to monopolize the sports pages. But these advantages would mean nothing unless Art produced a winner. "In Pittsburgh tradition," Havey Boyle pointed out, "local fans are waiting to be shown." Give them a team that beats quality opponents, he advised, and they will "turn out in a way to make many another place look ill by comparison." But, he warned, "All the ballyhoo in the world would not induce Pittsburghers to trail after a hopeless cause."

The signs were good. In the preseason, the Steelers rolled over the Trafford Alumni 49–0 before 4,000 fans whose price of admission was a contribution to the local police pension fund, then traveled to Erie to play the Chicago Bears in a benefit for the St. Vincent de Paul Society. Pittsburgh had been helpless before George Halas's Monsters of the Midway, not only losing every game they ever played but losing big. Halas took exhibitions—and just about everything else—dead seriously. But Art enjoyed yanking his chain. In the locker room before the game, as Arthur Daley recounted in the *New York Times*, Halas "was exhorting his monsters to perform gridiron mayhem on their rivals" when Art and eight-year-old son Danny walked in. Halas stopped with his mouth open and stared, flabbergasted. Lockers rooms were considered inviolable. The appearance of a member of the opposition was astonishing. "Say, George," Rooney drawled, "I hope you're giving them that keep-the-score-down talk." Halas was speechless, but a few chuckles started around the locker room until the Bears dissolved into laughter. "The Halas spell," Daley wrote, "was broken." Whether Art's remarks took away Chicago's edge is debatable, but Pittsburgh prevailed, 10–9. Art allowed himself to feel that this might be the year. A third triumph in a lopsided game against the Valley Giants from nearby Beaver Falls on Labor Day set the stage for opening day.

Art had mixed emotions. Opening day meant cutting players, a job he hated. His sons cried when they found out that Ed Karpowich, who had babysat for them during Miami vacations, would be released. Jerry Donnell, who had played for the Los Angeles Bulldogs the year before and hitched cross-country for a tryout, was also cut. Donnell came by the Fort Pitt Hotel, joking that somebody must have forgotten to write his name on the roster. He shook hands with Art and caught a bus back home. "I'm glad he didn't ask me to let him stay on," Art confessed afterward. "Kiesling would have had another problem." Rooney wasn't kidding. He had an awfully soft heart.

Coming off an undefeated preseason, Pittsburgh was positioned for its best start in years. Over 22,000 fans showed up for the opener against the Cardinals at home, a 7–7 tie. Pittsburgh also tied New York the following week at Forbes Field. Art was delighted with attendance. The club had drawn a combined 40,983 fans for its first two games; it had attracted a total of only 50,092 paying customers for five home games in 1939. Maybe this was the year.

A tie against the Giants was satisfying, but not nearly as rewarding as beating Detroit the following week. Art was ambivalent when he saw Whizzer White in a Lions uniform. He had traded White's rights to Detroit before the season and was getting pounded in the press for it. Bob Considine compared it to Boston's infamous trade of Babe Ruth to the Yankees for cash. Art laughed off Considine's barb, explaining that he had done everything possible to get White back after the war began in Europe. "I called Yale so often to talk to him they must have thought I was on the faculty there. I made him every kind of offer, but he was set on staying in school." A year later, Detroit approached him for the rights to sign White. "He wasn't doing my team any good, so why shouldn't I accept the offer? . . . I couldn't sign him, New York couldn't sign him, but Detroit, with a millionaire owner, could." Art felt vindicated when Pittsburgh rallied to beat Detroit.

The Steelers' next game, against Jock Sutherland's Brooklyn Dodgers, was their most anticipated contest since they had played Boston in 1936 for the East Division title. Sutherland, a local demigod, was returning to Forbes Field, where he had played his first football game, as a Pitt dental school student in 1914. Standing well over six feet tall, Sutherland had emigrated from Scotland as a teenager and worked at the American Bridge Works and on the police force of an Ohio River mill town. Enrolling at Pitt, he became an All-American for Pop Warner's national powerhouse. His players revered him, but his husky build and stern face led to his sobriquets as the "Dour Scot" or the "Sour

Scotsman," and opponents always expected a bruising encounter with his teams. Sutherland's arrival in the NFL was trumpeted as evidence that it had come of age. For Art, it was the next best thing to having Sutherland as his coach.

He hoped the game would achieve a longtime goal, selling out Forbes Field. Jock reserved four hundred seats for friends, and Brooklyn owner Dan Topping and his new bride, ice skating diva Sonja Henie, sat among them. Henie, dressed in a gray suit, black hat, and furs, threw out a football before the kickoff in a bit of ceremony borrowed from baseball. Art scrambled to accommodate press requests and to find his Buick, which somebody had stolen before the game.

Art didn't get his sellout. Only 26,618 fans—the third largest crowd for a pro game in Pittsburgh—rounded the turnstiles, far short of the crowds that Jock had once entertained at Pitt Stadium. Pro football still had a way to go. Brooklyn came out on top, 10–3, confirming sportswriter Claire Burcky's belief that a jinx bedeviled Rooney's teams: "An unhappy faculty of giving their poorest exhibitions before their greatest home crowds." The Steelers had gone into the game tied for the division lead, but the loss set them back on the road to perdition, with a match against Washington, the NFL's only undefeated team, on the horizon.

No team rivaled the Redskins, who brought their high-stepping one-hundred-piece marching band and a thousand diehard rooters to Pittsburgh, for pizzazz. George Marshall's marketing antics infuriated rivals, but he showed them sport's commercial future. A consummate showman, he had welcomed Sutherland to Washington that season with young women in kilts doing the Highland fling. Led by quarterback Sammy Baugh, Marshall's 1940 squad was rolling over its opponents on its way to the league's best record. Washington trounced Pittsburgh, 40–10, but at least the game drew well.

After Pittsburgh lost its third in a row, the season was looking more like the troubled campaigns of the past. Nonetheless the Steelers were drawing more attention. Both KQV and WWSW broadcast games, and Hollywood stars like George Raft and Mickey Rooney attended games.

Injuries compounded the team's woes. By the time Pittsburgh lost to Green Bay in late October, five players were sidelined with broken bones. The "fracture fraternity," as the team was tagged, was beaten down, but Art could not afford to sign reinforcements. Instead, he cut players, dumping salaries to reduce financial losses.

"The seamy side of professional football begins to reveal itself at this stage of the season," the *Washington Post*'s Shirley Povich argued after Washington demolished Pittsburgh in their second meeting. The game, he argued, cheapened the NFL. He called the Steelers who played at Griffith Stadium "a woeful gang" who made "a mockery of themselves and the league." Washington had a full complement of 33 players, Pittsburgh only 25 men. The Steelers were exhausted by the second half when the Redskins trampled them with waves of fresh players. "Art Rooney," Povich noted, "simply doesn't have the dough to keep substitutes on the payroll after pennant chances have gone." By going into the game short-handed, he figured that Rooney had saved $2,000 but damaged the integrity of the title race.

The loss to Washington was the sixth defeat in a row. Pittsburgh ended its season with two games against Philadelphia, with last place and the top draft pick at stake. Art and Eagles owner Bert Bell commiserated with each other every Sunday night. Art always asked Bert if he needed any money. "So after I turned him down three times in a row, I got a special delivery letter the next Monday," Bell told the *New York Times*' Arthur Daley. "There was nothing in the envelope except a check for $5,000. Do you wonder why I rave about the guy?"

Pittsburgh beat Philadelphia before a crowd large enough to break the 100,000 fan mark for the season. Pittsburgh had averaged 23,000 per game, three times what it had in 1939. The teams were set to play again in Philadelphia on Thanksgiving Day. Knowing that Bell expected a sparse turnout, Art phoned him. Disguising his voice, he pretended to be the head of the Westinghouse Social Club in town for the weekend and said he wanted to bring a thousand members to the game. What kind of discount would Bell give him? Whatever figure Bell gave, Rooney wanted something lower. Bell kept acceding to the demands until Rooney said, "Ah, forget it," and hung up. Bell got the last laugh when Philadelphia won the game.

Another Kind of Sellout

Art saved a better joke for Bell until the season's end. He decided the time had come to sell a franchise. Oddly enough, the franchise he sold was Bell's.

After the final game, Art announced that Kiesling would return as coach in 1941. His postseason analysis was simple; injuries had done in his squad. "I'm sure we'll have a contender next season." But on December 9, local papers announced that Art had thrown in the towel. They reported the sale of the franchise for between $160,000 and $185,000 to Alex Thompson, twenty-six-year-old scion of a Boston steel company family. The *Sun-Telegraph*'s Harry Keck called the outcome sadly inevitable. Art, he argued, had tried his hardest. "You can't blame the guy." But something about the deal did not sit right. Why had Art rejected offers by Pittsburgh interests seeking to buy the team and sold instead to a Boston combine? With reports circulating that Thompson would take the team to Boston, Pittsburgh fans worried that they had lost the franchise, not just local ownership.

Had Rooney betrayed Pittsburgh? Havey Boyle described Art as a boy from the wrong side of the tracks who sold his homemade wagon to the rich kid. After the meeting at which Thompson was introduced as Pittsburgh's owner, Art spent the night in a Washington hotel, richer but troubled. "It wasn't easy to do," Rooney confided to Boyle, "but I guess it had to come." He had made only $5,000 that season and was tired of the strain of keeping the team solvent. "I figured I gotta do something for the three kids and the set of twins," he protested. Though many people thought he showed little emotion, Art admitted cringing when Thompson assumed ownership.

Still, a cloak of mystery hung over the transaction, which became more baffling as its details dribbled out. Back in late November, the East-West Sporting Club, representing Thompson, had approached Bell seeking to buy the Eagles. Bell called Art, who said he would entertain an offer for the Steelers. Several days later, the Steelers' board of directors appointed Bell as its exclusive agent to sell the franchise. If Bell could negotiate a sale within thirty days, he would receive a twenty percent commission. Bell went back and forth between Thompson and Rooney, dickering over the price.

On December 9, 1940, Bell reached an agreement to deliver the Pittsburgh franchise and the contracts of twenty-four players—seventeen Steelers and seven Eagles—to the East-West Sporting Club for $160,000. For Bell, who was in a deep hole as the owner of a failing franchise, his $32,000 commission as middleman was manna from heaven.

Bell then went to the Eagles' board of directors for their approval because the deal involved some of their players. As compensation for the seven Eagles to be sent to Pittsburgh, eleven Steelers would be transferred to the Eagles. The Eagles board, which Bell controlled as the principal shareholder, unanimously approved. But the deal turned out to be much trickier.

The Eagles board then accepted the resignation of its vice president and approved his replacement: Arthur J. Rooney. It also doubled the number of shares of stock in the team and sold half of them to the Pittsburgh Pirates Football Club (which had never changed its name to the Steelers) for $50,000. Art was the sole shareholder. In other words, Art had bought half of the Eagles. Notes of the meeting indicated that the Eagles, in desperate need of working capital, intended to use half of the infusion of funds to pay off outstanding debts and bank the rest.

Art had never intended to get out of football. He had hatched plans to sell the Steelers but buy into the Eagles with the notion of making additional deals. So far, his plan was unfolding as anticipated. Keck reported that Art expected Thompson to move the club to Boston. He would then partner with Bell to run a team that split its home games between Pittsburgh and Philadelphia. They would christen the team the Keystoners.

But the NFL nixed splitting the franchise between two cities and Thompson wavered about his plans to move the Steelers to Boston. If Thompson stayed put in Pittsburgh, as he was now threatening to do, Art would own half of a football team in Philadelphia. He hadn't bargained on that outcome.

Alex Thompson held the key cards in the deal, and Art was stymied about how to play his hand. Thompson's background was more like

Bell's than Rooney's. His father, the president of the Inland Steel Company, had died when Alex was prepping at Andover, leaving the boy $6,000,000. Although he had played hockey and soccer, not football, at Yale, he hankered to own a pro football team. Thompson, who owned a cosmetic company in New York City, tried to soothe Pittsburghers' worries about losing their team. His partner Bill Mosle, another Yalie, said, "We feel Pittsburgh is a great football town and are confident of being able to produce a winner. I can assure you that we're here to get the Steelers out of the National League dog-house." But, Mosle confessed, they were considering relocating to Boston, which had lost its team when the Redskins left for Washington in 1937. While Pittsburgh fans worried that the club might end up in Boston, Art worried about being stuck in Philadelphia.

Philadelphia fans, however, were exhilarated. Bell, they said, could stand tall again, reinvigorated by the windfall he had received for brokering the deal and by having Art as a partner. One writer, hoping that Bell could persuade Art to move to Philadelphia, described Art as "the banshee of the bookies' existence . . . a two-fisted Hibernian" who had "more color than Helena Rubinstein."

The sale had spun out of Art's control, and he waited to see what Thompson would do next. Art asked Havey Boyle to explain what had happened to the fans who had stuck with the club over the years. "It was my baby," he sighed, "and I'm never happier than when meeting with the football players and the coaches and the owners and I guess that's one reason why when I decided to take the offer for the Pittsburgh franchise, I also made sure to make a tie-up with Bert in Philadelphia." Realizing that he sounded maudlin, Art laughed and asked Boyle, "Do you need any dough? I wonder what tracks are running." But Boyle found his humor forced.

Writers wondered about this new odd couple, Bell, the son of privilege, and Rooney, the saloonkeeper's son from the Northside. Bell, one wrote, had the demeanor of a hotel house detective and dined at the Racquet Club, while Rooney was always finding ways to excuse his coaches and players and preferred a "good sawdust joint." Nonetheless, the infusion of cash provided by Thompson meant that together, they could operate a sound franchise. Just one problem—at least for Art—it was in Philadelphia.

Thompson finally announced he was staying in Pittsburgh. He would change the team's name to the Iron Men and open offices in Pittsburgh by March 1, 1941. Havey Boyle wrote that the sight of Rooney—as native to Pittsburgh as coal and steel—on Philadelphia's sidelines trying to beat a Pittsburgh team would be grounds for treason on the Northside. Nobody felt that more keenly than Art.

An Ace in the Hole

While at the track in Miami that February, Art schemed. Thompson had announced that he would occupy his new Pittsburgh offices by March 1, but he had not followed through. When March 1 passed, Art made his move: He proposed they swap franchises. Rooney asked Thompson to let him stay in Pittsburgh in exchange for the Philadelphia territory.

Persuading Bert Bell to go along was easy. After all, Art had bailed him out of his financial difficulties and promoting pro football in Pittsburgh was more promising than in Philadelphia. Nor did getting Alex Thompson to agree prove difficult.

"It's funny the way it happened," Art explained. "When I sold the Steelers, Bell handled all the negotiations for me . . . The original proposition was that Thompson would buy the franchise and take the Pittsburgh club to Boston and Bell and I would pool our interests in a Philadelphia-Pittsburgh Club, splitting the home games between the two cities." But after the NFL vetoed splitting the franchise and Thompson decided to keep the club in Pittsburgh, Art's fallback plan was to trade cities. His execution of it would play to Thompson's Boston Brahmin sensibilities.

Art pitched the swap to Thompson at Owney McManus's saloon, a male bastion of sports and politics. McManus and Patsy Scanlon plied Thompson with Courvoisier and helped to convince him that Pittsburgh was not his sort of town. If McManus and Scanlon were any indication of what Pittsburghers were like, Thompson knew they spoke the truth. Philadelphia, they pointed out, was more genteel and closer to Broadway, where Thompson belonged. Before the evening was out, Thompson had succumbed to their persuasion. He swapped his Pittsburgh franchise for Philadelphia's, and Art was back as the owner of his city's team. "I know we've gone around in circles," Art said, "but I guess we're settled now. And by the way, the new name for the club, 'Iron Men,' is out. We'll still be the Steelers, and bigger and better, we hope."

After the league approved the franchise swap, Rooney and Bell finalized plans for operating in Pittsburgh. The two partners, who held all the shares, hired Bell as coach and Rooney as business manager, each with a ten-year contract for $7,500 a season. Bell would receive an additional $500 per season for living expenses in Pittsburgh. For the first time in his life, Art was on salary.

Having voted themselves a steady income for the next decade—contingent on the club making enough to pay them—Art and Bell had money left in their treasury. They purchased $17,500 worth of public utilities stock for the team and $50,000 life insurance policies for themselves. By August, however, the franchise was short of cash, and Art and Bert had to jump-start the season by lending the team $10,000. They did not get around to formally changing the name of the new Pittsburgh franchise back to the Steelers and would operate under the corporate name of the Philadelphia Eagles Pro Football Club, Inc. until 1944.

The press was bemused, calling the swap one of the strangest deals on record. "We always felt that Rooney never was very happy about this deal," Vic Wall wrote in the *Post-Gazette*. "His real place is Pittsburgh where he is . . . as much a part of the Smoky City picture as Pitt's famous Cathedral of Learning, Forbes Field, and other landmarks."

Rooney and Bell got the better of the swap. Although Philadelphia was a bigger city, Pittsburgh was the better football town. Bell often raved that Pittsburgh charged twice what Philadelphia did for tickets. The Steelers had also built a much larger season ticket base. "A winner in Pittsburgh undoubtedly would sardine the customers, but Philadelphia is an enigma," one writer suggested. Moreover, as the European war raged, Pittsburgh's economy was rebounding rapidly.

"We have the pick of the Philadelphia and Pittsburgh clubs," Bell contended. "We'll be able to put up a battle against the rich teams, like the Bears and the Giants and Redskins, who always had this bulge on us." But storms loomed on the horizon. "It is no secret that Rooney is delighted to be able to operate at home, and also that his partner, Bert Bell, is happy to be out of Philly," *Press* writer Chet Smith noted. Nevertheless, he wrote, "Mr. Bell is suffering from a case of war-jitters. He believes the league will have a difficult time of it for the next year or two." Bell was not alone. With Germany raging over Europe, many Americans worried that the war would spill across the sea. Alex Thompson might have cooperated in allocating players between the Eagles and Steelers, but Uncle Sam would not be so generous.

10

The World at War

1941–45

On a morning in late July 1944, the phone rang in Art's Fort Pitt Hotel office. It was the call he had dreaded. The naval officer on the line was bending the rules but he wanted to let Art know before the telegram arrived at his parents' home. His brother Tommy had been killed in the battle for Guam. Art called his sister Marie, who was living with her baby in Maggie and Daniel Rooney's house on the Northside. He told her about Tommy and said he would tell their parents. Art sat for a few minutes, gathering his thoughts, then walked slowly to his car.

Art had lost friends to the war, but his kid brother was like a son to him. The world had changed since Tommy—young, impetuous, and brave—had joined the Marines. Sport, for the first time in Art's life, mattered little. He was keeping football and boxing alive in Pittsburgh to raise funds for war relief and sustain morale on the home front. But winning and losing mattered little.

Before Pearl Harbor

Back in June 1941, while America was still at peace, Art's sons Danny and Art Jr. sat in the kitchen one evening. The two Rooney boys, aged eight and six, and several friends huddled around a radio, listening as Billy Conn fought Joe Louis at the Polo Grounds in New York. Most radios across the nation were tuned to the fight. At Forbes Field, the Pirates and the Giants stopped play in the fourth inning and piped the broadcast over the public address system.

Louis was black America's paladin. The heavyweight champ had beaten seventeen challengers in a row, but Conn, the Pittsburgh Kid with matinee idol looks, was a legitimate, if undersized, contender.

Danny and Art Jr. squirmed with excitement. Conn was a frequent visitor to their home and a favorite of their father. He had tossed a football around with the boys in the backyard and often picked them up after school. Mary Louise Smith, a pretty student at Our Lady of Mercy, was usually in the front seat.

Their father was ringside, along with Milton Jaffe. Thousands of Pittsburghers who had traveled to New York aboard Owney McManus's "Ham 'n Cabbage" Specials were scattered around the Polo Grounds. In the dressing room before the fight, Art and Milton had urged Billy on. Their bankroll was on Conn to take the title from Louis.

In a few months, Art would begin his tenth season in the NFL, but football had taken a back seat to boxing, and both were overshadowed by the war. Art's brother Dan, now Father Silas, had come home in March after five years in China. Silas had lost weight and his health while there. Riding back to his mission one night, a bandit had mistaken Silas for a soldier and fired at him. Silas's horse bolted and threw him. His foot caught in the stirrup, and the horse dragged him for several hundred yards, damaging his hip. Silas was to stay stateside for nine months to fatten up on Maggie's cooking and rest with his Franciscan brothers before returning to the mission in Hupeh Province. He had booked passage on a vessel leaving January 2, 1942. But as Japan consolidated its grip on China and began taking over Indochina, Silas's return was unlikely.

Reports from Europe were grimmer. The Germans had chased Allied forces off the continent at Dunkirk and pushed the British out of Greece. The headlines that June concerned Operation Barbarossa, Germany's three-pronged invasion of the Soviet Union. The effort to knock the Soviets into submission would prove to be Germany's fatal mistake. But with the nation still at peace, many Americans focused instead on the fight at the Polo Grounds.

Billy Conn

A month before the Louis-Conn fight, Rooney-McGinley had featured Conn in the city's biggest fight ever. Conn was the light-heavyweight champ, and that alone guaranteed a strong turnout at Forbes Field. But

Billy's charisma and the impending bout with Louis had fueled expectations. "There will probably be more women fans at tonight's fight than at any other this town has known," Harry Keck had speculated. "They've heard so much about what a handsome devil Billy is that they want to see for themselves."

For Conn, much had ridden on the Pittsburgh fight against Buddy Knox. He had been less than scintillating in recent bouts, and promoter Mike Jacobs had threatened to cancel the Louis–Conn bout. But Art had known that Conn was ready. At training camp, while they had been standing on a dock in the lake, Billy had reached down, scooped up a passing turtle, and bitten its head off.

Conn indeed had been ready; he flattened Knox in the eighth round. The gate shattered records for a local card, and the Pittsburgh Kid was guaranteed his shot at sport's most prestigious title. Art, normally reticent when it came to predictions, had touted his favorite afterward. "Wait'll this Conn catches up with Louis," he had proclaimed, maneuvering his cigar through clenched teeth. "If you want to make yourself look good—pick Billy Conn. It's the cinch of the century." It might not have been that, but it was shaping up as the fight of the decade.

Two days after beating Knox, Conn and Mary Louise Smith drove a few hours north of Pittsburgh to get a marriage license. Billy had met Mary Louise three years before when her father, Greenfield Jimmy Smith, invited him to their vacation spot at the shore. Billy, then twenty, was a popular athlete on the rise, and Smith was a well-known Pittsburgh sportsman. Smith never forgave Conn, or himself, for what happened next. Conn asked Smith if he could take Jimmy's fifteen-year-old daughter to dinner. Smith had no idea that before the night was over, the two would fall hard for each other. Conn told Mary Louise, a high school sophomore, that he was going to marry her. She was just as smitten.

Jimmy Smith had been what Frank Deford called a "good mouth, no hit" major league infielder best known for bench jockeying. During Prohibition, he had run speakeasies and a gambling joint called the Bachelors' Club in East Liberty. Smith's temper was legendary, as was his self-image as the toughest man around.

Smith ordered Mary Louise to stay away from this eighth-grade dropout pug. Art, who had played ball with Greenfield Jimmy, vouched for Billy, but Smith shipped his defiant daughter to a Philadelphia boarding school. His efforts proved futile. Mary Louise, now eighteen, and Billy got a marriage license before the Louis fight and began looking for a priest to marry them. When Smith found out, he barged in on the bishop and demanded that he block any diocesan priest from performing the sacrament.

Smith was not Conn's only concern; his mother Maggie was in a Pittsburgh hospital clinging to life. Conn visited her on his way to New York where a hotel of raucous Pittsburghers kept him up the night before the fight. The next day, he weighed in at 169 pounds, 30 fewer than Louis.

Art knew that Billy was notorious for starting fights slowly. When Louis pushed him around the first two rounds, Art wasn't concerned. Billy rallied and began inflicting damage. Louis was hurt, more so than in any previous title defense. In command after twelve rounds, Conn was ahead on two of three judges' cards and even on the other. His trainer Johnny Ray told Billy he had the fight won. All he needed to do was "stick and run" for three rounds. Across the ring, trainer Chappie Blackburn told Louis he had to knock Conn out to win.

Conn wanted to do more than stick and run. He wanted to kayo Louis and went right at him in the thirteenth round. But Louis busted through Conn's defenses, and caught him on the jaw. Conn was reeling when Louis struck again, sending him down for the count. Art was crestfallen. The Pittsburgh fans who had been on their feet cheering wildly slumped in their seats. In the locker room afterward, a subdued Conn muttered to Art, "What's the use of being Irish if you can't be dumb?"

Back on the Northside, Jossie White and another black friend quietly left the Rooney kitchen. Danny was so upset over Billy's defeat that it did not occur to him that his buddies had been rooting for Louis all along. After all, they had met Conn at the Rooney house. "I thought they were rooting the same as us," he recalled, "but as soon as Louis knocked Conn out, they smiled and got up and left." For Danny, the fight had nothing to do with race and everything to do with pride in

Pittsburgh and friendship with Conn. He didn't realize how much black America had invested in Louis.

Maggie Conn died several days later. After the funeral, Billy and Mary Louise were married in Philadelphia, beyond the range of Jimmy Smith's bullying. As the summer wore on, Art followed Joe DiMaggio's fifty-six-game hitting streak and Whirlaway's quest for the Triple Crown, hit the track, and went fishing in Canada and the Outer Banks. All the while, he watched the war spread.

Football Preseason 1941

On August 1, six weeks after Louis defeated Conn, camp opened in Hershey, the chocolate company town in central Pennsylvania. Bert Bell was Pittsburgh's new coach. Bell had not been his own first choice as coach, but he and Art could not afford to guarantee a contract when war might cut the season short.

Few players reported; several had enlisted rather than await their draft call-ups. Others looked at Pittsburgh's dismal history and declined offers to play. Nor did Bell inspire confidence as head coach. He was a likable, upbeat guy but in his eight years running the Eagles, the last five as head coach, the team had finished last four times and next to last the other four. Bell, however, was optimistic. "This is the finest squad I've ever worked with," he claimed, predicting that the team would finally give Pittsburgh a winner.

Chet Smith at the *Pittsburgh Press* figured that Bell would not rely so heavily on local players. "There were certain games," Smith chided Art, "when the Steelers resembled a reasonable facsimile of old Duquesne University teams."

Art arrived in Hershey with Danny and Art Jr. in tow. Watching the squad practice in new uniforms, he said, "They still look like the Steelers to me—in green jerseys." He should have been watching his sons. Danny broke his nose when he collided with the ground as a player twirled him around on the sidelines, and Art Jr. was badly sunburned. Daniel Rooney laughed that his grandson Danny now looked like all the other Rooneys, but Kass blasted Art for his negligence.

The team played an intrasquad game for soldiers from nearby

Indiantown Gap before beating Detroit and Whizzer White, who had led the league in rushing the previous season, in an exhibition at Forbes Field. Art was restrained; Bell was jubilant.

At dinner afterward, Art lobbied NFL commissioner Elmer Layden on behalf of small market teams. Clubs depended almost exclusively on ticket sales, and Art griped that small-market teams often lost money at home because of the $5,000 fee guaranteed visiting clubs. Instead of a guarantee, he contended that the visitors should get forty percent of the gate. That policy would protect smaller-market clubs at home and allow them to benefit on the road. Always the politician, Art laid the groundwork for future proposals even when they currently had little chance. Believing the key to Pittsburgh's long-term success was greater revenue sharing, he missed few chances to suggest it.

The preseason buzz dissipated after Pittsburgh lost its opener 17–14 in Cleveland. Pittsburgh had three chances to tie with a field goal, but Bell played for the go-ahead touchdown each time. While the Steelers regrouped, Art focused on the boxing card he was staging at Forbes Field.

Coaching Changes

The September show came at a transitional moment for the region's fistic fortunes. Four of Pittsburgh's reigning world champs had taken a beating in the ring that summer. Conn had relinquished his light-heavyweight title to fight Louis, Fritzie Zivic lost his welterweight belt to Red Cochrane, and Sammy Angott and middleweight Billy Soose lost nontitle fights. The Forbes Field card was intended to showcase Pittsburgh's return to the limelight, underscoring that its fight game was still second only to New York's.

A crowd of 25,000, including many politicians and the entire Pirates baseball team, paid a near-record $67,000 to attend. Part of the proceeds went to the Dapper Dan Club, the charity cosponsoring the event; the rest kept Rooney-McGinley going. Pittsburgh fighters—Zivic, McKeesport steelworker Mose Brown, and Harry Bobo—swept their out-of-town foes.

A few days later, Pittsburgh lost its home opener to Philadelphia. Bell was disconsolate. Few coaches worked as hard or cared more about winning. But being a hard-working nice guy did not win football games. Bell had failed to motivate his out-of-shape players. And he ran a single wing offense despite the success other teams were having with the pass-oriented T formation.

After the game, Bell fired himself. The press reported that Art wanted him to finish the season but Bell refused. He had lost confidence in his coaching abilities and said it would be in the team's best interest if he confined his duties to the front office. Another version surfaced later. After losing to Philadelphia, Bell was said to have proposed trading for players who could turn things around. "People in Pittsburgh are tired of our deals," Art retorted. "They always backfire." Bell asked, "What do you think we should do?" Not missing a beat, Art said, "Bert, did you ever think about changing coaches?"

Duquesne University's Buff Donelli replaced Bell. But there was a catch—Donelli would not stop coaching Duquesne. Buff Donelli had been an extraordinary athlete, playing in soccer's 1934 World Cup and starring in football at Duquesne for Coach Elmer Layden, now the NFL commissioner. When Layden left for Notre Dame in 1939, Donelli replaced him at Duquesne and led the team to a 17-1-1 record. Art approached Duquesne's president, the Rev. Raymond Kirk, and offered to pay Donelli his Duquesne salary if Kirk would permit the coach to direct both squads for the remainder of the season. Kirk agreed to the unprecedented arrangement.

The Steelers were thrilled. Donelli, one of college football's hottest coaches, addressed them at their Mountain View Hotel quarters near Greensburg, conducted practice, and then drove an hour to oversee Duquesne's workouts at Moore Field in the city's South Hills. That evening, Donelli returned to the hotel to explain the more advanced offense he would install.

Donelli's loyalties were clear: "I want it to be understood that my first interest always will be with these boys up here [at Duquesne]." But NFL commissioner Elmer Layden was miffed. Layden liked Donelli, who had captained his Duquesne squad, but he told him to choose one team or the other. In a ruse transparent to all concerned, Duquesne released

Donelli from his contract but allowed him to continue as an adviser. He attended practice and sat on the bench next to head coach Sam Sinko during games. But he, not Sinko, ran the team. Layden turned a blind eye—for the moment.

Donelli moved the Steelers into the city so that they could practice at Moore Field, where Duquesne trained. The players responded to his tougher workouts and sophisticated coaching. Although New York drubbed them in Donelli's debut, they outplayed Washington before falling 24–20 in the next game.

Art told the *Post-Gazette*'s Havey Boyle that the season had been tough at the gate, too. Ticket receipts were down over $5,000 per home game. "But, wait," Art said, "until I have a laugh. All we have to do now is go to Chicago to play the Bears." That elicited a chuckle. Boyle knew just how much Art thought of the Bears. "Why," Art joked, "I just wrote to Halas and told him we'd settle for a forfeited game, and forget about our guarantee, if he'd agree to a cancellation. Sending our little boys against those big Bears is just brutal."

Though losing money and games, Art professed to be encouraged. "In another year I'll bet Buff Donelli will be better than anyone in the league." Except for Halas, of course. "I know Bert Bell will agree with me when I say that if Buff had started out with us we'd have three games in the hamper right now."

The following Sunday, the Bears crushed the Steelers on a rainy, bone-chilling day. Rooney had never beaten Halas in the regular season. The Steelers lost their eighth straight a week later, but Donelli was making them competitive.

And then Commissioner Layden intervened. When Pittsburgh was to play in Philadelphia and Duquesne in San Francisco on the same week-end, Donelli made clear that he would head west with Duquesne, one of six unbeaten major colleges in line for a bowl game. Layden called Donelli's bluff: go to Philadelphia with the Steelers or quit the NFL. Calling Art a gentleman and a friend, Donelli resigned as the Steelers' coach.

Art took the turn of events with his usual equanimity. Just as he had in 1939 when Johnny Blood quit midseason, Art turned to assistant coach Walt Kiesling. It was a popular choice with the players, who after being abandoned twice in two months vowed to go all out for "Kies." They made good on their pledge by tying the Eagles in their next game, breaking a year-long losing streak.

A week later, they upset Jock Sutherland's Brooklyn Dodgers. The undermanned Steelers—playing three fullbacks in the secondary and a quarterback at center—won without throwing a single pass. Pittsburgh's last two games, however, were routs and the Steelers ended the season with only twenty-six players left in uniform.

Pittsburgh finished 1-9-1 in 1941, and Art dropped a sizeable bundle of cash, as home attendance fell twenty percent. The abysmal record brought them the first pick in the college draft, but Art wondered whether there would be a next year for the NFL.

Despite his preseason vow to sell the Steelers if they didn't start winning, Art indicated that he would keep them. It would have been a terrible time to sell, and as one writer pointed out, "The local owner is so wrapped up in the game he planted here it will take extra heavy losses to prompt him to sell." Art was convinced that he could build on the core of fans that had supported the club despite its inability to win.

If there was a draft, the Steelers were leaning toward Bill Dudley, the nineteen-year-old University of Virginia All-American who had led college football in scoring. Dudley could thrive in the T formation that Kiesling wanted to adopt. But Dudley indicated he was considering coaching at Virginia instead.

War Breaks Out

On Sunday, December 7, 1941, NFL games were interrupted by announcements over loudspeakers instructing soldiers to report immediately for duty. Japanese aircraft were pounding Pearl Harbor. The ensuing declaration of war deflected attention from football. The Rooneys rallied to the nation's defense; soon Art, his father, and brothers Jim and Vince would be the only Rooney men left in town.

Father Silas was determined to return to China. After Pearl Harbor, he enlisted, assuming that with his language skills and knowledge of China, he would be sent to the Pacific as a chaplain. "China," Father Silas had written his mother, "is the ideal place for one who has vowed himself to God's work." When he had returned home that spring, Silas was so weak and gaunt that Art outweighed him. But Silas held far more spiritual sway. While in China, Father Silas had rescued unwanted twin girls from being drowned in the Yangtze River and stared down warlords who invaded his sanctuary. He told the Father Silas Rooney Club, whose monthly luncheon feted him in Pittsburgh, that he would eventually return to China and continue his work. No one doubted Silas's resolve, but he had not reckoned with military logic. The Army sent him to Europe.

Jim Rooney also tried to enlist, but the injuries from his 1933 car wreck made him 4-F. Vince, with five children, damaged hearing, and a job with the Office of Price Administration, was unlikely to be accepted in the military either. But John, 34, was in the army before the end of 1942, and Tommy, only 21, knew immediately what he was going to do. He joined the Marines.

Art was forty when the war broke out. With five sons to raise and two businesses to run, he was uncertain about what to do. "Who is it that doesn't feel the urge when he hears a band strike up?" Art asked. "And who wouldn't if he had a chance?" Art discussed enlisting with Father Campbell, Dan Hamill, and several military men. They told him he would be more useful staging sporting events to boost spirits on the home front. Art knew he was past the age where he would see combat, but he didn't like other men fighting in his place. After arguing with Kass, Art went to recruitment headquarters and signed up. It quickly became clear how ill-suited he was for military discipline. As Art handed in his papers, a recruiter began badgering him. "You're no big shot now!" he shouted in Art's face. Art grabbed his papers and tore them up. "I never took the oath," he told Kass.

The war touched most families in Pittsburgh. Wherever it took them, the Rooneys found men from the Ward. Art tended to those left behind. He found people waiting for him in the Fort Pitt Hotel lobby every morning. Many counted on Art to intercede on their behalf or reach into his pocket. After the line of supplicants dwindled, Art corresponded with his brothers, friends, and players in the service. He went by to see his parents daily and checked on siblings' families. On the way home,

Art visited wakes. If there was a sporting event, he attended with Dan Hamill.

Art's father began working at the office. Daniel was suffering from depression and the aftereffects of his broken hip, but one morning he arrived chuckling. The previous evening, he had been on the streetcar back to the Northside when the motorman said, "I had a strange thing happen to me today. Some damn fool came up and handed me a $20 tip so I would let him off between stops." Daniel asked, "Did that damn fool walk with a limp?" The driver said, "Yeah, do you know him?" Daniel replied, "That damn fool is my son Jim."

Boxing and Football

While Pearl Harbor jeopardized football's future, the onset of war did not immediately derail boxing. Rooney-McGinley hosted more fight cards than ever through the summer of 1942. Art found something in boxing that had eluded him in football—success. Boxing sustained his household and underwrote his team during the war. "Boxing carried the football team from 1939 to 1945," Art's son Dan remembered. "No question about that."

Amid ongoing speculation that Mike Jacobs would abdicate his position as boxing's czar, writers talked of Art filling the void. Jacobs liked Art's style. "Rooney," he observed, "has the gambling instinct a real promoter has to have. He's the kind of a guy who can win or lose thousands without batting an eye." Art's potential was evident. Rooney-McGinley staged cards every other week, featuring local fighters, drawing large crowds, and giving part of the proceeds to war charities.

With the war going badly, Art was philosophical about football. "He has a suspicion," Havey Boyle wrote, "not shared by most of his brother magnates, that there will be no professional football next season, but he does not see this as an unmixed evil."

Most teams drafted cautiously that December, picking players who might be around for the 1942 season. Bill Dudley, the Steelers' top choice, was their only well-known pick. Otherwise, Bell and Kiesling selected married men with high draft numbers. "If the war continues and the National League operates next autumn, Bert and Kies will have had the right dope," Art said. "However, I would have liked to have grabbed all the big names possible, take a flier on the war being over and having the greatest roster in our history."

At NFL meetings, Rooney and Bell tried to convince their peers to limit the 1942 season to nine games, reduce rosters, and play only on Sundays. They objected to night games, pointing out that defense work might cause blackouts. "Bell and I are not in favor of trying to go whole hog in times such as these," Art declared. But the owners voted to stay with an eleven-game schedule and thirty-three-man rosters.

Boxing Booms

Art did persuade fight fans to fill Duquesne Gardens that winter. Staging shows around patriotic themes, Rooney-McGinley admitted servicemen for free and sold war bonds between bouts. One night, the crowd pitched in $700 to help "Buy a Bomber for Uncle Sam." Luring boxers to Pittsburgh proved easy; Art paid well and treated them fairly.

Billy Conn could have set attendance records, but he was fighting for the army, which was unlikely to release him except for a much-anticipated rematch with Joe Louis. In the meantime, Harry Bobo's bout with Len Franklin, billed as the best between black boxers since Sam Langford fought Jack Johnson in 1906, set indoor attendance records. Bobo came off the mat to floor Franklin three times before knocking him out. The sensational knockout set up Bobo to fight either Abe Simon or Bob Pastor, with Conn or Louis in the offing. Conn–Bobo in Pittsburgh would break the bank.

Art also stumbled upon a rising star. When the army denied ex-champ Ken Overlin a furlough to fight Charley Burley, Ezzard Charles replaced him. Charles, a Cincinnati high school student, looked like a lamb being led to the slaughter against Burley, a seasoned pro on a twenty-six-fight winning streak. Fritzie Zivic headlined the card, but the lamb's toppling of Burley was the showstopper. Charles adopted Pittsburgh as his second home, and Rooney-McGinley had a dazzling new boxer to promote.

Art was looking forward to two fights that summer: the "Fight of the Century" at Yankee Stadium between Louis and Conn on June 25, and his own card at Forbes Field, a title fight between light-heavyweight champ Gus Lesnevich and Mose Brown. After heavy advance sales, Rooney-McGinley estimated a $75,000 gate, with ten percent designated for war relief. It would be Brown's best payday ever.

But Art promoted a private fight first, on May 11 in a Squirrel Hill kitchen, with Billy Conn in the main event. Conn was home on furlough for the christening of his son, David. Art was the baby's godfather. After the ceremony at St. Bede Church, Art, Milton Jaffe, friends, and family returned to the Conns' home. Jimmy Smith, who boycotted the event, called Art on the phone there and asked him and Milton to come over.

They found the new grandfather mollified by the baby's christening. Milton called Billy to say that Art had persuaded Jimmy to bury the hatchet, and the Conns went over to Smith's home. Jimmy proffered his hand to Billy. "I shook it and was glad to," Conn said later. "This was the second time I'd tried to make up, and the other time he told me to get to hell out . . . This time everything was okay so we had a drink on it." The peace was short-lived. Smith cornered Conn in the kitchen and began to roar. Billy countered, "You don't scare me, Jimmy."

Smith reared back and swung at Billy, who instinctively hit back. As soon as his hand smacked Smith's skull, Billy knew he had made a mistake. Grabbing Billy in a clinch, Smith clawed at his face. A brief scrum ensued before they were pulled apart. But it was too late; Billy's hand was broken. He left for Mercy Hospital to have it set. Mary Louise's face was scratched and Milton Jaffe banged up from falling down the steps. Asked later where Art was during the fight, Billy laughed. "Rooney? I don't know where the Prez went."

"I had my back turned to them," Art said, "when I heard a few snarls and a scuffle." He could not believe how so much blood had spattered on the ceiling and walls so quickly. Smith wouldn't let it go. Later that night, he pounded on the Conns' door with a baseball bat, demanding they open up. Billy called the police.

"The in-law scuffle between Billy Conn and Greenfield Jimmy Smith on Sunday night may have been a family affair," Al Abrams wrote in the *Post-Gazette*, "but its reverberations are being felt all over the boxing world." With his hand broken, Billy's million-dollar rematch with Louis was off.

"I don't want people to say, 'Oh, he's a fighter who goes around socking people,'" Conn protested. "I was attacked and was merely defending myself." When asked about the Louis fight and his $150,000 cut of the purse, Billy joked, "I'm not worried about getting in shape for Louis. I'm going to get into shape for Smith now."

The fiasco was the first of several disappointments for local boxers. Harry Bobo was hit the hardest. His bout with Abe Simon, which could have gotten him a title shot, was nixed when the New York slugger retired. Mose Brown then had his title bout cancelled when Gus Lesnevich was ordered back to base. The news came hours after rain had postponed another Rooney-McGinley show. Art and Barney were stunned. In short order, they had lost two big cards, a smaller show, and the excitement of Conn's rematch with Louis. "Everything happens for the best," Art rationalized before going fishing in Michigan with Owney McManus and Walt Kiesling.

Rooney-McGinley soon rebounded. Their biggest card featured ten hard punchers with proceeds going to Camp O'Connell, a summer camp for kids from the Hill. Harry Bobo, Mose Brown, Fritzie Zivic, Joey Maxim, and Ezzard Charles appeared on what writers called the nation's top card of the year. Worried about gas rationing, Art lamented that half of his customers lived too far out of town to get to Oakland by streetcar. But 19,000 fans turned out and the press acclaimed it the best show ever staged in Pittsburgh.

Boxing, however, was tanking elsewhere. Too many fighters were in the military. That Rooney-McGinley could stage any good fights went against the national tide. New York's Boxing Commission grilled Mike Jacobs about how Rooney could put on a first-class card in Pittsburgh while boxing in New York City was sinking. In truth, Art and his voluble matchmaker, Jake Mintz, were scrambling to put on cards. They cobbled together cards featuring young men from neighborhoods and mill towns that exploited natural rivalries. Each brought along a contingent of fans.

The Summer of 1942

Lt. Silas Rooney came home on a furlough that summer before heading overseas. Although Art had become the Rooneys' de facto patriarch, responsible for the extended family, Father Silas was the clan's heroic figure. He was a rugged man, and many Northsiders remembered him as a brawler with a hair-trigger temper. But ordination had elevated his stature, and his mission in China as a man of God counted mightily in Catholic Pittsburgh. The brothers had been virtually inseparable as teammates on the sandlots. Now Art treated Silas with a respect approaching reverence. Silas embodied the spirituality he sought in Catholicism.

Art watched the war pluck many men out of Pittsburgh with dismay about his own decision to stay home. Seeing Slim Silverhart, forty-two, who booked ball games and handicapped local elections, enlist bothered Art, who was younger and in better shape. Even Dan Hamill's nephew, seventeen-year-old Danny Lackner, who helped in the office, and Father Jim Campbell signed up.

The war was tearing apart NFL rosters, and Art wanted to cancel the 1942 season. By the time training camps opened, over 150 NFL players, including 12 Steelers, were in the service. The loss of so many players tightened competition, but Rooney and Bell did not exploit the situation. They signed few players and watched their top draft pick, Bill Dudley, enter the navy.

The war was providing the rationale to promote sport but making it frustratingly difficult to do so. At camp, which Bert Bell located in Hershey for the benefit of players working in Philadelphia defense factories, the team hardly had enough players to scrimmage. Prospects brightened when rookie Bill Dudley was given a furlough from the navy to allow him to play the season. He would report to camp after the college All-Star game.

Bell oversaw the training of a woefully thin roster in Hershey, and only sixteen Steelers entrained for East Liverpool, Ohio, for an exhibition against Cleveland to benefit civilian defense councils. It was a long train ride back for the Steelers after Cleveland, which had finished in last place the year before, routed them. Art was humiliated. "The Ol' Prez is mad," Eddie Beachler reported in the *Press*. "He's fed up on watching his Pittsburgh Steeler football team take it on the chin week after week, year in and year out." Art made his feelings clear about his sloppy and lackadaisical team. "I promise that if we have a losing team this year, it will be the last one."

Art had justified staying at home from the war to boost local morale, but the Steelers were only pulling it down. So he went on a recruiting frenzy that swelled the skimpy sixteen-man roster to sixty players. "We're going to have a payroll that will be exceeded by only one or two teams in the entire league," he maintained. "By gosh," he vowed, "we're going to win or else!" With Chicago coming to town, winning would wait at least another week.

The Chicago exhibition drew 20,000 fans to Forbes Field, testimony to the Bears' élan and the Dapper Dan Club's relentless promotion. Companies flush with war contracts bought blocs of tickets. The Westinghouse Electric Company Clerks Association purchased 4,000; the post office, IRS, and defense plants took thousands more.

While Chicago trampled Pittsburgh in the first half, the Steelers played them evenly afterward. Art thought it was a moral victory; Bell drew grander conclusions. He told Chet Smith that he did not see how Pittsburgh could lose more than a game or two all season. Art overheard that exchange and sighed, "Come out to our games and you'll see how." Smith reprised one of Art's most memorable lines: "I think the different jerseys are swell but the boys in 'em are still the same old Steelers." Yet this time, maybe not.

The Steelers were not the Bears, but they were no longer the pathetic team that Cleveland had clobbered in the preseason. They now included Bill Dudley, who reported after the College All-Star game. Dudley's debut in Pittsburgh's home opener against Philadelphia was an inauspicious start to a Hall of Fame career. Philadelphia dispatched Pittsburgh 24–14 before a disappointed crowd that included defense workers who had taken advantage of the late kickoff time to come after work. While *Press* reporter Cecil Muldoon complained that "the Steelers have stunk it out," his colleague, Chet Smith, packed a harder punch. The team's poor play, he wrote, "looks suspiciously like gold-bricking, lack of conditioning, poor management or a combination of the three."

Only Bill Dudley escaped the defeatism. He came up to Art afterward and said, "This club's going to win some games, Mr. Rooney." Art was touched. "From the tone of his voice I knew he had no doubt about it." Art liked the kid, who was about as old as his brother Tommy. Dudley's playing reminded Art of Whizzer White and of himself at that age: a tough undersized athlete who studied the game and anticipated the next play. Art took him golfing and home for meals.

Pittsburgh lost its second game when Washington returned a blocked field goal try for a touchdown. This time, George Marshall tried to boost Art's spirits. "Don't be a chump," Marshall scolded when Art said he was thinking of forfeiting the franchise. "If you can pull through this season you'll be able to sell the franchise for a good price. Don't throw it away for nothing."

Marshall was right. Nor were they the same sorry outfit they had been in the past. Dudley was why. In their first two games, Pittsburgh scored four touchdowns. Dudley ran 44 yards for the first, returned a kickoff 84 yards for the second, passed 15 yards for the third, and set up the fourth. "He's the best back we have had since I came to Pittsburgh," Kiesling proclaimed. "Yes, I do believe he is a harder runner than Whizzer White. He has a knack of picking openings almost before they develop."

"Whizzer White couldn't carry this boy's shoes," Art gushed. Given Art's feeling about White, his comments about Dudley were heretical. "He's tops in my book." Even allowing for the lowered level of play due to the war, Dudley was exceptional.

Danny Rooney, his buddies, and more than 4,000 Junior Commandos were guests at the Giants game. They had collected fifteen tons of scrap metal for the war effort. A newspaper photo of Danny and his pals sitting in barber chairs donated for scrap was captioned, "Hope they may help to give Hitler a close shave in some future battle." Settling scores with Hitler would take time, but the Steelers beat the Giants 13–10.

Meanwhile, the war was pulling more men out of sport and the Rooney family. In September 1942, Barney McGinley's son Jack, who had been working for the Steelers and Rooney-McGinley Boxing, was commissioned as a naval ensign. Before shipping out, Jack married Marie Rooney at Annunciation Church with Jim Rooney standing as best man. In October, Lt. Silas Rooney embarked for Ireland, prompting one wit to quip, "It took a Pittsburgh Rooney a long time to get to Ireland, but Dan finally made it by way of China."

Thousands of soldiers watched in Brooklyn as Dudley led Pittsburgh to victory in a game they won without completing a pass. For Bert Bell, the game was a milestone. In ten NFL seasons, his teams had never before won twice in a row. After the game, another two players enlisted.

If the Steelers could beat Philadelphia, they would almost certainly host the largest crowd in franchise history—possibly their first-ever sellout—against Washington a week later. A loss would mean business as usual. With Dudley, who led the league in rushing and kick returns, touching the ball on almost every play, the Steelers vanquished Philadelphia, their third win in a row. "Whizzer White may have had more natural ability than Dudley," Kiesling conceded afterward, "but Bill has more grit and determination than any ballplayer I've ever seen."

The division lead was now at stake against Washington. George Marshall, who never tired of bragging to the press, repeated his claim that he had kept Art from quitting football. Marshall said he had told Rooney that his own players feared Pittsburgh. "I lied gracefully . . . But I did want to give him a lift, and goodness knows, he needed it." Now, Marshall protested, he realized that his players really did respect Pittsburgh.

Marshall's flamboyance infuriated other owners, but Art enjoyed his showmanship, which he thought benefited the league. Besides, Marshall was easy to prank. Art once called his private number at midnight. "It's no fun calling him up if he isn't in bed," he explained. Marshall hated to be awakened. Disguising his voice, Art asked, "George, were you in bed?" "How dare you call me to the phone at this hour of the night!" Marshall barked. "Thank you Mr. Marshall," Art responded calmly. "We were having a little argument up here. Some of us contended you hadn't gone to bed as yet. Others were willing to bet you were already in bed. Now that I have it straight from you, the argument is settled. Pleasant dreams."

On game day, traffic snarled as a record 37,764 fans filed into Forbes Field. In years past, Pittsburgh had often padded its announced gate for appearance's sake, but Art did not need to inflate the numbers this time. The crowd whooped when Pittsburgh threatened, but Washington prevailed 14–0. Victory at the gate, however, meant more than defeat on the field. For the first time since Sutherland's glory years at Pitt, ropes were stretched around the field to accommodate fans. Harry Keck called it the day pro football came into its own in Pittsburgh. "And no one," he said, "enjoyed the transformation more than the patient Rooney, who was able to look about him from his seat on the Steelers' bench and take in the panorama his venture had wrought."

"Instead of ducking down alleys and tying to sidestep my pals, I'm walking down the main street again," he said. It got even better. The Steelers entered terra incognita, winning their next four games. Out-of-town writers called them the surprise of the season.

Columnist Bob Considine sat beside Art during the streak. Rooney, he joked, found winning too much to bear. Making a run for the title had turned the happy-go-lucky Rooney into "a graying, cigar-chewing, nervous wreck who now dies a thousand deaths each Sunday afternoon worrying about his first good team . . . Every play now counts, whereas it used to be that the only suspense at a Pittsburgh game was the number of points by which his team would be beat. Poor sucker!"

In the midst of the streak, the Steelers raised $35,000 to build a USO canteen near the Pennsylvania Railroad Station by playing the Fort Knox Bombardiers. John Moody, from Freeport, an Allegheny River town, was black college football's top scorer the last two seasons and led Fort Knox.

The presence of African Americans on military squads begged the question: Where were they in the NFL? The white press didn't ask. In the nation's leading black paper, the *Pittsburgh Courier*, Lucious Jones hailed the integrated Bombardiers for their All-American cast. "That's the stuff of which the Four Freedoms are made. That's what our white and colored boys are fighting for—a victory at Home as well as Victory Abroad!"

The war was pushing open other barriers. Pitt had never allowed a

Rooney team to sully its sacred athletic sanctum, Pitt Stadium, but the USO benefit induced the university to host the game. Art also finally walked into the Duquesne Club, the city's elite WASP bastion, to promote the benefit. Perhaps the most unusual bow to the war effort was that reporters, players, and officials all paid their way into the game. Only servicemen were admitted free.

The Steelers won easily, but Moody was the top performer. "That boy Moody sure is a ballplayer," Kiesling acknowledged. Several coaches said he could start for the Bears. "No higher praise could come to him," Harry Keck observed.

Riding a four-game winning streak, Pittsburgh played Green Bay, a team they had never beaten, to end the season. On a frozen field in sub-zero weather, they came close, losing 24–21. Art finally had a winning season. Pittsburgh, 7–4, finished second and made a profit. It was a bittersweet moment for Art. As delighted as he was, he saw the war as what really mattered. "We might finish out the 1942 football season, but I certainly can't see any hopes for 1943," he said. "Neither can any of the other owners." Smith predicted that the NFL would be more popular than ever after the war, perhaps overtaking the college game. But the war's end was not in sight and many players enlisted after the season.

Chilly Doyle wrote an ode to Pittsburgh's premier sportsman that ran on the last day of 1942 in the *Sporting News*. Rooney, Doyle said, "holds that one of the less worthy forms of charity is to make a donation and then tell somebody about it." But groundbreaking for the USO canteen had provoked a public salute. "It may be a rare case, [but] Art Rooney really is a prophet with honor in his own country." For Art, money was just a means for philanthropy. "Look straight into his eyes," Doyle wrote, "and you don't know whether he has a nickel or $10,000 in his pocket." Building the canteen, where Art and Kass frequently visited, was some solace. But it seemed as if every man he knew was joining up—even Kiesling took his physical—and Art remained uneasy with his decision to remain a noncombatant.

War's Distraction

At the postseason meetings, Art unsuccessfully sought suspension of operations in 1943. He knew that his 1942 team would never reunite and was more concerned about the fate of friends at the front than football.

Art was an inveterate correspondent, and players kept him posted on their whereabouts. He went over war dispatches each morning to see what his brothers, friends, and players were facing. By early 1943, Tommy was in the Pacific, Silas in England, and John poised to land in Italy. John's letters were matter of fact and sought to soothe anxieties at home. He wrote that he was playing ball in camp and would be sending a little extra money home because the cards had favored him. Silas's letters sounded a deeper chord. "My lads, in general, are grand and worthy. Some things are distasteful. Guess I try to do the sweet and hard things with equal vim and vigor. Anyway, I try and hope. There is always hope and when God calls, there is eternity." Art read and reread his brothers' missives. They made football seem trivial.

Boxing Tanks

The war breathed a second life into Pittsburgh's aging steel industry and put money in fight fans' pockets. Rooney-McGinley did better than fight clubs elsewhere, promoting thirty-four cards during the war's first year. With gas rationing kicking in, they relied on fans who came by streetcar or on foot and capitalized on local rivalries Most of all, they had Fritzie Zivic. That would take them through the first year of combat.

Billy Conn entered the ring only three times in 1942, never in Pittsburgh, and would not fight again until after the war. However, Rooney-McGinley had Zivic, the nation's top draw, on a card almost every other month in 1942 and 1943.

Fritzie gave his all in the ring, and the fans loved him for it. He had gone toe-to-toe with Billy Conn, Charles Burley, Sammy Angott, Henry Armstrong, and Ray Robinson in a pro career that began as a featherweight in 1931. Upsetting Armstrong to win the welterweight crown in 1940, he was written off after losing the title a year later. After all, he had fought almost 150 times in his twelve-year pro career. Few fighters had given or taken so many blows in the ring. His nose was flattened and bumpy, and scar tissue protruded around his eyes.

Zivic had earned his reputation as a dirty fighter. His fight with Bummy

Davis at Madison Square Garden prompted Red Smith's famous appraisal: "When it came to refinements such as inserting a thumb into an adversary's eye, drawing the laces deftly across the mouth, employing the skull, the elbow or the shoulder as a weapon, treading firmly on the opponents' feet and kneeing briskly in the clinches, no fighter was more polished than Fritzie Zivic." After his match with Beau Jack sold out Madison Square Garden in an hour, the third time Zivic packed boxing's mecca in eighteen months, he was called the "Box Office Kid."

Zivic, unbeaten in Pittsburgh since 1937, was a terrific draw. Rooney-McGinley promoted his two brawls with Jake "The Bull" LaMotta during the summer of 1942. LaMotta, who would do a stretch on a Florida chain gang, fought with an animalistic fury. Coming straight at foes, he wore them down with a relentless barrage of punches. His bouts with Zivic were box office godsends for Art, who was so worried about gas rationing that he considered retrenchment for the duration.

By the end of their first fight, LaMotta had one eye closed and the other bloodied. As ring announcer Joe Tucker started reading the judges' decision, LaMotta ducked through the ropes, leaving the ring to Zivic, whom he believed had won. When Tucker announced that LaMotta had won a split decision, Jake froze. His mouthpiece fell to the floor, its thud audible as he muttered in disbelief. The crowd erupted, roaring disapproval and throwing newspapers and burning cigarettes into the ring. Fritzie "gave Jake a boxing lesson, nothing less," Harry Keck wrote, "and Jake himself knew it. He didn't have to be told." A member of LaMotta's entourage agreed, admitting that "Fritzie beat our brains out—and we're sure thankful the referee and one of the judges weren't looking." LaMotta was hurting so badly that he canceled his next match. Fritzie was unscathed, but he lost a grand he had bet on himself to win.

Rooney-McGinley promoted their rematch a month later. LaMotta, figuring that Zivic would tire in a longer fight, insisted that it be a fifteen-rounder. Pittsburgh had not hosted a fifteen-rounder since Conn–Bettina for the light-heavyweight title in 1939, and over 15,000 fans turned out. This time, Fritzie won.

Zivic's appeal, Chet Smith argued in the *Press*, had outdistanced both Harry Greb and Billy Conn. A brutal fighter in the ring, Fritzie was easygoing and affable outside it. One writer described Fritzie as talking in rushed paragraphs, coming up for air only twice a day. "He has a rather high, shallow voice and his words pop out endlessly in a series of little, staccato explosions, like he's swallowed a string of Chinese firecrackers." Zivic fought often to cash in on his box office appeal while it lasted. He knew his legs were going and that he could be drafted at any time.

Rooney-McGinley also had Cincinnati's Ezzard Charles and Harry Bobo to promote. Pittsburgh had embraced Charles as if he were a native son. In September, he became the first fighter to knock out Mose Brown and then beat Joey Maxim, his sixth consecutive win for Rooney-McGinley. Bobo was also a big draw, but after Gus Dorazio thumbed him, he lost sight in one eye and had to retire. Art had a soft spot in his heart for ex-pugs. He had seen Harry Greb and John Henry Lewis lose vision and pushed the boxing commission to require periodic examinations of fighters. He offered to finance the reform but could not sell the idea. By November 1942, the draft boards had called up so many boxers that few good matches could be made. "Interest in this so-called sport here is practically nil," Harry Keck wrote.

Weathering the War

While Art managed the logistics of everyday life on the home front, Father Silas set the family's moral compass from abroad. When the press profiled Lt. Edgar Malin as he recuperated at Butler's DeShon Army Hospital from wounds incurred in North Africa, Malin protested the attention. "If you've got to write a story about a hero you ought to put in a plug for Father Rooney," he insisted. "There is one of the greatest chaplains in the Army . . . He's always around when a guy needs a friend."

Women now occupied the center of the Rooney clan. Art had not lived in such a feminine world since moving into Grandma Rooney's boarding house when he was a toddler. His mother was sick for much of 1943, and his father was increasingly withdrawn. Jim, although ever-lovable, was unreliable and dissolute. His lack of discipline stood in contrast to Silas's steely resolve. Silas embodied manly virtue. He refereed boxing matches among his lads, heard their confessions, and sent more than a few off to die.

The Steagles

For the rest of the war, Art was buffeted by forces beyond his control. He would sacrifice his team for the sake of the league and sport for the sake of the nation. The 1943 season turned out to be full of irony. Before leaving for the April owners' meetings, Art had been blunt: "The Steelers will go through the motions although I am not very optimistic about the National League operating next autumn." A third of its players had enlisted, and more were being called up each week. Yet Pittsburgh was coming off its best season ever, and the war-driven economy was guaranteeing clubs a profit. Paradoxically, the NFL would set attendance records despite fielding mediocre squads, and Art would profit on the season even though he hardly had a team to call his own.

By June, with only five players on his roster, Art acknowledged talk of combining the squad with Alex Thompson's Philadelphia Eagles. He figured that home games would be split evenly. "That way we could keep pro football alive in both cities." Art conferred daily with Bert Bell, who had written to more than 250 players without signing one of them. In June, the NFL dropped to eight teams, adopted a reduced schedule, and hammered out a Pittsburgh-Philadelphia merger. Although upset that Pittsburgh would get only two games, Art did not complain to the press.

Bell did not mind that the Steagles—as the merged squad was known in Pittsburgh—were based in Philadelphia. He lived there; so did most of the players, who had defense jobs and trained after work. But the merger was tough on players with jobs in Pittsburgh. They worked out on their own and showed up for games.

Art had decided to play in 1943 to keep Pittsburgh in the NFL, but Pittsburghers would see little football. Defending Art's decision, Harry Keck said the alternative was fielding a weak team and squandering the goodwill he had built during the 1942 season. Besides, Keck pointed out, Philadelphia was full of war workers with money to spend. He was right about that. A week later, 32,000 watched the Steagles play in

Philadelphia. But the deal bothered Art, especially when Philadelphia announcers called the club the Eagles, not the Steagles.

Feeling more like a visitor than an owner, Art hung around the field during practice. When players organized an impromptu drop-kicking contest, Art jumped in. Whoever could kick a ball over the crossbars from the 20-yard line the most times would get a dollar from the others. Despite wearing street shoes, Art split the uprights eight times to win. He had added pounds to his frame but still had an athlete's reflexes. Art had some fun, but he hardly knew the guys.

The absentee owner of an absent team, Art worried more about family and friends overseas than football. Ensign Jack McGinley had been cited for heroism in the landings at Sicily and Salerno. His vessel had sustained heavy fire, but Jack downplayed it when he wrote home, "We caught them asleep; they never took the bat off their shoulders!" John Rooney was with a chemical warfare unit in Italy, Tommy was in the Pacific, and Silas in England.

Pittsburgh fans—like those everywhere—looked to football for distraction from the war. Even without its best players, the NFL was attracting record crowds, except in Pittsburgh, where the Steagles did not play until Halloween.

By November, Art no longer concealed his displeasure with the merger. War or peace, Chet Smith of the *Press* wrote, Art would not extend the arrangement. "He has become even more determined to operate the Steelers under their own name and on their own field in 1944."

The Steagles finished 5-4-1 and their combined attendance in Philadelphia and Pittsburgh was tops for both cities. Not only had the NFL prospered in 1943, Art had outnegotiated Philadelphia owner Alex Thompson. When profits were apportioned, the *Sun-Telegraph*'s Harry Keck observed, "the big end came to Pittsburgh" even though the Philadelphia team had been "wagging a Pittsburgh tail." But profits were not enough. Pittsburgh had been shortchanged. If the team could not provide fans distraction from the war, then why play?

Art bellyached about the merger as a way to release the grief and anxiety he rarely revealed. That December, his old teammate, Moo O'Malley, died from wounds suffered at Salerno. Moo, whose brother Pat was one of Art's closest cronies, had played for Hope Harvey and the Majestics. Even though Moo disliked guns and had never carried one while working as a constable, his reputation as a scrapper was legendary.

When Art arrived in Chicago for league meetings in January 1944, he had six players signed. "We have tried to line up new material, but had no success," he announced. "It will be almost impossible to secure the necessary players without a merger." Art was open to one if half of the home games were played in Pittsburgh, but no decision was made.

Boxing and Politics

For the first time in his life, sport took a backseat. Art dropped football that spring and told a *Detroit Times* writer that he was through with racing, too. He was fed up with pari-mutuel betting. Of course, when he went upstairs to the horse room in the Fort Pitt Hotel, he was betting against bookies, not the pari-mutuels.

Even boxing was crashing. Rooney-McGinley kept it alive by capitalizing on local rivalries. The first outdoor bout of the season featured former champs, now Private Fritzie Zivic, Coast Guard Lt. James Braddock, and Merchant Marines Lt. Benny Leonard, selling war bonds. Fans pledged $100,000. Busloads of servicemen recovering at DeShon Army Hospital were guests at fights, and when the *Sun-Telegraph* came up short in its effort to give a Christmas present to every serviceman in a district hospital, Rooney-McGinley made up the difference.

Art also played politics. The GOP was slipping further out of power in Pittsburgh, and its factions duked it out in the 1942 primaries. There was talk of running Art for county commissioner on a ticket brokered by James Coyne. Instead, Coyne persuaded him to run for the registrar of wills. Labor unions endorsed his candidacy, but Art narrowly lost the primary when Coyne's slate foundered. He had dodged another job he did not want and went fishing in Canada.

The Republicans may have been out of power, but Art was the treasurer and a top strategist of the Republican 32 Club, a caucus of the party's thirty-two ward chairs. He could still help constituents get jobs, including his father, who was appointed to the voter registration committee.

Merger Redux

At the April meetings, the league asked Art to combine with the Chicago Cardinals for the 1944 season. While their owner Charles Bidwill was Art's racetrack buddy, the Cardinals had gone winless in 1943. "You know, if we don't watch ourselves," Kiesling joked, "we'll be arrested for polygamy." Art reluctantly consented, rationalizing that it was in the NFL's best interest. Besides, he could not have fielded a team himself. "We could have put a weak team on the field and so could Chicago, but together we are sure to be fairly strong," Art speculated.

Pittsburgh would get only three home games and two exhibitions in 1944. If the NFL continued to slight Pittsburgh, sportswriter Harry Keck warned, the city would be fertile soil for a rival league to plant a franchise after the war. Keck foresaw a new golden age for sport, especially for the pros, when the fighting ended. But the war was far from over.

War Hits Home

During the long-awaited invasion of Western Europe in June 1944, Jack McGinley's ship ferried troops across the English Channel. He had made it through North Africa and Italy unscathed, but three days after D-Day, a German torpedo sank his craft 20 miles off Cherbourg. Only seven of the twenty-four men in his unit survived. Jack and his mates spent hours in a lifeboat until they were rescued.

But bad news followed quickly. Before Jack got home on furlough to meet his eight-month-old son, Jackie, Art had to take the agonizing drive to his parents' house with the news of Tommy's death on Guam. Tommy, the youngest of the nine Rooney children, had been twenty-one when the war began. A prep school star, Tommy was tall, athletic, and fair-haired. He had enlisted in the Marines after Pearl Harbor and shipped out before Christmas 1943.

Silas had done his best to reassure Maggie Rooney about her youngest son. "Tommy certainly picked out a grand spot," he wrote her in February 1944. "I spent a few weeks there in 1941." The South Pacific might have struck Silas as paradise when he passed through on his way back from China, but for Tommy, it had been a hellhole. "I can say that I have been in action and that I am safe," he had written. The censors did not allow him to elaborate. Tommy had not slept in five or six days—he had lost track. "Your prayers have been surely answered, Mother. It was many times during those days and nights that I never thought I would be writing this letter." Tommy held up a brave front, but the family sensed his trepidation.

Tommy peppered his letters with "gee" and "swell" and reassured Maggie that he was going to Mass, taking the sacraments, and swimming in the ocean. But his tone darkened in April 1944. "There may be some time go by between this letter and my next," he explained. His next correspondence came weeks later, thanking sister Marie for prayers that "brought me out of three battles." Tommy had taken part in hard-fought landings on the Marshall Islands.

"I have a cot, tent over my head, and the food is starting to come in," he wrote his parents. "As long as I have these three things I will be satisfied till all this mess is over." Tommy confided to his sister Margaret that he had once thought of following Silas into the church. "I have never told this to anyone but I some time think that the great call was given to me and I passed it up." When Art wrote him that Vince had stopped drinking, Tommy was delighted. "He will get ahead without that stuff." Mostly, Tommy wrote longingly of coming home. "It will be the greatest day of my life." Then in May he wrote that he would not be able to write for awhile. "All I can say is keep me in your prayers and I will come out on top."

But Tommy did not come out at all. The Rooneys heard two versions of his death. One was that he was hit as he got off a landing craft, fell into the water, and drowned. The other was that a sniper shot him as he was using his flamethrower. He was buried on Guam.

Silas consoled the family in a way that Art could not. "He is in heaven," he wrote from England. "He was the kind that was sure of Eternal Salvation." The family was devastated. "I don't know that they had the war's full impact until Tommy got killed," Art's son Dan explained. "That's when it hit them. That's when they felt the power of this war."

Car-Pitts

Art stayed strong to support his grieving family and the cause for which Tommy had died. But his world was a drab and joyless place.

When the Car-Pitts, or Carpets, as sportswriters dubbed them, arrived in Waukesha, Wisconsin, for camp in August, they were undermanned and untalented. More than a third of the roster had been discharged from the military for medical reasons. Still, the Allied advance toward Germany and gains in the Pacific boded well for the war's end. Art anticipated a strong postwar comeback for sport, knowing how it had surged after the last war.

With college football reeling, the Car-Pitts offered the best hope for local fans, but that reed was too thin to grasp. The closest they came to winning in 1944 was their opening 30–28 loss to Cleveland.

Art worried more about friends and family than the shellackings his team endured. Both Silas and John Rooney remained upbeat in their letters. Silas took part in six campaigns, including Normandy and the Ardennes, and was promoted to captain. He said Mass for Tommy weekly in French villages with the men in his unit from St. Peter's. "Know he is in heaven, Mom. These departed lads who have gained heaven are so much better off." John Rooney was with Allied forces retaking Europe. Like Tommy, he pondered his future and thought he might complete school to become a pharmacist. Both he and Silas were stunned by the war's devastation and longed for its end. "The French people have suffered severely," Silas wrote. "Wherever the Germans invaded they brought misery and destruction." Silas kept abreast of enough news to know the Car-Pitts were having a miserable season. "Art has a bum team," he wrote his sister Margaret.

At home, Art wished he could bring his long-enduring fans a winner. "And no one," Carl Hughes wrote, "is pulling more for Art Rooney to have that winner than the fans he's trying to please."

Falling Apart

Art was close to his players, taking them to the track and naming horses after them. They in turn were near unanimous in their respect and affection for him. But as losses on the field mounted, the team fell apart.

The first signs of trouble came in October. Coach Kiesling and half-back Johnny Butler had butted heads since camp. After one loss, Kiesling fined Butler, Johnny Grigas, and Eberle Schultz $200 for their lack-adaisical attitude. When the coaches came into the locker room for the next practice, they found the players seated in their street clothes. They said the fines were unjust. Kiesling stood his ground. The players could appeal to the commissioner, he said, but anybody who wasn't ready to practice should leave. Most did. Those who stayed suggested a meeting with Art.

At the meeting, Kiesling accused Butler of "laying down on the job." Butler protested that he had played to the best of his ability. Other players said Kiesling was abusive in practice. Art intervened and said he would discuss the fines with the three men. The next day, Schultz and Grigas returned to practice, while Butler quit. Although the fines remained in place, Art returned the money at season's end.

The season's "highlight" was a fight. When a Car-Pitts player tackled a Redskin and threw him roughly out of bounds, a horde of Washington players and coaches intervened. The Car-Pitts ran to their teammate's aid. Art started out with them, but he stopped halfway when he realized how undignified it would be for an owner to join a brawl. He clenched his fists and watched from midfield. A veteran of many fracases, Art delighted in his players' intensity and agreed to pay their fines. "If we have that spirit versus the Lions next week, we'll win." But they didn't. At halftime, Lt. Commander Jock Sutherland sold war bonds. Art thought for the umpteenth time how good Jock would look as the Steelers' head coach.

As the season deteriorated, Art gave away thousands of tickets. At the start of the season, he had set aside five hundred tickets per game for Junior Commandos. He expanded the giveaway to youth groups that participated in scrap drives. By season's end, just about any kid in town could get in for free.

On December 3, Art hit bottom. As dropping temperatures froze Forbes Field's turf rock hard, Johnny Grigas, second in the league in rushing, slipped out of his room at the Webster Hall that morning. He left a letter for Art. "Think what you may of me, but I sincerely believe that in all justice it is for the best." Grigas had been beaten down. "Money was not my primary aim, but to play ball as a sport and have a little fun in a successful season." He had had neither fun nor success. Having played for the Cardinals the year before, he was on a twenty-five-game losing streak. Grigas, the team's workhorse, said he was "ready for the stud farm."

Grigas's departure left the team with only twenty-two players, the minimum to avoid forfeit. Fewer than 10,000 fans, a quarter of whom were kids, saw Chicago win 49–7, their tenth straight win over Pittsburgh. Art hosted their coaches for dinner at the Lotus Club on the Southside afterward, but he was just going through the motions.

With a 0-10 record, the franchise was winless for the first time. "We just didn't have it," Art stated. "It wasn't because of bad breaks, the ball bouncing unfavorably." They had simply lacked the talent to compete. The armed forces had taken Art's best players, including Bill Dudley, who had averaged almost 10 yards a carry playing for a military squad.

After the season, Chet Smith of the *Press* took Art to the woodshed. Art, he argued, should have rejected the league's shotgun weddings. "The Steelers were the tail on the Philadelphia Eagles' kite in the combine of 1943," Smith said. Rooney and Bell should have tried harder to stay independent. "Art and Bert are as nice a pair as you'll find on any bench in the National League," he declared. "Art's fault is in being too good-hearted to get tough at the right time." Neither Art nor Bert had enough larceny in his heart to make tough decisions.

Art could see that Smith was on the mark. He was adamant that Pittsburgh would not be a party to another merger in 1945, but he had little choice. "I will agree to a merger only if the League demands it," Rooney said, "and then I will insist that half of the League games be played at Forbes Field." Art was down and it showed. After Tommy's death and a 0-10 season, he figured things could not get any worse.

11

The Sutherland Years

1946–47

Art Rooney was not alone in taking stock at the end of the war. While he confronted a football team that had redefined mediocrity, Pittsburgh faced problems threatening its viability as a major metropolis. The Steelers had won only two games in two years, their fan base had crumbled, and neither players nor coaches stuck around for long. The war had extended Pittsburgh's aging factories' lease on life, but now the city's future, like that of the Steelers, was uncertain.

Smoky skies and intermittent flooding had long plagued the city. Its urban landscape was visibly weathered, its social fabric coming undone. The sense of unity forged during the war fractured amid layoffs, work stoppages, and racial tensions. At the end of 1945, a quarter of a million workers walked picket lines in what verged on class warfare. Even the Pittsburgh Pirates voted to strike.

Art's friend David Lawrence became the city's mayor in January 1946. No Pittsburgh mayor ever confronted more daunting problems. Lawrence looked for ways to renew a dying city, Art to revive a comatose football team. While Lawrence oversaw a rebuilding that became heralded as the Pittsburgh Renaissance, Art's Steelers helped to knit together a fractious city. In decades to come, the team would embody Pittsburgh's identity as a gritty, hard-working town.

Postwar Bumbling

Art eschewed a quick fix after the traumatic 1944 season. He was less concerned with the next season than with building a team that could ride the crest of sport's postwar boom. That vision required letting go of the past, a task that had never been easy for him. He refused to undercut the loyal Kiesling, who had twice stepped in when the team was left in the lurch. Kiesling made it easy for him by resigning. Relieved, Art renewed his pursuit of Jock Sutherland.

The Steelers played on their own in 1945, with assistant Jim Leonard serving as coach. Hoping to field a credible squad, Art sent business manager John Holahan to search for players. Holahan talked with semipros, discharged vets, and almost anybody looking rugged enough to play. He came up short. After Boston Yanks owner Kate Smith sang the national anthem at the season opener, her players routed the Steelers in Boston. A week later, the Giants humiliated the Steelers by scoring three touchdowns in 35 seconds. Few fans saw Washington hand Pittsburgh its third straight loss the following Sunday, but one trained observer watched from the press box. Lt. Commander Jock Sutherland was appalled by what he witnessed but intrigued at the challenge to remake such a terrible team.

Bill Dudley's homecoming after he left the service offered some hope. Dudley, a pilot instructor during the war, was still the best player on the field. He scored twice and anchored the defense as the Steelers won their first game at Forbes Field in almost two years. Despite Dudley's contributions, Pittsburgh won only two of ten games. But Art soon achieved the coup he long had sought.

Felicitous Times

A few days after Christmas 1945 and seven years after leaving the University of Pittsburgh, Jock Sutherland signed a five-year pact to coach the Steelers. The announcement came at the Pittsburgh Athletic Association, where Jock had lived for over twenty years. Art had not been inside the stately stone edifice since beating Olympic champion Sammy Mosberg there in 1920. In truth, Art was not especially welcome at the club that personified the city's old guard. Some graying members still suspected he had been behind the burglary that occurred the night of the Mosberg fight. But it was a homecoming for Jock.

Sutherland's arrival would be followed by Bert Bell's departure to become the NFL commissioner and Lawrence's inauguration as mayor. While Sutherland reshaped the Steelers and Lawrence jump-started Pittsburgh,

Bell would steady the league when a new war broke out. The All-America Football Conference (AAFC) challenged the NFL's monopoly in 1946. More important, African Americans returned to pro football that season, adding momentum to America's postwar racial reconfiguration.

Each of these shifts would be felicitous for Art. Sutherland, whom he had chased for years, was not only the most successful coach in the history of Pittsburgh sport, he was revered. Bell was neither. Although the likable Bert had been a mediocre coach and owner, he would prove to be a remarkably effective commissioner and the leading protagonist in pro football's evolution into America's major sport.

Art adored Bell as a pal but was better off with Bert as commissioner than as his partner. Bell trusted Art implicitly, and their friendship became the fulcrum on which the league shifted toward policies encouraging parity among teams and recognition of the players' union. Bell's focus on building a league in which small-market teams could compete would become the cornerstone of its success. More favorable league rules kept Art in football and created the preconditions for his team's eventual success. Having Lawrence as the mayor and Bell as commissioner meant that both city hall and the league looked favorably on his team.

Jock's return not only electrified the city, it transformed the team's fan base. His imprimatur legitimized the Steelers to fans who had worshipped him at Pitt. Overnight, his presence brought Protestant Pittsburgh into the fold to root for the same club that the region's Catholic, Jewish, and Eastern Orthodox working classes had long considered their own. Sutherland's arrival brought another bonus for Art: it allowed him to redirect his energies to racing. In the decade since "Rooney's Ride" had made him a legendary figure at the track, losing streaks, the war, and pari-mutuel betting had limited his involvement. With the war over and Jock in charge, Art was free to do what he did best—play the horses.

Jock Comes Home

When Art had been a boy on the Northside, Jock had been an All-American guard on Pop Warner's championship squads at Pitt. Under Sutherland, who coached Pitt from 1924 through 1938, the school was acclaimed the national champion six times, appeared in four Rose

Bowls, and best of all, beat Penn State twelve times in a row. But Jock left in 1938 after falling out with an administration bent on deemphasizing football. Students threatened to strike on his behalf, and Pitt fans felt as if their hearts had been ripped out. So did Jock. "Sutherland," sportswriter Joe Williams observed, "got something out of the university that was close, intimate, almost spiritual." Although Art had offered him the Steelers' helm then, Sutherland needed to distance himself from Pittsburgh.

After Pearl Harbor, Sutherland enlisted. But Art never lost hope that he could persuade Sutherland to return to Pittsburgh and approached him late in the war. Sutherland said he would decide after the 1945 season. His former Pitt colleagues were skeptical about Rooney. "I guess they felt Jock was coming into the den of iniquity," Steeler publicity director Ed Kiely reflected. "Art loafed with a bunch of people that Jock didn't approve of," Pat Livingston, Kiely's predecessor, recalled, "while Sutherland was a fancy guy who lived in the PAA." Separated by religion and peer groups, Sutherland and Rooney found common ground in Pittsburgh and football. "After he got to know him," Livingston observed, "Sutherland really became a Rooney fan."

Sutherland's $27,500 salary was a record for Pittsburgh. Plus, he would receive a quarter of the profits—if there were any—and hold an option to buy part of Bell's stake in the team. Unlike Rooney's first eight coaches, for whom contracts were verbal agreements sealed with handshakes, Jock requested a written accord. That was how the Doctor did things.

The Steelers opened new offices in the Union Trust Building, separating football operations from boxing. It would not do to ask Sutherland to share space with the rowdy crew that loafed at the Fort Pitt Hotel. "That would be like putting a skilled surgeon into a dog clinic," Jack McGinley said. Sutherland was all about football; the card games and schmoozing at Rooney-McGinley headquarters would have unnerved him. Bell would remain the team's president and Art its vice president, but Jock would set its course.

Sutherland's hiring was widely acclaimed as the tonic for Rooney's perennial losers. The hallmark of his stewardship was an intense focus on every detail—from finding talent to game-day strategy. In that regard, Jock was Art's antithesis. Art never focused exclusively on football for long, delegated what he could, and stayed in the background.

In his *New York Times* column, Arthur Daley pictured "those droll characters," Art and Bert, gleefully slapping each other on the back. "They know—and everyone else in football knows—that the acquisition of Jock means that Pittsburgh will soon be challenging . . . for Eastern supremacy." Daley cautioned that not even Sutherland could turn the Steelers around overnight. "But it will happen," he assured his readers. "The grim-visaged Scotsman will build the way he's always built, soundly, solidly, and from the ground up." Aloof, austere, and intimidating even to hard-boiled sportswriters, Sutherland was every bit the coach that Daley thought him to be.

Sutherland's teams, Daley observed, operated with "the cold-blooded efficiency of a dentist working with a drill. Nothing fancy, you know, but dreadfully effective." Jim Rooney could attest to that. Jock's modus operandi—the single wing—had not changed since Jim played for him at Pitt. His pounding style of play exacted a toll on opponents and his own players.

Sutherland, like Rooney, prized loyalty. He could have had any number of jobs, but his allegiance to Pittsburgh drew him back. Since arriving in 1913, Sutherland had embraced the city, which in turn placed him atop a pedestal. Sutherland moved back into his old room at the PAA, across the street from the University of Pittsburgh's Cathedral of Learning. "Everything I have, I owe to Pitt," he said. "Believe me, I didn't want to leave." Signing his contract, he declared, "I'm back home."

Ticket orders surged. Suddenly, the team that had never played to a packed house at home was threatening to sell out its entire 1946 home schedule. Jock downplayed expectations. "Frankly, I couldn't win with the squad which ended the past season. I saw several of the late games, you know." His goal was to build an organization capable of sustained excellence, precisely what he had done at Pitt.

Commissioner Bell

Arriving in New York for the winter league meetings in 1946, Art accepted the congratulations of his peers, who were pleased that he could

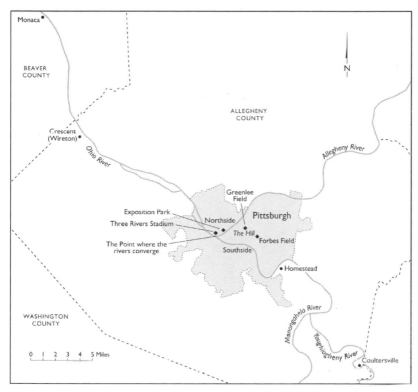

1. Map of Pittsburgh.
(By William L. Nelson.)

2. Maggie Murray Rooney, around
the time of her wedding in 1899.
(Art Rooney Jr. Collection)

3. Rooney family gathered at the Rooney Inn in Crescent. Art Rooney, age seven or eight, is in the middle row on the far right. In the top row (*left to right*) are Catherine Rooney, Dan Sheehan (family friend), and Mary Ellen Rooney Foreman and Agnes Rooney Brooks (Catherine's daughters). Middle row (*left to right*): Daniel Rooney, Maggie Murray Rooney, and immediately in front of them their children Jim, John, and Art. Front row (*left to right*): Arthur and Edward Foreman (Art's cousins), Danny Rooney (Art's brother), and Helen Ward (Art's distant cousin). (Mary Ellen Davisson Collection.)

4. Dan Rooney Café and Bar, July 4, 1918. Daniel Rooney stands under the pointed pennant with his arms around Vincent, eight, and to the right of John, ten. (Kathy Rooney Collection.)

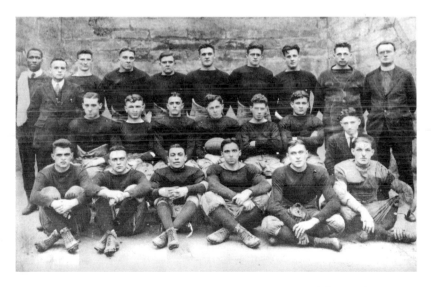

5. Duquesne Prep team. Middle row: Dan Rooney (*second from left*) and Art Rooney (*fifth from left*). (Kathy Rooney Collection.)

6. Daniel Rooney, Art Rooney's father, about 1920.
(Art Rooney Jr. Collection.)

7. Art Rooney was one of the nation's top amateur welterweight fighters in 1920. (Pittsburgh Steelers Collection.)

ART
ROONEY   RED
REESE   DEORGE   SULLIVAN   TOOTS
KLEIN   DEORGE   DAN
ROONEY

HOPE HARVEY
PITTSBURGH PA

8. The 1923 Hope Harveys on Phipps
Field on the Northside. Art Rooney
(*second from left*), Dan Rooney (*tenth
from left*), Jim Rooney (*second from
right*), and Vince Rooney (*seated*).
(Pittsburgh Steelers Collection.)

9. Brothers Art and Dan Rooney starred
for the Wheeling Stogies in 1925.
(Pittsburgh Steelers Collection.)

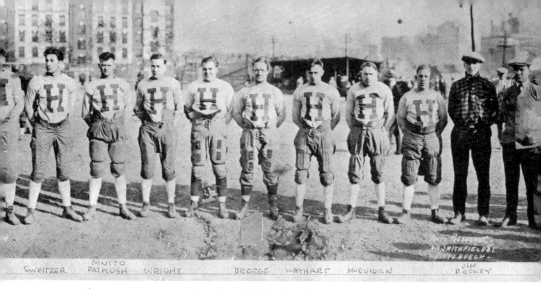

SWEITZER   MOTTO PATKOSH   WRIGHT   GEORGE   WAYHART   McGUIGAN   JIM ROONEY

10. Kass and Art Rooney on their honeymoon in 1931.
(Pittsburgh Steelers Collection.)

11. Jim Rooney's campaign poster in his race for state legislature.
(Pittsburgh Steelers Collection.)

12. Art Rooney soon after joining the
NFL. (Pittsburgh Steelers Collection.)

13. John "Blood" McNally, about
1934. (Pittsburgh Steelers Collection.)

14. Art Rooney holds the twins, John and Patrick, with (*left to right*) Dan, Tim, and Art Jr., in 1939. (Pittsburgh Steelers Collection.)

15. Whizzer White (*center*) and Art (*right*) with an unidentified friend on August 10, 1938, the day White signed his contract. (Pittsburgh Steelers Collection.)

16. Walt Kiesling, longtime player and coach. (Pittsburgh Steelers Collection.)

17. Eagles coach Greasy Neale, Art Rooney, and Eagles owner Alex Thompson in 1943, the season their teams played as the Steagles. (Pittsburgh Steelers Collection.)

18. (*Left to right*): Barney McGinley, Jack McGinley (U.S. Navy), Tommy Rooney (U.S. Marine Corps), and Art Rooney. (Pittsburgh Steelers Collection.)

19. Father Silas Rooney in France during World War II. (Pittsburgh Steelers Collection.)

20. Art's friend Bert Bell was co-owner
of the Steelers before becoming NFL
commissioner in 1946. (Pittsburgh
Steelers Collection.)

21. Steeler fans often traveled to away
games on Ham and Cabbage Specials.
Vince Rooney, wearing a white shirt,
is fourth on the left. (James P. Rooney
Collection.)

22. Art, Kass, and their five boys: (*left to right*) twins John and Pat, Art Jr., Dan, and Tim. (Pittsburgh Steelers Collection.)

23. Daniel, Maggie, and their children, about 1950: (*back row, left to right*) Jim Rooney, Marie Rooney McGinley, Daniel and Maggie Rooney, Father Silas, Margaret Rooney Laughlin; (*front row, left to right*) Art, John, and Vince Rooney. (Kathy Rooney Collection.)

24. Art Rooney is lifted up by (*back row, left to right*) George Halas, John Michelosen, Pete Rozelle, Buddy Parker, and Father Silas, with Johnny "Blood" McNally and Bill Dudley (*front row*), at the 1964 Saints and Sinners banquet. (Pittsburgh Steelers Collection.)

25. At league meetings in the 1950s: (*back row, left to right*) George Halas, Tex Schramm, Ted Collins, Charles "Stormy" Bidwill, Victor Morabito, Walter Wolfner, Jack Mara, and Don Kellett; (*front row*) George Preston Marshall, unidentified, Joe "Jiggs" Donoghue, Bert Bell, Edwin Anderson, and Art Rooney. (Pittsburgh Steelers Collection.)

26. Art bred and boarded thoroughbreds at Shamrock Farm. (Richard Stack, The Sunpapers, Baltimore.)

27. Shamrock Farm became Art's retreat after World War II. (Richard Stack. The Sunpapers, Baltimore.)

28. Portrait of Art Rooney, 1965.
(Pittsburgh Steelers Collection.)

29. Art Rooney with his grandson Art II,
who became the Steelers' third president
in 2003. (Pittsburgh Steelers Collection.)

30. In late April 1968 ground was broken
for Three Rivers Stadium. Art, sixty seven,
kicked a field goal as son Dan held the ball.
(Pittsburgh Steelers Collection.)

31. Art and his son Dan pick Terry
Bradshaw in the 1970 draft. (Pittsburgh
Steelers Collection.)

32. Art watches his team in 1972. He was
concerned about television's effect on the
game. (© *Pittsburgh Post-Gazette*, 2008, all
rights reserved. Reprinted with permission.)

33. Art Rooney with one of his favorite players, Joe Greene, in 1972, the season Pittsburgh won its first division title. (Pittsburgh Steelers Collection.)

34. Art Rooney chats with Franco Harris in the locker room. (Pittsburgh Steelers Collection.)

35. Terry Bradshaw lights Art's cigar. (Pittsburgh Steelers Collection.)

36. Art confers with his five sons in 1975: (*left to right*) Art Jr., John, Tim, Pat, and Dan. (Pittsburgh Steelers Collection.)

37. Clutching the game ball, Art Rooney accepts the Lombardi Trophy from Pete Rozelle after Pittsburgh wins its first Super Bowl, 1974. (Pittsburgh Steelers Collection.)

38. Art and Dan Rooney on the sidelines at Super Bowl X, as Pittsburgh beat Dallas 21–17 in Miami. (Pittsburgh Steelers Collection.)

39. Art and Dan Rooney in the Orange Bowl prior to Super Bowl XIII, in which Pittsburgh beat Dallas 35–31. (Pittsburgh Steelers Collection.)

40. Art on the field. (Pittsburgh
Steelers Collection.)

41. Arthur J. Rooney, 1901–88.
(Pittsburgh Steelers Collection.)

42. Curt Gowdy and Art Rooney,
probably in Miami at Super Bowl XIII.
(Pittsburgh Steelers Collection.)

43. Steelers coach Chuck Noll
(*left*), Art Rooney, and Miami
Dolphins coach Don Shula.
(Pittsburgh Steelers Collection.)

now field a respectable team. That evening, Art caucused with owners intent on ousting commissioner Elmer Layden. George Marshall, George Halas, and Green Bay Packer founder Curly Lambeau wanted to fire Layden and lobbied Art to join their ranks. Counting votes and realizing that Layden's lack of support would hamstring him in the looming battle with the AAFC, Art joined the insurrection. He also deduced that Bell, a man with whom all the owners were comfortable, would replace Layden.

Hiring Bell was ironic. His career record of 10 wins, 46 losses, and 2 ties was the worst of any coach with at least five seasons in the NFL. Bert had done no better at the box office, and Art had bailed out him more than once when the Philadelphian had run short of cash. But instead of thinking that Bell's abysmal record disqualified him from running the league, Art argued that it helped him understand what it was like to struggle. "That's what made him such a good commissioner," he later explained.

Bert called his seven years with Art his happiest in football. "I never in all my life," he said, "met a finer, a more honest, a more generous or a more delightful person than that Rooney." Still, it wasn't hard to persuade him to surrender his stake in the Steelers for the $20,000-a-year job as commissioner. Bell, who had taken the train from Philadelphia the night before games and slept on a cot in the office, had never made Pittsburgh his home.

Bell took over as the NFL entered a war with the formidable All-America Football Conference. The rival league boasted of deep-pocketed owners, fielded teams in four NFL cities, and aggressively pursued players. After the meetings, Art headed to Miami reenergized. With Sutherland coaching his team, Bell running the NFL, and Lawrence leading his city, he settled back into old routines. He felt even better after he got to Florida.

The Sport of Kings and Characters

Horse racing roared back after the war; so did Art. During the conflict, his two favorite West Coast tracks—Tanforan and Santa Anita—had been used to intern Japanese Americans. Elsewhere, gas rationing crippled attendance, and tracks were plowed under to plant victory gardens. When the war dragged into 1945, the government shut down racing for the duration. Only Hitler's suicide rescued that year's Kentucky Derby.

Florida's tracks were handling record wagers by the time Art arrived in January 1946. Jimmy McGee, who trained Art's thoroughbreds, immediately alerted him to an opportunity. Morris Wexler, an Ohio sportsman for whom McGee also trained, had hit a rough patch. Wexler, known as Moishe or Mushie, owned the Theatrical Grill, Cleveland's best-known club, where celebrities like Joe Louis and Frank Sinatra mixed with racketeers, sportswriters, and athletes. Wexler had been part of the gang that ran Cleveland's gambling wire and was one of Browns owner Mickey McBride's "tough boys" during the city's taxicab wars. But the New York Jockey Club was forcing Wexler out of racing because of his gambling ties.

Jimmy McGee brokered the sale of Wexler's horses to Art for $100,000. Horses were expensive to breed, train, and race, but Art always said that except for Kass, thoroughbred racing was his greatest romance. He now owned several well-known horses, including Air Patrol, British Buddy, Plebiscite, and Westminster. Art also paid $40,000 to buy Darby Dieppe, the third-place finisher in the 1945 Kentucky Derby. While Darby Dieppe turned out to be a bust, four of the horses Art bought from Wexler and three he already owned were stakes winners; that is, they won at the sport's highest level by competing in races their owners paid to enter. With seven stakes winners adding to his legendary history as a bettor, Art's fame in racing surpassed his reputation in football.

British Buddy had the highest upside, but Air Patrol was Art's steadiest winner. A handsome chestnut with a disposition sweet enough to tolerate a child in the saddle, Air Patrol finished in the money most times out. "I rode a lot of good horses," said jockey Ira Hanford, who had ridden Bold Venture to victory in the 1936 Kentucky Derby, "but Air Patrol was one of my favorites because he was so consistent. He never ran a poor race." An upset winner in the 1946 Capital Handicap at Laurel, Art Patrol paid $56.30 on a $2 winning ticket. Art took home the $10,000 purse, plus whatever he stung the pari-mutuels and book-ies for. Air Patrol's winnings topped $52,000 by spring.

British Buddy had arrived with a besmirched reputation. He had been disqualified after winning the 1945 Maryland Handicap when his sa-liva tested positive for caffeine. As a result, Jimmy McGee, who trained him, was suspended from racing for a year. McGee was embarrassed by the incident, although it was not necessarily his fault. Grooms and exer-cise boys often carried mugs of coffee around the stables. One spill onto British Buddy's feed could have caused the positive test.

Art never looked askance at McGee. He liked Jimmy, a wiry man with leathery skin and a crooked Dick Tracy nose. McGee had grown up in Baltimore's St. Mary's Industrial School for Boys, an orphanage and reformatory, where an older boy, George Herman Ruth, kept the bullies from picking on him. When the Babe left St. Mary's to play base-ball, Jimmy ran away. He took refuge at the track, changing his name from Gray to McGee to dodge the St. Mary's brothers looking for him. After meeting Art in 1944, McGee took him to Louisville to show him a prize yearling. Art bought the horse and named him Little Harp after Harp Vaughan. When Little Harp broke his maiden at the Narragan-sett track, Art said it was like winning the Kentucky Derby. McGee took that to mean that Art won as much on Little Harp as a Derby winner, $100,000. A few of Art's other horses, especially Plebiscite, did well, but none as well as Westminster would in January 1947.

Coach Sutherland

Sutherland was realistic about turning around a team that had won two of its last twenty games. Figuring he could build around Dudley, he de-cided to open camp early to squeeze in extra practice.

Jock, who commanded exceptional loyalty, reassembled his inner cir-cle. John Michelosen, Ralph Dougherty, and Mike Nixon (whose name had been Nicksick until Jock suggested he Anglicize it) had played for him at Pitt. Michelosen, a star back during the 1930s, was Jock's prin-cipal assistant. Nixon also was an assistant. Dougherty, an All-Amer-ican center who became a surgeon, signed on as the team physician, and Dr. Ray Sweeney became the trainer, the job he had done for Jock in Brooklyn. Brue Jackson, the team's sole black employee, was let go. Brue, a Northsider, blamed Jock for his firing, believing it was racially motivated. But he remained friends with Art.

Art knew well enough to leave Sutherland alone. For Jock, football was a twelve-month-a-year operation. Sutherland signed the Scranton Miners and Richmond Rebels as farm teams, scheduled exhibitions, and embarked on a three-week swing to visit college coaches. Meticulous and organized, Sutherland suffered no foolishness. Off the field, he favored gray pinstriped suits and vests. He parted his hair in the middle and slicked it back. Well over six feet tall, Sutherland stood ramrod erect and commanded attention. He walked briskly for several miles each morning from the PAA in Oakland to Steeler offices downtown. Art was ten years younger than Jock, but his once-lithe body had grown portly. His handball games with Dan Hamill were infrequent, and he rarely golfed any more.

Jock oversaw every detail, from ticket sales, which set records, to plans for a marching band. He picked through phone bills, questioning particular calls, and approved the photos adorning the team's new offices, which he directed from a glass-enclosed room.

Jock pitched the Steelers to a new constituency. It was an easy sell. His Pitt fans were already transferring their loyalties to the Steelers. Jock's evenings were given over to speaking engagements, which generated slews of season ticket orders. A group of men who had studied dentistry at Pitt purchased 265 season tickets, while the Westinghouse Clerks Association bought 1,500. Tickets sales approached a season sellout, but Sutherland was also spending at record speed. Competition for players from the AAFC pushed Pittsburgh's weekly payroll to $20,000, up from $1,300 in 1933. Art asked the Pirates to erect temporary seating on the field to accommodate more fans but was turned down. "We may not wind up with much money even if we sell out," Art concluded, "but we sure are going to handle a lot of it for awhile, anyway. It will be fun even if we just break even." He meant it; a winning team that broke even would have delighted him.

Having shored up the roster and fan base, Jock took a break to visit his mother in Scotland, whom he had not seen since before the war. While there, he stayed up late to listen on the radio as his friend Billy Conn finally got his rematch with Joe Louis. The June 19 fight was an anticlimax; Louis knocked out Conn in the eighth round. Billy, Harry Keck wrote, looked like a zombie, not the savage fighter he had been before the war. Art and Bill Dudley went to Conn's dressing room afterward. Conn, sprawled on a table, said, "Bill, how much is Arthur paying you?" When Dudley answered, Conn said, "Hell, I earned that much in a second tonight." But Conn's career in the ring was almost over.

Sutherland grew restless in Scotland, worrying about the challenges awaiting him. As he sailed back, Art joked, "If the captain of that boat is a two hundred–pounder and is pretty fast, I'll make a prediction some steamship agency is going to lose an employee. I never saw anybody jump into a job the way Jock has with us." Art kept a low profile with the press to avoid upstaging Sutherland and to tamp down expectations. "Well, I think that in two or three years under Jock we may have something," he allowed. "But I feel pretty sure now, after stumbling around over the years, we are on the right track. And that's because we've got Jock to head this up."

Presciently, *Post-Gazette*'s Havey Boyle tied the postwar boom for sport to Pittsburgh's anticipated renaissance. The Steelers, he argued, were part of efforts to improve city infrastructure and promote its renewal. Sport made Pittsburgh more livable. "The work-a-day guy wants something to root for in the athletic world and something to be proud of. A good baseball or football team can help develop community spirit, cooperation and pride." Boyle predicted that the Pirates' new owners would find a city on the move in sports. No one better understood the role sport could play in the city's rebirth than David Lawrence, the driving force behind Pittsburgh's renaissance.

Sutherland embraced the challenge: "I can't remember ever coaching a poor team, and I don't expect to start at this late date." When pressed, Sutherland said he was operating on a five-year plan to take the team to the top. But he would only be able to implement its first two years.

"Pittsburgh has been kicked around considerably," Jock observed. "I certainly hope we won't be kicked around this year." He made his expectations clear. Players who did not put out completely would be gone in short order. Sutherland was visibly upset when Bill Dudley showed up late on the first day of camp. Dudley, who assumed he was only due to report but not practice that day, brimmed with enthusiasm until he faced Sutherland's wrath. "Dr. Sutherland was a little bit miffed," Dudley recalled. "I think he got the impression I had a big head." Although Dudley was the team's star, Sutherland made it clear he was the boss.

The players were older and more serious than ever. Although many had seen combat, few had faced a training regimen as demanding as Sutherland's. Jock strove to build physical and mental toughness. Awakened by reveille at 7:30 a.m., players assembled for a chalk talk and practiced until noon. Jock preached conditioning and fundamentals—blocking, tackling, and running plays as diagrammed. Players stretched, did calisthenics, and ran wind sprints to exhaustion. They executed plays, drilling on footwork, timing, feints, and blocking. Jock exerted total control. Because he saw too much hydration as a sign of weakness, he mixed oatmeal with drinking water to develop a Spartan edge. After lunch, players listened to another lecture and drilled for the rest of the afternoon. Following supper, they convened for more meetings. Lights were out at ten.

The writers drank in the lounge each evening, but Jock kept his coaches away from liquor and the press until Friday nights. He demanded formality and decorum, a far cry from when Bert Bell ran camp and dictated correspondence to Jack McGinley late at night as he sat in his underwear.

Sutherland, who had rarely lauded a Pitt player until he had graduated, went out of his way to praise Dudley. "Sure, go right ahead and print that I consider Dudley one of the greatest backs I have ever coached," Jock declared. "He's only a fair passer, but we believe we have found the defect in his style and that he will improve. Best of all, he has the right spirit. If he were only as big as some of our other backs he would be in a class all by himself."

But Dudley was not exempt from Jock's ire. Sutherland lashed into him that week. "I wasn't a real good passer," Bill explained. After throwing an interception at practice, Dudley complained about the offense and defense wearing the same colors. Sutherland overheard. "Are you coaching the team?" Sutherland demanded. "No, sir, I'm not," Dudley replied. "Well," Sutherland snapped, "you have to take orders here like everybody else." Dudley, abashed by the dressing down, stood his ground. Sutherland abruptly ended the exchange: "You're either going to do it our way or you're not going to do it at all."

Dudley, upset, went to see John Holahan to demand his release. Holahan remonstrated with Dudley, a conscientious young man who had considered studying for the ministry, until he was nearly in tears. Dudley stayed, but he was troubled by his relationship with Sutherland. A few days later, he unloaded to Art. "He just listened," Dudley recalled.

On the fifth day of camp, eleven men were released; seven more left over the next three days. Some couldn't take it; others fell below Sutherland's standards. Jock commended the "fine bunch of boys" that remained and gave them Sunday off. "We still have a long way to go," he cautioned.

Back in Pittsburgh, even though it was baseball season, people were talking football. Hershey became a popular stopping place for Pittsburghers that summer. Art showed up every few days. He had dropped off Danny, Art Jr., and their friend Jackie Hart when camp opened and left them there while he visited eastern racetracks with Jim Rooney, Mayor Lawrence, Barney McGinley, and Dan Hamill.

Danny, fourteen, who attended his first camp when he was five, had spent every summer since visiting or working there. His earliest memory is standing on the sidelines as a horde of players crashed out of bounds. "One of the players picked me up—I was just a skinny little kid—grabbed me just before they fell on me. It was like I was part of the action." He was now a ball boy.

Sutherland commanded respect but remained an enigma to most people. "He has an aloof, austere manner that scares most of them away," Arthur Daley wrote in the *Times*. Even as a boy, Danny could see this. "He was not like my father, at ease with every crowd," he remembered. But the boy brought out something nurturing in the Scotsman, and Jock made Danny his protégé. He showed him that coaching meant creating an organization and attending to its every detail, not just strategizing with Xs and Os.

Sutherland controlled every aspect of the franchise. "It is said," Havey Boyle wrote, "that he insists his players tie their shoe laces with a uniform knot he learned from his navy days." Sutherland even instructed players how to dress off the field. At the end of one lecture before a trip, he glanced at the scruffy Rooney boys and Jackie Hart, then turned to Holahan: "And, John, when we get to town, buy three new shirts for the Rooney kids and their boyfriend."

When Sutherland saw Danny experimenting with his Christmas present, a motion picture camera, he appropriated it to film practice. In return, Jock complied when Danny asked to film him. To the amazement of reporters, he took Danny's direction along the sidelines. Later in camp, when the blackboard used to diagram plays disappeared, Jock entrusted Danny to drive to town to buy a replacement although he did not have a driver's license.

To Art Jr., a shy and cautious boy of eleven, Sutherland was a stern face at the end of a tall body. His workouts were so tough, Art Jr. recalls, that many players—even battle-hardened ex-Marines—quit camp. Art Jr., who had blond curls and a dreamy nature, explored the nearby Hershey amusement park but always kept sight of camp. Doc Sweeney, the team physician, Frank Scott, the equipment manager, and players with "guard dog instincts" kept their eyes on them. Danny and Art Jr. spent more time there than Art did. Both of them fell in love with football during those summers and chose to make it, at least subconsciously, their life's work.

Sutherland's attention to detail impressed Danny, who watched Jock scold the equipment manager for not counting "the whites"—the jocks, socks and tee shirts—before sending them to the laundry. "The man was a perfectionist, a guy who did things right, and the players had tremendous respect for him—he demanded it," Dan recalled. Attention to detail would become the hallmark of Dan's approach during his transition from ball boy to club president.

The first time Art saw his son quarterback North Catholic's varsity, Danny played well but broke his arm. Yet Danny's leadership qualities were apparent. He told Kass, "He runs that team the same way he runs the kids that come here to play in the yard." Danny was already taking charge.

Pittsburgh writers liked what they saw in Hershey. After Dudley ran a punt back 54 yards in an intrasquad game, the *Post-Gazette*'s Jack Sell proclaimed, "They are not the same old Steelers, but he still is the same old Dudley." The ranks of players thinned, but those who survived Camp Sutherland were in terrific shape. "Jock always has been a stickler for two things," the *Sun-Telegraph*'s Harry Keck observed, "conditioning and fundamentals, and he isn't letting down now." Pittsburgh fans devoured news of the most eagerly anticipated Steelers squad ever.

In August, they ran roughshod over the Scranton Miners on Chuck Cherundolo Night, as the Pennsylvania coal town honored its native son, who anchored the Steelers line. The Newark Bombers, Richmond Rebels, and the Patterson Panthers were next to fall. Sutherland avoided NFL clubs during the preseason, but by executing their game plan against semipros, the Steelers proved to themselves that they could win playing the way Sutherland demanded.

Dudley was unstoppable. Pittsburgh scored over 200 points while almost shutting out their opponents and attracting crowds bigger than those at regular season games before the war. Sutherland wanted perfection; despite their 42–0 rout of Newark, he lit into his players for committing 21 penalties.

The NFL's biggest 1946 preseason game was the College All-Star Game in Chicago. The game was noteworthy for its audience. A half million people, the largest midwestern television audience ever, saw its broadcast. Taverns with televisions were jammed, those without were empty. Families with sets hosted neighbors, and fans gathered by appliance store windows to watch sets tuned to the game. It was a historic moment for football, but Art, who was there, had little inkling of how television would reshape the game.

He focused on the crowded stands at Forbes Field. The Steelers, who emerged from Pittsburgh's sandlots, were heirs to its self-organized working-class sporting tradition. But Jock was drawing new constituencies into the fold—middle-and upper-class Protestants looking for an alternative to Pitt football, which had collapsed after Jock left.

"The day they signed Sutherland as coach is the day that everything changed for the Steelers," Pat Livingston attested. "All the Pitt fans became Steeler fans."

Sutherland's ability to bridge Pittsburgh's ethnic and religious divides reflected his enormous stature, as well as a nation in flux after the war. The chasm separating white, native-born Protestants from Catholic, Jewish, and Eastern Orthodox immigrants and their children was narrowing. Since the 1924 Quota Act choked off immigration from Southern and Eastern Europe, their offspring had Americanized. Sport facilitated that process, as did FDR, the New Deal, and the CIO. Returning stateside after the war, the sons and grandsons of white immigrant America found more tolerance of nationality and religion. The postwar shakeout in American sports delivered one more favor to the Steelers. Before the war, more people had attended sandlot games each weekend than Pirates or Steelers games. But in the late 1940s, suburbanization, integration, and television sucked much of the life out of community sport. The Steelers, who had begun on the sandlots as the Hope Harveys, picked up that fan base, too. Only one major gap remained. While the sandlots featured interracial play, professional team sports were still segregated. That, too, was about to change.

End of an Era

In March 1946, Art's friend, Cumberland Posey Jr., died of cancer. A fierce competitor, Posey excelled as an athlete and a promoter. His Loendi and Monticello basketball teams were national black champions; his Homestead Grays defined excellence in the Negro Leagues.

Art's teams had played—and usually lost to—Posey's Grays, but both teams benefited at the gate. Art's success had surpassed his mentor's, whose horizons had been limited by segregation and access to capital. Art had helped Posey overcome his chronic underfinancing. "Every spring, Uncle Cum used to go to the Northside and get the seed money so that the Grays could go to Hot Springs for spring training," Posey's nephew Evan Baker remembered. Spring training for the Grays entailed playing in the South to raise operating funds. "Cum, being a barnstormer, didn't have the financial wherewithal till the cash flow turned his way," Baker explained. "Getting that money from Mr. Rooney was life or death to us." He doubts that his uncle ever paid Art back. Baker asked Art about it over lunch. "Mr. Rooney acted like he never heard what I said. He started talking about the carrots instead. There wouldn't have been a Homestead Grays," Baker stressed, "if it hadn't been for Art Rooney."

Art watched the Grays at Forbes Field from a seat behind their dugout. At Posey's home, the two men sipped root beer and talked politics and sport. When Cum died, Art paid his respects. "Everybody was on pins and needles because Mr. Rooney was coming," Baker recalled. "He was the most important man in Pittsburgh. An hour before he came, the florist brought a baseball made of carnations with red seams in it that took up the whole front room."

Art and Josh Gibson, the Negro Leagues' greatest hitter, were honorary pallbearers. Posey's death, a body blow to black baseball, was followed by Gibson's demise at thirty-five in January 1947. If Posey's death was strike one and Gibson's strike two, black baseball's third strike came in April when Jackie Robinson took the field for the Brooklyn Dodgers. After a half-century of segregation, the majors reintegrated. That long overdue victory was the death knell for the Negro Leagues. The Grays, the Negro National League's best-ever franchise, did not survive integration. Ironically, the collapse of independent black sport would allow Rooney's Steelers to become black Pittsburgh's team.

Art never forgot Posey and campaigned for his induction into baseball's Hall of Fame. "I don't know of any other promoter-manager who deserves to be in the Hall of Fame more than Cum," he argued. "He's long overdue for it. What has to be done is to tell the people who Cum Posey was and what he was." Sixty years after Posey's death and almost twenty after Art's, Posey was finally enshrined in Cooperstown.

Art also remained close to Gus Greenlee, who suffered from a crackdown on the numbers game. The IRS was "taking everything he had," according to his brother, Dr. Charles Greenlee. During the worst of Gus's troubles, Charles was sitting with his brother at the Crawford Grill one evening when Art came by. Dr. Greenlee recalled that Art said, "Here, mate, I hear you're in trouble," and threw his brother a paper bag. "We took the bag upstairs, and it was $20,000."

Pro football had integrated in August 1946, when coach Paul Brown brought Marion Motley and Bill Willis to the AAFC Cleveland Browns' camp. About the same time, the NFL's Los Angeles Rams signed Kenny Washington and Woody Strode. The Rams knew they needed to integrate in order to play in the city-owned Los Angeles Coliseum.

These breakthroughs and Art's own longstanding ties to black sport make it hard to understand why he did nothing to integrate the Steelers. Art's sandlot clubs had included black players, and African American Ray Kemp played for his first NFL squad. Art's friends Cum Posey and Gus Greenlee were Pittsburgh's leading black sportsmen, and few if any whites were held in higher regard than Rooney by the city's African Americans. "Mr. Rooney practiced civil rights before it became fashionable," Evan Baker declared. But Art did not sign an African American until 1952.

Art's failure to integrate his team drew little attention. Only the *Pittsburgh Courier*, the city's black paper, raised the question. Noting that six clubs had signed black players for 1947 and calling Art a friendly, liberal man free of prejudice and known "to give a guy a square shake at all times," the paper asked, "What about the Steelers, Mr. Rooney?"

Perhaps the best explanation for Art's inaction was deference to the league and his coaches. At least one owner, Washington's George Marshall, feared that integration would damage his lucrative southern market. Sutherland's racial attitudes were also questionable. Dan Rooney believes that Jock was so bent on winning that he would have been willing to break in anyone he thought could help. But there were few black players at the college powerhouses Sutherland scouted, and black schools were off his radar.

The 1946 Season

Although he failed to cross the color line, Sutherland jockeyed for every other competitive edge. Anticipating that the Cardinals, in the midst of rebuilding, would improve as the season progressed, he pressed Art to move their game from December to September. Bert Bell consented, and Art persuaded Cardinal owner Charley Bidwill that the game would draw better as Sutherland's Steelers debut.

On opening day, Art had already sold $185,000 worth of tickets for the season, nine times his previous best. He had been up late handling ticket orders. "I've never seen anything like it," he said. "We have had them waiting in line for days, and I remember, not so long ago, when we used to be happy to deliver two tickets to any customer, even at his house, just so he would buy them." Art, who had handed out thousands of passes in past seasons, watched scalpers getting $15 a pop.

Local bookies favored the Cardinals, who fielded eight former All-Americans, including Marshall Goldberg, who had starred for Jock at Pitt. An all-day rain soaked the crowd of 32,000 and inundated the field. Many stood to avoid wet seats, while boys watched from trees overlooking the leftfield wall. Art had his first sellout.

With Jock on the bench, Art moved to an unfamiliar perch, the press box. Pittsburgh scored twice, capitalizing on Chicago errors, and held on to win 14–7 after Dudley intercepted a pass to end the game. When the final gun fired, fans delivered the sweetest ovation Art had ever heard his team receive. Water streamed off the brim of Sutherland's fedora and he repeatedly wiped his glasses free of condensation, but he smiled slightly as he strode off the field through a gauntlet of fans. The crowd savored his homecoming and a new era of Pittsburgh football.

Some began calling Pittsburgh the Cinderella team of the year, but Cinderella never absorbed this much punishment. Most pro teams had abandoned the single wing for the T formation. Not Jock, for whom football was less a matter of deception than execution. His single wing offense pounded the ball down opponents' throats. Even teams that beat Sutherland's squad came away battered. And Jock's style took a toll on his own players, especially Dudley, one of the smallest men in the NFL. Dudley rarely left the field; he ran with the ball, threw it, caught it, kicked it, returned kicks, and played defense.

Sutherland's controlling nature weighed heavily on Dudley. In an early game, the Steelers had the ball inches from the end zone. As Dudley prepared to receive the snap, guard Nick Skorich signaled him to run his way. Skorich had noticed something that convinced him he could open a hole for Dudley to score. Dudley abandoned the play called to follow Skorich into the end zone. When the team watched film of the game, Sutherland stopped the film before Dudley's touchdown and asked, "Bill, what play was called?" Dudley said it was an off-tackle run. Sutherland followed up, "What play did you run?" Dudley said he ran over the guard. Sutherland's tone was menacing: "Would you mind telling me why?" Dudley replied that Skorich had motioned him to run that way. It was clear that Sutherland had not seen Skorich signal Dudley during the game and did not believe him now. "I caught hell," Dudley recalled; then Sutherland advanced the film. To Sutherland's embarrassment, everyone could see Skorich signaling Dudley on the film.

Other teams keyed their defense to containing Dudley. Green Bay held him to a touchdown, a point after, and two interceptions to beat Pittsburgh in October. Washington, however, failed when Dudley scampered 80 yards after intercepting Sammy Baugh to upset the defending champs 14–7 on a glorious Indian summer day. It was, Jack Sell exulted, the greatest day in local pro football history as "the silent Scot's eleven adopted the Sutherland tradition of late-season invincibility." After the Pirates finally permitted seats on the field, attendance hit a record 39,080.

Pittsburgh led the league in attendance. Selling out Forbes Field was all the more impressive given the strikes by streetcar, power, and hotel workers that inconvenienced the city. "Blame the crowds on one man," Art laughed. "Dr. Jock Sutherland. He made us what we are today." Sutherland countered that the ticket frenzy was the result of "free-spending times in a football-hungry city." They were both right.

In their last home game, the Steelers came from behind, as they had been doing all season long, to beat Philadelphia and keep their pennant hopes alive. As a rule, no one cheers in the press box, but Al Abrams noted that colleague Jack Sell "jumped around like an excited freshman" when Dudley booted the winning kick. Afterward, Philadelphia's coaches joined Art at the Lotus Club. Candidly appraising the Steelers, Greasy Neale claimed no Steeler would upgrade his Eagles. But, he said, "that Dudley is a marvel. He makes up his mind he's going to do something and then does it. You can't beat a guy like that."

"Few teams bear the imprint of their ace player more," Havey Boyle said. "Dudley is not unusually big; he is not unusually fast; but he probably is the best defensive backfield man in the league, and he has a will to win exceeding probably any contemporary." But the season was taking a toll on Dudley. Knowing Pittsburgh rarely passed, opponents stacked the line of scrimmage against him.

The night before the Giants game, Art and Jock took a crew of reporters and coaches, including Shirley Povich and Bob Considine, to Toots Shor's in Manhattan. Everyone agreed that if the Steelers could beat the Giants the next day, they would be favored to win the division. But they lost.

Pittsburgh played opportunistically, scoring more points from their adversaries' turnovers than they did on their own. "No professional team ever 'put out' more than the Steelers of 1946," Havey Boyle concluded. "It was a college team wearing the whiskers of the professionals. Which is another description of Dudley."

The Steelers had a slight chance to win the title when they played their final game, in Philadelphia. Down 10–0, they scored and got the ball back. On fourth down, Dudley dropped back to pass. He fell to the turf after releasing the ball, and a teammate, pushed backward by two defenders, came down on him. Dudley writhed in agony. The ligaments in his right leg were torn and he was carried off the field. It wasn't the first time he had been hurt, but this ended his season, and as it turned out, his time in Pittsburgh. "I know my limitations," he confessed. "I'm just not big enough to take such a beating as this league calls for in a key player."

The "gallant Dudley," Havey Boyle underscored, was more than a spectacular offensive player. "Until someone better comes along he will be known as Mr. Pittsburgh in professional football circles." Dudley's pass defense was so spectacular that Art claimed that some coaches fined quarterbacks who threw passes anywhere near him.

Dudley, who had a year left on his contract, wasn't the only Steeler contemplating retirement. Even with the rival All-America Football Conference bidding up salaries, football pay was paltry. Art was unfazed. "It has been my experience," he said, "that the boys quit every December but are right back in uniform the following August." Besides, he had Sutherland. With the season over, players sought work. Bob Davis sold insurance, Jack Wiley helped on his father's farm, and Johnny Clement headed for the oil fields. Jock and Art went to New York for the championship game.

Although the Steelers did not reach the postseason in 1946, they had turned the corner on a dismal past. The fans certainly thought so; twice as many as ever before—177,854—attended games. Art could hardly contain himself as advance season tickets sales for 1947 doubled to 21,120.

The NFL season, however, ended on a disquieting note. The night before the Bears–Giants title game, Art, Jack Sell, and Jack McGinley were returning to the Commodore Hotel from Dinty Moore's, one of Art's favorite New York sawdust joints. As they stood in the elevator, Bert Bell entered. "Something terrible has happened," he whispered. Once inside Art's suite, Bell said that two Giants had been offered $3,500 to fix the game. They discussed Bell's options. Art considered it incredibly stupid for anybody connected with the NFL to bet on games. He had warned buddies who bet football not to travel with the Steelers. On the basis of the available evidence, Bell ruled fullback Merle Hapes ineligible but allowed halfback Frankie Filchock to play.

Chicago won the game, which took place on the last day of Bell's first year as commissioner. Before leaving New York, Art and Barney McGinley held a dinner party for Jock and presented him with a diamond-studded platinum watch.

The Steelers, who finished 5-5-1, were the league's best defensive unit, which helped considerably because they were also one of the lowest scoring teams. They were underdogs in most games, but Dudley had compensated for their deficiencies. He led the league in rushing, interceptions, and punt returns, and was voted its MVP. His 1946 performance was the greatest single season by a Steeler ever.

Art's worries were hardly over. He had lost money on the season despite record attendance. The NFL-AAFC rivalry was inflating salaries and costing both sides plenty, with no end of that war in sight.

Westminster

The Rooneys' winter excursions to Florida, infrequent during the war, were shortened afterward because the boys were in school. Art drove Kass, her sister Alice, and the boys back to Pittsburgh, turned around, and headed south again to watch his horses run. He thought little of jumping in the car with a friend or three and driving through the night. In Miami, Art, Dan Hamill, Father Campbell, Walt Kiesling, and Sam Leone fished, golfed, played cards, and went to the track.

His son Dan remembers driving to Miami with Hamill and Campbell when he was twelve. They said the rosary before launching into a discussion of *The Lives of the Saints*, a book Hamill had brought along. When they quizzed young Dan, he wowed them with his knowledge. Dan didn't let on that he had received the book as a Christmas present.

At the track, Art had his eye on Westminster, a horse he had acquired from Moishe Wexler. The biggest event at Coral Gables' Tropical Park was a rare double event, in which two handicapped stakes races were held in January 1947. Westminster, Bull Dog's six-year-old son, was among the entrants. A big reddish-brown bay, Westminster was ornery enough to have been gelded. On the track, he liked to open up an early lead but could be erratic. "If a good horse caught up with him, he would give up kind of quick," Donnie McGee, the trainer's son, remembered.

Shortly before the double event, Westminster lost to Eire, a huge upset. Although Westminster rebounded to win his next race, he had faded in the homestretch. His disappointing performances turned out to be a godsend for Art. When writers handicapped the field for the double event, Westminster was an afterthought. Instead, they focused on Statesman, who had won several races at Tropical, and False Move, who was coming off a dazzling workout. Ted Atkinson, the first jockey to earn a million dollars in purses in one year, was atop Apropriado, while Eternal Reward had won the $100,000 American Derby.

Nobody but Art thought Westminster had a chance. As a result, he carried less weight and went off at 16-to-1. Westminster liked hard, firm tracks like Tropical and stayed close to the leaders. When jockey Bobby Martin let him go at the top of the stretch, he shot past Statesman and won going away. He tied the track record for a mile and a furlong, paying $33.40 on a $2 bet. Over $814,000 was bet at the track that day, much more with bookmakers.

Westminster breezed home first in the backend of the double event, too, clipping two-fifths of a second off his own track record. It was closing day at Tropical Park and bettors wagered a record $907,000. The odds were shorter this time, paying only $3.90 on a $2 ticket.

Art did not go down to the winner's circle, but he made a killing on Westminster. If Art had told Martin to hold Westminster back in his last two races before the double event to get better odds or a lighter weight, it would have been a clever, if unethical, move. Nobody in racing who knew Art thought that he had done so, although stories of Art painting a horse to conceal his identity were oft-told fables. Nor did anyone suspect McGee. In all likelihood, Westminster ran the race of his life in the first leg, upsetting a field in which nobody gave him a chance.

The double event was probably Art's biggest score, although it never acquired the legendary stature of his 1937 ride. In 1972, Red Smith wrote in the *New York Times* that "legend says Art cleaned up just under a million" on the pair of victories. Legend was likely fact. Both Joe Tucker, the Steelers' announcer, and Pat Lynch, the *Journal American*'s racing editor, concurred that Art made a million on Westminster. Characteristically, Art disclosed nothing. He never boasted about his winnings nor bemoaned his losses.

If Art did make a million on Westminster, he was betting with bookmakers as well as the track. After the war, pari-mutuel betting, run by the states, was the only legal option. Art resented pari-mutuels because if he bet heavily on a horse, he pulled down his own odds. Studies of gambling speculate that three times as much was bet with illegal bookmakers as pari-mutuels in the late 1940s. Art contributed substantially to those calculations.

Art's talent as a horseplayer steadied him through down times. Even when his team was more down than up, he usually won at the track. "My father had a knack," Tim Rooney observed. "He had tremendous information, but he also had a tremendous ability to play faces and judge the information he was getting." "Playing face" meant judging who was credible and who was not. Art told Pat Lynch that he could look at a face and know if it was a "player's" face, one he could trust. Plus, Lynch said, "Art Rooney had the greatest sense of chance I've ever seen in a man."

Given his facility with numbers, Art juggled complicated odds with ease. "He might look at a 6-to-1 shot and think this horse ought to be 15-to-1 and not bet him," Tim Rooney said, "but see a 6-to-5 that he really liked because he thought the horse should have been an even bigger favorite." When Art saw odds he liked, he bet big.

His sons believe that Art made more from racing than any other venture through the early 1960s. Tim figures that his father cleared several hundred thousand a year at the track. Only Art and his little black book knew for sure.

Jack McGinley joined Art at the Jamaica racetrack on April 30, 1946, when he bet $2,000 on King Pretty, one of entertainer Louis Prima's horses. King Pretty, a 13-to-1 long shot, won but a foul claim was filed. As Art waited for the claim to be adjudicated, a racetrack habitué named Memphis sidled over and said, "I'll give you $10,000 for your bet." Art, who had seen the finish, felt confident that King Pretty had not fouled. He turned Memphis down and pocketed $26,000 when the claim was rejected. Before McGinley returned to Pittsburgh that evening, he accompanied Art to the New York Hotel where two men handed Art a valise of money that he asked Jack to count. "They were all hundred dollar bills," McGinley remembered. "I was pretty good counting money from working in the ticket office. There was $75,000 there, money Art had won from them on the horses." Art asked Jack to take the money back to Pittsburgh for him. "I wrapped it in a newspaper and carried it under my arm, got a roomette on the train, and went straight to the Fort Pitt Hotel when I arrived," McGinley recalled. "I didn't sleep much that night."

Art's horses ran well in 1947. His only major disappointment was Darby Dieppe, who had finished in the money at the Derby and the Preakness in 1945 when Pirates owner John Galbreath owned him. Art thought he could make back his $40,000 price by putting Darby Dieppe to stud, but his trainer, Jimmy McGee, had inexplicably gelded him.

Art was a racetrack celebrity again. His horses ran against steeds owned by Samuel Riddle, who owned Triple Crown winner War Admiral, in races before grandstands packed with the likes of former ambassador to Great Britain Joseph Kennedy and automotive magnate Walter Chrysler Jr. In this world, the Steelers were an afterthought.

Back to Football

The tension between Sutherland and Dudley that had smoldered during the season ignited afterward. Dudley, saying he could not sustain the pounding, announced that he would no longer play for Sutherland. Because the single wing ran through Dudley, he was tackled more than any other Steeler. On defense, he often did the tackling. Undersized and rarely off the field, Dudley had played hurt during the season. Besides, Dudley recalled, "It wasn't much fun playing for someone who didn't respect me."

Dudley and Sutherland had kept their mutual antagonism from affecting the club during the season. Sutherland had called Dudley one of the most remarkable players he had ever coached, but Art had known trouble was brewing. "Dudley liked to play Dudley's game instead of Sutherland's," he observed. Art took Bill to the Kentucky Derby and he tried to persuade him to return. Dudley refused to play for Sutherland, but he agreed to be traded. That summer Art sent him to Detroit.

"I was never upset with Art," Dudley affirmed. He understood how much Sutherland meant to Art. But for Art, losing Dudley, his favorite player, was difficult. They remained friends, and Dudley, a Protestant, would accompany Art on retreats to Gethsemane, a Catholic monastery near Louisville.

The Sutherlanders—as the press called them—trained for the 1947 season at Alliance College in Cambridge Springs, north of Pittsburgh. Many were veterans of the war. Dudley's absence was alarming when the team struggled to score during its exhibition opener in Erie. After the game, the team went to the Bartlett Hotel for a late meal. Art, not always attentive to his sons, was distracted by his team's performance. Tim, ten, gobbled down dinner and sacked out on a couch in the lobby.

The team departed, leaving Tim behind. A night clerk found him later and arranged his return to camp.

The Steelers found their rhythm, walloping the Norfolk Shamrocks 48–0 and the Richmond Rebels 35–0. Art was overjoyed to see big crowds turning out. It augured well for the season. They capped the preseason by beating Green Bay for the first time in a Dapper Dan Club fundraiser for victims of the Greek civil war.

Sutherland was uncharacteristically upbeat. When pressed on what Dudley's absence would mean, Sutherland smiled tightly. "Sure, Bill was a grand player," he conceded, "but we'll be all right." Slinging a back-handed slam, he said, "The spirit is much better than it was last year . . . No prima donnas, no individualism."

The 1947 home opener against Detroit carried the additional baggage of Dudley returning to play against the coach he had renounced. Pittsburgh fans, some standing behind ropes stretched around the field, watched Dudley play with his customary élan. According to one possibly apocryphal account, Art cheered Dudley on when he ran for a touchdown. But Pittsburgh rebounded and won. With scant time to savor the victory, the team entrained for Los Angeles, where the Rams demolished them 48–7. The defeat was Jock's worst ever, reprising memories of his Pitt team's humiliation in the 1929 Rose Bowl. The game was noteworthy for another reason—Kenny Washington played for the Rams, the first time that Pittsburgh had faced a black player since 1933.

After Pittsburgh lost again, fans wondered if the loss of Dudley would be insurmountable. Their doubts dissipated as Pittsburgh embarked on a record six-game winning streak, which ended in Chicago with a 49–7 drubbing. Pittsburgh had not beaten Chicago in eleven regular season encounters.

The Chicago game reminded fans that Sid Luckman, whose exquisite passing led the Bears, had once been Pittsburgh property. Art had drafted Luckman in 1939, only to trade him to Halas for the all-too-forgettable "Eggs" Manske. Art, limiting his financial losses, had not always drafted the best player but the one who fit his payroll. Luckman became a Hall of Famer, but not in Pittsburgh.

Pittsburgh lost the next game but rebounded to beat Boston and reach the playoffs for the first time in franchise history. They had two weeks to prepare for Philadelphia. When Art said he wanted to pay the players for practicing during the off week, Sutherland objected. "Some of them don't get paid very much," Art pointed out. Sutherland, who carefully monitored costs, retorted, "The ones who don't get paid very much happen to be the ones who need the practice." Jock won the argument, but not the game. Some felt that the lost payday contributed to their defeat.

Returning home, Art threw a party for the team and left for Chicago for the championship game. The night before the game, Jock had a drink with Jack McGinley. Near midnight, Jack decided to attend Mass. To his surprise, Jock asked if he could tag along. Although Jock was a Presbyterian, he knelt during services, contributed to the collection, and warmly thanked Jack afterward. The Cardinals won the title game the next day but the victory was bittersweet. Charley Bidwill, their owner and Art's good friend, had died earlier that season and did not witness his club's first championship.

Art returned to Florida, confident that Pittsburgh would contend in 1948. After all, one of the game's greatest coaches led his team, and the 1947 squad, the highest scoring, most offensively accomplished in franchise history, had won more games than any previous team.

Jock came to the office to inspect the books because his contract entitled him to a quarter of all profits. Thanks to selling out its home games, drawing well on the road, and playoff revenue, the franchise had broken the million-dollar mark in revenues and cleared a record $50,000. Sutherland's bonus was $12,500. Fran Fogarty, who handled the business end of the team, and Jack McGinley had the books ready. "The Doctor came in the door," McGinley recalled. "He never took his hat and coat off. He asked, 'Have Arthur and Bernard [McGinley] seen these books?'" Fran confirmed that they had. "Then send me my check," Sutherland said, turning around and walking out. McGinley could not help but think how far the relationship between Sutherland and Rooney had come, from substantial suspicion to unqualified trust.

Challenges

While the Steelers had turned a profit, the war with the AAFC was driving up salaries. The fight with the rival league bonded the owners as much as the hard times they had experienced during the Depression and the war. Although the tensions that flared among George Halas, Tim Mara, and George Marshall could be exasperating, the owners stuck together. Art was their emotional and political center, the owner with whom every other man stayed friends. "Art became the mediator," reflected Ed Kiely, who sat in on meetings and listened as Art worked the phones. "If Bell got in trouble with one of the owners, he would come to Art. He had a way he could talk to them."

Art was relieved that Bert Bell held the commissioner's job. The hallmark of Bell's tenure was his indefatigable effort to create a league in which the small-market clubs could compete. His priorities, like Art's, put the league first.

Art's political savvy kicked in as he lobbied fellow owners before votes. "He was a master of that," Kiely attested. "Not all of those guys were oriented to that. They just thought they could make a speech and sway the audience. Art knew you'd have to have the votes."

Other owners came to Art with problems. "They'd call him and he would go to work," Kiely explained. Art could even reason with the willful Marshall, who was most infuriating during fights over the schedule. Who played whom, when, and where greatly affected a team's record and gate. Scheduling was invariably contentious, with owners arguing over who was getting what they wanted and who was being abused. "The owners who had the staying power were the ones who came away with the decent schedules," Art explained. "The guys who snuck out to get some sleep or go nightclubbing wound up getting murdered the next season because when they weren't there to defend themselves, we'd give them all the dates we didn't want."

Once, several days of dickering produced a schedule acceptable to everyone but Marshall. Marshall, who often slept in, had come to the meeting in his bathrobe and slippers. Arising from his seat, he sauntered to the blackboard and erased the schedule. His colleagues roared when they realized that nobody had copied it down. But Art could laugh at Marshall, knowing that when an issue really mattered, he could find the votes to defeat him. "When Marshall had some hare-brained schemes he wanted to get approved, he would get up and walk up and down, going on and on," Ed Kiely recalled. "Finally, Art would say, 'Let's vote.'" Marshall knew that once Art did that, he was defeated. "Arthur," he acknowledged, "you always have the votes."

After two fruitless days of haggling after the 1947 season, the owners entrusted Bell with devising a 5-year schedule. The AAFC rivalry made them realize that, more than ever, they needed to maintain unity and assist vulnerable teams. To start the season, Bell scheduled weaker clubs against each other and stronger clubs against each other to keep as many in contention as long as possible and boost attendance. Parity had become his—and Art's—article of faith.

With Sutherland at the helm, the Steelers had suddenly become a million-dollar business, and Art needed to change his approach to the organization. He could have run the business himself, but that would have meant downplaying the track and politics. Not about to do that, he relied on Fran Fogarty.

Fogarty meshed Rooney's old office crew with Sutherland's hires. He combined an astute sense of business with an inherited understanding of Pittsburgh sport. His grandfather, from County Cork, Ireland, had worked at Exposition Park, down the street from Rooney's saloon, and his father was Forbes Field's head groundskeeper. Fran was from Oakland's Irish section on the slopes of the Hill. An All-American hockey player at Duquesne, he had joined the organization when nobody had job titles. "You just showed up and did your work," Ed Kiely explained. Pat Livingston did publicity, Joe Carr handled tickets, Jack McGinley managed boxing, and pretty, young Mary Regan was the receptionist. When Sutherland and Livingston started butting heads, Pat went on the road to scout, and Kiely took over public relations.

Fran kept the books—for football, boxing, and horse racing—often in his head and always with discretion. Like Art, he rarely talked about himself. Few knew that Fogarty had been captured during the war, shot during an escape, and had hidden for months with a French family.

Art and Fran, who were second cousins, talked shop every day. Art trusted Fran implicitly. Fogarty kept his under-financed team afloat—often by restraining Art's free spending. Although Fran's brother was vice president of the ushers union, Fran controlled costs by curtailing staffing for games and fight cards. Art invariably added more men, arguing that they needed Thanksgiving turkeys or money for Christmas.

Fogarty sometimes told Art, "Don't cut that guy; he still owes us money." Gene Hubka, at camp in 1947 after leaving the Marines, requested a $2,000 loan. Art asked if he had a problem. No, Hubka explained, but he had never owned a car. New ones were rolling off assembly lines, and he wanted to buy a Mercury. "Art took out his checkbook and started making it out," Hubka recalled. "Then he looked up and said, 'By the way, what's your name?'" Hubka got the car and job security.

Sudden Death

By 1948, Art had made his peace with Tommy's death, at least as much as he ever would. He never talked about it. But he found solace at Mass and in the sacraments. After losing friends during the war, he was about to lose another.

In late March, Sutherland left town for his annual excursion to renew contacts in southern football circles. On Easter Sunday, he fell out of sight. Jack McGinley was at work a few days later when he got a call from the sheriff in Bandana, Kentucky, asking, "Do you people have a coach named Sutherland working for you?" Jock had been found wading through a field in the backwoods. His car was mired in mud nearby. "I am Jock Sutherland," he told the sheriff, but he could not account for his whereabouts during the past week. Visibly confused, Jock said he was hungry and his head hurt.

The sheriff thought it was amnesia, while doctors in Cairo, Illinois, where Jock was taken, diagnosed a breakdown. In Pittsburgh, Marion Sutherland confirmed that her brother had not been well when he left town. John Michelosen, Ralph Daugherty, and John Holahan flew to Paducah, the nearest airport, on Weirton Steel president Thomas Millsop's plane. While Holahan drove Jock's car back to Pittsburgh, the other men brought Jock home.

Jock went directly into surgery at West Penn Hospital, where Art and Mayor Lawrence stood vigil. After two long surgeries revealed a malignant and inoperable brain tumor, Jock died on April 11.

His death cast a pall over the city. Lawrence ordered the city to place its flags at half-mast; so did the University of Pittsburgh. An honor guard of men who had played for Jock at Pitt stood around his bier, which lay in state at Calvary Episcopal Church. Mourners spilled out of the church and accompanied the casket to Homewood Cemetery. Young Dan Rooney was among those outside the church. "The football world lost one of its greatest leaders," Art said. "Pittsburgh lost one of its leading citizens and I lost one of my finest friends." Jack McGinley agreed. "His death was a great loss. He was the best I ever saw. Had he lived, we would have won a million championships." Sutherland's death was the most devastating setback Art had encountered professionally. As he often did when distressed by football, Art returned to horse racing. And now, he had a horse farm of his own to which he could retreat.

12

Shamrock Farm

Soon after Jock Sutherland's funeral, Art headed for Maryland horse country. He needed time to himself. At Shamrock Farm, he could escape the line of supplicants that formed wherever he went. Art normally controlled his expectations, but his sense of possibility had soared after Jock took the squad into the playoffs for the first time. Art—and Pittsburgh—had dared to hope for the title.

That dream had turned to dust. Art mourned Jock more than he did his team's diminished fortunes. Approaching fifty, he had lost in short order his brother Tommy, friends Martin Flanagan, Moo O'Malley, and Charley Bidwill, and now his coach. He found solace in the Church and with Jim Campbell, who had returned to St. Peter's after the war, but Shamrock became his sanctuary. Art had purchased the run-down dairy farm for $40,000 before Jock's death. Within an hour's drive of three racetracks, it was a five-hour trek from Pittsburgh. As Art walked his farm that spring, he took stock.

Jock's death had cast a pall on football but darkened racing less. Since purchasing Moishe Wexler's stable of thoroughbreds in 1946, Art had needed somewhere to board and breed his horses. During Jock's first season, Art had used training camp in Hershey as a jumping-off point to East Coast tracks. Driving through Maryland horse country, he idly scouted for a farm to stable his horses. Jimmy McGee was even more eager than Art to find something. The trainer figured that if he managed a horse farm for Art, he would have a place to live.

"It was Jimmy McGee's idea that I should own a farm in Maryland," Art said. So I told him: 'Okay, maybe I'll get one some day.' Next thing I knew, I owned this farm, and Jimmy was living on it." McGee collected per diem fees for horses under his care and ten percent of purses when they won. Like most horsemen, McGee bet, but discreetly. "He wouldn't tell the Pope what he was betting," laughed trainer Tuffy Hacker. "But when he got off to himself during the race and got to chewing his gum, he was betting."

The four-hundred-acre farm near Sykesville in Carroll County gave Art ready access to Pimlico, Laurel, and Bowie. He could breed horses there and take in boarders to defray racing's considerable costs. Other locations would have been better investments. "My father looked at another farm that was on the ocean in New Jersey," Dan Rooney explained. "Had he bought that one, it would have been worth a fortune." Tim Rooney concurred. "If my father had bought any other farm than the one he did, he would have been able to sell it later as an enormous investment when development and sprawl took over the region." But Art wasn't looking to turn over the property.

Shamrock's white frame farmhouse with dark shutters at the end of a long, straight driveway looked almost stately. The house had a grand entrance with an overhang and second-floor porches that gazed over the surrounding countryside. But it was primitive on the inside and only partially heated. The McGees occupied the heated side; the Rooneys slept in the unheated part when they visited. "It could get pretty cold, let me tell you," Tim Rooney recalled. The cold did not deter Art. "My dad always loved the place," Tim emphasized. "There really was nothing in the world he enjoyed more than going to the farm."

Art, who had raced horses under the colors of Shamrock Stables since 1938, named his property Shamrock Farm. He renovated the old barns and built a few new ones. Dan, handier than his dad, took up hammer and saw and helped out. Thinking they would spend considerable time there, Art and Kass planned to remodel the farmhouse. But they never did. Five sons with sporting commitments made long stays difficult. Instead, they usually came for weekends. On Friday afternoons, they packed up the two Buicks that they had bought from Kass's uncle and drove east on the Pennsylvania Turnpike through the Alleghenies to Breezewood, then headed south to Hancock, Maryland, along state roads clogged with trucks.

Art raced along the turnpike as if driving were a competitive sport, constantly scanning the radio dial in search of a ball game. "When we were going through those mountains, the radio was horrible," Tim said, describing his father's fiddling with the tuner. "You would have thought he was in the Second World War trying to find some message about the invasion of Normandy." Art's speed made his distractions all the more worrisome. "He was a ninety-mile-an-hour guy," Jack McGinley said, "and often was stopped by the cops." Kass drove the younger boys and their friends in the second Buick. When the boys fought—which was most of the time—she restored order by steering with one hand and whacking whoever was in reach with her purse.

When his sons began driving, Art relinquished the wheel. He began trips by leading the rosary, then settled back to read the paper and racing form, smoking his cigar with the window open no matter the weather. The Rooneys were old hands at road trips. In the 1930s, they had traveled to Atlantic City, Miami, and Quebec. Now, Shamrock became their regular destination. Stopping in Hagerstown for dinner, the family arrived at the farm late in the evening.

Like their Northside home and Ligonier cottage, which they had owned for several years, Shamrock opened its doors to guests. The boys' friends squeezed into the backseat; so did Jim Rooney, Alice McNulty, and Sam Leone. Players sometimes visited or worked there for a while; Art figured it kept them in shape. Tip O'Neill, Art's old buddy, was living on a Congressman's modest budget in Washington. On weekends, he brought his kids to Shamrock and headed to the track with Art.

All the boys enjoyed the farm, but only Tim and the twins, John and Pat, picked up their father's passion for horses. Dan was sixteen years old, Art Jr. thirteen, Tim eleven, and the twins nine when Art bought Shamrock. Pitching in with the chores, they learned racing from the bottom up. Shamrock and sorties to the track marked their coming of age.

"When we got there on Friday night," Tim remembered, "no matter how late, first we went to check out the horses. We were always hoping to see a horse foal. And first thing in the morning, we went to look at the horses again." After Mass and breakfast, they went racing. Afterward, they stopped at Getz's Restaurant outside Baltimore for dinner.

With one last look at the horses on Sunday morning, they left for Mass in Libertytown on the way home. Although the family usually visited on summer weekends, Art began taking refuge there on Sunday nights in the fall, after especially gruesome defeats.

Family Values

Art left daily intervention in his sons' lives to Kass. "If you had a big problem," Dan explained, "he was the guy to go to. If you had a little problem, you went to mom. She smoothed things over." Art taught more by example. "You knew how he thought you should act," Dan said. That was usually enough.

At the track, they watched him treat people with the respect that governed all his interactions. He approached betting in a disciplined, thoughtful manner, arriving long before the first race. As the usher pocketed Art's tip and found him the seat of an absent patron, Art pumped him for information. He then spread the racing form on his lap and sifted through what he had heard from touts. Between races, he studied the data. If he was betting the next race, Art eyed the odds and calculated how much he liked his horse. "I knew the tote board value of a horse," Art said matter-of-factly. "I knew what price it should pay. And I was never impatient to get even on days when I was losing." If a race had little appeal, Art hung out with his buddies.

Tim, who often accompanied Art to the track, watched men approach with information. They were, he remarked, "the ones you would want to get a tip from." At Laurel, Art once had tips on eight different horses for the first race alone. "He was always getting more info than anybody else," Tim recalled. As was the custom, Art graced touts' palms with a few bucks. He gave one guy $25 for advice about a horse that went off at 15-to-1 and won. After Art collected his winnings, the tout cornered him. "You son of a bitch," he yelled. "What the hell did you do that for!" Perplexed, Art shrugged. "If you gave me $5," the fellow explained, "I would have bet it on the horse, but I wasn't going to bet $25. I held on to it. You cost me!"

Although treated akin to royalty at racetracks, Art never had his own box. "He'd just duke the usher," Tim explained. In general, the Rooneys lived comfortably, not luxuriously. Art rarely pampered himself or the boys, who knew they were well off by Northside standards. Despite the vagaries of Art's income as a horseplayer, they never lacked for anything. Dan, the oldest, could recognize when his father was on a losing streak. "He didn't talk a lot about it, but I was old enough to know what was going on." Whatever their income flow, neither Art nor Kass spent lavishly. One of the boys' favorite stories involves the family's old beat-up station wagon. Its bumper and a door were taped on. Dan was driving Art and his brothers home via the Hill District after a dispiriting defeat at Forbes Field. When Dan got to the base of the Hill, he turned the car around, put it in reverse, and started backing up the street. When Art asked in disbelief what he was doing, Dan explained that the car didn't have enough power to climb the hill in drive. Art shook his head, muttering, "The team stinks. The coach stinks. The stadium stinks. The fans stink. The city stinks. And now I have to back this stinking car up the hill. This organization is a disgrace!"

"He was always telling us not to spend money," Dan recalled. Art wanted the boys to appreciate the value of a dollar, but he also made it clear that money and possessions were secondary. His father was motivated more by "the thrill" of the venture than the lure of money or prestige, Dan attested. Putting on airs was never tolerated in the Rooneys' world. Social status and job titles meant little—a person's word everything. Bookmakers could be honorable people, those from high society bums.

Art's lack of pretension—and intolerance of phoniness in others—stemmed from his belief that good fortune was a blessing given, not merely earned. He never hoarded wealth; the hand blessing others was often his own. Art's benevolent reputation was widespread in racing. Tim remembers a horse trailer that maneuvered down North Lincoln and stopped by their house. The driver was broke, but he needed to get his horses to Kentucky and knew Art would help him get there.

Art's humility, like his generosity, was rooted in his religion. He went to Mass daily, said prayers regularly, and kept a rosary next to his bed. In the evening, Art whistled to whoever was playing in the backyard to come inside and say a rosary. If any kid protested that he was not a

Catholic, Art cupped a hand around the back of his head and barked, "Come on. It won't hurt you." He expected his sons to show reverence. "He had such power," Art Jr. recalled, "that he could demand that his teenage boys kneel down each night and say the rosary even when he was out of town. I suppose we could have not done it and lied to him about it, but we didn't dare do that." Art kept a bowl of rosary beads on the dining room table. "We'd gather around every night to say them," remembered his niece, Tricia Jesek, who lived with the family for several years. "Our friends would be afraid to come in. They'd look in the window before they knocked on the door. If they came in while we were saying the rosaries, he would make them sit down and join in." While intimidated by the household's religious discipline, youth were drawn there.

"You didn't have to be a big shot or a big shot's kid to be with Mr. Rooney," remembered Northsider Baldy Regan. "If you could jump in the family station wagon, you could go where the family went and be treated just like the family. If they were going to a football game or a racetrack, you went with them. If they ate lobster, you ate lobster. Do you know what it's like to a poor kid who grew up in the projects to be treated the same as everyone else just because you were a friend of the family? It makes you feel like a million dollars."

Art knocked down a garage to expand their Northside backyard for football. In the winter, the boys flooded the yard, installed goals, and put in lights so they could play hockey. Pat lost two front teeth there. "When the kids were growing up, we would toss a football out the back door, lock the gate and let them go at it," Art said. "Aside from a few yards of adhesive tape and maybe a bottle or two of arnica, they were practically no bother at all."

In the basement, the boys flailed at a speed bag when they weren't whacking each other. "We were stumbling around, trying to hit it one day," Tim recalled, when Art, in his fifties, entered the basement. "Get out of the way," he said. Although he had not worked out on a bag in decades, Art hit it with rhythmic dexterity. The boys, who had only inklings of his athletic background, gaped in astonishment. "He hadn't hit a speed bag in thirty-five years, and it was unbelievable. He hit it like he was doing it every day," Tim said.

But Art rarely took the time to watch his sons play, much less to teach them. He had little patience for nurturing. When Art hit ground-balls to his sons, his athletic instincts took over. "He thought we were gold glove guys," Dan recalled. "He would hit the ball so hard that we would say we didn't want to play." They remember when Tim, twelve, raced to first base after making contact. Thinking an infielder had caught the ball, he ran hard to first. Reaching the bag, Tim ran past it, not realizing that the ball had gotten into the outfield and that he could have turned and made it to second. Art was unforgiving.

"My father," Tim recalled, "yelled at me and said 'Don't you know you turn to the left?'" Tim yelled back, "You don't do that anymore, that's when you played. Those days are over." Art retorted, "You guys don't know anything about the game. That's a basic. If you're that dumb and you don't know that, I don't want to watch you play." With that, he went home and never watched them play baseball again.

"It frustrated him that we didn't know how to play the game like he did," Tim said. "My father was a real student of the game." A gifted athlete who had approached sport with preternatural focus, Art was glad his sons enjoyed sports, but he could not bear to witness their shortcomings.

Dan quarterbacked North Catholic's freshman team. Although lacking Art's athleticism, Dan was fast, tough, and heady, like his father. He played varsity ball as a sophomore until rheumatic fever hospitalized him for nineteen weeks. Sidelined his junior year, Dan became a de facto assistant coach. He soon knew what every member of the team was supposed to do on a play. He hit stride as a senior, starting at quarterback.

Art was relieved by Dan's recovery. "He was such a sick kid last year—there were times we wondered whether he would pull through—that of course we're tickled to death to see him playing football." Art even bragged a little. "They tell me he is a good quarterback. Has a sense for calling the right play at the right time. Likes the going tough and all that sort of thing. Just a chip off the old block."

Kass told Art to give away her Steeler tickets for games that conflicted with North Catholic contests. She has "gone batty about football and Danny," Art said. "It was never quite like this before." Now, Kass talked football during dinner. "We get quarterback sneaks with the fruit cup, handoffs with meat courses, and jump passes with the dessert," Art chuckled. Dan led North Catholic to the city Catholic championship by beating St. Justin's, whose quarterback was a gangly boy from Mt. Washington named John Unitas.

Art's sons were ball boys at Steeler camp and played football at North Catholic. Tim and Pat also played on a baseball team called the Allegheny Shamrocks that Dan and Baldy Regan coached. They followed in their father's and uncles' footsteps. "In the first four games," Baldy said, "we had five runs and six fights." Pat was the best baseball player, but none of them displayed Art's enormous talents for sport.

The boys spent summers at the Ligonier cottages, where the air smelled of mown hay and the fresh water that tumbled down stony Loyalhanna Creek. The Rooneys roughhoused with their cousins, the five Laughlins and six McGinleys, under the watchful eyes of Kass Rooney, her sister Alice, and Art's sisters, Margaret Laughlin and Marie McGinley. Keeping track of this wild clan of sixteen cousins left the women weary. Once the police stopped Margaret for speeding while she was driving a carload of jostling cousins. She rolled down the window and told the officer, "I hope you plan to put me in jail, officer. I sure could use the rest." The families bonded here amid the fun and fights. If any of the children perceived a threat from the outside, it was one for all and all for one. "All the kids in Ligonier would say, 'You better not ever mess with a Rooney, a Laughlin, or a McGinley,'" Margaret Laughlin recalled.

Shamrock Farm became an extension of the cottages, another pastoral counterpoint to the gritty Northside where the Rooneys lived cheek by jowl with people struggling to survive. Tim, Pat, and John saw their father more on trips to Shamrock and the track than in Pittsburgh. They witnessed a side of him that the public rarely encountered. "He could be tough," John reflected. "He wasn't mean, but he wasn't trying to be your best friend. At times, it seemed like he had two emotions, either laughing or yelling at you." Once, Tim was driving home from a New Jersey track with John beside him. Art read the paper and gave directions from the back seat. They approached an interchange where three routes converged, and Tim took the wrong one. "The Chief started screaming at Tim," John explained. "Tim turns back to the Chief and says, 'If you hadn't been reading that paper while you were giving me directions, I wouldn't have made a mistake.'" Art told him to pull over and get out. As Tim stepped outside, Art ordered John to take the wheel and drive away. "I said, 'Tim isn't in the car.' He said, 'Leave him.' So he left Timmy, about eighteen years old, four hundred miles from home to hitch home. That's what I mean by tough. You didn't give him any lip."

The Clubhouse

Art went to Shamrock frequently to get away from football and Pittsburgh. He watched the thoroughbreds and wandered through the woods, much as he meandered along Northside streets at home. But no one approached him for a favor here. The sweet smell of hay and fruit blossoms mixed with a whiff of composting manure. "It's so quiet and restful that I can relax almost at once," Art said. "Horses don't talk back, you know, and that can be a great relief when you spend most of your life around sometimes temperamental football players."

But life in the hustle and bustle more closely suited Art's nature. He moved in the company of men and was rarely alone. In part, Jack McGinley pointed out, Art needed somebody watching his back. A well-known bettor with cash rolled in rubber bands in his pockets, he presented a tempting target. Tim, who delighted in counting Art's roll as a boy, tallied as much as $25,000.

Art's buddies, nephews, and sons made Shamrock into their clubhouse. Most tell farm stories. Vince Rooney's son, Timmy, recalled stopping for a jug of buttermilk on the way to the farm. "Buttermilk is the leitmotif that weaves its way through the Rooney family," Jamie Rooney pointed out. "You'd be traveling someplace with my uncle Art, and he always knew where to stop to get buttermilk." Cousins Tim and Timmy were passing the jug back and forth with Sam Leone between them in the backseat. "Sam," Timmy explained, "was always immaculately dressed, closely shaven, and good looking. He even smelled good and was the nicest man in the world." Sam eyed the passing buttermilk with apprehension. Sure enough, the boys spilled it all over his beautiful camel's hair coat. "He was so upset that he cried," Timmy remembered. "He was mortified." While Sam, the dandy, wailed, Art—who rarely bothered to press his trousers—cracked up. "I can see him leaning out the window with a cigar, laughing."

The next day, Timmy was exploring the paddock when Sam sidled up to him. "Sam was always working a deal," Timmy observed. After crooning how wonderful Shamrock was, Sam said, "Maybe you can talk to your uncle and tell him that Sam would like to stay down here a long time." Timmy, feeling bad about the buttermilk, dutifully approached Art. Art had heard it before. Sam, who eked out a living on the fringes of society, was angling for a free room near the track. "Art said, 'Don't worry about it. I'll take care of Sam,'" Tim recalled.

One summer in the 1950s, Art took Steeler safety Jack Butler to Shamrock. At the track the next day, Art had Butler place his bets. Butler, aware of Art's reputation, put up his own money alongside Art's. But it was not Art's day, and Butler was soon busted. When Art left the next day, he suggested that Butler stay at Shamrock and lend a hand until he returned. Butler, a city boy taken with the farm's bucolic beauty, naively agreed. He never asked what farmhands did or how long Art would be gone. Awakened daily at 4:00 a.m., he mucked stables and cut fields for a month. "Boy," Butler recalled, "I was in good shape for camp."

Shamrock was a no-frills working farm, a far cry from Kentucky bluegrass country. In addition to breeding horses, Shamrock stood two stallions at stud: British Buddy and Lion Rampant, a descendant of Man o' War. Other owners brought their mares to be impregnated for a fee.

Making the Rounds

To Art, all parts of life—the sacred and the profane, high and low society—were beads on the same rosary. He loved his racing routines just as he loved to say the decades of Hail Marys around the circular strings of beads. He based his life on the rhythms of racing, football, and Catholicism. His year started at Florida's tracks. Come spring, he frequented East Coast venues. The Kentucky Derby in May and the Belmont Stakes in June were annual rituals, and he usually attended the Preakness.

Art stayed close to the team during football season, but on road trips he invariably visited the track. "My mother lived in that North Lincoln house much more than my father did," John Rooney commented. "He lived at the Bellevue-Stratford in Philadelphia. In New York, it was the St. Regis and the Warwick." In the summer, Art showed up at the cottage in Ligonier, but rarely stayed for long.

Playing the horses was Art's vocation, what he did better than anything else professionally. From the time Art and Kass hit the Belmont Stakes on their honeymoon in 1931, their lives revolved around racing almost as much as football. They never missed the Belmont Stakes as long as they were alive. Summers included pilgrimages that began at Shamrock and mixed racetracks with religious shrines. The boys referred to the tracks as Our Lady of Laurel and Our Lady of Aqueduct.

St. Anne de Beaupré, where the Jesuits built a chapel to honor the mother of Mary, was also an annual destination. The magnificent basilica near Quebec City was Art's favorite shrine. He collected holy oils and waters there, mixed them together, and rubbed the potion on his horses' legs. His horses bore the names of saints, football players, and friends.

Art had regular haunts almost anywhere he went. At the Kentucky Derby, he stayed at the Galt House and attended Mass at the Cathedral of the Assumption on Saturday mornings. After the races, he ate at Hasenour's Restaurant. "Rooney," columnist Vincent Flaherty wrote, "always knows the little out-of-the-way sports hangouts where one is likely to run into the kind of sports people he likes best." In Louisville, that was Marty Yurrell's tavern. The ex–steeplechase rider pulled the shades down and locked the door while Rooney and Damon Runyon, another regular, talked through the night. "Rooney doesn't care much about nightclubs and shows," Flaherty observed. "He takes his entertainment with him, in the persons of [Owney] McManus and [Patsy] Scanlon, two little guys who carry a lot of energy and conversation with them . . . Mr. Rooney, however, just sits and listens and chortles a little and fondles a big cigar that is usually a foot and a half long."

Art made friends everywhere. At racetracks, he greeted parking lot attendants and ushers by their first names. A person's status meant little to him. "He'd get up so early that nobody would be outside except the doorman," his son John recalled. "He'd stand there talking to the guy for hours." John recalled a time when his father encountered several prostitutes on the boardwalk. "He knew what they were and looked over at them and said 'Good evening, how's business?' To him, it seemed a legitimate business. They were out making a living and he wasn't looking down his nose at them."

The Player

As Native Dancer, Swaps, and Nashua debuted after the war and television boosted racing's audience, attendance far surpassed any other sport. Sportswriters touted Art as a racing icon. Art, writer Pat Harmon declared in 1951, was racing's Taj Mahal—a living shrine. "Some people yearn to get close enough to touch his coat-sleeve, just for luck." Even his losses became legendary. Art had once placed a bet in the men's room, standing at a urinal next to a bookmaker named Frank, Harmon wrote. Art asked about a horse in the next race and Frank offered 10-to-1 odds. Art said, "I'll take $50,000," to which the bookmaker replied, "A bet." Art's horse lost, denying him a half-million-dollar payoff. Another time, Harmon wrote, some bookmakers approached Art at the track and said, "Settle an argument for us. Did you or did you not once bet $100,000 on a jumper?" He had. According to Harmon, the 8-to-5 favorite finished second.

A new generation of turf writers rediscovered Art. Stories about his casual comportment missed the seriousness of his approach. For Art, betting on horses was a profession requiring constant attention. "Those who think they can be a success as a horse player and make a living off of betting without knowing every angle of the racket are sheer fools," he argued. "Horse playing is the toughest of professions."

Tight-lipped, Art never divulged his picks. During contract talks, quarterback Bobby Layne once said, "Don't give me a raise. Just give me a horse." Art growled, "When I have a horse, I don't even tell my wife." He camouflaged wagers to prevent his odds from dropping. Because he was recognized at pari-mutuel windows, he split the money to be wagered among several people, often the twins and their friend Gerry Lawrence, the mayor's son. The young men refrained from betting until the last minute so that other bettors would not notice that big money had been placed on a horse until it was too late for them to react. "John," Art instructed, "you hit the hundred-dollar window at the south end of the first floor. Pat, you hit the hundred-dollar window at the far end of the second floor. And Gerry, you go to the window on the first floor and tell him to hit it until the bell. Just keep betting until the bell rings."

One day Art went to the $50 window. When the clerk looked up, he called down the line, "Rooney's betting on his horse." The other clerks stopped handling customers and started betting for themselves. Art had to interrupt the man to get his own bet down. Eventually, Art's sons lost their anonymity, too, and had the same problem. "I went with instructions that I was only supposed to bet at the last minute," Dan said. "When I went to the window with just a few seconds left and put the money down, the guy yelled: 'He's betting on his horse.' He didn't even say 'Rooney.'" Ignoring Dan and their other customers, the clerks began betting for themselves.

Art devised another gambit to throw bettors off his trail if he was hot. "If there were a couple of races in a row that he didn't much care for," John explained, "he bet a couple of hundred dollars on a horse he was confident would lose." Figuring that Art had cooled off, other players lost interest in his wagering and he resumed betting as he wished.

Bookmakers

Although the states had outlawed bookmaking, it thrived and, like bootlegging during Prohibition, was widely tolerated. Art and Kass were a steady foursome at Triple Crown races with David and Alyce Lawrence, but the mayor had to keep some pretence of upholding gambling law. Art was once seated between them in the backseat when the mayor began telling Art about the arrest of a local bookmaker. Alyce elbowed Art and whispered, "Get him off that subject. I bet with that guy."

While searching for subversives, real or imagined, in the 1950s, the

FBI gave bookmaking a pass. FBI director J. Edgar Hoover was an avid horseplayer who frequented Pimlico. Highly secretive about how much he bet or with whom, Hoover and his companion, Clyde Tolson, always took the same table in the Pimlico clubhouse, facing the door with their backs against the wall. Hoover talked horses with Art at Pimlico and took him and Ed Kiely to dinner afterward. Art's friend Dan Hamill was on a first-name basis with the powerful FBI chieftain, but Art, skeptical about the anticommunist witch-hunts of the 1950s, was less enamored. At dinner, "they talked about horses," Kiely recalled. "They didn't talk politics."

Eventually, the federal government passed the Interstate Wire Act of 1961 to criminalize the use of the telephone or telegraph for sports wagers between states. While the law targeted bookmakers, not bettors, Art backed off betting with bookmakers.

He grudgingly adjusted, protesting, "You put a big bet on a horse at the mutuels and you knock your own price down." But he took out the required government gambling stamp and scrupulously reported his earnings to the IRS.

Unlike bookmakers, the pari-mutuels required bettors to be present at the racecourse, so Art was often on the prowl for proxies. When John Rooney married on a Saturday in 1970, Art called the room where he and JoAnn were staying in New York City about 7:30 a.m. on Monday. John could hear his mother shouting, "You're talking to Johnnie, you stupid ass! He's on his honeymoon." Art answered, "It's not going to hurt him to go out to Aqueduct and make a bet for me." The newlyweds obediently hopped on the subway and headed to the track.

Art missed the old days. "Racing's not the same," he said in 1963. "All the romance is gone. They took away the characters when they brought in the pari-mutuel machines. Ah, the bookies, they were wonderful people."

Art had another reason for limiting his betting by the late 1950s. He had moved into a new part of racing: owning tracks. While playing the horses was more profitable for Art than breeding or owning them, owning tracks proved the most lucrative.

Unsteady Stables

By the 1950s, Art's stable was slipping. Air Patrol, Westminster, and Little Harp were old; Best Reward and Lady Gunner, clipped from behind in races, broke their legs and were put down. Art had not replenished his stable. Thoroughbreds were costly, and he knew the perils that befell anybody who approached the business as a dilettante. He purchased a yearling or two a year and occasionally an older horse but let Shamrock decline.

Art held on to the farm as his pastoral retreat. But his difficulties with Shamrock were reminiscent of his problems with the Steelers. He went through farm managers as frequently as he went through coaches. While trainer Jimmy McGee got Art's horses into the winner's circle, he was less proficient at managing a farm. McGee hired men from nearby tracks to work there, but men accustomed to the racetrack were not suited for a farm. The Rooney boys found liquor bottles when they played in the hayloft. The McGees often took care of the boys while Art was at the track. Art, in return, looked out for the McGee boys. Father Silas helped Donnie McGee, who later trained horses for Art, get into St. Bonaventure.

After a couple of seasons at Shamrock, McGee returned to training full time. Pat McGuire, the Irish horseman who succeeded McGee, did well but did not stay for long. Like McGee, McGuire was a trainer, not a farm manager. Elmer Duncan might have been effective, but he was shot dead by a jealous husband. Johnny Bill Linton took over next. Unkempt, his clothes stained with tobacco, Johnny Bill rarely shaved and paid more attention to his dogs than the farm. "Johnny Bill," Tim exclaimed, "can't keep his own face clean. How is he going to take care of the farm?" Kass took to calling the farm Green Acres, after the television comedy about a run-down farm. When Johnny Bill quit, Art's impulse was to sell Shamrock. Tim retorted that he should go to church instead and give thanks that Johnny Bill was gone. Tim's logic prevailed. Arnold Shaw, who came to Shamrock in 1971, put the farm on a business footing, before running out on his wife five years later. Tim assumed a larger role at that point and hired Jim Steele. Like the appointment of

Chuck Noll as the Steelers' coach in 1969, Steele brought both stability and success to the farm.

Boxing's Last Hurrah

Art still promoted fights. But while racing had surged after the war, boxing had collapsed. Boxing's problem was that it was ideally suited for television. When Gillette began broadcasting the Friday night fights from Madison Square Garden and extended its "Cavalcade of Sport" to other nights of the week, fight clubs around the country went down for the count. Art watched television kill what he liked best about the sport—the gyms where boys learned to box and the clubs where they displayed their courage. Television's effect on boxing prepared him for its impact on football.

Jack McGinley took over the fight club. "Affable Jack McGinley couldn't have taken over as matchmaker for the Rooney-McGinley Boxing Club at a worse time," sportswriter Carl Hughes worried in January 1947. "The cauliflower crop is the worst in years." McGinley fought a rear-guard action, keeping boxing alive and relatively profitable until 1953.

Because of Rooney-McGinley, Pittsburgh was on a par with Chicago and Philadelphia, lagging only New York as a fight town. Boxing, long considered the red-light district of American sport, often exploited its athletes, but Rooney-McGinley's reputation was solid. Fighters here, Havey Boyle testified, usually got better terms than elsewhere and were treated on the up and up.

Fighters and boxing's eccentric characters were like bookies to Art— a dying breed. While boxing paid the rent at their Fort Pitt Hotel offices, Art and Barney drew only minimal salaries. "They ran it more like a hobby than a business," Jack McGinley attested. Except for a few nice paydays, Rooney-McGinley was a pastime now.

Art used his connections to help Jack make matches but let him handle the logistics. McGinley liked boxers, too, but kept his focus on the finances. "We never lost any money," he said. "I could tell within a thousand dollars what we were going to draw." That margin worked for Art, who was satisfied to break even and occasionally make a few bucks.

Pittsburgh still had good local fighters but none ready for a title shot. Billy Conn considered a comeback to redeem himself for his sorry showing against Joe Louis in 1946, but Art discouraged him. Nor was Fritzie Zivic still a viable headliner.

Their top draws were out-of-towners like Sugar Ray Robinson. Sugar Ray traveled with an entourage that included a barber and a golf pro. "When he came down the aisle to the ring, he had a big white robe over his head," Jack McGinley recalled. "He'd jump into the ring, and he didn't have to throw a punch. You just knew he could fight." Few disagreed. Many consider Robinson the best fighter, pound for pound, ever.

With Rooney-McGinley's help, Robinson pushed against Pittsburgh's de facto segregation. Boxing had broken the color line before most sports, but racial boundaries persisted outside the ring. White fighters trained at the Pittsburgh Lyceum, African Americans at the Centre Avenue YMCA on the Hill, where they stayed at Bailey's Hotel and dined at black restaurants, unable or unwilling to penetrate the white downtown. Robinson crossed that line by staying at the Fort Pitt Hotel after Rooney-McGinley made the arrangements. Nobody would say no to Art and the McGinleys.

Robinson fought three times for Rooney-McGinley in 1946. Each time, the crowd was bigger and more impressed. In his third Pittsburgh fight, in October, Robinson beat Ossie Harris at Forbes Field before 15,000 fans. Two months later, he won the welterweight title. In 1947, Rooney-McGinley promoted cards at Duquesne Gardens, Hickey Park in Millvale, and the Heidelberg Raceway. "We didn't have sensational fights," McGinley remembered, "we had good ones. You just couldn't go into Forbes Field anymore with what we had."

Charles-Walcott

In 1951, Rooney-McGinley promoted its biggest fight—the heavyweight championship. After Joe Louis retired, Ezzard Charles beat Jersey Joe Walcott to win the vacated title. When Louis came out of retirement, Charles beat him, too. Charles had fought for Rooney-McGinley since he was in high school and made his reputation in a dozen fights they staged. When Rooney-McGinley matchmaker Jake Mintz began comanaging

Charles, he said that if Charles ever won the title, he would fight for Art in Pittsburgh. Mintz kept his word.

To promote the fight, Rooney-McGinley joined with Jim Norris, whose International Boxing Club had become the most powerful entity in boxing. They signed Joe Walcott to fight Charles. Although Charles had beaten Walcott twice, the fights had been close. A third bout promised to attract a good gate.

The fight was set for Forbes Field on July 18, 1951. Charles trained in Ligonier near Art's cottage, Walcott at McKeesport's Rainbow Gardens. Charles had a Pittsburgh following, but the underdog stole their hearts. "Pappy" Walcott was at least thirty-seven years old and had fought professionally for twenty-one years. His dogged, unprecedented fifth attempt to win the heavyweight throne touched people. He had lost twice to Charles and twice to Joe Louis. Walcott, a Sunday school teacher, befriended ten-year-old Jimmy Slater from White Oak, who tended his water bucket during workouts and ran alongside him when he did his roadwork. He went to Jimmy's ball games and had dinner with his family.

Few writers gave Walcott a chance, but the world championship electrified Pittsburgh. Rooney-McGinley offices stayed open till midnight the night before the fight, and the next day's weigh-in was mobbed. While city detective Fritz Campbell set up the ring on the infield, Art walked through the stands pasting numbers on seats. About 3,500 seats were on the field, with ringside seats costing $25.

The forecasted rain held off, and vaudeville acts and preliminaries warmed up the crowd of 29,000. Former champions Billy Conn, Fritzie Zivic, Teddy Yarosz, Primo Carnera, Joe Louis, and one future champ, Rocky Marciano, were ringside. Pabst sponsored the radio broadcast, and television reached a potential audience of sixty million, the largest ever for a fight. It was blacked out locally, and Art pocketed $100,000 for television rights without sacrificing the record gate.

Right before the fight was to begin at 10:00 p.m., Charles's manager, Jake Mintz, objected to a judge because he lived near Walcott's hometown of Camden. Insisting that all three judges should be Pittsburghers, the excitable Mintz tried to pull Charles from the ring. Boxing commissioner John Holahan, the Steelers' business manager during the day, carried Mintz away.

The fight started slowly, with Charles holding the edge. Walcott took over in the third round and fought the fight of his life. Ahead on all judges' cards in the seventh round, Walcott feinted with a right hook and shot a devastating left to Charles's jaw. It traveled barely six inches but dropped the champ. Charles flopped around, trying to rise, but he made it only to his haunches before referee Buck McTiernan called him out. Charles was carried to the locker room, where he was hazy about what had just happened. Walcott, the oldest man to ever win the heavyweight title, almost fainted. He fell to his knees and was so overcome with emotion that he couldn't speak when network reporters stuck microphones in his face.

Art felt bad for Charles but was thrilled for Walcott. The boxing world was stunned and writers stretched to find a comparable upset. Harry Keck wrote that Walcott was more of a Cinderella Man than James Braddock, a barely employed dockworker who defeated Max Baer in 1935 to become champion of the world. Other writers reached back to James Corbett's twenty-first-round knockout of John L. Sullivan in 1892.

Charles and Walcott were graceful afterward. Charles, consoled by his biggest payday ever, $100,000, said that if he had to lose, he was glad it was to Walcott. As challenger, Walcott received $50,000.

Jack McGinley was walking through the deserted stands, winding down, when he was paged to come ringside, where Jim Norris gave him a $100,000 check. After expenses and the Dapper Dan Club's $27,000 cut, Art and the McGinleys split $25,000. It was their most profitable boxing card, but among their last.

Televising the fight was profitable, but bittersweet. "The Gillette fights on television weren't bad at first," Jack McGinley explained, "but they started to go every night. If they could have stayed with one night, we could have survived." It became hard to charge for something that television gave away for free. "Television killed boxing here," McGinley concluded. People stopped attending live bouts. Between 1952 and 1959, over 250 of the nation's 300 neighborhood fight clubs closed.

Even Madison Square Garden hardly drew crowds. Rooney-McGinley closed up shop in 1953.

Barney McGinley died later that year at the age of sixty-four. He and Art had been partners since the 1930s, and when Bert Bell became NFL commissioner in 1946, Barney bought his stock in the Steelers. His wife, daughter Rita, and son Jack took over his shares, but Art had lost one of his closest friends.

Art was apprehensive about television's impact on football. As the number of sets soared from one million in 1948 to 14 million in 1951, television devastated attendance. By 1957, when 47 million American homes had sets, minor league baseball and sandlot sport were crippled. Football, Art knew, would have to confront the one-eyed monster. But first, he had to make sure that the NFL survived its war with the AAFC.

13

Same Old Steelers

1948–56

By the late 1940s, Art was slouching into middle age and his Steelers were slipping back into mediocrity. After Jock Sutherland's death, many Pittsburghers wrote Art off as a cheap and hapless loser. Some thought he looked the part. He packed 180 pounds on a 5-foot-7 and a half-inch frame topped with bushy gray hair. Thick black eyeglasses and an ever-present cigar defined his face.

The balance of Art's nature appeared to be shifting. He had always been shaped by countervailing traits. On the one hand, his competitive eyes—sharp as an eagle's—could sweep across the field of play, sense his opponents' strategy, and outmaneuver them with speed and cunning that overcame what he lacked in size and strength. Art had applied that ability to think ahead of the play as a promoter, gambler, and owner. This visionary quality pulled Rooney toward the future and made him take risks.

But there was an even stronger element of his character: an intense loyalty grounding him in the city of his youth. Once Art planted his faith in the people, habits, and institutions that had molded him, he never budged. These loyalties steadied his gambler's hand and kept the eagle from flying into the sun.

Entering middle age, Art might have felt discouraged, even depressed, after so many defeats. The loss of Sutherland—in whom he had invested his dreams—hit particularly hard. Art settled into a new equilibrium, pulling back in football and boxing and limiting his risk-taking to the track. He seemed less committed to his enterprises, less willing to stick his neck out.

In the past, when ambition had collided with loyalty, he remained loyal. He had kept his franchise in Pittsburgh when other cities beckoned and stayed a Republican after the party collapsed in Pittsburgh. People came first, and Art increasingly set priorities by his relationships. He had never hired farm managers or coaches with the same cool calculation he picked horses. As a result, the fates of Shamrock and the Steelers rode on men of wildly uneven skills. Art lived more and more in the familiar habits and friendships that had always sustained him.

He sensed his own aging; the evidence was inescapable. His brothers Silas and Jim were permanently hobbled: Silas from being dragged by a horse in China, Jim from his car wreck. They lived with a daily quotient of pain, dealing with it in different ways. Silas internalized the discipline of a Franciscan; Jim became the life of the party. Art's buddies bore the trauma of sport—scar tissue around the eyes, arthritic knees, crooked backs. Art remained in good health, but his diminishing abilities frustrated him. He had stopped drinking but did little to control his appetite, and his spreading waistline showed it.

Awards and anniversaries, a sure hallmark of middle age, came frequently. His parents celebrated their golden anniversary in 1949. Father Silas sang mass for Maggie and Daniel, who knelt to renew their vows in front of seven children and nineteen grandchildren.

Silas had returned to St. Bonaventure after the war to become athletic director. Locking horns with its powerful boosters club, he reined in the costly football program. Silas could never completely suppress his hot temper underneath a Franciscan's robe. He had a running battle with another priest, who was playing golf one day while Silas rode the lawnmower and said his rosary. Spotting his nemesis, Silas took a U-turn on the mower and ran over the priest's clubs without missing a bead. As part of his monastic duties, Silas monitored the Franciscans' cocktail hour. He disapproved of the practice, but accepted it as a ritual among the priests. "If a priest had a little too much to drink or was a little loud or finished his drink after six," a brother recounted, "Father Silas rode the elevator down with him. I can remember going down the steps and hearing a banging from the elevator. You never wanted to take an elevator ride with Father Silas."

Jim Rooney, on the other hand, would have you laughing on the way down. He and George Quinlan ran the Allegheny Sportsmen's Club. Ever the bon vivant, Jim regaled patrons for hours. Quinlan liked to tell about the time Jim called from a speakeasy because he couldn't pay his tab. After Quinlan settled up, Jim asked him for another $20, which he handed to the hatcheck girl. When Quinlan said, "What are you giving that to her for? You don't even have a hat!" Jim smiled: "Yeah, but she's a nice girl." Jim, Quinlan claimed, never went to bed without having spent or given away all his cash that day.

Art's brother Vince worked in the Steelers' ticket office; John, a Duquesne grad, drove a cab. Both had growing families. So did Margaret and Marie, who spent summers with Kass and their children in Ligonier.

Despite these blessings, Art was unsettled. He felt uncomfortable with sport's increasingly commercial orientation and his part in the pageant. Jock's death had hit Art at a sobering moment—and not only because it left him without a coach and reminded him of his own mortality. The NFL was in turmoil, facing competition from a rival league.

Several of Art's buddies were under attack. After hearing testimony from hundreds of witnesses, a grand jury investigating corruption indicted 66 Pittsburghers. It was a reprise of the Prohibition probe that had indicted 167 in 1928. Art knew many who were charged, including numbers baron Woogie Harris and bookmaker Slim Silverhart. The most awkward indictment was that of George Quinlan, Jim's partner. Although Jim was not named, the grand jury called his Allegheny Sportsman's Club a screen for gambling. The Fort Pitt Hotel, meanwhile, was cited for housing a major horse room that Art frequented. Little came of the indictments, but they troubled him.

The Michelosen Years

The Steelers fell into a prolonged slump after Jock. The problem was limited resources, compounded by one stubborn coach, another with diabetes, and a third who grew impatient with anyone not sharing his Hall-of-Fame grasp of the game. Moreover, Art sometimes sacrificed the Steelers' fortunes to focus on the league, which was facing the rival All-America Football Conference, television, and a players' revolt. Although none of this was easy to foresee, by working closely with Bert Bell and helping his sons become men, Art was laying the foundation for the league's ascent, his sons' success, and the Steelers' ultimate triumphs.

First, Art needed to fill the chasm left by Sutherland's death. Without considering anybody else, Art made John Michelosen the youngest head coach in the NFL. Jock had intended to coach for five seasons and turn the team over to Michelosen, his heir-apparent. But Jock's death after two seasons had truncated Michelosen's apprenticeship.

Although Art had few illusions regarding the magnitude of the loss, he believed that Michelosen, thirty-two, was ready. A local hero from Ambridge, where his father worked at J&L Steel, Michelosen had played for Sutherland's national championship teams at Pitt and enjoyed his mentor's unqualified support.

Art's next concern was skyrocketing salaries fueled by bidding wars with the AAFC. "I remember when I bought this franchise in 1933 for $2,500," he reminisced. "I never really thought it would develop into the big business it is today. Or the losing business it is, either."

Refusing to plunge deeper into debt, he trimmed salaries. "I don't blame the players for getting all they can while the getting's good," he said. "But there has to be a stop somewhere. Whether this leads to joining up with the All-America Conference, or the Conference breaking up, I don't know. Somebody or something simply has to give." On the field, the transition to Michelosen was rocky. Pittsburgh stumbled through a 4-8 campaign in 1948.

Battered in 1949

Art lost $40,000 in 1948. Rather than lose even more in 1949, he let players defect to the AAFC and asked others to take pay cuts. "I'm not interested in making a profit," he claimed. "All I want to do is come close to breaking even this season so I can stay in business a few more years." Ten players held out when camp began and another jumped leagues. When Art was attacked as cheap, he didn't bother defending himself. He had heard it all before.

Despite its depleted roster, the squad won four of its first five games in 1949. But Pittsburgh's fan base was shrinking to a core of deeply committed loyalists. Both Owney McManus and Art's brother-in-law Johnny Laughlin organized train coaches to the Washington game. McManus's Ham and Cabbage Special and Laughlin's Shamrock Special (named after his Northside restaurant) featured bands. The five hundred men aboard wore black beanies with "Rooney U" emblazoned on them in gold and drank freely. "When our fans return from a game," Art chuckled, "nobody knows whether we won or lost."

Michelosen emulated Sutherland and scrimmaged players during practice, which meant that they hammered each other on weekdays in addition to the banging they took on Sundays. "No other team did that," remembered staffer Jim Boston. Making matters worse, Michelosen stuck with the single wing, which was more physically demanding than the T formation. The Steelers were the league's sole single wing stalwarts, determined to win the Sutherland way. Nobody looked forward to playing Pittsburgh, but the Steelers were increasingly battered as the season progressed.

Sutherland's approach wasn't working for Michelosen. "You just can't follow Jock," Art cautioned. But Michelosen wouldn't budge. "John was stubborn," reporter Carl Hughes reflected. "As a result, the team just went downhill." "He was a great guy," Jim Boston said, "but there was only one Sutherland, and these guys didn't take too kindly to the discipline that they might have taken from Jock." "Scrimmage in the morning, scrimmage in the afternoon—five days a week," Boston remembered. This was bruising, workmanlike football. "You had to be a tough guy to play for the Pittsburgh Steelers," Boston said with understatement.

No Steeler was tougher than Ernie Stautner, who chafed at losing. "We had the most brutal training camp you ever saw," he maintained. One summer, they scrimmaged twenty-one days in a row. But Michelosen knew only one way to ready a team—the way Jock Sutherland had. When you played for Jock, players had said, Sunday's game was your day off.

Bell's Counsel

Surprisingly, Pittsburgh contended until late in the 1949 season, but Art's enduring success came inside the NFL. His political touch, molded by Ward politics, had not faded. Art's forté was resolving disputes. The NFL confronted the ongoing problem of competitive balance between richer and poorer teams, as well as three conflicts: war with the AAFC, television contracts, and unionism. Rooney and Bert Bell herded the owners—an unruly lot—through a delicate set of decisions that would ultimately lead to football's coronation atop American sport.

Bell and Art teamed up to defend the most vulnerable franchises, as they had since entering the league in 1933. Both believed the league was only as strong as its weakest teams. In January 1947, Art won approval of a measure he had long championed: the league agreed to give visitors forty percent of the gate, protecting weaker teams at home and benefiting them on the road.

Comrades in battle, Bell and Art's friendship deepened. They spoke daily, and after the winter meetings, spent a week at Bell's home in Margate, New Jersey, rehashing the season. "When my dad would sit down at the table after dinner during the season," Jane Upton Bell recalled, "the first owner he would call was Mr. Rooney, then Halas and Mara." Bell was closest to Art. "If my dad wanted to do something," Bert Bell Jr. explained, "Art was always for it. He didn't have to spend time convincing him."

By refusing to admit new franchises after the war, the NFL had provoked the creation of the AAFC. The two leagues were now locked in a savage dogfight, kicking salaries upward and attendance into free fall. The results were disastrous for both leagues. In 1948, Art had grossed more than $900,000 but lost $40,000. He expected to bring in a million dollars in 1949 and lose even more. "A screwy business," he reflected. "But it's the kind that gets in your blood."

Pittsburgh wasn't the only team hurting. Even the AAFC's Cleveland Browns, who had set pro football attendance records, were losing money. Cleveland coach Paul Brown was the team's star, so popular that the club was named for him. Brown had won fame coaching at Massillon High School and Ohio State. His allure was so strong that the Browns' arrival had scared the NFL's Cleveland Rams into leaving. Despite winning the 1945 NFL championship, the Rams fled to Los Angeles rather than compete with Brown.

Art watched the Browns tear through the AAFC, winning its first four titles. Though committed to the NFL, he recognized the potential of a Pittsburgh–Cleveland rivalry. He knew Cleveland owner Mickey McBride, who had run the bookmaking wire and a taxicab company in Cleveland, from the track, and kept lines of communication open.

Bert Bell was battening down the NFL's hatches as its losses mounted. Bell's father, John Cromwell Bell, had helped to craft the reforms that saved college football when it was thrown into turmoil by scores of deaths in the early 1900s. His son, confronted by his own challenge at midcentury, refused to let the NFL succumb. Yet his stance toward the rival league, like Art's, was evolving.

In the NFL, only Chicago and Washington were making money, strengthening Halas and Marshall's resolve to fight the AAFC. But Art, tired of losing money, sought compromise. He no longer sold out Forbes Field, season ticket sales had plummeted by half, and attendance was down a third.

At the same time, costs were exploding, as players became the objects of competitive desire. Salaries, the biggest expense, had quadrupled since 1941. "They're way out of line," Art protested. So were travel and taxes, which had jumped from $20,000 to $175,000 after the city imposed new mercantile fees. Any way Art sliced the numbers, he saw lean years ahead. Realizing how costly the league war had become, he sought resolution short of the AAFC's capitulation.

Merger

"We can't help but make peace this year," Art declared after the 1949 season. "There are only two owners in our league who can afford to take the losses." Those two, Halas and Marshall, had blocked efforts that Rooney and Bell had made the year before to end hostilities.

The two leagues' combined losses over four seasons climbed above $9 million. The Steelers, by slashing salaries, were $15,000 in the black in 1949, but the next season's outlook was poor. "They say there's no business like show business," Art joked. "I guess you could apply that to pro football."

Bell, with Art's knowledge, began meeting secretly with AAFC representatives. In December 1949, they reached a deal, admitting three AAFC franchises—the Cleveland Browns, Baltimore Colts, and San Francisco 49ers—into the NFL. The remainder of the AAFC dissolved. Bell was retained as commissioner and given a ten-year contract.

Art, who spoke with Bell three times on the day the settlement was consummated, was ecstatic. The war had ended on terms favoring the NFL, leaving it the sole pro league and on steadier footing. At the meeting ratifying the pact, Art delivered a heartfelt appeal for concord. When the merger almost fell apart over how to create two new divisions, Bell delivered an ultimatum—reach an agreement or find another commissioner. The league quickly adopted a new configuration.

It split into two six-team divisions with a thirteenth club, Baltimore, playing each team once. Art rejoiced over his good fortune. He kept traditional rivals Philadelphia, New York, and Washington, and added Cleveland. The games with Cleveland, pro football's top draw, were likely to bring defeat on the field but pack the stands. Cleveland's proximity to Pittsburgh would boost attendance for both teams and be the difference between losing or making money.

The merger, *Pittsburgh Press* sportswriter Chet Smith argued, had come just in time. "One more season of the reckless nonsense that has been going on since the Conference moved in and everybody would have gone broke." Smith commended Art's foresight in lopping off salaries before they bankrupted him. "During the salary-clipping process at least one club owner expressed his envy of the Steelers' gumption. 'I wish I had the nerve to do it, but I'm afraid of the consequences at the gate,' he told Rooney. 'You'll be getting around to it,' Art answered, 'and in the meantime we're gaining a year on you.'" Art had balanced his books, stayed in contention, and kept football in Pittsburgh.

Same Old Steelers

In November, Art's brother John died at the age of forty-three from pneumonia, leaving a wife and two daughters. With a degree in chemistry from Duquesne University, John had dreamed of becoming a pharmacist, but he was injured by poison gas in Italy and never fully recovered his health. He had spent the years since the war driving a taxi.

After a miserable start in 1950, Pittsburgh won four of its last five games to finish 6–6. Bill Dudley cost them a winning season. Now with Washington, Dudley scored twice and intercepted two passes in a game at Forbes Field. In the play of the game—maybe the season—Dudley fielded a punt over his shoulder, slid in the mud, eluded tacklers by using an official as interference, and scooted 96 yards for a touchdown. Even Art had to smile as the play unfolded.

Cleveland routed Pittsburgh twice that season. Nobody could stop the Browns, who romped to the title, but the Cleveland games pushed Art $25,000 into the black for the year.

The late-season surge sparked hope for the 1951 team, which Art predicted would be the best in Pittsburgh history. When it fell far short, fans clamored for a new coach. Art defended Michelosen. "Why, last year," he protested, "they were talking about giving Michelosen the Coach of the Year Award." His club was fiscally stabile, but its competitive decline was evident. Art urged Michelosen to adopt the T. Even Halas encouraged Art to make the change. "The single wing takes too much out of your players," he said. "I know we take a physical beating whenever we play you . . . [But] in the long run your team is the team that suffers most from the single wing."

The refrain of "same old Steelers" echoed through Forbes Field. They limped into Washington to end the season. Trailing 10–0, injuries forced Michelosen to put Jim Finks at quarterback and let him pass—at last. Finks rallied Pittsburgh to victory on a snow-covered field and that was it for Michelosen. Art could no longer ignore what was so evident. Pittsburgh had to abandon the single wing, and that meant getting rid of Michelosen, who gracefully retired. The Sutherland era was finally over.

Although the Steelers were a bust, the postmerger NFL had rebounded. The NFL would next come to terms with television—the new monster devouring sport—and learn that bargaining with its players was better than embittering them. By the end of the 1950s, the NFL would be poised to become the nation's principal sporting spectacle. The Steelers, meanwhile, revisited their past, twice.

Back to Bach

With Michelosen out, Art searched for his fourteenth coach in twenty seasons. No longer thinking ahead or even with the play, Art brought back Joe Bach. He had regretted letting Bach go in 1936; it didn't take long to regret bringing him back in 1952. Art didn't know Bach had diabetes until after he hired him. "He was just as good a coach as ever," Art later said, "but his stamina wasn't as great." Stamina mattered mightily in a league where coaches were becoming workaholics.

The Steelers had a new complexion, too. They finally integrated, drafting Alcorn A&M's Jack Spinks and Lincoln University's Willie Robinson. They were behind the curve. Jimmy Joe Robinson had broken the color barrier at Pitt in 1945 and Cleveland had integrated the AAFC in 1946, breaking the color line that had marred pro football since 1934. Kenny Washington reintegrated the NFL the same year, but black players were still scarce.

The coaches, however, were skeptical about Spinks and wanted to cut him. One complained that Spinks, from Toomsuba, Mississippi, had never traveled: "He doesn't know anything. He doesn't even have a coat to wear when we go on the road." Jim Rooney retorted, "This guy is as good as the other guys that you're keeping. He can have my coat." Taking off his jacket, Jim found Spinks and gave it to him. The rookie had no idea what motivated the gift; he was just happy to make the squad.

Robinson, who had grown up on the Northside and played with Dan Rooney, was a long shot. Art had to insist that the coaches bring him to camp. They grudgingly conceded, but Art had to intervene again.

"We're wasting our time with him," protested Walt Kiesling, who was back as an assistant coach. "All I'm asking is for you to put him in on the kickoff and we'll see what he can do," Art responded. He called Giants coach Steve Owens before the next exhibition. "These coaches won't give the kid a chance and I want to see what he can do. I got him on the kickoff team. Would you see that your guy kicks the ball to him?" Owens, glad to oblige, asked, "Do you want him to go all the way?" Art chuckled and said that wasn't what he had in mind. He just wanted Robinson to get a chance.

He did. The Giants kicker drove the ball deep into the end zone where Robinson caught it. A teammate shouted at him to down the ball, but Robinson, figuring this was his only chance, ignored him. He was 2 yards out of the end zone when he realized his teammate was right and retreated back across the goal line. But it was too late. Once he had left the end zone, he could not return, and the Giants tackled him for a safety. "I told you he couldn't play," Kiesling crowed. Robinson was cut the next day.

Once the Steelers brought black players aboard, Art tried to smooth the bumpy road to integration. In 1956, when Pittsburgh played an exhibition in Jacksonville, the backlash against the civil rights was felt as soon as the team landed. Jacksonville officials sent a caravan of cars to the airport to parade the team through town, but motorcycle cops harassed black players and excluded them from the parade. Later, they were denied rooms at the team's hotel. "That day," Lowell Perry recalled, "we were practicing at the Gator Bowl and Art Rooney, who had come on a later plane, told all of the black players, 'I promise you, this will never happen to one of my teams again.'" The following year, realizing that his players would be segregated during a visit to Atlanta, Art cancelled the game.

Kidnap?

The 1952 season opened against a sinister backdrop. On August 13, Art received a poorly spelled letter saying that if he valued the lives of his thirteen-year-old twins, he should gather $10,000 in small bills and place a note in the *Pittsburgh Press* classifieds indicating his compliance. "Do as we say if you love them or we will kill them."

Art went to the FBI, who advised him to follow the instructions. The Bureau watched his office, but would not safeguard the boys. Figuring the best place for his sons would be with the team, Art sent them to training camp, where they went on a road trip under their brother Dan's supervision. "I was the only one in the family who knew besides mom and dad," Dan recalled. "They thought sending them to training camp was like hiding them out, but it became the world's worst road trip." From Hershey, the team went to St. Bonaventure, then Buffalo,

Chicago, and Des Moines. In Des Moines, the team could not find enough hotel rooms for everybody and the boys roamed the streets that night. "It was brutal," Dan said, but nobody harmed his brothers, who were oblivious to the danger.

Pittsburgh's FBI bureau exchanged a flurry of urgent teletypes with Director J. Edgar Hoover, who knew Art from the track. Pirate slugger Ralph Kiner also received a letter warning "You'll make a good target in left field," with instructions to leave $6,200 in a taxi outside Ambridge High School. So did food magnate H. J. Heinz II: the target was his young son, future senator John Heinz III.

A month later, a more ominous letter arrived. "Rooney," it read, "Kiss the [twins] goodby because now they will die. Somewhere someplace we will get them. We warned you to pay, remember you are responsible for their death. Calling the FBI will do no good. They are doomed."

While Art waited and worried, H. J. Heinz II got a letter telling him to leave $20,000 in a package under a bench in West Park on the Northside. FBI agents staked out the park and made the drop, but nobody picked it up. Five more letters led to similar stakeouts with similar results. Finally, on the evening of December 18, an agent posing as Heinz left the package under a bench. When two girls picked it up, the FBI quickly grabbed them. One was fourteen, the other fifteen. They both confessed to the Heinz threat, and the fifteen-year-old took responsibility for the Rooney letters. No other arrests were made; because they were juveniles, they received probation.

The 1952 Season

Pittsburgh lost its first four games in 1952. "I've had some clubs with bad luck before," Art lamented, "but none this bad." Bach liberated Pittsburgh from the single wing and incessant scrimmaging, but opening up the offense could not compensate for a porous defense. By winning three of the last four games, Pittsburgh finished 5-7.

Dan Rooney, who was around the club as much as his father, could see that Bach's strength was waning. "He just wasn't with it." Pittsburgh finished the season on the West Coast, where Bach was too depleted to put in a defensive game plan. "Finally," Dan explained, "the players went out into the parking lot and Kies put in the defense." Nevertheless, Art brought Bach back in 1953. Pittsburgh played erratically and finished 6-6. His diabetes worsening, Bach did not return in 1954.

Kiesling Redux

To contend, Art needed a coach like Sutherland who could build the organization from the bottom up. But instead, he again tapped his pal, Walt Kiesling.

Few men had been around football longer than Kiesling, who had debuted as a player with the Duluth Eskimos in 1926 and would win election to the Hall of Fame in 1966. He was also an inexpensive choice. "Kiesling understood my father's financial limitations," Dan Rooney explained. But his third time as coach was no charm.

Kiesling knew football better than he knew people. Stinting in praise, he had trouble teaching players who lacked his finely tuned football instincts. A strong-minded man, Kiesling evaluated players by his own metrics. If a man didn't measure up, Kiesling shut him out. And when the 280-pound Kiesling stood his ground, he was unmovable. Although Kiesling and Art did not see eye to eye on players, Art invariably deferred to him.

Kiesling's Steelers won four of their first five games, including their first win over Cleveland, whom they crushed 55–27 at Forbes Field. They lost only to Philadelphia, their biggest rival, after two questionable penalties allowed the Eagles to kick a game-winning field goal. Sportswriter Pat Livingston called it "an open and blatant jobbing," and Ed Kiely became so agitated that he was kicked out of Bert Bell's box. It had been a typical, bone-crushing Eagles–Steelers contest. A vicious forearm to Jim Finks' face knocked him out of the game.

When the teams met again two weeks later, a record 45,000 fans jammed Forbes Field. Finks fastened a catcher's mask onto his helmet to shield his broken jaw. Ahead 3–0, Pittsburgh had the ball at midfield and needed a yard for a first down. With everybody expecting a run, Finks faked a handoff and passed to Elbie Nickel who easily scored. Fans began dreaming of a title.

But Pittsburgh—and Philadelphia—came out of the game banged

up, and the season spiraled downward. The physical style for which the Steelers became famous was one that they could not sustain. Adoption of unlimited substitution in 1950 meant that most teams played two platoons, with players specializing on offense or defense. To compete, teams needed deeper—and more expensive—rosters.

When the Steelers lost players, they could not replace them. "I think we had thirty-two guys when the season began," safety Jack Butler said. "We might end up with twenty-four." Pittsburgh lost six of its last seven games. "I felt sure we would win that year," Art later admitted. "That might have been the best team we ever had." The following season, Pittsburgh reprised the ups and downs of 1954, winning four of its first five games, losing the last seven.

Daniel Rooney succumbed to cancer in February 1956. An engaging storyteller at the center of the Ward, the former steelworker and saloon-keeper had lost his platform with Prohibition. A near fatal fall, pneumonia, and finally cancer robbed Daniel of vitality. In his later years, he walked with a cane, told fewer stories, and spent hours staring out the window of his Perrysville Avenue home. Born in the iron-making town of Ebbw Vale, Wales, Daniel died in the steelmaking metropolis of Pittsburgh at the age of eighty-three.

Hi Diddle-Diddle

Kiesling's coaching was so predictable that everybody knew his first play would be to run Fran Rogel up the middle. Mocking Kiesling, sports-writer Bob Drum coined "Hi diddle-diddle, Rogel up the middle." Although Kiesling's stubbornness troubled Art, he didn't interfere. But before one game in 1956, he told Kiesling that he wanted him to call a pass on the first play. Kiesling objected, but Art was adamant. Standing next to Drum in the press box, Art hinted that Rogel would not carry on the first play. With fans yelling "Hi diddle-diddle," Drum said he would bet dinner that Rogel did. When the Steelers got the ball, quarterback Jack Scarbath faked a hand-off to Rogel, stepped back, and threw to Goose McClairen who ran untouched into the end zone. Drum was stunned. "You're buying dinner, Bob," Art hooted. But Pittsburgh had been offside, nullifying the play. Drum turned to Art and said, "I knew

Kies would come through." On the next play, Rogel ran up the middle. Afterward, Art confronted Kiesling: "I thought I told you what I wanted." Kiesling barked, "Nobody's going to tell me how to run my football team."

Nobody needed to tell Kiesling to play rookie Lowell Perry. Perry, who had captained the University of Michigan team, electrified fans with two 90-yard kickoff returns and a long touchdown catch. Although Jack Spinks had lasted only a season in Pittsburgh, Perry was now one of several black Steelers. Against New York, Perry was sandwiched between defenders on an end-around. When he fell to the turf, the Giants' mammoth Roosevelt Grier crashed down on him. His pelvis fractured and his hip dislocated, Perry was hospitalized for months. Art was his first visitor. "I remember that day like it was yesterday," Perry recalled later. "Mr. Rooney was, and will always be, one of the most fair and honest people I have ever known. He told me, 'Lowell, as long as I own the Pittsburgh Steelers, you have a job in my organization.'" Art kept Perry on payroll, making him the NFL's first African American coach in decades, and facilitated his admission to law school.

Kiesling's health was declining, and Art asked Bill Dudley whether he should fire him. Dudley responded, "Boss man, I'm not after anybody's job, but Kies is not going to give you a winner." Art knew that, but loyalty outweighed winning. Even when Kiesling was hospitalized, Art said, "Walt will be my head coach as long as he wants to be, and even if he doesn't want to be." Pittsburgh stumbled through another 5-7 season, and though Kiesling's health was still an issue, he was back in August 1957.

Drifting

Though the Steelers rarely humiliated themselves, they faded against better clubs. "I don't think they were really geared to be a winner," Jim Finks reflected. "They just closed down shop and sent everybody home in the off-season."

Yet Finks—and most players—adored Art. Halas might have won more games, but some players considered him cold-hearted and mean-spirited. Nobody thought that of Art. "The happiest seven years of my life were the years I spent there," Finks attested. But he saw that football was Art's hobby, not his business.

Art would have agreed; he had grown up when each sport had its season. Football, however, had become a year-round operation, and most owners managed their teams closely or appointed someone who did. But Art never focused on only one endeavor. His time was scattered among horse racing, politics, St. Peter's, friends, and family, and the Steelers suffered. Nor was Art willing to break the bank to win. Art did not mind losing a few thousand dollars a season—profit was not his god—as long as he kept the team going in Pittsburgh. But his reserves were limited.

"The Steelers," Finks reasoned, "were just sort of drifting along, having a nice time, while the winners in the league were really buckling down." Finks considered Kiesling too conservative in his play selection and too abusive on the sidelines. He routinely cursed Kiesling in the huddle. During practice in Portland in 1955 before an exhibition, Finks was tormenting the defense and rubbing it in. Kiesling exploded, "Get the hell out of here and don't come back."

Finks wanted to quit. "Kies was a bullheaded Dutchman, and I was a bullheaded Irishman," he said. But Fran Fogarty would not advance his fare back to Pittsburgh. Instead, Fogarty called Art at Shamrock Farm. Art insisted that Kiesling patch things up, but Finks retired after the season. If he had left in August, the Steelers could have filled his spot by keeping rookie John Unitas.

Nothing symbolized Pittsburgh's failure to pursue excellence as much as player development. Pittsburgh neither employed full-time scouts nor systematically evaluated players. Undertaker Ray Byrne, who directed scouting, did little more than subscribe to football magazines and stop by the train station for out-of-town papers.

As a result, the team routinely let talented athletes slip away, bypassing them in the draft or prematurely cutting them. In 1953, Pittsburgh was poised to select Joe Schmidt, Pitt's relentless All-American linebacker. Assistant coach Kiesling, sitting with Byrne at the draft while Joe Bach was hospitalized, was wary of Schmidt because the Pittsburgh native had injured his knee and suffered a concussion. Still, Kiesling was ready to take him after Detroit, which chose before Pittsburgh, picked another player. Then Byrne did something that cost him his job and the Steelers a great player. Detroit had inadvertently selected a player who was still a junior and thus ineligible for the draft. Rather than let it slide, Byrne objected to Detroit's choice. Allowed to choose again, Detroit picked Schmidt, who became a Hall-of-Famer. Byrne soon returned to his Northside mortuary.

The pick that haunted Art the most came in 1955. He had first encountered Johnny Unitas in 1949, when Dan's North Catholic team played St. Justin High School on Mount Washington. Dan was runner-up to Unitas, the son of Lithuanian immigrants, as the Catholic all-city quarterback that season. But Unitas attracted little interest from colleges. Notre Dame thought that the 145-pound Unitas was too small, and while Pitt offered a scholarship, he failed the entrance exam. Unitas attended Louisville, and Pittsburgh, which loaded up on local players, chose him late in the 1955 draft.

Unitas was a long shot to make the team. Finks was setting records and Ted Marchibroda, the top pick in 1953, and Vic Eaton were capable backups. Eaton could punt and play defensive back, which gave him an edge over Unitas. Besides, Kiesling thought that Unitas wasn't smart enough to play quarterback. The Steelers had adopted football guru Clark Shaughnessy's complex offense in which the quarterback called formations and blocking assignments. Its terminology required study and repetition. But Unitas mostly sat during practice. When he got on the field, Kiesling found flaws in his play. Unitas needed coaching and practice time; instead, he puzzled out the offense on his own while the veterans ignored him. "Most of the time they acted like I wasn't there," Unitas said.

The only ones who believed in Unitas were Art's sons. Unitas threw to Tim and the twins. "He would tell them to run as far and as fast as they could," Art Jr. said, "and he'd hit them on the head with the ball. His accuracy was incredible. I'd watch him throw for hours and it made me sick to think Kies wasn't giving him a look." Tim wrote his father a fifteen-page letter touting Unitas. Art replied from the track that Tim should leave coaching to the coaches. But he talked to Kiesling. "My boys tell me the best passer in camp is Unitas. Are you giving him a good look?" Kiesling responded, "Unitas is too dumb. He can't remember the plays." Kiesling cut Unitas without playing him in a game. "Kies had his funny little foibles," Art later acknowledged, "and you weren't about to change him if he felt some way about somebody."

That fall, Art, Kiesling, and sons Dan and John were driving along West Liberty Avenue when John spotted Unitas in another car. Art told Dan, who was driving, to pull alongside. Art rolled down his window and said "John, I hope you become the best quarterback there ever was," while Kiesling squirmed in the back seat. Unitas worked construction and played for the semipro Bloomfield Rams that fall. Then the Baltimore Colts received a postcard plugging Unitas. He would lead Baltimore to NFL titles in 1958 and 1959 while Finks, Marchibroda, and Eaton soon retired. Joe Tucker later wrote that Art, believing Unitas deserved a better shot than Pittsburgh had given him, had sent the postcard.

Art had better luck with the ponies. After a game in Milwaukee in August 1955, Art, Tucker, and Pat Livingston drove to Chicago to watch Swaps duel Nashua. Art had seen the magnificent Arabian stallions in the Kentucky Derby. Swaps had won, but fans clamored for a rematch. Livingston was accustomed to seeing Art get hot, but he was in awe that day. Nashua won the $100,000 winner-take-all rematch while Art ran the table, picking every winner. Art broke his habit of leaving before the last race to beat the crowd. "I got to bet Little Harp," he insisted. Little Harp, one of his favorites, won, paying $31.

But Art kept losing on draft day. Since 1947, the first pick each year had gone to a team selected by lottery. Once a team got the bonus, it was excluded from subsequent draws. In November 1955, only three teams were eligible for the selection. Bert Bell put paper slips with the three teams' names in a hat and designated Dan to pick the winner. Dan could see the one that had Pittsburgh written on it; he thought that Bell had planned it that way. But Dan hesitated, knowing that Kiesling would use the bonus to select Colorado A&M safety Gary Glick. He pulled Pittsburgh's name out anyway.

Dan implored his father to use the pick for another player, but Art countered, "You've got to let the coaches make the pick." Kiesling, who liked to load up on defense, bypassed future Hall-of-Fame running back Lenny Moore for Glick, although no Steeler scouts had seen him play. Sportswriter Bob Drum confronted the coaches: "Harry Stick! Where the fuck did you get this guy?" After watching film of Glick, the coaches went to see Art. "Nobody says a thing," Dan recounted. "My father finally said, 'He didn't look very good, right?'" They had squandered their bonus pick.

In 1957, the Steelers passed on running back Jim Brown and picked quarterback Len Dawson, who languished on their bench and found stardom only after leaving Pittsburgh. The Steelers did hang on to some standouts, but they could not replace key players sidelined by injury. Despite their shortcomings, no opponents considered the Steelers a pushover. They might beat them, but they were bruised and battered for the effort.

Dan Rooney

In 1952, Bert Bell suggested that the Steelers relocate to South Park, outside the city. Forbes Field, unable to accommodate large crowds, had never been a good venue. But Art would not consider leaving the city, even for the suburbs. He vehemently dismissed Bell's suggestion: "Pittsburgh is the greatest sports town in the country, and as long as I can do so I intend to keep the Steelers in operation right here. I had offers when things were bad to move the franchise to other cities but I would never think of such a thing. This is my hometown and here's where I stay."

If Art had been pulled down by loyalty to the past, the team's future was standing nearby. Dan Rooney had never displayed his father's sporting aptitude, but he possessed attributes that Art lacked—business acumen, organizational skills, and penetrating focus. Dan had been born into the game. In high school, he sat on the roof at Forbes Field during games with coaches who called plays down to the bench. Even when working construction during the summer, he reported to camp when it opened. There, he held every job from ball boy to camp manager. Best of all, Dan hung around the coaches, picking up football from the inside. He learned the game and the business.

While in college, Dan revamped the Steelers game-day program and convinced NFL teams to share artwork, advertising, and stories, boosting revenues to $10,000 for the 1952 season.

Fran Fogarty, Joe Carr, and Ed Kiely mentored Dan, who soon understood the business of football better than his father. Dan had considered studying medicine or architecture, but after graduating Duquesne in 1955, he rebuffed efforts to push him into another profession. "I knew that football was what I wanted to do." By then, Patricia Regan, who dated Dan, was working in the office. Father Campbell, who knew Pat from St. Peter's, recommended her to Art. She and Dan soon wed and began their brood of nine children.

Dan focused on football in ways that his father had not. He had studied Sutherland and saw men stumble when they refused to adjust to changes in the game or commit to it fully. He knew the Steelers needed to revamp their internal workings. The selection of Gary Glick in 1956 on the flimsiest of scouting had opened Dan's eyes to his father's shortcomings. "But I didn't draw conclusions till the 1960s," he reflected. He and his brothers, however, absorbed their father's deep sense of loyalty to players and Pittsburgh. They saw the respect, trust, and even adulation that he won in return.

Television

For years, Dan Rooney watched his father balancing the politics of self-preservation with those of the NFL's common good. Television would sorely test the sense of collective self-interest he had helped to build. During the 1950s, it devastated sport's landscape. Sandlot ball all but disappeared, baseball's minor leagues contracted violently, and major league ballclubs that allowed unlimited broadcast of home games saw their fans vanish. Television posed a dilemma: It generated income but savaged attendance. The stakes were apparent by decade's end, when most households had sets. Learning from other sports' woes, the NFL hesitated before hitching its future to television.

Bert Bell had negotiated the NFL's first television deal, a West Coast broadcast of the 1949 championship. But the rights to regular-season games, and their revenues and risks, belonged to individual clubs. The results proved instructive. While some clubs sold their rights for small change, bigger-market teams made far more. With admirable foresight, the Rams negotiated a pact with Admiral Television that provided compensation if attendance dipped below 1950 projections. When it fell by half, Admiral coughed up $307,000. The Rams' experience was a cautionary tale. In their next contract, they allowed broadcast of away games but blacked out Los Angeles for home games. They pocketed their rights fees and watched attendance snap back.

Bell urged other teams to black out home games, but the federal government brought suit against the league for restraint of trade. Few issues consumed more of Bell's time or caused him more angst. In 1953, he won a tremendous victory when a federal court allowed clubs to black out home games and block telecasts of other NFL games into their markets when they played at home. Teams could now reap broadcast fees without sacrificing attendance.

Television subsequently pumped ever more money into team coffers, and attendance almost doubled. But Art worried that television was unbalancing team revenues, allowing teams with large metropolitan or regional audiences even greater competitive advantages.

Bell, with Art at his side, had so far steered the NFL through the Scylla and Charybdis of television and the courts. "Everything that my father did, he would consult first with Art," Jane Upton Bell emphasized. The cornerstone of their approach was to minimize competitive imbalance. Since pushing for the draft in 1936, they had believed that the league was best served by buttressing its weaker franchises. As a result, the NFL shared more revenue than major league baseball. Art had lobbied hard and long for the forty percent of the gate that visiting clubs received. Visiting baseball clubs, on the other hand, received only a pittance for each ticket sold. Art and Bell now wanted to make sure that television revenues did not destroy this fragile competitive dynamic. Art proposed that the league divide television revenue 60–40 between home teams and visitors. When big-market clubs balked, Art told his fellow owners he could live with that. "I'm satisfied to take my chances in the open market." But he had laid the groundwork for approaching television revenues differently.

Pittsburgh's broadcast deals earned between $55,000 and $150,000 per year in the mid-1950s, the second lowest in the NFL. For Art, what mattered more was that Pittsburgh had not sacrificed attendance, which was rebounding. As television showcased the NFL, ratings and advertising revenues climbed, and the networks and the league crafted a win-win relationship.

Inside the NFL, however, all teams were not rising on the same ratings tide. Owners dreamed in dollar signs when CBS Sports Director Bill MacPhail addressed their February 1957 meetings. CBS was ecstatic with NFL programming, which had reached more homes than college football in 1956. Those ratings were especially gratifying for Art and other owners who remembered when the colleges had scorned the pros. Underscoring CBS's success, MacPhail offered $1 million for exclusive television rights to show all NFL games on CBS. Confident of the league's draw, CBS was willing to challenge college football on Saturday afternoons. The owners listened intently but deferred action. The money was tempting, but the question of how to divide it was a minefield. Sharing revenues equally would mean substantial boosts for some teams, but losses for others. In the meanwhile, the players were planting their own land mines.

Unionism among the Players

Although NFL attendance and revenue hit highs during the 1950s, salaries did not rise proportionately. The salary bumps players enjoyed during the NFL-AAFC war had receded after the merger. Players complained that contracts blocked free agency, lacked pensions, and did not cover injured players. A majority supported formation of a union.

Most owners were aghast. Not Art. Unionism was an article of faith for the Rooneys. Art had grown up in a pro-union household in a working-class neighborhood in a city that was a labor stronghold. His grandfather Arthur had been a union activist and his mother's family was filled with United Mine Worker partisans. During the 1930s, Pittsburgh's workers swelled the ranks of labor. They were Art's neighbors, his team's fans. "If there was ever trouble in Pittsburgh," Tim Rooney recalled, "there was no question whose side you were on."

But unionism was a hard sell to Bell and owners reluctant to surrender unilateral powers. In 1956, the NFL Players Association (NFLPA) asked the league to recognize it and bargain collectively. Striking a concilia-tory tone, the NFLPA sought a minimum salary, pay for training camp and injured players, the provision of all equipment, and meal money on the road.

Bell tried to deflect formal recognition by announcing that the league would implement several minor demands, but he rejected a minimum salary, an injury clause, and union recognition.

The owners' united front was cracking. They did their best to con-ceal these divisions, holding discussions at private sessions that went unreported in league minutes. But the *New York Times* reported that six owners favored recognition, while four objected to any accord, with Marshall and Halas the most vehemently opposed.

In February 1957, the U. S. Supreme Court intervened. In a case brought by William Radovich, a player blacklisted after jumping leagues, it ruled that football, unlike baseball, fell under antitrust law. The Court determined that Congress should resolve football's antitrust status. As a result, Bell found himself in front of Chairman Emmanuel Celler's House Antitrust Subcommittee in the summer of 1957 seeking legis-lative relief.

Bell argued that if the draft, reserve clause, powers of the Commis-sioner, or territorial rights were deemed to be unreasonable restraints of trade, pro football would lose its competitive balance and face ruin. The draft and the reserve clause, which allowed clubs to renew a play-er's contract for an additional year, had saved the league by leveling the playing field, he said. Bell did not mention that they also held salaries down because players could not shop their services.

"I think the ballplayers that we have got are the greatest kids in the world," Bell said. But they needed guidance. "I try to treat and teach them as if they were my own boys." His comments dripped with pater-nalism, and his usual savvy and charm failed to persuade the Congress-men that the owners had the players' best interests at heart.

His plea for congressional relief without union recognition fell on deaf ears. Unions were at high tide, representing more than one of three American workers. Chairman Celler chastised Bell: "It leaves a rather bitter taste in the mouths of us here when we find that the owners re-fuse to recognize the players." Celler's ultimatum was clear—if the NFL wanted to retain the draft and reserve clause, it would have to recog-nize the NFLPA.

A chastened Bell soon returned to tell the committee he was prepared to recognize the NFLPA. The difficulties in implementing Bell's declara-tion became apparent as soon as George Halas followed him before the subcommittee. When pressed as to whether he would negotiate with NFLPA representatives, the combative Bears owner hedged. An exasper-ated Celler responded that Halas was "chipping away" what Bell had just said, causing NFL counsel Clinton Hester to intervene. Bell, he ex-plained, could not formally recognize the union until ten of twelve own-ers voted to enter into a binding contract. Three owners could squash the deal. This drama would come to a head after the 1957 season with Art playing a critical role in its denouement.

Go-to Guy

Art had respect and was well connected in high places. But in Pittsburgh he was now known as a truly good guy stuck with a wretched football team. Art had a gift for reaching people where they were and forming genuine bonds. He cared little about his public persona, disdained put-ting on the dog, and showed his valor in the quiet, private comings and goings of everyday life.

Just about everyone Art met—unless Art judged him a "chump"—became his friend. A bevy of people hovered around his office. After hir-ing Sutherland, Art had opened a more dignified office for the Scotsman in the Union Trust Building on Grant Street. The fight club held on to its street-level headquarters across town at the Fort Pitt Hotel. Art pre-ferred its eclectic mix of characters. Vince Lombardi or Mayor Law-rence might show up and run into the bishop or somebody looking for a handout. Regulars, impatient with the roundabout trek through the lobby, climbed through the office windows along Penn Avenue. After the offices moved upstairs, Pie Traynor stopped coming by. When asked why, the Pirate Hall-of-Fame third baseman said he was afraid he'd for-get they were on an upper floor and step out the window.

A few men or women—bookies in over their heads and people with problems—usually waited for Art in the lobby. He invariably helped them. When encountering young people, Art asked if they had made their Easter Duty. If they said yes, he handed them a twenty. One boy named Hymie, who knew the routine, assured him that he had. When someone pointed out that Hymie was Jewish, Art laughed, "That's all right. He's a good boy."

Jack Butler's fortunes illustrate Art's web of generosity. Art had played ball with Jack's father, Pat "Happy" Butler, who had run liquor during Prohibition. When Jack graduated high school in 1947, Happy sent him to talk with Art about college. Jock Sutherland recommended VMI, but Jack nixed that when he found out that the "M" stood for "military." Art had Silas get Jack into St. Bonaventure.

Jack's roommates, ex-servicemen on football scholarships, talked so much about football that Jack, who had never played organized ball, decided to try out. When he asked for a uniform, the equipment manager told him, "Scram!" Jack sought help from Father Silas, and thus began an improbable career.

Underweight and inexperienced, Jack could not even put his uniform on properly. "I got the hell beat out of me in practice for the next two years," Butler confessed. But he loved football. "I even loved to practice."

Silas kept an eye on Jack and put him on scholarship. Jack accompanied Silas to a gambling concession at the golf course near campus each Monday. "They had a room with the one-armed bandits in it and we'd clean all the machines out. My pay was what I could grab with a handful."

After Butler graduated, Silas asked Art to bring him to camp. Art convinced John Michelosen to keep him even though the rookie had never seen the single wing before. He soon started at safety. "I never had so much fun in my life," Butler recalled. He loved riding the train, watching Art's buddies carry soft leather suitcases with clinking bottles inside. A game in New York meant a train to Grand Central Station and a night at the Governor Clinton Hotel. "In the mornings, we would get a dime from Fran Fogarty, walk out of the hotel, get on the subway, and get off at the Polo Grounds." Afterward, they got back on the subway.

Art's collection of friends was ever-expanding, but he never neglected his closest buddies. For years, Art played poker regularly at the Fort Pitt Hotel with Father Campbell, Dan Hamill, and businessmen Alan Reynolds and Charlie Delehanty. The room thickened with cigar smoke as stories were told and retold. No one ever won or dropped more than a thousand dollars.

Campbell, from Pennsylvania's anthracite coalfields, was a rugged, charismatic man who shared Art's appreciation for sport and faith. "Father Campbell was a street guy," recalled Jim Boston, "and Art's closest friend." They went to the track and sat together during games.

After the war, Campbell hired a pro to run St. Peter's bingo game. Soon, Art said, "What do we need this guy for?" They did it themselves. By then, St. Peter's was known as Rooney's parish, and its games became the diocese's biggest. Bingo and Art's patronage carried the parish even as its membership shrank and grew poorer. Jim Boston and the Rooney boys sold bingo cards and delivered prize money, while Pete Flaherty, who would become mayor in 1969, handled the money. Art usually strolled in halfway through the evening. He took over for the cashier or sat in the kitchen, talking. The kitchen was a de facto meeting hall where aldermen, union business agents, and politicians gathered. They were heirs to the men who once had gathered at Daniel Rooney's saloon. Art, who maintained the whip hand over ward politics, often settled disputes. When bingo was over, he walked home.

Although Art had achieved national celebrity, loafing at bingo was a favorite way to spend time. His lack of pretension reinforced his populist identity. "You knew he was a special guy," Jim Boston explained. "You knew that from everything he did, especially the way he handled people." People often gave Art cigars. "Some might have cost a dime, some five bucks," Boston recalled. "But even if it was a cheap cigar, he'd say 'This is one of my favorite brands,' to make you feel good." Art had that effect. "He'd make you feel warm when you met him," J. D. Fogarty recalled, "like you knew him all your life."

The Press and Other Friends

Art was not oblivious to his status with reporters or their importance to his success, but his friendships with them were genuine. "You have to understand," Carl Hughes attested, "Art loved what he called 'the newspaper guys.'" And they loved hanging out with the "Prez." Coming back from Green Bay, sportswriters sat in Art's coach drinking. The beer ran out, and Art asked the porter to get more. When the dining car didn't have any, Art said, "We got to do something about this. We can't let these guys go thirsty. Have the conductor stop at the next bar." "The next thing I know," Hughes recounted, "we stopped at a crossing and the porter in his white jacket ran across the rails into a bar that still had its neon sign on and brought back a couple of six-packs, and we were on our way."

Art no longer drank. Although alcohol had never been a problem for him, it was for his brothers Jim and Vince. Dan remembered the last time he saw his father drink. Art had downed a few beers after playing golf in Ligonier. Driving the boys back to the cottage, he swerved off the road making a turn. Art took the near miss as a signal to stop drinking, and he quit easily. His appetite for food was another matter.

The night before a game in Detroit, Art asked reporters, "Anybody hungry? Let's get some fried chicken." They got a taxi and told the driver what they wanted. The cabbie objected, "You can't get any fried chicken this time of night except in the colored district." Art said, "Take us to a good place there." When the driver protested, Art said, "Don't worry about it." Soon they were at a place that looked like a speakeasy. When they knocked on the door, a guy slid the tab open and said they did not serve white people. Art asked for his boss. After inquiring if he knew Gus Greenlee, Art said, "Call him and tell him you have Art Rooney outside waiting for some fried chicken." The man soon returned. "Mr. Rooney," he said, "everything's on the house."

Art charmed reporters, and his door was always open. "Rooney is good copy," Prescott Sullivan gushed to San Francisco readers. The out-of-town scribe was awed. "While he certainly is not to be confused with any of the Mellon or Carnegie heirs who are the 'big money' hereabouts, to many a man in the street Rooney is Pittsburgh's leading citizen." Noting that Art controlled the "Irish" vote on the Northside, Sullivan concluded that people thought Art could take care of anything. While Sullivan sat in Art's office, the telephone rang constantly and Billy Conn came in through the window. One caller needed help getting a boy into an orphanage, another sought to "square the beef" for a teenager arrested with firecrackers, and a third asked for a donation to a parish ballclub.

Sullivan quickly realized that Art was the go-to guy in Pittsburgh. "People were always calling him to get jobs, find something for their kid, get a promotion in the fire department or public works," Boston explained. Schooled in politics, Art asked how supplicants got along with their ward chairmen. "He never stepped over people," Boston affirmed. "He knew every ward chairman in the city and insisted you talk to them first." If priests had a good student for North Catholic whose family couldn't afford tuition, Art paid it. Scores of students attended Duquesne University the same way.

Art made time for rich or poor and blurred the boundaries between them. When crooner Bing Crosby became part-owner of the Pirates, Art ribbed him about mingling with the upper crust. "Why don't you come over to our joint and meet the boys?" Rooney asked as he walked Crosby over to Johnny Laughlin's Shamrock.

Art's public persona cast him as the good loser, but few roles made him angrier. *Sports Illustrated*'s Mort Sharnik raised the matter. "Art had the stub of a cigar in his mouth when I asked, 'What's it like to be seen as the epitome of a good loser?' I thought he was going to swallow his cigar. 'Good loser?' he said. "I hate it!'"

Jim Boston saw what those close to Art knew—he was a terrible loser. On Mondays after a loss, Art was uncharacteristically quiet. He read the papers and absorbed the abuse heaped on his team. "It really bothered him inside," Boston remembered. But Art did not take it out on anybody at work. Instead, he took a day or so to rally. "He was always upbeat around the team, saying, 'Don't worry, we're going to be all right this week.'"

If Art revealed his anger anywhere, it was at home. There, nobody talked football, especially at dinner, if the team had lost on Sunday. "We had a standing rule," Art said. "Nobody was allowed to mention the Steelers for two days after we lost. That's how much it bothered me." His boys took losing hard, too. But they had plenty of experience with it.

14

Buddy, Bobby, and Bert

1957–59

Walt Kiesling was more likely to lead the Steelers back to the sandlots than to a championship, but Art would not sack his pal. With the NFL prospering, Art had made money in four of the last five seasons, his best financial run ever. But winning was elusive. As Kiesling whistled camp open in Olean, New York, Art's expectations for his 1957 squad were minimal. He was spending more time conferring with Bert Bell about whether Halas and Marshall would block recognition of the union than he was running the Steelers. Then serendipity struck.

On August 12, Buddy Parker finished his drink and stood up to address Detroit fans gathered for their boosters' banquet at the Statler Hilton. After leading the Lions to back-to-back NFL titles, the tempestuous coach was adored in Detroit. As fans, players, and owners pushed their plates away and sat back to hear Parker talk football, he got to the point. "When you get a situation where you can't handle football players," he began, "it's time to get out and that's what I'm doing tonight. I'm through with football in Detroit." Calling his players zombies, Parker told the stunned audience that he could no longer reach them. Maybe somebody else could get more out of them. Parker sat down and the banquet dissolved in confusion.

Art was watching practice with his brother Silas at camp when the story broke. He denied interest in Parker, even though they had talked about the Steelers job the year before. "My man [Kiesling] is healthy, and he's happy, too," Art quipped. "At least until Saturday night when we play the Chicago Bears."

Predictably, Pittsburgh lost to Chicago, but each Steeler received $50 for the game. Although the league had not recognized the union, Art had incorporated its demand for exhibition pay into contracts. After the game, he shrugged when asked about a story out of Detroit that he would hire Parker: "It's all news to me."

But the next day's headlines announced Parker's hiring. The press took a rare shot at Art for his dissembling. "The Steelers," Al Abrams jabbed, "have borrowed a leaf from the Pirates' book on how to alienate friends and make for bad public relations." Abrams hit Art's weakest spot. "While the move was a smart one on Rooney's part, this is only the first giant step toward building a championship club." Pittsburgh, he argued, needed a strong general manager. "Rooney, a man . . . who places loyalty and friendship above common sense in business, has more or less run things haphazardly with the aid of well-meaning but incapable friends." Pittsburgh, Abrams argued, should build through the draft and stop letting talented athletes slip by. Abrams, however, was overlooking Parker's disdain of the draft.

The next day, fans lined up to buy tickets for the upcoming season. Few were ruffled by Art misleading the press or concerned about his stewardship of the Steelers. Parker was a winner, and for the first time since Sutherland's death, fans had real hope. While the new head coach traveled to upstate New York, the old one quietly returned, with some relief, to an assistant's role.

Parker sized up the team. Its defense was strong, led by All-Pros Jack Butler and Ernie Stautner, but the offense was in shambles, with Ted Marchibroda and rookie Len Dawson contending at quarterback. Parker quickly traded a player and two first round draft picks for quarterback Earl Morrall and prepared for opening day.

Parker was a players' coach. "He had no rules," Butler explained. "As long as you won, you could burn the city down." Stautner noticed a difference immediately. "I guess you could call it a winner's aura." But Parker's personnel moves unsettled the players. "Nobody was what you'd call secure with Buddy around," Stautner observed.

The Steelers began the season with promise, winning four of their first six games. They ended it, however, like the "Same Old Steelers," losing four of their last six. Candidly assessing Pittsburgh's offense as the league's worst, Cleveland's Paul Brown said that Parker should have been coach of the year for winning six games.

Parker, who had few illusions about his players, began remaking the team. The coaching staff studied film that Art's brother Vince shot during games and evaluated individual players. "We can save time when we get around to the offensive backs," Parker said coolly. "There aren't going to be many of them around next season." Chet Smith hailed "the great Parker Purge," which, he joked, almost took out Art and the doorman at the Roosevelt Hotel where the club had moved its offices.

The Players' Union

With Parker running his team, Art refocused on league matters. Union activists had escalated their campaign for a contract in November, threatening to file an antitrust suit seeking $4.2 million in damages. Bell pleaded for time, arguing that his statement to Congress that summer had constituted recognition of the union. But to complete an agreement with the NFLPA, he needed the votes of ten of the twelve owners. "We'll get that at our meeting," Bell promised. He conferred daily with Art and counted on his buddy's quiet politicking to deliver those votes.

Bell's statement before Congress recognizing the NFLPA had plunged the owners into turmoil. Some were willing to accede to specific demands, but Halas and Marshall needed only one other holdout to nix recognition.

Art, the most pro-union owner, already acted within the union's parameters. No Steeler made less than the union's minimum demand of $4,000, and injured players were paid. He argued that recognizing the union was the right thing to do. Moreover, failure to do so would provoke a Congressional backlash.

Though his influence was cloaked to the public, Art was the consummate politician inside the NFL. He persuaded the owners to compromise, to sacrifice immediate and personal interests for the long-term collective good. Patient and affable, he crafted deals across political divides. Although Halas and Mara were rivals and Marshall exasperated everyone, Art befriended them all. He was the league's emotional and political center, the one with whom every owner stayed friends.

When it came to football, Art's sense of loyalty and his visionary abilities worked in harmony. He could garner his peers' votes because he had earned them. Almost everyone in the room owed Art for past favors. Rooney had bailed Bell out when he owned the Eagles, finally bringing him on board as the Steelers' co-owner. In 1936, Art had taken a second game with Halas's Bears, allowing Mara's Giants to play a weaker team and improve their title chances. The resulting loss knocked Pittsburgh out of the playoffs. Halas had picked his pocket for Sid Luckman and Bobby Layne. Nor had Halas hesitated to call on Art for a personal favor. When Ed McCaskey, a student at Penn and a nightclub singer in Philadelphia, began courting Halas's daughter Virginia, the Bears owner asked Art to check out his prospective son-in-law.

At the same time, Art could sell the other owners his vision of a healthy, competitive NFL that fed their long-range self-interest. They knew that Art put the league first, even if it meant sacrificing the Steelers' welfare.

Art handicapped votes and assessed egos the way he read racing forms. Halas and Marshall vied with each other for authority. "Marshall thought he knew more than everybody else," Dan Rooney laughed, "and Halas thought he started the league, which he did." Art, on the other hand, could forge a coalition with the Eagles and Cardinals and pick up a few other owners. But union recognition required more than a simple majority. He needed near unanimity. It was time for Art to call in his chits.

With the antitrust suit dangling overhead, NFL owners convened on December 2, 1957. Art thought he had the votes. But when Colts owner Carroll Rosenbloom walked into the room with Marshall's arm around him, Art nodded in Marshall's direction, and whispered to Dan, "He knows who he can get." Bell told the owners that if they failed to uphold his pledge to Congress, the league would face legislative repercussions. Marshall objected, insisting that Congress had no right to interfere. "Whether they have the right to do it or not," Bell responded, "they'll do it." When Marshall and Halas voiced opposition, Art challenged them. "Wait a second," he said. "We have no problem with a union; we have no fear anyway. Let's recognize the union. We have to do it. If you don't do this, you'll wreck this business. I vote that we right now recognize the union."

His colleagues honored Art's conviction and passed the measure 10–2. They also agreed to pay $50 for exhibition games, a $5,000 minimum salary, and add an injury protection clause to contracts.

Several owners found negotiating with players with its intimations of equality galling. Ego repeatedly surfaced and, with it, an unwillingness to bargain over what owners considered their prerogatives. But Art—and later Dan—sought common ground. The Rooneys worked for win-win accords with the union, just as they would among the owners on the thorny issue of television.

The question of a league-wide television contract had been tabled while union recognition was resolved. Teams continued to negotiate their own broadcast deals while Bell boasted that the NFL had become television's hottest programming. Pete Rozelle, attending his first league meeting as the Rams' general manager, was taking it all in.

Cleaning House

While Art had herded cats at owners' meetings, Parker overhauled his team. The two men had shaken hands on a five-year, $100,000 contract, with Parker contending he needed that long to build a winner. Art set the financial parameters, Fran Fogarty maintained them, and Parker assembled the roster. A sportswriter visiting the office during the off-season expressed surprise to find it so busy. "Our coaches and everybody else works eleven months of the year," Art asserted. "There's no off-season for us. I've never known a coach who worked as hard as Parker. He lives, eats and sleeps football whether it's May or October."

Parker spoke candidly. "We just don't know how to win," he admitted. "We don't think like a winner." To Parker, a winner thought like his Detroit quarterback Bobby Layne. Parker doubted that Pittsburgh signal-callers Earl Morrall, Len Dawson, and Jack Kemp had the same determination.

Parker worked the phones, trading draft picks for veterans he thought could provide immediate help. "The year to take care of is the one you're living in," he argued. "When you get to next year, you'll take care of that." Parker made sure that the men reporting to camp in 1958 were not the "same old Steelers." Only five veterans reported to camp, but some contended Parker was trading away the team's future—in draft picks—as well as its past. Parker countered that he was accelerating Pittsburgh's success.

Parker, not done yet, traded another dozen draft picks for eight veterans during camp. To clear roster spots, he cut Jack Kemp, who had warmed the bench in Pittsburgh. Kemp later led Buffalo to consecutive AFL championships. In return for draft choices, Parker picked up veterans Tank Younger, Tom "The Bomb" Tracy, and Billy Ray Smith. Younger, who starred for Grambling, had been the NFL's first black college star, but he was nearing retirement.

A stream of college coaches eager to observe Parker attended practice, and fans thronged to scrimmages. The preseason fervor reflected football's deep roots in Western Pennsylvania, where high school football had boomed after the war. Groups in Monessen and Charleroi feted the Steelers before they left for the West Coast to open the season. While there, Parker picked up five more players.

For all his verve, Parker was drawn to odd characters and given to superstition. His old pal, "Boots" Lewis, became a constant presence. They had met at Centenary College in Louisiana, where Lewis had been the equipment manager. "That guy," Parker proclaimed, "is the luckiest crapshooter you ever did see." The players bankrolled Boots at crap games. "When Boots came back, he always had that folding money with him," Parker said. Boots, Parker's good luck charm in the pros, went on Pittsburgh's payroll. While not superstitious, Art was willing to pay Boots to be Parker's factotum and talisman.

But Boots's charm wasn't putting points on the scoreboard, and Pittsburgh lost its first two games. The second, a 45–12 pasting by the Browns, inauspiciously inaugurated the Steelers' new home field, Pitt Stadium.

Other owners, frustrated by what they made playing in Pittsburgh, had been after Art to leave Forbes Field, which sat fewer than 36,000, for Pitt Stadium, which held 59,000. The University had long resisted accommodating Rooney. But when the Dodgers and Giants moved to California, Mayor Lawrence pressured Pitt to let the Steelers play on campus in 1958, arguing that the team might not otherwise survive. Lawrence believed that sport was critical to reshaping the city's image. The *Pittsburgh Press* agreed. "Something has to be done and soon," it editorialized, "if we are to avoid the risk of losing one of the Nation's great sports spectacles." Rooney, the paper stressed, had never mentioned moving. "But we've been depending on Mr. Rooney's love of the game to keep pro football here. There isn't enough profit in it to justify the large risks in operating a pro team."

While endorsing the move to Pitt Stadium, the *Post-Gazette* argued that it was not a long-term solution. Instead, it proposed a new multi-purpose stadium on Monument Hill, near Art's home on the Northside. The idea went nowhere at the time.

Neither did the Steelers. After two games, Parker lost faith in Earl Morrall and had no patience with an untested Len Dawson. When Parker called Detroit coach George Wilson to arrange the exchange of game films of coming opponents, Wilson asked, "Would you be interested in a quarterback? Bobby Layne, for instance?" Realizing that Wilson meant it, Parker buttonholed Art and traded for Layne. Parker had his winner.

A reporter broke the news to Layne's roommate, Joe Schmidt. "You're out of your mind," Schmidt shouted. When the reporter suggested that Layne was washed up, Schmidt shrieked, "Washed up! He's the best blasted quarterback in this league. He's throwing better than he ever did."

Layne could have become a Steeler in 1948, when the team was set to draft the Texas All-American. But Art traded the pick to Halas for a player who lasted one season in Pittsburgh. Layne, subsequently traded to Detroit, led the Lions to the 1952 NFL title. With a last-second touchdown pass in the 1953 title game, he made it two in a row.

But Detroit thought he was too old, too expensive, and too beat up. Layne cost the Steelers two high draft picks and Earl Morrall, whom they had gotten the year before for Marv Matuszak and two first-round picks. "I'm not as smart as I thought I was," Art laughed after calculating what he gave to get Layne. "I'm lucky I didn't have to toss in a pint of blood." He would have given it; Layne was Art's kind of player.

Delighted to be out of Detroit and back with Parker, Layne grilled Dan Rooney about the team on the way from the airport to South Park. By the time they arrived, he was ready to take charge. Layne sensed that Pittsburgh had become comfortable with mediocrity. "The spirit on the team," he said bluntly, "was lower than last place."

Despite having little time to prepare, Layne played flawlessly as Pittsburgh beat Philadelphia that Sunday. The fans were euphoric, Parker confident. "Bobby Layne is the greatest leader I've ever been associated with," he said. "He'll set the pace for the rest of our players."

When Cleveland trampled Pittsburgh a week later, Art remained upbeat. "I've walked away from a lot of games feeling downright low," he said, "but it was a short ride home for me Sunday night. I felt that we had done our best against what is, in my opinion, the strongest team that Paul Brown has ever had." Layne was less sanguine. After another loss, Layne gathered his teammates at a tavern and hopped up on the bar. "Let's get down to business," he said. "This ball club is one-and-four, so what are we gonna do about it?" Layne, the NFL's highest-paid player, talked about winning and picked up the tab. He got his money's worth. The Steelers played the best football in the NFL for the rest of the season.

They won six of their last seven games and tied the other. Layne, perhaps the game's greatest come-from-behind quarterback, pulled off several wins on the last drive of the game. In a 31–24 win over Philadelphia, he accounted for all 31 points.

A leader off the field, too, Layne made sure that teammates stuck together. He reveled at postgame parties and Monday afternoon bowling sessions. "These are the things that make championship teams," Layne observed. "They build up team feeling, a sense of camaraderie . . . They didn't have it here in Pittsburgh, but we're getting it now."

But fans were not paying homage to this turnaround. Pitt Stadium was not the panacea Art had expected. Unlike Forbes Field, it had bench seating and no protection from rain. Fans had to climb up what students dubbed Cardiac Hill to get there. And while Forbes Field's limited seating encouraged season ticket sales, fans knew that they could get good seats at Pitt Stadium on game day. NFL attendance was booming, but not in Pittsburgh.

Governor Lawrence

In the midst of the 1958 season, Art celebrated a day he thought would never come: David Lawrence's election as governor. Lawrence often told Art that Pennsylvania was not ready for a Catholic governor, but after winning a fourth term as mayor in 1957, he succumbed to pressure to run.

For Art, friendship, class, nationality, and religion outweighed party affiliation. He went all-out for Lawrence; so did Republican county chairman Patrick McGrath Sr., who had played football at Duquesne with Art. "At that time," his son Patrick McGrath Jr. said, "the Irish all crossed the lines." They worked on both Democratic and Republican campaigns. "Irish Catholics," he argued, "transcended party."

For Art, politics was about people, not ideology. He remained loyal to Lawrence even when it was not in his best interests. Art accepted Lawrence's ten percent city amusement tax even though it placed a heavy burden on him. Dan Rooney opposed the tax because it came directly off the team's profits. "Paying that tax was ridiculous, but my father said we weren't going to fight David Lawrence."

On election night, early returns showed Lawrence trailing. Tim, who shared his father's attraction to politics, was at Lawrence headquarters. "It looked like he was going to get beat," Tim recalled. "I came home and told my father that it was looking very, very sketchy and my father had me drive him over there." Art, Lawrence often said, would stick with you even in defeat. But by the time they arrived, the election had turned. Satisfied that Lawrence had won, Art left without talking with him. He did not need to be there for the victory.

Religion had cost Lawrence votes in rural areas, but it helped him carry Pittsburgh and Philadelphia by larger than usual majorities to become Pennsylvania's first Catholic governor. As he left for Harrisburg, Lawrence said, "I will never have any doubts about where my roots are and where my affections are. I will be proud to tell the world that I am still a Pittsburgher—and always will be." When he attended a Philadelphia–Pittsburgh game, his advisers suggested he root for the Eagles one half and the Steelers the other. "Like hell," Lawrence responded. "I'm from Pittsburgh."

Several weeks after Lawrence's victory, the Steelers rallied when Jack Butler intercepted a pass. Two plays later, Layne hurled a 78-yard winning touchdown. Art savored the next win even more; he had been waiting for it since 1933. On November 30, with snow banked around the frozen turf at Pitt Stadium, Layne connected for two long scores and Pittsburgh finally beat Halas's Bears. Though it was also their fifth consecutive win, Art's elation was tempered. Attendance was terrible and the season ended before they caught the division leaders.

In December, Baltimore beat New York for the NFL championship, tying the score with seconds left to play and winning in sudden death overtime. The victory made an icon out of John Unitas, the Mt. Washington native whom Pittsburgh had cut in camp three years before. He would lead the Colts to another title in 1959. "When I saw Unitas quarterbacking the Colts in those championship games," Art said, "I'd think, 'Geez, that could be us there with that kid leading us.'" At least Art had Layne. "After our final game," Art said, "I heard from both Jim Lee Howell and Paul Brown, and they said we were the best team in the Eastern Division by the end of year. Imagine that. I had the best team in the division and wound up losing $40,000. It doesn't make sense, does it?"

No, it did not. The NFL had almost doubled attendance over the decade, while major league baseball was down sixteen percent. But the Steelers drew only 140,000 in 1958, down from their high of 243,000 in 1947. Bad weather and Pitt Stadium's lack of appeal undercut the best football the Steelers had ever played. Art figured he needed 28,000 fans per game to break even; he drew about 22,000. But he again dismissed any possibility that he would leave town. Few season ticket holders, however, wanted to return to Pitt Stadium in 1959, and Art persuaded the university to cancel his five-year lease.

Bobby

If the business of football bedeviled Art, at least he was having fun with his club. Layne was a swashbuckler with panache, the latest in a line of such men who endeared themselves to Art. Intelligent, focused, and fearless on the field, Layne refused to wear a face guard because it limited his vision, and did without pads in his pants to make it easier to run. Art was long past carousing with players, but he enjoyed Layne, who tempered his wild streak with street savvy and business acumen.

"I never saw an athlete like Layne in the last minute of a game," Art attested. And with the exception of Johnny Blood, he might never have seen another player quite like Layne off the field. "Aside from being the best poker player in west Texas," Murray Olderman wrote, "he's also a gambler on the football field, a devil-may-care long ball thrower." Teammate Doak Walker once said, "Bobby never lost a game. Some days, time just ran out on him." Layne said Art was one of the best things about coming to Pittsburgh. "I had heard about Mr. Rooney all my life and what a great guy he was. Everything said about him is true."

Layne was a sociable man who brought others in on the action. No matter what had happened on Sunday, the team gathered at a bowling alley near South Park on Mondays. They broke into teams, bowled, then headed into town to drink, often at Layne's expense.

Layne was a cheap drunk, recalled Jim Boston, his designated driver. "People thought he drank whiskey twenty-four hours a day. It wasn't that; Bobby just didn't hold his liquor good." Drunk or sober, he led the team. "Once he got started drinking, he got on the pulpit," Boston laughed. "We just listened."

Layne's favorite nightspot was Bertie Dunlop's Hurricane in the Hill District. "Bobby was a great lover of jazz," Boston remembered, "and to hear jazz, you had to go into the Hill to the Hurricane and the Crawford Grill. Bobby became folklore there. Every black man in the Hill knew him. He had no worries there." Cum Posey's nephew, Evan Baker, knew why. He recalled evenings at the Hurricane. "Bobby would be dead smoke drunk, with his arms around a black girl who was performing, even kissing her, and nobody in the joint would say a thing to him because he was Bobby Layne, and Bobby Layne worked for Art Rooney."

Art skipped the December 1958 meetings, where the NFL held the draft's first four rounds. Parker had already traded their picks. He did go to Miami Beach in January for the remainder of the draft. As one columnist wrote, it had not been a happy semester financially at "Rooney U." When Jack Sell questioned Art about a story in the Miami paper that he would move his team there, Art retorted, "That's absolutely untrue. We're doing business at the same old stand." Six years before, Sell reminded readers, Baltimore was after the Steelers, then Buffalo, Houston, Louisville, and Dallas sought the franchise. Although attendance was down despite Pittsburgh's best record since 1947, Art wasn't going anywhere but the track.

Bert

After ending the season with a seven-game unbeaten streak, Art anticipated the 1959 campaign. But it became his toughest year in football, bedeviled by death and rancor over unionism and television. In February, Tim Mara died at the age of seventy-one. He was the second to go of the band of six who had led the NFL since 1933. Charlie Bidwill had died first, in 1946. Art had named a son after Mara, who had been like an older brother to him in football and at the track. Art attended services in New York. You can miss a wedding, he often said, but never a funeral.

Art took death stoically, finding solace in his faith. Bert Bell, who was anything but stoical, became agitated at Mara's funeral and suffered a mild heart attack afterward. The incident sped up his conversion to Catholicism. "My father," Jane Upton Bell explained, "was a blueblood Protestant who did not practice anything but had a great respect for religion." Bell's wife and children were Catholic, as was his best friend, Art. "I think my father was very impressed with Mr. Rooney's devotion," Jane said. "The way Mr. Rooney conducted himself as a man, as a Catholic, had to land somewhere in his brain and make an impression." After Mara's death, Bell took instruction and converted, his booming voice broadcasting his first Confession throughout the sanctuary.

Bell also buckled down to more secular concerns. Although the league had recognized the union, it had not negotiated a contract. While conceding the league's right to conduct the draft and retain the reserve clause, the players wanted a pension plan. Without a pension, they threatened to strike or file an antitrust suit. The owners resisted, and Carroll

Rosenbloom challenged the player reps during a January negotiating session to trust Bell or get out of the room. When the players backpedaled, the owners seized the initiative. Bell declared that pro football was a sport, not a business. "There isn't one owner in this League who is in football to make a living out of it," the commissioner proclaimed. "They are fans." With that, Bell dismissed the players.

The players subsequently accepted a modest pension system financed mostly by broadcast revenues. It did little for current or retired players but established a pension for future ones. The union's willingness to compromise on immediate concerns and its hesitancy to press more vigorously for change set the tone for years to come. The owners, not the union, held the upper hand.

The More Things Change

During the 1959 preseason, the Steelers continued to travel wherever Art could find paydays. After an August exhibition against the Cardinals in Austin, Bobby Layne went out with friends. They were driving around town, Bobby at the wheel, when he lost control on rain-slickened streets and smacked into a parked car. Bobby left the scene in a taxi but was arrested later for drunk driving, driving without a license, and leaving the scene of an accident. Although his companions claimed that Layne had only had a few beers, he spent the night in jail.

Layne's lawyer argued that Bobby had not been drunk, just hoarse with laryngitis. He had hit a parked car before, and this time it only enhanced his image as a carouser. "He doesn't savor his reputation for living high off the field," columnist Murray Olderman wrote, "but he says candidly, 'If I feel like a beer or two, I'm not going to sneak around some side alley joints. I'm going to go to the best place in town and walk in the front door.'" The incident faded, and the season began with promise when Pittsburgh beat Cleveland in a nationally televised night game.

North Lincoln grew quieter that fall. Art Jr. left for the Marines, the twins were attending St. Mary's College near the farm in Maryland, and Tim was at Duquesne. While Art was at the track during the off-season, Dan, twenty-seven, began assuming more responsibility for the Steelers. "Buddy Parker hated front office stuff," Dan explained. Nor did he have patience with the league office. "He thought they were bureaucrats and we should just play the game." As a result, Dan dealt with the commissioner's office and participated in league matters. "You can do it," Art told him.

Both the Rooneys and the Bells looked forward to Steeler–Eagle games. This year's contest on October 11 at Franklin Field featured the two teams Bert Bell had owned on the field where he had quarterbacked Penn. Jane Upton Bell, the commissioner's teenaged daughter, was keeping an eye on her father as per her mother's instructions. Frances Upton Bell was worried about Bert's health. He had survived a heart attack but suffered from high blood pressure, made worse by his round-the-clock devotion to the league. With 2 minutes left to play, Jane saw a commotion in the end zone seats where her father had moved to get out of the sun. "When I hopped over the fence and raced across the field," she remembered, "Mr. Rooney was already there." Bell, sixty-five, had suffered a massive coronary. Firemen rushed over with oxygen and an ambulance hustled him to University Hospital just blocks away. Art ran after it and had to be yanked out of the way of a trolley car. But nothing could be done for Bell, who died minutes after he was admitted. Art was in shock; he had lost his best friend in football.

The NFL was shaken. Bell had brought stability, wisdom, and patience to the league since 1946, commanding it through battles with the AAFC and skirmishes with the Canadian Football League. Staving off congressional interference, Bell had won a home blackout policy from the courts that helped the NFL craft sport's most successful approach to television. With Art's help, he had persuaded the owners to recognize the players association. "No matter who we'll pick," George Marshall said, "we'll never find a commissioner as good as Bell." For once his colleagues were in total agreement. "Professional football lost its greatest missionary, evangelist, and plain hard-working cop on the beat," Chet Smith wrote in remembrance.

Arthur Daley said goodbye in his *New York Times* column. "No commissioner in any sport," he eulogized, "was better equipped than he for the handling of his appointed task because he brought to it a matchless blend of intelligence, courage, background and personality." Bell's secret, Daley said, was that he was more than a great man. He was a great guy. Daley highlighted the contrast between baseball and football. The NFL had concluded that competitive balance was essential and that it could harness television. "Unlike baseball, which hides fearfully under the rug while TV destroys it," Daley argued, "Bert boldly fought in the courts for the right to black out home games. He won and now television is pro ball's most industrious servant, not its master." After his death, it was revealed that Bell had been planning to retire and buy back the Eagles for himself and his children.

Overwhelmed, Art could hardly talk to reporters. In the St. Margaret's sanctuary where Art had stood as Bert's sponsor while he received his first communion, Art was now his pallbearer during the funeral Mass.

Art kept his thoughts private. But their friendship had been the closest among the owners, and a profound grief gripped him. The two men had met at the track at Saratoga in the 1920s and entered the league together in 1933. As friends with struggling franchises, they quickly adopted a common agenda. They had savored their time together on train rides, in league meetings, and at Bell's home in Margate each February. The loss of his friend mattered more than what Bell's death would mean for the NFL.

Time for that would come. Their friendship and mutual self-interest had defined the NFL, marking the league's structure and ethos in ways that fostered collective over individual success. Art never said he was on a mission to fulfill Bell's vision of the NFL after his death. But that's what he accomplished. Art accompanied the family to the cemetery and stayed in close touch with them afterward. Hardly a day had gone by since 1933 that Art and Bert had not spoken or seen one another. For the remainder of the season, Art watched his team play with a pain no game could take away. Any number of times he must have started to pick up the phone to call Bert. It would be a lonely off-season.

Playing Out the Season

The Steelers were 2-4 when Detroit came to town in November 1959. Layne rallied Pittsburgh to a tie with a late touchdown but most fans had already given up. Parker was taken aback by the crescendo of boos showering his sputtering team. "Man, this is a tough town," he complained. "They don't give you a chance, do they?"

A core of fans, however, stayed loyal. Before the Detroit game, they presented hometown boy Jack Butler with a station wagon stuffed with gifts and feted him afterward. A week later, 10,000 Pittsburghers, including Governor Lawrence, saw Layne bring Pittsburgh back to beat Cleveland on the road in the closing seconds. Throwing his hat in the air, Lawrence shouted, "That was the greatest play of all time!" Disgusted by his team's second loss to Pittsburgh that season, Paul Brown complained, "Take [Layne] away from the Steelers, and they're nothing." Al Abrams happily countered that Pittsburgh had outplayed Cleveland on both sides of the line of scrimmage.

When Pittsburgh beat Philadelphia 31–0, Layne contributed to all 31 points with four touchdown tosses, four extra points, and a field goal. The win, however, was costly. Jack Butler was carried off the field in agony. The paltry crowd outraged Pat Livingston. "Pittsburgh, a city which once boasted it was a good sports town, can hang its head in shame," he scolded. "The crowd was a joke, the biggest laugh in the NFL this year!" Referring to talk of a new stadium, Livingston concluded, "It would be more appropriate to build a new morgue."

Pittsburgh's only loss in the last five games came in Chicago amid bitter complaints about the officiating. "I'll sure be glad to see Halas retire," Buddy Parker snapped. "Then maybe you'll be able to beat the Bears in this town." Halas was notorious for badgering officials. "When we play Halas again," Parker added, "I'm gonna get Rooney down on the field and let some of those officials see him once in a while. Maybe they'll start to figure Art got a vote, too." It wouldn't have helped. Art never browbeat officials; Papa Bear, on the other hand, bullied them shamelessly. The loss left Pittsburgh 6-5-1 for the season.

Two years of "Buddyball"—Parker's wholesale trading of draft picks for veterans—had left the Steelers prematurely aged. In a league where most players had retired by twenty-seven, teams declined quickly if they did not replenish themselves with younger players. Although Jack Butler did not know it, he had played his last down. Infection developed in his mangled leg. Despite several operations, Butler could not play in 1960. Art suggested he take a coaching position with Buffalo in the newly formed American Football League. He could return to play if he got better and coach for the Steelers when he retired. Butler went to Buffalo but soon returned to Pittsburgh to coach.

The AFL

In 1960, the NFL faced a new rival. The absorption of the AAFC in 1950 had left only the Canadian Football League to challenge the NFL, but it had become merely a minor irritant after Bell negotiated a no-raiding agreement in 1955. The very success of the NFL, however, reprised an old dilemma. When groups in seven cities had sought admission to the league in 1957, owners voted 8-3-1 against expansion. Art was among the minority. He and Halas comprised the league's expansion committee, but as long as NFL rules mandated that new franchises receive unanimous approval, they had no business to conduct.

But the NFL could not prevent the men they had spurned from forming a league of their own. Their leader was Lamar Hunt, son of one of the richest men in the world, oilman H. L. Hunt. Unable to buy a franchise or persuade the league to expand, Lamar Hunt rounded up several deep-pocketed would-be owners and created the American Football League.

Bert Bell had told the House Judiciary Subcommittee in 1959 that he favored the new league. But privately, he was distressed by the competition and spent much of his last few months of life trying to contain it. Hoping to avoid another war, Art tried to preempt the rival league by persuading NFL owners to amend their constitution to allow expansion with the vote of ten of twelve owners.

Rooney and Halas, the NFL expansion committee, finally had something on their agenda. In Houston for a preseason game, the pair recommended admitting a pair of franchises in Texas in 1961. Not coincidentally, two AFL franchises would be based in Texas. Their recommendation was too little, too late. The AFL did not fade away; instead, it gained momentum after securing a television contract with ABC. The five-year, $8.5 million deal gave it financial stability and the money to compete for players. It also introduced a new style of revenue sharing to sport—television income would be divided equally among the teams. That got Art's attention.

At the December 1959 meeting, only two owners opposed expansion. The rest, mindful of the painful AAFC war, voted to grant franchises to Dallas and Minneapolis. But the AFL marched on. Many NFL draft picks took the new league's money, including Pittsburgh's second-round selection, North Texas State halfback Abner Haynes.

Bobby Layne would have been an invaluable commodity for the AFL, especially if he were to play in his home state of Texas. But Layne ignored the AFL's blandishments. Instead, Pat Livingston reported in December 1959, the "devil-may-care Texan with a philanthropist's disregard for money" signed a two-year, $50,000 deal that both Art and Bobby hoped could run longer. About to set NFL career records for passes completed and touchdowns thrown, Layne would remain a Steeler. "This is my last stop," Layne said. "I'm going to end my football career here in Pittsburgh." The AFL could not entice him at twice his salary, he said.

Like Rooney, Layne valued trust and loyalty. He never actually signed a contract; Art's word was enough. Layne also credited Parker with resurrecting his career. He trusted Parker to tell him when to retire, and repaid him by playing brilliantly. "Let me tell you about Parker," he said. "If all the players in the league who want to play for him were allowed to, there wouldn't be enough left over for all the other teams."

Not everyone shared Layne's enthusiasm for Parker, especially when he drank. "A lot of people thought he was drinking all the time," Dan Rooney reflected, "but that was not so. Parker only drank two times, both the worst times to drink. He would drink after games—win, lose, or draw. If he won, he was in a jovial mood. If he lost, he was in a bad mood. The other time is when he had to make a speech. He dreaded making speeches."

The Steelers had benefited when a tipsy Parker had announced his abrupt departure from Detroit in 1957. But Parker's tippling was their liability now. After one loss, he telephoned Bert Bell and roared, "They all stink. Put my whole team on waivers. I don't want any of them." Bell ignored him. So did Pittsburgh writers when Parker said he was resigning after losses. "When we lost a game," Dan Rooney recalled, "the players would try to hide because he would cut them." Dan told players to stay out of sight until Parker sobered up. He usually forgot his threats by the morning.

Most players forgave him, but not Jack Butler, one of the most affable men on the team. "I played for him for three years and I don't think he ever said a word to me," Butler recalled. Parker could coach, Butler acknowledged, but he became abusive after games. "By the time we got from the ballpark to the airplane, he'd be drunk." On one flight home, Parker started at the front of the cabin and worked his way down the aisle, berating players. He told one player he was a bum and asked the next one who ever told him he was a football player. Parker belittled All-Pro tackle Frank Varrichione: "Frank, I thought you were a good football player. I had a chance to trade you. What a mistake I made!" When he reached Billy Ray Smith, he shouted, "Billy Ray, you're a terrible football player. You can't play a lick." Billy Ray said, 'But, Coach, I didn't play today. I had my knee operated on." Undeterred, Parker got to Butler and Ray Mathews in the back of the plane: "Look at these two. They've been here a long time and never won anything." Mathews responded, "You're right, Coach, and we've been here for three years with you and we still haven't won anything."

But players never tired of Art. "He'd be down in the locker room after the game if we lost, saying we did the best we could," Butler recalled. "Mr. Rooney never raised his voice." Art had played enough football to know when men were trying hard. He was comfortable with players and got to know them and their families. "There was no fear, no intimidation with Mr. Rooney," Butler asserted. "He treated you with respect."

The NFLPA asked Butler to become the Steelers' player representative. "I went to Mr. Rooney and said, 'I don't know anything about unions.' Other people would say get the hell out of here. He said, 'Jack, do what you think is the right thing to do.' He was absolutely sympathetic to the union."

A New NFL Commissioner

When the owners convened at the Kenilworth Hotel in Miami Beach in January 1960, the room had a different feel to it. Going into a meeting without hashing over the agenda with Bert Bell or seeing him and Tim Mara in their usual seats unsettled Art. New, younger owners and their lawyers had taken their places. Almost sixty, Art was no longer the kid in the room. He, Halas, and Marshall were the three remaining patriarchs.

The owners faced two crucial issues: electing a new commissioner and negotiating a television contract. For the time being, the union was the dragon sleeping under the table. Art had too many other interests to pursue the commissioner's job himself. Nor did he want it; he functioned better in back rooms. But Art was committed to steering the league on the course he and Bell had set. Through all the owners' fractious and interminable league meetings, no one had ever picked up his football and gone home.

One marker of the NFL's commitment to consensus was that it required ten of twelve votes on major matters, including the election of a commissioner. Consensus had been central to the owners' success, but Art sensed that newer owners did not necessarily share that commitment.

They were already divided into camps. Seven voted for San Francisco 49ers attorney Marshall Leahy on the first ballot, but four—Art, Marshall, Rosenbloom, and Eagles owner Frank McNamee—supported acting commissioner Austin Gunsel. Halas abstained. Art was determined not to let this issue drive them apart. There were other prickly issues to address and Art was worried that Marshall, who had been on the losing side of the union and expansion fights, was becoming alienated. He was fond of Marshall and valued his Washington connections.

Concluding that neither Leahy nor Gunsel could win, Art worked to quash both candidacies and open the door to alternatives. On the second ballot, he switched to Leahy knowing Leahy would not get the required ten votes. He then nominated Colts general manager Don Kellet. Marshall and Rosenbloom, who had felt betrayed by Art's defection to Leahy, quickly followed his lead. The master politician had not lost his chops. He had simultaneously moved Marshall and Rosenbloom off Gunsel and deflated Leahy's chances.

On subsequent ballots, the Fearless Four—Art, Marshall, Rosenbloom, and McNamee—nominated Pittsburgh judge Samuel Weiss and former baseball commissioner Happy Chandler. Their candidacies went nowhere. Leahy's backers, mostly newer owners, held firm. The only decision they could agree on was to attend opening day at the Miami Beach Kennel Club.

Twenty-two ballots later, Wellington Mara suggested to Art they back Pete Rozelle, the Rams' thirty-three-year-old general manager. Art hardly knew Rozelle, but he saw an opportunity to placate the younger owners. Dan Rooney, who had befriended Rozelle, enthusiastically endorsed him. "That may have been the meeting where my father started to listen to me," Dan reflected. Art then reached out to Philadelphia's Frank McNamee, who responded, "Who the hell is Pete Rozelle?" Art admitted his own ignorance, but offered, "If Well [Mara] says he's okay, that's good enough for me." Late in the evening on January 26, the owners elected Rozelle. A new generation had gained a foothold without disenfranchising the old guard or demolishing its values.

Television

Soon afterward, Art attended a meeting in Colts owner Carroll Rosenbloom's Central Park apartment to discuss a television deal. The NFL's relationships with the networks were evolving. CBS had monopolized regular season telecasts during the 1950s, but ABC, still a fledgling network, had signed a groundbreaking contract with the AFL in 1960. Now NBC wanted in on the action. In 1959, before Bell's death, the Peacock network had offered to package Pittsburgh and Baltimore's games for a national audience. After his election, Rozelle tried to discourage the deal. Art, who was losing money, shook him off. "My father," Dan Rooney recalled, "said we had to do it." So he, Dan, Rosenbloom, and NBC's Tom Gallery hashed out NBC's offer at Rosenbloom's apartment.

NBC wanted the national rights to broadcast a weekly game, alternating the two teams. Coming off three winning seasons, Pittsburgh brought a long tradition and a good schedule to NBC. Baltimore was an even better draw. Winning two of the last three titles, the Colts had seared the game into the nation's psyche with their sudden death defeat of the Giants in 1958. With Unitas at quarterback, the Colts were a terrific attraction. Rosenbloom raised the most important question yet to be resolved:

How much would NBC pay? When Gallery answered $900,000 per year, Rosenbloom interjected, "I have to have $575,000." That would leave Pittsburgh with just $325,000. Art glared at him. "I thought we were partners," he said. But Rosenbloom would not budge. Gallery backed away, saying how they divided the money was not his concern.

Art and Dan stepped into the next room. Angered by the unequal split and Rosenbloom's bullying, Dan told his father, "Forget it. Let's get out of here. We're not taking less." Art told him to calm down, pointing out that they had only made $125,000 from television in 1959. Dan fumed. "This bum is taking advantage of us," he argued. "I wouldn't let him do this." Art listened, then went back in the room and shook hands on the $325,000. "I would have never made that deal," Dan later explained. "I would have cut my nose off to spite my face, but I would not have made that deal." But the deal boosted Pittsburgh's bottom line and meant that it made more from television than most teams. Accepting less was a characteristic move by Art. He rarely fought for the last dollar, even if it allowed somebody to gain an advantage.

The NFL still faced the daunting task of forging a league-wide television agreement. In March 1960, the owners reconvened. Their ability to solidify Bell's share-alike approach lay on the line. Rozelle's negotiating abilities were untested, and the wrong deal could kill the smaller clubs. Art navigated between his team's and the league's interests. CBS controlled the rights to all teams except for Pittsburgh and Baltimore, which had signed with NBC, and Cleveland, which operated independently. CBS's Bill MacPhail wanted the whole pie. He approached Rozelle with an offer of $10.5 million over three years in exchange for exclusive rights to all NFL games. Otherwise, CBS threatened to drop several smaller-market teams from its coverage. The offer did not specify how the money would be distributed. If split evenly, Pittsburgh, Baltimore, and Cleveland would receive less for their television rights than they were getting with independent contracts. If the bigger markets took a disproportionate share, revenue imbalance would become more acute.

In Art's eyes, Rozelle looked too eager to consummate a contract with CBS. "They had this association with CBS and wanted to stay with them," Dan Rooney reckoned. Most owners favored CBS, but Art would not renege on the two-year deal he had signed with NBC. He demanded that the other networks be allowed to bid on the rights. Otherwise, he would block any CBS agreement. "My father held out that TV had to be a biddable package," Dan explained.

Other owners berated Art, and Rozelle insisted that the CBS deal was "in the league's best interests." Art held his ground. "Pittsburgh is going on NBC," he declared, "and I'm sure the league will be satisfied." When Rozelle asked if Pittsburgh would enter into a package plan in a year if the terms were satisfactory, Art turned Rozelle's language about "the league's best interest" back on him. An open bid, he said, "would be for the best interests of the league." Art had slowed Rozelle's rush to sign with CBS. As a result, when CBS, NBC, and ABC bid on broadcast rights a few years later, the competition maximized revenues. The time gap also allowed Art to press for equal division of television revenues.

Jockeying for position began immediately after the meeting in the bar at the Seaview Hotel in Miami Beach, where Rams owner Dan Reeves lobbied Dan Rooney. Reeves suggested several ways that the league could divvy the dollars. Still smarting from negotiations with Rosenbloom and NBC, Dan sputtered, "There's only one way to do it, and that's to divide the money equally." When Reeves replied that the big market clubs would balk, Dan exploded, "Then there won't be any television in this league." Pittsburgh, he reminded Reeves, had the right to block visiting clubs broadcasting from its home venue. "When the Rams come to Pittsburgh, there aren't going to be any games going back to L.A." Reeves protested that if that happened, Pittsburgh wouldn't get anything. Dan cut him off, "Then neither will you." Both Rooneys were resolved that the money be split evenly.

War with the AFL, which had signed a five-year pact with ABC, lent urgency to sharing television revenues evenly. The bigger-market NFL owners recognized that they needed smaller-market teams to survive if they were to outlast the AFL. If Green Bay or another small club failed, the entire league would suffer. Eventually, the Giants, the biggest market with the most to lose from the equal distribution of television dollars, accepted that approach.

During the 1960 season, Pete Rozelle hammered out a forward-looking television policy. On January 27, 1961, the owners voted to negotiate an exclusive television contract and divide revenues equally. A few clubs would sacrifice for the league's sake.

In January 1962, after allowing all three networks to bid on a new contact, Rozelle negotiated a new two-year, $9.3 million agreement. The winner, CBS, paid substantially more than it had offered two years earlier. Echoing Bell, Rozelle told the press that equal distribution of television income would preserve a balanced league. Most owners were staggered by the deal, which had been ratcheted up by the competitive bidding that Art had demanded. Subsequent deals surpassed their wildest fantasies. Despite the windfall and the victory for a principle he had championed, Art remained apprehensive. Coming back from the 1962 meeting at which the contract was ratified, he told Dan, "You'll rue this day." Art welcomed television's dollars and needed them to survive. But he foresaw the interference that the networks and other outsiders would impose on pro football.

15

Renaissance for Pittsburgh, Not the Steelers

1960–64

October 13, 1960

Art Rooney hunched down into his seat at Forbes Field. The New York Yankees had just taken a 7–4 lead in the top of the eighth inning of the seventh game of the 1960 World Series, and gloom had enveloped the city. Art had sat with David Lawrence in a cold rain at Forbes Field the last time the Pirates had played in the seventh game of the Series. On that October day, the Pirates rallied in the bottom of the eighth inning to beat Walter Johnson and the Washington Senators in the 1925 World Series. Since then, neither the Pirates nor the Steelers had won much of anything.

David Lawrence was hurting even more than Art; he was far away from Forbes Field that afternoon. The governor hated missing the game, but the final presidential debate between Richard Nixon and John Kennedy would occur that evening. With the election weeks away, Lawrence could not abandon the campaign trail.

Art's mood brightened when the Pirates scored twice in the bottom of the eighth and soared when Hal Smith's three-run homer put Pittsburgh up 9–7. The underdog Pirates had come from behind all season long. But when the Yankees abruptly tied the game in the top of the ninth, a hush descended over the city. Pirate second baseman Bill Mazeroski stepped into the batter's box to lead off the bottom of the inning. He took the first pitch for a ball and drove the second deep to left center. Art rose to his feet as Yankee outfielder Yogi Berra turned his back to home plate, took a few steps, and sagged despondently when the ball cleared the left-field wall. Mazeroski galloped around the bases, hardly touching earth, as jubilant fans poured onto the field. The Pirates had won the World Series. The *Pirates* had won the World Series!

Church bells rang out, traffic stopped, and passengers hopped out to boogie in the streets. Office girls snake-danced downtown as workers hurled a blizzard of confetti from windows. Trolleys stalled on tracks covered with debris. With a horde of celebrants rushing toward downtown and no place left to put them, police blocked the bridges and tunnels into the city. It was too late to stop the biggest outpouring anyone could remember. Pittsburghers reveled through the night, and bars ran out of liquor. The delirium, Art said, far surpassed the 1925 celebrations. "Not many people had automobiles in 1925 and not many women went to ball games. And you didn't have the enthusiasm building up for a whole year."

The World Series was the crowning moment of Pittsburgh's renaissance, the symbolic capstone to the city's physical rebirth. "It is the same spirit," the *Post-Gazette* crowed, "that moved the city to pull itself up by the bootstraps in the nation's outstanding example of postwar reconstruction."

After the game, Steeler coach Buddy Parker entered the Pirates' locker room and asked manager Danny Murtaugh for his golden wand. He left empty-handed. Comparisons with the Pirates must have irked Art even as he cheered them on. His team had the sorry distinction of competing the longest in the NFL without winning a title. Until they did, Art would have to settle for the Pirates' championship and another astounding upset, the election of an Irish Catholic senator as president of the United States that November.

Irish Hour

As far as Art—and many Pittsburghers—were concerned, David Lawrence was a miracle worker. After the war, as deindustrialization eroded the steel industry and ravaged the coal mines that fed it, Pittsburgh began falling into rusty decline. Lawrence arrested that decay and became midwife to the city's rebirth. He negotiated his way through a tangle of naysayers, contentious unions, and arrogant corporate leaders to revitalize a stagnant industrial metropolis. Since becoming mayor in 1946,

Lawrence had cleansed the skies, made the sun shine, and tamed the flooding rivers that had forced Art to escape his boyhood home on the Northside in a skiff. By curtailing the use of soft coal that left a sooty haze over the city, lobbying Congress to build dams upriver, and rebuilding the Point, Lawrence had refurbished Pittsburgh's image.

Lawrence believed that sport was at the center of Pittsburgh's rejuvenation. It was civic cement and the catalyst to rally a city coping with decline. The 1960 baseball season had borne out his contention. When the Pirates brought down the Yankee Goliath, their victory shouted that Pittsburgh could climb out of its smoky past.

Lawrence had successfully crossed the city's historic ethnic, religious, and class divides. Art Rooney had also bridged these divisions in sports and politics. Like the Pirates, the Steelers were becoming Pittsburgh's team.

Ironically, the Pirates were no longer as rooted in Pittsburgh as they had been during the forty-seven years that Barney Dreyfuss and his family owned them. The team's current owner, real estate magnate John Galbreath, lived in Columbus, Ohio. How much sweeter it would be for Pittsburgh if Rooney, the son of its sandlots, and the Steelers, the lineal descendents of that sporting tradition, could lead its sporting rebirth.

Eager for the Steelers' success and anxious about keeping them in town, Lawrence had initiated plans for a municipal stadium in 1955. He steadfastly backed Art's endeavors and "knew more about sports," Art attested, "than any laymen I ever knew." Lawrence might have said the same about Art's grasp of politics.

Art never felt compelled to subscribe to party positions he did not share nor endorse candidates he disliked. He had criticized the anticommunist hysteria ginned up by Senator Joseph McCarthy, whom he knew from the track, and was an early critic of intervention in Vietnam. "I think maybe it was Art Rooney who taught me that all Republicans aren't right, all Democrats aren't bad," Elsie Hillman reflected.

Hillman, who entered politics as a Republican ward chair in Pittsburgh, became a powerful national figure. "To get things done," she reasoned, "you just work with whoever is there to work with." Both Republicans and Democrats wanted to work with Art, she said, because he provided access to other people and did so without fluff and wasted time. "He slaughtered the King's English, yet was in the court of kings." Democratic Congressman Tip O'Neill knew that about Art and came by to confer before the 1960 spring primary.

A buddy since Art had beaten O'Neill's pal Tansey Norton in the 1919 AAU boxing nationals in Boston, Tip now held John Kennedy's old seat in the House of Representatives. Valuing Art's counsel about politics as much as he did about horses, O'Neill came to ask him how Kennedy could win Pennsylvania's delegates to the Democratic Party convention.

O'Neill's dilemma was David Lawrence. "Art," Tip said, "we've got to get Lawrence for Kennedy, but he doesn't think that a Catholic can win." That wasn't news to Art. He knew that Lawrence did not believe that the country was ready for an Irish Catholic president. "They had an awful time selling him that Kennedy could win," Art later reflected.

The Irish in Pittsburgh—and throughout the Northeast—had been gaining power over the century. Now, as they trembled on the brink of their greatest success, they scarcely dared to acknowledge that their hour had arrived. Lawrence and Rooney had come of age in an era when their friend Senator Coyne had been forced to bow before the Mellons. But the Scots-Irish Presbyterian hold on Pittsburgh had waned as Catholic political muscle waxed. During Pittsburgh's renaissance, Lawrence had formed a collaborative partnership—not a subservient relationship— with Richard King Mellon, the Mellon family's latest scion.

O'Neill quizzed Art about mayors and representatives he might target, but Art interrupted, "Tip, you are going about this the wrong way. They are not the people that are going to get delegates elected." Talk to "Clarkie" in Philadelphia, Art said. "He's the biggest politician in the state. He's the guy that gets these people you are talking about elected." James Clark, Art advised, could outmaneuver Lawrence.

Clark, a politician and sportsman, had led the "100 Brothers," men who had put up $3,000 apiece to buy the Eagles in 1949. He and Art shared more than a passing interest in the April primaries. Alongside the presidential ballot, fourteen counties would decide whether to allow harness racing. Both men hoped to operate a track if a county close to home voted yes. Art called the Philadelphia boss to say that O'Neill would be in touch. A few days later, Art checked in with O'Neill. "Joe Kennedy is having dinner with him tonight," O'Neill reported. Art, an old friend of the elder Kennedy, smiled.

While Lawrence tried to keep the state's delegation uncommitted in case Adlai Stevenson ran again, O'Neill cultivated Clark and his Philadelphia organization. They helped Kennedy score a smashing primary victory.

Both Governor Lawrence and Mayor Barr supported harness racing during the campaign, and Art became the initiative's public advocate. Some Protestant pulpits in Western Pennsylvania condemned the measure during the campaign, and Art clashed with a Congregationalist pastor in the press over racing's propriety.

On election day, Allegheny County decisively voted down harness racing. Although Pittsburgh voters backed the measure, they could not overcome resistance in the rest of the county. The measure also lost in surrounding counties. Clark, however, carried the day in Philadelphia. Cartoonist Cy Hungerford caricatured a frowning Art in the *Post-Gazette* with a cigar clamped in his mouth. He sat on a fence with Lawrence and Barr, a trio of dejected railbirds watching a sad-looking trotter go by as the governor commented, "It Doesn't Pay to Bet on Horses!"

Art took defeat in stride. "I'm probably not as disappointed as a lot of people," he observed. "I probably saved money." He knew thoroughbreds, not trotters, and confessed to reservations about harness racing. What rankled him were the denunciations of horse racing people as underworld denizens. "Art Rooney, as most of his friends know, is a man slow to anger," *Post-Gazette* sports editor Al Abrams observed. "But, as they also know, once his fuse simmers near the danger mark, he can explode higher than most short-tempered gents." Rooney was near detonation. "Those charges that only thieves and racketeers run the sport are nothing but a pack of lies," Art fumed. Fed up with politicians who had jumped on the vote-no bandwagon, he charged, "These kind are nothing but hypocrites and phonies."

Art's frustration was tempered by his delight over Kennedy's primary victory. After Stevenson declined to run, Lawrence broke for JFK.

While O'Neill worked the Pennsylvania delegation, sitting among them on the convention floor, Lawrence huddled with the major players. He helped persuade Kennedy to offer the vice presidential slot to Lyndon Johnson.

Art, who supported Kennedy in the general election, was a New Dealer at heart, seeing government as a tool to deliver jobs and help people in need. "Franklin Roosevelt," Art often said, "stole our thunder." He relished the prospect of his friend Joe Kennedy's son in the White House.

Lawrence stumped for Kennedy so unstintingly that he missed the seventh game of the World Series. That November, Catholics in Pittsburgh and Philadelphia helped JFK carry Pennsylvania comfortably in a tight presidential race. Years later, after O'Neill became the Speaker of the House, Dan Rooney was on Capitol Hill lobbying him on the NFL's behalf. When ushered into a room full of military brass, Dan said his business could wait. O'Neill would not hear of it and insisted on telling the generals how Art Rooney had put JFK into the White House. "Tip always talked about my father as the guy that elected Kennedy," Dan Rooney recalled. "He made it bigger than it was."

Back to Football

But Art was not seen as a kingmaker in Pittsburgh, where the Pirates' success reinforced the public's tiresome take on Art as a feckless loser. But he could not escape the record. In the twenty-seven years from 1933 to 1959, his team had six winning seasons and an overall record of 116 wins, 182 losses, and 12 ties. Art never saw himself as a loser, nor defined himself exclusively by football; nonetheless, losing chafed.

He tried to right his team during the off-season, acquiring fullback John Henry Johnson. A punishing blocker who relished inflicting pain, Johnson broke jaws, bloodied faces, and ended careers. Running backs absorb more than their share of punishment, but Johnson could not abide with the treatment he received from opponents. "They jump on me after the whistle," he said. "They scratch my eyes—that kind of thing. All them things annoy me a little bit." In his first season as a pro, Johnson had his cheekbone fractured, ribs broken, and teeth knocked out. The injuries only made him fiercer. "The rougher they get with John Henry," a teammate observed, "the rougher he gets with them."

During the 1960 preseason, the Steelers played the Eagles in Hershey. The night before, Jack Butler, now an assistant coach, visited former teammates Nick Skorich and Chuck Cherundolo, who coached for Philadelphia. He returned around midnight, spoke briefly with Buddy Parker, and turned in. "Next day," Butler recalled, "we get our butts kicked." At the hotel bar afterward, the coaches gathered in a booth, and Butler wound up next to Parker, the last place he wanted to be after the ear-beatings he had seen Parker inflict on assistants. After several drinks, Parker turned on Butler: "Where were you last night? I know! You were down there cavorting with the enemy. I'm not so sure I want you on my staff." Butler stood up. "Coach, you don't have to worry," he said. "As of now, I'm no longer on your staff. I'm done." Although Parker apologized later, Butler had had his fill of him. Art convinced him to stay with the team and work in personnel.

The Steelers began the regular season with a 35–28 win over the expansion Dallas Cowboys. Bobby Layne, a Texas legend, was responsible for all 35 Steeler points. But it would be their only road win that season. Decimated by injuries, the team sank in the standings. "With the Steelers," Layne observed, "we only had about sixteen men who could do a first-class job, and any time one of them got hurt, it put us out of commission." After three winning seasons, the Steelers came up short, finishing 5-6-1.

Art added another bruising, high-living player during the off-season, defensive tackle Eugene "Big Daddy" Lipscomb. The former Baltimore Colt All-Pro was thirty when he joined the Steelers. At 6-feet-6 inches, the 285-pound Lipscomb looked as if he could grab a handful of players and toss them aside until he found the man with the ball. One of the biggest men playing, Lipscomb was absurdly fast for his size. Baltimore had capitalized on his fury to win two titles but tired of his off-the-field behavior. Parker, who made his career by acquiring other teams' veteran discards, figured that the larger-than-life Lipscomb would fit in on the Steelers. He fit in well enough to become a cult figure. Pittsburgh fans embraced him.

The league did the Steelers no favors with their 1961 schedule. After a season in which they lost all but one away game, the team played three of its first four on the road. They lost all four. When Layne, who had taken his share of hits, was injured in one of the losses, fans booed as he left the field. Ernie Stautner, the squad's senior member, snapped. "I'm not happy playing in Pittsburgh," he snarled. "This is a lousy sports town, and if Art Rooney had any sense he'd get out of it." He called Pittsburgh a graveyard where coaches threatened to send underperforming players.

Art kept his equanimity, at least in public, and the players regained theirs. At the team's late-season vaudeville show, which Layne emceed, they all shared a laugh when Big Daddy Lipscomb did the twist and joined John Henry Johnson in a soft shoe routine.

Late in the season, Layne threw four touchdown passes to tie Sammy Baugh's career NFL record. Early the next morning, he broke another career record—for parked vehicles struck while driving. With characteristic flamboyance, he nailed a streetcar. After returning from a game in Washington, players gathered at Dante's, their favorite club. Layne arrived late and left early. As he wrote in his memoir, "I wanted to start this book by saying: 'I was driving down the avenue early one morning, alert and happy, when a parked, swerving streetcar ran into me head-on.' But who would believe it?" Layne was on Wylie Avenue when his car's wheels stuck in the city's ubiquitous trolley tracks. "It was a slippery night," Layne explained, "so when I jerked the steering wheel to get out of the tracks, I headed straight on into a streetcar facing the other way." Layne smacked into his car's windshield and was stitched up at Mercy Hospital.

Art knew that Layne drank. "No doubt about that," he laughed. "He said to me the next day, 'Shoot, if I was drunk, I would have never hit that car. I'm only a bad driver when I'm sober. I don't have that much practice at it.'"

The Steelers finished below .500 again, despite the presence of Layne, Stautner, and Johnson, three men who were bound for the Hall of Fame. Lipscomb would have joined them if his own personal demons had not bested him. But they had become an old team, even by Parker's standards. "If I ever felt we had hit bottom," Art later said, "that was the time."

During the off-season, President Kennedy nominated Byron White to the Supreme Court. Feeling like a proud father, Art recalled Whizzer's rookie year. While most players played cards and drank beer aboard the Sullivan day coaches they rode, White had buried himself in books. "He knew where he was going," Art reflected. "He'd play cards a bit and then he'd read."

In 1962, Parker's aging giants rallied. Worried about Layne's health, Parker acquired quarterback Ed Brown from Chicago. The trade was the least Halas could do after all the lopsided deals he had made with Art. Other acquisitions solidified the offensive line, which now complemented the Steelers' imposing defensive line of Lipscomb, Ernie Stautner, Joe Krupa, and John Baker.

Pittsburgh's record was 3-4 at midseason. Layne was playing hurt, with one side of his body badly battered. He had the trainer tape him up and the doctor shoot him up before games, but he was miserable afterward. In their tenth game, Pittsburgh trailed Washington 21–6. Going back to pass, Layne was sacked. Fans booed mercilessly as he lay on the ground injured, unable to continue, and Ed Brown replaced him. Angry at the Redskins and their own fans, the Steelers rallied and won 23–21 on Lou Michaels' last-second field goal. With Lipscomb rallying the defense and Brown leading Pittsburgh to three wins in the next four games, they finished the season 9-5.

Pittsburgh played Parker's old team, Detroit, in the Playoff Bowl, a game featuring the league's runner-ups that the NFL had begun in 1960. It was Pittsburgh's first postseason appearance since 1947. Detroit played tough, physical football, and Parker started Brown to save Layne the punishment. He wanted Bobby to retire afterward. But with Detroit leading 17–10 late in the game, Parker put in Layne to see if he could pull off one last comeback. Layne moved the team to Detroit's 23-yard line, but when Buddy Dial couldn't hold on to a fourth-down throw, the game was over. So was Layne's career; he begrudgingly announced his retirement. Having thrown and completed more passes for more yards and more touchdowns than anybody in NFL history, Layne called "not winning a championship for Mr. Rooney" his biggest disappointment.

Art hated to see Layne retire; he felt worse in March when Eugene Lipscomb was found dead in his Baltimore apartment. The coroner's verdict: death from a heroin overdose. Lipscomb, thirty-two, was fond of drinking and famous for womanizing, but Art rejected the verdict. Art knew that Lipscomb did everything to excess but did not believe he had done drugs while in Pittsburgh: "The players would have known and they didn't." Art had kidded with Lipscomb on the telephone two days before he died and sent him an advance on a contract that Lipscomb was to sign the following week. His death was sobering. Art and Dan were the only NFL personnel to visit the funeral home. "Gene was a fine young man and deserves our respect now," Art declared, "as he always did."

Art often said he never had a player he didn't like, but a few tested his patience. Other owners would have shown John Henry Johnson the door. "John Henry was something of a thorn in our side," Dan Rooney acknowledged. "My father could handle it better than the rest of us, but John Henry drove us crazy." Johnson came into the office one day and nervously asked for Mr. Rooney: "I've got to talk about my salary." Johnson had out-rushed Jim Brown for the first time that season. "He was very proud of that," remembered Hugh Carr, who was waiting there for his father Joe. "He hated Jim Brown and once put himself in on defense so that he could tackle him." Although reasonably well paid, Johnson had only a few years left to cash in. Half an hour later, Johnson emerged from Art's office. "Art has his arm around him," Hugh Carr explained. "John," Art announced, "is going to be leaving us." Turning to Johnson, he said, "John, you've really been a great player." Startled, Johnson protested, "Wait a minute, Mr. Rooney. I don't want to leave." At that, Art said, "Well, come on back, we'll straighten this out." Johnson ended up signing for what Art had originally offered.

Evan Baker Jr. could testify to Art's affectionate forbearance. "I was with John Henry one night, about four o'clock in the morning. We were out fooling around, drinking, chasing women, when we ran out of money." Johnson called Art, left, and returned with $500. "Now how many guys," Baker laughed, "could call you up at four o'clock in the morning just because they worked for you so they could get drunk?"

Commodities and Tracks

Art applied his instincts and dexterity with numbers to the commodities market, as well as at the track. He and his friend Jerry Nolan established a short position in soybeans, betting a bumper crop would cause futures to fall. "Riding home from New York," Art explained, "I read a little item in the *Times* about floods in China." He asked Silas Rooney, now the superior at St. Anthony's, a Franciscan house in Boston, to speak with the Chinese priests there. Although the 1949 revolution had expelled the Franciscans from China, they had retained connections to the Chinese countryside. "Sure enough," Art recalled, "floods were playing hell with the soybean crop. I called Nolan in Chicago, and we switched our positions from selling short to going long. We made a nice score."

Later, Art and a few partners began cornering the cocoa market. "He had more chocolate than Hershey's," Dan Rooney said. Their heavy buying drove up prices and attracted the attention of several major traders. Upset at the intrusion into their territory, they warned Art to abandon his position. "They didn't want him fooling around with their ability to buy," Dan explained. Art took heed and bailed out, making a tidy profit. Those who held their positions were wiped out when the major traders caused prices to collapse. Art's approach to commodities was similar to the way he bet horses. "If he thought it was going good," Dan said, "he shot the moon." But Art also knew when to back off.

Horse racing offered a good deal more romance than commodities. Art held the license to manage Cleveland's Randall Park Racetrack in the 1960s. Tim Rooney ran the operation, but when Edward DeBartolo, a Youngstown, Ohio, developer who owned nearby Thistle Downs, began consolidating control over Ohio tracks, Art sold him Randall Park's rights. But Randall Park had convinced Art that running a track was good business. Racing was growing in popularity, and the federal crackdown on bookmaking was generating more action at the track. As a racetrack operator, Art would benefit from the pari-mutuel system that had impeded his betting career. He would receive the stipulated percentage of the handle—the amount bet on a race—that went to the track. Operating racetracks would prove more profitable and secure than his other ventures. Nor would it stop Art from betting on horses at tracks he did not operate, or from breeding and racing them.

While Allegheny County had prevented Art from running a local track by rejecting the April referendum, he was eligible for a license in counties where the measure had passed. Art, however, refrained from approaching the governor out of concern that it might create the appearance of a conflict of interest. Eventually, David Lawrence broached the subject. "You are the only guy that I can trust to go into this business," John Rooney remembered Lawrence telling his father. "I know that you would run a good, clean operation."

With Lawrence's approval, Art negotiated with Jim Clark, who held the license for Liberty Bell outside Philadelphia, to run half of its meet. He then formed the William Penn Associates and sent his twenty-four-year-old twins, John and Pat, to Philadelphia to manage it. John had taught high school and Pat had worked as a copper salesman, but they happily switched and learned the racing business from the bottom up. Gerry Lawrence, the governor's son and the twins' friend, joined them in Philadelphia, where racing began in June 1963.

Tagging along behind their father at the track, John and Pat had begun placing bets for him as soon as they were old enough to do so legally. John and Gerry Lawrence had once gone to Aqueduct for Art to bet $2,000 on Lou Michaels, a horse named for a Steeler. "We didn't have ten cents between us; we couldn't even buy a hot dog," John recalled. "I'm looking at the odds when we bet, and I see we were going to win $100,000 if it came in. That was a lot of money back in those days." When Lou Michaels lost in a photo finish, they had to scrape up fifty cents to pay the toll to get across the bridge and back to Philadelphia.

Art schooled his sons in how to survive in racing. "He was very analytical," John reflected. "He knew if a guy was good or not such a good person the minute he met him." That ability to read people was critical in horse racing. But for all his tough talk, Art did not always heed his own advice. John and Art were at Liberty Bell when an old race hand passed by: "My dad said, 'Has he ever asked you for money?' and I said, 'Yeah.' He said, 'Did you give him any?' and I said, 'A couple hundred.' He said, 'You idiot! He'll never pay you back.' Just then the guy came up and said to the Chief, 'I'll get you back that $2,000 I borrowed.' Man, did I feel great."

While Art let his sons run the track without interference, he checked in nightly. "I asked him what I should do one time," John explained, "and he said, 'You're there. You know more about what is going on than I do. Make your own decision.' That's how he was. He'd say, 'Do anything you want, just don't make a mistake.'" Art had little cause to complain. William Penn Associates did more business than the Steelers, netting $3 million dollars a year during the 1960s. Racing was far more profitable for the family than football.

The 1963 Season

At camp, Buddy Parker regretted pushing Bobby Layne into retirement and asked Ernie Stautner to talk him into returning. "Buddy knew we had the players to make a run at the division," Stautner recalled, "but we needed the take-charge guy in the driver's seat." Layne, however, had already made other commitments. "So that was that, and I believe that was all that kept us from winning the championship."

Ed Brown took over at quarterback. "Eddie Brown had some great games for us that year," Stautner observed, "but Bobby had the extra something that made the difference in close games. He could make a team play over its head." Brown played well at home, where the Steelers won five games and tied two, but he was ineffective on the road. "This is a funny team," Parker admitted. "It seems any time the pressure's on, they fold up. They choke. Not everybody, of course, but just enough to wreck the rest of the team." Art knew they missed Layne.

Against Cleveland, Pittsburgh held Jim Brown to 6 yards rushing in the second half and tackled him in the end zone for a safety to win 9–7. With his team in contention, Art anticipated a full house for Chicago. The November 24 game was a possible preview of the NFL championship.

But on November 22, President Kennedy was assassinated in Dallas. Art was shaken, at a loss for words when the press asked for comment.

The next day's Pitt–Penn State game was postponed, while Pete Rozelle debated whether the NFL should play on Sunday. "Pete," Dan Rooney said, "we shouldn't play." But Rozelle called Pierre Salinger, Kennedy's press secretary, who said, "Do it; it will be good for the country. The president would have wanted you to." Art disagreed. At church Sunday morning, he told tackle Joe Krupa, "There's no way there should be a game today." But there was.

While the networks did not televise the games and Rozelle would regret his decision, the local press raised little criticism at the time. Most writers saw football as a brief respite from painful news. Dan was listening to coverage of the assassination on a transistor radio at the ballpark Sunday morning when Jack Ruby shot alleged assassin Lee Harvey Oswald. "It was surreal," he recalled.

So was the game. Stautner and other vets verbally ripped George Halas, who stood nearby working the refs for calls. Pittsburgh could not tackle Chicago tight end Mike Ditka, the former Pitt All-American, who brought Chicago back to tie the game.

The game mattered little against the backdrop of Kennedy's death, but it figured importantly in the standings. The Steelers had played opportunistically that season, capitalizing on opponents' mistakes. They also benefited from league rules that based the standings on winning percentages. Because ties did not factor into that percentage, the Steelers found themselves in the division race with Cleveland and New York with two games left, even though Pittsburgh's record was 6-3 3, while the two other clubs were 9-3.

When Pittsburgh played in Dallas two weeks later, Art went to the spot near the Texas Schoolbook Depository Building where Kennedy had died. "To my recollection," Art Jr. said, "he never went back to Dallas again for a game. He always had an excuse."

After beating Dallas, the Steelers went to New York on December 15. They were 7-3-3 and the Giants 10-3, but a win would give Pittsburgh a better winning percentage and a spot in the championship game.

The night before the game, Art held court at Toots Shor's. "Boys, I'd like to win this one," he confessed. "It's been a long time." Art's cronies did their best to buck him up, and he acknowledged their toasts with uncharacteristic bravado: "We are going to give them holy hell," Art proclaimed. "We are going to bring home the bacon to Pittsburgh." He had reason to be confident; the Steelers had destroyed the Giants 31–0 in Pittsburgh in the September. But league MVP Y. A. Tittle had missed that game. Toots Shor kidded Art. "Every time the Giants score a point," Toots said, "I'm going to take a little nip against the cold. I expect to be loaded by the middle of the third quarter." Even Art laughed.

After Mass, Art went to Yankee Stadium, where 63,000 fans huddled against chilly gusts blowing off the East River. New York was playing for a third straight division title, Pittsburgh its first.

Ed Brown, who had played well during the season, fell apart on the icy field and so did his teammates. When Pittsburgh fumbled on the first play from scrimmage, the Giants recovered and scored. Brown missed open receivers and threw three interceptions; his teammates fumbled twice. But Pittsburgh mounted a comeback and trailed by only 6 points with New York facing a third and eight at its own 24-yard line. If the Steelers stopped the Giants, they would get the ball back with momentum. Tittle dropped back to pass under pressure. When he released the ball, few thought the intended receiver, Frank Gifford, could catch it. But Gifford made the catch of his life, grabbing the ball with one hand and holding on as he slammed into the turf. The Giants won 33–17.

Years later, Stautner maintained that Pittsburgh could have won the game and the title if Layne had played. "A game like that, with everything riding on one roll of the dice, was Bobby's meat." Stautner, a tough, cerebral man who had been exhilarated at kickoff, was devastated afterward. "I was terribly angry at our quarterback, Ed Brown . . . I was angry at Buddy Parker, too, because he was the man who made Bobby Layne retire."

The inimitable writer Myron Cope put his own spin on Brown's performance. "To the utter dismay of those who know their Steelers best," Cope wrote, "quarterback Brown, a strapping former Marine buck sergeant, took the big game too seriously. On the Wednesday preceding the showdown, he disappeared from his favorite saloon. He went into training." Cope had spent enough evenings at Dante's to lend credibility to his hyperbolic account. "His body well rested, his insides dry as a temperance union president's, his head disgustingly clear, [Brown] totally lost his timing and sangfroid."

Art never blamed Parker, criticized Brown, nor bemoaned the absence of Lipscomb. In the locker room, he quietly consoled players: "I was proud of you today. I'll always be proud of you." Still, he hurt. "I thought for sure that it would be 1963," he admitted later. "That game is a sore spot. And that's the closest we've come. The closest. We should've won that day and then we'd have come up against George Halas's Bears and who can tell? We could've done it." Instead, he watched New York play for the championship and smiled stoically when acquaintances offered condolences.

Saints and Sinners

After a life spent trying to think ahead of the play, Art had begun to sense that the play was getting ahead of him. Sport was becoming ever more a business, sweeping away much of what he loved about it. Nor had losing become any easier. On January 19, 1964, a month after the defeat in New York and days before his sixty-third birthday, Art looked on stoically while Pittsburgh's Saints and Sinners feted him with a $15-a-plate stag affair at the Hilton Hotel.

He had agreed to the event only because it benefited Children's Hospital. "All through the parade of speakers, which embarrassingly at times extolled him last night," Pat Livingston wrote, "Art Rooney, the guest of honor, sat impassive, immobile, stone-faced and imperturbable." He failed to crack a smile when pals as disparate as David Lawrence and Johnny Blood celebrated his virtues. Brought up to believe anyone caught "putting on the dog" deserved a pummeling, Art was uncomfortable with the litany of praise. He was also troubled by the intimation that he and the sporting life of his youth had one foot in the grave.

The fifteen hundred men who packed the ballroom had come to lay laurels at the feet of a man each considered a friend. Collectively, these men had created the sporting life that propelled Pittsburgh's emergence as a citadel of sport. But big-time professional sports were paving over the sandlots and burying the fight clubs of their youth. Art was deeply ambivalent about these changes. Despite his misgivings, he wanted the

339

Steelers to succeed in sport's brave new world. So did many who were present, including some who used the event to lobby on Art's behalf for a municipal stadium.

By the time the speeches started, most attendees had downed a drink or three and lit cigars. The tributes to Rooney were spiked with politics. The opening speakers, Mayor Joe Barr and County Commissioner Dr. William McClelland, were locked in combat over whether to build a municipal stadium for Pittsburgh's pro teams. Barr, a stadium booster, tied Art's loyalty to the city's welfare: "By keeping the Steelers in Pittsburgh these many years, he has zealously protected our big league image." Art had dug into his own pockets even while being branded as a loser, Barr pointed out. "We're counting on him as we proceed with our plans on the new Northside stadium."

Most applauded Barr's remarks linking Art, civic patriotism, and a municipal stadium, but not Commissioner McClelland. The crotchety maverick was an antitax, antigovernment Republican long at odds with Barr and Lawrence. McClelland was savvy enough not to pick a fight at the banquet, where support for Art and the stadium ran deep. Nor would he risk alienating those listening to the tribute on KQV radio. Instead, he reminisced about the day at Forbes Field when Chicago had offered Art a contract. That evening, Homestead Grays ace Martin Dihigo struck Art out four times. After the last strikeout, McClelland said, Art trudged away muttering, "Maybe I should have signed with those Chicago Cubs."

David Lawrence, currently an assistant to the president, gave a rousing keynote address. "Pittsburgh has been wanting to say something like's been said tonight for many, many years," he intoned. Lawrence, born within the shadow of the hotel where he now stood, boasted that he had known Art as long as anyone present, since they were boys playing at Phipps Field and Expo Park.

Lawrence pushed open the door that Mayor Barr had cracked regarding the stadium. "Athletics," Lawrence stressed, "is a very important part of any well-rounded city. That's why the battle was put up here for the stadium. We didn't want the Pirates, we didn't want the Steelers, to leave Pittsburgh." To Lawrence, Art and the Steelers were an integral part of the community, at the heart of Pittsburgh's renaissance.

Art's life connected baseball, football, boxing, and horse racing, America's four major sports, but he also had ties to the places where these men had grown up and played. He had fought—in or out of the ring—against several of them, including two former coaches, and played with or against hundreds of others.

Speakers paraded to the podium. Some knew Art as a rough and tumble ballplayer and an even tougher opponent in the ring. Elmer Daley, who had run the Mid Atlantic League when Art and Dan had played for Wheeling, remembered Art as a thief who had stolen 58 bases in 109 games in 1925, a record that lasted for twenty-seven years. Daley called the brothers "rugged boys and great competitors" who belonged on any MAL All-Star team. Surveying the forces that had largely wiped out sandlot and minor league baseball, Daley lamented that sport was changing and not for the better. The culprit, he implied, was the pursuit of business over sport, and the review of Art's life made those financial forces visible. They were the same forces that now made a new stadium necessary for the Steelers to succeed.

Other speakers touted Art as a promoter who had sustained independent teams and given fighters a fair shake. They recognized Art as one of the best handicappers who ever stood by the rail as horses flashed down the backstretch. "The most important thing that racing has ever done for me," trainer Carl Hanford testified, "was to bring me and Mr. Rooney together." That was high praise, given that Hanford trained Kelso, the horse of the year for four years running. He called Art "the grandest man" he had ever known. "If you're considered one of his friends, it just enhances your life a thousand fold."

And everyone there knew Art as one of the dwindling number of pioneers who had nurtured the NFL into a multimillion dollar business. Another of those pioneers, George Halas, noted that the NFL had made two of its greatest moves in 1933: "We put the goal posts on the goal line and Rooney in the National Football League." He thanked Art for his uncommon willingness to place the league's collective interests ahead of his own.

Ernie Stautner, speaking for the team, wished they could have brought Art the title. "As is typical of his selflessness, Mr. Rooney wanted this championship not only for himself, but more so for Pittsburgh and for us." Art squirmed as Stautner said, "Art, we not only respect you for being an owner, we love and admire you for the man you are, a regular guy and a friend of each of us."

A frisson of anticipation went through the hall when Buddy Parker approached the podium. Parker, who dreaded public speaking, had belted down a few drinks to steady himself. "Arthur," Parker slurred in his Texas twang, "you've never sent me a play, never helped me on personnel, ordered a substitution, and not once did you ever come up on a fourth and one situation." A chorus of Art's other ex-coaches present—Jap Douds, Luby DiMelio, Joe Bach, John Blood, and John Michelosen—uttered an amen. "If character and fairness would determine the breaks that a football team should get," Parker said, "I think the Steelers have about ten pennants stored up for them in the future."

Parker had kept his composure but worry rippled through the audience when John Blood rose to his feet. The Hall of Famer was hammered. Dan Rooney blanched when Blood asked Bishop Wright to stand up, too. "We were all scared to death," Dan said. With His Excellency on his feet, Blood brought down the house when he announced, "You now see a saint and a sinner, and there's not much difference between us." Blood said he was fortunate that Catholics believed in the forgiveness of sin. "If Arthur didn't have the capacity to forgive, I wouldn't have lasted five minutes."

Bishop Wright rejoined that Blood, not he, represented the saints. "If I said I was a saint I'd be lying; if I said I was a sinner I'd be bragging." Wright said he would speak for the one group not on the program, "the men on the street." While they made sport—and religion and government—possible, Wright argued that they were often forgotten. But Art Rooney, he said, never forgot the men in the street because he was one of them.

Father Silas Rooney brought word from Maggie Rooney on the matter of saints. "My mother read some newspaper stories about the dinner, and she said they are trying to make my son a saint. He is not one—yet," Silas assured the crowd.

Picking up on David Lawrence's comment that Art was a man who stayed loyal to his friends even when they lost, Dick McCann said, "Absolutely right. Mr. Rooney was always with his friends when they lost, and he generally had given them the horse." McCann, director of the recently opened Pro Football Hall of Fame, elicited the most laughs of the evening when he said, "With everybody else getting introduced here, I wonder if all the former bookies from the Northside would please stand."

Never had so many sportsmen gathered in Pittsburgh. Their stories wove a narrative about sport and Pittsburgh and a man who symbolized both. Sport, like steel, demanded sacrifice, rugged strength, and stubborn fortitude. To these men, sport represented the city's tough and resilient persona, and Rooney was its champion.

While class, topography, nationality, race, and religion had long riven Pittsburgh, sport provided common ground where many could shed tribal loyalties to forge a more inclusive identity. Competition had brokered their sporting fraternity. For generations living in the smoky city, sport was an elixir, the pastime that brought them together.

The speakers reflected how sport bonded Pittsburgh. A Gentile and a Jew shared master of ceremony duties: Bob Prince, the voice of the Pirates and a notorious prankster, and Joe Tucker, the voice of the Steelers and Art's racetrack companion, kept the speakers rolling and the mood loose. Unable to attend, Pittsburgh's leading reform rabbi, Solomon Freehof, entrusted his spiritual brethren, Catholic Bishop John Wright and Episcopalian prelate Dean Moore, to speak for him. Many of the longstanding class, religious, and ethnic chasms that had divided the city for decades were submerged under a common allegiance to sport, personified by Art.

But the limits of sport's diversity were also apparent at the affair. That night, most of the blacks and all of the women in the room were waiting on tables. Nobody mentioned this fraternity's racial or gender exclusivity. That would be a topic in future years.

Finally, Art spoke, picking up threads from what others had said.

"I would like to tell Buddy [Parker] that I had the experience of sending in a play one time and that was enough." Art recalled how fans had serenaded the Steelers with "Hi diddle diddle, Rogel up the middle," prompting him to ask Kiesling to begin a game with a pass. It went for a touchdown but was called back because a player was offsides. When the laughter stilled, Art said, "I've had a number of coaches during my career, and I can sincerely say to you and to them and also to the ballplayers that have played for Pittsburgh that I have never had a ballplayer play for us that I sincerely wasn't fond of."

He admitted that he had been moved more than his expression belied. But, he added, "I suppose you're tired of hearing of Rooney." He referred briefly to the elephant in the room, the crushing loss to the Giants. Reminding the gathering that the event was for Children's Hospital, Art concluded by thanking God for the opportunity to participate in this charitable endeavor. As one writer put it, "Everyone of the 1,500 diners knew Art meant it."

A band played "When Irish Eyes Are Smiling" and the men, mixing tears with smiles, stood to applaud Art one last time. Art recognized that this sort of event was reserved for men past their prime. And while he was not about to give up on the Steelers, he had begun handing the ball off to his sons. They had come of age in a sporting world their father had helped to create and were ready and eager to play their parts in it. Art might never overcome the sorry distinction of having gone the longest in the NFL without winning a title, but these men appreciated him as a loyal friend who never put on airs. Bishop Wright closed the evening with his benedictions.

The More Things Change . . .

Art could hardly wait to get out of town afterward. "He was always on the go," his sister Margaret marveled. "He had fun, and so did Kathleen." Fun for Art was, as it had always been, a restless pilgrimage from one sporting event to the next, in the company of the saints and sinners with whom he had shared his life.

In March, he saw Duquesne play basketball at Madison Square Garden and attended opening day at Aqueduct. Art was more at ease among the throng of 48,000 horseplayers than on the Saints and Sinners dais. He knew hundreds of people there and thousands knew of him. At Toots Shor's restaurant that evening, talk turned to Cassius Clay's (soon to be known as Muhammad Ali) upset of Sonny Liston in February. Art, who maintained that Joe Louis could have beaten either of them, joked about Liston's recent arrest for speeding and carrying a pistol. "The way he fought Clay," Art told Toots, "he *should* carry a pistol."

Art owned the rights to show a closed-circuit broadcast of the fight in Pittsburgh, and Dan Rooney and Ed Kiely had organized the event. They had shown old fight films, including Billy Conn's first bout with Louis, before the main event. Art had taken Conn's son, Timmy, and Timmy's grandfather, Greenfield Jimmy Smith, to dinner before the show. The old man's animosity toward his son-in-law, which had turned into a bloody brawl after Timmy's baptism, lingered. "We had just about finished our coffee," Art told Shor, "when Jimmy looked at his watch. Turning to Timmy, Smith said, 'C'mon boy. It's getting late. I'm taking you to see your old man get knocked out.'"

When Art was on the road, he kept in touch by telephone and correspondence. "He'd get himself a mittful of those cards that hotels gave out," Ed Kiely said, "and at night, he'd sit in his room and write cards to everybody back home." One reporter called Art "America's most prolific postcard writer."

Art's network extended to the grave. He lived all the Corporal Works of Mercy but took most seriously "bury the dead." Kiely checked the obituaries each morning and drove Art, when he was in town, to funeral parlors in the evenings. "That was a way to keep your constituency," Kiely explained. If someone else was laid out in the same funeral home, Art went to see those mourners, too. "The people were so delighted that he would come. He didn't really know the guy, but it was an old political way of doing things."

Art called on his sons, nephews, and his friends' sons to serve as pallbearers or to chauffeur him to wakes. When a homeless or poor person died, priests knew they could ask Art to handle expenses and see that somebody attended the Mass. Art was no longer an athlete, although he could show up at a golf course without playing in a year and best his foursome. He still had a powerful motor and an inordinate amount of energy. Grandchildren, nieces, and nephews were now part of his entourage. They joined him on trips to shrines, Shamrock Farm, and about town. They saw his generosity and felt his irascible temper. "My uncle Art was great on the needle," his nephew Jamie Rooney recalled, "and the closer you were related to him, the worse you got it."

Art usually relinquished the wheel to others. "He liked to read while someone else drove," Jim Boston recalled. "He could open up the *New York Times* and three hours later say, 'Where we at?' Then he'd look out the window, and say 'Oh, I know where we're at, we're only a half hour away.' He knew all the highways in the eastern United States."

"One of the worst things that could happen to you was to have to drive my uncle Art someplace," Jamie chuckled, "because if you made a wrong turn—man, oh man! He could be a very demanding guy." Art hated crouching to get in and out of Jamie's MGB, a low-slung British sports car whose muffler needed replacing more often than the oil needed changing. Art often scowled at Jamie whenever he saw him and asked if he still had "that car."

"But he couldn't have been more generous," Jamie added. He was an attentive uncle, staying abreast of the lives of his many nephews and nieces. Art had acquired the nickname "The Chief," after the twins said he looked like Perry White, the newspaper editor in the television version of *Superman*. But to nephews, Art was "The Bull."

Art had one more day of limelight to endure before the 1964 season. In September, he was inducted into the Hall of Fame. When the Hall had opened in Canton, Ohio, the previous year, its inaugural class had included Art's dearest friends in the game: Bert Bell, Tim Mara, George Halas, Johnny Blood, and George Marshall. Now it was Art's turn, and though he hated being fussed over, his selection was gratifying. Columnist Charlie Powell captured the essence of Art's election, calling him "the man who has given integrity and dignity to the sport."

Canton welcomed a contingent of Pittsburghers to the ceremony. Father Silas gave the opening prayer, and David Lawrence presented Art for enshrinement. Art spoke briefly and joined his brother and Lawrence afterward to watch Pittsburgh play Baltimore in the Hall of Fame exhibition. The game was a disaster. John Unitas embarrassed the Steelers 48–17. The defeat left them with a 1-3 preseason record and without their All-Pro defender Myron Pottios, who was lost for the season with a broken arm. At least Art, Silas, and Lawrence were not on the team bus that broke down on the way back to Pittsburgh.

16

Not the Same Old Steelers—Worse

1965–68

Toward the end of the next season, *Times* columnist Arthur Daley caught up with Art. Yankee Stadium was subdued, absent the electricity of the year before, when the Giants and Steelers had played for a berth in the 1963 NFL championship. This year, it was a clash between last-place teams. "Maybe we better cross it off as just a bad year," Art said, his eyes twinkling over a saucy grin. "This best-natured of men," Daily observed, "is a true sportsman, able to treat those two imposters, victory and defeat, with the same disdain." At least Art took a wad of cash home, thanks to a crowd of 63,000. But he was right: 1964 had been terrible.

The Steelers had surrendered. Buddy Parker's strategy of trading draft picks for vets had run its course; the team was old and dispirited. Two new NFL franchises, larger rosters, and the AFL had doubled demand for players, slashing the supply of veterans. Parker, who had surrendered well over half of Pittsburgh's top draft picks since taking over in 1957, had nothing left to deal. The Steelers finished 5-9, their worst season in nine years, and stalwart defender Ernie Stautner retired afterward.

Buddy Parker gave no signs that he would follow suit. Art, who had no designs to force him out, made a show of faith by signing Parker to a new three-year contract worth $80,000. The contract required Parker to run all trades by the Rooneys. But when the Steelers lost three of four 1965 preseason contests, the man who had coached Pittsburgh longer than anyone triggered his own exit. Parker impetuously tried to trade two defensive starters for Philadelphia's back-up quarterback King Hill. Art was at the track, leaving Dan Rooney in charge at camp. Dan, weary of Parker's proclivity to recklessly trade players after a loss, suggested the coach sleep on it. They would talk in the morning. But

Parker, who might have listened to Art, instead offered his resignation. Dan accepted on the spot.

"Now wait a second," Art protested when Dan reached him. "We've got to think this out." But Dan had thought it out. He had had his fill of Parker. "This guy's gone," he told his father. Art knew Dan was right. "He lasted eight years here," Art reflected, "and he quit every time we lost, but our newspaper guys knew enough not to take him seriously. Parker would coax them, even beg them, to write it, and they never did."

Although Parker's resignation abrogated his contract, Art paid him anyway. "Be sure to put in the paper," Parker instructed reporters, "that Art Rooney is one of the greatest fellows I ever met." Art appreciated the accolades, but he was relieved to see Parker go. The coach had closed him out of decisions, and his binges and irascible disposition made him volatile in defeat. Dan did what Art's sense of loyalty had kept him from doing: fire Parker.

Parker's ouster confirmed the changing of the guard. Art, almost sixty-five, had begun handing off duties to Dan in the late 1950s. He, commissioner Rozelle, and other owners recognized that the younger Rooney was reliable and totally dedicated to football. While sharing Art's values, Dan gave the Steelers more attention than his father ever did.

Art Jr. was also making football his life's work. After graduating as a history major from St. Vincent's in 1957, studying acting in New York, and serving in the Marine reserves, Art Jr. had returned home to promote ticket sales. "My mother made my father hire me," Art Jr. laughed. He then moved into scouting. "It was the safest job in the world, because Buddy Parker didn't hold on to many draft picks." Diligently studying how scouts evaluated talent, he soon headed the department. But when it came time to draft in the spring of 1965, he twiddled his thumbs until the late rounds. Parker had traded five of their first six picks. Chicago used Pittsburgh's top pick that year to take Dick Butkus, who became one of the game's legendary defenders. The Steelers got bubkes in return. Frustrated, Art Jr. vowed to change how Pittsburgh assembled its roster.

Art was apprehensive about his sons working for the club. "The NFL was still shaky," Art Jr. recalled, "and my father was not drawing a salary from the team. He worried about me supporting a family." Nor was Art so sure about family members working together in a business. "He said, 'Nothing but trouble comes out of these things.'"

Art grudgingly acknowledged that his sons could give football the monomaniacal attention required to win. "I never was one much for details," he confessed. "When it's time for meetings and the draft and such, I'd just as soon be out shooting the breeze with the sportswriters." His sons would be more hands-on, but Art was not about to slip into his dotage. "The Chief was still the chief," Art Jr. attested. He vetted issues and made the final decisions. Ed Kiely watched him school his sons. "Art was a plan-ahead guy. When he got mad at you, he'd say 'You have to think ahead of the play.'" Art never let his sons forget that or how to be tough when need be. "He was good to everybody," Kiely asserted, "but I bet he told Danny many a time, 'I'm not going to let these guys break me—players, agents, anyone.'"

None of them broke Art, but he remained football's all-time loser. "The public knew three things about us in those days," Art Jr. shrugged. "They knew we were Rooneys, they knew we were dumb, and they knew we were cheap." Art could handle the abuse coming his way, but he hated hearing that he had bequeathed a legacy of losing to his sons and his city.

To do anything about it, Art needed to solidify the team's fiscal foundation. For that to happen Pittsburgh needed to fulfill the sporting component of its renaissance, and the NFL had to regain its equilibrium. Securing the first required a municipal stadium; the second meant an end to the costly war with the AFL. Together, these changes would allow his sons, his team, and his city to shed their losing image.

Stadium Games

Where the Steelers would play might have been the most important question they faced. Always the tenant, never the landlord, they were at a disadvantage to clubs playing in municipal parks with more favorable leases. While the Steelers paid $100,000 annually for Forbes Field in the late 1950s, the Colts paid but $12,000 for Baltimore's municipal stadium.

The difference in costs hurt; so did Forbes Field's limited capacity. Moreover, the Pirates were difficult landlords. They denied Rooney a cut of concession revenues but charged for cleanup costs. Baseball also took precedence when it came to scheduling games or practices. The Steelers were forced to settle for abysmal practice facilities in South Park, where locker room toilets lacked seats, reinforcing their second-class image.

Historically, owners built ballparks. In 1909, Pirates owner Barney Dreyfuss constructed Forbes Field for $2 million in four months. But in the 1950s, cities took over as the authority constructing new ballparks. David Lawrence first proposed a municipal stadium in 1955. Boston, New York, and Brooklyn were losing teams, and he resolved that Pittsburgh would not suffer the same fate. Joe Barr, who followed Lawrence as mayor, shared his commitment. But it would take Pittsburgh $55 million and fifteen years to build Forbes Field's replacement at the headwaters of the Ohio River.

After the University of Pittsburgh purchased Forbes Field in 1958, a new ballpark became more urgent. Pitt leased Forbes Field back to the Pirates, who sublet to the Steelers, for five years. The agreement bought time to build a multiuse stadium that could generate increased revenues and keep both teams in Pittsburgh.

But when the Forbes Field lease expired in 1963, the new stadium was still only a vision. Mayor Barr prevailed upon Pitt to let the Pirates remain at Forbes Field and the Steelers to divide games between Forbes Field and Pitt Stadium, a classic football bowl. The stadium, a disastrous venue for the Steelers in 1958, proved far more attractive this time. Attendance averaged 46,000 a game there, twice what Forbes Field attracted. Overall attendance surpassed a quarter of a million in 1963. But while drawing as many fans as during Sutherland's tenure, the team badly lagged the league average. And Pitt, intent on expanding into the Oakland community, was unwilling to indefinitely accommodate both teams.

The Allegheny Conference on Community Development, which advanced corporate Pittsburgh's agenda, agreed with Lawrence that professional sport was integral to the city's "big league" image. It funded planning and design. A dozen sites were studied and several models proposed, including one on a deck spanning the Monongahela River between downtown and the Southside.

By the early 1960s, all parties agreed that the Northside was the optimal location, returning pro sport to its original venue on the floodplains of the Allegheny. The difficult question was who would pay for it. Art had never squawked about the city's stiff ten percent amusement tax nor threatened to leave town. "I had many tempting offers," he acknowledged, "but I always was afraid to even mention the thought to the governor." Now, it was Lawrence, Mayor Barr, and Pittsburgh's turn to reward Art's loyalty.

Recognizing the teams' regional appeal, Governor Lawrence enlisted Allegheny County's commissioners. The postwar flight to suburbia meant that a majority of season ticket–holders for pro teams now lived outside the city, which was bleeding population. Lawrence ensured state funding and used his influence with the Kennedy administration to secure federal appropriations to help with site preparation. Plans called for an auditorium authority to finance construction by issuing bonds guaranteed by the city and county. The ballclubs would, in turn, commit to forty-year leases to secure the bonds.

But the city-county government alliance crumbled in January 1963. Although Mayor Barr endorsed the funding proposals, two of Allegheny County's three commissioners, William McClelland and John McGrady, balked. They insisted that the Steelers and Pirates pay half of construction costs—a deal-breaker for both clubs. McClelland would praise Rooney at the Saints and Sinner tribute in January 1964, but political enmity between them stemmed back to McClelland's feuds with Coyne and Lawrence. McClelland was up for reelection, and stadium opposition played well with those who disliked public funding or an expanded government role—both sizable constituencies in the land of the Whiskey Rebels. When the county pulled out, the city took complete responsibility for the ballpark and established a Stadium Authority to issue bonds to fund construction.

But McClelland's intransigence delayed the bidding process until mid-1966. By then, inflation had riddled initial budgets and bids came in $12 million over the $26 million estimates, jeopardizing the project. "It would be the greatest mistake this city ever made," Art warned, "to let a few million dollars stand in the way at this point."

While Art used his savvy and connections to keep the stadium initiative alive, Dan focused on design questions. Redesign cut costs and got the project back on track. Part of the savings sacrificed the stadium's signature element, an opening in centerfield so that spectators could look out onto the three rivers. But Art would finally get his stadium.

Meanwhile, Art's protégé, Tom Foerster, unseated McClelland in 1967. Foerster had played football at North Catholic with Dan Rooney and coached the sandlot club on which Art's nephews played. Art had backed the young Northsider when he ran as a Democrat for the state legislature in 1956 against incumbent Harp Vaughan, a member of his first NFL club, and later in his race against McClelland. "Tom Foerster," Jamie Rooney chuckled "lit a candle to my uncle every day of his life."

Television Again

The NFL soared to new heights during the 1960s, while the Steelers sank to new lows. By decade's end, pro football had become America's most popular sport, and Pete Rozelle was anointed the greatest commissioner in sport history. But Rozelle stood on Bert Bell's shoulders. Bell's triumphs, in turn, had been coauthored by Rooney, Mara, Halas, Marshall, and Bidwill, men who worked toward a common end. The ethos and structure they bequeathed to Rozelle were his greatest assets.

Art remained a league stalwart, even while turning over duties to Dan. Sitting by the hotel pool during the 1965 winter meetings in Palm Desert, he discussed Rozelle's tenure. In a concession to California, Art unbuttoned his collar and loosened his tie, but he refrained from putting on sunglasses. Like the man himself, his blue suit, black socks, and black shoes fit in better back East. He puffed on his cigar, squinted into the sun, and spoke frankly. "Here we are, in a plush joint with guys playing golf and soaking up the sun by the pool. It's not surprising that we're stretching the meeting over a week. In the old days, we used to meet day and night so we could get our business over with fast and cut down the hotel tab."

Rozelle had relocated league offices from Philadelphia to Manhattan, a decision reflecting football's evolving relationship with Madison Avenue, and greatly expanded staff. Art neither opposed these changes nor rejected football's growing revenues, but he and the rest of the dwindling old guard—Halas, Marshall, and Tim Mara's sons Jack and Wellington—vigilantly guarded the league's soul. Art had become the league's conscience, and the other owners respected him for it. Nowhere was this clearer than in their dealings with television.

When the league had signed its richest television contract ever, Art sounded a cautionary note. "I honestly feel we would be better off if TV hadn't given us so much money," he reasoned. "It has the players stirring and has other things unsettled and has our budgets geared to taking in this much or more forever. What if television drops us?" he asked. "TV is a hot and cold business which drops guys all the time. Then we have to rip out the whole system, and start over again. Since most owners in this league don't need football for eating money, it might have been better if our success had come more gradually."

Network bidding for NFL rights, a rivalry that Art had fostered, pushed revenues skyward. When the 1964 CBS deal tripled each team's cut of the national package to more than $1 million, the owners were stunned. "Pete Rozelle is a gift from the hand of providence," Art exclaimed publicly. Privately, he told Dan, "You are going to rue the day. This is going to change the business. It's going to bring all kinds of different interests. The television people are now going to start telling you what to do."

After losing the NFL to CBS, NBC negotiated a five-year, $42 million contract with the AFL. The deal secured the new league's future. "No one recognized the new situation faster than Art Rooney," Arthur Daley wrote in the *Times*. "When the news broke, Rooney nodded his head knowingly. 'That does it,' he said. The AFL is here to stay and they no longer have to address us as mister.'" With rapprochement inevitable, Art began working behind the scenes to speed that day.

Racing

After Pennsylvania approved thoroughbred racing in 1967, Art began racing thoroughbreds alongside trotters at Liberty Bell. The twins took charge, with Pat running the thoroughbreds and John handling harness racing. Despite their youth, Pat, John, and Tim were proving to be the most financially savvy members of the family. Of Art's five sons, only Tim, a broker, worked outside the family's growing sport business. Tim, however, shared his father's romance with horses and lent a hand at the farm.

Shamrock was not on a strong business footing, nor had it bred the champion Art wanted. "You can see from this place that I've operated economically," he told a visitor. "Nothing for show." Nevertheless, Art was enamored with the farm. "I think when I retire that I'll move down here to Maryland. Mrs. Rooney loves this place." Seated at the kitchen table on a spring morning, devouring a breakfast prepared by his farm manager's wife, Art was more than content. "I envy the guy with the thoroughbred breeding farm who makes a successful living out of it," he said. "To me, that would be right next to heaven."

Talk of retirement, breeding horses full time, and leaving Pittsburgh was just talk. But with his sons operating his enterprises, Art was freer to indulge his passion for thoroughbreds. He took advantage of state programs to encourage breeding, raced horses, and kept others at Shamrock, including stallions whose stud services could be purchased. Ironman Rogel was named after halfback Fran Rogel and Bill Burns after a KDKA newsman. A third was *Piave, a stallion Art bought from breeder Hughie Grant that he hoped would sire a great horse. Despite his bloodlines, *Piave never panned out; Art called the investment his biggest mistake in breeding.

But, as with football, he was willing to absorb the losses. "It would be hard to say that football isn't my favorite sport," he acknowledged, "but racing is near the top."

Art was part of racing's mythology now, with Rooney stories told and retold. In Dave Anderson's account of the story of the priest with the leaking roof, Art gave a ride to a priest waiting for a bus near the Bowie racetrack. As they chatted, the priest mentioned that a fire had destroyed his church's roof. Art, flush with winnings, asked, "How much would it take to fix it?" When the priest said $7,500, Art peeled off seventy-five $100 bills. The astonished priest exclaimed, "I hope you came by this money honestly." Art replied, "Don't worry, I won it playing the horses. Just say a prayer for me." But Ed Kiely and others, contending that Art knew every con game in the book, doubt that he would have handed over so much cash without establishing the priest's bona fides.

Art himself told the tale of Winnie the Weeper. After cashing winning tickets at Narragansett, Art noticed a bereft elderly woman dressed in black. "She was standing against a wall, crying bitter tears. I walked over and said, 'Ma'am, are you ill? Can I do anything for you?' She turned to me, the tears streaming down. 'No, sir,' she said, 'Nobody can help me now.'" Art enjoyed this story so much that he added texture to it over the years. The woman told Art she could not afford her rent or medicine for her tiny grandson, who was stricken with whooping cough. "I came out to the track, praying that I would have a winner to buy medicine for the little tyke. But my horse lost by a lip, and now I don't know what to do. But it's all right, sir. I'll get by somehow." She told Art to go enjoy lobster and champagne with his winnings. Art gallantly handed her a $100 bill. "Take this, my dear lady," he said. "Say a prayer, and I'm sure something good will turn up for you." When Art told a tout about the sad lady, the man howled. "I thought he would laugh himself sick," Art remembered. "He said, 'You've been taken by Winnie the Weeper. That old doll has been hanging around the $50 cashier's window and working that act with strangers for years.'" Art would grin sheepishly at this point of the tale, before concluding, "I still think The Weeper deserved the money. She gave a great performance."

Art was behind the wheel during a trip to Shamrock with Dan Hamill when their car had a flat tire. Hamill had never driven a car in his life, and Art had never changed a tire. They were struggling to get the wheel off when a woman hanging laundry nearby shouted that they were turning the lug nuts the wrong way. Seeing their confusion, she walked over and changed the tire for them. Art reached in his pocket and peeled a $50 note off his roll, saying, "Lady, I don't know how to thank you." The woman looked at them skeptically and replied, "What are you two, hoodlums? I don't want your money." It was one of their last laughs together. Hamill died not long afterward.

Merger

During the 1965 postseason, Art hired a coach and pushed his colleagues to end their war with the AFL. Buddy Parker's precipitous resignation before the start of the 1965 season had left the Steelers leaderless. The Rooneys promoted assistant coach Mike Nixon to get them through the season, but he was in over his head. Pittsburgh dropped its first five games, won two, and then totally fell apart. Losing the last seven games, Pittsburgh finished 2-12. Remarkably, fans kept coming. Although the Steelers drew well below the league average, ticket sales and television dollars kept them profitable.

Mike Nixon said his only regret was not doing a better job for his boss: "Art Rooney, to me, is one of the greatest men that ever lived." Dan Rooney winnowed the pool of fifty candidates for the head coach position to five men. They interviewed Bill Austin first. The session with Austin, who had crafted Green Bay's offensive line for Vince Lombardi during the Packers' run of titles, went well. When Art called Lombardi afterward, the coaching great endorsed Austin. Art told Dan to offer him the job. Dan protested that they should conduct more interviews, but Art disagreed: "I don't need to talk to them. Lombardi says he's our man."

Meanwhile, Art conferred with owners in the AFL about ending hostilities. "I have good friends in the other league," he acknowledged, mentioning the New York Jets' Sonny Werblin, the Buffalo Bills' Ralph Wilson, and the Boston Patriots' Billy Sullivan, whose uncle had printed forms for Art's racetracks. No NFL owner was more willing to end the war. It was in Art's best interests to do so, because Pittsburgh, more than most teams, could not compete for players, especially good backups, as salaries escalated. But Art also believed it was in the NFL's best interests. With the AFL's survival guaranteed by NBC, Art escalated talks—as he put it—"casually and informally, but without authority."

"When the AFL came into being," Art said, "I figured it was here to stay. I was one of the few that did. I felt that television would keep it in business." Art, Roy McHugh wrote, had "seen the handwriting on the balance sheets. Pete Rozelle saw the handwriting, too, and in the spring of 1966, pro football's landscape was redrawn. The two leagues agreed to merge and play a championship game—what became the Super Bowl—in 1967.

"It was inevitable," Art said. He endorsed interleague play and the new championship as win-win solutions. The NFL was launched on a trajectory to become the nation's preeminent sporting pastime. The Steelers, however, slunk back to their losing ways.

Coach Austin

Bill Austin reignited hopes of a turnaround. A disciplinarian, he advocated Lombardi's simple but overpowering offensive style. Scrimmages had not been so demanding since John Michelosen coached the team. "He wants us to hit hard," linebacker Bill Saul said. "He doesn't only want us to make the tackle but to shake the other man up when we do."

Austin forbad players to drink at bars and instituted a curfew with bed checks. Pat Livingston was shocked that the notoriously freewheeling Steelers were adapting to the new regime. Parker's "anything goes policy" was out. All members of the team's traveling party now wore coats and ties on the road. Nobody told Art, who found himself in violation of the policy when he met the team at the airport after they broke camp. He sheepishly borrowed a tie from reporter Jack Sell.

Austin cleaned house. The new coach was spared one headache when the team released John Henry Johnson, now thirty-six, before camp. After Johnson pulled a ligament in the previous season's opener, his year was effectively over. The only Steeler to ever gain over a thousand yards rushing in a season, Johnson ranked third in NFL career rushing attempts. Nobody had delivered as many punishing blocks. But Johnson, unhappy with his salary, wrote the Rooneys repeatedly seeking to renegotiate. "John Henry would tell us in these letters he couldn't play football unless he was happy and we knew he wasn't going to be happy," Dan said. Unwilling to reopen Johnson's contract, Dan released him. Never one to dissemble, Dan added, "He always has been a guy that's dissatisfied. And he's not going to help us that much." Johnson was just as frank. This was business, he said, not personal. Years later, Johnson had Art present him for enshrinement into the Hall of Fame.

Art said his team would surprise opponents in 1966 but cautioned patience. "With the breaks, we could have a winner inside of three years." The key was staying healthy. NFL seasons were campaigns of attrition, and Pittsburgh had faltered when Art could not replace injured players. "One of the biggest things [Austin] has to overcome," Art emphasized, "is the defeatist attitude and losing complex around here."

The NFL scheduled Pittsburgh's first three games at home, and more than 37,000 fans came to the Pitt Stadium opener, twice as many as the pennant-contending Pirates drew to Forbes Field that afternoon a few blocks away. The contrast reflected a phenomenon still not widely recognized: football was surpassing baseball as America's favorite game. After surrendering a 14-point lead and settling for a tie against the Giants, the Steelers beat the Lions in their second game—their first win over Detroit in seventeen years. The defense basked in the approbation of the fans, who delivered thunderous ovations every time it left the field. "I've never seen a Pittsburgh crowd act this way before," defensive back Jim Bradshaw exclaimed. "It was a great, wonderful thing." But not for long. Pittsburgh lost the next five in a row and finished 5-8-1.

"Austin deserved a second year," Dan Rooney reflected, "but after that we would have been better off firing him." Austin could not be Lombardi any more than Michelosen could channel Sutherland. Austin delivered inspirational pregame talks, but Lloyd Voss, who had played for Lombardi, told teammates, "That's the exact speech Vince Lombardi gave in Green Bay. I've heard it five times." Austin could not do what Lombardi had done in Green Bay—win. "Austin was a foolish taskmaster," Dan Rooney concluded. His treatment of players troubled Art. "My father established something that I tried to follow," Dan said, "in that we treated everybody here fairly, as a human being." Art watched out for players' welfare in ways that few owners matched. After Pitt halfback Paul Martha, the team's top draft pick, said he intended to become a doctor, Art encouraged him to pursue his studies while he played. When Martha realized that studying medicine while playing ball wouldn't work out, Art proposed law school. "The next day," Martha said, "I get a call from the dean of law at Duquesne telling me that I was enrolled. He said, 'You start tomorrow night.'"

359

Austin did not share Art's concern for players. Their values worked at cross-purposes, which might have been tolerable, even invigorating, if the team had been winning. As it was, the players kept their affection for Art, but lost respect for Austin.

Rookie Rocky Bleier, a sixteenth-round draft pick from Notre Dame, was among the disillusioned. He enjoyed Art, who invited him to breakfast his first morning in town, but thought that Austin had lost control of the team. Rocky's season ended prematurely when he was drafted into the military in December. Art sent him game clippings along with notes wishing him well.

Austin's dismal three-season record was 11-28-3. Not even Art, and certainly not Dan, would accept a .282 winning percentage, especially with gate receipts down $150,000 in 1968. Austin's contract was up, and he was gone. Bidding the coach farewell, Roy McHugh acknowledged that Austin had turned the Steelers from a rowdy, beer-guzzling bunch into a disciplined and dutiful group. "The trouble was," McHugh concluded, "they were well-behaved losers."

Race

Austin had another liability: he got along poorly with African Americans. By the time Austin arrived, black power politics had radicalized the civil rights movement, and just about everything, including football, was viewed through the lens of race.

Although the NFL was under scrutiny, Art's past insulated him from criticism. *Pittsburgh Courier* sportswriter Ric Roberts offered Art an unsolicited testimonial: "The Negro players on the team, to a man, swear by the veteran owner." While "accepted wisdom" held that African Americans were neither intelligent nor composed enough to play quarterback, Art declared that "color has nothing to do with individual capabilities in any endeavor, and [I] wish it understood that the Steelers will use any brilliant quarterback we can recruit, regardless of color." Roberts believed Art without qualification: "Certainly the most popular and beloved of all NFL owners, especially with reference to newsmen, coast to coast, Mr. Rooney has many lifetime Negro friends and acquaintances."

That became apparent in April 1968 when Pittsburgh went up in flames. More than five hundred fires blazed over a five-day span after Martin Luther King Jr.'s assassination in Memphis. Gangs took to the streets of the Hill, Homewood, and Art's Northside. While many Pittsburghers succumbed to fear, Art remained unperturbed. His part of the Northside had gotten poorer and blacker over the years, but he and Kass stayed put. Art, who took neighborhood kids to ball games and refereed their pickup games in the street, felt totally secure there.

Jack O'Malley was the priest at St. Joseph's in Manchester, a black neighborhood abutting Art's street. "After King's assassination," he recalled, "it was very dangerous. I'd come home late at night and Art would be out there with a cigar, walking around the block by himself." O'Malley, known for his courage and activism, worried about Art, who had played ball with his father. "I thought, 'Man, this is dangerous.' But Art was so endeared to the people and to the kids especially, I don't think that anyone would dare touch him. He was one of the few white untouchables in that neighborhood."

Wanting to be proactive regarding race, Dan Rooney asked sportswriter Ric Roberts why his editor at the *Courier*, Bill Nunn Jr., rarely came around. Nunn responded, "Tell him as long as the Steelers have the approach they have to black athletes, they never have to worry about me being down there." Dan mulled Nunn's comments over, then asked him to lunch with Art. Nunn was willing to take the Rooneys seriously because of Art's friendship with his father, William Nunn Sr., the *Courier*'s former managing editor. Art had tangled with Nunn on the sandlots when Nunn played for the Homestead Grays and talked politics and sport with him, Gus Greenlee, and Cum Posey at the Crawford Grill. During the 1950s, Nunn Sr. had found housing for black Steelers on their trips into the segregated South. His son, a standout athlete at Westinghouse High and West Virginia State, became sports editor in 1950 after Wendell Smith, the first African American journalist elected to the baseball Hall of Fame, left the *Courier*.

Bill Nunn's critique of the Steelers went beyond a coach with a bad attitude. The Steelers, Nunn argued, were indifferent to black colleges. The *Courier*, a flagship paper for the black press, selected a team of black All-Americans each year and feted them at a banquet in Pittsburgh. When Buddy Parker was coach, he had attended the *Courier* banquet and stayed half the night talking football. But Austin and the rest of the organization skipped the affair.

Nunn had covered black football and cultivated close relationships with coaches. At Grambling, he stayed at coach Eddie Robinson's home. At Morgan State, he was the president's guest. He knew what black colleges thought about the Steelers and spelled it out for the Rooneys. When Nunn finished his litany of slights, Dan asked, "Why don't you help change it? Why don't you come and work for us?" Nunn said he had a job, but Dan countered that he could work part-time. Nunn began scouting black college football during Austin's final season.

"Art Jr. was not too anxious for me to come on board," Nunn remembered. But as scouting director, Art Jr. realized that the organization needed to adapt. Pittsburgh had ignored black schools, focusing on higher profile conferences. Nunn guided Art Jr. beyond that paradigm, and the team began tapping the talent at black colleges the NFL had previously overlooked.

Few men had higher credibility or better contacts in black football. "Bill Nunn," Dan Rooney reflected, "gave the Steelers a total leg up on everybody." The Steelers were immediately welcomed where they had been scorned. Though he had limited experience with football, Nunn could identify exceptional athletes. "One doggone thing in Western Pennsylvania," he exclaimed, "you've seen good athletes coming up."

After the season, the Rooneys asked Nunn to work full time. He requested time to think it over. As managing editor of the *Courier*, he had one of the most prestigious positions in the black press. But the black press was slipping as the mainstream press integrated. When an out-of-town chain bought the *Courier* in 1970 and asked Nunn to relocate to Chicago, he balked and joined the team full time. "A lot of people figured I wasn't making that much of an upward move by leaving the paper," Nunn recalled.

Nunn's arrival catalyzed larger changes. "I felt that we had to go out and bring African Americans into the organization," Dan explained.

"It was a conscious effort that we should have black coaches, black scouts, and front office personnel." And he followed through, Nunn confirmed.

Nunn's hiring solidified Art's reputation in black Pittsburgh. A generation of black sandlot athletes already regarded Art as a fair-minded, progressive man who had never tolerated racial abuse at games. Some referred to him as a Robin Hood, as willing to help African Americans as whites. When the Steelers were criticized, the *Courier* resolutely defended him: "The Negro stars who played for him, like Brady Keys, Perry, John Baker, et al., go into rhapsodies about Prexy Rooney . . . 'My life would have been nothing,' vows Attorney [Lowell] Perry, 'had God not given me the privilege of having him in my corner.'" The *Courier* noted that Pittsburgh would welcome twenty black players to camp in 1968, including three of its last four top picks.

Loss and Grieving

Art lost more than football games in the late 1960s. In April 1967, state troopers stopped Art on the Pennsylvania Turnpike to tell him that his mother had been taken to Divine Providence Hospital. Maggie Rooney, eighty-seven, had collapsed at her home on Perrysville Avenue. She died that evening.

In 1968, former coaches Luby DiMelio and Joe Bach died. Bach dropped dead following his induction into the Curbstone Coaches Hall of Fame, moments after Art had left the ballroom. But the death that shook Art the most came in November. While David Lawrence was speaking to a Democratic Party rally at the Syria Mosque near Forbes Field, his heart went into arrest. He fell into a coma and did not recover. Art was stunned; their friendship had been a constant of his life. Since leaving office, Lawrence had served Kennedy and Johnson as head of the President's Commission on Equal Opportunity in Housing. Tributes poured in from across the country, but Art, who had recently celebrated Lawrence's seventy-seventh birthday with him at the racetrack, delivered his eulogy privately to Lawrence's family. This loss was too personal to discuss publicly.

Back on Track

While his older sons shouldered responsibility for football, Art played the horses and alighted for a spell on two new interests: hockey and soccer. Art's connections with hockey were limited. The great Canadian hockey player, Lionel Conacher, had suited up with the Rooneys on Duquesne's football team in the 1920s, and Art had toyed with bringing a pro team to Pittsburgh in 1932.

But in June 1965, the NHL announced it would expand from six to twelve teams. Despite having only one American player, the NHL was setting attendance records and believed that expansion would generate a network television deal.

Ten cities, including Pittsburgh, sought franchises. State senator Jack McGregor led Pittsburgh's syndicate. Art had helped McGregor win election in 1962. "He had a huge following that was ready to be primed every election day," McGregor remembered. "Every member of his family seemed to have legions and legions of loyal friends." But Art declined McGregor's entreaties to join his syndicate.

"Mr. Rooney told me he would not mix sports," McGregor said, "but would try to help us out." Art knew two of the NHL owners on the expansion committee: Chicago Black Hawks owner Jim Norris, and his half-brother Bruce, who owned the Detroit Red Wings. Jim Norris, a horseman whose International Boxing Club had dominated boxing after the war, had copromoted the Charles–Walcott championship in Pittsburgh. McGregor came to Art's hotel in New York and listened as he lobbied the brothers over the phone. "He leaned real hard on them," McGregor remembered. "He told them that this would be a big shot of adrenaline for the city." According to McGregor, Buffalo had been the likely choice for the sixth franchise. Art turned it around. "The clincher was Art telling the Norrises: 'You owe it to me.' I never asked him why."

McGregor could not have asked for a better reference. Art lent his voice in public, arguing that the team would thrive in Pittsburgh. "He changed the odds around completely," McGregor said. Pittsburgh got its franchise, and Art bought season tickets for the new team: the Pittsburgh Penguins.

His other new venture was soccer. Although the game had once flourished in Western Pennsylvania's mining patches and immigrant communities, Art knew little about it. Other sportsmen, however, were willing to see if the most popular game in the world could catch on in the
United States. With prominent investors, and CBS offering a multimillion dollar television deal, they created the National Professional Soccer League in 1967. The Rooneys bought the Philadelphia franchise and
named it the Spartans.

"Dad thinks this league has a better chance than the NFL did in 1933,"
club president John Rooney told the press. But Art knew the investment was risky. "Right now we don't even have a coach, a player or
even a soccer ball," John admitted. Art traveled with the team and was
intrigued by the players, who spoke limited English. "The Chief loved
it," John explained. "He came to every game and kept saying, 'This reminds me of the old days.'" The front office and the players ate and
traveled together the way clubs had in the 1930s. "You ran it from your
vest pocket, like he must have run the Steelers," John said.

The Spartans finished tied for first in their inaugural season, 1967,
but were shut out of the title game on a tiebreaker. The club lost money,
and the Rooneys convened at the Roosevelt Hotel to discuss its future.
Art and the twins, especially John, loved the sport. But, unlike football,
where he had sustained losses for decades, Art was unwilling to subsi-
dize the Spartans. He pushed to terminate involvement. "Let's vote,"
he demanded. "Let's get this over with. We've got the votes." Art, despite having become hard of hearing, caught Pat muttering, "Don't be
so sure." His father snorted, "Listen, you, we've got the votes or *you*
won't have a vote." The vote went Art's way.

Déjà Vu

Late in April 1968, as Pittsburgh sorted out the disturbances following Marin Luther King Jr.'s assassination, ground was broken for the
new stadium. In deference to the cold, raw day, the ceremony was brief.
Olympian Jesse Owens, mindful of the outbursts, delivered the featured
remarks. "As long as men of all color and creeds can play baseball and
football together here," he said, "as long as they share the team spirit,

this hallowed ground is worthwhile under the eyes of God." To that, Art said amen.

Many at the groundbreaking missed David Lawrence. Mayor Barr and Commissioner Foerster had urged the stadium authority to name the stadium in his honor, but it opted for Three Rivers Stadium. Barr strove to capture Lawrence's vision of the project. "What we begin here today," he said, "is more than a stadium, although a great stadium it is to be. It is a part of a common denominator. For as the inscription on the shovels read—it is on this ground that every citizen will know that 'He will always have a ball game to watch and a home team to cheer.'"

Art felt a sense of déjà vu. The stadium would stand on the site of Phipps Field, where he had played after moving to the Northside. It was minutes away from his North Lincoln Avenue home. With Dan holding a football, Art, sixty-seven years old, attempted a field goal. Wearing street shoes and declining to take off his suit coat, he barely missed as winds swirling off the Allegheny River altered the ball's trajectory. Future kickers on the site would suffer similar indignities. Unfazed, Art tried again and the ball split the black-and-gold wrapped goalposts.

The More Things Change . . .

As the Steelers crumbled during Austin's final season, Art's inability to win went from embarrassing to intriguing. No one got better press than Art, who represented a sporting culture dissolving before the onslaught of television, advertising, and merchandizing. But the persistent subtext was that he was a loser and always would be. "Little Art Rooney," sportswriter Morton Moss wondered, "will he ever win?" Art never dodged the issue. "My gosh, it gets worse all the time," he admitted. "The desires and frustrations are terrible. Besides, people . . . must think a guy who can go so long without winning must be pretty dumb. They have to think you don't know how to get in out of the rain." Art, Moss wrote, was troubled by "the erosion of the human element, a bygone personal touch that has evaporated with the advance of scientific management."

Art put it differently. "Everything moves so fast now. We old guys, you know, we live in the past and our loyalties and friendships are to the past. It used to be that you had some time to sit around and talk to people when you came to town." For Art, getting there was a communal endeavor. He preferred trains to planes. "The way it's become, you're in and out of a town before you know it. I like to get to town and renew old acquaintances. There's such a speedup. I miss the companionship we had. That's true in all sports. Something is missing from the human side of it." At the same time, he could not deny that television's bounty and the stadium would make the future brighter for his team.

But nobody predicted a dramatic turnaround, and everywhere the Steelers played, stories contrasted the weakness of Art's teams with the strength of his character. "Art Rooney deserves a title," Rich Koster wrote in the *St. Louis Globe-Democrat*. "If sentiment and the law of averages were considered in the determination of NFL titles, the Pittsburgh Steelers would surely be lopsided favorites." Francis Stann observed in Washington's *Sunday Star* that "Art Rooney is the kind of man that people have in mind when they use the cliché, 'If I couldn't win, I'm glad he did.'"

Jets owner Sonny Werblin chimed in. "You have one of the finest men in sports anywhere," he said of Rooney at Toots Shor's one evening. "If he would only let his head dictate decisions instead of his heart." When the Steelers played Cleveland, Benny Marshall wrote, "His presence honored our city," even if his team stunk out the joint. Art blamed himself for the Steelers' woes. "If I had started out paying much attention to it," he acknowledged, "we could have won. I had these other businesses, and maybe I spent too much time at the racetrack." Marshall spoke for many: "Thirty-five years, going on thirty-six, and it hasn't happened, but this Rooney will go on trying, and hoping, and I can think of nothing which would please me more than for the lightning to strike just once."

Art protested the notion that he was a gracious loser. "It hurts too much to laugh," he said, "and I'm too old to cry." Art kept his emotions as close to the vest as his picks at the track. But losing, he said, never stopped hurting. "When I get home after losing a game, I don't want to talk football. I don't want to watch reruns, and most of all I don't want to read the morning paper." He could not duck the tag of sport's "most popular loser."

367

17

Changing History

1970–71

The press had Art's obituary as America's lovable loser ready to roll. A chorus of Pittsburghers hardened by defeat would have shouted amen to that. But Art wasn't through yet. His glasses were thicker, his hair whiter, and his body pudgier, but he was just beginning a decade in which a lifetime of loyalty would be rewarded. After hitting bottom in 1968, the Steelers sailed into the unknown. Their ensuing voyage would make them a more enduring symbol for Pittsburgh than steel. Along the way, Rooney became the patron saint of sport, heralded throughout the land as the nice guy who finished first.

Hiring Noll

After the 1968 season, Art undertook the familiar task of hiring a coach. He had gone through eighteen since 1933, but only Sutherland and Parker had compiled winning records. Dan took the lead this time, and he was determined to get it right.

At the team party, Art suddenly decided that Ara Parseghian was the man for the job. Within minutes, Art Jr. was on the phone with Notre Dame's coach, who graciously answered that he was happy in South Bend. When his son reported back, Art said, "If it had worked out, that would have been great. But no matter, every time you go to Notre Dame from now on, you'll get a real nice reception."

Next, the Rooneys courted Joe Paterno over breakfast in Miami where Penn State was preparing for the Orange Bowl. Art brought Vince Lombardi along to persuade Paterno to jump to the pros. When conversation turned to how faith sustained them in crisis, Art told Paterno about his brother the Franciscan while Paterno countered with his mother, who prayed daily to the Infant of Prague for Penn State's success. According to Paterno, Art upped the ante, claiming that his sisters were nuns who prayed constantly for the Steelers.

A few days later, Penn State rallied from a 14–0 deficit against Kansas. On the game's last play, a Penn State touchdown made the score 14–13. Playing to win rather than tie, Paterno went for a 2-point conversion. It failed, but Penn State got another chance when Kansas was penalized for having twelve men on the field. This time, Penn State converted and won 15–14. Art wired Paterno, "WILL TRADE MY BROTHER AND TWO SISTERS FOR YOUR MOTHER."

Paterno turned down the trade and the job. Dan then interviewed former Eagles coach Nick Skorich and Colts assistant Chuck Noll. The Rooneys knew Skorich, who had played and coached for them, and had glowing recommendations about Noll. Art Jr. heard his name mentioned every time he asked scouts for suggestions. But Dan was skeptical of old boy endorsements after his father had been swayed by Lombardi's recommendation of Bill Austin. Dan would decide, with Art's counsel, after conducting his own interviews.

Dan promised Baltimore coach Don Shula he would not interview Noll until after his team played in Super Bowl III on January 12, 1969. The game featured two Western Pennsylvania native sons. John Unitas, who played in black high-top shoes with a no-nonsense approach, epitomized NFL tradition. Joe Namath personified sport's increasingly flamboyant future. Broadway Joe, who had guaranteed a Jets victory, delivered a 16–7 upset. The next day, Dan and Noll talked in Miami. Impressed, Dan asked Noll to meet his father.

Chuck Noll had played for Cleveland's Benedictine High School and cocaptained his University of Dayton team, where his nickname, "The Pope," testified to his "infallible" grasp of the game. Browns coach Paul Brown drafted the undersized Noll and used him at linebacker and as a messenger guard relaying plays to the quarterback. "After a while," Brown confessed, "Chuck could have called the plays himself without any help from the bench. That's how smart he was." Seven seasons later, Noll made a smooth transition to coaching.

In Pittsburgh, Dan, Art, and Noll sat at the Roosevelt Hotel restaurant table where Art conducted business. Art knew that Noll, thirty-seven, would not raise hell like Johnny Blood nor pick ponies like Walt Kiesling. No matter; he wasn't looking for a new buddy. Art's questions were more personal than programmatic. But Dan, who was writing an organizational manual for the Steelers, focused on Noll's vision of how to build a team. Noll, thoughtful and straightforward, asked the Rooneys if their goal was the championship. They said it was. It was the only answer Noll would have accepted, although he cautioned not to expect a quick turnaround.

A third Rooney crashed the interview. Art Jr. had come by the office to prepare for the draft. "I elbowed my way into the meeting," he recalled. Art Jr. had his own agenda and was not shy about raising it. Three years younger than Dan, he was a bigger, more physically imposing man, and by now, thoroughly invested in the team. Learning scouting from the ground up, he had developed confidence in his ability to identify talented athletes and the conviction that Pittsburgh had to change how it built its roster.

Art Jr. had been feverishly preparing for the draft. For the first time in years, the Steelers had kept most of their picks. At Jack Butler's suggestion, they had ranked players by their abilities regardless of position. They wanted to select the best athletes available. Meanwhile, Bill Nunn had opened Art Jr.'s eyes to the pool of outstanding black players that had formed as black youth shifted from baseball to football. Art Jr., who was beginning to know his way around Morgan State and Grambling, immediately challenged Noll regarding black players and the draft. "My father and brother were shooting me looks," Art Jr. remembered, "but I was on a quest for finding good football players and building from the draft." Noll did not flinch. He didn't care about race or religion. He wanted men who could become great players, meaning smart, coachable, and athletic. Noll also valued the draft. Although put off by Noll's professorial style, Art Jr. found him absolutely straightforward. "I never got the idea he was telling us what he thought we wanted to hear."

Noll was adamant that he would have the final say on players. "I didn't like that at all," Art Jr. recalled. As scouting director, he wanted to make those decisions. "I wanted to get right into it with him. Dad finally put me in my place and shut me up." The tension evaporated and the interview continued. Afterward, Art Jr. complained, "I'm doing the work out there. I'm the one on the road all the time and I want all the responsibility, too." Art disagreed. "You're in charge of scouting and getting ready for the draft," he said. "The coach decides on players." To Dan, Art said simply, "I was impressed with him. Keep him on the list."

After a sleepless night, Dan offered Noll the job. At a press conference introducing the Steelers' nineteenth head coach, a reporter joked that Pittsburgh's teams were all on losing streaks. "This is the City of Losers," he told Noll. Without missing a beat, Noll responded, "We'll change history."

Rebuilding

Noll was impatient to end the press conference. He would not sleep that night. With the draft in the morning, he had film to watch and data to study. Noll and the Rooneys stood by the blackboards in Art Jr.'s narrow office where players' names were listed with scouts' ratings, their speed, height, weight, and school. Noll listened intently as Art Jr. evaluated them. "Afterward," Art Jr. remembered with satisfaction, "Dan told me it was my finest hour."

The upside of Pittsburgh's dismal 2-11-1 record in 1968 was that it had the fourth pick in the draft. Everyone agreed that if North Texas defensive lineman Joe Greene were available, he would be their pick.

Pittsburgh selected Greene, Notre Dame quarterback Terry Hanratty, who was from nearby Butler, and Oklahoma lineman Jon Kolb, who would anchor the offensive line, in the first three rounds and Arkansas A&M's L. C. Greenwood in the tenth. The Steelers almost missed out on Greenwood. Though his kids were sick, Art Jr. had flown to Arkansas to evaluate a player. A&M's coaches showed him film of Greenwood, a tall, slender player who flew around the field, running players down. At camp that summer, Art Jr. said he saw little potential in Greenwood. On the contrary, Noll responded, if he remained healthy, L. C. could be something special. The draft began turning the Steelers around.

Nobody counted on Rocky Bleier being anything special. He had played sparingly before his induction into the military late in the season. Rocky came through Pittsburgh in April en route to Vietnam. He had missed the last three games in 1968 but figured he would ask Fran Fogarty if the Steelers would pay him anyway. Before Fogarty could answer, Art shouted from the adjoining room, "Fran, give him what he wants." When Fogarty replied that NFL rules prevented the team from paying the salary, Art said, "Then give him his bonus." Bleier was eligible for a $1,500 bonus if half of his playing time had been at running back, which it had not been. Fogarty slipped it to him anyway.

Rocky was in Vietnam during the preseason when the Steelers went to Green Bay. Rocky's parents owned a restaurant in nearby Appleton. Bleier's Restaurant was jammed for Friday night fish fry, people two deep at bar, when Art approached Ellen Bleier and said, "You're too young to be Mrs. Bleier." They chatted about Rocky, who was in his fourth month in Vietnam, and Art said they'd like a table. He told Rocky that his mother smiled and handed him a number. For years, Art teased Rocky about his mother telling his boss to take a number— whether or not it happened.

Later that month, North Vietnamese forces ambushed Rocky's unit near Khe Sanh. Rocky was hit in the thigh; a grenade shattered his right foot and shrapnel pierced his legs. When Art got Rocky's letter telling him what had happened, he looked at Art Jr. and said, "Rocky says he got hit by a grenade but he can still play." Art paused: "Yeah, he can still play." Art didn't believe it. As one surgery led to another, nobody but Rocky thought he would play again, and Rocky wasn't so sure, either.

The New Era

The Steelers had a few solid players. Ray Mansfield, picked up for the $100 waiver fee in 1964, was a steady presence at center, and four teammates played in the 1968 Pro Bowl, including linebacker Andy Russell.

Russell had never planned to play professionally; he had a ROTC commitment to fulfill after finishing college in 1963. During exam week, somebody congratulated him for being drafted. Thinking he meant the military draft, Russell said his ROTC commitment precluded that. To Russell's surprise, Pittsburgh had drafted him in the sixteenth round.

After realizing that he could play the season before entering the military, Russell signed. Buddy Parker, however, let Russell know how little he thought of him at camp. Rookies, he yelled, lost games. Absorbing Parker's disdain, Russell realized that he was training camp fodder for the vets. But he made the team despite Parker's aversion to rookies. On opening day, starting linebacker John Reger convulsed and swallowed his tongue. When his replacement turned an ankle, Russell went in. He would make the All Pro Rookie team.

Russell spent the next two years in the military and returned to play for Bill Austin, who made him defensive captain. He was a link to Pittsburgh's last winning season in 1963. When Noll asked him to come by, Russell figured his new coach was going to congratulate him for making the 1969 Pro Bowl.

Instead Noll said, "I've been watching you on game film. Frankly, I don't like the way you play." Noll thought that Russell played too aggressively. By trying to make the big play—an interception or sack—he was often out of position, allowing opponents to capitalize on his mistakes. Noll told Russell, "I'm going to change the way you play."

Not every player was ready for Noll's blunt assessment. Some, habituated to losing, smirked that they had been here before Noll came and would be here when he was gone. "We would talk about what was wrong with us," Russell said. "We felt that we had talent. Why couldn't we win? We figured it was lack of effort."

Noll disagreed, "I can tell you why you're losing. It's because you're not very good. It's not that you're not trying, but your technique is poor and you're guessing too much on the field. If your strategy and techniques are flawed, it doesn't matter how hard you try. You're destined to fail." Noll wasn't looking for heroics. Winning, he said, resulted from playing intelligently, with proper technique, within a system. I'm going to teach you how to play this game to the numbers. But," he concluded, "I'm going to have to get rid of most of you."

At practice afterward, players were making lots of noise, straining to impress Noll. "Quiet," he said, "I don't want any noise. You don't win games with noise. We don't need any pseudo-chatter." Noll expected players to motivate themselves. "He was able to pick guys who were driven to succeed," Russell reflected. "He'd teach them, but they would bring their own motivation."

Confrontation: August 1969

During training camp, protests shut down the Three Rivers Stadium worksite. The Black Construction Coalition had been pressing building trades unions to open their ranks to African Americans and contractors to hire them. Few changes had been made. Gathering at the worksite, demonstrators marched on to the Manchester Bridge, where some of them battled construction workers and police. Hundreds were arrested and scores injured. When Mayor Barr persuaded builders to declare a five-day moratorium, white construction workers, upset by their loss of pay and what they saw as capitulation to the protesters, stormed city hall.

During the crisis, Nate "Available" Smith, a former middleweight who rarely ducked a fight, came to see the Rooneys. Art had often called him the day of a Rooney–McGinley card to say, "Come to Duquesne Gardens tonight and bring your trunks. If someone doesn't show, we'll put you in the ring." Smith had been on the undercard for the Charles–Walcott title bout in 1951 as a fill-in. His bout would occur if another fight was needed to allow the championship to begin in prime time. Smith never got into the ring, but he gave tickets for the fight to a union representative. In return, Smith got a membership card in Local 66 of the Operating Engineers. He was among its first black members.

A charismatic activist committed to redressing workplace discrimination, Smith trusted Art. "At holidays, he'd make sure I had a turkey on my table," Smith remembered. "I'd call him up if I was broke and he'd take care of me." But this meeting was emotional. He told the Rooneys that they should refuse to play in the stadium unless African Americans were hired to build it. The Rooneys knew that black men were excluded from the trades. Getting a coveted union card often required having a relative on the job.

"We'll do what we can," Dan said. Smith said that they had to do more than that: "You have to make a statement." Recognizing that Smith was right, Dan and Art drove him to Latrobe to address the players.

Fearful of splitting the players along racial lines, the Rooneys said the only way they would do anything was as a team. Smith talked with the black players and then the entire squad. "Our players didn't know what to do," Dan reflected. But they emerged from the meeting in agreement; Dan and safety Paul Martha would write a statement for the team arguing that black workers deserved a chance. That satisfied Smith. When a halt in federal funding led to the Pittsburgh Plan, which would bring 1,250 blacks into local union ranks over the next four years, the Steelers returned to football.

Marshall

That August, George Preston Marshall died at the age of seventy-two. He had been sick for months, partially paralyzed and unable to speak. Rooney and Halas went to see their comrade one last time. "He couldn't take part in the conversation, so we had to talk in front of him," Art said. "It was very hard," especially given how vocal Marshall had been. "Finally Halas asked the nurse for a drink. She brought a quart of whiskey and Halas took a water glass full." Art, who had not had a drink in twenty years, abstained. "[Halas] was not a drinking man, but he drank it down, and now he got loose, real loose, talking to Marshall about a lot of things that happened in the past, and pretty soon Marshall was laughing and crying." That reduced all three men to tears. "I told Marshall I'd need his wheelchair to get Halas home and he laughed some more. I was real proud of Halas that day."

Now, only Halas and Rooney remained of the old guard, and Art was feeling his own mortality. His hearing was deteriorating, and cataracts made reading difficult. He lost his friend and coworker when Fran Fogarty died hours after his daughter's wedding.

Joe Greene

Noll built around defense, with Joe Greene the keystone. A 6-foot-4, 275-pound defensive tackle from North Texas State, Greene's physical talents were enormous, and his will to win was even more imposing. So was his anger at losing, which the Steelers did all too often his rookie season.

They won their first game in 1969, but lost with mind-numbing regularity from then on. Still, Greene played well, even in defeat. After Cleveland beat Pittsburgh, Browns guard Gene Hickerson praised him: "That seventy-five. He's going to be great." Hickerson didn't know yet that "seventy-five" was Greene. "He's strong as a bull and so blasted quick. I don't know how anyone's going to handle him in a year or two." Greene's frustration, however, mounted with each defeat. When opposing linemen tried to stop Greene by illegally holding him, he lashed back. Against Minnesota, Greene committed two personal fouls and was ejected. "It's like a nightmare," he said afterward. "Everything goes against us, and there's nothing we can do." Art was stoical: "Heaven knows, the law of averages ought to be working in our favor."

In late October, Pittsburgh played Washington, whose coach, Vince Lombardi, was dying from cancer. It was Steeler alumni weekend, and former players were introduced on the field. Although he didn't consider himself an ex-player, Rocky Bleier attended. It was his first time in Pittsburgh since Vietnam. "When I was wounded," Rocky recalled, "Art wrote, 'The team's not doing well. We need you.'" That cheered him up. So did the ovation he received as he limped on to the field using crutches.

In the visitors' locker room, Bill Austin, now a Redskins assistant, cursed at Pat Livingston and commanded the sportswriter to leave "his dressing room." When Livingston stood his ground, Austin grabbed him in a hammerlock. They tussled until Lombardi intervened, shouting, "Stop it, Bill! Don't be so childish." Livingston deadpanned, "Now you might understand why he was a 2-11 coach."

The season's most important contest was a game between two clubs going nowhere—Pittsburgh, 1-7, and Chicago, 0-6. The Bears played like contenders, smacking the Steelers from one end of Soldier Field to the other. "Our team looks horrible," Art muttered in the first quarter. Pittsburgh looked worse by game's end. But at season's end, it turned out to be the best loss in franchise history: it would give the Steelers the number one draft pick.

Though they kept losing, players did not lose respect for their coach. "Noll drove me crazy," recalled Andy Russell, "but he made me a better player." In November, the Steelers played St. Louis. Early in the game, Russell bit on a play-action pass and surrendered a touchdown. "I'm the first guy to know that I made a mistake. I came off the field expecting to get ripped, but Noll didn't say a word." Russell paced back and forth until Noll approached him. "He said 'Andy,' instead of 'thirty-four" or 'Russell,' which is how he usually called me. 'What was your thought process on that play when we gave up a touchdown?' He didn't say 'you,' he said 'we.'" Russell replied that St. Louis invariably ran off tackle from that formation. "Coach," Russell said, "I can't believe they ran play action without setting me up first with the run." Noll paused, then smiled. He told Russell that it was good to know opponents' tendencies. "But instead of guessing, if you had read your keys, you would have seen the tackle was back on his haunches getting ready to pass block." Russell absorbed Noll's point. "I said to myself, I want to play for that guy." In the fourth quarter, as Pittsburgh fell behind 47–10, Art sighed, "They ought to refund these people their money."

But "Rooney U" finally had a professor at the helm and was playing better by season's end. After Dallas beat Pittsburgh, Cowboys coach Tom Landry appraised them. "With Greene, they're something else. Greene's as good a football player as has come into this league in years."

Art had befriended Greene when he first came to town after the draft. "What's the problem?" Art asked when he saw Greene, who was upset about contract talks, hanging around the office. When Greene answered that he and the team were $10,000 apart, Art shouted to Dan, "Give it to him. He's worth it." Greene said he often thought about that moment. "That easy gesture made me want to be worth it, whether I was or not."

Greene fought through the disheartening season. "Sometimes it gets discouraging," he admitted. "But we always have that next game to look forward to. We feel like Pittsburgh is the team of the future." Art realized that Joe needed something Noll could not give him. "He was a very angry guy," Dan Rooney remembered. "When he came here, he didn't trust us at all." While it took Dan and Joe years to establish trust, Art quickly became Joe's friend. "My father respected him and saw that he was a person of class," Dan said. Greene's rage made him special. "To become a great player," Dan recalled, "he had to channel that anger."

Greene's play and Noll's coaching encouraged Art about the future. When a reporter asked whether hiring Noll was a mistake, Art exclaimed, "No, sir! . . . Chuck never once lost his poise and he didn't lose the ballplayers. I turned to my sons and said, 'Well, you've got yourself a coach. This guy's got it.'"

Realignment

The NFL began its second half-century in 1970 by realigning itself into two new conferences and selling rights to ABC for *Monday Night Football*. Both proved wildly successful.

When the NFL and AFL merged in 1966, owners deferred realignment into two new, balanced, divisions because no NFL team would join a conference of AFL clubs. Art's epiphany about joining the American Football Conference (AFC) came in Art Modell's hospital room, where he, Dan, and Wellington Mara were talking realignment with the Cleveland owner, who was being treated for bleeding ulcers. Realizing that Cleveland and Baltimore were willing to jump, Dan exclaimed, "Under no circumstances will the Steelers move." Art countered, "Danny, you can stay in the National Conference. I'm going with Art Modell to the American Conference." In January 1970, Pittsburgh, Cleveland, and Baltimore joined ten AFL clubs to form the thirteen-team AFC. To sweeten the shift, each team switching conferences would receive $3 million.

"I could see that it was going to be the final solution," Art said later. Dan was less sanguine. He saw joining the AFC as a loss of status. But his father overruled him, just as he had when Dan balked at accepting less than Baltimore in the 1960 NBC deal. "When it finally came down to it," Art said, "I couldn't have done it unless Modell had come, too." Steelers–Browns games were their best paydays. The two teams drew 80,000 fans, including thousands of Pittsburghers, when they played in Cleveland's stadium on Lake Erie; Cleveland fans, in turn, caravanned to games in Pittsburgh. For Art, the rivalry was a financial lifeline. The Steelers weren't going to contend in 1969, but Art was thinking ahead of the play. The shift of Cleveland and Baltimore—two championship franchises—and Pittsburgh with its long history—legitimized the AFC. The $3 million Art received for switching conferences and the revenues Three Rivers Stadium would generate would stabilize his finances. Although nobody predicted a title, the Rooneys finally had the wherewithal to build a contender.

But a strike by veterans during camp jeopardized the 1970 season. Pat Livingston, as much a fan as a sportswriter, criticized striking players for hurting the team. The next day, receiver Roy Jefferson and Joe Greene confronted him at camp. Jefferson chastised Livingston; Greene spat in his face.

A feisty reporter comfortable with confrontation, Livingston asked editor John Troan to ignore the incident. Livingston's sense of loyalty to Art was paramount. Pat's wife Elsie had died in 1960, on their daughter's third birthday. On Christmas Eve, Jim Boston arrived at Livingston's home with a carload of gifts for his girls from the Rooneys. "I was scared to death I wasn't doing right by them," Livingston remembered. "But Art and Kass had not forgotten. They took care of everything." Publicizing the spitting incident would subject Greene to league discipline and damage his reputation. Unwilling to risk Greene's career or harm Art, Livingston told the Rooneys that if they would talk with Greene, that would satisfy him.

While the veterans stayed out of camp, rookies, not yet eligible for union membership, practiced. Rocky Bleier, recently discharged from the military, was among the strikers. He had played a season, but to make the team, he needed to be in camp. Instead, Bleier moved in with fellow Notre Dame alum Terry Hanratty and trained with the veterans during the strike. Badly hobbled by his wounds from Vietnam, Bleier ran off kilter. Though he worked out relentlessly, few thought he had a chance. When the strike dragged on, the vets gave Bleier their blessings to report. The walkout ended soon afterward.

Noll called Rocky into his office before the first game to tell him he had been waived. "Go home. Do what you need to do to get yourself in shape and come back next year." Bleier was crushed; he argued with Noll, whose only concession was to let him practice that day.

Rocky was still feeling miserable when Dan Rooney called the next day.

"He said he'd talked things over with Noll and his father. The Steelers would put me on the injured reserve list instead of waivers. Mr. Rooney wanted me to have another operation, then I could rejoin the team later in the season." It was never clear to Bleier whether it was Art's or Dan's idea. "The apple," he said, "did not fall far from the tree. It's part of the culture of who they are. They take care of players."

Art told Art Jr., "Get Rocky involved in scouting. He'll probably be good at it, and he might like it. In case his foot doesn't get better, let's see if we can find a place for him in the organization." Surgery removed troublesome shrapnel and broke up scar tissue that had hindered running. Rocky dedicated himself to the painful and uncertain process of reconstructing his body.

Bradshaw

While Joe Greene anchored Pittsburgh's defense, Terry Bradshaw stepped in at quarterback. They were both Southerners, but as different as black and white, and their careers took contrasting trajectories. For Greene, the AFC rookie of the year, stardom was readily apparent. Bradshaw, though, struggled and was often benched. What they shared was a common friend and mentor—Art.

That Pittsburgh ended up with Bradshaw was ironic. Nobody had beaten Art on the field or abused him in trades as often as George Halas. Art finally got even in 1969. By losing to Chicago that season, the Steelers and the Bears wound up with identical 1–13 records. On January 9, 1970, two days before Super Bowl IV, Dan Rooney and Halas's son-in-law Ed McCaskey met in New Orleans to flip a coin for the first pick. Art said that when flipping coins, let the other man make the call so that the pressure would be on him to make the right one. Dan told McCaskey, "Go ahead, you call it." McCaskey called heads, the 1921 silver dollar came up tails, and Pittsburgh got Bradshaw.

A college All-American, Terry Bradshaw stood 6-foot-3, weighed 215 pounds, and had set a national high school record by throwing a javelin over 244 feet. But he had played at a small school, Louisiana Tech, and had not learned how to read coverages or find secondary receivers. He had never watched film to prepare and was not the sort of student of the game that Chuck Noll prized. He was also thin-skinned. Some players could block out jeers and catcalls, but not Bradshaw. He played poorly in his first game and was replaced by Terry Hanratty, who quickly threw for a touchdown. Bradshaw sat in his car afterward and cried. Mistakes punctuated his season more than success, and Noll frequently yanked him from games.

Football wasn't the only issue troubling Bradshaw. "Coming to Pittsburgh was a shock," he remembered. A product of southern segregation, Bradshaw was bewildered by the city, where he saw blacks and whites playing and working together. "I didn't know anything about black people. I didn't know their dress codes, their music. I'd never been around them."

Bradshaw's black teammates sensed good faith and taught him how to avoid offending. Joe Greene, especially, made Bradshaw feel that he belonged. On the field, his ferocious play took pressure off the rookie. If Bradshaw didn't give the game away, the defense could win it for them. "I will always love Joe," Bradshaw swore. "I was scared to death and needed somebody to reassure me of my place on this Steeler team because it was going to be a bumpy ride." Greene told Bradshaw, "You're going to be all right. You are our leader, the man we're going to win it with." He warned reporters off Bradshaw and became his best friend on the team.

Art took on that role off the field. When Art invited him into his office and gave him a cigar, Bradshaw was flattered. "He took a kindness to me, a simple kid who didn't really know what he was getting into," Bradshaw recalled. Overwhelmed by football, Pittsburgh, and the expectations he faced as the top draft pick, Bradshaw took comfort in Rooney's welcome. Art knew the odds confronting Bradshaw, the eleventh quarterback taken first in the draft's thirty-five years. Only one, Paul Hornung, became a star, and he did so at halfback.

Three Rivers

The Steelers began playing at Three Rivers Stadium in August but did not move into their new offices there until later that season. Unlike the Fort Pitt Hotel's cramped quarters, where no amount of fresh air or soap could remove the remembrances of cigars, these offices were spacious, clean, and modern. No wayward souls paraded through on their way to the horse room upstairs or crawled through the window, as they had at the Fort Pitt Hotel.

Three Rivers was a five-minute walk from Art's North Lincoln home, but it took him a while to grow comfortable there. His new walnut desk was as big as his old office and he was uncertain about the contemporary décor. "This is a sports office?" he harrumphed when Pat Livingston came by. That morning, a young decorator had displayed an assortment of paintings for its walls: psychedelic riots of colors and more prosaic framed schedules of past seasons. Art wanted neither. "He's trying to do what's right," Art said about the decorator, "but this is a sports office. Sports are people. It's humans. He came in here with a pile of cardboard."

Pointing at a quilted tapestry covering a lobby wall, Art snorted, "I just discovered it's the play where Elbie Nickel caught a pass to beat the Eagles back in 1954. It looks like a Chinese puzzle to me."

"Sports is a history of people," Art argued. "Those are the kind of pictures I want." And that's what he got, photos of Bell, Halas, and Marshall. "If I can get pictures of Harry Greb, Billy Conn, and Fritzie Zivic, I'm putting them there," he gestured. "They were world champions. And I'm going to put pictures of five Pirates under them—Pie Traynor, Honus Wagner, Paul and Lloyd Waner, and Danny Murtaugh. They were world champions, too."

To Art's relief, Dago Sam, Uptown Dougie, and Iggy Borkowski were not put off by his new digs. Nor were city leaders. After former Mayor Barr left one day, a down-on-his luck Northsider came in. "Look, Art," he scolded, "I been waiting around twenty minutes for that other guy to leave." Art hid his smile, slipped him a twenty, and apologized for the wait.

While Dan ran the club, Art spent time with players. They worked out at Three Rivers now, ending their South Park exile. They had graduated from the league's worst facilities to possibly the best. "When we were at the other park," Art ruminated, "we just weren't first class. When we moved into Three Rivers Stadium, it brought all of us closer. Our offices are here. We practice here. We play our games here." The Rooneys got to know players even better. "If there's a secret, I think that's it."

On the other side of the stadium, the Pirates' complex separated training facilities from the front office. The Steelers, however, welcomed visitors into a lobby where players, coaches, and employees interacted during the day. Dan Rooney had designed the setup. The lockers were roomy, the weight room and facilities expansive. Dan and Art felt it was imperative that the players feel like winners. "We were going first class," Dan stated. "Before, we were transients." Three Rivers had the desired effect. "When we went into the new stadium," Ray Mansfield said, "we got a new image. It was a turning point for me. I thought that maybe, finally, I had a chance to be with a winner."

Greene and Bradshaw

Art, an unlit cigar in hand, walked around the field for exercise while players loosened up. "He'd pat you on the back afterward and chat," Andy Russell recalled. "He gave it a family atmosphere." Art knew all the players, but he paid particular attention to Greene and Bradshaw. He invited Joe back to his office, gave him a cigar, and showed him the photos on his wall. He told him about Bill Dudley and Billy Conn, Senator Coyne and Governor Lawrence. Most of all, he listened to Joe, who trusted Art, not because he was the owner, but in spite of that. Art never told him what to do, but he was there if Joe wanted to talk. Greene relished the opportunity. "Whatever that man talked about, I took it as part of my education. I had me a wonderful teacher."

Art invited Terry Bradshaw back, too. "I used to sit in there and just listen to him. I mean, I would have been foolish not to—he was an original, a connection to the past and the beginning of the NFL." Bradshaw relaxed while Art worked the telephone. "There was always somebody calling, and he was always, 'Don't you worry, I'll take care of that.'"

Bradshaw interrogated Art. "I wanted to know as much as I could about him." But Art rarely talked about himself. "We talked about handicapping horses," Bradshaw remembered. "We talked about the old NFL and his relationships with Paul Brown and Papa Bear Halas, and we talked a lot about family." But their conversations rarely centered around the Steelers. "I understood that my relationship was not as an employee with him," Bradshaw reflected. "I worked for Dan Rooney. I didn't work for Art Rooney, but I respected who Art Rooney was, and he was my friend."

Art bucked up Bradshaw, especially when he played poorly. "He'd say to me, 'You're the best, you're going to be great.'" A tense relationship with Noll rattled Bradshaw's already fragile ego. "My father was very concerned about Bradshaw," Art Jr. remembered. "He'd tell him, 'Terry, I've been around the great ones—Ruth, Conn, Man o' War, Jack Dempsey—and you're right in there with those guys. You're like Babe Ruth, you're like Conn.' Terry needed somebody pumping him up. My father did that."

"He loved Bradshaw." Rocky Bleier reflected. He called Brad the 'big guy.' He either saw Brad's insecurities or had been around enough athletes and people to know what Brad needed."

If Terry was troubled, he went to Art's office. "Sometimes I wouldn't say much, but he knew. He always knew." Art insisted that Bradshaw would excel. "When I was struggling," Bradshaw emphasized, "he was the one person who I knew really cared." North Lincoln became Bradshaw's refuge, especially after bad games. "Just me and Art," Terry recalled. "We'd eat in the kitchen. Mary Roseboro, his maid, did the cooking. God, what a sweet lady!"

Joe Greene often joined them. "One of the things that I remember most," Art's nephew, Tim V. Rooney, recalled, "is that when Bradshaw was going through hell in the early '70s, Joe Greene is the guy who really stepped in for him. When times were tough, they were eating at Art's house every night." And for Bradshaw, there were many tough times.

You didn't have to be a top draft pick for Art to care. Ground crew veteran "Dirt" DiNardo was on the Houston trip in 1970. Art made sure each groundskeeper took at least one road trip a season. Dirt had grown up near Forbes Field and often received tickets from Art. "Funny thing about Art Rooney," Dirt explained, "once he met you, he never forgot you. He remembered almost everything about everybody." Art was asleep Sunday morning when he got a call from an acquaintance on the Houston police force. "We've got one of your guys here," the cop said, thinking a player had been arrested. It was Dirt, who had been enjoying himself at a club before getting into it with another patron. Art bailed him out and said nothing about it. "Anything you do with Art Rooney stays with Art Rooney," Dirt said. "No questions asked, no favors demanded in return; he just did it and that was that. Who am I? Just a common working man, a groundskeeper, but that never mattered to him." Art was fond of the crew. On Mondays, he had the Allegheny Club send hams down for lunch, and when they worked nights changing the field over from football to baseball, Art brought coffee and doughnuts. They were his people.

When Art missed a Monday night contest because he was hospitalized, Howard Cosell, Frank Gifford, and Don Meredith mentioned it on the air. The following afternoon, the hallway outside Art's room was a jungle of flowers and plants. A florists' group sent a display to the announcers thanking them for the business.

Getting Better

The team began 1970 the way they had finished 1969. "We're going to explode one of these days," Noll predicted after Pittsburgh's fifteenth straight defeat. He repeated himself a week later. But then, the Steelers did erupt, beating Buffalo and Houston. Winning four of five, the Steelers evened their record to 4-4 and tied Cleveland for the division lead before losing five of their last six games.

In the final game, Joe Greene played spectacularly while Terry Bradshaw struggled. Bradshaw handled punting duties, but his first kick was blocked and returned for a touchdown. Greene, however, registered four sacks despite Eagles linemen holding him on every play. Joe threatened retaliation if they kept doing it. When they did, he struck back. First one, then a second, Eagles lineman had to be helped off the field. That didn't stop a third from trying the same tactics. Infuriated that the referees were not calling holding penalties, Greene picked up the football as the Eagles approached the line of scrimmage. He turned to a referee: "If you can't see these guys grabbing me, this game is over," and slung the ball out of bounds. When an official got another ball and placed it on the ground, Joe took that one, too. "I told you, man. You either start calling this holding or this game is over." Greene ignored warnings that he would be ejected. A ref asked Andy Russell to intercede, but he could not calm Greene, who held the football in one hand and gestured to the crowd. "Come on, you want this ball?" he bellowed. "Come and take it." As Philadelphia fans hushed, Greene pitched the ball into the stands and stalked off the field.

Pittsburgh finished 5-9. It was quite a bump up from the previous season, and Bradshaw had shown flashes of promise. But while throwing 6 passes for touchdowns, he had 24 intercepted. Chuck Noll's two-year record was 6-22. Nevertheless, after the season, Dan Rooney extended his contract and declared that he would coach Pittsburgh for as long as he wanted.

Racing

While Noll, Dan, and Art Jr. were overhauling the Steelers, the twins were expanding the family's racing operations. When Art heard that John Boggiano's Palm Beach Kennel Club was in play, he told Boggiano, "I'll send my boys down to look at it." "Boggiano was an old New York guy and the Chief knew him from gambling," John Rooney explained. After a long pause, Boggiano replied, "No, we don't do business like that anymore." Art chuckled, "I'm not talking about *those* boys; I'm talking about my sons." In September, they bought the dog track for $7 million.

Tim was the only son outside the family businesses. If he had stayed in Pittsburgh, he probably would have entered politics. Instead, he left for the New York Stock Exchange. But his heart belonged to racing. While in school, Tim had often joined Art at Aqueduct for the day. They rode back into Manhattan afterward with *Times* writer Lou Effrat, ate at Toots Shor's, attended Mass at St. Patrick's, and flew home.

Tim had kept Shamrock's books since Fran Fogarty showed him how to do them in the early 60s. When farm manager Johnny Bill Linton quit in 1971, Tim intervened. Johnny Bill was an unkempt character with tobacco-stained clothes. Art wanted to sell Shamrock, but Tim argued that Linwood's departure was a godsend. He pitched in at

Shamrock, arriving at the farm on Thursday nights and cutting hay till late at night. Tim brought in a veterinarian, mucked stables, and returned home on Monday night. By Tuesday morning, he had washed the smell of horses off and was back on Wall Street. He pulled double duty until Arnold Shaw took over and turned Shamrock around. Meanwhile, Tim's romance with horses intensified. Soon, like his brothers, he was thoroughly engaged in the family's sporting empire.

Bonds at Three Rivers

Art set the tone at Three Rivers. "If somebody was sitting in the lobby when he'd come in after practice," Joe Gordon said, "he'd go over and say 'What's your name? My name's Rooney.'" Art would engage in Pittsburgh geography, figuring out who they knew in common. "If he had nothing else to do, Art would say 'Come on back.' He'd take him in his office and give him a cigar, show him the photos on his wall. The guy would be flabbergasted."

As a boy, Joe Gordon had waited outside Forbes Field for Tim Rooney to give out passes before kickoff. "So much of Art Rooney was legend," Gordon remembered. He jumped at the chance to work for the Rooneys.

Joe shared Art's love for baseball. Art watched batting practice from the dugout after work, then wandered up to the press box to chat with reporters. "More baseball players, managers, and coaches knew him personally than knew the Galbreaths, who owned the Pirates," Gordon claimed. "They were in their Eiffel Tower, but Art was down in the dugout, smoking his cigar, kibbitzing with people. He knew them all— Don Zimmer, Joe Torre, Whitey Herzog." They always asked if Art had a horse he liked.

Art watched games from his box. It was nothing fancy, just bare concrete floor and chairs, without windows to keep out the elements. Sometimes, neighborhood kids joined him. Other times, Art sat with Richie Easton, a *Pittsburgh Press* truck driver who drove for him, or with Gordon's father, Manny, a former Homestead barkeeper who had played minor league ball in Oil City.

Art was more than a friendly face at Three Rivers. A sounding board for sons, employees, and players, he led by example and a few words of counsel. "He could be tough," Gordon cautioned, "but at the same time, he was totally fair." He expected employees to act accordingly. "You would always ask yourself," Gordon explained, "is this right or wrong. If it's right, you do it. If it's wrong, forget it. That's how he lived his life."

But employees felt free to disagree with Art. "If you could convince him you were right," Gordon remembered, "he didn't stand on ceremony. It wasn't an ego thing with him."

Art was tougher with his sons. "The only time I would ever hear him raise his voice was when he would get in an argument with Dan," Gordon remembered. But Art was never tougher on anyone than he was on himself. "He was enormously self-disciplined," Gordon observed. "He was the most mentally tough person I've ever known."

His generosity was legendary and was becoming his legacy. Gordon and trainer Ralph Berlin quickly experienced it. After Berlin began work, Dan asked when his family would join him. Berlin said he had to sell his house in Kentucky first; he couldn't handle two mortgages. Dan asked how much he needed. When Berlin answered $10,000, Dan had Fran Fogarty write a check. Flabbergasted, Berlin asked if he should sign for it. Fogarty shrugged: "I know you got it and you know you got it." Berlin asked about the interest on it. Just pay the $10,000 back when the house sold, Fogarty replied. "Dan," Berlin concluded, "was in his father's mold."

At the end of 1969, six months after he had been hired, Gordon was astonished to receive a bonus. "I thought it was a mistake. It was such a huge percentage of my salary, and they weren't making any money then." Years later, when players struck during the 1982 season, teams laid off staff or cut their hours. "Not the Steelers," Gordon said. "We had nothing to do, but we came in every day. At the end of the year, the Christmas bonus was exactly the same as it was the previous year. And that's how they've always been." Art set the standard without issuing mandates. "You just lived and functioned by the way they lived and functioned."

Father Figure

By steering the NFL toward competitive parity and moving to Three Rivers Stadium, Art had created the conditions for Noll and his sons to make the Steelers into contenders. He settled into a different role, circumnavigating the locker room daily and asking players about themselves and their families. Art did not act like other owners. "The Rooneys didn't come over here with a silver spoon in their mouth," Dwight White said. "This guy rolled his sleeves up, socked a few people in the nose, and probably got socked a few times in the nose himself. This was my kind of guy." The players knew that the Steelers belonged to Art, even if Dan was running the show. "The Chief," White emphasized, "was the man."

That June, he invited Ray Mansfield and Andy Russell to the Belmont Stakes. "I felt so honored," Russell recalled. "The hatcheck girl, the ushers, everyone knew the Chief." The Belmont was attracting extraordinary attention because Canonero II, a Venezuelan horse, was one win from the Triple Crown. "I bet a dollar on the favorite to win," Russell remembered. "Art bet on Pass Catcher, a 30-to-1 long-shot." Pass Catcher was a late addition to the field, but after a quick surge in the backstretch, he passed Canonero II and won, paying $71 on a $2 bet. When Russell asked why he bet Pass Catcher, Art said he liked the name.

During the 1970 draft, Art let his sons and Noll handicap prospects while he regaled reporters with tales of how he had approached scouting. "I used to leave Miami after the winter racing season and stop off at the various colleges to talk to the coaches," he said. "A lot of those coaches were horse players. I used to see them at the track. I knew they were my kind of people. If they told me a college player was a good pro prospect, I believed them."

Things were different now, Art Jr. reflected, because of Noll. "Our methodology was in place, but he made the difference." Noll knew the kind of player he wanted, and made sure that scouts did, too. After selecting Greene, Kolb, and Greenwood in 1969 and Bradshaw and Mel Blount in 1970, Pittsburgh picked Penn State linebacker Jack Ham, East Texas defensive end Dwight White, and Western Illinois safety Mike Wagner in 1971. They were crafting a competitive squad.

Art listened as Noll raved to reporters about the Steeler picks. "This reminds me of horse owners talking about their two-year-olds before they have raced," Art cautioned. "They all look like Kentucky Derby winners." Art wanted to see how they performed before evaluating them. "I don't believe I have a winner until I see the red board go up at the track." Art was seventy, but he was not talking retirement. "I live five minutes from the new stadium and walk to the office every day. I put in a full day, mostly because I take pleasure in being around the operation. Dan still has to get my approval before any major trades are made, but otherwise I leave him alone to run things."

Art appreciated how much football had changed. "I never dreamed the league would become what it is. It was a tough, rugged league then, made up of rugged football players who forgot everything else when they were on the field. They were players who got maybe $100 for a game." Now, some Steelers were making almost $100,000 a season.

Art had concerns about the league. "It doesn't seem too long ago when we could settle every pro football problem in a quick discussion around a table," he reflected. "The guys who ran the league were Bert Bell, Tim Mara, George Marshall, George Halas, and myself. We ran it pretty well, too." Now, owners came with an entourage: "A squad of lawyers, accountants, tax experts, and more advisers than I can even name. When we were struggling to survive, pro football was a fun thing. The bigger we get though, the less fun there is in it."

In August 1971, Rocky Bleier came to camp fighting to make the team. He heard talk that he was there only because of Art's intervention. "Art thought I was a nice kid," he reflected. "I grew up in a bar. He grew up in a bar. He probably said, 'Let's take care of him.'" While Bleier had been incredibly dedicated to building his body back, the process was excruciating. At the end of camp, he was placed on the reserve squad and played on special teams a few times. "Last year, he was a cripple," Art Jr. said. "This year, he's just bad."

Dwight White, however, quickly cracked the lineup. "I grew up in the South during a period of boycotts, with the perception that things were so much better in the North," he explained. In Texas, White attended segregated schools and rarely interacted with white people. He realized that he faced a steep learning curve in Pittsburgh, as did white teammates who had little history with men from black colleges. "I figured the Rooneys must be good white folks," White remembered. "They were Catholics and religious; certainly that was a good thing." But he knew little about Art.

White learned quickly. "He used to call me 'Dwight White,' in that low tone of his, while smoking a cigar. I can proudly say that I think that I was one of his favorites. I think there was some chemistry there." White quickly discovered that others shared that feeling. "I'm over on the Mexican War streets on the Northside one evening after practice with some guys messing around and here comes Mr. Rooney and Father Silas riding up the street. The only problem is that it's a one-way street and they're coming up the other way. Guess what? People are yelling 'Hey, Mr. Rooney!' and waving hello. I'm thinking this guy must be pretty big. He can go up a one-way street and nobody says anything about it. And these were black folks." White breakfasted with Art at a Northside diner. "I thought that was so cool, for a guy of his stature to be able to walk around in that community. There was a sense of him just being a regular type of guy, and from what I heard, he was very regular."

The 1971 season began the way the previous one had ended, with a frustrating defeat. Chicago came back to beat Pittsburgh by returning a fumble for a last-minute touchdown. Joe Greene, who had played brilliantly, took his helmet and rifled it toward the stands in disgust. It smacked into the goalposts instead. The Steelers won six games and lost eight that year, with five of their wins coming at home. Bradshaw looked great in some games, self-destructive in others. Some collapses defied diagnosis, Pat Livingston concluded, but there was no doubt about the underlying problem: Bradshaw had not acquired a winner's poise. Art stayed close to his young friend. Despite the setbacks, the mood on the team was changing. The Steelers were on the rise.

18

1972

In 1972, Rooney's team came together on and off the field. So did Pittsburgh, which finally embraced the Steelers totally and unequivocally. With the steel industry entering its death throes, sport triggered a decade-long makeover of the city's identity. Since Jock Sutherland's arrival in 1946, the Steelers had belonged to white Pittsburghers, whether they were blue- or white-collar workers, Catholic, Jewish, Eastern Orthodox, or Protestant in faith, Irish, Italian, or Slovak in background. Now they became black Pittsburgh's team, too. From tony suburbs to struggling mill towns, the Steelers unified the people of the region as well as the far-flung Pittsburgh diaspora. Football would tell their story to the world.

Art had put the pieces together—Dan to run the organization, Art Jr. to head scouting, Noll to coach, and a loyal cohort to work for them. They were finding, training, and teaching the most amazing collection of players in NFL history. Art, as always, mixed business with pleasure. He played cards with Ralph Berlin, counseled Greene and Bradshaw, and traveled to Shamrock Farm and the track. All the while, he schooled his players and employees.

Timothy V. Rooney saw his uncle in action after joining the personnel department in 1972. "Danny was running the team," he explained, "but Art was ever-present, tuned in to what was going on." Nor had the game passed Art by. "He knew everything—strategy, personnel, rules." But what struck Tim the most was Art's wisdom. "That wisdom could be found not so much in him telling you what you should do, but in telling you what might happen: how people might react, what consequences might result."

It was the wisdom Art had used to build consensus within the league.

"He was not in the front part of the argument," said Tim, who studied him at meetings. "He'd be on the back part and bring it together." His wisdom had earned the other owners' trust, his sacrifice their respect. "For my uncle, the Steelers weren't first, the league was first." That attitude gave Art unparalleled moral authority within the NFL.

And among the sporting world at large. Writers like *Times* columnist Red Smith, who accompanied him to Aqueduct that spring, found Art irresistible. At a time when sport was becoming Madison Avenue's handmaiden, Smith cherished Art as an icon of a more authentic epoch. But Smith, who had come of age when racing vied for the nation's heartstrings, knew that Art's purchase of the Yonkers Raceway made him much more than a nostalgic reminder of sport's past. For Art, the venerable track evoked déjà vu as the place where he began his most heralded score, when it was called Empire City. The Rooneys paid $52 million for Yonkers, with a taxi company and some New York real estate thrown in. Off-track betting and Atlantic City casinos, however, had cut Yonkers' handle and imperiled its future. Tim Rooney took over Yonkers, with Art a phone call away.

Defying History

"We're thinking championship," Chuck Noll announced when camp opened in Latrobe that July. Noll meant it, and he wasn't alone in predicting success. Veterans Andy Russell and Ray Mansfield could sense a difference in their young teammates. "We felt that we could win with them," Russell said, especially at Three Rivers where the crowds were bigger and more intense than at Pitt Stadium. "You'd look up at the stands and think those fans are not going to let us lose."

Art hosted an outing at the Churchill Valley Country Club when camp opened and brought along former Homestead Gray star Vic Harris, an old sandlot adversary. When Harris had been arrested at Forbes Field for fighting at a game between barnstorming teams led by Dizzy Dean and Satchel Paige in 1934, Art persuaded the judge to drop the charges. Art, seventy-one, had not swung a golf club in years, but after watching his players hack away, he vowed, "I'm going to play next year. I didn't see anyone out there who could play any better than I can."

At camp, Noll raised the bar. "We've grown up a lot," he observed. "It could happen this year; it may take another year or two, but we're on our way." Art's expectations had been dashed so often that he dared not voice any, but he could see that Noll and his sons had built a contender. Art's efforts to create parity within the league, to build Three Rivers Stadium, and to shift to the AFC had made the Steelers viable.

Bill Nunn was also playing a part. While Bill Austin had ignored the men Nunn found at black colleges, Noll developed their talents. "Bill," Noll told Nunn, "you were an athlete. I want you to go out and find me athletes." Noll, who had drafted a league-high eleven black collegians since arriving, thoroughly integrated the club, but not as a matter of policy. "Chuck Noll was color-blind," Dan Rooney attested. "Me and my father, we would say we weren't color-blind because we were trying to bring blacks in. But Chuck didn't care who you were if you could play."

As anticipated, Southern University cornerback Mel Blount and Grambling receiver Frank Lewis were the fastest men at camp. The surprise was Rocky Bleier. After spending a year on the reserve squad, he reported in better shape than anyone imagined possible. Rocky's 4.5-second 40-yard run was among the fastest posted. "The best 40 he's ever run," Noll exclaimed. "It looks like he's put all of his injuries behind him."

"I heard I was around because the Old Man liked me, that I was the club untouchable," Bleier told columnist Phil Musick. "And honestly," Musick added, "Art Rooney's paternal feeling toward him might have been a part of the reason." But Rocky no longer needed Art's intercession. He excelled on special teams, where he had played some in 1971. "This year," Bleier said, "my goal is to prove I can play running back in this league."

If Bleier was the biggest surprise, Franco Harris was the key addition. One of nine children born to an African American sergeant and his Italian war bride, the Penn State fullback was expected to relieve the pressure on Steeler quarterbacks. Tennessee State quarterback Joe Gilliam, taken in the eleventh round, was an afterthought. "I didn't envision Gilliam even making the damned team," Art Jr. said about the skinny, pass-happy coach's son. "He was a Bill Nunn guy." Though they had

Bradshaw and Hanratty, Gilliam was an enticing choice. Even if he did not make the team, his selection solidified Pittsburgh's standing at black colleges. So did their approach to camp, where Nunn roomed players alphabetically to forge cohesion. His son, Bill III, and Dan Rooney's oldest boy, Art, both ball boys, roomed together.

Dwight White was back for his second year. After his rookie season, the defensive end had settled in Richardson, Texas. A black man in a white town, he didn't last long. "Those people ran me from around there," he recalled. White and his line mates had been born into a South stamped by sharecropping and segregation, grown up during the civil rights movement, and come of age as black power politics radicalized the struggle for equality. They became close; White and Joe Greene even roomed together one season. "That," White laughed, "would never happen again; we were like two pit bulls living together."

What surprised White, however, was how much they shared with white teammates. "You had one guy from Penn State—Jack Ham from Johnstown—who ends up meshing with Ernie Holmes from Hempstead, Texas, and Texas Southern. You got Terry Bradshaw, a cracker out of Louisiana, who *ain't* never been around no black folks, handing the ball off to a biracial guy, half-black and half-Italian, and then one Audie Murphy sports hero, Rocky Bleier." What they had in common, White argued, was prodigious talent and determination.

Pittsburgh swept through the preseason. "Pro football is a question of having the people," Noll observed. "We have the people now."

The Steelers were scheduled to play an exhibition in Memphis featuring southern icons Terry Bradshaw and Archie Manning. Art asked Joe Gordon when he was leaving to advance the game. "I'll make you a deal," Art offered. "I'll go with you, but we have to go to Philadelphia first on Monday because there's a game I want to see. We'll watch half the game, then drive to New York because I want to go to Belmont Tuesday." Gordon was ecstatic. Having Art advance a game "was money in the bank. All you have to do is walk into the newspaper with Art Rooney and school's out."

Art, Joe, and Jack Butler drove to Philadelphia on Monday and left for New York at halftime. Art wanted to be fresh for the next day's races.

In the morning, Joe met Art and Jack after Mass and drove to Belmont. "Every single person there knew him," Gordon remembered. "At valet parking, it was 'Mister Rooney! How ya doing? Haven't seen you for a while.' Same thing at the turnstile, with waitresses in the clubroom."

In Memphis, Art took Joe to a dog track in Arkansas that the family was considering purchasing. "Arkansas," Gordon recalled, "felt like a foreign county, but people came over and said, 'You're Art Rooney, aren't you?'" Back in Memphis, they made the rounds of the local media. "It was like the Pope came to town."

In the fourth quarter, with Pittsburgh crushing New Orleans, Joe Gilliam drove the team to two touchdowns, prompting one sleepy employee to gripe, "What's he throwing for? We won't get home until four o'clock." Art retorted, "What's wrong with throwing the ball? That kid's trying to win a job. He can throw it all night as far as I'm concerned . . . I've been on too many of these trips when we've had to make the long trip home." He meant returning after a loss. The 1972 Steelers, Pat Livingston observed, were making Art young again.

The 1972 Regular Season

Pittsburgh sport was on the rise. The Pirates had won the World Series in 1971, when Roberto Clemente led their dramatic comeback to beat Baltimore. Clemente, the series MVP, was finally heralded as a great player. Art had advanced the date of his cataract surgery to better see the Series. With an office at the stadium, he watched more baseball than ever. The Pirates were playing well again, and Clemente was nearing his 3,000th career hit.

With over 51,000 fans at the opener primed for a fast start, the Steelers did not disappoint, beating Oakland 34–28. "We can play with the best," Dwight White proclaimed afterward. Noll gushed about the crowd; the press was jubilant. "The Steelers of 1972 are for real, baby," crowed Sam Bechtel of the *Beaver County Times*. "The longest prayer vigil in the history of football may have ended yesterday," Phil Musick added. "This long-suffering burg can get off its knees."

One game, however, did not persuade Pittsburghers, especially after the team lost the next game. Deep psychic wounds lingered. "Noll chafes under the burden of history," Phil Musick observed. "'I am not interested in the past,' he says. And says. And says. And the city does not really listen, perhaps because the Steelers and their inadequacies have belonged to it far longer than they have belonged to Noll." Skepticism concerned Noll. "A team lives in a city," he said, "not in some type of sterile environment. The players are affected by the city's reaction to them."

Art understood what Noll meant. He knew a crowd could dampen even committed athletes. He had heard fans boo sandlot legend Mose Kelsch and Hall-of-Famer Bobby Layne. He saw how much they hurt Terry Bradshaw.

Art played a surrogate father to Bradshaw, but he knew his limits. "He didn't cross those boundaries," Bradshaw observed, "but he would get to the fence and you'd be face to face and you would know that he was hurting for you." Bradshaw never felt that Art was building him up for the team's sake. "He was just concerned about me." Art enjoyed this young athletic Adonis and took him to the track. "I didn't know how to bet so he said he'd do the betting for me," Bradshaw recalled. "I won every race!" Art also brought Terry, who had ridden horses as a boy, to Shamrock Farm. "I loved it there."

Art kidded Bradshaw. "He loved to tease me about girls—girls I was dating, my wife, even my mother. If he found something in the game, he'd tease me about that. It was all good-natured; he just liked to mess with me." Art knew what he was doing. "There were difficult times," Art said. "I'd kid Terry a lot and sit with him on the team bus. So often he'd be sitting by himself. He seemed to be down. I didn't give him much advice—I try to stay out of people's way—but I remember telling him to have patience and things would work out." Terry teased Art back by taking his cigars. "Ralph Berlin and the other guys knew me and the Chief were tight. So they'd all say 'Run down there and get us some cigars.' They didn't have the nerve." Only Bradshaw could charm his way past Mary Regan, Art's secretary.

In October, Art appeared before a Senate Subcommittee. Congress, under pressure from President Nixon, was considering legislation to end home blackouts of games sold out in advance. The presidential election was weeks away, and though war in Indochina dominated debate, Nixon sought to burnish his suspect populist credentials by talking football. The league opposed the bill, and Pete Rozelle wanted Art, who knew several committee members from racing, to make the NFL's case.

Art was dead set against ending home blackouts. The Steelers had made a record $3.3 million in 1971 ticket revenue. But if not for payments received for shifting to the AFC and expansion fees, they would have lost money. Art argued that local broadcast could devastate attendance. When the only way to see the game was to buy a ticket, he said, football was the thing to do. "If we show fourteen games on the television, I am afraid that it will get to be the thing not to do."

Rhode Island senator John Pastore asked what could be done for fans unable to buy tickets. Art conceded that he had no answer. "The president has said he would like to sign this bill before we go home this session," Pastore said. Art was unswayed by Nixon's desires. Despite his fears, Congress authorized local broadcast for games sold out seventy-two hours in advance, beginning in 1973.

Back in Pittsburgh, Noll called their comeback win over St. Louis in game three a turning point. "It showed what kind of capabilities we have." It was only Noll's third road win in three and a half seasons. But after a loss left them 2-2, Bradshaw, the hero of the St. Louis comeback, was jeered during introductions at Three Rivers. Many fans favored native son Hanratty. They stopped heckling when Pittsburgh romped over Houston. Despite facing a defense geared to stopping him, Franco Harris ran through and over gangs of defenders.

The defensive line—Joe Greene, L. C. Greenwood, Dwight White, and Ben McGee, with Ernie Holmes pushing for playing time—began to dominate opponents. Greene was indomitable; White was playing like a Pro Bowler, and Greenwood was proving Noll's initial assessment correct—he was something special. They held Houston to 7 points and then New England to three. Next up, O. J. Simpson and the Buffalo Bills. Simpson, picked first in the 1969 draft, had received a record $300,000 salary, while Greene, taken fourth, got much less. "If O. J.'s a $300,000 running back," Greene reasoned, "it takes a $300,000 tackle to stop him." Simpson rushed for 189 yards and Buffalo scored 21 points, but

Pittsburgh scored 38 and Greene thanked each offensive player afterward. "They bailed us out," he admitted.

After beating Cincinnati, the Steelers were 6-2 and great fodder for columnists. "Steeler fans," *Beaver County Times* writer Dick Stilley opined, "are western civilization's experts at living with a loser." He sketched their habits—mumbling 'Same Old Steelers' and griping that the Rooneys were cheapskates. "If a relative from Cleveland came to town, you changed the subject." Such defensive mechanisms were no longer necessary.

The horde of fans that traveled to Buffalo evoked memories of Ham and Cabbage specials. Pittsburgh won and returned home to vanquish Cincinnati and Kansas City. Art took *Philadelphia Inquirer* sportswriter Jim Barniak around before the Kansas City game to meet "some of my boys." Barniak thought Art meant his sons. Instead, Art took him into the locker room. Barniak was incredulous. "Why, in Philadelphia," he wrote, "a writer is forbidden privy to the Eagle sanctum." Art chuckled, "Some places this is a taboo, I guess. But this isn't the Pentagon I own here. Goodness, it's only a football team."

The game witnessed the debut of Franco's Italian Army. East Liberty baker Tony Stagno came with second-generation Italian Americans from his neighborhood. Carrying banners and wearing army helmets inscribed with "Franco's Italian Army," they marched inside Three Rivers and established a beachhead under the press box. Although Harris identified himself as black, he had embraced his mother's Italian culture and given Stagno his blessings.

"We've been a team in the process of turning the corner," Greene told Barniak. "We've been sort of tiptoeing up and peeking around to see what it's like around there. Well, today, we got a pretty good idea and baby, it's nice." Barniak looked for Art after the game but he had left to beat the crowds and catch the later game on television. Besides, Art had to answer a barrage of phone calls from well-wishers.

The Steelers took a 7-2 record to Cleveland, who trailed them by a game in their division. A win would put them ahead by two games with only four left. Steeler fans went berserk after Franco galloped 75 yards for a go-ahead touchdown in the freezing rain. Their celebration was premature; Cleveland kicked a field goal with seconds left to win 26–24.

Like many of his colleagues, the *Times'* Dave Anderson had waited for years to feature Art as a winner in football. He reprised Art's comment about the NFL. "Whatever I lost in money with the Steelers," he had said, "I was lucky to be able to lose it. I'd pay to lose it, to keep in this game. I love it that much." Anderson noted the crowd's ardor and the aura enveloping Rooney. "But the fans and Art Rooney's charisma as the NFL's most lovable owner can only do so much. The fans and Art Rooney have been here for decades, but it wasn't until this season that the Steelers had enough players to win, players such as Franco Harris and a defensive unit that has everything but a reputation." The reputation was coming.

Pittsburgh defenders surrendered only 15 points in the remaining four games. "I'll tell you," Joe Greene said, "when the Steelers drafted me, it *should* have been the happiest day of my life, but I couldn't be happy about it. I couldn't find anything good about it. And in my rookie year, 1969, we were 1-13, and it was awful. But the next year I could see something happening. And now I wouldn't want to be on another team." Greene, who had listened intently to Art's stories, appreciated the significance of the Steelers' turnaround. "This is history happening," he said. "You grow to love this team. Every year Mr. Rooney knows every rookie's name, and he's the owner. There's a lot of owners can't do that. That's why even if we get in the playoffs as the wild-card team and win the Super Bowl, it won't be the same unless we win that first division championship."

To do so, Pittsburgh would need to win its home rematch with the Browns, who had won their last four road games. "This is the biggest game I've ever played," Andy Russell said before kickoff. "We're at a point where we can right everything for all the bad years." Russell, the lone player left from the 1963 squad that had contended for the division title, said, "I've been waiting since 1963." A teammate added, "One game and we can erase history."

Because the NFL still imposed a seventy-five-mile blackout of home games, thousands of Pittsburghers drove into Ohio and Maryland to watch at bars and in hotel rooms. Members of Franco's Italian Army gathered at Vento's pizzeria that morning to stuff hoagies with capicolla and provolone and hollow out loaves of bread to smuggle bottles of wine into the stadium. They paraded inside with banners exhorting Franco and shook *corno*, a red pepper–shaped medallion with a small hunchback inside, to ward off the *malocchio*—or evil eye

Jack Ham's fan club called itself Dobre Shunka. "Dobre Shunka" meant "good ham" in Polish, but the men and women from the Blue Rock Club in Port Vue, a Monongahela River town, translated it as "Great Ham." The second-year linebacker played at that high a level. Brothers Ted and Dan Majzer had formed Dobre Shunka with other blue-collar workers with Eastern European roots, many of whom worked at National Tube in McKeesport. They had grown up on the sandlots where Art once roamed.

So had Gerela's Gorillas, who had embraced Steeler kicker Roy Gerela. Their leader, Bob Bubanic, wore a gorilla costume. The men—many of whom were Ukrainians from Port Vue—unfurled bed sheets in the stands with messages designed to distract Cleveland kicker Don Cockcroft.

The game itself was anticlimatic; Cleveland crossed midfield only once; Andy Russell recovered two fumbles, and Jack Ham one. After Franco's second touchdown, his army danced atop stadium dugouts, waving banners and flags. "We've put the evil eye on the Browns," rejoiced four-star general Tony Stagno.

Franco had rushed for over 100 yards in the last five games. Only Jim Brown had ever put together a six-game, 100 yards-per-game, streak. With a 27–0 lead, Noll told Bradshaw to give Franco the ball until his fullback and offensive line had matched Brown's mark.

The ninth win, the Steelers' first shutout in a decade, tied their all-time mark for victories. The frenzy at Three Rivers was matched by jubilation in homes where fans listened on radios. In Zanesville, Ohio, outside the blackout zone, hundreds of fans who had taken a bloc of rooms to watch on television emerged en masse when the game ended, tossing beer bottles and each other onto the motel lawn.

Art, who had remained silent during the game, soaked in the cheering in the stands and quietly congratulated players afterward. Art Jr.

brought *Sports Illustrated* writer Mort Sharnik and Sharnik's sons into the locker room, only to be confronted by equipment manager Jackie Hart, who barred children from his fiefdom. Art Jr. and Hart squared off and Hart ended up in an ice cooler. Art, who had been in enough fights not to be perturbed, made them shake afterward.

That evening, Ed Kiely drove Art to Cleveland to pay their respects to the late Browns' owner Mickey McBride. Kiely recalled his favorite McBride story: Turning to McBride after a Cleveland touchdown, Art said that the play would be reversed. Sure enough, an official called a penalty that nullified the touchdown. McBride, who knew racing better than football, stared at Art in awe and said, "Geez, you've got the referees, too."

Pressed on his reaction to closing in on his first title, Art deadpanned, "I don't think I could have done it so soon, without a combination of brains and hard work." Asked what had been the smartest thing he had done, Art replied, "I put my son Artie in charge of the scouting. The draft has turned us around in five years." Art reflected on success. "You have to be lucky," he acknowledged, and "you need a coach who believes in what your personnel department is trying to do." Attitude mattered, too. "Last year our team was about as good as this one, but it didn't think it could win. It just waited to get beat. This year they believe. The town believes, the newspapers, the owner, everybody in Pittsburgh is a believer now."

Losing still stung. "When you come home from a losing trip," Art said, "it's like there's a body on the plane." Football had been more exciting in the old days, he laughed, with the biggest thrill coming Mondays—making payroll. Football encourages dedication, he argued. "I see it in my boys, Danny and Artie. They're determined to make the Steelers a success, and nobody has contributed more than Danny." When asked how he could run the team and the tracks, he said, "It's the three younger boys who have the tracks, Tim, Pat, and John. The other two, Danny and Artie, spend so much time on football they don't know the difference between a horse and a donkey."

Pittsburgh had a one-game lead with two games left. Its injury-riddled defense held Houston to 3 points in the next game as rookie Joe

Gilliam, substituting for an injured Bradshaw, led Pittsburgh to a 9–3 victory. Cleveland won, too, preventing Pittsburgh from clinching. On the flight home, trainer Ralph Berlin treated thirteen injured players. Andy Russell commandeered the plane's intercom when it reached altitude. "We decided to award the game ball to a guy," he announced, "who is so outstanding that much of the time his play is taken for granted." He handed the ball to Joe Greene, who had played with uncommon ferocity, sacking the quarterback four times and blocking a field goal. It was the sixth time that the defense had not surrendered a touchdown. Art passed around handmade Jamaican cigars after games. At home, the phone rang all night.

As people jumped aboard the bandwagon, a legion of sportswriters paraded into town. "They've made Franco's Italian Army, Gerela's Gorillas, and Dobre Shunka," Pat Livingston declared, "as well known along the Eastern seaboard as they are in Pittsburgh." The networks, loving the Cinderella story, featured Pittsburgh. Even the old guard was pulling for Art. Halas called every Sunday to let Art know that if he could not win the title, he was pulling for his oldest friend in football. He wasn't the only one.

"Getting the owners of the 26 NFL teams to agree unanimously can be difficult," *Football News'* Jim Haughton wrote. "But on one point there is full agreement. Ask them what owner—besides themselves—they'd like to see grab the marbles and the Super Bowl and chance would be it's Arthur J. Rooney."

Art seemed unfazed. "The public is clamoring to see the Steelers," Livingston argued. "But Art Rooney acts no different today about his team than he acted in the past." But Art did feel different. "Maybe it's worth it, waiting all those years," Art mused. "If we had won in those years—in 1936, 1947, 1963—maybe the thrill wouldn't be so great right now." He even dared to think about the postseason. "We've beaten everybody—or feel we can beat them," he said quietly.

Colonel Sinatra

The Steelers headed west early for their final game in San Diego. While Noll figured that Palm Springs would be more conducive to practice, the front office and beat writers savored the reprise from winter. Dan Rooney stayed behind, but Art was relieved to get away. The stream of out-of-town reporters, each dredging up Art's history as the game's quintessential loser, was wearing thin. "It's not up to me to be confident," he replied when asked if this would be the year. "The coaches and the players are the ones who have to be confident. All I do is go to the game and root." He conceded—again—that losing had hurt. "But I wouldn't trade it for anything. Owning a team here in Pittsburgh has been a great experience." Writers questioned players and ex-players about him. "He is always so considerate," Joe Greene said softly, "and he takes personal interest in each one of the players." Supreme Court justice Whizzer White put it simply: "Art Rooney is the finest person I've ever met."

That week, the Rooneys bought Green Mountain Racetrack. Although it was Vermont's only track, Art was skeptical about the $8.6 million purchase. "That was the only thing he advised us not to buy," John Rooney recalled. "He said this place has more cows than it does people. We never were successful there except maybe the first year."

In Palm Springs, a party of newsmen and employees dined at Lord Fletcher's, a pub on the outskirts of town. "And all of a sudden," Jim Boston remembered, "who walks in with his entourage but Sinatra." Frank Sinatra, accompanied by former baseball manager Leo Durocher, golfer Ken Venturi, a tall brunette, and a bodyguard, entered a private room. Myron Cope leaped into action. He had been trying to find Sinatra, who had a home in Palm Springs, to induct him into Franco's Italian Army. Scrawling a note on a cocktail napkin, Cope called the waiter over. When the waiter hesitated to deliver it, Cope said, "We're with the Steelers. You know who we are. We're like him." The waiter reluctantly left with the note. A few minutes later, Sinatra strode over to their table.

"Cope jumps up," Boston laughed. "You know Cope; he takes over and says we're going to get you deputized in the Italian Army." Sinatra replied, "Groovy, I'd love to. Is Mister Rooney with you people?" Cope said, "Yeah, we'll introduce you to him. We'll get you a cigar." Pat Livingston described the Sinatra-Cope exchange as one between "the best voice and the worst voice in the English-speaking world." Promising he would attend the next practice, Sinatra asked about Bradshaw's injured finger. Cope interpreted that as confirmation of rumors he bet heavily on football. After Sinatra left, the waiter returned with cases of Pommard St. Vincent and Pouilly Fuisse. "Mr. Sinatra's compliments. He said you can have more if you want it."

Cope called Patsy Stagno, reaching the army commander at his bakery. "Get out here as quick as you can," he barked. "You have to personally induct this guy." Stagno and Albert Vento grabbed an assortment of wines and cheese and caught the next plane. It was Stagno's first flight.

At practice the next day, Jim Boston was on the phone with Joe Gordon, who asked if Sinatra was there. Boston laughed: "No. Sinatra never showed." Just then a voice behind Boston piped up, "Who didn't show up? I said I'd be here, didn't I?" Sinatra, in checked trousers, white pork pie hat, and orange golf sweater, had been watching from the stands. He had held back, knowing his presence would disrupt practice.

When Art heard that Sinatra wanted to meet him, he growled, "What does he want to meet me for?" But he went over, stuck out his hand, and said, "I'm Art Rooney." Sinatra grabbed it. "Mr. Rooney, one thing in my life that I always wanted to do, I wanted to meet you. You know that you're a legend." Art was flustered. "His face started to get red, and his cigar was twitching," Boston recalled. "He's blushing. That's the first time I saw him get like that, like he was trying to hide under a table. The whole thing got him shook up."

Sinatra lathered on the flattery. "There's nobody in Las Vegas that doesn't know you. Any time I go to Las Vegas, all those big shots, they always say to me, 'You mean to tell me that you don't know Art Rooney?'" Milton Jaffe, who managed the Stardust Casino, had given Art a Vegas profile. Although not interested in Vegas shows or gaming, Art visited frequently, staying with Milton and catching up with old friends. Pittsburgh expatriates ran the city's powerful sport betting industry.

After chatting awhile, Sinatra told Art that he had come to meet him. "But where's Franco at? I'm joining the army." When told that Sinatra was waiting to meet him, Franco demurred. But Noll beckoned him to the sidelines, where Patsy Stagno commissioned Sinatra as an officer. Afterward, Stagno called his wife: "Honey, it was for real. I kissed him on both cheeks. It was like kissing God." The induction initiated a life-long friendship. Sinatra sent Art boxes of Cuban cigars and Art sent him footballs and jerseys. "Sinatra fell in love with him," Boston said. "Art had Sinatra's number at home. He could always get ahold of him."

The Steelers were bemused by Sinatra but worried about the game. They were badly banged up, and players watched part of Cleveland's game on television before leaving for the stadium. With Cleveland winning, they realized that they would not back into the title. They had to win. Those on the team the longest felt the most pressure. On the bus, Ray Mansfield tried to unfasten the top button of his shirt to relieve the tightness only to find it was already open. Andy Russell was in comparable turmoil. "I told myself, 'Christ, here we are. We've had a great season and now we can screw it up, then that stigma of the losing Steelers will still be there.' That's what my heart told me. My brain said, 'Hell, we should win this game because we're the better football team.'" Joe Greene, however, was unfazed and unequivocal. "Even if we go to the Super Bowl, it won't be the same if we don't win the division. We'd like to get that title. It means a lot to [Art]," he told Phil Musick. "Art Rooney seems to have a special rapport with the black players," Musick reflected, "or maybe it's just that he treats everyone the same, like he thought you were really important. Or maybe that rapport seems to exist because when he was a kid at the turn of the century on the Northside, the gentry spit on Irishmen."

Art sat with the press, uncharacteristically second-guessing play selection and smoking not one, but two, cigars. In the stands, sailors waved "Franco's Italian-American Navy" signs. Several thousand Pittsburghers were there, along with those who had left the city years before but retained their allegiance.

The game was one-sided. After Bradshaw put Pittsburgh ahead 24–2 with 6 minutes left, sportswriters closed in on Art. "It was a long time coming," he reflected. As the game ended, Dwight White stood on the sidelines, chuckling, "Same Old Steelers."

When Art entered the locker room, Dan took his hand and said, "We made it." They had rarely talked about the team's chances, no matter how often they thought about them, during the season. In truth, they didn't want to jinx themselves. Before Art got to his players, a phalanx of media surrounded him. When he escaped, he told Livingston, "If I knew so many people were going to talk to me, I'd never have gone in there." When pressed as to his low-key demeanor, Art shrugged: "It's just my nature. I never show my enthusiasm."

Art said he had felt that this team could win the division since losing the season's second game. "A team that can lose a game and not worry about it is a team that believes in itself. And that's all this team had to do."

The plane was over the Sierra Nevada when Art got out of his seat and slowly made his way down the aisle. He thanked each member of the team and organization, including the grounds crew. He shook their hands, expressed his gratitude, and received their congratulations in return. "Why congratulate me?" he asked when he reached reporters in the back. "Those fellows up there are the ones who should be congratulated."

After Art sat down next to coach Lionel Taylor's wife, Loren, Andy Russell got on the intercom. "I don't want to sound maudlin or sentimental," Russell began, "but I speak for every member of the team when I say that this ball goes to a great guy . . . We all respect this man and we love to play and work for him. He's waited a long time for this and this is just the first of many to come." Russell brought the game ball to Art as cheers thundered through the cabin. Art could not find words, and his glasses misted over. When he recovered his composure, he took the intercom. "This is the best gift I've ever received." Many of those listening had tears slipping down their cheeks. Art took the ball home and kept it there. "From now on," Dan said, "whenever they say 'Same Old Steelers,' it won't hurt any more. They'll be referring to winners."

Despite frigid weather and Dan's refusal to give out their arrival time to prevent chaos at the airport, 5,000 fans were waiting when they touched down after midnight. Before dawn, lines had formed for tickets to Saturday's playoff game against Oakland. An afternoon editorial cartoon featured Rooney as a leprechaun, his cigar as long as his torso, sliding down a rainbow into a pot of gold. Steelers' coverage overshadowed Nixon's resumption of the air war in Vietnam and a devastating earthquake in Nicaragua.

At noon the next day, Father John Duggan celebrated a Mass of thanksgiving with Dan Rooney and Ed Kiely serving as altar boys. Art deflected attention when cornered afterward. "I didn't do anything different this season than I did in the other thirty-nine," he remarked. "Our players, our coaches, our scouts and our organization made this year a success." But reporters insisted on reprising Art's folkloric status. Charley Feeney teased an admission from Art: "We used to have teams that waited to get beat. I became part of it. I sat in the stands and waited to get beat, too."

Another old friend, *Post-Gazette* sports editor Al Abrams, joined the salute. "No owner, I am sure, in the history of sports has stood up to failure with as much patience and fight as this stocky, venerable resident of the Northside. He took all the howling, the insulting letters, the unwarranted charges that he is cheap to the point of being miserly." Abrams recalled the 1963 Giants game when a parade of writers came by wishing Art well. Even New York writers had pulled for him. "I doubt if there is an owner in sports today who is better known to sports writers the country over." Abrams knew that Art was deeply pleased but pointed out that he had changed little from when he was broke and his team losing. "They were happy days, too," Art reminded Abrams. "I think we had more fun when our office was in the Fort Pitt Hotel, and you fellows would rather come through the window than walk all the way down the lobby to the door."

Race

While Art was the Steelers' patriarch, Franco Harris became the poster child for a team overcoming racial division. Both white and black Pittsburghers laid claim to the handsome young rookie. Some African Americans, however, resented what they saw as white appropriation of a black athlete. Army member Ben Elisco countered that while celebrating Harris's Italian heritage, he did not discount his African American background. "I realize [Harris's] greatest contribution to Pittsburgh—and maybe the country—won't be made on the football field. It will be made on the streets, in the way people treat each other." Harris's quiet dignity, he said, had done much to break down racial prejudices. Many waving Italian flags, Elisco noted, were black.

The Steelers were composed almost equally of white and black players. "So many of us had come out of situations that were less diverse," Dwight White explained, "but everybody rose above that." Race, he recalled, came into play only when they socialized in public. Some white players were more comfortable with black teammates than others. "Gerry Mullins was from usc," White said. "He was a little more worldly, a different animal from Bobby Walden from Stone Mountain, Georgia." But White felt that most teammates gradually ditched their racial baggage. "We used to have fish fries that were some of the greatest times," he remembered. Given the competitive nature of their work, there were tensions. "But I never felt that a white player didn't like me because I was black," White concluded. "He might not like me because I run my mouth, or I'm a pain in the butt, but not because I was black. Winning breaks down a lot of barriers."

The Rooneys, White argued, made the team feel like "a mom and pop type organization." Coaches and staff ate at a stadium cafeteria. So did the players after White saw Myron Cope eating there. "If a sportswriter could fix a sandwich," he figured, "I can fix me a sandwich. The Chief would be there with Rich, his driver, and we'd be sitting around talking. It was family."

The younger players hung out together. Ben McGee and Chuck Hinton, who had played at black colleges, owned the Peyton Place Clubhouse in East Liberty. "We would eat dinner over there and chase girls," White recalled, "or they'd chase us." Many made their homes in Pittsburgh. "I never thought I would live up here," White explained. "In Texas, you were either black, white, or Mexican. Wasn't no Jew, wasn't no Polish person, weren't no Italians. You were just a honky. In Pittsburgh, I learned diversity, for better and worse." White recalled his surprise when Karen Farmer, the African American woman he married, called her Italian American girlfriend her very best friend. In Texas, that was beyond the realm of possibility.

The Immaculate Reception

The Friday before the playoff game with the Raiders, Art hosted the Steelers' Christmas party. Handing out gifts to children, he chatted with Terry Bradshaw's wife, Melissa, a former Miss Teenage America from Pittsburgh. That night, Art visited funeral homes and wound up at the wake of a friend from the Ward.

The next day, Father John Duggan was tossed out of the Raiders practice. When he protested that he knew nothing about football and could do Oakland no harm, a Raiders official said, "You're a priest, aren't you? That makes you dangerous. Art Rooney has every priest in the country pulling for him." Duggan couldn't argue with that.

The Kilkenny native was a fixture at games. Art's sons had met the young priest in Ireland and invited him to see Pittsburgh play during the 1970 preseason. The Steelers won every game Duggan saw but started losing again after he departed. Two years later, Duggan arrived in Boston to pursue a doctorate and reconnected with the Rooneys, who persuaded him to accompany the team. Duggan missed two games, both losses, but Pittsburgh won eleven of the twelve he attended. The only defeat came against Cleveland. "They had a man with more experience on their side," Duggan rationalized, "a Jewish rabbi." Art was religious, not superstitious. Still, he ordered his sons, "You get that priest down here for every game. I don't care what the cost is." Duggan, who worked diligently to understand American football, held Mass before games, blending scripture with prayers for the players' health and Pittsburgh wins.

On game day, convoys streamed out of town as fans searched for television sets beyond the blackout zone. Moose and Elks lodges chartered buses to Meadville and Erie to watch at fraternal branches. Although Mayor Pete Flaherty had filed suit to void the blackout and President Nixon complained about it, the NFL would not waive its longstanding rule. "What else but an issue like the televising of a football game," Roy McHugh pondered, "could divert Richard Nixon from his preoccupation with dropping bombs on North Vietnam?"

Art went to the stadium from Mass. He saw Oakland coach John

Madden inspecting the field and said "Hi, I'm Art Rooney. I wish you all the luck in the world, except for today." Pirate owner John Galbreath and his son Dan came over to buck him up. The Pirates had won their division that year but lost in the playoffs on a wild pitch.

Sportswriter Gene Ward interviewed Art before kickoff. "I'm happiest for the fans," Art said. "They really deserved it, and I only hope they won't be too disappointed if the Raiders beat us today, which, with the injuries to our guards, could happen." Sam Davis and Bruce Van Dyke had missed several games. They would play, but Art wondered for how long.

By the time the game began in balmy 43-degree weather, Art was in his spartan box on the third level of the stadium with Father Campbell, Father Flanagan, and Richie Easton. Below him, Bob Bubanic, the leader of Gerela's Gorillas, wore his gorilla mask and a Santa Claus outfit, hoping for an early Christmas.

While Art fretted about his team's health, fans worried about stopping Oakland's high-powered attack. Eight Raiders, seven on offense, had made the Pro Bowl. But for the first 58:47 of play, Pittsburgh held Oakland scoreless. The Raiders could not move the ball. Andy Russell intercepted a pass early in the game but the Steelers could neither capitalize on that turnover nor on a fumble Russell caused. The game was scoreless at halftime.

Pittsburgh finally scored on a Gerela field goal. In the fourth quarter, after Ken Stabler replaced Daryle Lamonica at quarterback for Oakland, Joe Greene and Dwight White forced a fumble, which led to another field goal. Art said little during the game and recited the rosary at the beginning of the fourth quarter. Pittsburgh led 6–0 with 3:50 to go, but Art had been around football too long to feel comfortable.

With under 2 minutes to play, Stabler drove the Raiders to the Steelers 30-yard line. He dropped back to pass as Pittsburgh blitzed. Russell got caught in a scrum of players and Stabler scooted down the left side of the field. He slithered around Craig Hanneman, and raced untouched into the end zone to tie the game. Western Pennsylvania native George Blanda, the oldest man in the league at forty-five, kicked the point after to put Oakland ahead 7–6 with 1:13 left to play.

When the kickoff went into the end zone, Pittsburgh began on its own 20-yard line. Bradshaw completed passes to Franco Harris and Frenchy Fuqua to get to their 40-yard line, but his next three attempts fell incomplete. On two of them, defensive back Jack Tatum blasted the intended receiver hard enough to break up the play. The Steelers faced fourth and ten from their own 40-yard line with 22 seconds left to play. They needed to gain about 25 yards to attempt a field goal. But even if they gained a first down and put Gerela in range, they would have to kill the clock before time expired.

As sportswriters composed their epitaphs for Pittsburgh, Art stood up and left his box, followed by his friends. Nobody spoke. They trudged over to the elevator, where Pirates announcer Bob Prince held the door so that Art could get inside for the ride to the locker room. "I figured we had lost," he later explained, "and I wanted to get to the locker room early so I could personally thank the players for the fine job they'd done all season.

On the field, Bradshaw had one last chance. Noll sent in 66 Circle Option, a play designed to hit rookie receiver Barry Pearson down the middle and get within field goal range. Bradshaw dropped back under a heavy rush. "I felt pressure coming from one side," he said later, "so I moved to the other side. Then I got some pressure over there so I started to scramble." A Raider grabbed him around his shoulders, but he twisted away. Frenchy Fuqua curled into the center of the field, deep enough to give Gerela a shot at a field goal if the pass could be completed and time stopped by downing the football. But another Raider lurched toward Bradshaw, forcing him to unload the ball. "I saw Frenchy and I didn't see anyone around. Then I don't know what happened," Bradshaw said. "I guess I got knocked down."

The football, Frenchy Fuqua, and defender Jack Tatum converged at Oakland's 35-yard line. The ball bounced off Fuqua, or Tatum, or both of them, and ricocheted backward. Fuqua fell to the turf, dazed. He had not seen Tatum coming. "He gave me a good lick; everything was dizzy . . . I saw this dude at the 5-yard line and I couldn't figure out why." The dude was teammate Franco Harris.

"I was supposed to stay in and block a linebacker if they blitzed, but they didn't," Harris said later. "I knew Brad was in serious trouble so I went downfield in case he needed me as an outlet receiver. I was always taught to go to the ball, so when he threw it, that's what I did. The next thing I knew the ball was coming right to me." Grabbing the football at his shoe tops before it hit the ground, Harris streaked down the left side of the field. He eluded one Raider at the ten and managed to stay in bounds as momentum pulled him toward the sidelines. Myron Cope, half Franco's size, stood by the end zone shrieking, "C'mon Franco, c'mon!" Harris crossed the goal line with 5 seconds on the clock.

Fuqua arose. "I hear people cheering. I can't imagine what happened." Nor did those on the sidelines. All they saw was Franco in the end zone clutching the ball.

While the play unfolded, Art was slowly descending to the ground floor. Silent since leaving the box, he grappled with what he would tell his players. Then the stadium suddenly reverberated. "We heard a wild scream from the crowd," Art said later. "It could only mean one thing but no one in the elevator dared believe it."

As Art got off the elevator, a stadium guard came rushing toward him, shrieking, "You won it! You won it!" "I asked him if he was kidding and he screamed, 'No! Listen to the crowd!' I heard all the shouting and cheering, but I still wasn't sure what happened." Art entered the locker room, deserted except for trainer Bobby DeMarco and club photographer Marty Homa. "They didn't know what had happened either."

Art pieced together that the Steelers had somehow scored. But as time passed, his uncertainty soared. "I was waiting in the locker room and I couldn't figure out where the players were. Then we heard there was a question about the touchdown. I was dying while we waited to find out."

Fans had swarmed the field after Harris crossed the goal line while officials huddled to determine what had happened. If Fuqua had touched the ball without a defender also or subsequently touching it, then Harris's catch would be nullified. Head referee Fred Swearingen conferred with umpire Pat Harder, who had the best view of the play, and the back judge. They agreed that both Fuqua and Tatum had touched the ball. Before ruling, Swearingen got on a baseball dugout phone with NFL

supervisor of officials Art McNally, who was in a booth upstairs. Mc-
Nally asked, "How did you rule?" Swearingen said, "I called it double-
touching. Touchdown." McNally said, "That's right."

By then, five achingly long minutes had expired. Art stood by a locker,
chewed his cigar, and waited. The longer the delay went on, the less sure
he was of anything. "I started to suspect that whatever good had happened to us would be disallowed." Then, on the field above, Fred Swearingen raised his hands to signal touchdown and the stadium erupted
again. Art didn't know what had happened but the crowd's primal
scream sounded wonderful.

It took another 10 minutes to clear the field and allow Gerela to kick
the point after. There were 5 seconds to play and Pittsburgh kicked off.
Stabler threw one long incomplete pass from his 20-yard line and the
game was over. Raiders coach John Madden ripped the telephone off
the dugout wall while fans retook the field. Most were giddy, their euphoria mixed with disbelief. The Steelers, giddy themselves, poured inside the dressing room. Kicker Bobby Walden rushed over to Art, enveloped him in his arms, spun him around, and shouted, "We won!" Chuck
Noll knelt in the middle of the locker room and led a prayer.

Franco Harris tried to reconstruct what had happened. Rambling
on, he summed it up with one word, "Beautiful." Ray Mansfield, who
had initiated the play by snapping the ball to Bradshaw, said, "I went
from the depths of despair to the apex of ecstasy." Tackle John Brown
added, "Tomorrow morning when I wake up and read the paper I still
won't believe it's real." Father Duggan smiled and said, "I knew the
ball would bounce that way." He said he had a premonition when he
opened his Bible that morning to a passage that read, "Stand firm and
wait for the Victory of the Lord."

For Jack Ham, the unbelievable ending had a familiar feeling. He had
played in the 1969 Orange Bowl, when a penalty called on Kansas for
having twelve men on the field allowed Penn State a second chance at
a game-winning 2-point conversion. Penn State coach Joe Paterno had
watched the Raiders–Steelers game in New Orleans, where he was preparing for the Sugar Bowl. He told writers about breakfasting with Art
before the Orange Bowl. After Penn State's miraculous reprieve, Paterno

said, "Mr. Rooney, who had two sisters who are nuns and a brother who's a priest, told me he would trade them straight up for my mother." He declined the trade. "After I saw Franco Harris catch that rebound last week against Oakland, I wired Mr. Rooney. I said, "It's a deal. You can have Mom. Send me your sisters and your brother.""

Joe Greene peeled off his dirty uniform. "Don't know why anybody wants to talk to me," he smiled. "I ain't about to take any credit for this one. 'Bout time somebody else gets the headlines. I don't mean to knock victory, but we didn't win this one. Fate or luck did it. Or maybe it was the Man, you know, the main Man."

In Oakland's locker room, there was little talking. "It seems unfair," John Madden muttered. He had more to say after viewing film of the game on Christmas Eve. Seething and convinced that officials had botched the call, Madden insisted that Tatum had hit Fuqua from behind as the ball hit Fuqua's shoulder, causing the ball to carom back. If he was right, Harris's catch should have been nullified. Furthermore, he claimed that officials missed Steeler John McMakin clipping Raiders linebacker Phil Villapiano after the catch. Madden argued that Pittsburgh fans had intimidated the officials. "There was no way they were going to call it any other way with all those people out on the field," he said. "Somebody would have been killed."

If anybody knew for sure if the call was correct, it was Frenchy Fuqua. When reporters demanded an explanation and he hesitated, Andy Russell intervened. Pulling Frenchy aside, he explained the rules. With that, Frenchy said that he was done talking. "I'll tell you after the Super Bowl," he smiled. "I'm not chopping down any cherry trees but no comment."

As Myron Cope prepared for his evening radio show, he received a phone call from Sharon Levosky, who said her friend Michael Ord had called the catch "The Immaculate Reception." Cope used the tag on the air that night and it stuck. Fuqua later said that he told only one person, Art, what had happened. Art replied, "Frenchy, let it stay immaculate." Art Jr. summed up the play. "That catch wasn't good scouting," he reflected. "It wasn't good coaching, it wasn't good playing. It was seventy-two years of good Christian life on the part of my father."

The city was in bedlam. Unlike the disturbances following King's assassination in 1968, this upheaval was a happy riot of multiracial release. "In the raucous streets," Red Smith wrote, "Frenchy's Foreign Legion honked at Bradshaw's Brigade, Gerela's Gorillas hailed Ham's Hussars, and foot soldiers in Franco's Italian Army waved red, white and green flags . . . not since Braddock was ambushed at Fort Duquesne had the town known a day like this."

The national press held Art in higher esteem than ever. Art had never enjoyed such uncritical adulation in Pittsburgh—not that he had wanted it—but now he was the city's favorite son. A few writers detected capriciousness in Pittsburgh's response. Art was no longer labeled a cheapskate and the Steelers sad-sack losers, but Roy McHugh would not allow Pittsburghers to forget the abuse long leveled at Art. "The whole town is mawkish about the Steelers, after 40 years in which the predominant feeling toward them was scorn," McHugh wrote. "Art Rooney is now being acclaimed by everybody for all the good qualities he had in the same abundance when his hired hands were losing."

Dan Rooney was less concerned about the slings and arrows hurled their way in the past. "The big thing about this year is that we've overcome our history," he said. "We don't have to relive it. Even though we were having a great year, and had won more games than any other Steeler team, if we hadn't won the championship, it still would've looked like history repeating itself." The Same Old Steelers could be buried.

Arthur Daley spoke with Art after Christmas. "We've had a fine Christmas," Art said straight-faced. "Everyone here is starting to believe in miracles. As for me, I'm embarrassed to say that I'll have to take their word for it. I didn't see the miracle. I missed the play." Daley paid homage. "That he should be the most respected and beloved man among his fellow owners is not surprising," the dean of *New York Times* sportswriters reasoned. "But the players and the sports writers feel the same way about him, and that sets apart this white-haired, over-sized leprechaun with the quick smile and the warm personality because they rarely agree with anyone, especially each other . . . Rooney has never changed as he carried on his love affair with Pittsburgh . . . 'These are my people,' Rooney had once said, 'and this is my town, and it does my heart good just to be here.'"

Almost

Before the AFC championship versus Miami, Red Smith wrote that Tim Rooney had his hands full at Yonkers. Hot Horse Howie Samuels' off-track betting (OTB) business was clobbering the Rooneys. "Art Rooney and his five sons are no green peas in sports promotion," Smith noted. "They couldn't have gone into the Yonkers deal with their eyes shut." Tim responded that New York state law provided for OTB to cover short-falls if betting and attendance dropped below 1969 levels. "With the assurance that business couldn't go below that minimum," Tim said, "this figured to be a sound investment." Smith wasn't convinced. The Rooneys conferred daily about their most lucrative enterprise and its vulnerability to competition for gambling dollars.

In Pittsburgh, few cared about Yonkers. Still buzzing over the Oakland game, fans were concerned about their team's health. Badly worn down, the team's psychological and physical reserves had been tested during the last eleven games. Although Pittsburgh had won ten of them, each had been a draining, must-win affair. Dwight White was playing on bad knees, guards Clack and Davis were in and out of the lineup, L. C. Greenwood was banged up, and all three quarterbacks had been sidelined. Prior to the December 31 AFC championship, influenza hospitalized Bradshaw and Larry Brown and weakened Greenwood, Holmes, and Greene.

Pittsburgh's opponent, the undefeated Miami Dolphins, featured an impressive attack and the league's leading defense. Franco's Italian Army dropped thousands of leaflets from a plane over the William Penn Hotel, where the Dolphins were staying, guaranteeing safe passage out of town. The wind, however, carried most of the leaflets into the river. Coming after the Immaculate Reception, the contest was an anticlimax. This was Miami's year, and Cinderella was left by the roadside, her carriage a pumpkin again.

Although Pittsburgh scored first, the Dolphins regained momentum when Larry Seiple faked a punt and streaked 37 yards to the Steelers

12-yard line. Miami scored to tie the game. After Gerela put the Steelers ahead with a field goal, the Dolphins regained the lead. Bradshaw, vitiated by the flu, endured a hard hit that pinched a nerve and forced him off the field. He came back in with the Steelers trailing 21–10 and brought them back to 21–17 with 5 minutes left to play. But Pittsburgh did not score again. In the locker room, no player blamed anybody but himself. Each vowed the Steelers would be back next year. But Miami, not Pittsburgh, was going to the Super Bowl.

New Year's Day 1973 dawned sadly in Pittsburgh. Pittsburghers awoke to the news that Pirate right fielder Roberto Clemente had disappeared in an airplane accident. Clemente had managed Puerto Rico's team in the Mundiales, the world amateur baseball championship, the previous month in Nicaragua. After he returned home to Puerto Rico, an earthquake rocked the Central American nation, and Clemente spearheaded relief efforts. When he found out that Nicaraguan dictator Anastasio Somoza's National Guard was looting relief supplies, he decided to fly there himself on New Year's Eve. Clemente's plane disappeared into the waters off San Juan after takeoff; his body was never recovered.

Roberto Clemente, Honus Wagner, and Josh Gibson were the three greatest baseball players ever to grace Pittsburgh fields. Art had played against Wagner and Gibson and watched Clemente during his eighteen seasons in Pittsburgh. Although they chatted during batting practice, Art did not get to know the proud, enigmatic right fielder the way he had Wagner and Gibson. Still, he had admired Roberto, a strikingly handsome man who played with drive and elegance. Art knew what it took to excel at baseball, and he relished watching Clemente, who was as complete a player as could be found. Pittsburgh, Puerto Rico, and fans across the Americas were in mourning. "It is just as well the Steelers didn't beat the Miami Dolphins on Sunday," Pat Livingston acknowledged. "In light of developments that night in the skies about Puerto Rico, nobody would have cherished the memories of the city's football celebration."

The 1972 season, the most exciting one in the Steelers' forty years, was over. Though it ended short of the Super Bowl, Art was accorded a winner's status. That belated recognition amused, even angered, those who knew Art had been a winner—on the sandlots, in the ring, at the track—his entire life. Art, for his part, showed little emotion. Only those close to him knew how profoundly happy he was. It wasn't so much that he was called a winner, but that his sons, his team, and his city were. Besides, it was time to head for the track.

19

Football's Promised Land

1973–74

Even as the chasm in age, race, and culture widened between the seventy-two-year-old owner and his twenty-something Steelers, Art grew closer to them. He was old enough to be their grandfather, a role for which he had ample experience. A friendly, nonjudgmental figure, Art was reassuring in a gruff way. Players found his rootedness in family, Pittsburgh, and football comforting. Their trust in him deepened their commitment to the team. While Joe Greene and Terry Bradshaw developed special relationships with Art, many Steelers felt deep loyalty to their stocky, graying owner.

Art knew firsthand what it meant to play hurt and to hurt because you could not play. Dwight White's bad knees and Terry Hanratty's battered ribs were not abstractions. He had experienced the physical pain they endured and the psychological stress they faced. He knew how tough it was to leave the game and how much a man paid the rest of his life for a career of contact.

Art had mellowed, easing up on his sons, on whom he had always been toughest. "At home," John Rooney stressed, "he was great, but he was your father; he was not your friend. By no means was he your friend." Never a micromanager, Art had entrusted his sons with considerable responsibility. They had done well and not just with football. John, Tim, and Pat had turned racing into the family's cash cow. Art talked shop with his sons daily, helping them to negotiate racing's maze of constituencies and the flotsam drawn to gambling. Speaking from experience, he pulled no punches. As Pat Livingston observed about the Steelers, but was true for the tracks, "Dan Rooney does not command the final, irrevocable word on major decisions. His dad is still a vigorous, active overseer."

Ernie Holmes

While the boys tended to business, Art endured the public makeover triggered by the Immaculate Reception. He embodied the luck of the Irish again, and his team was a "feel-good" tale for a country roiled by Vietnam. Dan was voted NFL Executive of the Year, and Art Jr. was heralded for drafting Greene, Bradshaw, Blount, Ham, and Harris. Roy Blount Jr. profiled the Rooneys for *Sports Illustrated* in July; Myron Cope followed with another feature in August. Blount stuck around to write a book about the team, while author James Michener, embarking on his next opus, a study of sport in America, visited camp intending to feature Art. Art talked horses with Michener but dismissed being preserved for posterity.

His players were feted throughout the region. Jack Ham and girlfriend, teacher Joann Fell, thanked his Dobre Shunka fan club by visiting the Blue Rock Club in Port Vue in March. Nobody minded that Ham did not know how to polka.

While Ham watched his girlfriend polka in Port Vue, Ernie Holmes resided on the tenth floor of the Western Psychiatric Institute, out on bail for three counts of intent to kill. Holmes, a fourteenth-round draft pick in 1971, had not stuck with the club that season. After making the team in 1972 and playing well, he was expected to start in 1973.

But Holmes had tumbled into free fall during the off-season. Calling the Rooneys for help, he arranged to meet with Dan. Holmes drove to Pittsburgh on March 16 but arrived after the office had closed for the day. He turned around, sat in traffic on the Fort Pitt Bridge, and began a slow burn. By the time Holmes was on Interstate 80 in Ohio, he was ready to blow. Convinced that truckers were trying to run him off the road, he grabbed his pistol and began shooting. A chase ended when his car careened into a ditch and he fled into the woods. Holmes had sacked quarterbacks before; this time he brought down a police helicopter, wounding its pilot. Cornered, Holmes surrendered before the troopers fired back. "We could've killed him a dozen times," one officer said. "I didn't want to hurt anybody," Holmes contended. Nevertheless, he had shot a trooper.

The incident occurred outside Salem, near where Art had played sandlot ball. Most organizations would have immediately released Holmes. Instead, Dan, Chuck Noll, and Ralph Berlin went to Salem while Art returned from Florida. Holmes was released into their custody with the proviso that he enter a psychiatric institution.

Art visited daily for the next two months. Holmes was scared and confused. "I was having some hard times," he remembered, "but Mr. Rooney was always there. He came to my aid like a father to a son." Art listened to Holmes and assured him that he would stand by him. "He made you feel it would work out," Holmes said.

While he appreciated Holmes's value to the team, Art's solicitude was for the man, not the player. "I know it's going to be okay, Fats, old boy," he said, steadying Holmes. "This is a guy I'd go into war for," Holmes emphasized. "I'd rush Bunker Hill for him."

If ever there was a time to shoot at truckers and wound a trooper, Holmes had found it. The Steelers' success and Art's status gave Holmes a chance to stay out of prison. While awaiting trial, he worked out at Three Rivers and returned to Western Psych afterward. At the trial, a psychiatrist testified that Holmes had been suffering from "acute paranoid psychosis." Pleading guilty to assault with a deadly weapon, he received five years of probation. In July, Holmes arrived at camp with a new nickname, Quick Draw.

The rest of spring proved less eventful. Art met with his sons about their corporate interests and attended NFL meetings. The boys persuaded Art to trade the wad of cash he carried for a credit card. When he used it to pay for their rooms after a meeting in Acapulco, the hotel rejected it. Art savored the moment; he preferred cash and handshakes to credit cards and contracts. In Acapulco, he opposed Pete Rozelle's proposal to require overtime for tie games. Overtime was appropriate for title games, Art said. "But if a regular season game ends up tied, let it be a tie." His reasoning was classic Rooney. "I was thinking in particular of those teams in that icebox division. Can you imagine asking those guys to play overtime in the kind of weather they're subjected to?" The owners agreed.

Art's sons were gaining stature in the league. Dan began chairing the expansion committee, a role Art once played, and everybody was trying to replicate Art Jr.'s scouting mojo. Art visited his tracks in Philadelphia and Yonkers, as well as a few where he could make a bet, and then headed to Palm Beach for the Kennel Club's closing weekend.

The 1973 Preseason

"The monkey's off," Pat Livingston crowed when camp opened. Instead of lugging the baggage of perennial losers, players and coaches arrived with air conditioners, stereos, and perceptible swagger. "Last year I got a sip of paradise, and man, I can still taste it," Dwight White said. Chuck Noll was almost as enthusiastic, declaring, "Bradshaw is on the verge of a dramatic development."

After four months at Western Psych, Ernie Holmes was delighted to be at camp. Two-a-day drills and dormitory living beat the psychiatric ward and an uncertain future. Holmes would discuss only football and Art: "If it was possible to add an additional person to your family, I'd like to add him to mine." As for the shooting, "If you want to talk about [it], you'll have to talk with my attorney," he said.

When a helicopter flew overhead at camp and Tom Keating yelled, "Don't get anxious, Fats," even Holmes laughed. After a rookie guard held him in practice, Holmes bellowed, "Son, you keep holding me like that, and we're gonna have another Ohio Turnpike out here." Then, he broke into a huge smile. "All my teammates have been great," Holmes remarked. "It is just like being in a family." His roommate, Joe Gilliam, was prescient. "I'll tell you something," the wiry quarterback said. "I feel sorry for whoever is playing in front of him this year."

Art remained circumspect at camp, letting others talk while he greeted a parade of visitors. He breakfasted with New York's Terence Cardinal Cooke the morning of the first exhibition game, then hosted the Steelers Alumni Association. Fifty men, including John Blood and Jap Douds, attended the game. That night, Art joined them on Mt. Washington, where they closed down the LeMont Restaurant.

Art never interfered with his coaches, but he paid close attention to his players, especially Bradshaw. Frustrated by his quarterback's lapses,

Noll excoriated him on the sidelines during a preseason game. Bradshaw had thrown three interceptions, including two returned for TDs. On one, he had done precisely the opposite of what Noll had instructed. Art corralled his young friend afterward and helped Bradshaw keep his sense of humor about it. "I got it pretty good, today," Terry said. "I guess it's one of my development stages."

Art knew better than most people how besieged Bradshaw had become, especially as his marriage unraveled. The media relentlessly probed Bradshaw's psyche, asking him on camera to answer criticism that he wasn't smart enough to play quarterback. "I was dumbfounded," Bradshaw remarked. "Nothing bugs me more than people going around saying I'm stupid . . . I hear it, my wife and my family hear it, and it's starting to make me sick."

"I suppose I'd purposely seek him out. He was going through a tough time," Art acknowledged. Still, Bradshaw had won more games in his first three seasons than Joe Namath, and Art left no doubt that he stood behind him.

The New Season

By March, every Steeler ticket for the 1973 season had been sold, including two season tickets that Franco's Italian Army bought just to store provisions on the seats. The advance sellout meant that fans without tickets could watch on television. The NFL had ended blackouts of home games sold out seventy-two hours in advance. Congress exacted a quid pro quo, permitting it to skirt antitrust law and hold the draft, and also allowing the public financing many clubs sought for new facilities.

Art was on the money predicting the end of blackouts, but he was dead wrong about their impact. So was Roy McHugh, Pittsburgh's most astute sportswriter, who argued that Congress was giving football away like food stamps, at the expense of the NFL and ticket holders. Rooney and McHugh had assumed that too much television exposure would damage the gate the way it had for boxing, a sport for which they shared an abiding passion.

Their angst was unwarranted. Pittsburgh rolled over Detroit in the opener with few no-shows. Week two, they demolished Cleveland as

Fats Holmes found redemption on the field. He was in the quarterback's face for the whole game; Noll awarded him the game ball.

Pittsburgh leaped to a 7-1 record, but while the Steelers were winning games, they were losing players, especially quarterbacks, to injury. Noll, despite predicting that Bradshaw would have a breakout season, benched him if he struggled. And Bradshaw struggled mightily.

In game seven, Pittsburgh played Cincinnati. The score was tied in a brutally hard-hitting game when Bradshaw ran a sneak. He made the first down but was whacked so hard that he was forced from the game. As Bradshaw walked off the field, listing to one side from a separated shoulder, many fans cheered. Art was appalled: "It almost made me sick." Joe Greene was incensed: "You could hear it loud and clear. He hadn't taken two steps and he was holding his shoulder, obviously in pain, when that shit started. I'd be lying if I said *he* doesn't tick me off sometimes, but that was vicious." Terry Hanratty rallied the team, throwing for a touchdown on his first pass. It was the third time he'd done that in seven games. But later in the game, a blitzing linebacker savaged Hanratty. With Bradshaw en route to the hospital and Gilliam already injured, Hanratty had to stay in. At practice that week, Greene was still upset. "They don't know what it's like to bust your butt out there and take all that, and then hear something like people cheering when a guy has been hurt."

Steeler quarterbacks weren't the only ones having a rough season. Two native sons destined for the Hall of Fame came to town. The first got off lightly. Beaver Falls native Joe Namath stood on the sidelines due to injuries and flirted with fans as the Jets lost to the Steelers. But Mt. Washington's John Unitas, now forty, took a beating when he led woeful San Diego on to the field. Unitas was football's icon, but San Diego's line could not protect him, and his arthritic body could not evade Pittsburgh's relentless pass defense. "I hate to see a legend being tarnished." Joe Greene said afterward. "All he's gonna do is get killed."

Christopher R

After Art's breakout NFL season in 1972, he finally had the horse he had awaited in 1973. In 1969, trainer Hugh Grant had offered his champion

Loom as a stud for a mare of Art's choice. Tim Rooney selected Rita Marie, whose father Cavan had won the 1958 Belmont Stakes. Art named their foal Christopher R after a grandson.

Art thought highly of Christopher R's lineage but risked him in a $5,000 maiden claiming race so that he could bet on him. In a claimer, any owner who has a horse running at the meet can put in a claim—in this case for $5,000—to purchase any horse in the race. Art lost his bet on Christopher R but won an even bigger gamble when the colt went unclaimed. Art then turned him over to Beverly "Tuffy" Hacker to train.

In 1936, fourteen-year-old Tuffy Hacker had left Kentucky to become a jockey. He got his nickname when his trainer's daughter saw him scrapping with another jockey and drawled, "We got ourselves a toughie." Hacker had ridden for Art and been atop Westminster, the horse who hit the jackpot by copping the Double Event at Tropical in 1947.

A few years later, Hacker took note of a horse named Seabang that he figured Art was holding back until he found a race where he could bet big on him. When Art entered Seabang in a claimer, Tuffy claimed him. Art found Tuffy in a bar the next day. He told Tuffy he wasn't angry at losing his horse but he had spent considerable time on Seabang. "I know this is a business," Art said. He would appreciate Tuffy letting him know when he was running Seabang to win. Tuffy obliged and Art placed bets on Seabang for them both.

After becoming Christopher R's trainer, Tuffy ran him in a $20,000 claimer. He was leading at five-eights of a mile before fading. Nevertheless, Tuffy liked what he saw. "After that, I never ran him in another claimer." The next time out, Christopher R was in front until late in the race. "He stopped so bad," Hacker recalled, "I could have outrun him. But he was an awfully fast horse." Tuffy then found a maiden race, one in which none of the entrants had yet won, and told jockey Billy Passmore to rein in Christopher R until the top of the stretch. Passmore had Christopher R in fourth and when he raised his whip, the stallion took off before he brought it down and won easily. Tuffy said to himself, "Shoot, I can win the Tri-States Futurity with this horse."

Owners can nominate horses for a futurity by paying a fee when the horse is bred and continuing payments until the race. Believing Christopher

R's bloodlines warranted the investment, Art had nominated him for the Tri-States Futurity, a stakes race open to horses from Maryland, Virginia, and West Virginia, and kept up payments for two years.

Art showed up for the race at Shenandoah Downs in West Virginia on Friday, November 2, 1973, with his driver Richie Easton and Roy Blount, a writer "loafing," as he put it, with the Steelers that season. Art, Easton, and Blount had embarked on the four-day road trip to Shenandoah Downs after the Steelers–Bengals game. Before leaving Pittsburgh, others braced Blount about traveling with Art. Chuck Noll warned him to take a gas mask for Art's cigars, while Easton suggested, "You better take a can to pee in." Art rarely stopped once he was on the road.

After hitting Liberty Bell in Philadelphia on day one, Art won enough at Aqueduct the next day to pay for the trip. The men spent the night with Tim and June Rooney in Scarsdale, began day three at Yonkers, and ended it at Shamrock Farm. Along the way, they helped themselves to a stash of cigars in the glove compartment and talked football, horses, and Watergate. While at Shamrock, Art inadvertently ignited the locust tree in front of the farmhouse. After the fire was extinguished, Art sheepishly asked, "You don't think it was the toby I put in that hollow place at the bottom, do you?"

At Shenandoah Downs, Art watched from the clubhouse. He was quiet during races, as he was during football games. Christopher R's chief rival was an unbeaten filly, but he got out of the gate in front and was ahead by five lengths at the turn. He won going away, setting a Futurity record of 1:12 for six furlongs.

Art stepped into the winner's circle for the photo, something he usually avoided. He posed with Tuffy Hacker, a small man in a bow tie and windowpane suit, Shamrock Farm manager Arnold Shaw, and the magnificent Christopher R with Billy Passmore aboard. Art looked solemn, wearing a blue-gray suit and a bright white shirt and holding a cigar. Christopher R, a handsome bay with a star on his forehead, towered over him. Art deferred to Tuffy, who was reticent with the press. "I'd rather not answer any questions," Tuffy said. "I just live from day to day and I just train from day to day." But Tuffy was enamored with his steed.

427

"A perfect gentleman, one of the nicest horses I ever had." Having won $57,000 that season, Christopher R's prospects were excellent.

Leaving after the race, Art and his companions reached Pittsburgh as dawn broke over the Northside. A road-weary Blount wondered how Art, twice his age, had weathered the trip better than he had. Art was already thinking about Monday night's game against Washington.

Not This Year

Despite Art's misgivings about injuries, Pittsburgh won. Terry Hanratty taped his broken ribs, and when he was knocked out of the game, Joe Gilliam came in. Art caught some grief from Kass afterward because he had put Bobby Layne and his uproarious buddies in her box, but he laughed it off.

A week later, the Steelers traveled to Oakland, where John Madden, his Raiders, and fans were still smoldering about the Immaculate Reception. It was a bizarre game. When Ray Mansfield bent over to snap the ball on the first play from scrimmage, he found expletives scrawled on it. Later, somebody sent a badly underinflated football into the game before Gerela attempted a field goal. Several Raiders coated their jerseys in Vaseline so that Steelers could not grab hold, and the Steelers suspected that their locker room had been bugged. Art was bemused; he had seen worse. While Oakland's owner Al Davis was considered the most obnoxious man in the NFL, he was no George Halas when it came to gaining a competitive edge. Pittsburgh won anyway.

But injuries and emotional letdown caught up with the Steelers. Joe Greene, who hadn't missed a play or practice due to injury in five seasons, sprained his back and played sparingly in a loss to Denver. It was the first defeat that Art had witnessed at Three Rivers in fourteen games. He saw another loss a week later in Cleveland; so did thirty-seven busloads of Franco's Italian Army who made the trip. Pittsburgh's divisional lead was gone for good after a third defeat, to Miami. Joe Gilliam could not complete a pass—except for three to Dolphins—and Miami led 30–3 at halftime. Bradshaw, despite a bad shoulder, almost pulled off a comeback, but Pittsburgh lost 30–26. Bradshaw was learning to cope with hostile Steeler fans. "Right now," he said, "I don't care if they hate my guts."

Pittsburgh stumbled into the playoffs as a wild card team and returned to Palm Springs to prepare to play Oakland. The team stayed at the Gene Autry Hotel; Art always did like westerns. He sat poolside and joined players in the whirlpool. "He leaves you with the impression," Sam Bechtel wrote, "that he surely is the youngest seventy-two-year-old kid in the world." Art was relaxed, even contemplative. Some of the excitement, he confessed, was missing. He expected to win now, and knew he would sell out Three Rivers even if the weather was crummy.

But Art was inordinately excited about Dan. "Knowing that he handles himself properly, does the kind of job I'd like, keeps his feet on the ground, and is not a know-it-all guy gives me a lot of satisfaction," he said. A younger cohort was running the league now, and Art was okay with that. He stopped by Dan's suite, where writers and league men were arguing about labor negotiations. It reminded him of past sessions. But, he said, "We didn't do it in a fancy room like you guys were in. We did it in saloons."

The morning of the game, Art shook hands with John Madden at midfield. It was the last moment of good will.

A fierce Oakland crowd greeted Pittsburgh with a cacophony of abuse; Harris and Bradshaw were the most reviled. Pittsburgh surrendered a season-high 33 points in defeat. Bradshaw, upset by the loss and the realization that his marriage was over, ducked out of the locker room afterward and missed the flight to Pittsburgh. Art played gin on the ride home. "Wait till next year," was all he said.

To make matters worse, twelve harness drivers at Yonkers and Roosevelt Raceway were indicted that weekend. Prosecutors alleged that they and coconspirators had pocketed $3 million rigging races. Tim Rooney ordered his staff to analyze hundreds of races to spot irregularities and strategized with his father about how to defend the track's credibility.

Art headed south, but the death of venerated *New York Times* columnist Arthur Daley soon brought him to Manhattan. Art attended Mass for his friend at St. Patrick's Cathedral and went to the Frank

Campbell Funeral Parlor to celebrate the life of the Pulitzer Prize winner. "We're here at this place too often," he told the *Washington Post*'s Shirley Povich.

The Draft

Not all signs trended downward. Art Jr.'s scouting machine was hitting on all cylinders, and that January the Steelers pulled off the greatest draft in NFL history, choosing four men who became Hall-of-Famers. In the first two rounds, they drafted USC receiver Lynn Swann and Kent State linebacker Jack Lambert. They had traded their third pick, but took Alabama A&M receiver John Stallworth and Wisconsin center Mike Webster in the next two rounds. The Steelers also signed safety Donnie Shell and tight end Randy Grossman as free agents.

Swann came from a high-profile school, but Lambert and Webster were undersized and Stallworth relatively unknown. When Nunn received game films of Stallworth, Pittsburgh scouts were mesmerized. They delayed returning them to limit Stallworth's exposure to other teams, and gambled that he would last until the fourth round. Pittsburgh snagged Shell, even though other teams offered more money, because of Bill Nunn's friendship with South Carolina State coach Willie Jeffries. Under Noll, no team had drafted more black collegians. Shell became a key contributor; so did Grossman, the only Jewish player in the NFL, who had played at Temple.

At the winter meetings, the referees asked to be included in the pension plan. Art had strongly favored recognizing their association when it formed in 1968 and had helped several, including Jerry Bergman, get jobs with the league. Bergman and association president Ed Marion made their case to the owners and entertained questions. A man needed ten years to vest in the plan, and Vikings general manager Jim Finks asked, "What if we release a guy after nine years so he wouldn't vest?" Marion answered, "That would be on your conscience, not ours." After another question, he and Bergman left the room. "Before the door was closed," Bergman recalled, "Art Rooney rose to his feet and said, 'I move that we grant them a pension.'" The motion passed unanimously. The owners took Art as their moral compass; if he thought something was the right thing to do, they often agreed.

New Challenges

In March, Father Jim Campbell died. The rugged pastor from Pennsylvania's anthracite coalfields had been Art's constant companion since the 1930s. A highly decorated armed forces chaplain who had been wounded in the Pacific, Campbell returned to be St. Peter's pastor after the war. His death left a void in the box where Art watched Steeler games and a much larger one when Art sought confession.

The business of sport worried Art. Returning from the Kentucky Derby, Art warned, "The game is in a lot of trouble." The league faced two threats, a new rival called the World Football League and a "freedom strike" by the NFL Players Association. A battle-scarred veteran of football wars, Art counseled the league to stand firm against the WFL. His team was in its best financial shape ever and could afford rising salaries. Still, he told Dan to be judicious. Concerned with rising ticket prices and the saturation of sport on television, Art doubted revenues could climb much higher. "We're at the top now," he cautioned. "I see nowhere to go but down."

The WFL debuted with a splash, signing Larry Csonka, Jim Kiick, and Paul Warfield, who left without giving their team, the Miami Dolphins, a chance to make a counteroffer. "You can bet your last nickel," Sam Bechtel wrote, "that had the three in-limbo Dolphins played for the Pittsburgh Steelers, they would not have refused to talk to Arthur J. Rooney."

Terry Bradshaw didn't need to talk with Art. "I'll never jump for money," he said. "I have a real close relationship with the Rooney family." Despite problems with fans and an ongoing quarterback controversy, Bradshaw trusted Art. Terry Hanratty also rejected the WFL after Noll said he would have a shot at starting. Frenchy Fuqua was the first Steeler to sign with the WFL, but his deal would not begin until 1976, after his Pittsburgh contract expired.

The WFL sought bigger game than Fuqua. The Birmingham Americans signed L. C. Greenwood while the California Suns pursued Dwight White and Joe Greene. "They were trying to raid the Steel Curtain," White said, "to pick us off one by one." When White had signed in

1971 for $16,500, he made twice what his father, a mailman raising a family of four, earned. After White was selected to the Pro Bowl his second year, his salary jumped to $32,000. "I'm in hog heaven now," he laughed. But the WFL would pay even more.

"Joe," White told Greene, "I've got to look at the money. I got to go." But White went nowhere. "Art Rooney was the one who sat down and convinced me to stay," he explained. After receiving a WFL offer, White called Dan Rooney that morning. He was on a plane to Pittsburgh that afternoon, met Dan at the Hilton Hotel that evening, and signed a new contract in the morning. White received a huge raise and signing bonus. "It was the Chief," he said, "who got me paid." According to White, as he signed Art said, "'Dwight White,'" and I said, 'Yeah, Chief?' He said, 'That's a lot of money.' I said, 'I know.'" With that, Art took his cigar and left the room.

Joe Greene rejected the WFL outright. "I'm a Steeler and I'm going to stay a Steeler," he told the Rooneys. When WFL teams urged Greene to use them to force Pittsburgh into offering more money, he responded, "I won't do that to these kind of people."

Art was especially fond of Greene. "Joe Greene really meant something to my father," Dan explained. "He was a special guy." Joe became special to Dan, too, and vice versa. "Joe said that the best thing I ever did for him," Dan remembered, "was that I told him no when he asked to renegotiate his contract early in his career. I stood toe-to-toe with him and said, 'You still have a contract and you're going to live by the contract.' He said it taught him to grow up."

The "freedom strike" was more vexing than the WFL. Football salaries lagged those in baseball and the NBA. The WFL gave players leverage, but the absence of free agency undercut bargaining power for those who stayed in the NFL. Clubs were allowed to keep players an additional year at the end of contracts by renewing them at ninety percent of current pay. If a player played out his option year and switched clubs, the club losing him received compensation—players or draft picks—from his new team. If clubs could not determine compensation, the commissioner decided for them. Compensation—known as the Rozelle Rule— was such a disincentive to sign free agents that players rarely played out contracts and went elsewhere. Moreover, careers were short, averaging under four seasons.

The players struck in July 1974, picketing camps in shirts reading "No Freedom, No Football." They wanted their salaries guaranteed and the draft and option clause eliminated so that players could begin their careers as free agents. While the veterans displayed spirited solidarity when the strike began, they faced a unified ownership.

The College All-Star game became the strike's first casualty. "It's a black eye for the game," Art complained. "I'm worried about the future of our league." The NFL, he reasoned, had survived challenges from four rival leagues. That sort of competition was business. But the strike troubled him because he felt that the league had negotiated in good faith. "You know," he said, "I carried the ball for recognition of the NFLPA to help negotiate for the best interest of the game. But I do believe the players are way out of line with their demands." Art said he would sacrifice the season to keep the option clause and the Rozelle Rule to maintain the competitive balance he and Bert Bell had fought to achieve. His stand sobered players who knew that Art was the most sympathetic owner.

Star players, Art said, would survive the strike. But fringe players not vested in the pension were vulnerable. "I told Franco that he doesn't have to worry. But what about those players who have three years in the league and need two more to make the pension plan? That's who I'm really worried about."

Art wanted the players to hear him out. "The NFL has come a long way because everyone has been treated fairly," he argued. "The freedom issues are bunk, and I'm violently opposed to yielding. Of course," he conceded, "Ed Garvey on their side is as strong in his opinion as I am in mine."

Garvey, the NFLPA executive director, respected Art. "If there were more owners like the Rooneys and coaches like Chuck Noll," he stated on Myron Cope's show before the walkout, "we probably wouldn't be faced with the threat of the player's strike."

Dan Rooney was as annoyed as Art. "You build a team up to this point and then this happens," he sighed. "We were thinking this was our year to really make a run at the Super Bowl." But the Rooneys were also looking beyond the strike. "There is definitely not going to be any retaliation after the strike is over," Dan vowed.

Though their players backed the strike, they appreciated the Rooneys' goodwill. "The Pittsburgh management has been out of sight," player representative Preston Pearson maintained. Dan let the veterans address the rookies, who were not yet eligible to join the union. "Some other clubs are running their teams like a concentration camp," Pearson said. "The Dallas Cowboys have told their rookies, 'Keep your heads down— Don't look at the pickets when you pass by.'" The Rooneys, though, kept a sense of humor. When Father Duggan, the team's Irish good luck charm, called to say he was coming to camp, Dan instructed him to stay home. "I told him he was the chaplain for the veterans, not the rookies, and since the veterans were on strike, he was on strike, too."

Joe Greene agonized. "People say I deal with everything emotionally," Greene observed. "I don't want to carry a picket sign against the Rooneys. They're the nicest people I know. If the other owners were like the Rooneys, there wouldn't be a strike."

Sportswriters were generally sympathetic to the players, fans less so. Angry callers deluged talk radio complaining that athletes were overpaid ingrates. Many protested that Rocky Bleier was only on the team because the Rooneys felt sorry for him. One night after Myron Cope received several vituperative calls slamming Bleier, Art phoned Rocky. "Rock," Art said, "I was in the car this evening, listening to the radio. Somebody called in and questioned your allegiance to the Rooneys. He said you owed us more loyalty than you're showing during this strike, because we supposedly carried you after your Vietnam experience. I just want to tell you that's not true. You've been an asset to us, both on and off the field. We don't want you ever to think you owe us anything. Whatever debt you feel you might have had, you've paid it." Bleier was relieved. "I wasn't Joe Greene or Terry Bradshaw; I was a special teams guy trying to make the club. I didn't know that Art had a pro-union background, but then you saw that when the grounds crew was on strike in January. It was cold and Art went out with Steelers sideline parkas for them." Art's final words were, "All I have to say is this—if you feel that

434

what you're doing is right, that's fine with me. Carry on." That week, a few players were holding a lonely picket on the road leading to camp when Art arrived with cold beer. "Thought you fellows might be awful hot out here."

Christopher R

As the strike dragged on, Art found relief at the track, where Christopher R was racing again. Tuffy Hacker had shut the stallion down after the Tri-States Futurity because of problems with his ankles. It had frustrated Art to have bred a stakes winner and not be able to race him, but Christopher R was healthy again.

Art and Tuffy spoke frequently. "Anytime I get beat," Art said, "I call Tuffy and he'll pep me up some way." With Tuffy, the NFL was irrelevant, and he made sure Art knew when he had a horse running at a good price. "He didn't like to bet favorites," Tuffy pointed out.

Tuffy adored Art. "He's the finest man I ever met," he testified. "Before that, the finest man I ever met was General Eisenhower, over in Europe." Tuffy appreciated Art's laissez-faire approach. "He's the kind of owner everybody's looking for. He don't bother you. When you train for him, it's just like you own the horses." That was a good thing, Tuffy laughed, because "Art didn't know horses. He didn't know the head from the tail." But Art knew betting, even if Tuffy found his approach baffling. "He had some kind of system," Tuffy explained, "but I didn't really understand it." "I'm a figure man, Tuffy, I bet the figures," Art told him. Although Tuffy clocked morning workouts, he had little faith in numbers. He was more intuitive. "Mr. Rooney," he said, "the only time that times matters is when you're in jail.'"

Christopher R resumed racing in August. A front-runner, he won seven races, placed second twice, and was out of the money only once in 1974. He was selected Maryland's champion three-year-old male of the year.

Back to Football

The strike gave rookies valuable playing time, and a few vets who were worried about being replaced crossed the picket line. So did Ernie Holmes. "I had to come," he said. "You could call it loyalty, but it's really more than that. Let me ask you. Would you be loyal if I saved your life? Sure, you'd be willing to do anything that was possible to please me. And I guess that's what I'm doing. Art Rooney is a beautiful fellow. I dig the guy the utmost." Holmes said he would repay his debt to the Rooneys by helping Pittsburgh win the Super Bowl. Quarterback Joe Gilliam also crossed. Despite his scrawny physique, Gilliam had a strong arm and loved gunning the ball downfield. Noll appreciated Gilliam's field vision and quick release as he led the Steelers through an undefeated preseason.

After a federal mediator ordered a truce in August, the players returned to camp. Once back, they stayed and in the end won little from the strike. Most veterans reclaimed their starting jobs, but not Bradshaw. Injuring his forearm, he fell behind Gilliam, who became the first African American to start at quarterback in a season opener.

Only four players remained from Noll's first season in 1969. The roster, rebuilt through the draft, featured an exceptional group of rookies. Pittsburgh was deeper and better than ever. Moreover, it came out of the strike with little rancor. Tackle Tom Keating, the NFLPA vice president whom Pittsburgh waived, was the notable exception. "This is the owners' way of undermining the union," Ed Garvey charged. "I thought the Rooneys were above that, but I guess not." Keating, slowed by injuries and age, had missed much of camp. Noll deemed him expendable.

Winning

"This is the championship season." Chuck Noll proclaimed before the opener. With Joe Gilliam starting the first six games, Pittsburgh went 4-1-1. When Gilliam was on, he was superb, and *Sports Illustrated* featured the flashy pass-slinger on its cover. But he frustrated Noll, who preferred to control the game by running the ball, especially with his magnificent fullback, Franco Harris. Against Denver, Gilliam threw fifty passes. While Gilliam delighted in throwing the ball, Noll chafed and Bradshaw suffered on the bench.

"Terry hit bottom," Art Jr. recalled. "I'll tell it to you straight," Bradshaw told reporters. "I'd love to be traded. I'm just eating my heart out here every day knowing I'm not going to be starting Sunday . . . I don't feel any allegiance toward the Steelers, that's for sure." But after talking to the Rooneys, Terry retracted his comments. He said he felt sick about being portrayed as disloyal to the Rooneys. "Hell, I'm not crying, going around feeling sorry for myself. Joe Gilliam's done a great job. He deserves to start." Bradshaw denied saying he did not owe the team his allegiance. "I said that I loved the Rooneys; that we have a great football team here." The press battered him anyway. "The golden boy with the golden arm reaffirmed our worst suspicions," reporter Dave Ailes wrote. "He has a wooden head that ruins whatever physical attributes God gave him." Though it hurt Bradshaw not to play, he did not quit on himself. He grew a beard and came to the stadium early to throw to members of the ground crew. "Terry was out there working his ass off," Art Jr. said.

"Terry," Andy Russell remembered, "was a super, genius player, with the best physical talent I had ever seen at quarterback, but he was struggling." Russell was skeptical whenever Bradshaw was forced off the field by injury only to return as if nothing had happened. He once mocked Bradshaw by giving him a trophy for the most theatrical performance of the season. Only later did Russell appreciate the personal issues Bradshaw faced.

Russell wasn't the only one doubting Bradshaw. "Chuck Noll was tough on Bradshaw," Timothy V. Rooney added. "The fans were tough on him, too. The players liked Hanratty; the players liked Gilliam, except for Joe Greene. Joe hated Gilliam. He didn't trust him, and he was right about that." While Greene backed Bradshaw in the locker room, Art massaged his psyche. "I talked about my personal problems with him," Bradshaw explained. "You're going to be all right," Art assured him. "Just try not to worry." Art was right. Terry smoothed the rough spots in his life while Gilliam played himself out of the lineup by ignoring Noll. With a fierce defense and a strong running game, Noll knew his team did not need to rely on passing. "But Joe always wanted to throw," Art Jr. said. "He was a mad bomber."

Even with the lineup in flux, Pittsburgh kept winning. They were a young team, with fourteen rookies on the forty-seven-man squad. Greenwood and Fuqua, who were playing out their options before jumping to the WFL, performed well, especially Greenwood. "He has been excellent," Dan Rooney attested. "There's been no animosity because of his signing."

Injuries, however, hampered the offense. When it faltered, Noll changed quarterbacks. Gilliam's inexperience was evident, while Hanratty, whose commitment to the union had kept him out of camp longer than Gilliam or Bradshaw, seemed the forgotten man. Fans and the media fueled a quarterback controversy. In game three, against Oakland, the crowd chanted for Bradshaw when Gilliam struggled in the 17–0 defeat. They finally got Bradshaw in game seven, a Monday night win. But Noll went back to Gilliam when Bradshaw stumbled, and even gave Hanratty a surprise start.

The defensive line was playing inspired football, and linebacker Jack Lambert was a contender for rookie of the year. "We've got a rookie who's so mean, he doesn't even like himself," assistant coach George Perles cracked. After beating Kansas City, Fats Holmes shaved his hair into an arrowhead. He said it was his mother's suggestion. When asked about his play, Holmes said, "I'm still repaying the Rooneys for treating me so well when things went bad for me two years ago."

When Noll started Bradshaw in game seven against Atlanta, Franco was unleashed and ran for 141 yards. Franco benefited from Rocky Bleier's addition to the backfield in the fourth game. Rocky, who had labored for years to regain strength, agility, and speed, paved the way for Harris with his blocking.

While the switch to a white quarterback infuriated some black fans, the players knew that Gilliam had fallen out of favor because he wouldn't listen to Noll. "The transition was made and it didn't cause a ripple," Dwight White said. "We have a bunch of guys with intelligence and understanding." The organization had won credibility with black players. Under Noll, the Steelers had chosen a black player first in the draft every season but one. Pittsburgh had integrated the front office better than most teams and featured African Americans at middle linebacker, guard, and quarterback, the so-called thinking positions that racists claimed blacks were incapable of playing.

Meanwhile, Pittsburgh kept winning. The stadium authority even approved raising ticket prices, the league's lowest. Though Three Rivers Stadium was a better venue than Forbes Field or Pitt Stadium, it did not generate the revenues the Steelers could have received elsewhere. Even with the price hike, a string of sellouts, and a new television contract, Dan feared that escalating salaries and soaring costs caused by the energy crisis would trigger losses.

Bradshaw began playing with confidence and consistency. After beating New England to clinch their second title, the Steelers waited until they were flying home to pop champagne bottles and salute each other. Even then, they were relatively subdued. "We've been here before," Chuck Noll said. "We'd like to go a little further this time." In the final game, when Bradshaw was forced out with an injury, fans stood and applauded him, a change from the year before when some had cheered because a Bradshaw injury meant he could *not* play.

Pittsburgh faced Buffalo in the playoff opener. When Art got to the stadium that morning, an usher handed him a telegram that read, "Eat 'em up . . . Love and Kisses Francis Albert Sinatra." They won 32–14, with Bradshaw playing his strongest game yet. "I enjoyed it," he said, "but ovations don't last long if you don't produce. I've been booed, too, remember?"

The national press rallied behind Art as Pittsburgh headed to Oakland for the AFC championship. As Pittsburgh native Murray Chass pointed out in the *Times*, the matchup pitted one of the best-liked men in sport, Art Rooney, against one of the least liked, Al Davis. The Steelers were confident; so was Art: "Our ball club is good enough to do it." Anybody who watched Art during a game saw a stoic. "You know, I never root when I'm watching a game. I never say a word," he said. "Sometimes it's embarrassing. They tell me to smile and I can't smile. But I'm smiling with my eyes." Art had felt good for the past four seasons: "Our defense has always been one of the best. This year I think they're a Super Bowl offense, too." Indeed, the defense had allowed the fewest points and yards in the AFC and led the league with 52 sacks and 47 interceptions and fumble recoveries. They led the league in penalties, too.

The man who had convinced Art that the Steelers had the offense to win came up to him during breakfast on game day. Nothing in Terry

Bradshaw's demeanor suggested that a cat burglar had rifled his hotel room the night before. She had also lifted Ron Shanklin's wallet and was in Lynn Swann's room when he awakened and scared her away. Bradshaw evinced confidence, even though Oakland had won the last two times they played. "Are you ready for a lot of publicity tonight," Bradshaw teased Art, "because we're going to win?" Art retorted, "Nobody comes out to see me; they come out to see you. *You* better be ready." Art took heart in seeing Terry ebullient before the biggest game of his career. It wasn't only Bradshaw who boosted Art's spirits. Joe Greene approached Art, enveloped his hands in one of his own, and confided, "We're going to get 'em." That's when Art knew they would win. "That was an emotional moment. I never had a moment like that."

At halftime, with the score tied, Greene stood in the locker room and told his teammates, "We're going to win this game." But Oakland led in the fourth quarter before Pittsburgh tied the game on a long drive. After Jack Ham intercepted a pass and returned it to the Raiders' 9-yard line, Bradshaw threw to Swann for the go-ahead touchdown. The defense, which held Oakland to 29 yards rushing, stood firm. "We had a bunch of guys who knew it was going to happen eventually," Chuck Noll said afterward. "That," the *Times*' William Wallace added, "was what the elder Rooney kept telling everyone in Pittsburgh for several decades."

Art hardly spoke during the game. When Pittsburgh pulled away, he surrendered his seat to a friend and stood at the back of the windswept press box. He told Ed Kiely he would speak to the boys on the flight home. He did so over Nevada. Joe Greene found Art outside the locker room and said, "Enjoy yourself now." "That Joe Greene," Art told reporters. "He takes you. I've never seen a player lift a team like he does. I just hope he plays out his full years. He's the type of player who wouldn't want to be associated with a team that didn't play all out." Art didn't overlook his other favorite. "Bradshaw can do everything," he said. "He can throw and he can run." "And he smokes cigars," somebody added.

Wearing his brown herringbone topcoat and a plaid cap, Art spoke quietly with writers. His lips were puffy, chapped, and specked with blood from furiously chewing cigars during the game. Art acknowledged that he was close to his players. *Newsweek*'s Pete Axthelm said it was more than that. "It is difficult to imagine another pro club on which the stars would punctuate their victory celebrations as Greene and bearded quarterback Terry Bradshaw did last week, by shouting, 'We told the Chief we'd win this one.'" Art accepted congratulations with a proviso: "You have to win the Super Bowl to be the champion now. You don't hear too much about the guys in the Super Bowl that lost." It was, he said, his greatest day. He had been confident even when Pittsburgh fell behind. "I still thought we'd win. You get that feeling sometime. When I go to the track, I get that feeling."

On to New Orleans

In Pittsburgh, frenzied fans overran downtown, and a few prisoners tried to capitalize on the commotion to break out of the county jail. Before the Steelers' flight was over the Rockies, crowds had overwhelmed the airport. Art was first off the plane. A band played "When Irish Eyes Are Smiling" as he walked down a red-carpeted ramp, shaking hands and beaming through his fatigue. When he stepped on to an airport balcony, the crowd erupted. Ernie Holmes pumped his fists in the air and displayed his arrowhead haircut. "I tell you," Art said, "it brought a tear to my eye."

Myron Cope provoked as much response as any player. "Here comes Myron!" fans shouted. One yelled, "You're better than Cosell!" The diminutive Cope was knocked around like a beach ball as he braved the gauntlet. A cop finally intervened when teenagers started ripping his suit off.

Art heeded Joe Greene's advice to savor the moment. He could hardly open the newspaper without reading hyperbolic estimations of his contribution to humanity. "They just don't make 'em like Art Rooney anymore," sportswriter Milt Richman gushed. "He's God's gift to the human race." Art's phone rang every time he replaced the receiver. "I heard from Whizzer," Art said when asked about the Supreme Court justice. "He was among the first to congratulate us on our victory over Oakland. You never know he's as big a man as he is." And if the impending Super Bowl wasn't enough, Christopher R was running in the Bowie

Handicap. "For the better part of an otherwise fruitful and rewarding life," Pat Livingston observed, "Art Rooney, one of the world's happiest septuagenarians, has been denied two things that mean much to him—a football championship and a super horse. But now in the October of his years, both will be in his grasp." Tuffy Hacker was enraged that Christopher R was a relative nonentity to the public. "You don't know these people," Art said. "They're not interested in horses. They don't even know who Secretariat is." Tuffy could not tolerate that; Christopher R had won six consecutive races, earning more than $150,000 for Art.

Art invited a few players to dinner before the Super Bowl. He sat at the head of the table, Joe and Agnes Greene on one side, Dwight White and Franco Harris on the other, while Kass and Mary Roseboro prepared salad, steak, corn, and peas. The room was lit by candles and a cut glass chandelier. Everybody felt good and, despite the pressure of the upcoming game, relaxed. Franco reported that his family said a special grace because there were nine kids. "In the name of the Father, the Son, and the Holy Ghost," he intoned, "whoever gets here first eats the most." The Rooneys let their guests do the talking. They reminisced about college, and Franco talked about winning his first daily double. Eventually they turned to football. "I believe if we can hold this club together," Art said, "we will be a strong ball club for five or six years. We might not win every time, but at least we'll have the team that can do it any year." They knew how tough it was keeping a team together. Nobody had forgotten how the WFL and the strike had jeopardized the season. Joe Greene looked at Art, but spoke to his teammates when he said, "I think *he'll* hold the key for awhile."

Super Bowl IX

On New Year's Day, Art handed out cigars in the locker room at Three Rivers Stadium. The city was giddy, and Pittsburgh bettors, who had battered the bookies by betting big on Pittsburgh to beat Oakland, were wagering heavily on them to win the Super Bowl.

The press deluged Art. For many newsmen, he was the story. Each Super Bowl, Dave Anderson argued, was linked to a particular participant: "The plot of this Super Bowl belongs to Art Rooney." A colleague wrote, "They have dubbed this 'Art Rooney's Super Bowl.'" Most agreed with sportswriter Chuck Heaton that "The people's choice among almost all those connected with the NFL championship, with the exception of the rabid Minnesota rooters, is Arthur J. Rooney." "Everybody, and I mean everybody, is pulling for Art," San Diego owner George Pernicano affirmed. "There is widespread rejoicing today," Red Smith wrote, "because Art Rooney's Pittsburgh Steelers, after 41 years of disappointment, are playing here tomorrow for the world championship." The *Times* ran a photo captioned "Rooney & Sons: A Dynasty. What the Kennedys have been in politics, the Barrymores in the theatre and the Rockefellers in finance—that's what the Rooneys of Pittsburgh have become in sports."

Art's celebrity meant an unbelievable number of ticket requests. "I've had those ticket problems all my life," he laughed. Art's problem in the old days was that he could hardly give Steeler tickets away. Pittsburgh's allotment was 12,000 tickets. "I needed a couple of thousand myself to be sure I took care of my friends," Art admitted. "I got 'em. I would have been an awful rube if I didn't." Every employee, including the ground crew, and the players' wives, went to New Orleans on Art's tab. Art wasn't sure about girlfriends. "I don't know what Noll is going to do about that," he chuckled. "Some coaches don't even want the wives around, but I never believed in that. I believe the greatest thing for a player is being with his family. I never thought if a guy was with his wife the night before a game that it bothered him. All he had to do was take a glass of milk and he was strong again."

In New Orleans, reporters searched for Art, who did not show until long after his team. "He didn't want to upstage the players," *Times* columnist Dave Anderson confided. A *Washington Post* reporter asked Art if waiting so long had given him the patience of Job. "Hell, no," Art said, indulging in a rare expletive. "It was terrible to be considered an inept owner, a patsy who couldn't put together a good football team. Trying to win a championship for Pittsburgh became my obsession." Art added that he knew all the alleys in Pittsburgh. "I had to. They were my hiding places."

Pittsburghers had swamped New Orleans before Art was spotted in the French Quarter. "I promised if we ever made it to the championship," he said, "I would invite all my friends to the game. We've got 'em scattered in hotels all over town. I probably will be the first owner ever to lose money on the Super Bowl. But I don't care. It's a great day for all of us." One charter carried players, another held priests, buddies like Sam Leone, Billy Conn, and Iggy Borkowski, and 192 stadium workers and their families. "Everybody's coming," Art laughed. His sons arranged charters from Philadelphia, Yonkers, and Vermont.

The day before the game, Christopher R ran in the Bowie Handicap. He was a heavy favorite, but Selari Spirit caught him in the backstretch. It was a bad omen, and it worried trainer Tuffy Hacker, but he had no time to dwell on it. After the race, he hurried to New Orleans.

When Art walked into NFL headquarters in New Orleans, he greeted writers he knew and introduced himself to those he did not. They led him into a room where he sat, a brown plaid cap on his lap, answering questions. "I lost so long, my frustration is longer," he told them. Some of the writers had known Rooney for decades, and to others he was wispy legend. They asked about his 1937 ride at the track, Whizzer White and Johnny Blood, and hustling to meet payroll. They laughed when he mentioned an owner demanding his guarantee in cash at halftime. "Nobody lost much money, but nobody made much either," Art said. One asked him when he had turned the team over to Dan. "I didn't turn this thing over to him," he protested, "he just took it. Dan and Artie have done the job, but I'm there all the time. They probably wish I wasn't."

Art had flown to New Orleans with Vikings owner Max Winter. They met the press jointly and spent evenings together. "It was a tough week for Winter," Pat Livingston noted. "The sporting press, to whom Art Rooney has long been a favorite, is actively pulling for the Steelers with all the partiality that ethics will allow." Even Winter could not consider losing to Art a crushing disappointment. Art had facilitated his entry into the league. "If we have to lose," Winter said, "I'd rather lose to Art than any owner in the game."

On the eve of the game, John Macartney, the Rooneys' racing partner, brought them the deal of their lives. Avis, the car rental company, was in bankruptcy. Macartney's financial acumen enabled him to put together a $5 billion bid that the Rooneys could finance with relatively little cash. All they needed was Art's signature on the offer to take to the bankruptcy judge. The sons were ready to execute the deal when they realized that it would hit the newspapers the morning of the Super Bowl and deflect attention from their father. This was his moment and they believed they could wait a few days. But somebody else got Avis. Macartney figured that he and the Rooneys would have made $2 million each if the deal had been consummated.

Tulane Stadium, January 12, 1975

In the locker room before kickoff, the players knelt in concentric circles to pray or reflect. Art was among them, on one knee next to Donnie Shell, Ray Mansfield, Mel Blount, and Franco Harris. Dwight White, devastated by pneumonia, had talked his way out of the hospital and back into the lineup. He was not going to miss this game, even though he was weak and had lost weight. "I won't have any problem getting that back," he joked.

The Steelers and the Vikings entered the field from the same portal. Steeler safety Glen Edwards, 5 feet 9 inches tall, wedged himself between Minnesota's huge linemen Carl Eller and Alan Page. Looking up at them, he said, "You guys better buckle up!"

Art headed to the press box. When a young boy brought him a cup of coffee, Art tipped him a buck. The day before, he had handed the Super Bowl Handicap Cup to the owner of Grocery List—who wore Minnesota's colors. "I told my wife about it . . . She's very superstitious, you know . . . and she told me that was a bad sign according to old Irish folklore." Art shrugged it off. "I've always lived with hope," he said. "I think over the years we've had top teams. I thought they were the best, but they never did." This year, his players did, too.

The weather in New Orleans was uncharacteristically cold, and players slipped and fell on Tulane Stadium's slick artificial turf. Equipment manager Tony Parisi, anticipating rain, was the unsung hero. He had found a Montreal shoemaker who provided the team with footwear that gave them traction.

Whether it was traction or better players, Pittsburgh's defense dominated Minnesota. Trying to capitalize on Dwight White's illness, Minnesota ran seven of their first eight running plays his way but gained no yardage. The Steelers scored first when White tackled Fran Tarkenton in the end zone for a safety.

Art watched silently. "The only discernible response from Rooney during a tight spot," a reporter observed, "issued from his cigar. The end turned red. A billow of smoke wafted past my head." With the Steelers deep in their own territory, someone asked Art what he would call. "We run a pretty conservative game," Art replied, "but I would throw it as far as I could." The game was interrupted near halftime when Sandra Saxton, the French Quarter's Champagne Queen, ran across the field wearing a G-string and pasties. Pittsburgh led 2–0 at half time. While the players retreated to the locker room, Grambling's marching band warmed up fans.

Minnesota fumbled the second-half kickoff, and Pittsburgh scored a touchdown. The Vikings could not budge Greenwood, Holmes, White, and Greene—who intercepted a pass and recovered a fumble. With Pittsburgh leading 16–0, Minnesota finally scored after blocking a punt. Overall, Minnesota gained 17 measly yards, while the Steelers ran for 249, including a Super Bowl record 158 by Franco Harris. The final score of what Red Smith called the most one-sided NFL championship yet was 16–6.

Art sat in press box as the clock wound down. Newark sportswriter Jerry Izenberg said, "It looks like you are going to do it, Mr. Rooney. Congratu . . . " Art cut him off. "Shhh, we're not there yet." At the two-minute warning, he and Dan left for the locker room. On the field, Jim Clack said to Ray Mansfield, "I bet the 'Burgh looks like Hiroshima." When the gun sounded, Mansfield, who was born in a migrant labor camp, went searching for the game ball. It was lying on the turf as players fled the crush of fans rushing the field. "All of us had been fighting for it so long and now it was just lying there," Mansfield mused. "It looked kind of sad." He grabbed the ball and gave it to Andy Russell. A reporter asked Joe Greene what he was thinking about when the game ended. Greene answered he was thinking about Mr. Rooney. Rocky Bleier entered the locker room first and embraced Art."

As captain, Andy Russell was about to award the game ball to Greene, when he saw Art standing against the wall, out of the spotlight. "It hit me," Russell explained, "I had to give it to him. He was the man." Players hoisted Art up on the platform and Russell said, "This one's for the Chief," as teammates cheered. Art was overwhelmed, but kept his composure. "Thank you," he told his team. "I'm proud of you, and I'm grateful to you."

Art kept the game ball in the crook of his arm as Pete Rozelle handed him the Lombardi Trophy. He cherished the ball more than the trophy. "I didn't want to accept the trophy," he protested. "Dan Rooney and Chuck Noll deserved it. I guess they just wanted me to be a big shot for a day."

So did the Steelers. "That's the greatest man who ever walked," Terry Bradshaw maintained. "Winning this for him was the big thing." The entire team, Gerry Mullins added, dedicated their effort to Art. "Everybody in this room is happy for him." Ernie Holmes knew what he owed the Rooneys. "I will always remember Mr. Rooney for what he did."

A few tears lubricated Art's cheeks and helped him regain his equilibrium. "I try never to get too excited and I try not to get depressed," he explained. "I thought right from the beginning of the game we were the strongest ballclub." He paused. "If we had lost, that trip back home would have been disastrous." Art had been on enough trips like that.

NFL representatives escorted Art to a press tent, where he unwrapped a cigar and spoke from his heart. "This is the biggest win of my life. I don't think I could top it even if we won next year again." It didn't matter much what Art had to say. Many reporters had been waiting a lifetime to file copy about Rooney winning the title.

Art stayed so long in the locker room that he missed the limo back to the hotel. As he stood on the sidewalk with Roy McHugh waiting for a cab, Art asked, "What do they want me to do, dance a jig? I didn't want to show any emotion. I was afraid I would start crying." On the way back to the hotel, he said he preferred taxis anyway. "I've always felt uncomfortable in a limousine."

Aftermath

While the team partied at the Royal Sonestra Hotel, delirious fans occupied downtown Pittsburgh, ignoring snow and subfreezing temperatures. Though 223 were arrested, Sheriff Eugene Coon pronounced the celebration less rowdy than the tumult following the Pirates' World Series victory in 1971. On Monday, over 100,000 people jammed the airport and downtown to greet the team. Thousands had waited for hours; for some, the wait had been four decades long. The entire squad was there. Joe Greene and Franco Harris had intended to go straight to Miami for the Pro Bowl and Terry Bradshaw was headed to California, but Art persuaded them to return to Pittsburgh first, for the fans' sake. As their caravan came through the Fort Pitt tunnel, a roar began that lasted until the last vehicle made its way through an hour later.

His first day back at work, Art heard a receptionist answer the phone, "Good morning, World Champion Steelers." He told her to drop the "World Champion." They were still the Steelers—if not the same old Steelers—and that was good enough. Art spent a few days writing notes to players that went with their $15,000 playoff checks and left for the track, where he was back in the winner's circle. Although Christopher R had been upset in his race the day before the Super Bowl, he won the Stryker Handicap two weeks later at Bowie. "Another success," the *Times* said, "for the eminently popular sportsman, Art Rooney."

The season over, players parted ways. Dwight White, who had played with pneumonia, spent a week at Divine Providence Hospital, near Art's home. "I was in bad shape," White recounted. "I remember the Chief came by the hospital to see me. He was just that type of guy, came by a couple of times. That really makes you feel—you can't describe that. The season is over, we won the thing, and he should be out there doing the media stuff." Instead, Art visited White and made sure he was receiving the best care possible.

Franco Harris, who had refurbished an old house on the Northside, headed to Manhattan with his parents to receive a car from *Sport* magazine as the Super Bowl MVP. His mother Gina intrigued reporters. During the war, she had hid in the mountains with her father when the Germans occupied their village near Pisa. One day, they saw smoke rising from the town as German troops annihilated those who had not fled. "It was not my destiny to die that day," she said. "It was my destiny to live. Just like Franco's destiny was to play for the Pittsburgh Steelers."

20

Super Redux

1975

While his players scattered, Art returned to familiar haunts. On Mondays, he headed across the river for breakfast and visited his downtown tobacconist to stock up for the week. It took him three or four hours to get back to the Northside. People kept stopping him on the street. "So, I stop and talk," he chuckled. "I really enjoy that." For Art, schmoozing had intrinsic value. Art just moved along with the wind, Joe Greene remarked. He took neighborhood kids along to ball games, brought panhandlers home for a meal, and wore the flannel shirts he had long fancied.

Although Art had not changed, winning the Super Bowl made him realize how much the NFL had. "I'll tell 'ya, it's much bigger than I ever thought it was." At Hialeah, a turf writer told him that they had polled six hundred people—trainers, jockeys, workers on the backstretch—asking whom they wanted to win. It was not the lopsided tally, 598–2 in favor of Pittsburgh, that astonished Art. "Six hundred people at a race track interested in the Super Bowl?" he exclaimed. "That's unbelievable." He recalled Hialeah in the 1930s when hardly anyone had even heard of the NFL.

In March, Art dined with several sportsmen after Christopher R won at Pimlico. "They were guys about town," Art explained, "and they told me that never in the history of Baltimore—outside of their own team winning—was that whole city as excited about anything as they were Pittsburgh winning the Super Bowl." Baltimore owed gratitude to Pittsburgh for allowing John Unitas to slip into the Colts' hands. "Maybe if we had won before it wouldn't mean so much," Art reasoned. "But there's no doubt in my mind that there's a great deal of difference between winning now and winning back then."

At the league meetings in Hawaii, Art and Kass dined nightly with the Halases and Maras. He told his friends he hoped they would experience what it was like to win now. "The Spadias and Morabitos, who've never won," he said with a hitch, "are very close to me and I know how they feel losing. I really hope they get a chance to experience what I'm experiencing." Art meant it, but he would not make it easy for them.

Being Art Rooney was a full-time job. Between forays to the track, Art attended banquets and talked with friends. Along with Mass and helping people out, these routines consumed most days.

His players, meanwhile, savored their celebrity. Ray Mansfield and Rocky Bleier embarked on a USO tour in Asia, while teammates accepted awards and made appearances. Terry Bradshaw ducked the spotlight and retreated to his ranch in Grand Cane, Louisiana, where he lost twenty pounds working out. Dwight White, released from the hospital, began putting that much back on.

At the Dapper Dan banquet, *Post-Gazette* publisher Bill Block presented Art with a reproduction of the front page from the morning after the Super Bowl. The crowd rose to its feet, an ovation Art tried to quell by talking over it. Although several Steelers were lauded, Joe Greene was bathed in the brightest limelight. Introducing clips of Greene wreaking havoc on opponents, Art proclaimed, "That's the best football player in the game." Handing him the Sportsman of the Year Award, he said, "I wish you a lot of happiness all through your life." Greene replied in kind: "It's very easy to work for a man like that," he said of Art. "He and his son Dan are two of the finest people I've ever met." Greene was just getting going. "We're a family," he told the hushed crowd. "There's love in our dressing room . . . We knew some bad times, and they make the good times so much better. We showed the world what togetherness could do." The Rooneys, he stressed, set the tone. "Seeing Mr. Rooney accept that Lombardi trophy was a great thrill," Greene said as his voice quavered. "And I felt a part of it."

That week, Art appeared before the National Gambling Commission, which was considering whether to legalize sports betting, something the pro leagues adamantly opposed. Art, testifying first on behalf of the league, argued that the scope of illegal gambling on NFL games was exaggerated. Legal wagering, he warned, would be far more destructive. When asked why he bet on horses but not football, Art responded, "Horses are animals, football players are human beings." They were vulnerable to pressure.

Meanwhile, Dan happily avoided publicity. He testified on Ernie Holmes's behalf in a suit brought by the trooper he had shot, but otherwise stayed out of sight. "Dan Rooney is destined," Phil Musick observed, "to remain the old man's kid: to have no substantive image as the architect of the current Steeler success. Which, to a large degree, he is."

Art Jr. took the same tack. Like his father, he deflected credit. But, Sam Bechtel noted, "Art Rooney Jr., perhaps the least known member of his family, has had just as much, if not more, to do with the rise of the Steelers as has anyone." The *Times*' Dave Anderson wrote that his 1971 draft list of Ham, White, Holmes, Wagner, and three other starters should be bronzed. "Some teams don't draft seven starters of that quality in seven years. The Steelers did it in one." Although it was not yet apparent, Art Jr. had surpassed himself in 1974, crafting the best draft in NFL history. His sons' humility warmed Art. "I'm proud of the way they are," he said, "proud of the way they don't put the dog on and the way they try not to let people know who they are."

Ireland

After paying his respects to Hialeah, Bowie, and Yonkers, Art visited Ireland. An agitated Tuffy Hacker admonished him that they were killing each other over there. "Tuffy," Art laughed, "they've been doing that for centuries." He assured his trainer that he would be far from the violence.

Ireland reminded Art of the Northside during his boyhood, full of amiable, talkative people. He had seen names and faces like these in the Ward. People had a similar self-deprecating sense of humor and even said "youse" instead of you, just like Pittsburghers. "They're so friendly and humble." Art often thought about humility in the wake of the Super Bowl. He had never been more visible and the celebrity was wearing. Art abhorred being held above others. He relished regaining his anonymity in Ireland, at least when he slipped away from the established itinerary.

Art was always aware of his Irish roots, even though his paternal grandparents had left the island during the 1840s. Only his grandfather Michael Murray had been born there. After sojourns in Canada and Wales, the Rooneys arrived in Pittsburgh in 1884 with few ties to Ireland intact. Art had a passing grasp of Irish politics but did not know what to expect when he arrived in April. His sister-in-law Alice McNulty, who could dance an Irish jig, knew more about their ancestral land than Art. "If my father got out of line when he talked about the Irish," Dan recalled, "Alice got on him, saying: 'You don't know anything about the Irish.'" Art knew she was right. Ireland was largely an abstraction to Art. "He was never a professional Irishman," prone to Irish affectations, *Sports Illustrated*'s Mort Sharnik remembered. But Art's sense of Irish history, acquired in his father's pub and at Duquesne University, made him relish their underdog status.

His sons reconnected with Ireland first, but their curiosity came from Art. "I gained an interest in Ireland from my father, going way back," Dan explained. The family joined the Irish American fraternal scene, with Art in charge of decorations at Knights of Equity banquets. "How he ever got that job," Dan smiled, "I don't know because that was not his forte by any means." Dan had hung shamrocks at Hibernian affairs and decorated a station wagon for the St. Patrick's Day Parade with a sign reading: "Bring the Luck of the Irish to the Steelers." The boys threw little footballs into the crowd from the car.

Tim and June Rooney escorted Art and Kass to Ireland. Tim knew his way around its breeding industry and had met many of the Republic's power brokers. They went to Limerick, Tipperary, Kildare, and Galway, looking at farms to breed thoroughbreds but found nothing suitable. Art didn't mind; he relished driving around the countryside. "I would love to come back here for a long vacation and I intend to do that," he professed.

Although the Rooneys were only there a week, Heinz Corporation CEO Tony O'Reilly, known as the "Golden Boy" of Irish rugby, horseman

Vincent O'Brien, and Waterford industrialist John Mulcahy feted them. Art endowed the Rooney Prize in Irish literature at the University of Dublin and was honored by the Royal College of Surgeons, for whom he was a benefactor. The Rooneys had tea with President Cearbhall O'Dalaigh. "I've known a lot of Irish politicians in my days in Pittsburgh," Art said, "but this guy wasn't like them. He was a real dude. He even poured the tea for my wife, Kathleen, and me, and he looked up our names in a big book of Irish heritage."

Art felt more at home in pubs, chatting with the locals. To them, he was another American coming home. "The men were drinking and talking, which they seem to do a lot of," he said with admiration. "I don't drink anymore myself so I had water or pop. I was the greenhorn there." The absence of pub fights surprised him. "Back home it wouldn't be like that," he said. When he bought a round at a pub and asked the whereabouts of the racetrack, someone asked if he was a horseman. "I'm a player," he responded. "What's a player?" they wanted to know. "I bet my money," he replied. "They thought they had a live one," Art laughed.

At racetracks, he was thrilled to see bookmakers standing by their slates, barking out the odds, while punters milled around, figuring their plays. "Do you understand the odds?" someone asked as he sized Art up. "I understand them," he answered casually. "Betting odds with bookmakers was the greatest part of my life."

He wrote Ed Kiely from Ashford Castle on Lough Corrib, where John Ford had filmed *The Quiet Man* with John Wayne and Maureen O'Hara. Wayne played a Pittsburgh prizefighter returning to Ireland after leaving the ring. Art was dazzled by the castle and County Mayo's countryside. "I cannot begin to describe the splendor of this place—the architecture, the massiveness, and the beauty. Yesterday I sneaked into town and stopped in the local pub. I just wanted to remind myself where the real people are." Art engaged in a brief exchange in Gaelic at church one day. "I didn't know you could speak any Gaelic," Tim said in disbelief. "Oh, I can't," his father told him. "That's just a phrase that everybody knows."

The press caught up with Art in Dublin. He and Tim, the "Visiting Yanks," were photographed standing by the Charles Parnell monument on O'Connor Street. Over breakfast at the Gresham Hotel, Art raved about the food. He was expansive, talking politics and history, but rarely sport. Recalling slights Irish Catholics encountered when he was young, Art said that Pittsburgh had been known as the Belfast of America. "But we were tough enough to fight against it," he said. "I lived in an all-Irish neighborhood and there were no big problems except that people just found it hard to get work." Art praised Irish Americans for coming up the hard way. "I've often thought that they're more Irish than the Irish." He regretted that Irish Americans were so cut off from Ireland, as had been the case for his family.

After an interview about racing, Art said, "You never asked me anything about the Super Bowl." The reporter responded, "What's the Super Bowl?" Art exclaimed, "Man, oh man, am I glad to talk to you." The only discordant note he sounded concerned religion. Although impressed by the Lady of Knock shrine, he was troubled by its commercialism. "That's the big problem with a lot of shrines like that," he reflected. "I think it is a great pity."

The Rooneys returned via London, Paris, and Rome, where Art visited racetracks and horse farms. In England, he hired a driver to take him to Newmarket, where he passed time talking with an old bookmaker and making $17 bets. In Italy, he played trotters, beating the daylights out of a bookmaker. Art wanted to leave before he wiped him out, but the bookmaker pleaded for a chance to get even. Art was embarrassed when he knocked him out of business for the day.

"The best part was seeing the bookmakers operating," Art remarked. "I got a big kick out of them. It was like turning back the pages of time." Art rarely missed a chance to express his admiration. "Those bookies were part of the romance of horse racing years ago. They were honorable people."

Art was knackered by the time he got back to the States but had little chance to rest. "In sports," Dave Anderson joked in the *Times*, "the price of fame is always high, in calories." Rooney, he said, had attained the stature of the cigars he relished. "Both are now in great demand after dessert." Art graced the dais at the Waldorf Astoria ballroom in New York three times over six days in May. He attended Iona College's sport banquet and a luncheon hosted by the American Iron and Steel Institute, whose logo adorned Steeler helmets. Then he was the guest of honor at a $150-a-plate dinner in support of Ireland's Royal College of Surgeons, St. Michael's House, the Gleneree Center for Reconciliation, and the Rooney Prize for Literature.

The dais at the Irish affair included Tony O'Reilly, Ethel Kennedy, and eighty-nine-year-old James Farley, who had held New Deal Democrats together for FDR. Pete Rozelle, George Halas, Tim Mara, columnist Bob Considine, and Andy Russell balanced politics with sport. Art squirmed in his tux, lace-front shirt, and black bow tie as O'Reilly lauded him. "Not only do we pay tribute to an extraordinary person, Art Rooney, who has proven that nice guys do finish first, but we also pay tribute to the special, warm feelings that Americans have for Ireland and her people." O'Reilly and Dan Rooney were forging a strong relationship of their own. They created the Ireland Fund as an alternative to Noraid, which raised money for the Irish Republican Army. The nonsectarian fund instead fostered cooperation between Catholics and Protestants. New York Governor Hugh Carey, referring to New York City's fiscal crisis, joked that "Mayor Beame and I have decided to give Art Rooney a million dollars to bet on a horse for us so we can balance the budget."

"Gosh," Art replied, "I didn't know you became such a big shot after you win once." He talked about how much the Irish reminded him of the unpretentious people who had lived in the Ward. "I was just a little boy around my father's saloon, but the Irish were like that when they came over, until they got hip to everything. After a month, they thought they were the only Americans there. What changed them is what changes everybody after things start coming easy. I just hope winning the Super Bowl doesn't change the Steelers."

Art was determined not to let that happen. In Pittsburgh, he asked Joe Gordon, "You know that thing you give the media?" Gordon was confused. "You know," Art said, "that book." Joe guessed the media guide, which came out when camp opened. "This year," Art instructed, "I want you to make Danny the president in there." When Gordon asked how Art wanted to be described, he said, "What's that thing they call it—the chairman of the board?" Had he discussed this with Dan? "I don't have to talk to Dan about this," Art snorted. "Just do it." There was no announcement and nobody realized that the presidency had changed hands until later that summer. That was just how Art wanted it.

Racing

Art was feted for months. In May, he went to the White House. When Gerald Ford, who had become president when Nixon resigned, appointed Lowell Perry to chair the Equal Employment Opportunity Commission, the ex-Steeler invited his old boss to the Rose Garden ceremony. Art was not asked for identification at the White House; the guard was a Northsider. After brief remarks, Ford greeted his guests. Spotting Art, the president plowed through the crowd, grabbed his hand, and proclaimed, "I've always wanted to meet you, Mr. Rooney." Ford, who had played football at Michigan, told Art how impressed he was with the Steelers. Art was no stranger to presidents; he had met them all since FDR. Ford kept talking football until Art gently suggested that the president should attend to his other guests. "There's nothing phony about this guy," he said, paying Ford his highest accolade. "He impressed me as a regular guy."

When the hoopla became overwhelming, Art escaped to the track, where his standing had little to do with football. But at Belmont friends coaxed Art to display his championship ring, which he kept in a trouser pocket with his rosary beads and bankroll. *Daily Racing Form* writer Barney Nagler kidded him that the ring had more inscriptions than the Rosetta Stone and was heavier than a bookmaker's slate. Art wasn't sure what to do with it. Kass suggested that it would make a nice brooch. "I don't like rings," Art said, "but what I may do with it is make it into a tie clasp."

Art was concerned about Christopher R's health that summer. So was Tuffy Hacker. After Christopher R's defeat before the Super Bowl, he suspected something was wrong. The vet scoping Christopher R discovered a paralyzed vocal chord that prevented him from running long distances. "I had to sprint him from then on," Tuffy said. Christopher

R adjusted well; he won six stakes races over the next four months and was voted Maryland's horse of the year.

The stallion's emergence heralded better times for Shamrock Farm. His winnings and potential as a stud made the break-even operation profitable. "All you need today is one good horse," Shamrock manager Arnold Shaw observed. "With Christopher R running for us, Mr. Rooney's horse operation will show a substantial profit."

Art had never complained when Shamrock failed to produce a top horse. Enjoyment, he reckoned, was not about money. Art could now plow Christopher R's earnings back into the farm. "This horse came along at just the right time," Shaw said. He replaced the termite-infested farmhouse and built new paddocks. Art sprinkled holy water he had collected on pilgrimages to St. Anne de Beaupre over them.

Art became, as he saw it, a recreational bettor. He recorded bets on his program, marking "TW" or "TL" for total won or lost each day, and transferred the figures to his black book for tax purposes. His bets were bigger than most plungers, but he no longer put $20,000 down on a horse. His wagers were rarely more than $200. "I go to the racetrack a lot now, but I only go to see my friends," he said. "I don't play much." Old habits, though, were hard to break. When Art went to the track, he was at work, studying the racing form and trolling for information. "He'd say you really had to be at the track every day to know the horses," Shamrock manager Jim Steele, recalled. "You just can't fly in and out. It was business." And while Art was still more likely than most men his age to jump into a car and drive through the night when he got a hunch about a horse, he had slowed down. He no longer grabbed a pal and drove nonstop to Miami just to make a bet.

Art had another reason for holding down his betting. Although few knew, his eyesight was deteriorating. His cataract surgery in 1971 had not worked, and reading had become difficult. Sam Leone, Tim Rooney, and others read the *Daily Racing Form* to him, but Art hesitated to bet without being able to see for himself.

Christopher R had rekindled interest in Art as a bettor. Now that he no longer saw himself as a gambler, Art opened up about his history as one of the best. "I'm not saying this to be boastful or anything," he acknowledged, "but I was probably as big a player as there was. I was as good as any of 'em."

While Art fielded questions about betting, Tim Rooney rebuffed charges that the Rooneys were milking Yonkers by taking excessive profits from the raceway. Tim received a $250,000 salary as president and his brothers and father made $100,000 a year for their role in Ruanaidh (Gaelic for "Rooney") Associates, the corporation that ran the track. "People are confused about who the milkman is," Tim retorted. "The milkman happens to be in Albany." Ruanaidh, he said, had not taken dividends since its $47 million purchase of the track in 1972, but had paid $36 million in taxes the previous year. "We didn't come into town on a white charger for charity," Tim said. "We're businessmen and our aim is to make a profit."

And profit they did. "I've owned race horses and I've owned racetracks," Art said, "and let me tell you, it's a lot easier owning racetracks. You make a lot more money." The Steelers were marginally profitable; not the tracks. The Rooneys would draw far more compensation from racing than football until the 1980s.

Tim, John, and Pat were engineering Ruanaidh's highly profitable expansion. As the tracks prospered, the younger brothers began playing with house money that they invested elsewhere. Yonkers alone cleared $3 million annually. The only non–family member of the Associates, their shrewd, deal-making partner John Macartney, quickly sized up the senior Rooney. "Art Rooney was as smart a man as I've ever met," he testified. "He knew everything." And not just about racing. "He had a knowledge of people, especially of people not on the square."

Ruanaidh was more powerful than ever, and Art still called the shots. "He had the final vote," Ralph Berlin argued. "If it was five to one and his vote was the one vote, his was the final vote."

Art's authority was evident when the Rooneys signed a letter of intent to purchase a jai alai fronton in Bridgeport, Connecticut for several million dollars and the assumption of an $11 million mortgage underwritten by the Teamsters pension fund. Art foresaw problems. Jai alai was notorious for fixed matches, the Teamsters were mobbed up, and Art had testified against legalizing sport gambling before a federal commission reviewing gambling policy. He made an exception for horse racing but nixed jai alai. Although several sons favored the deal, Art overruled them.

The 1975 Preseason

At camp, reporters realized that Art had stepped aside as president. "Dad walked into my office and said, 'You're the president,'" Dan explained. "There wasn't a whole lot of fanfare involved. It's no big deal."

It was a bigger deal when L. C. Greenwood, free of his WFL contract, re-signed with Pittsburgh. Dan had handled negotiations, conferring with Art, who feared the contract could break the bank. Art also vetoed buying the Pittsburgh Penguins, believing that owning the hockey club could be perceived as a conflict of interest. "My sons and I looked at it," he said. "We've been hockey fans for a long time. But the NFL frowns on a team owner having an interest in another sport." Unlike baseball, the NFL barred corporate ownership and preferred that its owners focus on football.

Art's victory lap stretched into camp, where practices drew 5,000 fans. Art recalled Sundays when he had not drawn that many for a game. He greeted visitors, making each one feel special. Art fretted that his players might have lost their edge during a celebratory off-season, but they reported in terrific shape. Joe Greene came to camp lighter than he'd ever been as a Steeler, Terry Bradshaw had worked out on his ranch instead of cashing in on the banquet circuit, and Franco Harris looked like a Roman god. Camp was competitive. The NFL had cut rosters by four spots, and a Super Bowl ring did not guarantee a job.

In July, the Steelers played the College All-Stars. Delighted to finally play in the annual benefit, Art spent the afternoon at Chicago's Soldier Field watching practice. The game, as old as his franchise, faced an uncertain future. Most clubs opposed extending it because it kept top draft picks out of camp. In the past, Art had argued strongly for the game and, along with George Halas, mustered support to keep it alive. The game was the Chicago Tribune Charities' biggest fundraiser, and Art remembered how the paper had helped to legitimize the NFL during the Depression. "I feel we owe the *Tribune* a debt of gratitude. They stepped in when times were tough." But his sons could see the handwriting on the wall. "Probably the only guy left in the league that the game has any excitement for is my Dad," Art Jr. admitted. "He's been going there every summer and watching everybody else's team play. I think that's one reason the league's kept the game going. To give him a chance to get out there and see his team play in it."

Mayor Richard Daley presented Art with the Chicago Medal of Merit and thanked him for facilitating his son's wedding reception. When Richard M. Daley, a lawyer running for the state senate, and Margaret Corbett, the daughter of prominent Pittsburghers, were planning their reception at Pittsburgh's Hilton Hotel, they had encountered union problems. Hilton executives would not intervene, telling Daley, "The union in Pittsburgh has put a lot of hotels out of business." Daley called Art. "Mayor," Art replied, "let me see what I can do." He spoke with the local union president, who said, "I'll get it straightened out but tell them to keep their mouth shut." The Daleys could plan the reception they wanted—as long as they cleared it with Art.

The All-Stars proved tougher than expected, but Pittsburgh squeaked by due to Joe Gilliam. During the game, reporters came by to shake Art's hand. "Gilliam looked good out there tonight," he said. "People are going to start talking about the quarterbacks again." Arguing about who should play quarterback was becoming Pittsburgh's favorite pastime. Art knew how fickle fans were. Sure enough, when Gilliam sputtered next time out, fans scorched him. Pat Livingston chastised those who complained that the booing was racially motivated by whites preferring Bradshaw, their "blue-eyed, blond-haired hero." Livingston noted that the same crowd had frequently sent that "hero" to the dressing room fighting back tears.

Art preferred that fans direct their frustrations at him. "If I were sitting out there, I'd boo Art Rooney, too," he once said. He did not begrudge fans that outlet. "They are my people and this is my town and it does my heart good just to be here."

Terry Bradshaw had come to camp relaxed and feeling good. He had learned to play guitar and said he dreamed of singing at the Grand Ole Opry. Bradshaw had recommitted himself to Christianity and seemed calmer for it. Art teased him about the rock-star attention he drew on the road, especially from young ladies. Art was with him when Terry embarked from an airplane and was immediately embraced and kissed by a woman. "I remarked to him that of all the ladies I'd seen around him, that one was the nicest filly I'd seen," Art chuckled. "Then he told me it was his mother." Art could see that his young friend was better able to withstand what came his way.

Expectations sailed sky-high during the preseason, but injuries quickly sidelined several key players. Pittsburgh lost four of six exhibitions while Noll experimented with players, determined to give each man in camp a fair chance. When asked whether teammates had become complacent after tasting victory, Joe Greene scowled, "No people on this team are tripping on being world champions." Nobody posed a follow-up question. Noll, who found the press a distraction, seemed unconcerned. An enigma to writers, he had made no effort to cash in on the Super Bowl. "Publicity makes me uncomfortable" was all he would say.

In September, a Republican state senator charged that William Penn Raceway president John Rooney had made a $10,000 cash contribution in 1971 to help Democratic governor Milton Shapp with campaign debts. Although the contribution was legal, the senator claimed it was a payoff to induce Shapp to allow passage of a bill extending the harness meet. Art said that he, not John, had made the gift and that it had nothing to do with the bill. "The only thing I can say is I read in the newspapers that the governor was having trouble paying off his campaign debts . . . I wanted to help." Art was more interested in exculpating his son than protecting his own image. "The money was in an envelope. I gave it to my boy, Johnny, and told him to deliver it to the governor." Art took a few shots on editorial pages, but the matter blew over.

At a preseason game in Baltimore, Art spent the day accepting congratulations from old friends. Colts announcer Chuck Thompson, who had called Bill Mazeroski's 1960 World Series–winning home run on Armed Forces Radio, told Art that he had rooted as hard for Pittsburgh as he had when Unitas led Baltimore to the title.

Back in Pittsburgh, the Steelers Alumni Association feted the team. Art didn't feel much like celebrating; they had buried Patsy Scanlon that morning. Patsy, eighty, had been Art's sparring partner and road companion. A bantamweight who never lost his cocky, back-alley brawler's edge, Patsy had helped run Ham and Cabbage Specials and was in the thick of any fight that broke out.

Pat Livingston called Scanlon a civic chauvinist who never thought of washing the soot of Pittsburgh out of his hair. "It would have shocked some of—but not all—Rooney's friends among the owners," Livingston wrote, "had they known Scanlon ran a horse room . . . But Rooney never developed that puritanical intolerance toward an honest bloke whose only vicissitude was a desire to get in on the action." Patsy was not the sharpest bookie on the block. Upon hearing that Christopher R was a lock in a race at Pimlico, he gave a fellow loafing at his florist shop money to bet with another bookie. The runner placed the bet instead at Patsy's horse room across the street. Christopher R won, paying 15-to-1, "making Scanlon," Livingston said, "the first bookmaker in history to break his own bank."

While Art mourned Patsy and an era when sport was still rooted in neighborhoods, Pittsburgh's comeback was winning acclaim. "Pittsburgh's renaissance has gone far beyond the Golden Triangle," Dave Ailes wrote. "Once was the time when Pittsburgh was last in the National League, last in the National Football League and first in green river water. It still isn't a good idea to take a swig from the Mon, but it's safe to root for the Pirates and Steelers without getting mugged in the box seats."

Regular Season

A strike threatened the 1975 season, but few players wanted to walk out after the previous summer's defeat. The Steelers voted to continue negotiations while playing. They had come to trust the Rooneys more than NFLPA director Ed Garvey, even though negotiations were stalled and owners had suspended pension fund contributions. Common ground was elusive, but Pittsburgh could defend its title.

After the Steelers crushed the Chargers 37–0 in the opener, some Pittsburghers began making Super Bowl plans. But in game two, O. J. Simpson rushed for 227 yards, the most ever against the Steelers, and

463

Buffalo handed them their worst defeat in years. But they did not lose again until a meaningless season finale in Los Angeles.

Art had few official duties, but he greeted visitors to Three Rivers and counseled players and employees. He hosted George Halas when the Bears visited in October. Halas, whose passion to win was unequalled in NFL history, displayed grace in defeat. "He was a helluva guy before he was champion," Halas said of Rooney, "and it certainly hasn't spoiled him." Halas made sure that writers reprised the story of the two men almost coming to fisticuffs over the split of the gate decades ago.

Terry Bradshaw was flying high, dating Ice Capades skater Jo Jo Starbuck and covering Hank Williams in Nashville, but Joe Greene was hurting. He was ejected from a game for fighting and blasted for stomping a Denver player a week later. While Chuck Noll and Dan Rooney defended Greene from the press, Art took him into his office for a cigar. Greene was frustrated by his body's unwillingness to cooperate. Stumbling over a tarp in the preseason, Greene had twisted a knee and pulled groin muscles. He played hurt until late November, when he pinched a nerve in his neck. The injury was debilitating, and Greene was sidelined after playing in ninety-one consecutive games.

Joe often came by North Lincoln for a meal. His injury upset Art—he knew Joe's pride made not playing unbearable—and they became even closer. "My father would give Joe these baseball-bat sized cigars to smoke," Art Jr. recalled. "He was the only person who could put them in his mouth and it would look normal."

"After Joe got hurt," Ralph Berlin said, "he was a shell of his former self on the field. He still commanded respect in the locker room—he was still the boss. But he was never the same player again." Greene had long challenged teammates to match his intensity. "I remember once when he smashed his helmet against the goal post," Lynn Swann said. "That was a message that he was playing the best possible football that he could, but he saw some people around him who weren't. If you were giving less than 100 percent, he let you know." Some sought Greene out as their confidant; others learned not to trifle with his code. Ralph Berlin was in a stall in the lavatory when he overheard Greene confront a player who had bullied an employee. "Joe has the guy against the wall, telling him, 'If I ever hear you picking on him or anybody else, I'm going to beat the hell out of you.'"

Ironically, the defensive line began receiving its due at the moment when Greene was less able to play than at any time in his career. *Time* put Greene, Greenwood, White, and Holmes on its cover. The story, "Half a Ton of Trouble," called them the best front four in the game. Rarely, if ever, had defensive linemen been so extolled. "That Joe Greene," Art said, "I've never seen a player lift a team like he does." Neither had anybody else.

Art settled back into his routines. On Sundays, he rose by six, read the papers, attended Mass, and walked to the stadium. Arriving hours before kickoff, he visited the dressing room before seeking out ground crew and ushers. Kass arrived later, but she and Art rarely saw each other there and never sat together. "Why would I want my wife in there with me?" Art asked. "I'd never watch a game with my wife. Heavens, no." Art watched in silence while Kass had her own box where she watched and chatted with friends. "Pro football is no place to be talking," he declared. "We smoke our cigars and watch the plays. Maybe we'll chat at halftime, but nobody speaks when the plays are going on. That's too serious."

After Fathers Jim Campbell and Regis Flanagan died, Art wanted another priest in his box. When several were suggested, Art asked, "Is one of them quiet, not a cheerleader, not a screamer?" Father Richard Reardon, who had grown up in Swissvale and was friends with Art's sons, got the nod. Reardon quickly grasped the etiquette of the box. He and Art chatted before kickoff. "But once the game began," Reardon explained, "he did not like anyone talking and specifically did not like anyone saying this game is in the bag when the Steelers had a lead." Once, when someone did just that, Art said, "I wish you wouldn't say that." After Pittsburgh scored again, the man repeated himself. Richie Easton, Art's driver, said, "You'll never see that guy in the box again."

A lunch was provided at halftime, and late in the third quarter, Art brought out his rosary beads. "He stopped paying attention to the game," Reardon explained, "and he became at peace." After saying the rosary, Art resumed watching. He started to leave games at the two-minute warning. Easton brought the car around and Art and Reardon beat the crowd home. They had dinner in the kitchen and watched the second game. After Reardon left, Art took a walk and waited for a friend to bring over the bulldog edition of the paper. He liked to see what the other teams had done and devour the stats.

During the week, family and friends stopped by. Terry Bradshaw came for dinner, Ralph Berlin to play cards. "We'd play gin rummy," Berlin explained. "He could read cards and know what I had in my hand." Art often had two televisions on, one with football, the other basketball, while playing cards. "The sound is up on both of them," Berlin said, "he's talking on the phone, and he puts the phone down and knows exactly what was happening. That's how sharp he was."

Card games kept Art abreast of the team's internal dynamics. Berlin was close to many players, who spoke frankly as he tended their injuries. Berlin also played poker with Joe Greene, Franco Harris, L. C. Greenwood, and Sam Davis on Mondays and nights before games. "They accuse Ralph of being able to buy his house and put his kids through college playing poker with them," Dwight White chuckled. Berlin, in turn, confided in Art.

Art's office was within earshot of Dan's, and he was liberal with counsel. But Dan ran the team now. Just as Bert Bell had leaned on Art, Pete Rozelle depended on Dan to shape league policy on expansion and labor. Art reinforced Dan's belief that controlling salaries and limiting player movement would keep smaller-market clubs competitive.

The 1975 Playoffs

Pittsburgh finished a franchise-best 12-2, set club records for most points scored and fewest surrendered, and entered the playoffs for the fourth consecutive year. Bradshaw was playing his best football yet, and Franco Harris was amassing yardage like no back in team history. An unprecedented three linebackers made the Pro Bowl, and the defensive line finally acquired a nickname, the Steel Curtain.

The only cloud was Joe Greene's health. As Pittsburgh prepared to host the Colts, who were on a nine-game winning streak, Greene was doubtful for the game. "My body has taken a helluva beating," he admitted.

Art was not as upset about Greene's inability to play—Steve Furness was doing well in his place—as he was by his friend's pain. Art had long known what Greene was finding out: football was transitory.

Baltimore proved no match for Pittsburgh, whose next opponent was Oakland. That week, Ed Kiely told media, "Lay off the Prez for stories. He's too tired." When reporter Vince Leonard bumped into Art, he said, "I'm not supposed to talk to you." Putting his arm around Leonard, Art replied, "Why don't we go back to my office and shoot the breeze." But for the most part, Art kept a low profile.

Wind chill at Three Rivers Stadium dropped temperatures during the AFC Championship to 14 degrees below, and ice made footing treacherous. Greene, heavily taped, provided his teammates a huge boost by playing the first half. The Steelers fumbled five times and threw three interceptions, but Jack Lambert recovered three Oakland fumbles and Mike Wagner intercepted two passes.

When Lynn Swann was hospitalized after George Atkinson viciously tackled his head, John Stallworth replaced him. In the fourth quarter, his block allowed Franco to race 25 yards for a touchdown; Stallworth then caught a touchdown pass. With 17 seconds left to play, Oakland narrowed the score to 16–10. Recovering an onside kick, Oakland completed a pass to Pittsburgh's 15-yard line before the gun sounded. Pittsburgh was returning to the Super Bowl.

Super Bowl X

Art could not have asked for a more hospitable Super Bowl venue than Miami, where he had wintered since the 1920s. He spent the week making travel arrangements for friends, family, and employees, but he had trouble scoring tickets. The team's allotment of 12,000 seats was gone in hours. "I just can't do it any more," Art admitted. Joe Gordon defended his boss. "This is probably the first time in his life he has not had the number of tickets he wanted, and this is the man."

The Steelers were favored over their opponents, the Dallas Cowboys, and Terry Bradshaw arrived in Miami with an exuberance he had lacked in the past. Lynn Swann, however, had suffered a concussion in the Oakland game. When he returned to practice, he dropped balls he normally caught. "He couldn't catch a cold," Bradshaw remarked. More ominously, Joe Greene was not at full strength.

Pittsburgh had beaten Minnesota the year before by running the ball, so Dallas stacked its defense to stop Franco and force Bradshaw to pass. The Cowboys scored first, but a 32-yard reception by Swann showed that he had gotten over his concussion and led to a Randy Grossman touchdown that tied the score. Pittsburgh was down 10–7 in the fourth quarter when Reggie Harrison blocked a Dallas punt out of the end zone for a safety. Roy Gerela kicked two field goals and Bradshaw threw a pass to Swann that traveled 70 yards in the air to put Pittsburgh up 21–10. Bradshaw, clobbered as he released the ball, was helped off the field. He didn't realize that Swann had scored until regaining his senses in the locker room. Dallas pulled to 21–17 and had the ball on Pittsburgh's 38-yard line with time for one last play. But Glen Edwards' interception in the end zone sealed Pittsburgh's second Super Bowl win.

Art watched from the stands. The Orange Bowl was even more frenetic than usual because the crew of *Black Sunday*, a thriller in which terrorists attacked the Super Bowl, was filming at the game. Exhausted afterward, all Art could muster was, "Thank God the game is over." In the locker room, he asked Andy Russell to give the game ball to Dan, and stood aside as Pete Rozelle handed the Lombardi Trophy to Dan and Chuck Noll. At the team's dinner party that night, Art spoke confidently about the future. Before the game, he had said, "I think we can have a pro football dynasty here if we're able to keep our players together. We have a very young club and they're capable of winning it all for the next five years or so." He saw no reason to back off his prediction. "I think," he smiled, "they could win it again next year."

Celebration

Fans stormed downtown Pittsburgh after the game, but the police, experienced with championship mayhem, kept the revelry mellow. The next day, over 100,000 fans greeted the team's return. Pittsburgh, mired in a deepening economic slump, was far from jaded about winning. Steel jobs were disappearing by the tens of thousands, and the only smoke in Pittsburgh these days, one writer lamented, came from Art's cigars. A

teachers' strike and scandals involving Gulf Oil, headquartered downtown, thickened the malaise. But euphoria over the Steelers temporarily eclipsed all woes.

Sportswriters again buffered Art's image, but not to the extraordinary
sheen of the year before. "The last sportsman . . . the last of a breed. He
is an heirloom, not only of sport, but of America, of a time which has
passed," one wrote. "We're just plain, ordinary people," Kass Rooney
protested. "That's all." She made sure that Art never took himself too
seriously. His sons, however, were adamant that their father was special. "What you have to realize," Pat Rooney stated, "is that my father
is a great man. None of his sons are." Art demurred: "I am lucky. I am
lucky in life."

At the Dapper Dan banquet, Bob Prince, the recently fired Pirates announcer, led attendees in singing "Happy Birthday" to Art. "To make it
two in a row for Mr. Rooney was a big thrill," Terry Bradshaw said as
he received the sportsman-of-the-year award. Everywhere Art looked
at the banquet, he saw friends. Fritzie Zivic, Bill Dudley, and Buff Donelli were there; so was Cool Papa Bell, who had played with the Grays
and Crawfords. Art might have been the fastest sandlot player in Pittsburgh, but Bell was the fastest to ever play in the city. They reminisced
about Cum Posey, Gus Greenlee, and Josh Gibson.

Steeler employees surprised Art with a birthday party at the stadium
the next day. Afterward, Chuck Noll took his coaches and their wives
to a cay in the Bahamas. Terry Bradshaw married Jo Jo Starbuck, while
Georgia native Mel Blount campaigned alongside Jimmy Carter in Pennsylvania's presidential primary and Ernie Holmes attended a wedding
in Amarillo. At the reception, detectives charged into the restroom and
arrested Holmes for possessing cocaine. The police version of the arrest
was confused and contradictory, but Holmes was held for trial. Holmes
said a man asked if he wanted to buy a silver bullet. Holmes gave him
$20 and was examining his purchase when the police barged in. Only
then, Holmes said, did he find that the silver bullet contained drugs.
Holmes immediately called the Rooneys.

Joe Greene, after ending the season sidelined by pain, went through a
rough rehabilitation. Nerve and muscle damage had eroded his strength,

mobility, and peace of mind. "Don't let them write my obituary," he thundered after stories described him as finished. Joe Gilliam's stay with the Steelers ended. The talented but troubled quarterback had been the only Steeler not to play in the Super Bowl. Pittsburgh waived him that spring.

The Horses

Art, however, kept winning. Christopher R took the J. Edgar Hoover Handicap and came from behind to win the Sporting Plate Handicap, beating 1975 Eclipse sprinter of the year Gallant Bob. He won nearly every time out. His best win came in the 1976 Gravesend Handicap at Aqueduct when he again defeated Gallant Bob despite carrying more weight. But Christopher R lost his next two races, costing him the prestigious Eclipse Award for 1976. Tim Rooney was more upset about the Eclipse Award than Art. In five years of racing, Christopher R won 22 of 42 races, including 16 stakes races, and $400,000 in purses. In 1977, he went to stud.

By then, Arnold Shaw was gone. Shamrock's manager had a midlife crisis and ran out on his marriage shortly before Christmas in 1976. When Shaw left, Tim Rooney interviewed Jim Steele for the job. The University of Kentucky grad student transformed Shamrock into a first-rate horse farm. He understood breeding and worked closely with Tim, who Steele contended was the real expert in bloodlines.

Art purchased adjacent farmland, doubling Shamrock's size. A highly functional farm, it grew hay and grain, raised animals, and served as a stallion station and nursery.

Soon after Steele took over, Art asked him if the farm had any fighting birds left. A former trainer had kept gamecocks, turning them loose with the other chickens when they could no longer fight. Art told Steele about a cockfight, called a main, in which ten Shamrock birds fought those of another cockfighter. Put off by his opponent's boorish behavior, Art instructed his trainer to put his worst birds into the ring first. The other guy won the first bout and began bragging. Art increased his bet and lost again. He kept doubling the bet, and as the match went on, his better birds started winning. Art cleaned out the lout.

At the track, Steele enjoyed watching Art study the tote board before the race went off. "When the odds changed quickly and he saw a big bet made on a horse, he knew where the race was going, or at least where the money thought it was going." But what impressed Steele more was Rooney's understanding of people. "He had an incredible ability to size people up." Steele saw that Rooney stuck with people. "If you passed his test, you were good forever. I always knew my job was safe as long as Art Rooney was alive."

"Art won a lot of races and knew the pond he was playing in," Steele observed. "I don't think he ever aspired to win the Kentucky Derby." Art wanted Shamrock to breed stakes winners, but he also wanted it to break even. "You're racing for ribbons over there in Ireland," he chided Tim. "Here, you're racing for money." Tim did both, winning races and engineering hugely successful sales of horses he had bred. Like his father, Tim was seduced by the romance of horse racing.

Tim paid $65,000 for an Irish mare, shocking his father. "You sap," Art chided him. "You're really a sucker." But Tim was no sap. He sold her foals for a nice profit, prompting Art to exclaim "Get out!" in disbelief when he heard what they fetched. At times, Tim was as adept at breeding as his father had been at betting.

Shamrock was a haven, not a profit-maximizing venture. "There was no line of people waiting to see him," Steele said. Art walked through the woods, chewing a cigar and talking with buddies. "It was a retreat for him," Jim's wife Chris recalled. "Before I filled it with kids, he filled it with men," cronies like Richie Easton and Iggy Borkowski. The men had their routines. Art arrived at night and devoured the cookies that Chris left for him. He always walked down to the barns to look at the horses before turning in. Richie, whose broad, square face was covered with curly gray hair, got up first and made espresso in a little pot he brought along. They returned for breakfast after Mass and then headed to the track.

Few people knew when Art was there; Mary Regan was discreet regarding his whereabouts. "You didn't talk to him without going through Mary," Jim Steele explained. Once in the Pimlico Hotel men's room, a priest confronted Art at the urinal: "Aren't you Rooney? I've been trying to get a hold of you, but I can't get past your secretary, Mary. I can get to the pope, but I can't get to you!"

The Steeles were drawn into Art's embrace. "He made everyone feel special," Jim recalled. "You'd walk through fire for a man like him. With him, it was never how you screwed up. It was how you can do better."

Art bred a mare to Christopher R as a present for Terry Bradshaw after the Super Bowl. The foal was a fine mare, but Bradshaw's experience was with quarter horses. "I didn't know anything about keeping thoroughbreds," he confessed. The grass on his Louisiana farm was ill-suited and the weather too hot for her. "That old mare was barely to going to make it, but she had a baby. I kept the baby and I called Mr. Rooney and said, "Please take this mare back, because I don't know how to take care of her." The mare returned to Shamrock while Bradshaw held on to her filly. "She had a lot of heart, but I ended up trading her to someone in Maryland for a daughter of one of the great quarter horses." The filly earned half a million dollars in purses. "Half a million dollars!" Bradshaw howled when remembering the deal. "I didn't make that much in four years. Golly, Art laughed and laughed about that."

Bradshaw and Mel Blount, who loved to ride, visited Shamrock; other players worked there to get ready for camp. Art did not ride and knew little about breeding. But he could see the athlete in a horse and became attached to several.

Art didn't have to tell his sons much about running things anymore. They were sophisticated businessmen who had internalized his values. Just as Art had fought to include players and referees in the NFL pension fund, his sons found a way that fall to help racing's invisible workforce. The lack of a pension for those who worked along the backstretch had roiled racing, prompting a strike at Aqueduct. Art applauded his sons for creating a pension fund at Yonkers and Roosevelt. The tracks put up $100,000 a year to create a "backstretch pension fund" for grooms and stable hands. "Those who make up the backbone of racing will be cared for in their retirement years," Art Jr. said regarding the unprecedented commitment.

Aging

In Pittsburgh, Art spent days at Three Rivers. "When the lights are on at the stadium," he said, "I'm there." Ed Kiely took a call from a whiskey company running a campaign featuring distinguished gentlemen seated by a fire with a drink in hand. They would pay Art handsomely for a spot. "He doesn't drink," Kiely responded. The ad man replied, "That doesn't mean anything." Kiely snorted, "It does to him." The closest Art came to advertising was a United Way spot.

Art often lamented the change in football, as he had in racing when pari-mutuels pushed bookmakers aside. He felt that racing had become an industry, shedding the people who gave it character. Football, he said, was losing its romance. "It's all big business now."

After the Super Bowl, Art was on a plane with Ed Kiely, who took the aisle seat to shield him from interruption. It was a futile effort. After several people told him how great he was and what a great team he had, Art turned to Ed: "You know, when I was losing, they said I was a bum, that I was cheap. We're not doing anything different now than we did then, except we're playing better."

"My father," Pat Rooney said, "just doesn't understand that when some people wake up in the morning and look at their face in the mirror, it's not the greatest thing in the world." But Art was having a harder time seeing himself in the mirror and losing the ability to distinguish faces.

If he ever gave into depression, it was then. "I used to see him at home." John Rooney recalled. "I would see him lighting a match and he would keep doing it in the ash tray while looking at the fire. I think that was the only thing he could see." Art suffered silently, resigned to limited vision.

"This business of growing old gracefully is bunk," he complained when Dan found him in a chair wrapped in a blanket in Palm Beach that off-season. "He was just sitting there, doing nothing," Dan remembered, "concerned about not feeling good. He was definitely not himself." Dan confronted his father, and Kass, who was in better shape, got Art up and out. He began walking to Mass each morning, heading to the Kennel Club in the afternoon, and going out for dinner. From

Dan's perspective, his father's bout of depression, if it was that, ended quickly. But poor eyesight plagued him. Meticulously cleaning his eyeglasses did not help much.

Art was crossing the street one day when a man said hello to him. "I'm sorry, I can't see who you are," Art said. The man, an optometrist, identified himself. Art said, "It's cataracts. I can't see. I got operated on." The doctor responded, "Come see me, I think I can help." With new eyeglass lenses and treatments, the doctor restored much of Art's sight. Not long after that, Ed Kiely, John Rooney, and Art were at the track. Kiely was placing Art's bets when it dawned on John that his father was having one of his days. He asked Kiely, "What's he doing?" Kiely said, "He's doing all right." That was all John needed to hear. "I started chiming in and I ended up making $5,000 or $6,000 that day. That was really big money for me." Art was back.

21

City of Champions

1976–79

Cleveland, October 10, 1976

Art was horrified. Even Cleveland's partisan fans hushed. Terry Bradshaw lay face down on the turf of Municipal Stadium, his legs twitching. After dodging a Steeler lineman, Cleveland's Joe "Turkey" Jones had grabbed Bradshaw. Swirling him up and over as if the quarterback was a rag doll, Jones had spiked him into the turf neck first. Bradshaw bounced once, then splayed awkwardly on the ground. Art stood in the press box, petrified by the thought that Bradshaw's neck was broken.

The Steelers, already stuck 1-3 on the 1976 season, were losing again. Art could handle that; what scared him was Bradshaw. Both of his favorite players' careers were now in jeopardy. Joe Greene remained hampered by a pinched nerve and the toll of eight NFL seasons; Bradshaw might be facing paralysis. His neck braced, he was carried off the field.

The Steelers had gone to Cleveland feeling they had to win to right the season. Instead, they reached their nadir, the lowest point since Chuck Noll's first season. "It's frustrating, terribly frustrating," Art admitted the next day. "I feel bad, just as bad as the fans and the coaches and the players." Art was not so thick skinned and resilient any more. Bradshaw, however, had not suffered lasting impairment. "Anybody else's neck would have been broken," surgeon Dr. Paul Steele explained. "But Terry's neck bones are so much larger than normal." Bradshaw was sidelined, but his career would continue. "I feel I'm a lucky young man to be alive," he said, puffing one of Art's cigars a few days later.

Relieved about Bradshaw, Art worried about the season. He had felt since camp that the Steelers had lost their hunger. "It was a lousy training camp," Joe Greene admitted. "There was no zip." Art saw pervasive self-satisfaction, although not on Greene's part. The defensive stalwart had worked hard in the off-season to regain his strength. "Regardless of what you achieve," Greene observed, "it's always short-lived. You never arrive. If you maintain what you've got, then you become stale while everybody else is gaining."

Nobody was gaining faster than Pittsburgh's bitter rivals, the Raiders, who had beaten them 31–28 in the opener. The Steelers had been up by two touchdowns and were driving for another when Raider George Atkinson knocked Lynn Swann out with a vicious hit, blasting him from behind on a play in which neither was involved. The play reprised the 1975 AFC championship, when Oakland headhunting had hospitalized Swann with a concussion. Chuck Noll slammed the Raiders afterward. "It's football with the intent to maim," he charged. "We have a criminal section in every aspect of society and apparently we have one in the NFL."

The loss to Cleveland dropped Pittsburgh into last place. "I've learned something in this game," Art reflected. "The good teams that have the fewest injuries usually win. We have to get healthy and get the right bounce of the ball." Joe Greene said, "We're just not dominating teams any more." But he believed they would rebound. "No matter what, this is still the greatest football team ever put together."

Off the field, Raider George Atkinson took umbrage with Noll's comments about a criminal element and retained California legislator Willie Brown to sue the coach for slander. Art paid Atkinson little mind, but Pittsburgh's lackluster play concerned him. He attended each practice and spent more time in the locker room. In deference to age, Art had stopped making long road trips, but he would not miss another away game that season.

In the next game, rookie quarterback Mike Kruczek handed the ball to Franco Harris a record forty-one times, and Joe Greene played his best game in a year as Pittsburgh beat Cincinnati. Holding its next three opponents scoreless, Pittsburgh improved to 5-4. They were winning, but battered. Players spent more time with trainer Ralph Berlin than with their families. Their luck, Art rued, had turned.

On his nightly perambulations around the Northside, Art walked past the Kilbuck Station postal facility, where workers waited for him to talk politics and football. They wondered whether Pittsburgh would make the playoffs. "It would've been so easy if we would have just beaten New England," he muttered. "That was the game our season hinged on, only nobody took it too seriously at the time." Art had warned that the Steelers better not be nonchalant about the Patriots. They had been, fumbling six times and losing to an inferior club in September. "We can't expect help from other people," he told the postal workers. "We have to win all of them."

Although George Atkinson filed a $3 million slander and libel lawsuit against Noll and one against the Steelers, Pittsburgh kept winning. Eight consecutive victories pushed the Steelers' record to 9-4, but they would need help from an unlikely source—Oakland—to make the playoffs. They got it when Oakland beat Cincinnati in December. Art telegrammed congratulations to Al Davis and John Madden the next day. "Now we have life," he reflected. "People talked about the Raiders lying down. But I knew they wouldn't." By winning their last game, the Steelers made the playoffs for the fifth consecutive year.

Art prowled the sidelines at practice before the playoffs, buoyed by Joe Greene's return to Pro Bowl form. Greene had adjusted his game, playing within the confines of an extraordinary defense instead of freelancing on the strength of his exceptional physical abilities. "The best defensive game I've ever seen a man play," Art said, finishing one cigar and starting another, "was Joe Greene against Houston in 1972. We won, 9–3. I've never seen a lineman single-handedly dominate a game like that. It was like he was alone out there on the football field, eleven men against one." Art cared deeply for Greene. "He's been a great player for us." No Steeler defense had ever played better than this squad; it had shut out five opponents and allowed only 28 points in its last nine games.

Pittsburgh crushed Baltimore 40–14 to open the playoffs, but the win was costly. Franco bruised his ribs, Rocky hurt his big toe, and neither could play the next week. It could have been worse. Minutes after the game, a small airplane crashed into the upper deck where thousands of

Colts fans had been sitting. Because Baltimore was being blown out, the stands were empty.

Pittsburgh advanced to the AFC championship in Oakland but could not sustain a drive without Franco and Rocky. Oakland wore the defense down, winning 24–7. Art knew how gallant an effort his players had made that season. He and his brother-in-law, Jack McGinley, went down the aisle on the flight home, shaking players' hands and thanking them for their commitment. "A lot of teams could've quit with two stars like Franco and Rocky out," Art said. "But we didn't. Our team is every bit a winner as Oakland."

The 1977 Off-Season

In late December, Art attended Philip Iselin's funeral in New Jersey, where Howard Cosell eulogized Iselin, the president of Monmouth Park Raceway and the New York Jets. Art chatted with Joe Namath on the steps of Temple Beth Miriam afterward. Namath, football's highest-profile player, was nearing retirement. Rozelle had once asked Art to investigate rumors that Namath was gambling heavily on horses. Art figured that if he could no longer get a big bet down, neither could Namath. "If he is, I'm gonna start betting with him," he told his son John. After asking around, Art reported that Namath wasn't betting big. "If he's betting, he's betting a hundred bucks," Art reported.

These days, Pete Rozelle was more likely to turn to Dan than Art. He asked Dan to resolve the labor impasse that had left the NFL without an agreement for three years. Failure to reach a deal could eliminate the draft and imperil the Steelers. In the middle of the pack in terms of revenue, they could not afford the bidding war for players that would erupt without a contract.

Art shared a suite with Dan at the Phoenix NFL meetings. "They give me this place," he said, pointing to a mural of thoroughbreds, "'cause I like horses. In the old days we'd just have a room. On the train we rode coach instead of Pullman." He missed those days and the men with whom he had built the league. "There were only nine of us back then. We didn't have no lawyers with us . . . Now, there's so many people in there you don't even know." By the time he did know them, they were gone.

The old days had not been without rancor. "Oh they were bitter," he laughed. "At one time, Charlie Bidwill, the Chicago Cardinals owner, and I were the only ones who talked to everybody. The vote was always 5–4." Art still attended meetings, but, he laughed, "Halas and I never have anything to say." But Art told reporters that the draft and the Rozelle Rule limiting player movement embodied what he and Bert Bell had worked to achieve—competitive balance. Without them, football would suffer.

In February, Art went to Amarillo with Dan, Andy Russell, Franco Harris, and Jack Ham to testify as character witnesses at Fats Holmes' trial for possession of cocaine. The jury, skeptical of police accounts, acquitted him. Spectators applauded the verdict and Holmes effusively thanked the Rooneys. Holmes had dodged another bullet, but the trial left him indebted to the team for legal fees and sorely tested the Rooneys' tolerance.

Rozelle's confidence in Dan was well placed. Later that month, Dan brokered a five-year labor pact with the union. After NFLPA director Ed Garvey stormed out of negotiations in Washington, Dan surprised him by showing up at union headquarters ready to talk. He let Garvey vent and took him to a nearby steakhouse. "It was the first time we'd ever broken bread together," Garvey said. He realized what his predecessors had come to understand: the Rooneys were the owners most willing to work with the union. The meal jump-started negotiations, and a deal was reached that guaranteed survival of the union and the draft.

Dan was playing Art's old role now. Trusted by peers and the union, he was able to forge deals acceptable to both sides. Dan got along well with almost everybody except Al Davis. His father, though, could jolly Oakland's owner along. At the March meeting, Art and Davis went at it in the lobby. "There he is," Art intoned as Davis approached. "He's the biggest man in Pittsburgh. I've lived there all my life and he's a much bigger man than I am. All people ask me now is 'What's Al Davis really like?'" Art told them that Davis was really a nice guy and that he didn't grease his players' jerseys. Davis, who had grown up in Brooklyn, matched one-liners but showed uncharacteristic deference. Calling

Pittsburgh a Soviet satellite, he had Art howling. "It's behind the Iron Curtain. They don't tell people what's going on in the papers there." When Davis said he couldn't wait to drag Art into court for the suit against Chuck Noll, Art laughed, "Oh, we'll get that moved to Allegheny County."

Though many owners despised Davis, Art got a kick out of him. "I argue with him, but we like each other," Art said. "I'm one of the few guys in the league who does. He likes to think he's the devil, but he's not." When Davis's wife, Carol, was hospitalized after a stroke, Art wrote constantly. "I love that man," Davis said. "We get along because he's not afraid of me."

In March, Art bid farewell to Al Abrams, seventy-three, who had worked at the *Post-Gazette* since 1926. Art had named a horse for Abrams, and they celebrated when the stallion won at Aqueduct. Few of the reporters who had traveled with Art on the Pullmans were left.

Art's good humor was being undercut by sport's changing landscape. "Football was a lot more fun before the big money," he said. "The game was played for its own sake and a coach like Jock Sutherland would have spit his teeth into the camera if play had been stopped for a TV commercial." Prima donna players, agents, and hordes of accountants and lawyers at league meetings irked him. "The players had no fancy ideas," Art recalled. "They rode subways and trolley cars and ate in cafeterias."

Though football salaries were rising, the average major league baseball player made twice the average Steeler salary. Some Steelers argued that the club was taking advantage of them. Art disagreed, but left it to Dan to dispute their allegations. Pittsburgh's payroll was in the top third of all clubs, averaging $50,000 per player, with Greene, Harris, and Bradshaw topping $100,000. But Three Rivers' capacity was the second smallest in the league, and over a third of the roster made $30,000 or less.

During the off-season, Art and Kass had several players and their wives—Joe and Agnes Greene, Dwight and Karen White, Franco Harris and Dana Dokmanovich, and Terry Bradshaw and Jo Jo Starbuck—over for dinner. Art schmoozed with reporters on draft day and said goodbye to Andy Russell and Ray Mansfield, who retired. "You were good for us," he told Mansfield. As Mansfield watched Art walk away, he said, "That's great people. You know, I always felt like I would never be ripped off with this organization."

Distractions

Though the 1976 season had ended in defeat, Art took heart from Pittsburgh's noble comeback after a hideous start. His hopes for 1977, however, were dashed by a summer of discontent. As soon as rookies reported, Chuck Noll and Dan Rooney departed for San Francisco to appear in court. Art's sons talked him into staying home. When the vets arrived, Jack Lambert and Mel Blount were absent. Lambert wanted a new contract while Blount was furious with Noll. When asked in court if any Steeler had ever engaged in willful and wanton violence on the field, Noll had named Blount, Joe Greene, and Glen Edwards. Blount angrily declared he would file his own slander suit against Noll.

Art was the biggest no-show of all. Two weeks into camp, he had yet to visit St. Vincent's. "Never thought Art Rooney could stay away from a Steeler training camp so long," sportswriter Norm Vargo mused. "In fact, I could never imagine Art Rooney missing even a day of the preseason grind." While Art Jr. said his father was tending to business, Vargo wasn't buying it. He figured that Art was wounded by the squabbles and controversies. "The good Rooney name is being dragged through the mud," he wrote. "And you can bet the 'Old Man' doesn't care for it." Maybe Art was a no-show, Vargo concluded, "because he's just an old man who's been hurt by people he likes a lot." More likely, Art felt helpless to do anything about the acrimony troubling his team.

Dan, meanwhile, tried to keep the books balanced and the conflicts with Lambert and Blount from becoming too personal. Dan cared more about winning than making money but would not accept the deficits of earlier years. "Art was good to everybody, Ed Kiely recalled, "but he said, 'I'm not going to let these guys [agents and players] break me.' That's what he taught Danny."

In August, after rookie Randy Frisch's death in a car crash following a preseason game, the lawsuits and Lambert's holdout were finally resolved. Lambert reported after becoming the first Steeler to sign a multiyear contract worth over $1 million, and Noll was absolved of blame by the court in San Francisco. But Noll had missed much of camp, and the club stumbled through the preseason. Art feared the distractions would continue into the season. They did.

"Fats Holmes was absolutely wearing everybody out," Tim V. Rooney recalled. "He wore Chuck Noll out, he wore the front office out, he wore the position coaches out. But he never wore Art out. He liked Fats." Holmes owed the club much of his salary for having paid his legal fees. "There's no way I can thank the Rooneys for all of the help they've given me," Holmes said, "but, frankly, I expected more compassion . . . I'm not the patsy of the world."

When Tim, in personnel, was tasked with trading Holmes, Art watched with bemusement. Fats was a tough sell. When Tim announced that it was "ninety-nine to one" that he had a deal, Art interjected, "I'll take it." After the deal collapsed, Art howled, "Anytime you want to do that ninety-nine to one with me, I'll do it." "My uncle just had a way of understanding where things were going to come out," Tim explained.

As the regular season approached, Joe Greene challenged missing teammates to return. "We need our people back in there if we're going to go anywhere." A few days later, Mel Blount ended his fifty-six-day holdout and dropped his lawsuit against Noll. But as Blount returned, Ernie Holmes, distraught over his salary, walked out. "I can't hack it. I won't starve," he exclaimed before the opener. Art, standing in the rain at practice the next day, was annoyed. "This isn't like baseball," he observed. "Baseball is an individual game. You can have eight players who dislike each other and the management and they can still go up to the plate and hit. But this is a team game. They have to work together."

At least Bradshaw and Greene were ready. They had geared their off-seasons to the 1977 campaign. Bradshaw had shelved his singing career, adding muscle to withstand the pounding he would take, while Greene was an oasis of calm as rhetoric escalated. "I don't want to rock the boat," he said when asked about his inclusion in the "criminal element." "That's exactly what we don't need right now." Greene had started lifting weights regularly, slimmed down to enhance his quickness, and begun watching film of other players. He used to say, "I don't worry about the other guy; I let him worry about me." Now, he sought every edge.

Pittsburgh won its opener but then lost to Oakland, the defending Super Bowl champs, for the third consecutive time. Raider Phil Villapiano taunted Pittsburgh afterward: "The Steelers are history." Bad news abounded. Mike Wagner and backup quarterback Mike Kruczek were lost for the season, safety Jim Allen walked out over his salary, and when Bradshaw broke his wrist, rookie safety Tony Dungy was forced to play quarterback. The Steelers led the league in turnovers and penalties, and Joe Greene blew up over the officiating. "If I get half a chance," he warned, "I'll punch one of them." He was fined after threatening to "cleat one in the spine."

Pittsburgh's record fell to 4-4. "We are without question," Noll admitted, "at the bottom." Art watched the Denver game on television at home. He could make it out better that way. "It's always hard to watch your team lose," Art acknowledged. "These guys know they are up against it and that they can't afford to lose one more game." After Glen Edwards walked out to protest his salary, Art was visibly upset. "I can't remember one of our teams going through something like this," he said. "It almost doesn't leave any time to play football." Art had recently named two yearlings What's the Trouble and What Happened. "I hear those questions a lot," he said. "I wish I knew the answers."

Winning five of their last six games, the Steelers made the playoffs. But they were a dispirited club. Even Chuck Noll was injured; he fell on an icy sidewalk and broke his elbow. On the eve of the playoff game with the Broncos, Art appraised Denver's playoff jubilation. "It's a time the team should be enjoying because it's not nearly that way in Pittsburgh any more. You can keep the high for a few years, but now our fans have taken it for granted." Privately, he thought some players did, too. He rued the influence of agents who, he said, did not understand football. "The whole situation this year has kind of been a problem," he concluded with understatement.

The game was tied at halftime despite Pittsburgh's 183 to 44 edge in yards gained. But when Denver pulled ahead in the fourth quarter, Pittsburgh's season was over. Joe Greene's image took a hit after he slugged

Bronco Paul Howard in the stomach because Howard was holding him. The network replayed the punch endlessly; Greene would have been suspended for the next game if Pittsburgh had won.

The 1978 Season

During the off-season, cornerback J. T. Thomas was diagnosed with a season-ending blood disorder and Ernie Holmes was arrested for DUI in Arizona. Dan Rooney and Chuck Noll, determined to limit off-the-field distractions, finally unloaded Holmes, along with Jim Allen and Glen Edwards, for draft picks. Art told Dan that trading Holmes would add years to his life, but he was charitable about his troubled ex-player. Art liked him, he said, "despite all of his problems."

Of the 47 men who won Super Bowl rings in 1974, only 19 remained. After a two-year absence, Father John Duggan, the Dublin priest and good luck charm, reappeared. "It's a sure thing," said Duggan, when asked about the Super Bowl. Art, happy to see Father Duggan, was at camp awaiting his sandlot chum Jack Sell when word came of Sell's death. A charter member of the Pro Football Hall of Fame, Sell had written for the *Post-Gazette* for forty-eight years.

Art, seventy-six, could still take a hit. On the second day of camp, defensive back Ray Oldham was covering Bennie Cunningham on a pass play. Oldham separated Cunningham from the ball, then ricocheted into Art, who was walking along the sidelines. Art, his glasses, and cigar went flying. Everybody rushed over, but Art got up and retrieved his cigar. "Great play, Ray Bob," Art grunted. "You have to realize that this guy was tough," Ralph Berlin said.

So were the Steelers, who roared out of the gate in 1978. Dominating opponents, they won eight of their first nine games and finished 14-2 in the NFL's first sixteen-game season. Art kept a low profile. He was shy on camera but drew a crowd of players when he gave Jayne Kennedy, a stunning on-the-air reporter, a rare interview. Noticing the attention, Art smiled, "She ain't too bad, is she?"

On December 30, 1978, Pittsburgh hosted its first playoff game in three years, giving Art the chance to catch up with the national press. Many of his old friends were gone, but he made new ones. Art wandered around the stadium, peering into rooms and joining conversations. He introduced himself to young reporters, putting his hand forward and saying "I'm Art Rooney, how you doing?" Watching Art meander down the hall, one reporter commented, "It'll take Art a month to reach his office."

Pittsburgh beat Denver 33–10, avenging the previous season's defeat. "If we don't beat ourselves," Franco Harris said, "we're gonna be tough." They were very tough, crushing Houston 34–5 in the AFC championship. Houston fumbled six times, threw five interceptions, and lost most of the fights that erupted in a bone-chilling rain. The victory set up a Super Bowl rematch with Dallas in Miami.

Reporters now asked Art how he felt about winning instead of losing. "I knew I didn't have a championship team," he said about his team before Noll arrived. "Now we know for a fact, for a certainty, that we've got a good ballclub. In the old days, it was fun—but there's never fun in losing." Teams now felt more pressure to win. "Back then, in the sixties and before, after a day or two, you forgot the loss and you had fun." Those days were gone.

Art made few concessions to aging. He chewed cigars instead of smoking them, at least until evening, relied more on his hearing aid, and wore thick aviator-like glasses to block out the sun. He did not arrive in Miami until Friday. Once there, he hung out with grandchildren and watched practice. He sat on a bench with his granddaughter Duffy Rooney and let Terry Bradshaw fuss over him. Art looked forward to catching up with Halas. "I know his team will turn around soon," he said, "but I keep reminding him that we're the new Monsters of the Midway . . . If we don't lose somebody between now and then to sickness or something and the ball bounces evenly, I would be surprised if we lost." Art's biggest concern was accommodating ticket requests.

Bradshaw had played spectacularly during the season. As reporters dissected the decision to draft him, one wrote that it was Art who had demanded that they select Bradshaw instead of trading the top pick. Art said his epiphany about Bradshaw came at the track. "I'm in New Orleans watching my horses run. All of my railbird friends grooms, trainers, and owners—rave about the Louisiana Tech kid. So I told my staff

485

that if we got first choice, it had to be Bradshaw. No one fools those old hardboots from the racetrack."

Art also talked about luck and confidence. Sportswriter Bob Drum once told him, "'There's a black cat in this organization, a jinx, and I know who it is.' I said, 'Who?' He said, 'You, because you're the only one who has been around here the whole time.'" Buddy Parker had believed in jinxes, Art said. "I believe that the ball bounces." To him, confidence was key, and his players had lacked it. "They just waited to get beat and they got beat." But Art was feeling confident and lucky now.

Dallas was not. One play captured Pittsburgh's good fortune. On a third and three from the Steelers 10-yard line with Pittsburgh ahead 21–14 in the third quarter, Cowboy quarterback Roger Staubach spotted Jackie Smith open in the end zone. But Smith slipped as the ball hurtled toward him and it bounced off his chest. Dallas settled for a field goal and never regained the lead. Their other bad break was a questionable pass interference that led to a Pittsburgh touchdown. Fred Swearingen, who made the call, was the official who ruled that Franco Harris's Immaculate Reception was legitimate in 1972.

Bradshaw threw a Super Bowl record four touchdowns, and two late scores, 19 seconds apart, built a lead that withstood Dallas's furious comeback. "I've always had the old racetrack philosophy," Art said, "that it's better to take it all in a photo than to win by ten lengths. That way you have the thrill." Few games were more thrilling. "Finally a Super Bowl," the *New York Times* pronounced.

When Pete Rozelle presented the Vince Lombardi trophy, the Rooneys and Noll accepted it together. Art choked up while Chuck Noll observed, "I don't think we have peaked yet. I'm looking forward to bigger and better things." So was Western Pennsylvania.

The 1979 Season

In 1979, Pittsburgh was rechristened the City of Champions. Pittsburgh became more renowned for the Steelers than steel, and sport, not manufacturing, broadcast its identity to the world. After a glorious decade that included Clemente and the 1971 Series, the Immaculate Reception, Pitt's 1976 national football championship, and three Super Bowls,

Pittsburgh became the second city whose teams won the World Series and the Super Bowl in the same season.

Sport, especially football, was capturing Pittsburgh's gritty, unpretentious persona. A higher percentage of men in the region had played football—on the sandlots and scholastically—than in most of America. Many identified with Art, who had played on those sandlots and for those schools. And no Pittsburgher was less pretentious.

Art took enormous satisfaction in his team's unprecedented achievements, especially because of his sons' part in it. They had kept their cool and stayed resolute during walkouts, trials, and other distractions. Dan, who had dealt with the commissioner's office and handled business matters since Buddy Parker's arrival in 1957, had emerged from Art's shadow.

Comparisons with Art were inevitable. "My father's a people man. He's a politician," Dan explained. "His first reaction is 'What will people think?' My philosophy is that you have to do what is right and logical even if it is unpopular." Dan, forty six, relied on Art's counsel, but made his own decisions. "I guess it is one of those classic confrontations with the oldest son and the father being different," he offered. "We've had our disagreements, but I listen to what he has to say."

Pittsburgh had signed veteran tight end Jim Mandich late in the 1978 season. After the Super Bowl, Art wrote Mandich, thanking him for his contribution and enclosing a check for the incentive in his contract. Mandich had neither earned nor expected the incentive. Art's note said that the Steelers had reviewed films and felt he deserved the bonus. "I know I didn't," Mandich said. "It wasn't even close." He was retiring from football and knew that Art had acted without ulterior motive. "I don't know what impact I had on the Steelers but I know they made a hell of an impression on me."

Giving out incentives even when they were not due was one reason the Steelers lost money on the Super Bowl. Art's overflow guest list was another. But despite losing money in 1977, Art delighted spending 1978's profits at the Super Bowl.

In May, Speaker of the House Tip O'Neill presented Art an award from the Ireland Fund, which Dan Rooney and Tony O'Reilly had started in

1976 to promote reconciliation on the island. Art and Ed Kiely then went to Los Angeles for a memorial to Colts (and later Rams) owner Carroll Rosenbloom, who had drowned that April in Florida. The memorial, more of a party than a service, was held at Rosenbloom's estate. As the cabbie dropped them off amidst a fleet of fancy cars, Art said, "This guy must have been some big shot. "Yeah," the cabbie replied, "he owned a football team, the Rams. Hey, you must be a celebrity, too. Who are you?" Art deadpanned, "Wallace Beery," naming the rough-looking actor who had won an Oscar for his role in "The Champ."

Art was ambivalent about Rosenbloom. Years before, Rozelle had asked him to investigate whether Rosenbloom was betting on football. "Art had his own way of policing," *Sport Illustrated*'s Mort Sharnik recalled. "He'd talk to the bookmakers." After Rosenbloom swore he hadn't bet, Art voted to let him stay in the league. Although wary of Rosenbloom, Art did not feel a franchise should be lifted on hearsay. "Rosenbloom was a charmer," Sharnik observed. "He'd charm me, until I asked a probing question and then it was like watching a snake lower his lids."

Ill at ease amidst the glitterati, Art and Kiely were soon walking back down the driveway, where Art spotted columnist Jim Murray. They began talking about the Hollywood racetrack strike when a handsome couple approached and the man said, "Jim, the strike's over." Art asked how it had ended. Impressed by his command of the situation, Art asked if he worked there. "No," the man responded, "I'm on the board." Jim Murray introduced the men just as Art's cab arrived. In the cab, Kiely exploded, "Didn't you know that guy?" Art asked, "What's he do?" Kiely answered, "He's one of the biggest movie stars going!" It was Cary Grant. Art shrugged: "He was never in a cowboy show or I would have known him."

Art was more comfortable puttering around the stadium. Before one of his frequent lunches with nuns at Three Rivers' Allegheny Club, he rushed out of his office, apologizing for being late. The phone rang as they were leaving, and Art told Mary to take a message. "You've been waiting for this call," she replied. "It's Mr. Sinatra." Art excused himself: "Sisters, I have to grab this call." Art and Frank spoke regularly and dined together when crossing paths in New York. Jim Boston, who sat outside Art's office, saw the nuns exchange glances. One asked Mary, "You're not talking about Frank Sinatra, are you?" When Mary said yes, Boston recalled, "Their eyes got as big as saucers." Another said incredulously, "He's calling Mr. Rooney!" When Art returned, one nun asked, "Can you get us his autograph?"

That July, Art went to Canton for the Hall of Fame induction, where John Unitas headlined the new class. Art could finally laugh about cutting Unitas in 1955 and passing on Jim Brown in the 1957 draft, allowing the era's two greatest players to slip away. Winning had taken the sting away.

Cast as the patron saint of Pittsburgh sport, Art could hardly stand up in public without receiving an ovation. "You have to love him," said Pete Rozelle. To the perennially tanned and impeccably dressed commissioner who had advanced sport's marketing to unimaginable heights, Art was a quaint reminder of football's roots. "He uses a lovely term I'd never heard before—loaf— like when he'll say, 'Why don't you come over and loaf in my office?' And he's so honest and down to earth. He has a heart of gold." Pittsburgh cut against the grain of sport's marketplace orientation. "That the Steeler organization has not yielded totally to corporate incursion is a tribute to Arthur J. Rooney," *Times* reporter Alan Richman observed. "The organization is not so much under his control as under his aura." He asked Art whether he now dealt more with people who poured martinis than steel. "I don't," Art laughed. "My boy Danny does." But, Richman noted, Dan also preached simplicity. "Under him, the Steelers have remained perhaps the least merchandized, least promoted team in the NFL."

Super Bowl euphoria lasted until spring, when football was eclipsed by baseball. The Pirates showed a resiliency they had lacked in recent seasons. After an August swing along the West Coast, they climbed atop their division. Led by Willie Stargell, they became known by a Sister Sledge song, "We Are Family." Art was transfixed, capping days in his office by watching batting practice from the dugout and a few innings from the press box. Even though the Steelers won their first four games that fall, the Pirates garnered most of the headlines.

In the World Series, Pittsburgh fell behind Baltimore three games to one. During a broadcast, Howard Cosell discussed the two cities as exemplars of urban renewal and called Pittsburgh the City of Champions. Cosell's description of the city as "the cyclorama of the industrial revolution—a showcase of sport's excellence flanked by giant Seigfrieds shoveling slag into blazing taconite smelt furnaces" left heads spinning, but Pittsburgh embraced his tag line.

By the time the Pirates capped their comeback to win Game Seven, the Steelers were 5-2. They had just played their worst game of the season, losing 34-10 to Cincinnati. After watching film of the debacle with the team, Art mumbled to reporters, "Some game. Those poor guys are in there just shaking their heads."

Pittsburgh rebounded to win the next four games. Art was compensating better for his failing hearing and vision. "I'm not supposed to read too much," he admitted. "Doc says it's not good for my eyes." But his memory was as sharp as ever and his storytelling even stronger. Before the Cleveland game, Art held forth on the thirtieth year of play between the two cities, calling it the best rivalry in football. He had welcomed the challenge of playing Cleveland when it joined the league even though Pittsburgh would lose most times they played. The gate was worth it and the contests were primal. "We knew we'd beat them on Sunday," Cleveland's Jim Brown once said, "but we'd hurt like hell on Monday." Art recalled one inebriated Steeler fan who left Forbes Field, got on what he thought was a local bus, fell asleep, and woke up in Cleveland.

The Steelers had attracted a national fan base, including many with no physical ties to Western Pennsylvania. Fans of Pittsburgh's rugged persona, they helped make Joe Greene's Coca-Cola commercial that fall a sensation. In the 60-second spot, an exhausted Greene limped down a stadium runway, his jersey draped over his shoulder pads. When a young boy asked if he needed any help, Joe said no thanks. The boy persisted, offering his Coke. Joe declined but the kid handed it to him anyway. Joe downed the sixteen-ounce bottle in a gulp. As the boy walked away, Greene called out, "Hey kid, catch," and tossed him his jersey. It might have been the most popular sporting commercial in television history and transformed Greene's image into that of a simpatico giant.

Pittsburgh basked in sport's reflected glory. Frank Deford came to town to profile Lynn Swann for *Sports Illustrated*. "Pittsburgh still suffers its shabby old mill image," he wrote, "but it is a solid place, a heterosexual's San Francisco." It was a city that lavished as much attention on football's "grubbier wage earners," the defense, as higher profile players.

Despite injuries, Pittsburgh finished 12-4. As fans awaited the playoffs, *Sports Illustrated* hit the newsstands with Willie Stargell and Terry Bradshaw on its cover as Sportsmen of the Year. Ron Fimrite's accompanying story was titled "Two Champs in the City of Champions" and featured a photo of the duo flanked by steelworkers. "Pittsburgh is no longer the Smoky City," Fimrite observed. "Pittsburgh literally hosed itself off after World War II and ceased belching pollution. Still, it may take another generation or so for the city to free itself completely from an image that endured too long." David Lawrence would have been proud to see his city's renaissance capped by unprecedented sporting success. "In the old days," Art told Fimrite, "the lights never went out. We'd leave for school in the morning with clean clothes and get there covered with soot." But look at Pittsburgh now. Though its population was down to 520,000, Pittsburgh was home to sixteen Fortune 500 firms and still a manufacturing powerhouse. While it wasn't hard to find steelworkers to pose with Stargell and Bradshaw, the city was on the precipice of devastating decline. Sport would buoy the city throughout its crisis.

Before Christmas, Art was at Divine Providence Hospital visiting safety Mike Wagner, who was recovering from surgery, when Rocky and Aleta Bleier and Jack and Joannie Ham appeared, wearing surgical gowns and masks and pushing a cart with treats for Wagner. Several nights later, Art and Kass heard a commotion outside their home. Terry Bradshaw and Jo Jo Starbuck, Lynn and Bernadette Swann, and Gerry Mullins and his fiancée, were out front singing carols.

In the first round of the playoffs, Pittsburgh took revenge for the Steelers' 1972 loss to Miami in the AFC championship. The Steelers scored on their first three possessions and won 34–10.

Red Smith caught up with Art before the AFC championship versus Houston. "The Steel City," he wrote, "is a blue collar town, tough

491

as pig iron," just like Art. Calling Pittsburgh the capital of American sport, he paid homage to "Rooney, the great little man behind the cigar." Smith reprised old tales, especially the one he enjoyed the most, when Art "swept through the betting ring like Genghis Khan, leaving bookmakers wounded and dying in his wake" at Saratoga.

The Steelers looked like the Mongol horde against Houston, winning 27–13. "We are edging our way into history," Joe Greene said softly. "The rewards are greater now than they've ever been . . . The comparisons are real to the Packers as the greatest team of all time—provided things come through the way we want them to. Then we can lay claim to that." For Greene, history mattered.

Art savored each practice before the Super Bowl. Despite Arctic winds slicing through Three Rivers, he stopped to talk to players as he walked laps around the field. Enduring the cold longer than reporters did, he praised his players, who in turn, talked about him. Joe Greene described Art as a people's person. "He wants to make everyone feel good, and there ain't nothing wrong with that." Greene was closer than any other player to Art. "I just love listening to his stories, partially because he gets a kick out of telling them, but mostly I just like to hear them." He credited Art for their success. "The players look around and see him doing all those things . . . shoot, you can't help but be motivated . . . Mr. Rooney," Greene concluded, "knows what life is all about. That man is one of the reasons we want to keep on winning. Sure, we want to win for ourselves and Chuck, but we also want to win for him." Art dismissed such talk. "I don't know what I do here. I just try to stay out of everyone's way." Rocky Bleier disagreed, "What he does is keep everyone going. He's inspirational."

As the Super Bowl approached, two matters—one minor, the other consequential—troubled Art. The small matter was that the commissioner's office told Art that he would make the coin toss at Super Bowl XIV. Art didn't want to do it. Only Bronko Nagurski and George Halas had been so honored and Art did not put himself in their league. "I guess there's no way we can get out of it, is there?" he asked. Rozelle insisted. "Well, he's the boss," Art conceded. The serious issue was his brother's health. Father Silas was dying. "He's led a full life," Art said, "but he's fading badly." Art commuted to St. Petersburg, Florida, to spend time with Silas before the Super Bowl, not knowing how long he had. Faith cushioned his distress at watching his brother suffer a difficult decline with Lou Gehrig's disease. Silas, seventy-six, had been the Rooney clan's hero. Art knew it could be worse; he had recently attended services for Mugsy Halas, George's son, in Chicago. He did not show his pain in public. "My dad's really enjoying himself," Dan maintained. "I hope we have as many Super Bowl tickets as he's promised his friends. He called me at home Thursday night—I was in bed—and told me he had to get some tickets for the mailman. I told him he could do whatever he wanted to do with his tickets, but that he shouldn't be worrying about the mailman." After hanging up, Art walked over to the post office to drop off tickets.

Art, still fretting over the coin toss, did not go to Los Angeles until after the squad arrived. "I don't know why they selected me," he groused. "It was all right when George Halas did it last year, but it was a surprise when they picked me." Kass selected a suit for Art to wear, and he was driven onto the field in an antique blue Duesenberg Phaeton convertible. Over a hundred million watched on television. Puffing a cigar and moving smartly after exiting the car, Art handed the coin to referee Fred Silva to flip. "I just didn't feel comfortable about doing it," he said afterward. Art left to a huge ovation; reporters estimated that sixty percent of the record 103,985 people jammed inside the Coliseum were Steeler fans, even though the game was in the Rams' home city.

Although Pittsburgh was heavily favored, Los Angeles led 19–17 as the fourth quarter began. After Bradshaw hit John Stallworth with a 73-yard touchdown and another long pass to Stallworth set up a Franco Harris score, Pittsburgh prevailed 31–19. "Easily the best of the XIV played," *Sports Illustrated*'s Paul Zimmerman pronounced. Art thoroughly agreed. He laughed when Pete Rozelle whispered that they had to stop meeting this way as he handed him the Lombardi Trophy. By now an old hand at the postgame ritual, Art was more composed than in years past. "Those boys from Los Angeles," he said. "They should be proud, just as I am proud of my boys. These are the most gentlemanly fellows I ever had. None of them ever gets fatheaded." He said that Pittsburgh fans deserved the championship for their decades of loyalty. "This was a football team that had to overcome a lot just to get into the Super Bowl," he declared. "There's something special about winning this one."

Art wasn't the only one who thought that way. The *Times'* Dave Anderson argued that they were "the best team in history," surpassing the 1940s Chicago Bears, the 1950s Cleveland Browns, and the 1960s Green Bay Packers. After four Super Bowls in six years, few disputed the Steelers' place in history.

Art skipped the team's White House visit, where President Jimmy Carter described him as a man who kept his faith that Pittsburgh would become a city of champions. Art and his team, Carter said, had united a community by their toughness and togetherness. Art appreciated the sentiments but he had had his fill of hoopla. He spent his days at Three Rivers Stadium. "I might as well loaf here as loaf at my house," he said. "I was here when they were building the stadium and knew most of the people doing the construction. I probably know this place as well as anybody." He was sentimental about the hulking stadium, but miffed that it was prematurely aging.

Three Rivers was the venue that spring for filming *Fighting Back*, a movie about Rocky Bleier. Art met Art Carney, who was playing him in the movie, at a cast party. Jimmy Stewart, from Indiana, Pennsylvania, where Art had gone to school, had been considered for the part but Carney, who had impeccable proletarian credentials after playing Ed Norton in *The Honeymooners*, got it. "Art Carney's a good man," Art Rooney observed. "I've liked him ever since he played in that one show and ran around in his underwear with that crooked hat on." When Robert Ulrich, who was playing Rocky, told Art he was from Toronto, Ohio, Art spoke of playing there. That week, Art showed the crew around the stadium. Every time they passed a water fountain, Art pushed the handle. At the end of the tour, somebody asked why he did that. Art replied, "It's my business." He wanted to make sure things were working.

22

The Fourth Quarter

1980–88

Art was at Mercy Hospital the day before Thanksgiving 1980 for a checkup when Ed Kiely barged into the examining room. "Danny's been in an accident," he blurted out. "They just brought him in." On his way to work, Dan Rooney's car had spun out on an icy patch and collided with another car and a utility pole. The first person to get to him blanched at the blood streaming down his face. Dan's forehead was slashed open, his hip broken, and his knee bashed. When Art saw his son in the emergency room, he thought he would lose him. "They didn't think he had a chance in the world," Art said. "They thought he was a goner."

Dan looked worse than he was; much of the blood came from facial lacerations. He emerged from surgery with a steel pin in his hip, a plate in his knee, and stitches in his face. Dan stayed at Mercy for ten days as family competed for space in his room with fruit baskets and flowers. One day, the deliveryman warned Dan, "You better check this one out. It's from Al Davis."

The Steelers won the first game they played after Dan's accident and brought the game ball to him in the hospital. On crutches, then using a cane, Dan was back at work by Christmas. His return buoyed Art, who had spent days with Dan reciting the decades of the rosary by working his way around the ring he carried in his pocket.

But Dan's return could not right the season. Losing two of the last three games, Pittsburgh finished 9-7, out of the playoffs for the first time since 1971. As Dan recuperated, a debate raged. Had the dynasty crumbled? Was it time to start over?

The players with four Super Bowl rings were demigods in Pittsburgh, where the slogan had become "One for the thumb." But some questioned their ability to keep winning. "There is no escaping the fact," Carrie Seidman argued in the *Times*, "that a number of those household names are entering the autumn of their careers." A midseason losing streak provoked further introspection. "You sit back and look at our roster," Art Jr. reflected, "and you can't help but see some people who shouldn't be there. There's no question, we've got some dead weight."

Art Jr., whose job was to replenish the roster via the draft, often fought with Chuck Noll over whom to keep and whom to cut. At times, Art Jr. viewed Noll as a "know-it-all" while Noll looked at him as "a rich kid jerk." Few rookies made the team. "You didn't want to be drafted by Pittsburgh," Dwight White observed. "There was no place on the club for you." Art Jr. was especially upset when the team had waived promising defenders, but keeping them might have required cutting White or Greene.

"The real trouble," *Beaver County Times* reporter Rich Emert asserted, "is that Noll has hung on to some veterans too long. He is finding out the one more year he thought they had left isn't there." "We could be rotten like Dallas," Art Jr. observed, "They just go in and tell you it's over . . . That's not easy for us to do. It's hard to tell somebody who has helped you win four Super Bowls that they're through. Maybe we're too nice." But they always had been too nice; Art's compassion permeated the organization.

"I read in the papers that Joe [Greene] isn't playing like he used to," Art protested. "Well, I'll tell you what, even if he isn't, he's still as good as any other defensive lineman in football today. And maybe better. The trouble is, in his prime, Joe Greene was just so much better than anyone else who played the position." But the past wasn't winning games anymore. After Pittsburgh blew a lead against Cleveland, Art admitted that he had sensed they would lose. "You can sort of feel it in your bones," he said. "I really haven't had that feeling for years and years."

It was a bittersweet time. Dan rebounded and Art watched his granddaughter Kathleen wed Chris Mara, Wellington's son, after Christmas. Kathleen's father, Tim Rooney, had been born during Art's ride at Saratoga and was named for Tim Mara, Wellington's father. The two families, whose bonds had been forged at the track and in football, were now joined by marriage.

A funeral followed the wedding. On January 9, 1981, days before his seventy-eighth birthday, Father Silas was laid to rest. Silas, who had suffered with amyotrophic lateral sclerosis for a year, was buried at St. Bonaventure University. Family, friends, and priests surrounded Art in the cemetery, but he took the death hard. Once inseparable from his brother, Art had looked up to Silas as a man of faith and rectitude. So did all the Rooneys. "He belonged in a movie," the *Times*'s Dave Anderson wrote, "the legendary priest who was as tough as he was tender." Though Art was the oldest of nine siblings, four of them were dead. Only sisters Margaret Laughlin and Marie McGinley, and brothers Jim and Vince, remained. Jim still stood slightly askew on a leg that had never properly aligned after his 1933 car wreck. He talked in humorous asides, making people feel that he was sharing a confidence with them.

Art tried to find work for Jim and protect him from his own bad habits. When asked what he did, Jim smiled and said, "I'm with Arthur." Soon after Ralph Berlin joined the organization, he was sent to fetch Jim from Frenchy's Restaurant downtown. Ignoring the summons, Jim asked Berlin if he had any money. "Like a fool," Berlin said, "I gave him $10. He puts it on the bar and says, 'Bartender, when this is gone, throw us both out.'" He and Jim returned to the office "half smacked in the can."

By spring, Dan Rooney had worked himself back into shape and showed few ill effects of the wreck. He and Art bid farewell to Dwight White, Rocky Bleier, and Mike Wagner that off-season. Like several teammates, they stayed in Pittsburgh and built new careers. Their photos soon adorned Art's office.

In May, Terry Bradshaw pondered retirement. "I talked to him the other day," Art said. "He doesn't know what he wants to do." Art thought it best that Terry retire if his heart was no longer in it. He would have Art's blessings either way. By the end of the month, Terry decided to return for a twelfth season. Joe Greene, meanwhile, starred in an NBC special, *The Steeler and the Pittsburgh Kid*, based on his Coke commercial. And in a Pittsburgh courtroom, convicted killer Jack Siggson testified that he and three accomplices had plotted in 1977 to kidnap Art, tie a bomb to him, and demand millions in ransom. Afraid that Art might have a heart attack, they decided to kidnap Ryan Home founder Edward Ryan, instead. Neither kidnapping occurred.

Relieved by Dan's recovery, Art, eighty, and Kass, seventy-six, traveled during the off-season. They spent St. Patrick's Day on Maui at the NFL meetings, beginning the day at Mass with Wellington and Ann Mara. The Rooneys attended the Kentucky Derby in May and came home to celebrate their fiftieth wedding anniversary with a pomp they could never have imagined when they eloped to New York in 1931. After Art and Kass renewed their wedding vows at St. Peter's, the Rooney clan gathered on North Lincoln with a gang from the Steelers.

Tables laden with votive candles were draped with gold tablecloths and black napkins. Kass wore an azure cocktail dress and gold diamond necklace and pin, presents from her sons. Alice McNulty wore her traditional black, and their hairdresser and friend Angie fussed with the sisters' bouffant hairdos through the evening. In one corner of the now carefully landscaped and furnished backyard, a projector ran a continuous slide show of old family photos, some showing the same backyard as a muddy sea of boys playing football.

After dinner, Art and Kass cut the wedding cake, and Kass opened golden anniversary gifts. They capped their celebration by traveling to the Belmont Stakes, where they had gone on their honeymoon.

Invigorated, Art and Kass visited Ireland with son Tim and his wife June Rooney. Tim had been talking up a restaurant, Le Maribou, and its chef Sean Kinsella. When Art heard how posh it was, he was appalled. "He was telling us what saps we were to eat at such an expensive place," Tim recounted. "He said, 'Don't you dare take me to that place.'" Tim, however, took them there without telling Art where they were going. "He's seated at the far end of a long table and I'm at the other end because I wanted to have a drink," Tim recalled. "What am I, fifty, and still acting like that?" Art took one bite of a sliced mushroom appetizer and turned to June. "Is this the place?" He and Kass loved the meal. When Kass told Kinsella how much she liked lamb stew, he said he would make it for her tomorrow even though the restaurant would be closed. The Rooneys ate there three times. "Nobody liked food like my father," Tim said.

In County Kildare, Art watched Shergar, the magnificent thoroughbred owned by Aga Khan, win the Irish Derby. A year and a half later, Shergar was kidnapped, probably by the IRA. An IRA turncoat said that the kidnappers, unable to handle the spirited horse, had panicked and shot him. Shergar's body was never found.

Decline

"The lid blew off last year," Joe Greene admitted at camp. "We're not the kings of the hill." Art and the Steelers were a year older in 1981. Top draft pick Keith Gary opted to play in Canada, while Jack Ham broke his arm and tackle Ted Peterson had season-ending surgery for a tumor in his hip. A cacophony of voices declared the dynasty dead.

By the time Art returned from Europe, the preseason was ending. "I don't like to be out in the sun too much any more," he confessed after watching practice and seeking shade inside. Art, who had circulatory problems, was less inclined to come to camp when so many rookies were still there. "You get to know the kids," he explained. "Then I feel bad when they get released. It's difficult letting go."

Art was upbeat about the season. "I know we have some problems, but we've got a lot of talented players and I think we'll have a good team." But the Steelers lost their first two games, and their last three, finishing 8-8 in 1982 and out of the playoffs. "I felt really sad for our guys," Art said. "It really hit them hard, more so than most people realize." It troubled Art to see Terry Bradshaw, whose second marriage had dissolved, nearing the end of his career. "He's the best I ever saw," Art professed.

Two years out of the playoffs had increased pressure to clean house, but Art wanted no part in that. "I've always ducked out of sight when the coaches had to cut somebody," he confessed. "Then I'd write the guy and tell him how sorry I was." Veteran Sam Davis said there was nothing to feel bad about. "Loyalty is one thing," he reasoned. "Reality is another." Davis noted that the Rooneys had helped ease many players' post-football transitions. "They've had a lot to do with helping players make smoother adjustments into other fields." Enough Steelers had prospered after football to validate Davis's contention.

"I hope this isn't a decline," Art fretted. "I don't want to get back to that." He knew that once a team lost its edge, it could take a while to regain it.

Art visited Fritzie Zivic before Christmas. The former champ was dying, and they talked more about the past than the future. So did reporters who came by Art's office. Vito Stellino asked about the Al Abrams award Art would receive at the next Dapper Dan banquet. Art called Abrams a "racetracker" who believed that Pittsburgh was the greatest city in the world. Opening a 1933 ledger, he pointed to an entry that said, "Pittsburgh looked bad. Crowd hostile." Art chuckled, "The young people talk about the league today like it was always like this. It wasn't even a hop, skip and a jump from semipro ball. Maybe just a hop."

At the Super Bowl in Detroit, Art stood at the window of his eightieth-floor Renaissance Center suite with *Detroit News* columnist Joe Falls. "Boy, it feels good to be here," Art said, gazing at snow-covered Detroit. Art had pushed for Detroit to host the game, disputing those who favored warm-weather venues. "Snow?" Art said impishly, "Who cares about the snow? We've always played in the snow." Falls revered Art. When they had first met, Art had been embarrassed to discover a hole in his sweater. Kass had instructed Art to dress smartly for the interview. "Wait'll she finds out I wore this sweater. You won't tell her, will you?" Falls assured Art it would remain their secret. As Falls was leaving, Art gave him a cigar. Falls smoked it en route to the airport, then carefully placed it in his brief case and kept it like a religious relic.

In February, Art sat by Joe Greene as the most honored defensive lineman in NFL history retired. "I came into this league as a boy and I'm leaving as a man," Greene said, with a nod to the Rooneys. Surveying the exodus of players, Art declared he would miss Joe the most. Though he called Greene the best defensive tackle ever, Art thought that the Steelers might be able to replace him on the field. "There is always another fellow who comes along as good as the previous one." But they would not, he contended, find one who would lead like Greene. "It would be hard for you to realize what he meant to our team." Pittsburgh, he said, had never had many internal problems. "Joe Greene had as much to do with that as anyone else. If a player, particularly a black player, was moaning about something, like all players do, Greene would just stare and that would end it." And not just black players. "Greene was every Steeler's confidant," the *Times'* Dave Anderson stated. "When a teammate needed him, Greene was always available." "My father," Art Jr. said, "cared for Joe like he was his own kid."

Fifty Seasons

During the 1982 off-season, former coaches Buddy Parker and John Michelosen, both younger than Art, died, and the club announced plans to celebrate its fiftieth season. Art embraced the celebration as a chance to see old friends.

In March, a new broadcast agreement guaranteed each club $70 million over five years. Art's efforts to divide television dollars equally were paying ever-larger dividends. Pittsburgh had the league's second highest payroll but one of its smallest venues, and Dan was understandably appreciative of revenue sharing. "If it weren't for the NFL's policy of splitting such revenues equally," Dan acknowledged, "we would be in trouble." Art—skeptical of television's hold over sport—was less sanguine about the deal.

Like his father, Dan was troubled by the NFL's shifting sands. "Some of the ownership is changing," he lamented. "The value of a franchise has grown so much." The new owners had little background in sport but were eager to revel in its reflected glow. "Professional football is not their principal business," Dan observed, "and that sometimes takes something away." They had not internalized the values that Art and the founders had shared.

Nowhere were the changes more disturbing than in the NFL's dealings with the union, which scheduled a strike vote for March. "I really don't know what will happen," Art admitted. While baseball's strike the previous summer had created a void, Art pointed out that fans could replace pro football with high school and college games. "I think that the players and the owners better realize that."

Despite the labor impasse, players joined the Rooneys at a United

Way luncheon in April. Dan spoke for Art when he said, "I think the Steelers are a little different. I believe that we would sit at the same table for such an event even if our players were on strike. Sure, we've had differences over the years, but we've never lost respect for each other." Art adored his players—past and present. "They were all heroes to me," he claimed. "I've been so close to so many."

Art knew his influence was waning. "I still go to the office at 9 a.m. and stay until 5 p.m., and I go to almost all the practices," he shrugged. "I don't know how much I have to say in it anymore. I kid about the decisions, but I kid on the level. Maybe Danny wishes I'd stay home oftentimes. I tell them what I think and then they do whatever they want to do." He was okay with that, but he was at a loss to explain Pittsburgh's decline. The fans, he said, took winning for granted. "They got to the point where they thought the Super Bowl was part of our schedule."

That summer, City Council debated renaming Three Rivers Stadium for either Art Rooney or Roberto Clemente. The thought of his name on the stadium embarrassed Art, who had wanted to name it for David Lawrence. The Steelers urged leaving well enough alone. "We feel it is the most appropriately named stadium in the country," Joe Gordon said. "It's a beautiful name and highly identified with the Pittsburgh area, unlike the generic name of stadiums in other cities."

As the gathering labor storm muted anticipation of a new season, the club began its celebration of the past by introducing the eight surviving members of the 1933 team at a preseason game. "It's a splendid gesture," Ray Kemp said, "having us back like this, we guys from the Roman Empire. Art Rooney gave me an opportunity to play a little part in history." Pittsburgh pulled out two exciting wins to start the season before the strike halted play.

While Dan negotiated, Art spoke freely to reporters. He had a hard time understanding how owners and players had failed to avert the league's first midseason strike. "The money is there for both sides," he emphasized. But owners and players had crossed the Rubicon, he warned. "This could be bad. If it doesn't get straightened out very shortly, there won't be a football season." Art said that he feared that college and high school ball could once again surpass pro football's popularity. "The world is going to go on, just the same," he said. Fans would find alternatives. "This won't be like death."

Art sympathized with the players but not completely. "You better believe I grew up as a union guy," Art declared. "I used to listen to all the stories about my grandfather fighting the Pinkertons [during the 1892 Homestead Steel Strike]. Why, they say he stood right up there and fired a shotgun at them." Art had always known which side he was on. "I know what labor and unions are all about. My father's people were steelworkers and my mother's people were coal miners. But this is a little different. Back then, the people were fighting for their lives. They were fighting to put food on their table."

The strike was leaving a gaping hole. "I can see the stadium from my house," he said. "Every time the lights are on, I come down. Even if nothing is going on and they're just cleaning up, I come down and talk to the guys. What am I going to do? Sit around the house?"

Each week, more games were cancelled. While Art spoke with Halas, hashing out the strike, Dan negotiated. "Danny works hard for the game," Art said. "We talk, but he doesn't always listen." When players sounded him out, Art advised them to guard against resentment. "Bitterness," he said, "that can ruin a team."

"Ralph," he told trainer Berlin, "it doesn't matter what you pay Lambert. It doesn't matter what you pay Swann, Franco, Bradshaw, Webster, or Ham. You can never overpay the good athletes. Where you get in trouble in this business is when you pay the guys who can't play." The rules, he said, were not designed to protect the players from the owners or the owners from the players. "They're designed to protect the owners from the owners."

He confessed that he did not really understand the strike. Surely there was enough money for both sides. "I carried the ball for recognition of the players association when that wasn't the popular thing to do, and I believe there's a place for them." But he rejected their demands.

Fiftieth Anniversary

With football suspended, the staff plunged into the anniversary celebration. Dan dug through his parents' attic for photos, the Hall of Fame lent busts of eight Steeler inductees, and the club unearthed a trove of artifacts. Two stations announced they would broadcast the October banquet capping the celebration, and Howard Cosell received permission from ABC to miss a baseball playoff to serve as emcee. Fans selected an all-time Steelers squad, and television broadcast a special about Art. But the strike dragged on.

Admission fees to the David Lawrence Convention Center exhibit went to Dapper Dan charities. Fans and former players were overcome by emotion. "The thing I used to look forward to more than anything when we'd practice at Three Rivers," Joe Greene said, "was to sneak down to Mr. Rooney's office every once in a while to hear him talk about the old times, the train rides, the people who made the Steelers. The old days, there were never any bad ones, according to Mr. Rooney."

The exhibit overwhelmed Art. "I had no idea it would be this big a deal," he said. "I just thought we'd have a fiftieth year and bring in some old ballplayers." Art spent hours there revisiting his past. "I never thought about giving up, never," he stressed. "I came up in the sport. It's my life. And I wasn't the only one with my neck stuck out there; there were a lot of other guys in the same boat."

At the banquet, Howard Cosell stole the show. He called Myron Cope "the squeaky diminutive one" and captured the élan of the all-time team, but he lavished the most praise on Pittsburgh and the Rooneys. "This is still the City of Champions," he intoned. "The cheering has stopped in many NFL cities, but here the cheering will never stop. When you play Pittsburgh, you have to play the whole city." Cosell called the Rooneys the finest family in sport, the owners he respected the most. "I've always felt that way. And there's no reason to change. They are people of integrity and character." No team, he opined, had been more responsible for the success of ABC Sports and *Monday Night Football*. "Art Rooney is unique," he thundered. "Above all, he holds this franchise in trust for you, the people of Pittsburgh." Cosell underscored how rare Art was in contemporary sport. "There are few men in professional sports today who feel as Art Rooney does about his team, the people, and his city. He's made all of it a part of him."

Finally Art spoke. When the ovation stilled, he was humble and brief.

He introduced Kass, inadvertently calling her "my husband." What touched him the most was that so many current Steelers had attended despite the strike. "You present-day ballplayers who came tonight made me very, very happy." He said he could never understand why race and religion divided people. "I often thought of what God would think of us for thinking in such a manner."

The twenty-five hundred attendees dined on filet mignon and danced to Count Basie and his orchestra. "This is a tough town," Joe Greene mused, "an honest town, a good town. Its people are what the Steelers are all about." As delighted as he was with the banquet, Art was disconsolate that the strike showed no signs of ending.

Most days, Art walked to the stadium after Mass. Age had diminished his eyesight and hearing, but he was still a powerful walker. Art, who timed his walk to Three Rivers, was hardly slowing down. He stayed the morning, talking and corresponding. Reporters came by, and Art obliged their need for copy as the strike dragged on. The very popularity he had sought for the game was now causing problems, he told them. "The money we have gotten—that's the crux of all the problems."

One owner had written to tell Art he thought of him daily. "When we got our TV contract—not this contract, the one before—everybody was high and happy and I showed no emotion at all," Art explained. "When they asked me why, I said, 'I don't know if I will live to see the day, but some of the people in this room will see the day that greed will kill us, whether it is from the player, from the owner, or from an outsider.'" The letter said, "It looks like you're living to see the day."

Now that money fueled sport, Art's perspective seemed anachronistic. "There was a time when we didn't have enough money, and now we have too much," he claimed. "Too much is worse." Money, he said, had never lured him to Atlanta, Baltimore, Buffalo, or New Orleans when those cities offered a king's ransom. "I was a Pittsburgher all my life," Art stated, "my mother and father ahead of me, and that meant something. I'd rather stay in Pittsburgh and make a living than go elsewhere and be wealthy."

"I remember very well when Pittsburgh was considered a baseball town," he reflected. But he had never doubted that football would take hold. "I thought it would become just as much a football town because of the people of Western Pennsylvania. The people here are coal miners, steelworkers. They work hard and they play hard, and football would fit in just as well as baseball."

Within a few seasons, Pittsburgh would wonder if it was still a baseball town. After falling on hard times, the Pirates hired Jim Leyland to manage in 1986, a season in which they lost 98 games. "I'd be sitting by myself in my office," Leyland recalled, "down in the dumps and ticked off because we were losing, and there he'd be. It was uncanny. 'Hang in there,' he'd tell me. 'You'll be OK. I like this club. It's playing hard.' I'm convinced the only people who cared about the team in '86 were me, the players, the coaches, Syd Thrift, and Mr. Rooney."

Dan Rooney took over labor negotiations for the NFL and brought in Paul Martha, whom Art had set up at Duquesne Law School when he joined the team, to help negotiate. Their credibility with players broke the impasse, and an accord was reached in November. Dan was hailed as football's savior. The first day back, Art stood in the locker room, a foot-long cigar jutting out of his mouth, his hands behind his back, watching players suit up. "I'm very proud of Danny and Paul," he said. "They're both Pittsburghers. This is a laboring town, and they know what labor negotiating is all about."

Losing Kass

Art's joy at the resumption of play did not last long. Kass, seventy-eight years old and in better health than her husband, had fallen and broken her leg during the strike. She was in Divine Providence Hospital, Art at her side, when the Steelers played their first poststrike game. Kass came home but suffered a fatal heart attack on November 28. Patricia Rooney reached her husband, Dan, in the press box in Seattle where the Steelers were about to play. She put Art on the phone but he was too broken up to talk. Dan and Art Jr. informed the team after the game.

Art was stunned. "It was the worst I had ever seen him," Dan recalled. The house on North Lincoln was full of family but empty without her. Though a very private person, Kass was a public figure, and St. Peter's had not seen a Mass so packed since David Lawrence's death.

Kass's friend Father Henry McAnulty, Duquesne University's president, delivered the homily. Bishop Vincent Leonard was the principal celebrant, assisted by three bishops and fifty-four priests. Politicians, owners, players, her five sons and their wives, thirty-one grandchildren, and one great-grandchild heard Kass eulogized as an unpretentious, genuine, and loving woman. Five granddaughters took part in the offertory procession while six grandsons carried her casket. At the cemetery, Art noticed the gravestones that Dan and Patricia had erected near his and Kass's. "Why do you have your name on there already?" he asked. Dan replied, "You save a buck." Art managed a smile.

But he did not smile much after Kass's death. At first, he was angry. Art had never anticipated living without her. "That made him mad more than anything else," John Rooney reflected. "He wasn't prepared for it."

Kass and Art had traveled together for decades. Tall, slender, elegant, and shy, she had willingly tolerated Art's frequent absences and the constant company of his cigar-smoking buddies. Kass said she saw every racetrack in America and a few in Mexico and Canada on her honeymoon. Few women could have handled marriage to as footloose a character. "She was pretty spectacular about that," John Rooney recalled. "I can remember one time going to the airport with a bag of clothes for him. He'd fly in here, just take the bag and fly somewhere else. He'd give her the other bag to take home and clean." They had understood—and by all accounts adored—each other.

There would be other losses. Art's grandson James Patrick Rooney, John and JoAnn's fourth child, died in a car accident in 1983. His granddaughter Kathleen Rooney Miller, Dan and Pat's third child, died in 1987. These losses were tough, striking his grandchildren. Still, he was stoical. "Arthur always was very realistic," his sister Margaret Laughlin said. "When our son John died of lupus in 1986, he told me I shouldn't continue to waste my time grieving and making myself sick. He told me John had gone on to a better place."

Regaining his equilibrium, Art took care of other people as much as they did of him. Art looked after Alice McNulty, Kass's sister, who had lived with the family since the twins were born. It's what the Irish had always done, he said. "You always had an aunt living with you." Alice had kept Kass company, tended to the children, and allowed Art to maintain his frenetic traveling. Nor did Art retreat from public life; he kept his ward heeler's door open and made rounds of hospitals and funeral homes. "Art would come every day," Ralph Berlin recalled about a stretch he spent in Divine Providence. "He'd walk through the park at night even though it was bad in there." Art's appetite remained hearty. "If there was a box of candy here," Berlin laughed, "he would sit and eat the whole box."

Art gravitated to people whom others overlooked. The ground crew had long benefited from Art's generosity, going to Super Bowls on his tab and enjoying the coffee and doughnuts he brought late at night when they were changing the stadium over from baseball to football. After Dirt DiNardo's health deteriorated, Art hounded him to get proper care, sending Dirt to his own doctor and calling if he missed appointments. When Ralph Giampaolo was hospitalized after a kidney transplant, Art looked after his mother. "Even as a kid," Giampaolo said, "I heard what a great man Mr. Rooney was, but until I started working here, I thought no one was that good." When Giampaolo visited the Palm Beach Kennel Club, Art invited him to his box. Sports announcer Curt Gowdy was there. "I'll never forget the way he introduced me to the Gowdys," Giampaolo said. "'This is Ralph Giampaolo, a member of our organization.' Not a member of the grounds crew, not some rinky-dink bum, but a member of our organization. As far as Gowdy knew, I was a vice president of the team. Mr. Rooney made me feel ten feet tall."

The ground crew reciprocated when they could. When the NFLPA struck in 1987, the ground crew did not honor its picket line. DiNardo, their union steward, called the NFLPA an association, not a real union. "But," he added, "we crossed for Mr. Rooney. No way we wouldn't. He took such good care of us for years. He made sure our ground crew was on every Steeler trip. I can't imagine any other owner doing that or even talking to the ground crew. And remember, he helped the NFL union get started."

Art also befriended Gabriella Tamasi, a cleaning woman at league offices. While most owners hardly distinguished her from the furniture,

Art sent her gifts when he traveled. "He would never come to New York without finding me just to say hello," Tamasi said. "He's the kindest man I've ever known."

Another War

The 1982 strike-shortened season ended with a sixteen-team playoff. After blowing an 11-point fourth-quarter lead to San Diego in the first round, Pittsburgh's season was over. Lynn Swann and Jack Ham retired afterward, leaving nine players with four Super Bowl rings. The Rooneys lost $2 million that season.

But what upset Art was the creation of the United States Football League, a rival that would begin play in the spring of 1983. Its season would not conflict with the NFL's, but it wanted to put a franchise in Pittsburgh in 1984. Ed DeBartolo Sr., a Youngstown, Ohio, developer to whom Art had sold his Cleveland racetrack interests, was its prospective owner. The problem was not only that the USFL wanted to use Three Rivers Stadium but that DeBartolo's son, Eddie Jr., owned the San Francisco 49ers. The NFL limited involvement in other leagues, and Art saw the DeBartolos' owning teams in two leagues as an egregious conflict of interest.

The DeBartolos denied any conflict because different family members would own the teams. Art countered that it did not require an Ivy League education to see through that argument. Eddie DeBartolo Jr. acknowledged that Art, who had backed his bid to buy the 49ers in 1977, had reason to be upset. "The problem today," DeBartolo argued, "is that those basic things don't always make for the best business decisions." "He may be right," Art admitted, "but when you join a league you agree to do what's best for the league. When the New York Giants and the Chicago Bears agreed some years ago to share the TV revenue with the rest of the teams in the league, that wasn't the best business decision, either. But it made the league strong." Art was becoming livid and refused to back down. "It's hard to believe, at eighty-two, that he can get so riled up," Art Jr. said, "but he is."

"It's class," Art lectured. "Ever hear of the word? It's spelled c-l-a-s-s. It's in every business, whether it's sports or banking or being a horseplayer. It's as simple as that." Art said that if the USFL used Three Rivers, it would violate the Steelers' lease, which gave them exclusive rights to play pro football there. Art didn't say much at league meetings anymore. The new guys, he joked, didn't understand him. "I don't talk like those guys, or their lawyers . . . I use too many 'dems' and 'doses.'" But he blasted the DeBartolos, twice rising to his feet to rally owners to stand firm. Several of them, burned by costly court rulings when they tried to block the Raiders' move to Los Angeles, were leery of taking action; Wellington Mara, Buffalo's Ralph Wilson, and what was left of the old guard stood with Art. He declined to tell the press just what he said, but others did. "He didn't want to see [the league] disintegrate from within the ranks," Rozelle explained. "He got his point across, as he always does."

"Rooney made a great presentation," Mara said, "one of the most impressive showings I've ever seen at the meetings. It was nice to see he hasn't lost the hop on his fastball." Art and his cohort had constructed a league that worked for all, Wilson stressed. "Here's people like the Rooneys and the Maras and the Halases in big-city markets who agreed to share the TV revenues with the rest of us, to keep the Green Bays and Buffalos going. They made a big sacrifice. I think Mr. Rooney said it best. He spoke about class. Where is it in this case? Is it just the money now?"

Art had the moral high ground, but the NFL could not stop DeBartolo Sr. from owning the Pittsburgh Maulers. The Steelers lost two assistant coaches and a few players to USFL teams. The Maulers wanted Steelers' assistant Dick Hoak as their head coach but Hoak declined. "[Art's] the only reason I didn't take that job," he said. The Steelers sued over the stadium lease, but the issue died when the Maulers folded after a dismal season and the USFL followed suit a year later.

The 1983 Season

Pittsburgh picked twenty-first in the 1983 draft. Art lobbied hard for Pitt's homegrown All-American quarterback Dan Marino. "We've got to find a way to keep this kid in Pittsburgh," he growled. Assuming that Bradshaw would play several more seasons, Noll favored rebuilding the defense and chose Texas Tech defensive lineman Gabe Rivera, hoping he would become a cornerstone like Joe Greene.

"You should have taken Marino," Art barked at Art Jr. for years afterward. But his regrets did not dampen his warmth for Rivera. "If Rivera turns out to be as good as Ernie Holmes, or better, we've got something," he said. The night before the draft, a record six mares foaled at Shamrock. "That's great," Art chuckled, "but how many will turn out to be Kentucky Derby winners?" Someone asked if it was a good omen for Rivera. "I wouldn't go that far," Art answered. "I remember that Super Bradshaw was born the day Terry Bradshaw won us a Super Bowl and was named MVP. That horse started out by winning seven straight races, then lost it. I hope this guy does better."

Señor Sack, as the agile San Antonio native was called, got off to a good start in 1983. So did Pittsburgh. But in October, Rivera crashed his sports car in the rain and was hurled through the rear window. His spinal cord was crushed, his lungs and heart bruised. Rivera never walked again. His mother, Antonia, came to Pittsburgh. Art picked her up each morning and took her to Mass at St. Peter's, breakfast in the rectory, and the hospital. The Steelers could have terminated Rivera's contract because the accident was not football-related. Instead, they offered him a scouting position. "I don't know what I would have done without Mr. Rooney," Antonia Rivera said. "God gave me this person to help."

That fall, George Halas died. The NFL cofounder, eighty-eight, had been ailing when Art visited in September. "We talked for a while, then he asked me, 'How's the gate?' I told him, 'George, the gate is terrific. You can't buy a ticket.'" Halas smiled at that. They were the only two left from the band of brothers who had sustained the league since the Depression. They had sat together at meetings and talked daily. But after the September game, Halas became too ill to converse on the phone, and they talked only twice more. Art was watching the Monday night game on October 31 when Halas's son-in-law, Ed McCaskey, called. "Arthur," he said, "you've lost your friend."

"It's a big loss," Art reflected. "It was a long friendship and a loyal one." He called Halas one of the luckiest guys he knew, a Bohemian kid from the streets of Chicago who became the great George Halas.

Halas, who had fought to gain the slightest edge, had been an NFL loyalist. "He was always trying to do what was in the best interests of the NFL," Art commented, "whether or not it was for the best interests of the Chicago Bears at that particular time." Halas had backed the draft, revenue sharing, and expansion. And Art was in awe of the teams that he had fielded. "They *were* the Monsters of the Midway," Art stated. "Teams used to go in there and just want to come out alive." Art recalled a game when Joe Greene was getting into the Bears' backfield too easily to suit Halas. Art, whose box at Soldier Field adjoined Halas's, could hear him on the phone shouting at his coach: "Have someone hold that S-O-B!" When the coach answered they already were holding Greene, Halas retorted, "Then have three guys hold him!" Art called over, "George, holding is against the rules." "Rules!" Halas screamed. "Who are you to decide what the rules are? You don't know one rule from another!" Art said that Halas, the winningest coach in NFL history, never stopped being a regular guy. "It never got over his head." When asked if he would be lonely without Halas, Art replied, "The memories are so great that I don't think I will." But with Mara, Bell, Marshall, and now Halas gone, no one was left with whom Art had shared some of the best times of his life.

Art spent more time at Three Rivers, staying late most days. Alice McNulty was at home when he returned, and Mary Roseboro came by daily, but Art wanted to be around the team. Roseboro, an African American from the Hill with no children, had gone on vacations and to Super Bowls with the Rooneys. After thirty-eight years on North Lincoln, she said, "The Rooneys are my family." She and Alice took good care of Art.

The Homestretch

Art conceded little to age. He went to Churchill Downs in May 1984 for the Kentucky Derby as he had every year since 1926. "The Derby is something special," he mused before leaving, "but it sure has changed." Art recalled waiting with Joe Tucker and Bob Drum at a Chinese restaurant across the street from the *Post-Gazette* while Jack Sell wrapped up the sport section for the next day. "When he'd finish, we'd jump in the car and drive to Louisville. We stayed in some of the worst fleabags." Art no longer stayed in fleabags.

When Pirate manager Chuck Tanner asked who he liked this year, Art demurred: "I just don't follow it like I used to." In the past, Art said as much to avoid revealing his intentions. But now, he acknowledged, "I rarely go to the track anymore." Shamrock Farm was doing well under Jim Steele's stewardship, but Art had backed off there, too. "I haven't had a good horse in a long time," he said. "Racing isn't what it used to be for me. But you can't miss the Derby."

At Churchill Downs, Art assessed the race. He discounted the favorite, Althea, figuring that the filly would falter in the stretch. When he handicapped the field and Swale stayed at three-and-a-half-to-one, he bet $400 on him to win. "The Derby," Art smiled afterward, "came out this year just the way I thought it would." Art saw Swale win the Belmont, too, but the horse dropped dead a few weeks later. "I think his heart just stopped."

Art had not ceded full authority to his sons. "We may hold directors' meetings," Tim Rooney grunted, "but there is only one vote." Though the Rooneys no longer operated William Penn and Liberty Bell, they still ran Yonkers, Green Mountain, and the Palm Beach Kennel Club. Tim Rooney was breeding thoroughbreds in Ireland and trotters in the States. Asked why he was not involved in football, Tim replied, "Easy, when you're the third oldest, it's hard to find a place on the football ladder."

Although comfortable with his sons' oversight of racing, Art intervened when they considered casinos. Art realized that racing could not withstand competition from casinos. "Mr. Rooney," John Macartney explained, "knew there was no place in the country where their financial operations could coexist with casino gambling. He said it so simply: 'You don't have to wait fourteen, eighteen, or twenty minutes to find out whether or not you won or lost, the way you do in racing.'" At casinos, the outcome was revealed with a roll of the dice. But when offered a casino license, Art declined. He did not believe the family could own one as long as it was in football. "It would have been staggeringly more profitable to go into casinos," Macartney explained, "or have a few of the sons do so, but no deal." Though a majority of his sons favored the move, Art prevailed.

More Changes

Art gave up cigars for Lent but refused to quit smoking. If he only had a few years left, he would live them as he always had. He was worried, though, about Pittsburgh. Its mills were closing. "Things are changing," he conceded, "and I'm worried. I'm worried that we're not going to go back to the city we knew when this recession is over, worried that some of those mills are not coming back."

The Steelers rebounded in 1983 but Oakland clobbered them in the playoffs. Terry Bradshaw, injured most of the season, retired afterward. Another familiar face was missing when camp opened in 1984. Thirteen-year-veteran Franco Harris was holding out for a new contract. After gaining over 1,000 yards rushing in 1983, Franco was only 363 yards shy of Jim Brown's all-time rushing record. But negotiations over a new contract had become confused and acrimonious. After thirty-one days, the Steelers waived their greatest runner ever. Teammates and fans were stunned. There was little left on the field to connect the club with its Super Bowl glory.

Neither Franco nor the Rooneys were happy about how they parted ways. "I would do things differently if I had the chance," Franco said later. "I just never thought it would get to the point it did." For his part, Art called Franco's departure the most frustrating thing that had happened to him in sport. "Franco was a great player, and he was as great off the field as he was on it."

"I'm worried about our team," Art admitted. "When you had the Big Boy—Bradshaw—you always knew that if he stayed sound, you were going to be tough." The state of sport also unsettled him. "I hate to say it, but there's a lot of turmoil in the future of our business, the sports business. It's getting kind of out of line. Just imagine what it costs you to go to a sporting event if you're a working guy." He prided himself that the Steelers were a working man's team, but he wondered for how long. Pittsburgh, meanwhile, prided itself that Art was its native son.

He received twice as many votes as anybody else in a poll asking who in the city Pittsburghers admired the most.

"I know I don't have too long to go," he said. "I'd just like my boys to be good. They don't have to be champions, just be good and happy. For me, I'd like it to go just the way it's been going." It did, with one exception.

Ouster

The Steelers made it to the AFC Championship in 1984 before Dan Marino's four touchdown passes ended their season. They had losing records the next two years. In 1986, they started 1-6 and finished 6-10, prompting Dan Rooney to fire his brother Art Jr. as vice president of personnel. Reorganizing the front office, Dan gave Chuck Noll more say over personnel.

Art Jr. had presided over the most successful drafts in NFL history. Between 1969 and 1974, the Steelers selected nine future Hall of Famers—Greene, Bradshaw, Blount, Ham, Harris, Swann, Lambert, Stallworth, and Webster. The focus on building from the draft, selecting the best available athlete, and tapping black college players had laid the foundation for football's best team ever.

Subsequent drafts fell short. Finishing high in the standings meant drafting late in each round for a decade. From 1975 to 1986, only five picks became Pro Bowlers. "This was a once-in-a-millennium group of guys," Dwight White argued. "The coaches put the muzzles on. About ten minutes to one on Sundays, they took them off and got them back on as soon as they could afterward. You couldn't have reproduced that chemistry again."

Art Jr., fifty-one, was stunned. Though he remained employed by the club and handled other family businesses, he had lost a role that meant much to him. He tried hard to accept the decision without rancor. "You look at so many guys my age in Western Pennsylvania who lost their jobs and don't have any rich daddies to take care of them," he said. "The way I look at it is this: twenty-six years of being associated with the team is just phenomenal. How lucky can you get? It's a job you'd pay to have."

But he was devastated. Many saw his dismissal as fallout from a power struggle with Noll. Some felt Art Jr., whose personality differed dramatically from Noll's, had been a burr under the coach's saddle. NFL executives said that he could get a job immediately elsewhere. But for Art Jr., leaving the Pittsburgh Steelers would be difficult. The day after the shakeup, one of his draft picks, Joe Greene, was nominated for the Hall of Fame. "I didn't quit," Art Jr. said when pressed, "and I certainly don't believe I'm going on to bigger and better things . . . I don't know what I'm going to do. I'm a scout. I've been a scout all my life."

His father was staggered. "It knocked me out," Art admitted later. "It hurt me, hurt me badly, much worse than I ever let on. I saw it coming, but I didn't stop it. I blamed myself." Art knew that there was tension between Noll and his son, two men with strong egos. And he understood that Dan was under tremendous pressure to revive the club. "I tried several times but I did it in an almost apologetic way. I didn't call them together and say, 'This is the way it's going to be.' Because of the reputation of our family, a lot of people thought this could never happen to us. But I never thought that. I always knew it could happen. In any business, but particularly in sports, one man has to run it . . . Two can't do it. I've seen it fall apart in other families, and I saw it coming in ours."

Art retreated to Shamrock, but he found little solace walking alone in the January chill. John Rooney remembered his father calling the split a life-shortening experience. "Then it was like he caught himself. He sort of shrugged and said, 'Well, I guess maybe not *that* life-shortening.' Even then, he had his sense of humor about him. He knew it was ridiculous to say anything was life-shortening when you're eighty-five."

Wise and Humble

The stories that mark Art's last years carry familiar themes: wisdom and humility in the face of admiration nearing canonization.

His wisdom: People still sought Art's counsel. Pittsburgh voters had elected William Coyne, the nephew of Senator James J. Coyne, Art's old patron, to Congress in 1980. "He was Art's boy," Jim Boston laughed, "and the first thing Billy did after he got elected was to come and see him." Art immediately phoned Speaker of the House Tip O'Neill. "I've got a nice young Irish kid, Tip, just got elected. I want you to take care of him. The minute you see him," Art said, "you'll know he's one of us. He's going to be one of your best." O'Neill surprised Coyne by putting him on the powerful Ways and Means Committee a few years later.

"Time is starting to run out on me," Art wrote his sons in March 1987. Concerned that the distribution of Steeler stock to grandchildren would lead to arguments and jeopardize family control of the franchise, he urged his sons to regain control of all shares. "If this does not happen, down the road, there's going to be nothing but lawsuits." They took his advice, forestalling conflicts over ownership for the next two decades.

His humility: One summer afternoon, Art approached three black youths admiring the Super Bowl trophies displayed in the lobby. "How you guys doing? Want to see the field?" Art escorted them through the locker room and onto the field. Afterward, they thanked Art profusely. One asked, "Do you work here? Are you the janitor?" Ralph Berlin, who was waiting to drive Art home, watched him smile. "He never let on."

The admiration: At one of his last league meetings, Art arrived late. Entering through the wrong door, he found himself standing behind Pete Rozelle. Art quietly shuffled over to the Steelers' table across the room. "Then one of the most amazing things I have seen started to happen," Bears president Michael McCaskey recalled. "People started to clap. One or two at first, and then a few more tables. And then everyone in the room is applauding, a tremendous ovation, without one word ever being said or his name mentioned. The people in that room, almost every top executive in the league, seemed to all share the same feeling at the same time. And what everyone in the room felt for him just came out spontaneously."

Age Catches Up

Blessed with an athlete's physique and an even temperament, Art rarely worried about his health. He took illness and death in stride. The McNultys, Kass's side of the family, were more likely to get worked up over health than the Rooneys. "She's a McNulty," Art laughed, "they worry about being sick." A heart condition and circulatory problems got his attention but did not slow him down. "I always said he earned his keep to the day he died," Dan Rooney reflected. Art had a pacemaker installed in August 1985 but was loath to alter his diet or stop smoking cigars. "He asked the doctor, 'How long do I have left if I quit smoking?'" Ralph Berlin recalled. "The doctor told him eight or ten years. So The Chief says, 'And how long do I have if I keep smoking?' The doctor says six or eight years. The Chief says, 'Fine, you can keep the extra two years, I'm gonna keep smoking.'" Art stopped driving and let others carry his luggage, but he remained on the go. "The Chief always seems to forget how old he is," son John said. "He talks about events in the future with every intention of being there."

In March 1988, Art attended NFL meetings in San Antonio, where Mayor Henry Cisneros lobbied him in the coffee shop about an expansion franchise. In May, he went to the Derby, his sixty-third in a row, despite pains in his right arm. He arrived at Churchill Downs early that morning and returned to his hotel at midnight. Back home, he felt ill and called for an ambulance. Walking out of the house in his bathrobe, he dismissed efforts to put him in the back of the ambulance. "I'm all right," he said. "I'll sit in the front." At the hospital, Art was rushed into surgery to remove a blood clot in his arm. As soon as he finished surgery, he was impatient to leave. Art was shocked at the coverage he received. "Geez," he said, "they must have nothing else to do. Isn't Reagan still in Moscow?" Home days later, he made it to the Belmont Stakes in June. But his hip became troublesome, and when Pirates owner John Galbreath died in July, Art missed the funeral. "The doctor told me I could go if I went in a wheelchair. I asked him if he was kidding. There's no way I'm going anywhere in a wheelchair." He skipped the Irish Derby that summer.

But Art kept going to work. When his doctor told Art he was living dangerously, he asked him what he could do about it. "He said I could do a lot of things differently—eat right, sleep right, those kinds of things. I just told him, 'I've been around a long time. What's the use of bothering with those things now?'"

Art was not too concerned with football that summer. He spent part of Wednesday, August 17, 1988, talking with Lou Lamonde, the head ticket man at Three Rivers, whose mother had recently died. That afternoon, he told Dan, "I've put in my time; I'm going home." Suddenly dizzy, he slumped against the wall. Dan told Mary Regan to call 9-1-1, but Art said he would be fine and sat down. Mary called anyway. On the way to Mercy Hospital, they stopped to give him oxygen.

Art had had a stroke, his greatest concern. He was partially paralyzed and could not speak, but Dr. Theodore Gelet was optimistic that he would recover. On Sunday evening, Art could speak enough to tell Dan, "Get me my rosaries." He took the rosary ring, and after a while told Dan, "You can go. I'll be fine." Art prayed over the beads as he had thousands of times. "Holy Mary, Mother of God, pray for us sinners now and at the hour of our death." That evening, Rev. Jack O'Malley stopped by to visit his father's old buddy and anointed Art. He fell into a coma during the night. When Dan arrived in the morning, Art Jr. was there, but their father was in intensive care. Art recognized his sons but could not talk. Thousands prayed for Art's recovery, but his blood pressure dropped when doctors tried to wean him from the respirator. Art died that morning, August 25, clutching his rosary ring. It had to be pried out of his hand.

Tributes poured in. "He was a man who belonged to the entire world of sports," Pete Rozelle said. "It is questionable whether any sports figure was more universally loved and respected." Antonia Rivera sobbed that Art was "my angel from heaven." New England owner Billy Sullivan spoke of Art's role in ending the war between the NFL and AFL. "I think God was having a very good day when he made Art Rooney."

Green Bay president Robert Parins credited Art with keeping the Packers competitive. "He was one of the people who strongly supported the concept of revenue sharing, and that, of course, has made it possible for Green Bay to function as a franchise in the league." *Daily Racing Form* columnist Joe Hirsch said, "He was as close to a saint as we'll ever see around a racetrack." County commissioner Tom Foerster observed, "Everyone knows Mr. Rooney was our number one citizen. I'm fully convinced he did more for this city than R. K. Mellon did for the business community and David Lawrence and any of the mayors who followed him." But what Foerster remembered the most was that Art "was like a father to us on the Northside." Waitresses, truck drivers, and neighbors told tales about encounters with Art, the uncommon, common man they revered. "There weren't big people and little people to Mr. Rooney," Mary Regan said. "There were just people, and he wanted to help everyone. I never saw him say no to anyone in need."

"I go to see more dead people than probably anybody in Pittsburgh," Art had said. Now Pittsburghers paid their respects to him. Art's will stipulated that funeral expenses not exceed $1,000. That was ignored, but nobody dared move Mass from St. Peter's. "Art loved this church," retired Bishop Vincent Leonard said. "Jack McGinley, his brother-in-law, said, 'If we were to bury Art in another church, I don't think he would go.'"

On Friday, with flags in Pittsburgh at half-mast, over 5,000 people came to St. Peter's, where Art lay in an open coffin. Family members greeted each of them. The team practiced that morning, went together to St. Peter's, and departed for New Orleans, where they were to play the following evening. On Saturday, twelve hundred squeezed into St. Peter's for Mass; hundreds more watched on television in a hall downstairs. They were a mix of Pittsburghers and people from the sports world whom Art had touched. *Baltimore Evening Sun* columnist John Steadman said, "I couldn't have lived with myself if I had not come here today. I wrote today that if there had been a thirteenth disciple, his name would have been Arthur."

During the Mass, Bishop Donald Wuerl faced the congregation and said, "Let us offer each other a sign of peace." Pete Rozelle turned to shake hands with the person seated behind him and saw it was his bitter antagonist, Raiders owner Al Davis. They shook anyway. Bishop Leonard spoke the longest. After extolling Art's "old-fashioned Catholic ways," he smiled, "I'm not acting as a promoter of Art's canonization." After all, he pointed out, "A devil's advocate would have a field day with the life of a man who brought his wife to a racetrack on his honeymoon." Leonard had known Art for decades. "He was the friend of politicians, of thugs and thieves, of people good and evil," he said, "and the three qualities he possessed that left the most lasting impression were his humility, his courage, and his charity. He remained a simple person, a man who could speak to the little child as easily as he could a college professor." Leonard said that Art's comment that he never had a player he didn't like had stuck with him. "How many among us could say the same thing? I could not, not even of my fellow bishops and priests." When the laughter died down in the 150-year-old church, Leonard concluded, "Perhaps we shall never see his like again."

As Art's grandchildren carried his coffin out of St. Peter's, a plane flew overhead trailing a banner that said, "Bless you Chief—Glassport," a mill town down the Monongahela River. The funeral procession wended its way to the Northside Catholic Cemetery where Art was buried next to Kass. "The thing I remember," Dan Rooney recalled, "were the black families, whole families, along the way. They were outside, dressed in black and gold, holding signs. They said, 'We love you, Chief.' 'Thanks Chief, Goodbye.' This was a show of the real people."

When the Steelers played Dallas in the NFL opener, the Cowboys wore "AJR" on their helmets. "We're wearing it on behalf of all of the teams in the league," explained Cowboys' president Tex Schramm. "This will be the first game with no Art. It'll just be different."

The *Post-Gazette* captured the extraordinary degree to which Pittsburgh identified with Rooney. It argued that the smoky mills and other bygone landmarks branding Pittsburgh could be replaced. Pittsburgh's transformation into what Rand-McNally had called the nation's most livable city underscored its protean nature. But Art's passing created a void. "The Pittsburgh that Art Rooney takes with him is the city so many of its residents wished to be identified with and point to as being the essence of what the place was all about." Art personified Pittsburgh's unpretentious style, its roots in neighborhood and family, and its ability take a body blow but get off the mat. "That's the sort of man he was and, in living as he did, Mr. Rooney created an ideal for a city, a model of how Pittsburghers would like others to regard them." Art Rooney had become the story that many Pittsburghers would use to tell about themselves to the world.

Notes

1. Coming to Pittsburgh

Some of the sources are from Maggie Murray Rooney's scrapbooks. They often lack bylines, dates, and the names of the newspapers from which they were taken. The same problem exists with many articles from the microfilm archives of the Pittsburgh Steelers for their early seasons.

1   *Art's great-grandfather, James Rooney*: 1871 British census records for Ebbw Vale, found in Tredegar, South Wales, Public Library. The 1881 census lists James as a widower living with the Crotty family in Newtown. Years later, Catherine and Arthur's son Daniel told his children about visiting relatives in Newry when he was a boy in Ebbw Vale. Newry Parish records show that a James Rooney was born there in 1829, the only son of James Rooney and Margaret Connolly.

1   *Jonathan Swift had once*: Newry's port prospered so well during the eighteenth and nineteenth centuries that it outgrew Belfast, which came to use "Belfast near Newry" as its mailing address, according to Seamus Mallon and John O'Hare interview, October 31, 2002. While most of Ireland tied the vote to land ownership in the 1790s, Newry adopted a "pot walloper" rule that said every household with a separate kitchen fire and a pot to boil on it could cast a vote. Canavan, *Frontier Town*, 76 and 109; "Parish of Newry, County Down."

1   *While James trained*: Some of this research on the Rooney family's Irish roots was done by Og McAteer of Newry. We were unable to obtain independent verification of James Rooney's employment at the iron forge or the date of his departure from Ireland. John Gaydon, archivist and historian at Corus Steel, formerly the Ebbw Vale Iron and Steel Works, said that ironmaking was done on small charcoal-burning forges in Ireland at the time. John Gaydon interview, August 7, 2003.

2   *Newry's prosperity*: Kenny, *The American Irish*, 89–91.

2   *James found passage*: Passage at the time typically cost two to five pounds (each pound was worth about $5); lumber ships charged about half as much, according to Bernard Hagerty, historian at the University of Pittsburgh, personal correspondence, October 2003; see also Roberts, *Montreal*, and Cooper, *Montreal*.

2   *Like many Irish*: Information about the family's whereabouts during this period is sketchy. In the 1900 census of the United States, Arthur states that he was born in Canada. In the 1871 British census, taken when he was in Ebbw Vale, Arthur specified Montreal as his birthplace, although no baptismal record was found for him in that city. James Roney (as the name was often spelled) appears in the 1856/57 and 1858/59 *Mackay's Montreal Directory*. He lived at 36 Kempt, which is now Young Street, in St. Ann's parish. He listed his occupation as millwright, and his family shared the house with a widow Roney, presumably his mother. Both of these Montreal directories list a number of foundries and forges within walking distance of their home on Kempt Street.

2   *In 1851, James's wife*: The 1900 U.S. Manuscript Census lists Arthur Rooney, spelled Roney, as being born in May 1851. Other sources, including his gravestone, put his date of birth as 1850. Discrepancies in these dates of birth also occur for the other members of the family. In the 1871 census for Ebbw Vale, found in the Tredegar Public Library, James, Mary, and their son Arthur Rooney were living on Forge Row in Ebbw Vale. The family may have gone back to Ireland for a time or to Tredegar, Wales, a town some family members remember Arthur mentioning. We were unable to trace the family between 1857, when they were in Montreal, and 1871, when they were living in Ebbw Vale. Although there is no record of when Arthur started his apprenticeship, children as young as six or seven often went into foundries and coal pits in South Wales and worked twelve-hour shifts under dangerous conditions. Caswell, Gaydon and Warrender, *Ebbw Vale*, 78–79; Gray-Jones, *History of Ebbw Vale*, 113–14.

3   *Its paternalistic Quaker*: Gray-Jones, "Quaker Ironmasters," 90–91; Gray-Jones, *History of Ebbw Vale*, 120; Caswell, Gaydon, and Warrender, *Ebbw Vale*.

3   *Arthur and Catherine's children*: Gray-Jones, *History of Ebbw Vale*, 107. Baptismal records from All Saints Roman Catholic Church, retrieved by

Father Michael Hagerty in August 2003. The church began keeping records in 1874. No record could be found of Bridget's birth or baptism.

4   *Each working day*: Gray-Jones, *History of Ebbw Vale*, 154, 170; Keith and Irene Thomas, Ebbw Vale historians, interview, Ebbw Vale, August 6, 2003.

4   *While the Rooneys*: Caswell, Gaydon, and Warrender, *Ebbw Vale*, 23; John Gaydon, archivist and historian at Corus Steel, formerly the Ebbw Vale Iron and Steel Works, interview, August 7, 2003; Keith Thomas, Ebbw Vale historian, interview, August 6, 2003.

5   *In the 1870s*: In 1873, when Abraham Darby III retired as manager, the last "bonds of Quaker proprietorship, with its traditions and its honest even if limited concern for the workers" were broken. Gray-Jones, "Quaker Ironmasters," 90–95.

5   *James's son Arthur*: Many years later, Arthur's grandchildren would hear him called Cap, a sobriquet they suspected came from these seafaring adventures. The date of the Rooney immigration varies in different records. In the 1910 U.S. Manuscript Census, for example, Catherine Rooney reported her date of immigration as 1880. Daniel told the 1920 census enumerator that he had arrived in 1879. Kenny, *The American Irish*, 139–40.

6   *They rented rooms*: Walsh, "Across 'The Big Wather,'" 192.

6   *Arthur and Catherine found*: The name Ebbw comes from the Welsh *ebe*, or "beginning," and *wysg*, meaning "water," because the headwaters of the thin Ebwy River form at the northern end of valley and snake southward through the village and past the Ebbw Vale Iron and Steel Works. In Pittsburgh, two much larger rivers—the north-flowing Monongahela and the Allegheny coming south from New York State—join at the city's Point to form the Ohio River, which then heads toward the Mississippi. Caswell, Gaydon, and Warrender, *Ebbw Vale*, 5; Walsh, "Across 'The Big Wather,'" 192.

7   *Arthur Rooney fit*: Couvares, *Remaking of Pittsburgh*, 10, 32; Kleinberg, *Shadow of the Mills*, 50.

7   *Arthur started in*: Diffenbacher's *Directory of Pittsburgh and Allegheny Cities, 1884* lists Arthur Rooney as a laborer living at 1006 Bingham Street.

7   *Pittsburgh was not*: Kleinberg, *Shadow of the Mills*, is an excellent account of women's lives during these years; Gray-Jones, *History of Ebbw Vale*, 105.

8   *In Ebbw Vale*: Typhoid and scarlet fever alone caused 132 deaths in Ebbw
     Vale in 1882, one of highest rates in Britain. Gray-Jones, *History of Ebbw
     Vale*, 94, 102, 124.

8   *Similar conditions*: In 1900, other large U.S. cities had an average rate of
     typhoid deaths of 18 per 100,000, but in Pittsburgh the number was 145.
     Only Allegheny City, which would later be incorporated as Pittsburgh's
     Northside, had a higher rate. Kleinberg, *Shadow of the Mills*, 88–97.

8   *On May 16, 1884*: Baptismal records for St. John the Evangelist Church
     on the Southside, retrieved by Ken White, Archives and Record Center,
     Diocese of Pittsburgh, give this birth date and record her baptism on May
     25, 1884, with Daniel Sheehan and A. McDonald as her sponsors.

8   *Soon, however, a little*: Polk, *Pittsburgh City Directory*; Percy, *Metal-
     lurgy*. In Wales, Arthur Rooney had certainly been close to the puddling
     process, working alongside his father as an apprentice and rougher, al-
     though there is nothing in the records to indicate he actually trained as a
     puddler there. Fitch, *Steel Workers*, 33; Davis, *Iron Puddler*, 86.

8   *Arthur cleaned*: Percy, *Metallurgy*; John Gaydon, interview, Ebbw Vale,
     August 7, 2003; Davis, *Iron Puddler*; Gale, "Technology of Iron Manu-
     facture," 451–52.

9   *In 1886 after*: Pittsburgh workers, especially the skilled men, were better
     paid than those in most other cities. The mills here enjoyed some natu-
     ral advantages. The readily accessible Pittsburgh seam of coal and high-
     quality coke in nearby Connellsville reduced the costs of local produc-
     tion, which benefited both manufacturers and workers. The average wage
     for a roller was $10.69, according to Couvares, *Remaking of Pittsburgh*,
     16–17; Stromquist, "Working Class Organization," 173.

9   *The Rooneys moved*: Baptismal records for St. John the Evangelist Church
     on the Southside, Archives and Record Center, Diocese of Pittsburgh, re-
     cord the baby's baptism on February 14, 1886, with William Donovan
     and Maria Barry as her sponsors. "Some Pittsburgh steelworking fami-
     lies reused the name of a dead child [to keep] the memory of the child alive
     by retaining the name in the family. The name acted as living memorial in
     place of the cold marble that poor parents could not afford," Kleinberg,
     Shadow of the Mills, 114.

10   *The city's brotherhood*: A peripatetic artisan who later became a U.S. sen-
     ator and the secretary of labor, Davis hailed from Tredegar, a town just a
     few valleys west of Ebbw Vale. Like Arthur Rooney, Davis first settled in
     eastern Ohio and then came to ply his trade in Pittsburgh.

10   *Arthur Rooney was at home*: Couvares, *Remaking of Pittsburgh*, 34, 44–45, 59; Kudlik, "You Couldn't Keep," 51–63.

11   *In 1887, Catherine*: Baptismal records for St. John the Evangelist Church on the Southside, Archives and Record Center, Diocese of Pittsburgh, show that Agnes was born May 24, 1887, and baptized on June 5, 1887, with William Shean and Ellen Murphy as her sponsors.

11   *By the time Agnes*: Baptismal records for St. John the Evangelist Church on the Southside, Archives and Record Center, show that Arthur was baptized on August 25, 1889, and his sponsors were Michael Concannon, who would later marry Bridget Rooney, and Mary Regan, who was probably a sister or sister-in-law of Catherine Regan Rooney.

11   *But the family's*: Davis, *Iron Puddler*, 115.

12   *The Amalgamated Association*: The union represented only the skilled workers, about one-third of the workforce in the area's mills at the time, but their contract pulled up the wages of the remaining unskilled and mostly immigrant workforce. The Sons of Vulcan, the first union of ironworkers, had formed in Pittsburgh in 1862. In 1876, eight years before Rooney arrived in town, the Vulcans and other unions of skilled workers in iron and the incipient steel industry had joined forces to create the Amalgamated Association of Iron, Steel, and Tin Workers. In 1877, while the Rooneys were still in Wales, railroad workers staged a national insurrection. In Pittsburgh, workers had support from the city's middle classes and battled state militia brought in from Philadelphia to suppress the walkouts. More than a score of workers and some militia died, while millions of dollars' worth of rail yards, locomotives, and buildings were trashed and burned. Filippelli, *Labor*, 103–4.

12   *According to family*: The shotgun might have belonged to Arthur and Catherine's son-in-law, who worked in the iron and steel industry.

13   *The transition from iron*: Skilled trades were under assault in Pittsburgh. The reorganization of glassmaking and the metal trades meant workers lost the status that they had prized. A fifth of all deaths among men were now caused by accidents at work, leaving many mill-area households headed by widows.

13   *Arthur took the poor*: In fact, skilled Irish ironworkers and building tradesmen often went back and forth between mill work and saloonkeeping. Kenny, *The American Irish*, 185; Walsh, "Across 'The Big Wather,'" 223–24, 240–47; *usquebaugh*, the Irish word for whiskey, means "water of life." In Ireland, young men congregated in the shebeens, or taverns,

treating one another to rounds and brandishing their clan pride for a faction fight. Barrett, "Why Paddy Drank."

14   *The household above*: 1900 U.S. Manuscript Census. Two of the boarders worked in the mills as puddlers: William Williams, sixty, a Welsh immigrant, and Martin Jordan, a thirty-three-year-old Irishman. Charles Books, thirty, a stationary engineer, and John Ponz, a thirty-five-year-old laborer, were both born in Pennsylvania. James O'Neal, twenty-five, from Illinois, worked as a bartender. The mix suggests that by 1900, white workers—both native-born and émigrés from the British Isles—had blended together to a degree that would have surprised the more segregated Pittsburghers of the midcentury.

14   *In 1903, Arthur*: Only New York and Boston had higher pneumonia fatality rates in 1890. Kleinberg, *Shadow of the Mills*, 98.

14   *After working*: Within a year of Daniel and Maggie's wedding, Allegheny County property records show that Catherine and Arthur lost the property in a sheriff's sale. But in November 1900, Daniel and Maggie bought it back for $3,261.

15   *On January 9, 1899*: John and Mary Ellen Rooney, Daniel's brother and sister, served as the couple's attendants. Just how Daniel and Maggie met is lost in the folds of time. Older residents still recalled (in 2002) the Rooneys coming to visit the Drears, who were said to be related. Mary Ann Drear was the daughter of Robert Roney, which is how old Arthur sometimes spelled his name, and descendants believed they were part of the same Irish clan. The Drears lived in Alpsville, next door to George Bigley, a wealthy coal merchant, where Maggie Murray's mother and her aunts had worked as nannies, according to the 1900 census and Coultersville manuscript. So perhaps Arthur and Catherine's oldest boy Daniel first caught sight of the beautiful, auburn-haired Maggie visiting at the Bigley house.

15   *On January 27, 1901*: Baptismal record show that Arthur J. Rooney's godparents were Vincent Murray, his mother's brother, and Bridget Rooney Concannon, his father's older sister. Coultersville Book Committee, *Golden Memories*, 27–33. In his journals, Art Rooney Jr. recalls hearing the Rooney women tell the "golden boy" story when he was a child. Irishman Daniel Sheehan, forty-six, a distant cousin of the Rooneys with wiry dark hair and eyebrows, took a room and helped at the bar. James Sheehan had been godfather at the baptism of Daniel's brother John in Ebbw Vale.

15   *In the 1880s*: Annual Report, Geological Survey of Pennsylvania, 305.

The estimated wages for a fire boss at a mine with a capacity of 15,000 tons in 1886 was $3 per day.

15 *Murray's work*: Brophy, *A Miner's Life*, 38–50; 1900 census manuscript.

16 *At home, "Pap"*: Jackson, *Early Stages*, 24–25, 28, 54.

16 *In both the Rooney*: Early records show that the name was originally spelled Somers and Sommers, according to research done by Paul Greenaway, who is descended from Mary's sister Catherine Summers Greenaway. Mary Summers's first name is variously listed as Mary, Marie, Mary Ann, Mariam, and Marian Anna. Mary Ann Summers, the oldest of nine children, was born in Port Perry near Braddock to Irish immigrants Patrick Summers and Mary Betty Skillen. Patrick's parents were Moses Summers and Mary Retmond or Redmond, according to research done by Greenaway. The same research shows that Mary Betty Skillen's parents were Patrick Skillen and Bridget Dunn. Patrick and Mary Betty had been married in St. Peter's Church in McKeesport on July 15, 1855. In this marriage record, Patrick lists his residence as Osceola, probably the mine that employed him. He became a naturalized citizen in Allegheny County in 1860. Anne Jackson's book *Early Stages*, says that the Summers had strains of Scottish and English blood, but the 1900 census manuscript indicates that both her parents were born in Ireland.

16 *In her autobiography*: Jackson, *Early Stages*, 23–24, 199.

16 *Monday through Saturday*: Coultersville Book Committee, *Golden Memories*, 11–13; interview with F. Duane Brown, April 2003.

17 *But Coultersville's fortunes*: The area was then called Moon Township.

17 *Their property was*: Later called Wireton or Glenwillard.

17 *The move proved*: On Dec. 1, 1981, the *Beaver County Times* ran a picture of a fire at this structure with a caption: "An 80-year-old Monaca landmark, the former Colonial Hotel, was damaged by fire Monday afternoon . . . The old 22-room hotel . . . was scheduled for demolition by the borough . . . Once a popular speakeasy, the hotel was previously owned by the Art Rooney family of Pittsburgh."

17 *Their second son*: We will call this baby, Art's brother, Dan and continue to call their father Daniel.

17 *Art was three*: Margaret Laughlin Rooney interview, Pittsburgh, May 22, 2002. By the 1910 census, Catherine no longer ran the hotel, but she still had a full house. She had moved to Donora, a mill town twenty miles south of Pittsburgh along the Monongahela River. Her sons John, thirty-

two, a clerk, and Miles, nineteen, a machinist, lived with her. They shared the house with Catherine's brother Patrick Regan and an Irish boarder. Catherine had also taken in two children, who would remain part of the Rooney family for many years to come. In the census record, she lists John Ward, seventeen, and his sister, Ellen (later called Helen), thirteen, as her adopted son and daughter. Catherine's oldest daughter Bridget and her husband Michael Concannon and three of their children lived a block away on the same street. Michael was working as a roll hand in the steel mill.

17   *According to family*: John Rooney interview, June 22, 2003.

18   *When Daniel finally*: 1910 census tract and Polk City Directory; Margaret Rooney Laughlin interview, May 22, 2002.

2. The Young Athlete

19   *In a crinkled*: Daniel Rooney's granddaughter, graphic artist Kathy Rooney (whose father Vincent appears in the photo), has colored the flags red, white, and blue in her sketch of this photo. She had scanned the original and blown up each section in order to examine details such as the words on the poster that appears over Daniel Rooney's head and to the right in the window.

19   *An older boy*: Kathy Rooney, who found this image in a blowup of that section of the photo, thinks it may be Arthur or Dan, just pulling his head back into the apartment as the camera clicked. "It was like seeing a ghost," she said in June 2002.

19   *Though Daniel*: Miles returned from the war unscathed, but Wilmer Brickley, Art's football coach at Duquesne, did not survive a hydroplane crash. *Duquesne Monthly*, June and July 1918; *Pittsburgh Post*, November 13, 1918.

20   *Although Maggie*: Deed books, Allegheny County Recorder of Deeds, vol. 1801, 276.

20   *The saloon anchored*: Margaret Rooney Laughlin interview, June 6, 2001.

21   *The children internalized*: Margaret Rooney Laughlin interview, May 22, 2002.

21   *In these halcyon*: Margaret Rooney Laughlin interview, May 22, 2002.

21   *Spring brought floods*: Cope, *The Game that Was*, 124–25; Arthur Rooney Jr. Journal entry dated Nov. 15, 1995.

22   *Flooding had hurt*: Bonk, "Ballpark Figures," 52–70.

22 *"All the baseball"*: Cope, *The Game that Was*, 124; "A to Z Exhibit," Sen. John Heinz Pittsburgh Regional History Center.

22 *Maggie tried*: Interview with Arthur J. Rooney, Pittsburgh, July 30, 1980; Thorn et. al., *Total Baseball*, 2020, 2046–47, 2052–53.

22 *Until Pittsburgh*: John Canning interview, April 24, 2002.

22 *Parts of Allegheny*: Commission on Social Services, *Crime and Its Treatment*, 34–35; Hayllar, "The Accommodation," 79, 90–91.

23 *Maggie had*: Margaret Rooney Laughlin interview, June 6, 2001; Timothy Vincent Rooney interview, June 20, 2002.

23 *At the wagon's*: Arthur Rooney Jr. Journal entries.

24 *Art began exploring*: Benswanger, "Professional Baseball," 9–14; Lieb, *Pittsburgh Pirates*, 4–44; Ruck, "Sandlot Seasons," 352–60; Peterson, *Pigskin*, 26–29; Brynn, "Some Sports," 71–75; Kudlik, "You Couldn't Keep," 51–63.

24 *The Northside*: The Phipps family had once run a shoemaker's shop down the street from the Rooney's saloon. Although the shop was gone long before the Rooneys arrived, Art would later get to know the family at the racetrack. The family fortunes had risen with Henry Phipps Jr., who became Carnegie's partner as the Scottish entrepreneur built his empire of iron and steel. Like Carnegie, Phipps became a philanthropist. His "Phipps houses," model tenements designed to provide workers with ample light and sanitation, rimmed the playground he gave the Northside. The five-story yellow-brick apartments were among the nation's earliest model housing projects. Phipps, however, could not persuade immigrants—suspicious of the steel baron—to rent there. He had to prevail upon his own workers to inhabit his social experiment. Boegner and Gachot, *Halcyon Days*, 19–20; *Pittsburgh Post-Gazette*, September 23, 24, 1930; Arthur J. Rooney interview, July 30, 1980; *The Bulletin Index*, December 30, 1937.

24 *Art developed*: Ray Downey interview, September 13, 2001.

24 *Art moved rapidly*: Dan Rooney interview, August 23, November 1, 2001.

24 *"It wasn't anything"*: Cope, *The Game that Was*, 125–26.

25 *Art and his*: Arthur J. Rooney interview, July 30, 1980.

26 *Art's sporting baptism*: Chartered as the Duquesne University of the Holy Ghost in 1911, the school was the first Catholic university in Pennsylvania and the only one between Catholic University in Washington DC and Notre Dame in South Bend. Three of the six Rooney boys would attend

its high school and university during the teens and twenties; several of their children and grandchildren followed later. Rishel, *"Spirit that Gives Life,"* 1–5, 11–15, 27–28, 43. The name was shortened to Duquesne University in 1935.

26 *Students attended*: *Duquesne Monthly*, January 1919, July 1920.

26 *Art met all*: Rishel, *"Spirit that Gives Life,"* 11.

27 *In the spring*: *Duquesne Monthly*, June 1917; *Pittsburgh Post*, May 13, May 28, June 17, June 31, 1917.

27 *His first year*: While these grades might seem low, grade inflation had not yet boosted overall averages. Art enrolled in the shorthand course the next two years, pulling his grades up and doing especially well in European history, correspondence, and geography. With sixty as a passing mark, he averaged almost 69 for his seven courses. His grades during the 1917–18 academic year averaged almost 78 percent, which was also his average in fall 1918. In his third year, Rooney attended Duquesne only in the fall. His grades slipped in English and stenography but climbed to 90 in a course on the history of Rome and the West, and his best-ever high-school grade, 94, in civics. Rooney's education ranged from practical skills such as typing, stenography, and commercial law, to math, geography, English, and history. Duquesne University transcript for Arthur J. Rooney, January 7, 1920.

27 *While he had*: *Pittsburgh Post*, May 12, May 13, June 24, 1917; John Kennedy interview, October 30, 2001.

28 *"When I was younger"*: John Kennedy interview, October 30, 2001.

28 *By the fall*: *Duquesne Monthly*, October 1917.

28 *Students were dejected*: *Duquesne Monthly*, October 1917, January 1918.

28 *"Art Rooney has"*: *Duquesne Monthly*, December 1917 and January 1918.

29 *As soon as*: *Duquesne Monthly*, February and March, 1918; Ruck, *Sandlot Seasons*, 124–26.

29 *Midway through*: *Duquesne Monthly*, April-June, 1918.

29 *On the sandlots*: *Pittsburgh Post*, June 7, 15, 17, 30, 1918; Ruck, *Sandlot Seasons*, 42.

29 *Pittsburgh papers*: *Pittsburgh Post*, July 7, August 4, 17, 1918.

30 *Art played*: *Pittsburgh Post*, August 6, September 8, October 6, 1918.

30 *In the fall*: Christopher Snowbeck, *Pittsburgh Post-Gazette*, "1918 Memories," November 23, 2004, D1-D2; Arthur Rooney Jr. Journal entries.

30   *High school sport*: *Pittsburgh Post*, October 4, 5, 1918, June 18, 1919.

30   *The team's name*: Arthur J. Rooney interview, Pittsburgh, July 30, 1980; Cope, *The Game that Was*, 126–27; *History of the Allegheny Fire Department* (Allegheny, 1895); Patricia Bergman interview, November 1, 2003.

31   *Art preferred*: *Pittsburgh Post*, December 13, 17, 22, 29, 1918.

31   *Art, who had*: Robert Markus, Tribune Press Service clip in Steeler Notes, n. d.; Monsignor Charles Owen Rice, an Irish-born priest who spent most of his life in Pittsburgh, confirmed this use of language during an interview, August 16, 2001. He remembered "yellow bellies" as a term used to refer to the Orangemen, the people who changed their religion, "because they were yellow." He had not heard the term used for decades.

31   *Art battered*: Roy McHugh, "Ever-tough Dan Rooney a Hard-to-Beat Priest," *Pittsburgh Press*, January 11, 1981, and August 25, 1988; Cope, *The Game that Was*, 125; Ray Downey interview, September 13, 2001; Roy McHugh, "Boy Could They Fight," in "When Pittsburgh Was a Fight Town," unpublished manuscript; *Pittsburgh Sun*, January 24, 1920; *Pittsburgh Post*, February 12, 1922.

32   *Games often*: Ray Downey interview, September 13, 2001; McHugh, "Boy Could They Fight."

32   *The brothers*: These amateur clubs formed boxing's bedrock in Pittsburgh, with the Willow A. C., the Wilmerding YMCA, and St. Peter's A. C. the best of the lot. Lawrenceville's Willow A. C. had a national reputation, if only for the participation of the Zivic brothers, who won amateur, Olympic, and professional championships. On more than one occasion, the Zivics faced each other in the ring.

32   *The Pittsburgh Post*: *Pittsburgh Post*, March 7, April 6, 1920; Arthur J. Rooney interview, July 30, 1980; Timothy Rooney interview, December 8, 2001.

32   *Even while boxing*: Cope, *The Game that Was*, 125–26; quoted in *Pittsburgh Post-Gazette*, August 28, 1988.

32   *The Rooneys*: Timothy Rooney interview, December 12, 2001; Cope, *The Game that Was*, 126.

33   *"Rooney is"*: *Pittsburgh Post*, December 13, 15, 1918, January 12, 1919; *Pittsburgh Sun*, December 13, 14, 21, 1918.

33   *Boxing took Art*: *Pittsburgh Post*, March 19, 1919.

33   *The next week*: *Toronto Daily Star*, April 1, 1919, 21; *The Evening Telegram* [Toronto], April 1, 1919, 28.

34   *Two weeks later*: *Pittsburgh Post*, March 27, April 8, 9, December 28, 1919; *Boston Herald*, April 7, 8, 9, 1919; *Boston Globe*, August 26, 1988.

34   *Art got*: *Pittsburgh Post*, May 14, 1919; clips from Steelers microfilm archives, misc. years.

34   *Back home*: *Pittsburgh Post*, June 26, 1919.

34   *Art segued*: *Duquesne Monthly*, May 1919; *Pittsburgh Post*, March 23, June 1, July 15, 18, 22, August 7, 15, 16, 17, 21, 22, 31, September 21, November 2, 1919.

34   *Art returned*: Sperber, *Shake Down*, 90–91; University Athletic Director's Records 6/69 (September 19, 1920), University of Notre Dame Archives; Timothy Vincent Rooney interview, June 20, 2002.

35   *The preps*: Gradebooks of Normal School Students in Preparatory Subjects, Indiana University of Pennsylvania Archives.

36   *Indiana played*: AP, dateline Indiana PA; *Standard Observer* [Irwin PA], June 18, 1982; *Indiana Evening Gazette*, September 29, October 3, November 3, 9, 17, 1919; *The Normal Herald XXV*, November 1919.

36   *Meanwhile, Dan*: *Pittsburgh Post*, September 22, 1919.

36   *Back in*: *Duquesne Monthly*, December 1919. The best source for Rooney at Indiana State Normal is *The Instano IX* (1920) and *The Instano X* (1921), published annually by the senior class of the Pennsylvania State Normal School, Indiana, Pennsylvania. See also the *Pittsburgh Post*, October 26 and November 2, 13, 9, 16, 1919; *Pittsburgh Post*, June 10, 12, 1920; *The Normal Herald XXVI*, August 1920.

36   *His love*: The Woogie Harris anecdote was told by George Quinlan to Roy McHugh.

36   *Irish Americans*: *Pittsburgh Post*, April 17, May 5, 1921, and November 9, 1922.

37   *In the style*: O'Brien, *The Chief*, 93; Fair, *Give Him to the Angels*, 43–44, 71–73 86, 156, 183; *Pittsburgh Post*, March 21, 1922.

37   *Art skipped*: *Pittsburgh Post*, January 13, 24, February 8, 23, 25, March 7, 14, April 11, 18, 1920; *Pittsburgh Sun*, February 20, 1920.

38   *Four American*: *Pittsburgh Post*, January 19, 1920.

38   *Mosberg, a tough*: *New York Times*, August 20–25, 1920; "Sam Mosberg," International Jewish Sports Hall of Fame Web site, http://www.jewishsports.net/BioPages/SamuelMosberg.htm, April 23, 2009.

38   *Several accounts*: Timothy Rooney interview, December 8, 2001; Ruck, in "Art Rooney," is one of the writers to make this mistake.

38 *After the Olympics*: Timothy Rooney interview, Pittsburgh, December 8, 2001.

38 *Art's amateur*: *Boston Globe*, August 26, 1988.

39 *Instead of*: Chuck Klausing interview, September 14, 2001.

39 *Art was returning*: Chuck Klausing, who coached with Art's good friend and former teammate Steve Harrick, heard this story at the ceremony naming a residential hall for Rooney. Chuck Klausing interview, Pittsburgh, September 14, 2001; Bob Kravitz, *Pittsburgh Press,* January 27, 1985.

39 *As the 1920*: *Pittsburgh Post*, April 4, 1920.

39 *Daylight savings*: *Pittsburgh Post*, April 4, 1920; Ruck, *Sandlot Seasons*, 23–28.

40 *Highly sought*: *Pittsburgh Post*, May 20, 26, June 1, 9, 12, July 14, August 15, 1920.

40 *Dan, following*: *Pittsburgh Post*, August 22, 1920.

40 *At the end*: *Pittsburgh Post*, August 11, September 9, 1920; Harold Weissman, "Pittsburgh Story of the Rooney Brothers," article from unknown newspaper found in the *Pittsburgh Press* morgue files dated January 20, 1951 with a Philadelphia dateline.

40 *But Art changed*: Official transcript of Arthur J. Rooney, registrar's office, Duquesne University.

40 *Accustomed*: *Pittsburgh Post*, November 13, 20, 1920; *Indiana Evening Gazette*, September 18, 22, 24, 27, October 9, 18, 25, November 1, 8, 13, 19, 1920.

41 *Duquesne fielded*: In 1903, after several students were injured in a game with Washington & Jefferson College, Duquesne president Father Martin Hehir abolished varsity football. Students continued to play intramural ball but the college did not resume varsity play until 1913. Two years later, the school ended it again. High school football, however, continued uninterrupted. Rishel, *"Spirit that Gives Life,"* 8–11, 21–22; *Pittsburgh Post*, November 22, 1920.

41 *Duquesne's football*: *Duquesne Monthly*, July, November 1920; Indiana Evening Gazette, September 18, 1920.

41 *On October 15*: *Duquesne Monthly*, October 1920.

41 *Indiana repeated*: *Pittsburgh Post*, September 24, October 3, 4, 16, 17, 23, 1920; *Indiana Evening Gazette*, September 18, 22, 24, 27, October 9, 18, 25, November 1, 8, 13, 19, 1920. Although Art spent only a year and a half at Indiana and compiled an underwhelming academic record,

he left his mark. The school would award him an honorary doctorate in 1975 and later name a residential hall in his honor.

42 *After the season*: *Pittsburgh Post*, January 30, 1921. Arthur Rooney Jr. Journal entry, November 28, 1995. Yale had enticed All-American tackle James Hogan to enroll with the offer of free tuition, a suite of rooms, a ten-day trip to Cuba, and proceeds from the sale of game scorecards. The American Tobacco Company sweetened the pot by giving Hogan a commission on every pack of cigarettes it sold in town.

42 *Georgetown was a baseball*: *The Hoya*, March 10, 1921; *Ye Domesday Booke* [Georgetown University Yearbook] 1921, no page; *Georgetown College Journal*, April 1921.

42 *Art chafed*: Timothy Rooney interview, December 8, 2001, *The Hoya*, February 12, 1921.

43 *O'Reilly hired*: *The Evening Star* [Washington DC], April 11, 12, 13, 1921; *Pittsburgh Post*, March 30, April 3, 10, 13, 1921.

43 *Back at Georgetown*: Dan Rooney interview, August 23, 2001; *Georgetown College Journal*, April 1921; *Georgetown Today*, September, 1970.

43 *Art signed*: Bob Broeg, "Baseball's in Rooney's Blood," *St. Louis Post-Dispatch*, February 15, 1975.

43 *But the 1921*: *Pittsburgh Post*, February 27, July 17, August 4, 7, 14, 1921.

44 *Art and Dan*: *Pittsburgh Post*, May 18, 22, 24 26, 27, June 2, 7, 8, 16, 21, 27, July 17, August 30, 1921, April 2, 1922.

44 *Days before*: *Duquesne Monthly*, September 1921.

3. On Life's Learning Fields

45 *Prohibition*: Just four days earlier, the U.S. census taker recorded Daniel's occupation as "hotel keeper."

45 *For Art*: Margaret Rooney Laughlin interview, February 2, 2001.

46 *The Rooneys*: For information on the Irish as gatekeepers, Barrett and Roediger, "Irish Everywhere."

47 *Art grew*: John Rooney interview, November 30, 2001; Msgr. Charles Owen Rice interview, August 16, 2001.

47 *On their own*: Barrett and Roediger, "Irish Everywhere," 16.

47 *The Irish, as*: Riess, *Touching Base*, 170–71; Barrett and Roediger, "Irish Everywhere," 1.

48 *Art was so*: Arthur J. Rooney interview, Pittsburgh, July 30, 1980; John

Rooney interview, Pittsburgh, November 30, 2001; *Pittsburgh Press*, July 30, 1980.

48   *Art saw*: *Pittsburgh Post*, June 1, 1925.

49   *Wheeling played*: Former *Pittsburgh Leader* sports editor Dick Guy, who had been out of work after the demise of his paper in 1923, became a catalyst in creating the MAL. Guy, who years earlier had managed Rooney's brief professional boxing career and written to Knute Rockne on his behalf, now put him in the Stogie's starting lineup. MAL fielded six teams: Cumberland (Maryland), Scottdale and Johnstown (Pennsylvania), and Fairmont, Clarksburg, and Wheeling (West Virginia). A Class C minor league, the Middle Atlantic was the second level from the bottom in the four-tiered minor league pyramid that the majors built during the 1920s. But MAL was producing more than its share of major leaguers at a time when the game was more competitive than ever.

49   *The brothers*: Kramer, ed., *Middle Atlantic League*; *Pittsburgh Post*, June 25, July 1, 1925.

49   *But the Rooneys'*: A few years after the 1925 season, when Dan Rooney was finishing up his studies in a Washington DC seminary, he went to see Joe Cronin play at Griffith Stadium and waved to him from the stands. Cronin came over between innings. "Father," Cronin said, "I don't know you, but you put me in a mind of a tough Irishman I played against in the Middle Atlantic League. His name was Dan Rooney." Dan, who had taken the name of Father Silas, responded, "That's me." Cronin's jaw dropped. "Holy God!" he exclaimed. "You're a priest!" Roy McHugh, "Ever-tough Dan Rooney A Hard-to-Beat Priest," *Pittsburgh Press*, January 11, 1981.

50   *Art and Dan's*: In 1926, Art returned to his old standby, the Northside Board of Trade, and homered in the Traders' first game, a victory in early May at the Saltworks. At one point that summer, the three oldest Rooney boys played with the Traders: Art at centerfield, Dan catcher and first base, and Jim at shortstop or third. Art and Dan played again for the Traders in 1927. Art and Dan also played that year in Ohio for Honus Wagner's team. In 1928, Art played for the Northside Civics and Bellevue. He played and managed the Civics through the 1932 season. In 1933, he played for the Ottie Cochranes and then left the field for good.

51   *Art and Dan returned*: John Rooney was indicted by a federal grand jury in 1927.

51   *Art had patterned*: Posey used the name Charles Cumbert while playing

for Duquesne, probably to stay eligible as a college player while he was already getting paid to play baseball.

51   *"One time"*: Arthur J. Rooney interview, July 30, 1980.

51   *Indeed, he was*: Ruck, *Sandlot Seasons*, 126–27.

52   *He had played*: Ruck, *Sandlot Seasons*, 126–27.

52   *The biggest sandlot*: *Pittsburgh Post*, November 26, 1925.

53   *No team wanted*: *Pittsburgh Post*, November 15, 22, December 20, 1925.

53   *The Pittsburgh Post*: *Pittsburgh Post*, December 12, 1925.

53   *Despite*: *Pittsburgh Post*, November 25, 1925.

54   *Though the* NFL: Peter King, "NFL Landmarks," *Sports Illustrated*, August 30, 1999.

55   *Pitt's freshmen*: Maggie Rooney's Scrapbook.

55   *At the postseason*: Arthur Rooney Jr. interview, June 4, 2003.

56   USC *humbled*: *Pittsburgh Post-Gazette*, January 6, 8, 28, 29, 1930.

56   *Art Rooney saw*: *Pittsburgh Post*, November 25, 1925.

56   *Hope Harvey*: *Pittsburgh Post*, October 11, 14, 18, 1925.

56   *Sandlot backers*: *Pittsburgh Post*, October 8, 10, 11, 1926.

57   *Hope Harvey*: *Pittsburgh Post*, October 13, 18, 1926.

57   *"The Canton Bulldogs"*: *Pittsburgh Post*, December 4, 1926.

57   *The Bulldogs*: Cope, *The Game that Was*, 126–27.

58   *In October 1926*: *Pittsburgh Post*, October 13, 18, 1926.

58   *Art approached*: Dan Rooney interview, August 23, 2001.

58   *Despite Art's*: *Pittsburgh Post-Gazette*, November 29, 1928.

58   *For Art*: Jamie Rooney interview, May 2, 2002.

59   *Politics, like sport*: Cope, *The Game that Was*, 134; Dan Rooney interview, November 21, 2001.

60   *Around the dining*: Jamie Rooney interview, May 2, 2002.

60   *Daniel Rooney*: Jamie Rooney interview, May 2, 2002; Arthur J. Rooney interview, July 30, 1980.

61   *Lawrence was*: Weber, *Don't Call Me Boss*, 5.

61   *Lawrence's mother*: Weber, *Don't Call Me Boss*, 3–9, 27; Jerry Lawrence interview, April 23, 2002.

61   *Art's other*: Thomas Coyne interview, May 18, 2003.

62   *William Larimer*: Weber, *Don't Call Me Boss*, 14–15.

62   *These lieutenants*: Interview with Arthur J. Rooney, February 25, 1981; Ron Cook, *Pittsburgh Press*, August 27, 1988.

62   *Art could*: The source for this information is a clipping in a scrapbook

kept by Art's mother, Maggie Rooney. No newspaper or dates are on the clippings, but the approximate date can be surmised by their placement.

62 *Coyne's alliance*: Timothy Rooney interview, Pittsburgh, December 8, 2001.

62 *"Coyne was"*: Ed Kiely interview, Pittsburgh, January 4, 2002, Pittsburgh.

62 *Art told*: Timothy Rooney interview, December 8, 2001.

63 *Coyne earned*: Weber, *Don't Call Me Boss*, 25; Philip Coyne interview, June 3, 2002; see the clippings file on Coyne in the Pennsylvania Room, Carnegie Library of Pittsburgh. Newspaper accounts include *Bulletin Index*, December 1, 1932; *Pittsburgh Press*, March 12, 1933, July 26, 1954; *Pittsburgh Post-Gazette*, March 2, 1948; and several clippings without identification as to source.

63 *Coyne controlled*: Hayllar, "The Accommodation," 117; Philip Coyne interview, June 3, 2002.

63 *Art became*: Timothy Rooney interview, December 8, 2001.

64 *In Prohibition*: Hayllar, "The Accommodation," 79, 90–91; Commission on Social Services, *Crime and Its Treatment*, 34–35.

64 *Betting parlors*: *Pittsburgh Post*, July 26, 1926. Hayllar, "The Accommodation," identifies Ray Sprigle as the author of this story, but there is no byline in the paper.

64 *Little Canada*: *Pittsburgh Post*, July 26, 1926.

64 *Northside vice*: *Pittsburgh Press*, July 30, August 2, 1932; Hayllar, "The Accommodation," 106–7.

64 *Despite the*: Hayllar, "The Accommodation," 106–7, 112–15; *Pittsburgh Press*, July 30, 1932, August 2, 1932.

64 *As Coyne's lieutenant*: Commonwealth of Pennsylvania incorporation papers, filed November 21, 1923.

65 *Joe Carr*: Hugh Carr interview, May 7, 2002; Margaret Rooney Laughlin interview, February 1, 2001.

65 *A savvy*: John Canning interview, April 24, 2002; Weisberg, "An Irishman."

65 *Netty kept*: *Pittsburgh Post*, September 21, 1926.

66 *Sporadic crackdowns*: *Pittsburgh Post*, July 26, 1926.

66 *Local officials*: Hayllar, "The Accommodation," 95–100.

66 *That summer*: *Pittsburgh Post*, June 11, 1928.

67 *When the indictments*: *Pittsburgh Post*, June 11, 1928; *Pittsburgh Sun-Telegraph*, June 13, 1928.

67   *After FDR's*: *Pittsburgh Post-Gazette*, November 29, 1928; Ray Sprigle, *Pittsburgh Post-Gazette*, February 12, 1936.

67   *Half a century*: Arthur J. Rooney Jr. interview, June 20, 2003; James P. Rooney interview, March 1, 1982.

67   *Certainly*: Pegram, *Battling Demon Rum*, 85–86.

68   *During his*: Arthur J. Rooney Jr. interview, June 20, 2003.

68   *Jaffe was*: Margaret Rooney Laughlin thought that Jaffe owned it, but she wasn't sure of her brother's precise involvement, and no documents formally link Rooney to the enterprise.

69   *Docked on*: Arthur Rooney Jr. Journal entry; Margaret Rooney Laughlin interview, May 22, 2002; *Pittsburgh Post-Gazette*, December 2, 1933.

69   *"Milt had"*: Arthur Rooney Jr. Journal entry; Dan Rooney interview, August 23, 2001. Milt was married to Ruth Jaffe, whose father had been a Northside cop known as Bundles because he was on the take and often seen with a package under his arm. Ruth had dated fighter Harry Greb before marrying Jaffe. In later years, Art and Kathleen often socialized with the Jaffes.

69   *Art also*: Ruck, *Sandlot Seasons*, 137–69.

70   *The perennial*: *Pittsburgh Post-Gazette*, October 22, December 3, 1928.

4. Dreams, Depression, and Commitment

72   *Art courted*: *Pittsburgh Post-Gazette*, October 21, 24, 28, 1929.

72   *By kickoff*: *Pittsburgh Post-Gazette*, October 8, 1929.

72   *But that fall*: *Pittsburgh Post-Gazette*, December 27, 1929.

73   *During the off-season*: "Raid Halts Show Boat Gaiety," *Pittsburgh Sun-Telegraph*, May 15, 1930, 1.

73   *The Majestics*: Unidentified clipping in Maggie Rooney's scrapbook of press coverage.

73   *Unable to entice*: Clipping in Maggie Rooney's scrapbook of press coverage.

74   *The depression was*: *Value of a Dollar*, 182, 186, 187; Clipping in Maggie Rooney's scrapbook of press coverage.

74   *The conference*: Clipping in Maggie Rooney's scrapbook of press coverage.

75   *Art's reluctance*: Pegram, *Battling Demon Rum*.

76 *A cunning businesswoman*: Margaret Rooney Laughlin interview, May 22, 2002.

76 *As Father O'Shea*: Timothy V. Rooney interview, June 20, 2002.

76 *Tales of Dan's*: Some versions of this story say that it was Oscar Owens, another Grays pitcher, who knocked Dan Rooney unconscious with a pitch.

77 *After the 1928*: Sam D'Onofrio, *The Bonaventure*, May 20, 1949; clipping in Maggie Rooney's scrapbook of press coverage.

77 *Eighteen months*: Ron Cook, *Pittsburgh Press*, August 27, 1988; James P. Rooney interview, March 1, 1982.

77 *While at Pitt*: James P. Rooney interview, March 1, 1982; clipping in Maggie Rooney's scrapbook of press coverage.

78 *Hailing him*: clipping in Maggie Rooney's scrapbook of press coverage.

78 *In keeping with*: William Pfarr, "Sidewalks of Pittsburgh." The source for this undated newspaper clipping is a scrapbook kept by Margaret Murray Rooney covering 1930–32.

78 *Jim voted for*: Clipping in Maggie Rooney's scrapbook of press coverage. This story was datelined February 1931.

78 *"All in all,"*: Clipping in Maggie Rooney's scrapbook of press coverage.

79 *Editorials*: Clipping in Maggie Rooney's scrapbook of press coverage. The school board fight occurred during the first few months of 1931.

80 *After the slate*: Arthur J. Rooney interview, July 30, 1980.

80 *Meanwhile*: Hallyar, "The Accommodation."

81 *Some indictments*: Weber, *Don't Call Me Boss*, 38–46.

81 *"My father"*: Weisberg, "An Irishman."

81 *While Lawrence*: Weber, *Don't Call Me Boss*, 42–44.

83 *If Kass had*: Dan Rooney interview, April 17, 2001; Margaret Rooney Laughlin interview, September 24, 2004.

84 *The Rooney and Murray*: Margaret Rooney Laughlin interview, September 24, 2004.

84 *When Art and Kass*: Dan Rooney interview, April 30, 2002; stories from various Rooney relatives and Art Rooney Jr.'s journals.

85 *Despite taking*: Tom Birks, *Pittsburgh Press*, September 1932; Paul Kurtz, *Pittsburgh Press*, September 1932; Clipping in Maggie Rooney's scrapbook of press coverage.

85 *As Art had*: Tom Birks, *Pittsburgh Press*, September 1932; Clipping in Maggie Rooney's scrapbook of press coverage.

86   *Besides Jim*: Paul Kurtz, *Pittsburgh Press*, September 1932; Clipping in Maggie Rooney's scrapbook of press coverage.

88   *Art embodied*: Clipping in Maggie Rooney's scrapbook of press coverage.

88   *Art marshaled*: Cope, *The Game that Was*, 123–24; Timothy V. Rooney interview, June 20, 2002.

88   *As the season*: Harry Keck, *Pittsburgh Post-Gazette*, no date, in Maggie Rooney's scrapbook of press coverage.

89   *In Pittsburgh*: This clipping, headlined "$30,000 Reported Paid in Kidnapping of Jaffe," is in Margaret Rooney's scrapbook; no date and no paper, ca. spring or summer 1932.

91   *Meanwhile*: *Journal of the House of Representatives*, January 3, 1933, State of Pennsylvania.

92   *"Jim was"*: Timothy Rooney interview, December 8, 2001.

93   *Two months*: Hallyar, "The Accommodation"; *Pittsburgh Post-Gazette*, May 18, 1933.

93   *Until the 1930s*: Weber, *Don't Call Me Boss*, 33; Ray Downey interview, September 13, 2001.

93   *But the depression*: Clippings file on James Coyne in the Pennsylvania Room, Carnegie Library of Pittsburgh, especially *Pittsburgh Post-Gazette*, no date, 1954.

93   *Art shared Coyne's*: Weber, *Don't Call Me Boss*, 56–59, 120; clippings in Coyne file, November 23, 1934; *Pittsburgh Press*, July 26, 1954; Pennsylvania Room, Carnegie Library of Pittsburgh. In the spring of 1948, Coyne and Republican county chairman James F. Malone endorsed Art Rooney as a delegate to the Republican Convention from the 32nd Congressional District in an effort to block followers of Governor James Duff. Art was described as "a remnant of the organization once dominated by Coyne." *Pittsburgh Post-Gazette*, March 2, 1948.

5. Pittsburgh Joins the NFL

96   *When owners convened*: Halas, *Halas by Halas*, 150, 170.

97   *Art never worked*: Articles of Incorporation, Pittsburgh Pirates Football Club (in possession of the Pittsburgh Steelers). The team's directors included Dick Guy, the sportswriter who once had written to Knute Rockne on Art's behalf; Chris McCormick, a Northsider who had handled business matters for Art's sandlot teams; Martin Flanagan, a Duquesne alumnus and lawyer; John O'Donnell, Art's ward boss; and Jim Rooney.

98 *They settled*: Margaret Rooney Laughlin interview, September 24, 2004.

99 *A sensational-looking*: Jeremy Schaap, "Cinderella Man," *Sports Illustrated*, May 9, 2005, 57.

100 *On Wednesday, September 20*: Clippings from Steeler microfilm archives of 1933 season, no date or byline.

101 *A telling aside*: Smith, "Outside the Pale," 255–81.

101 *After Pittsburgh*: The newspaper article is from Reel-1933, microfilmed holdings in the Pittsburgh Steelers archives, no byline or date.

102 *On election day*: *Pittsburgh Post-Gazette*, November 8, 9, 1933; *Pittsburgh Sun-Telegraph*, November 9, 1933.

103 *The NFL had*: According to www.Kenn.com, the official Kenn Tomasch Web site, NFL average attendance in 1934 was 8,211 and grew to 12,041 in 1935. Its attendance probably exceeded the league average, but records were not kept until 1934. It is likely that 1933 attendance was less than the 1934 average.

104 *"Between you"*: James P. Rooney interview, March 30, 1982.

104 *Most of Art's*: A majority of the board of directors also hailed from Rooney's neighborhood, and so did those who worked for the organization.

104 *Art also signed*: See Cope, *The Game that Was*, 59–70, for an oral history with Blood.

106 *On the bright*: 2001 Media Guide, Pittsburgh Steelers, 265, and www.kenn.com. The newspaper article is from Reel One, microfilmed holders in the Pittsburgh Steelers archives, no date or byline.

106 *After the regular*: Halas, *Halas by Halas*, 178; Daniel Lackner interview, October 5, 2001.

107 *He also needed*: Davis, *Papa Bear*, 95–98.

107 *Art and Eagles*: Arthur Daley, "Bell's Monument," *New York Times*, February 1, 1973.

108 *Frances bankrolled*: Peterson, *Pigskin*, 112.

108 *Art challenged*: Peterson, *Pigskin*, 113.

108 *"Every year"*: As quoted in Arthur Daley, "Bell's Monument," *New York Times*, February 1, 1973.

109 *Mara and Halas*: Davis, *Papa Bear*, 130; Halas, *Halas by Halas*, 158–59; Peterson, *Pigskin*, 119–20.

109 *Instituting*: Harry Keck, *Pittsburgh Sun-Telegraph*, May 1, 1934.

109 *That winter*: Jack McGinley interview, August 14, 2001.

109 *Prohibition's end*: Hugh Carr interview, May 7, 2002.

111 *In September 1935*: Damon Runyon, September 17, 1935, Steelers Archives.

112 *On October 18, 1935*: Since the birth of the first known Arthur Rooney in Montreal in 1850, the names of the first-born male in the Rooney family have alternated between Arthur and Daniel, as each was named for his grandfather. The youngest is Daniel Rooney, son of Arthur J. Rooney II, current president of the Pittsburgh Steelers.

112 *Art and Bach*: Kowett, *The Rich Who Own Sports*, 33.

113 *Pittsburgh finished*: Ruck, "Art Rooney," 255.

113 *Hope dawned*: "NFL Draft Has Outgrown Tight Times," *Washington Post*, April 22, 1988.

114 *Ticket manager*: Hugh Carr interview, May 7, 2002.

116 *Before heading*: Pittsburgh Pirates Football Club minutes, January 7, 1937; stock certificate transfer August 18, 1937.

6. Rooney's Ride

118 *After listening*: Livingston, *Their Turf*, 146; Anderson, *Red Smith Reader*, 106–8. Smith writes that Rooney bet $20, not $200, but neither Rooney's betting history nor the odds and the payoffs on these races support the lower number.

118 *Mara's advice*: Bob Considine, no paper, July 28, 1937, Steelers microfilm archives.

118 *The year before*: Hillenbrand, *Seabiscuit*, 35–45; Livingston, *Their Turf*, 140–46.

118 *Undefeated since*: "Empire Track Mark Broken by Sea Biscuit," *Times Union*, July 25, 1937.

118 *Seabiscuit broke*: Bryan Field, "Seabiscuit Defeats Jesting in Record Time at Empire," *New York Times*, July 25, 1937.

119 *In the next*: Biederman, "Art Rooney"; *New York Times*, July 25, 1937.

119 *Art's day*: Bill Corum, *Journal American*, July 28, 1937.

119 *With Empire City*: Joe Williams, *World Telegram*, August 30, 1937. Given the frequency with which the same stories and comments are reported by multiple sports writers, it is difficult to know which writer broke the story and which ones are quoting what was printed elsewhere.

119 *Art and Buck*: Lardner, *It Beats Working*, 57–59; Mitchell, "The Markee," 20–26.

120   *"The next morning"*: Anderson, *Red Smith Reader*, 107; Wellington Mara interview, May 2001.

120   *Saratoga, one of racing's*: "Parade of Fashions," *Times Union*, July 25, 1937.

120   *After the workouts*: Wellington Mara letter to Rob Ruck, July 25, 2005.

121   *Art then settled*: Betts, *Across the Board*, 238–53.

121   *Saratoga had spent*: "Improved Saratoga Will Open Tomorrow," *New York Times*, July 25, 1937; Joe Williams, "Time When Rooney Cleaned Up," *Pittsburgh Press*, April 13, 1940.

121   *Before the first race*: Bill Corum, "It's Art But They Don't Like It," *Journal American*, July 27, 1937.

122   *"I had Tim"*: Anderson, *Red Smith Reader*, 107.

122   *In the fourth race*: Biederman, "Art Rooney."

122   *Art's pick, Quel Jeu*: Lardner, *It Beats Working*, 57–59

122   *"Rooney wasn't betting"*: Bob Considine, no paper, July 28, 1937, Pittsburgh Steelers archives.

123   *All of Saratoga*: Bill Corum, "Saratoga Springs," *Journal American*, July 28, 1937; Toney Betts, "Star Plunger backing Myer [sic] in Clubhouse," *New York Post*, June 2, 1938.

123   *In his Tuesday morning*: Bill Corum, "It's Art But They Don't Like It," no paper, July 27, 1937; Toney Betts, "Star Plunger Backing Myer [sic] in Clubhouse," *New York Post*, June 2, 1938, Pittsburgh Steelers archives.

124   *Syndicated columnist*: Bob Considine, no paper, July 28, 1937, Pittsburgh Steelers archives.

126   *Reporters and bookies*: Bob Considine, no paper, July 28, 1937, Pittsburgh Steelers archives.

126   *Damon Runyon*: Damon Runyon, King Features Syndicate, no date or paper, Pittsburgh Steelers archives.

126   *By Tuesday*: Biederman, "Art Rooney," 7–8, 52–53.

127   *Toney Betts revealed*: Toney Betts, "Saratoga Springs," *New York Post*, July 28, 1937.

127   *Art's traveling companion*: Toney Betts, *New York Post*, no date, Pittsburgh Steelers archives.

127   *A few writers*: Kent Hunter, *Evening Journal and New York American*, July 28, 1937.

128   *Art liked reporters*: Kent Hunter, *Evening Journal and New York Ameri-*

can, August 31, 1937; Prospectus, "How Rooney Cleaned up $100,000 in Single Day," no date or paper, July 1937, Pittsburgh Steelers archives.

128 *He stopped first*: Frank Ortell, *The Telegram*, August 6, 30, 1937; no byline, United Press, Pittsburgh Steelers archives.

129 *By Wednesday, August 4*: Frank Ortell, *The Telegram*, August 6, 1937; no byline, United Press, August 31, 1937.

129 *As Mara regaled*: W. S. (Bill) Farnsworth, *Evening Journal and New York American*, August 9, 1937.

129 *In two days*: Bob Considine, no paper, July 28, 1937, Pittsburgh Steelers archives; Joe Williams, *World Telegram*, August 30, 1937.

130 *On Friday*: Wellington Mara interview, May 2002. Tim Rooney's daughter, Kathleen, married Tim Mara's grandson, Chris Mara.

130 *The next day*: Frank Ortell, *The Telegram*, August 13, 1937.

130 *With his team*: Frank Ortell, *The Telegram*, August 30, 1937.

131 *It mattered less*: AP, August 31, 1937, Pittsburgh Steelers archives; Toney Betts, "Plunger Places Limit on Losses," *New York Post*, no date, Pittsburgh Steelers archives.

132 *To everyone else*: *New York Herald Tribune*, September 2, 1937.

132 *At the end*: Economic History Service, conversion tables, http://eh.net.

133 *Considine reported*: Al Abrams, "Sidelights on Sports," *Pittsburgh Post-Gazette*, no date, March 1943.

133 *Art's success*: Les Biederman, *Pittsburgh Press*, no date, Pittsburgh Steelers archives.

134 *While Art's story*: Toney Betts, "Those Daring Young Men," *New York Post*, no date, Pittsburgh Steelers archives.

134 *But Art's real edge*: Anderson, *Red Smith Reader*, 106; Wellington Mara interview, May 2002.

134 *Art often said*: Jerry Lawrence interview, April 23, 2002.

135 *Art's success*: Bob Considine, no date or paper, Pittsburgh Steelers archives; "Sports Stew," *Pittsburgh Post-Gazette*, July 23, 1937, Pittsburgh Steelers archives; Toney Betts, "Those Daring Young Men," *New York Post*, January 4, 1939.

7. Between the Races and the Fights

136 *The press*: Vincent Rooney, "Grid Pirates May Surprise," *Pittsburgh Press*, no date, September 1937, Pittsburgh Steelers archives.

136 *Blood still*: Jack Murphy, *New York Post*, November 6, 1937.

137   *Blood was*: David Condon, "In the Wake of the News," *Chicago Tribune*, November 25, 1967.

137   *After the*: Patricia Rooney interview, July 20, 2004.

137   *Blood might*: *Pittsburgh Post-Gazette*, October 27, 28, November 22, 1937. The Pirates' road attendance climbed from 11,250 to 17,071 per game.

138   *The Post-Gazette's*: Havey Boyle, "Mirrors of Sport: Hope Still Lingers for Pirates," *Pittsburgh Post-Gazette*, October 18–23, 1937.

138   *At this stage*: The best portrait of Byron White is Hutchinson, *Whizzer White*.

138   *Byron White*: Hutchinson, *Whizzer White*, 14–16.

139   *White had*: Hutchinson, *Whizzer White*, 55. Total yards include those gained by rushing, receiving, returning interceptions, and running back punts and kickoffs.

139   *The most talked about*: Havey Boyle, *Pittsburgh Post-Gazette*, May 18, September 6, 1938.

139   *It was no*: "Here's How and Why," *Buffalo Times* September, 1938.

140   *The publicity*: Shirley Povich, *Washington Post*, August 26, 1988.

140   *An early riser*: Al Abrams, *Pittsburgh Post-Gazette,* May 16, 1938.

140   *Art returned*: News clippings, no source or byline, March 17, April 19, 1938, Pittsburgh Steeler archives.

141   *Art had begun*: *Pittsburgh Press*, April 22, 1937.

141   *Though Art missed*: Claire Burcky, *Pittsburgh Press*, May 26, 28,1938.

141   *But it appeared*: Hutchinson, *Whizzer White*, 79–80, 90–93, 98; White's comment to *New Haven Journal-Courier* June 28, 1971, quoted in Hutchinson, *Whizzer White*, 98.

142   *The next day*: "Rooney Predicts Grid Crown After Addition of Whizzer," AP, August 2,1938, Pittsburgh Steeler archives.

142   *Columnists*: *Buffalo Evening News*, August 2, 1938.

143   *Art was also*: Cope, *The Game that Was*, 129.

143   *White emerged*: Hutchinson, *Whizzer White*, 99–100; *Pittsburgh Post-Gazette*, November 15, 1939.

144   *Frustrated*: "Sports Stew," *Pittsburgh Post-Gazette*, August 10, 1938.

144   *Although White*: Ray Ryan, *Buffalo Courier*, September 10, 1938; Bob Stedler, *Buffalo Evening News*, September 10, 1938; Frank Wakefield, *Buffalo Evening News*, September 10, 1938; Francis Dunn, *Buffalo Times*, no date, Pittsburgh Steelers archives.

144   *But reporters*: *Pittsburgh Press*, September 11, 1938.

144 *The Lions*: Francis Dunn, "Whizzer White Rates All Those Adjectives," *Buffalo Times*, September 10, 1938.

144 *Returning home*: *Pittsburgh Post-Gazette*, September 12, 1938.

145 *The Eagles*: September 17, 1938, no paper, Pittsburgh Steelers archives.

145 *A Buffalo*: "Here's How and Why," *Buffalo Times*, September 17, 1938.

145 *A few days*: Jack Sell, *Pittsburgh Post-Gazette*, September 19, 1938.

145 *"If I find"*: *Pittsburgh Post-Gazette*, September 20, 1938; "Rooney's Stand on His Grid Pirates," *Sun-Telegraph*, September 20, 1938; *Oil City Derrick*, September 28, 1938.

146 *For his part*: Henry McLemore, UPI, September 22, 1938, quoted in Hutchinson, *Whizzer White*, 110.

146 *In Pittsburgh's*: Gene Ward, "A Lone Buccaneer," *Daily News*, September 28, 1938.

146 *Ward's story*: Hutchinson, *Whizzer White*, 112.

146 *The blocking*: Cope, *The Game that Was*, 131.

147 *White played*: Hutchinson, *Whizzer White*, 122.

147 *His teammates*: Jack Sell, *Pittsburgh Post-Gazette*, October 5, 1938.

147 *The Pirates*: Jack Sell, *Pittsburgh Post-Gazette*, October 10, 1938.

147 *But hiring*: *Pittsburgh Post-Gazette*, September 30, 1938; *Pittsburgh Sun-Telegraph*, September 2, 1938.

148 *Incensed*: Jack Sell, *Pittsburgh Post-Gazette*, October 11, 1938; *Pittsburgh Press*, October 12, 1938.

148 *Art scoffed*: *Pittsburgh Post-Gazette*, October 12, 13, 1938; *Pittsburgh Sun-Telegraph*, November 16, 1938.

148 *Art argued*: *Pittsburgh Sun-Telegraph*, October 11, 12, 1938; *Pittsburgh Post-Gazette*, October 11, 13 1938; *Pittsburgh Press*, October 12, 1938.

148 *Rooney continued*: Claire Burcky, *Pittsburgh Press*, October 11, 1938.

148 *Perhaps Art*: Jimmy Powers, *New York Daily News*, October 14, 17, 1938.

148 *Even Bert*: The $35,000 estimate comes from Hutchinson, *Whizzer White*, 117.

148 *With so*: Claire Burcky, *Pittsburgh Press*, October 21, 1938; Jack Sell, *Pittsburgh Post-Gazette*, October 24, 1938.

149 *Nevertheless*: *Pittsburgh Post-Gazette*, October 31, 1938; Peterson, *Pigskin*, vii–viii.

149 *Rooney marketed*: H. L. McLemore, United Press, September 22, 1938, quoted in Hutchinson, *Whizzer White*, 110.

149 *"The hard-bitten"*: Chester Smith, *Pittsburgh Press*, November 3, 1938.

149 *Before the final*: Harry Keck, *Sun-Telegraph*, November 2, 1938; Jack Sell, *Pittsburgh Post-Gazette*, November 7, 1938.

150 *In the final*: Hutchinson, *Whizzer White*, 113, 117. A curious story appeared in Jack James's "Hit or Miss" column in the *Los Angeles Examiner* during the trip. James wrote about a Pittsburgh defeat in 1934 that he claimed had netted Art $20,000. James said that Art had bet $10,000 at even money that the New York Giants would not beat the Pirates by more than a touchdown and another $10,000 that the Pirates would score in the game. It looked as if Rooney would lose both bets when the Pirates fell behind 13–0 late in the fourth quarter. But on fourth down and 21 yards to go, Harp Vaughan threw a long pass for a Pirate touchdown, putting the Pirates on the board and covering one of Rooney's bets. On the kickoff, the Giants' Harry Newman caught the ball at the five-yard line and ran untouched for 93 yards. But Vaughan caught him from behind at the 2-yard line and thus, James alleged, won another $10,000 for Art. James wrote his column in a celebratory tone, not suggesting that Rooney had done anything improper by betting on his team. Ray Ryan had written something very different on the eve of the Pirates game in Buffalo in September two months before. He explained that Rooney "never has bet a dime on his Pirates and doesn't intend to. As frank as an old shoe, the Pirate boss told that he put through a league rule forbidding owners and players to wager on games with drastic penalties for all violations." Ryan's account is more plausible. Rooney always maintained he never bet on football. But with his image as the greatest plunger in America preceding him, Art was often portrayed as something he was not. Jack James, "Hit or Miss," *Los Angeles Examiner*, November 13, 1938; Ray Ryan, "Whizzer White Sparkles," *Buffalo Courier*, September 10, 1938.

150 *Pittsburgh had hit*: David Condon, "In the Wake of the News," *Chicago Tribune*, November 25, 1967.

150 *Blood missed*: Cope, *The Game that Was*, 130; *Pittsburgh Post-Gazette*, November 12, 1938.

151 *Before embarking*: Havey Boyle, *Pittsburgh Post-Gazette*, November 11, 21, 1938.

151 *On game day*: Cope, *The Game that Was*, 134–35.

152 *He told*: quoted in Hutchinson, *Whizzer White*, 113; *Baltimore Sun*, June 26, 1971.

152 *White's accomplishments*: Havey Boyle, *Pittsburgh Post-Gazette*, November 27, 1938, and undated article in late December 1938, Pittsburgh Steelers archives.

152 *Art told White*: Ray Hill, "The Sports Parade," no date or paper, Pittsburgh Steelers archives.

152 *Art protested*: Havey Boyle, "Whizzer Made No Kickback," *Pittsburgh Post-Gazette*, ca. February 1939, Pittsburgh Steelers archives. Dennis Hutchinson accepts the contention that White "refused for half of the season to accept his paychecks and absolutely refused to receive any proceeds from exhibition games." Hutchinson, *Whizzer White*, 115.

152 *Before sailing*: Jack Sell, *Pittsburgh Press*, no date, Pittsburgh Steelers archives.

153 *Art, boxer Billy*: Shirley Povich, *Washington Post*, August 26, 1988. Povich bases his remarks on comments from Bo Bregman, whom he described as a friend of both Rooney and Jaffe (mistakenly called Harry Jaffe). Other accounts suggest that Jaffe had already relinquished his shares; Timothy Conn interview, May 1, 2002.

8. Returning to the Ring

154 *If nothing*: David Condon, "In the Wake of the News," *Chicago Tribune*, November 25, 1967.

155 *As much as*: Copies of the telegrams are in the Pittsburgh Steelers archives, Reel-1939. Punctuation added to Rooney's telegram.

155 *Boxing, however*: *Pittsburgh Courier*, August 19, 1939, 15; Roy McHugh interview, March 1, 2001. We are heavily indebted to Roy McHugh and his manuscript on boxing in Pittsburgh, "When Pittsburgh Was a Fight Town."

156 *As a boy*: Jack McGinley interview, August 14, 2001.

156 *In March*: Chester Smith, "New Boxing Combine Welcomed Here," *Pittsburgh Press*, no date; Regis Welsh, *Pittsburgh Press*, "There Is Going to Be High-Class Fight Promotion Here this Summer," no date, both from Pittsburgh Steelers archives.

156 *Bernard McGinley*: Regis Welsh, *Pittsburgh Press*, no date, September and October 1, 1937; Eddie Beachler, "Sports Stew—Served Hot," *Pittsburgh Press*, August 16, 1938, Pittsburgh Steelers archives.

157 *Art saw*: Toney Betts, no date, Pittsburgh Steelers archives, Reel-1939.

158   *Conn soon*: John Henry Lewis, whom Gus Greenlee managed, had recently relinquished the title because of failing vision.

158   *Betts, who*: Toney Betts, no date, Pittsburgh Steelers archives, Reel-1939.

159   *Over a career*: McHugh, "When Pittsburgh Was a Fight Town."

159   *Charles Burley*: McHugh, "When Pittsburgh Was a Fight Town"; August Wilson interview, March 19, 1991.

160   *Only one discordant*: McHugh, "When Pittsburgh Was a Fight Town"; *Pittsburgh Sun-Telegraph*, July 26, 1938.

160   *Rooney-McGinley*: At $5,000 a year, the job was a political plum, and Art had called in several chits to help Boyle get it. Boyle would repay Art by hiring his sister Marie as his stenographer.

161   *Emerging*: Regis Welsh, *Pittsburgh Press*, no date, Pittsburgh Steelers archives; Havey Boyle, *Pittsburgh Post-Gazette*, July 18, 1939.

162   *Boxers fought*: A card generally scheduled between 32 and 36 rounds of boxing. Most of the time, three fights were slated for six rounds and two for four. The main event was always a 10-rounder.

162   *By the time*: By the late 1940s, prices had climbed to $1.50, $2.95, $3.95, and $6.00.

163   *The fighters*: Jack McGinley interview, August 14, 2001.

163   *In many cities*: Jack McGinley interview, August 14, 2001.

164   *Art wooed*: Chester Smith, *Pittsburgh Press*, January 13, 1937.

165   *He had no*: Jack Sell, *Pittsburgh Post-Gazette*, August 25, 1939.

165   *That summer*: Al Abrams, *Pittsburgh Post-Gazette*, July 12, 1939.

165   *Pittsburgh fans*: *Pittsburgh Post Gazette*, September 15, 1939.

165   *Green Bay*: Peterson, *Pigskin*, 116–17; Cope, *The Game that Was*, 130–31.

166   *After the Bears*: Harry Keck, *Pittsburgh Sun-Telegraph*, September 20, 1939; Claire Burcky, *Pittsburgh Press*, October 3, 1939; Marx, *Eighteenth Brumaire*.

166   *The national press*: Dan Parker column, no date or newspaper, Pittsburgh Steelers archives.

168   *With Coyne*: *Bulletin Index*, September 21, 1939.

169   *Antipathy*: Pittsburgh Steelers archives, Reel-1939.

169   *Art campaigned*: Frank White, *New York Post*, November 7, 1939; *Pittsburgh Post-Gazette*, November 15, 1939.

169   *The team's*: November 27, 1939, no date or byline, Pittsburgh Steelers archives.

169 *Art responded*: "Rooney Dizzy Denying Pirate Sale Rumors," *Pittsburgh Post-Gazette*, November 15, 1939; "Gets Offer For Pirates," *New York Times*, November 28, 1939.

170 *Bruised*: Claire Burcky, *Pittsburgh Press*, November 27, 1939.

170 *Art, who*: *Pittsburgh Press*, December 18, 1939.

171 *After New Year's*: Dan Rooney interview, December 5, 2001.

9. Season of Reckoning

172 *The Passionists*: *Pittsburgh Press*, January 29, 1940.

173 *Without Sutherland*: John Kieran, "Sports of the Times," *New York Times*, no date, Pittsburgh Steelers archives.

173 *On the other*: *New York Times*, November 28, 1939.

173 *Out of*: Art also began taking the family on an annual pilgrimage to St. Anne de Beaupre, a religious shrine in Quebec; Dan Lackner interview, October 5, 2001; "Easter Walk is Rite of Passage," *Pittsburgh Post-Gazette*, March 28, 2002.

174 *That weekend*: Dan Lackner interview, October 5, 2001, August 28, 2004. Other men at these retreats were Alan Reynolds, secretary to the president of Farmers National Bank; Martin Flanagan, a Northsider who served as attorney for the football team and whose brother was a priest; Jim Ferry; Charlie Delehanty, sales manager, U.S. Rubber Co. on the Northside; and Matt Pauley, of Pauley Construction.

175 *Calling his*: In Ebbw Vale, the mountain village in Wales where Art's father had been born and his great-grandfather and grandfather had worked as puddlers, the local rugby team, which formed long after the Rooneys had left, took the name Steelmen.

175 *Chet Smith*: Chester Smith, *Pittsburgh Press*, March 3, 1940.

176 *There were*: *Pittsburgh Post-Gazette*, June 26, 1940; Harry Keck, *Sun-Telegraph*, July 20, 1940.

176 *Art was*: *Pittsburgh Press*, June 23, 1940.

176 *Meanwhile*: Chester Smith, "Lesson 1, How to Get A Headache," *Pittsburgh Press*, no date, Pittsburgh Steelers archives.

178 *Jacobs never*: Regis Welsh, *Pittsburgh Press*, September 8, 1940; *Collyer's Eye and Baseball World*, September 14, 1940; *New York Times*, September 15, 1940.

178 *Art saw*: Havey Boyle, *Pittsburgh Post-Gazette*, July 26, 1940.

179 *The signs*: Chester Smith, *Pittsburgh Press*, July 31, 1940; Arthur Daley, "Sports of the Times," *New York Times*, December 28, 1940.

179   *Art had*: Havey Boyle, *Pittsburgh Post-Gazette*, September 4, 1940.

180   *Coming off*: Harry Keck, "Steelers Having Best Season," *Pittsburgh Sun-Telegraph*, no date, Pittsburgh Steelers archives.

180   *A tie*: Bob Considine, *Daily Mirror*, September 16, 1940.

181   *No team*: Chester Smith, "Grid's Larry MacPhail Here Tomorrow," *Pittsburgh Press*, no date, Pittsburgh Steelers archives.

181   *Injuries*: R. G. Lynch, *Milwaukee Journal*, October 25, 1940.

182   *"The seamy"*: Shirley Povich, *Washington Post*, November 6, 1940.

182   *The loss*: Arthur Daley, "Sports of the Times," *New York Times*, July 14, 1943.

183   *After the*: *Pittsburgh Press*, December 9, 1940; Harry Keck, *Pittsburgh Sun-Telegraph*, December 10, Chester Smith, *Pittsburgh Press*, December 10, 1940.

183   *Still*: The Steelers' corporate entity was still called the Pittsburgh Pirates Football Club, Inc.

184   *The Eagles*: Minute Book of the Philadelphia Eagles, December 11, 12, 1940, Pittsburgh Steelers archives; Minutes of the Pittsburgh Pirates Football Club, December 2, 11, 12, 28 30, 1940, Pittsburgh Steelers archives.

184   *Notes of*: Minute Book of the Philadelphia Eagles, December 30, 1940, Pittsburgh Steelers archives; Minutes of the Pittsburgh Pirates Football Club, January 8, 9, 10, 13, April 2, 1941, Pittsburgh Steelers archives.

184   *But the* NFL: Harry Keck, *Pittsburgh Sun-Telegraph*, December 10, 1940.

184   *Alex Thompson*: *Times Herald*, December 10, 1940.

185   *Philadelphia*: Bill Dooly, "Bert Bell Beaming Again," *Philadelphia Record*, December 11, 1940.

185   *The sale*: Havey Boyle, "Thoughts on the Local Football Sale," *Pittsburgh Post-Gazette*, no date, Pittsburgh Steelers archives.

186   *Thompson*: The first article has no date or paper attached; Havey Boyle, "Mirrors of Sport," *Pittsburgh Post-Gazette*, no date, Pittsburgh Steelers archives.

186   *Art pitched*: *Pittsburgh Press*, April 4, 1941; "'Iron Men' Out, Local Pro Gridders Back to Their Old Steelers Name," *Pittsburgh Sun-Telegraph*, April 8, 1941; unidentified Philadelphia paper, April 4, 1941, Pittsburgh Steelers archives; Pat Livingston, *Pittsburgh Press*, September 4, 1975.

187   *After the*: Minutes of the Pittsburgh Pirates Football Club, April 1941, Pittsburgh Steelers archives.

187 *Having voted*: Minutes of April 1941, and August 9, 1941, special meeting of the board of directors of the Eagles held in Hershey PA, Pittsburgh Steelers Archives; Minutes of Philadelphia Eagles Pro Football Club, Inc., September 21, 22, 1944, Pittsburgh Steelers archives.

187 *The Press: Pittsburgh Post-Gazette*, April 4, 5, 1941.

187 *Rooney and Bell*: Unidentified Philadelphia paper, April 4, 1941, Pittsburgh Steelers archives; Lewis Burton, "The Lowdown," *Sun-Telegraph*, no date; Vic Wall, "All Angles," *Pittsburgh Post-Gazette*, no date.

187 *"We have"*: no date or byline, Pittsburgh Steeler archives, Reel-1941.

188 *"It is no"*: Chester Smith, *Pittsburgh Press*, April 5, 8, 1941.

10. The World at War

190 *In a few months*: Harold Weissman, no date or paper, Pittsburgh Steelers archives.

190 *A month*: Harry Keck, *Pittsburgh Sun-Telegraph*, no date, May 1948, Pittsburgh Steelers archives.

191 *For Conn*: Jacobs had threatened to substitute Buddy Baer for Conn in the June 18 title fight; "Uncle Mike Got Break When Baer Stood Up," *Pittsburgh Press*, no date or byline, Pittsburgh Steelers archives.

191 *But Art*: *Pittsburgh Sun-Telegraph*, May 28, 1941.

191 *Jimmy Smith had*: Frank Deford, "The Boxer and the Blonde," *Sports Illustrated*, June 17, 1985. Smith's club had been busted by federal agents in the same raid that closed James Coyne's Monaca Club in Oakland.

192 *Back on the Northside*: Dan Rooney interview, October 1, 2004. The newlyweds went to Hollywood, where Conn starred in *The Pittsburgh Kid*, a film about a fighter from Pittsburgh. The movie was less than an artistic success, and Conn joked that when he didn't like a visitor, he would take him to his basement and show him the film. Conn could have stuck around Hollywood and played the lead in a movie about Gentleman Jim Corbett, but he had little interest in acting. The part went to another ex-prizefighter, Errol Flynn.

193 *On August 1*: Chester Smith, "Recess Ends for Boys of Roo-Bell Tech," *Pittsburgh Press*, no date, Pittsburgh Steelers archives.

193 *Few players*: Claire Burcky, "Sports Stew," *Pittsburgh Press*, no date, Pittsburgh Steelers archives.

193 *Chet Smith*: Chester Smith, *Pittsburgh Press*, "Recess Ends for Boys of Roo-Bell Tech," no date, Pittsburgh Steelers archives.

193   *Art arrived*: "Rooney and Bell Views Differ After Early Look at Steelers," no date or byline, Pittsburgh Steelers archives.

194   *At dinner*: Havey Boyle, "Mirrors of Sport," *Pittsburgh Post-Gazette,* no date, Pittsburgh Steelers archives.

195   *After the game*: McCambridge, *America's Game*, 45.

195   *The Steelers*: Eddie Beachler, *Pittsburgh Press*, September 25, 1941.

195   *Donelli's loyalties*: Harry Keck, *Pittsburgh Sun-Telegraph*, September 25, 1941; Clair Burcky, *Pittsburgh Press*, September 27, 1941; Alan Donelli interview, October 2, 2002.

196   *Donelli moved*: *Pittsburgh Post-Gazette*, October 20, 1941.

196   *The following Sunday*: Havey Boyle, "Mirrors of Sport," "Along the Pro Front," no date, *Pittsburgh Post-Gazette*, Pittsburgh Steelers archives.

196   *And then*: Al Abrams, *Pittsburgh Post-Gazette*, November 6 1941.

196   *Art took*: Clair Burcky, *Pittsburgh Press*, November 12, 1941; Harry Keck, *Pittsburgh Sun-Telegraph*, November 17, 1941.

197   *A week later*: Jack Sell, *Pittsburgh Post-Gazette*, November 10, 1941.

197   *Pittsburgh finished*: Chester Smith, "Steelers Want Collegiate Draft Postponed," *Pittsburgh Press*, no date, Pittsburgh Steelers archives.

197   *Despite his*: "Steelers Call It A Year," no date or byline, Pittsburgh Steelers archives.

197   *If there*: Clair Burcky, "Pros and Cons," *Pittsburgh Press*, no date, Pittsburgh Steelers archives.

197   *Father Silas*: Letter from Silas Rooney to Maggie Rooney, August 20, 1938.

198   *Art was forty*: Arthur Rooney Jr. interview, January 2, 2005.

199   *While Pearl*: Al Abrams, *Pittsburgh Post-Gazette*, December 2, 1941.

199   *Boxing sustained*: Dan Rooney interview, October 1, 2004.

199   *With the war*: Harry Keck, "Mike Jacobs Getting Ready to Bid Adieu to Boxing," *Pittsburgh Sun-Telegraph*, December 17, 1941.

199   *Most teams*: Jack Sell, *Pittsburgh Post-Gazette*, December 21, 1941.

200   *At NFL meetings*: Chester Smith, "Rooney and Bell Want Sunday Games Only," *Pittsburgh Press*, no date, Pittsburgh Steelers archives.

200   *Art was looking*: Bill McElwain, "Charles Snaps Burley's Streak," *Pittsburgh Press*, May 25, 1942.

201   *"I had my"*: Pat Lynch, *New York Journal American*, March 20, 1954; Harry Keck, "Billy Conn Breaks Hand Fighting Father-in-Law," *Pittsburgh Sun-Telegraph*, May 1942.

201   *"The in-law"*: Al Abrams, "Injury Delays Billy Conn's Title Bout," *Pittsburgh Post-Gazette*, May 12, 1942.

202   *The fiasco*: No byline, "Simon Quits Ring, Bobo Fight Off," April 20, 1942; Al Abrams, "Lesnevich Forced to Cancel Fight," *Pittsburgh Post-Gazette*, no date, Pittsburgh Steelers archives.

202   *Rooney-McGinley*: Jack Sell, *Pittsburgh Press*, March 10, 1942.

202   *Worried about*: Chester Smith, "The Village Smithy," *Pittsburgh Press*, July 28, 1942.

203   *The war was tearing*: John P. McFarlane, "The Sports Front," *Pittsburgh Post-Gazette*, June 10, 1942; United Press, "War's Effect Seen In Fewer Players," August 8, 1942; Jack Sell, *Pittsburgh Press*, July 11, 1942.

203   *At camp*: *Pittsburgh Post-Gazette*, June 11, 1942.

204   *Art had justified*: Eddie Beachler, "Sports Stew—Served Hot," *Pittsburgh Post-Gazette*, no date, Pittsburgh Steelers archives.

204   *With Chicago*: Chester Smith, *Pittsburgh Press*, September 5, 1942.

204   *The Chicago*: Cecil Muldoon, "R-B-K Mean Business," *Pittsburgh Press*, September 4, 1942.

204   *The Steelers were*: Cecil Muldoon, *Pittsburgh Press, September 14, 1942*.

205   *Pittsburgh lost*: Harry Keck, "Pro Football 'Arrives' With Overflow Crowd," *Pittsburgh Sun-Telegraph*, no date, Pittsburgh Steelers archives.

205   *"Whizzer White"*: Jack Sell, "Dudley Rated Tops By Kiesling and Rooney," *Pittsburgh Press*, no date, Pittsburgh Steelers archives.

205   *Meanwhile, the war*: Charles Doyle, *The Sporting News*, December 31, 1942.

206   *If the Steelers*: Jack Sell, *Pittsburgh Post-Gazette*, October 1942, December 31, 1942.

207   *On game day*: Elmer Layden ended the deception of padding when he became commissioner.

207   *The crowd whooped*: Harry Keck, "Pro Football 'Arrives' with Overflow Crowd," *Pittsburgh Sun-Telegraph*, October 26, 1942.

207   *"Instead of"*: Al Abrams, *Pittsburgh Post-Gazette*, no date; Chester Smith, *Pittsburgh Press*, no date, Pittsburgh Steelers archives.

207   *Columnist Bob Considine*: Bob Considine, "Rooney Has Winner; Care-Free Days Gone," no date, Pittsburgh Steelers archives.

207   *The presence*: Lucious Jones, *Pittsburgh Courier*, September 18, 1943.

208   *Riding*: Cecil Muldoon, *Pittsburgh Press*, November 30, 1942; Tom Birks, *Pittsburgh Press*, December 7, 1942.

208   *Chilly Doyle*: Charles J. Doyle, *The Sporting News*, December 31, 1942.

208   *At the postseason*: Chester Smith, *Pittsburgh Press*, December 15, 1942.

209   *Art was*: Ed Beachler, *Pittsburgh Press*, no date.

209   *By early 1943*: Letter to Maggie Rooney from Silas Rooney, January 6, 1943; letters from John Rooney to Maggie Rooney, March 13, April 16, 1943.

209   *Fritzie gave*: Pete Zivic fought professionally for eleven years, Jack for ten, and Eddie for nine. Only Joe never turned pro.

209   *Zivic had*: Bummy Davis was no choirboy either. When Zivic aroused Bummy's ire in the first round, Davis resorted to repeated low blows. The ref disqualified Davis, who started kicking Zivic, a prelude to total mayhem. Policemen had to enter the ring to separate them. After the fight, Davis was suspended from boxing for life, although his enlistment led to reinstatement. Red Smith, *New York Times*, November 18, 1979; *Pittsburgh Post-Gazette*, February 13, 1943.

210   *Zivic, unbeaten*: "Local Boxing Hanging on the Ropes," no byline or date, Pittsburgh Steelers archives.

210   *By the end*: Harry Keck, *Pittsburgh Post-Gazette*, June 11, 1943; Eddie Beachler, *Pittsburgh Sun-Telegraph*, June 11, 1943; Chester Smith, *Pittsburgh Press*, June 12, 1943.

210   *Zivic's appeal*: Chester Smith, *Pittsburgh Press*, December 1942.

211   *Rooney-McGinley*: Harry Keck, *Pittsburgh Sun-Telegraph*, no date; Chester Smith, *Pittsburgh Press*, no date; Harry Keck, *Pittsburgh Sun-Telegraph*, November 1942; Bill McElwain, *Pittsburgh Press*, August 7, 1942; John P. McFarlane, "The Sports Front," no date or paper, Pittsburgh Steelers archives.

211   *While Art*: Letter from Silas Rooney to Maggie Rooney, August 20, January 6, November 1, 1943; Letters from Silas Rooney to Marie McGinley, no date.

211   *When the press*: No byline or date, Pittsburgh Steelers archives.

211   *Women now*: Letters from Silas Rooney to Marie McGinley, January 6, November 1, 1943.

212   *For the rest*: Jack Sell, *Pittsburgh Press*, April 8, 1943.

212   *By June*: Harry Keck, *Pittsburgh Sun-Telegraph*, July 8, 1943.

212   *Art had decided*: Havey Boyle, "Mirrors of Sport," *Pittsburgh Post-Gazette*, September 10, 1943.

213   *Feeling more*: Harry Keck. *Pittsburgh Sun-Telegraph*, September 11, 1943.

Al Abrams, *Pittsburgh Post-Gazette*, no date, Pittsburgh Steelers archives.

213 *The absentee owner*: *Catholic Review*, January 15, 1943.

213 *By November*: Chester Smith, *Pittsburgh Press*, November 1943.

213 *The Steagles*: Jack Sell, *Pittsburgh Post-Gazette*, October 1943; Cecil Muldown, *Pittsburgh Press*, December 7, 1943; United Press, December 8, 1943.

213 *When profits*: Chester Smith, *Pittsburgh Press*, December 6, 1943; Harry Keck, *Pittsburgh Sun-Telegraph*, no date, Pittsburgh Steelers archives.

214 *Even boxing*: *Pittsburgh Press*, February 15, 1943.

214 *The first outdoor*: *Pittsburgh Press*, April 30, 1944; *Pittsburgh Post-Gazette,* May 16, 1944.

215 *At the April*: United Press, April 20, 1944.

215 *"We could have"*: Chester Smith, *Pittsburgh Press*, August 2, 1944; *Detroit Times*, August 18, 1944.

215 *Pittsburgh would get*: Harry Keck, "Latest Pro Merger No Bargain for Local Fans," *Pittsburgh Sun-Telegraph*; Havey Boyle, *Pittsburgh Post-Gazette*, no date, Pittsburgh Steelers archives.

215 *Keck foresaw*: Harry Keck, *Pittsburgh Sun-Telegraph*, July 1944; Paul Gardner, "Sports Set for Post-War Boom," Universal Service, New York, July 29, 1944.

215 *Silas had done*: Silas Rooney letter to Maggie Rooney, February 10, 1944; Tommy Rooney letters to Maggie Rooney, February 23, March 2, 14, 1944.

216 *"I have a cot"*: Tommy Rooney letters to family, March 28, April 1, 19, May 19, June 2, July 11, 1944; E. J. McKiernan letter to Rooneys, September 8, 1944.

216 *But Tommy*: Dan Rooney interview, October 1, 2004.

216 *Silas consoled*: Silas Rooney letter to family, September 27, 1944.

217 *With college*: Harry Keck, "To Take a Safety or Not," *Pittsburgh Sun-Telegraph*, September 26, 1944.

217 *Art worried*: *Detroit Times*, August 18, 1944.

217 *At home*: Carl Hughes, *Pittsburgh Press*, August 27, 1944; John Rooney letters to Maggie Rooney, August 1944, November 11, 1944; Silas Rooney letters to Rooneys, August 5, 19, 26, October 15, 1944, September 14, 1945.

218 *The first signs*: United Press, October 18, 1944.

218 *At the meeting*: Carl Hughes, *Pittsburgh Press*, October 19, 1944.

218 *The season's highlight*: Jack Sell, *Pittsburgh Press*, October 31, 1944.

218 *On December 3*: Tom Birks, *Pittsburgh Sun-Telegraph*, December 4, 1944; Jack Sell, *Pittsburgh Post-Gazette*, December 4, 1944.

219 *After the season*: Chester Smith, *Pittsburgh Press*, December 4, 1944.

11. The Sutherland Years

220 *Smoky skies*: Weber, *Don't Call Me Boss*, 208–27.

220 *Art eschewed*: Jack Sell, *Pittsburgh Post-Gazette*, January 27, 1945; Tom Birks, *Pittsburgh Sun-Telegraph*, January 27, 1945.

221 *Bill Dudley's*: Jack Sell, *Pittsburgh Post-Gazette*, April 8, October 21, November 12, 1945.

222 *When Art*: Joe Williams, no date or newspaper, Pittsburgh Steelers archives. Several sporting publications selected national champions in these years, often resulting in seasons in which there was no consensus choice.

223 *"I guess"*: Ed Kiely interview, January 4, 2002.

223 *"Art loafed"*: Pat Livingston interview, April 5, 2001.

223 *The Steelers*: Harry Keck, *Pittsburgh Sun-Telegraph*, December 29, 1945.

224 *In his New York*: Arthur Daley, *New York Times*, January 9, 1946; Chester Smith, *Pittsburgh Press*, December 30, 1945.

224 *Sutherland*: Chester Smith, *Pittsburgh Press*, December 30, 1945.

224 *Ticket orders*: Harry Keck, *Pittsburgh Sun-Telegraph*, December 29, 1945.

225 *Hiring Bell*: Musick, *Game of Passion*, 321–22.

225 *Bell took*: Arthur Daley, *New York Times*, July 14, 1953.

225 *Horse racing*: Howland, "Spit the Bit"; Devereux, *Gambling*; Bishop, "And They're Off."

226 *Florida's tracks*: Donnie McGee interview, June 7, 2005; U.S. Senate, Special Committee to Investigate Organized Crime in Interstate Commerce, Report #725, 82nd Congress, August 31, 1951; Mosbrook, "Jazzed in Cleveland"; Steve Bossin, personal correspondence, May 17, 18, 2005.

226 *Jimmy McGee*: Jerry Lawrence interview, April 23, 2002.

226 *He now owned*: Timothy Rooney interviews, April 26–27, 2005. John Galbreath, a real estate magnate and horseman who bought part of the Pittsburgh Pirates a year later, owned Darby Dieppe in 1945.

226 *British Buddy*: Ira Hanford interview, June 6, 2005.

227   *Art never*: Donnie McGee interview, June 7, 2005.

227   *A few of*: Tommy Trotter interview, June 7, 2005; Mike Hopkins interview, Maryland Racing Commission, June 6, 2005; *New York Times*, October 7, 18, 1945, October 3, 1946, January 2, 26, April 2, May 27, November 20, 1947; Timothy Rooney interview, April 26–27, 2005.

227   *Sutherland*: Bill Dudley interview, March 10, 2005.

228   *Brue Jackson*: Yvonne Lewis interview, September 7, 2001. When Bell became the league's commissioner, he was required to divest his shares in the Steelers. Sutherland declined to exercise his option to buy them, and Art, short on cash, persuaded Barney McGinley to increase his interest in the team to forty-two percent. Art resumed the chairmanship of the board and club presidency but, according to Pat Livingston, later regretted not buying Bell's stock himself. "Art said the worst mistake he ever made was that he didn't know finances at that time. He didn't realize that he could have borrowed the money and made debentures, bonds, or issued new stock. He sold his share at a hell of a bargain to Barney McGinley." Pat Livingston interview, April 5, 2001.

228   *Art knew*: In one of their last handball games at the Keystone Club with Hamill, Dan caught Art in the eye as he made a corner shot. "It looked like Billy Conn laid one on him," Hamill's nephew Dan Lackner recalled. Art told everyone "Hamill hit me." Daniel Lackner interview, October 5, 2001.

228   *Jock oversaw*: Ed Kiely, *International News Service*, July 26, 1946.

228   *Jock pitched*: Havey Boyle, "It's Fun—But Expensive—To Field Pro Football Team," *Pittsburgh Post-Gazette*, August 13, 1946.

228   *Having shored*: Harry Keck, *Pittsburgh Sun-Telegraph*, September 25, 1946.

229   *Sutherland grew*: Havey Boyle, *Pittsburgh Post-Gazette*, no date, Pittsburgh Steelers archives.

229   *Presciently*: Havey Boyle, *Pittsburgh Post-Gazette*, August 9, 1946.

229   *Sutherland embraced*: Jack Sell, *Pittsburgh Post-Gazette*, August 6, 1946.

229   *"Pittsburgh has been"*: Les Biederman, *Pittsburgh Press*, August 6, 1946.

230   *The writers drank*: Jack McGinley interview, January 20, 2005.

230   *Sutherland, who had rarely*: Jack Sell, *Pittsburgh Post-Gazette*, August 14,1946.

230   *But Dudley*: Bill Dudley interview, March 10, 2005.

231 *Dudley, upset*: Bill Dudley interview, March 10, 2005; Jack Sell, *Pittsburgh Post-Gazette*, August 13, 1947; Les Biederman, *Pittsburgh Press*, August 13, 1947.

231 *Danny, fourteen*: Dan Rooney interview, November 1, 2001.

232 *Sutherland controlled*: Havey Boyle, *Pittsburgh Post-Gazette*, November 26, 1946.

232 *Sutherland's attention*: Dan Rooney interview, August 23 and November 1, 2001.

232 *The first time*: Dan Rooney interview, November 1, 2001; Les Biederman, *Pittsburgh Press*, August 17, 1946.

233 *Pittsburgh writers*: Jack Sell, *Pittsburgh Post-Gazette*, August 18, 1946; Harry Keck, *Pittsburgh Sun-Telegraph*, August 19, 1946.

233 *In August*: Les Biederman, *Pittsburgh Press*, no date, Pittsburgh Steelers archives.

233 *The NFL's*: *Chicago Sunday Tribune*, August 22, 1946, Pittsburgh Steelers archives.

233 *He focused*: Pat Livingston interview, April 5, 2001.

234 *Art's teams*: Evan Baker interview, October 2, 2001.

235 *Art never*: Randolph J. Harris, *Homestead Daily Messenger*, April 13, 1974.

235 *Art also remained close*: Charles Greenlee interview, June 18, 1980.

236 *Pro football*: Smith, "Outside the Pale," 255–81; McCambridge, *America's Game*, 17–20.

236 *These breakthroughs*: Evan Baker interview, October 2, 2001. Underscoring the role that Irish Catholics played as the gatekeepers for other nationalities and minorities in Pittsburgh, Baker concluded that in his experience, Irish Catholics were "the most empathetic people that I've ever met. The reason is that they got their ass kicked so they had this empathy because they had experienced it."

236 *Art's failures*: "What About the Steelers, Mr. Rooney?" is a clip without a byline that is most likely from the *Pittsburgh Courier*; Pittsburgh Steelers archives.

236 *Perhaps*: Thomas G. Smith, citing a letter from Art Rooney, January 15, 1988, "Outside the Pale," 260.

236 *Although*: Jack Sell, *Pittsburgh Post-Gazette*, July 11, 1946.

237 *Local bookies*: Sec. Taylor, "Sutherland A God," No paper, September 1946; Al Abrams, "Sidelights on Sport," *Pittsburgh Post-Gazette*, no date, Pittsburgh Steelers archives.

237 *With Jock*: Livingston had fallen under Art's spell when Art came to St. Frances of Loretto to make arrangements for training camp in 1938. Coach Jim Leonard asked Pat, editor of the college paper, to escort Art to dinner and a boxing show. At the show, Art was asked to pick the winning ticket for a $1,000 raffle out of a hat. He selected Livingston's mother's ticket and helped Pat celebrate at a tavern afterward. "I was just a kid and he treated me like Jim Leonard," Livingston recalled. "He was that way all his life." Pat Livingston interview, April 5, 2001; Frank Noll, United Press, September 21, 1946.

237 *Some began*: *McKeesport Daily News,* November 23, 1946 and September 25, 1946; Pittsburgh Steelers archives.

237 *Most pro teams*: Tom Shriver, AP, no date, Pittsburgh Steelers archives.

237 *Sutherland's controlling*: Bill Dudley interview, March 10, 2005.

238 *Pittsburgh led*: Havey Boyle, "Mirrors of Sport," *Pittsburgh Post-Gazette*, November 6, 1946; Les Biederman, *Pittsburgh Press*, October 24, 1946; AP, October 17, 1946.

238 *In their*: Jack Sell, October 21, November 13, 18, 19, 1946; Al Abrams, *Pittsburgh Post-Gazette*, no date, Pittsburgh Steelers archives.

239 *The night*: Vincent Flaherty, *Los Angeles Times*, November 26, 1946.

239 *Pittsburgh played*: *Pittsburgh Press*, November 29, 1946; Havey Boyle, *Pittsburgh Post-Gazette*, November 26, 1946.

239 *The "Gallant Dudley"*: Tom Birks, *Pittsburgh Press*, December 2, 1946; Havey Boyle, "A Tribute to a Great One," *Pittsburgh Post-Gazette*, December 3, 1946.

239 *Dudley, who*: Jack Sell, *Pittsburgh Post-Gazette*, December 3, 1946.

240 *Although the*: Season ticket sales information provided by Joe Gordon, Pittsburgh Steelers.

240 *Chicago won*: Jack Sell, *Pittsburgh Post-Gazette*, December 16, 1946.

241 *At the track*: Donnie McGee interview, June 7, 2005.

241 *Shortly*: *Miami Herald*, January 4, 1947.

242 *Westminster breezed*: *New York Times*, January 5, 17, 1947; *Miami Herald*, January 16, 17, 1947.

242 *Art did not*: In a handicapped race, the track stewards assign weights to each horse to level the field. Statesman carried 126 pounds, Westminster only 117. Westminster was not an unknown in 1947; he had been winning races for years. Sports writers referred to him as the "hero" of the 1945 Narrangansett Special, his biggest win prior to the Double Event.

242 *The double*: While the size of the purses his horses won is a matter of

public record, it's harder to determine how much Art made betting on them. Art disdained pari-mutuel betting, where the odds were based on the amount bet on each horse in a race and constantly refigured until post time. "You put a big bet on a horse at the mutuels," he complained, "and you knock your own price down." He was much more likely to bet with a bookie, but nobody kept records of these transactions for long. Pat Harmon, *Cincinnati Post*, July 25, 1951.

242 *If Art*: *Pro! Magazine*, 1972.

242 *Studies of gambling*: King, *Gambling*, 65; Clark Gardner interview, April 28, 2005.

242 *Art's talent*: Barney Nagler, *Daily Racing Form*, August 15, 1952.

243 *Jack McGinley*: New York Times, May 1, 1946; Jack McGinley interview, January 20, 2005.

243 *Art's horses*: John Webster, *The Philadelphia Inquirer*, August 2, 1947; William Boniface, *Baltimore Sun*, September 9, 1947; *New York Times*, April 2, May 27, August 2, 13, November 14, 20, 1947.

244 *Art was*: New York Times, December 18, 31, January 5, 17, February 6, 1947; Red Smith, *New York Times*, April 2, 1972.

244 *Dudley and Sutherland*: Harry Keck, *Pittsburgh Sun-Telegraph*, November 22, 1946; Havey Boyle, *Pittsburgh Post-Gazette*, January 23, 1947: George K. Leonard, no paper, April 1947, Pittsburgh Steelers archives.

244 *Art had known*: Jack Sell, *Pittsburgh Post-Gazette*, no date and August 6, 1947, Pittsburgh Steelers archives.

244 *The Sutherlanders*: Al Abrams, *Pittsburgh Post-Gazette*, August, 25, 1947.

245 *Sutherland was*: Al Abrams, *Pittsburgh Post-Gazette*, August, 26, 1947.

245 *The 1947*: Jack Sell, *Pittsburgh Post-Gazette*, September 22, 1947.

245 *After Pittsburgh*: Jack Sell, *Pittsburgh Post-Gazette*, October 20, November 10, 1947.

246 *Pittsburgh lost*: John Wiebusch, "Winning Isn't the Only Thing," no date, 1972, *Gameday*, National Issue XV, 1972, reprint 1984.

246 *Returning home*: Jack McGinley interview, January 20, 2005.

246 *Jock came*: Jack McGinley interview, January 20, 2005.

247 *Art's political*: Ed Kiely interview, January 4, 2002.

247 *Other owners*: McCambridge, *America's Game*, 39–40, citing Didinger, *Great Teams*, 120.

247 *Once, several*: Ed Kiely interview, January 4, 2002.

248   *Fogarty meshed*: Ed Kiely interview, January 4, 2002.

248   *Fran kept*: J. D. Fogarty interview, April 16, 2002.

249   *Art and·Fran*: Fran was Art's cousin on the Murray side of his family.

249   *Fogarty sometimes*: Gene Hupka interview, November 17, 2001.

250   *His death*: *New York Times, Pittsburgh Sun-Telegraph, Pittsburgh Post-Gazette*, April 8, 1948, through April 14, 1948; Jack McGinley interview, January 20, 2005.

12. Shamrock Farm

251   *That dream*: John Webster, *The Philadelphia Inquirer*, August 2, 1947; William Boniface, *Baltimore Sun*, September 9, 1947; Snowden Carter, "Art Rooney's Shamrock Farm in Carroll County," *The Maryland Horse*, March 1966.

251   *"It was"*: Snowden Carter, "Art Rooney's Shamrock Farm in Carroll County," *The Maryland Horse*, March 1966.

252   *Like most*: Tuffy Hacker interview, June 2, 2005.

252   *The four-hundred-acre*: Dan Rooney interview, May 11, 2005; Timothy Rooney interviews, April 26–27, 2005.

252   *Shamrock's*: Marty McGee, "In the Tradition of 'The Chief,'" *Thoroughbred Times*, March 24, 1989; Timothy Rooney interviews, April 26–27, 2005.

254   *At the track*: Robert Markus, *Chicago Tribune*, no date, Pittsburgh Steelers archives.

254   *Tim, who often*: Timothy Rooney interviews, April 26–27, 2005.

255   *"He was always"*: Dan Rooney interview, December 5, 2001.

255   *Putting on airs*: Dan Rooney interview, November 12, 2001.

255   *Art's lack*: Timothy Rooney interview, December 8, 2001.

255   *Art's humility*: Dan Rooney interview, November 12, 2001; Pittsburgh Steelers Public Relations, *Steelers Notes*, no date.

256   *"You didn't"*: Pittsburgh Steelers Public Relations, *Steelers Notes*, August 1988.

256   *Art knocked*: Chester Smith, *Pittsburgh Press*, 1949. Arnica, an herbal remedy derived from a plant that is commonly called leopard's bane, can be rubbed on the skin to soothe and reduce the inflammation of bruises, sprains, arthritis, and muscle or cartilage pain. Herbal Information Center, http//www.primary.net/~gic/herb/arnica.htm.

257   *"My father"*: Timothy Rooney interview, December 8, 2001; Dan Rooney interview, November 1, 2001; Roy Blount Jr., "An Unsentimental Education," *Sports Illustrated*, July 16, 1973.

257 *Art was relieved*: Chester Smith, *Pittsburgh Press*, no date, 1949, Pittsburgh Steelers archives.

258 *Art's sons*: Dan Rooney interview, December 5, 2001.

258 *Tim and Pat*: Timothy Rooney interview, December 8, 2001; Dan Rooney interview, November 1, 2001.

258 *Shamrock Farm*: John Rooney interview, November 30, 2001.

259 *Art went*: John Dorsey, "Horses Don't Talk Back to the Steelers' Boss," *Baltimore Sun Sunday Sun Magazine*, October 27, 1963; Dan Rooney interview, May 11, 2005.

259 *But life*: Dan Rooney interview, May 11, 2005.

259 *Art's buddies*: Timothy V. Rooney interview, June 20, 2002; Jamie Rooney interview, May 7, 2002.

260 *One summer*: Jack Butler interview, June 17, 2002.

261 *St. Anne*: John Rooney interview, November 30, 2001.

261 *Art had*: Bill Fidati, *Bulletin Sports*, August 19, 1973.

261 *In Louisville*: Vincent X. Flaherty, *Pittsburgh Sun-Telegraph*, May 8, 1947.

261 *Art made*: John Rooney interview, November 30, 2001; Bill Fidati, *Bulletin Sports*, August 19, 1973.

262 *As Native*: Pat Harmon, *Cincinnati Post*, July 25, 1951.

262 *A new generation*: Bud Spencer, "Found: A Horse Player Who Won't Die Broke," *San Francisco News*, December 5, 1952.

263 *Art devised*: John Rooney interview, November 30, 2001.

263 *Although*: Gerry Lawrence interview, April 23, 2002.

263 *While searching*: Hack, *Puppetmaster*, 370; Demaris, *The Director*, 17–18.

264 *Hoover talked*: On another occasion, Bob Strauss, the Democratic Party chairman and Washington power broker, wanted to meet Art. He approached Kiely at a Florida track and asked if he would introduce him to Art. "That's no problem," Kiely said. "You'd enjoy him because he's interested in politics. He'd be able to give you a conversation. 'Politics!' Strauss said. 'I don't want to talk politics. I want some tips to get even.'" Ed Kiely interview, January 8, 2002.

264 *Unlike bookmakers*: John Rooney interview, November 30, 2001.

264 *Art missed*: Pro! Magazine, 1972.

264 *Art had*: Bishop, "And They're Off"; Tuffy Hacker interview, June 2, 2005.

265 *By the 1950s*: Donnie McGee interview, June 7, 2005.

265   *After a couple*: Jim Steele interview, May 26, 2005.

266   *Jack McGinley*: Carl Hughes, "Sports Stew," *Pittsburgh Press*, no date, 1947, Pittsburgh Steelers archives.

266   *Because*: Havey Boyle, "Mirrors of Sport," *Pittsburgh Post-Gazette*, July 25, 1948.

266   *Fighters*: Havey Boyle, "Mirrors of Sport," *Pittsburgh Post-Gazette*, July 25, 1948.

267   *Pittsburgh still*: Zivic lost his last fight in Pittsburgh, a decision to Ossie Harris in the summer of 1945. He fought until 1949. Harry Keck, *Pittsburgh Sun-Telegraph*, September 25, 1946; Carl Hughes, "Sports Stew," *Pittsburgh Press*, no date, 1947, Pittsburgh Steelers archives.

267   *With Rooney-McGinley's*: Jack McGinley interview, August 14, 2001.

267   *Robinson fought*: He fought twice more in Pittsburgh, including the final bout of his career, in which Joey Archer beat the forty-four-year-old in ten rounds in 1965. Art was at the fight but had stopped promoting by then.

269   *Jack McGinley*: Jim Norris called a few months later and asked them to stage a fight as a favor to him. He was committed to a bout between Ezzard Charles and Rex Lane, but neither Madison Square Garden nor his Chicago arena was available. Jack McGinley said they would be happy to promote the bout but doubted it would do much business because both of the principals had recently been knocked out. Charles had been knocked out by Walcott, Lane by Rocky Marciano. Norris didn't care, just as long as the fight came off when scheduled. To sweeten the deal, he threw $50,000 of television money into the pot. But even with the broadcast revenue, Rooney-McGinley made little on the bout.

269   *Televising*: William O. Johnson, "TV Made It All A New Game," *Sports Illustrated*, December 22, 1969; Ruck, *Sandlot Seasons*, 195–96.

270   *Art was*: Ruck, *Sandlot Seasons*, 195–99.

13. Same Old Steelers

272   *Silas*: Timothy V. Rooney interview, June 20, 2002; Mike Abdo, *Times Herald*, no date, January 1981; Sam D'Onofrio, *The Bonaventure*, May 20, 1949; Dave Anderson, *New York Times*, January 18, 1981.

272   *Jim Rooney*: Carl Hughes interview, May 11, 2001; Roy McHugh, *Executive Report*, May 1990.

273   *Several*: Weber, *Don't Call Me Boss*, 294–97; *Pittsburgh Press*, September 15, 30, October 1, 1948.

274 *Refusing*: Les Biederman, *Pittsburgh Post-Gazette*, no date, Pittsburgh Steelers archives.

274 *On the field*: Jack Sell, *Pittsburgh Post-Gazette*, December 13, 1948.

274 *Art lost*: *Bulletin*, August 8, 1949; Elaine Kahn, AP, August 19, 1949; *New York Times*, August 17, 1949; Harold Weissman, *New York Mirror*, August 18, 1949.

275 *Sutherland's approach*: Carl Hughes interview, May 11, 2001.

275 *"He was a great"*: Jim Boston interview, November 11, 2001; *New York Tribune*, October 31, 1949.

275 *No Steeler*: Didinger, *Great Teams*, 134, 167.

276 *Bell and Art*: Musick, *Game of Passion*, 324; Jane Upton Bell interview, May 14, 2005; Minutes, NFL Owners Meetings, January 24, 1947, Pro Football Hall of Fame archives.

276 *Comrades*: Bert Bell Jr. interview, May 12, 2005; Jane Upton Bell interview, May 14, 2005; Upton Bell interview, April 19, 2005.

276 *By refusing*: UPI, December 15, 1948.

276 *Pittsburgh wasn't*: McCambridge, *America's Game*, 46–50, provides a good overview of the NFL-AAFC war.

277 *Art watched*: No byline, December 21, 1949, Pittsburgh Steelers archives; Brown, *Paul Brown Story*, 192

277 *In the NFL*: *Pittsburgh Post-Gazette*, October 18, 1948.

277 *The two leagues'*: Al Abrams, *Pittsburgh Post-Gazette*, January 23, 1950; UPI, December 24, 1949; Billy Kelly, *Buffalo Courier Express*, no date, Pittsburgh Steelers archives.

278 *Art, who spoke*: no date, no byline, Pittsburgh Steelers archives; UPI, January 25, 1950.

278 *The merger*: Chester Smith, "The Village Smithy," *Pittsburgh Press*, no date, Pittsburgh Steelers archives.

278 *In November*: Patricia Rooney Moriarty interview, June 5, 2007.

279 *After a miserable*: Jack Sell, *Pittsburgh Post-Gazette*, December 3, 1950; Jack McDonald, *Call-Bulletin*, December 1952.

279 *The late-season*: Pat Livingston, *Pittsburgh Press*, no date, 1950, Pittsburgh Steelers archives.

279 *Even Halas*: Didinger, *Great Teams*, 168.

279 *The refrain*: Harry Keck, *Pittsburgh Sun-Telegraph*, no date, Pittsburgh Steelers archives; Al Abrams, *Pittsburgh Post-Gazette*, October 27, 1951.

280 *The coaches*: Dan Rooney interview, November 12, 2001.

281 *He did*: Dan Rooney interview, May 22, 2002.

281 *Once the*: Mike Freeman, "Forgotten Pioneer: Black Coach Recalled," *New York Times*, October 29, 1997; Richard Goldstein, *New York Times*, January 11, 2001.

282 *A month later*: *Pittsburgh Post-Gazette*, September 29, 1952.

282 *While Art*: Federal Bureau of Investigation Freedom of Information Act Release, Subject: Arthur J. Rooney; Dan Rooney interview, November 1, 2001; *Pittsburgh Sun-Telegraph*, December 20, 1952, *Pittsburgh Post-Gazette*, December 20, 1952; John Rooney interview, July 11, 2005.

282 *Pittsburgh lost*: Didinger, *Great Teams*, 72.

282 *Dan Rooney*: Dan Rooney interview, October 1, 2004.

284 *When the Steelers*: Dan Rooney interview, July 1, 2005; Jack Butler interview, June 17, 2002; Pat Livingston, *Pittsburgh Press*, September 7, November 7, 1972.

284 *Kiesling's coaching*: Carl Hughes interview, May 11, 2001.

285 *Kiesling's health*: Didinger, *Great Teams*, 174; Bill Dudley interview, May 9, 2005.

285 *Though*: Didinger, *Great Teams*, 107.

285 *Yet Finks*: Didinger, *Great Teams*, 108.

286 *"The Steelers"*: Didinger, *Great Teams*, 110.

286 *Finks wanted*: Tucker, *Steelers' Victory*, 105–6; Didinger, *Great Teams*, 111.

286 *Nothing*: Didinger, *Great Teams*, 107–8.

286 *As a result*: Davis, *Papa Bear*, 139.

286 *In 1953, Pittsburgh*: Didinger, *Great Teams*, 170.

287 *The only ones*: John Wiebusch, "Art Rooney At Super Bowl XIV," in Steelers media notes.

288 *That fall*, Dan Rooney interview, July 1, 2005; John Rooney interview, July 11, 2005; Espn.go.com/sprtscentury/features/00016574.html; Art Rooney Jr. as told to Didinger, *Great Teams*, 171–72; Tucker, *Steelers' Victory*, 101–8.

288 *Art had better*: Pat Livingston interview, April 5, 2001.

289 *In 1957*: Dan Rooney interview, July 1, 2005; McCambridge, *America's Game*, 88.

289 *In 1952*: Al Abrams, *Pittsburgh Post-Gazette*, September 9, 1952; "Organized Professional Team Sports," House of Representatives Antitrust Subcommittee of the Committee on the Judiciary (USGPO, Washington: 1957), 2562–64.

290 *Fran Fogarty*: Dan Rooney interview, July 1, 2005.

290 *Dan focused*: Dan Rooney interview, July 1, 2005.

290 *Bert Bell*: Chafe, *Unfinished Journey*, 107; McCambridge, *America's Game*, 69–74. McCambridge offers the best analysis of the NFL's postwar evolution.

291 *Bell urged*: *New York Times*, October 12, 1959; Jane Upton Bell interview, May 14, 2005; Upton Bell interview, April 19, 2005.

291 *Television*: McCambridge, *America's Game*, 101, 131.

291 *The cornerstone*: Minutes, NFL Owners Meetings, January 21, 1951, Pro Football Hall of Fame archives.

291 *Pittsburgh's broadcast*: Jack Sell, *Pittsburgh Post-Gazette*, October 29, 1951; *New York Times*, October 29, 1951; "Organized Professional Team Sports," House of Representatives Antitrust Subcommittee of the Committee on the Judiciary (USGPO, Washington: 1957), 2562–64.

292 *As television*: Patton, *Razzle Dazzle*; McCambridge, *America's Game*, 131–32.

292 *Inside*: Minutes, NFL Owners Meetings, January 2, February 1, 2, 1957, Pro Football Hall of Fame archives.

292 *Although*: Minutes, NFL Owners Meetings, January 22, 1951, January 29, 1954, Pro Football Hall of Fame archives.

292 *Most owners*: Arthur J. Rooney interview, July 30, 1980; Tim Rooney quoted in Roy Blount Jr., "An Unsentimental Education," *Sports Illustrated*, July 10, 1973.

292 *But unionism*: *New York Times*, December 30, 1956; "NFLPA History, The Early Years: 1956–67," NFLPA Public Relations Department, typescript, in NFLPA Files, Pro Football Hall of Fame archives. See also "National Football League Players Association: History" in same archives.

293 *The owners' united*: Minutes, NFL Owners Meetings, January 22, 1951, January 31 to February 3, 1957, Pro Football Hall of Fame archives; *New York Times*, February 3, 1957.

293 *In February 1957*: Lomax, "Conflict and Compromise," offers a solid analysis of changing labor relations.

293 *"I think"*: *New York Times*, January 29, February 3, 1957; "Organized Professional Team Sports," House of Representatives Antitrust Subcommittee of the Committee on the Judiciary (USGPO, Washington: 1957), 2497–99, 2505–10, 2519–23.

294 *A chastened*: *New York Times*, August 1 and 2, 1957; "Organized Professional Team Sports," House of Representatives Antitrust Subcom-

mittee of the Committee on the Judiciary (USGPO, Washington: 1957), 2588, 2691–92

295   *A few men*: Father Francis Lackner interview, Pittsburgh, August 14, 2001.

295   *Jack Butler's fortunes*: Jack Butler interview, June 17, 2002; Rooney quoted in an article, no date or byline, Pittsburgh Steelers archives.

296   *Campbell*: Jim Boston interview, November 11, 2001.

296   *After the war*: Jim Boston interview, November 11, 2001.

296   *Although Art*: Jim Boston interview, November 11, 2001; J. D. Fogarty interview, April 16, 2002.

297   *Art was not*: Carl Hughes interview, May 11, 2001.

297   *The night before*: Carl Hughes interview, May 11, 2001.

297   *Art charmed*: Ed Kiely interview, January 4, 2002.

298   *While Sullivan*: Prescott Sullivan, *San Francisco Examiner*, September 7, 9, 1950.

298   *Sullivan quickly*: Jim Boston interview, November 11, 2001.

298   *Art made*: Commissioner Kenesaw Mountain Landis had nixed the performer's previous efforts to become involved with baseball because he owned racehorses. But after Landis died, baseball accepted Crosby as well as black players.

14. Buddy, Bobby, and Bert

300   *On August 12*: *Pittsburgh Post-Gazette*, August 13, 1957.

300   *Art was watching*: Jack Sell, *Pittsburgh Post-Gazette*, August 14, 1957.

300   *Predictably*: *Pittsburgh Post-Gazette*, August 27, 1957.

301   *But the next*: *Pittsburgh Post-Gazette*, August 30, 1957.

301   *Few were ruffled*: Jack Sell, *Pittsburgh Post-Gazette*, August 28, 1957.

301   *Parker sized*: Didinger, *Great Teams*, 12.

301   *"He had no rules"*: Didinger, *Great Teams*, 34; Jack Butler interview, June 17, 2002.

302   *With Parker*: *New York Times*, November 22, 1957.

302   *Art, the most*: "Organized Professional Team Sports," House of Representatives Antitrust Subcommittee of the Committee on the Judiciary (Washington: USGPO, 1957), 2640.

302   *Though his influence*: Ed Kiely interview, January 4, 2002.

304   *His colleagues*: Dan Rooney interviews, November 1, December 5, 2001; *New York Times*, December 3, 1957; *Pittsburgh Press*, December 3, 1957.

304 *The question*: Minutes, NFL Owners Meeting, December 2, 1957, January 29, May 18, 1958.

304 *While Art*: No byline or date, Pittsburgh Steelers archives.

306 *While endorsing*: Tucker, *Steelers' Victory*, 126–29; *Pittsburgh Press*, January 29, 1958; *Pittsburgh Post-Gazette*, August 19, 1958.

306 *Neither did*: Arthur Daley, "Sports of the Times," *New York Times*, October 26, 1958.

306 *A reporter*: No byline, *Pittsburgh Press*, October 1958, Pittsburgh Steelers archives.

306 *But Detroit*: Murray Olderman, no date or paper, Pittsburgh Steelers archives; Arthur Daley, "Sports of the Times," *New York Times*, October 26, 1958.

307 *Delighted*: Layne, *Always on Sunday*, 124–25, 141.

307 *Despite*: Pat Livingston, *Pittsburgh Press*, October 13, 1958; Didinger, *Great Teams*, 13.

307 *When Cleveland*: Didinger, *Great Teams*, 17.

307 *But fans*: Al Abrams, *Pittsburgh Post-Gazette*, November 17, 1958; UPI, no date, Pittsburgh Steelers archives.

308 *In the midst*: Weber, *Don't Call Me Boss*, 345–46.

308 *For Art*: Patrick McGrath Jr. interview, November 18, 2002.

308 *Dan Rooney opposed*: Dan Rooney interview, April 30, 2002.

308 *On election night*: Timothy Rooney interview, December 8, 2002.

308 *Religion*: Weber, *Don't Call Me Boss*, 346–47.

309 *Several weeks*: Al Abrams, *Pittsburgh Post-Gazette*, November 24, 1958; Pat Livingston, *Pittsburgh Press*, December 1, 1958.

309 *In December*: Didinger, *Great Teams*, 16.

309 *The NFL had*: Jack Hand, AP, February 7, 1958; Clark Nealon, *Houston Post*, no date, Pittsburgh Steelers archives.

310 *"I never saw"*: Layne, *Always on Sunday*, 131.

310 *Layne was a cheap*: Jim Boston interview, November 11, 2001.

310 *Layne's favorite*: Evan Baker interview, October 2, 2001.

310 *Art skipped*: Jack Sell, *Pittsburgh Post-Gazette*, no date, Pittsburgh Steelers archives.

311 *Art took death*: Jane Upton Bell interviews, May 14, August 21, 2005.

312 *The players subsequently*: Minutes, NFL Owners Meeting, January 22, 1959; Lomax, "Conflict and Compromise," 20–21.

312 *Layne's lawyer*: UPI, Aug 26, 1959; Murray Olderman column, no date, Pittsburgh Steelers archives.

312   *North Lincoln*: Dan Rooney interview, July 25, 2005.

313   *Both the Rooneys*: Jane Upton Bell interview, May 14, 2005; Upton Bell interview, April 19, 2005; *New York Times*, October 12, 1959; Pat Livingston, *Pittsburgh Press*, October 12, 1959.

313   *Arthur Daley*: Arthur Daley, *New York Times*, October 13, 1959; Jane Upton Bell interview, August 21, 2005.

314   *Overwhelmed*: Jane Upton Bell interview, May 14, 2005.

314   *The Steelers were*: Pat Livingston, *Pittsburgh Press*, November 9, 1959.

315   *A hard core*: Jack Butler interview, June 17, 2002.

315   *Two years of*: Jack Butler interview, June 17, 2002.

316   *Rooney and Halas*: *New York Times*, August 30, 1959.

317   *Bobby Layne would*: *New York Times*, December 11, 1959; Pat Livingston, *Pittsburgh Press*, December 1959.

317   *Like Rooney*: Bob Collins, "Hard to Name An Equal for Layne," *Indianapolis Star*, January 31, 1982; Chester Smith, *Pittsburgh Press*, no date, December 1959, Pittsburgh Steelers archives.

318   *Most players*: Jack Butler interview, June 17, 2002.

318   *The NFLPA*: Dan Rooney interview, May 22, 2002; Jack Butler interview, June 17, 2003.

319   *Concluding that*: Pat Livingston, *Pittsburgh Press*, January 20, 22, 1960.

319   *On subsequent*: *New York Times*, January 23, 26, 1960.

320   *Twenty-two ballots*: Dan Rooney interview, July 25, 2005; McCambridge, *America's Game*, 149–50.

321   *Art and Dan*: Dan Rooney interviews, December 5, 2001, July 1, 2005.

321   *The NFL*: Minutes, NFL Owners Meeting, March 11, 12, 29, 1960; Patton, *Razzle-Dazzle*, 53.

321   *In Art's eyes*: Dan Rooney interview, July 25, 2005.

322   *Other owners*: Minutes, NFL Owners Meeting, March 29, 1960.

322   *Jockeying*: Dan Rooney interview, August 4, 2005.

322   *During the 1960*: Patton, *Razzle-Dazzle*, 55–56.

323   *In January 1962*: Dan Rooney interview, July 25, 2005; *New York Times*, January 11, 1962.

15. Renaissance for Pittsburgh, Not the Steelers

325   *Church bells*: Vince Johnson, *Pittsburgh Post-Gazette Sun-Telegraph*, October 14, 1960.

325 *The World Series*: *Pittsburgh Post-Gazette Sun-Telegraph*, October 15, 1960.

325 *As far as*: Weber, *Don't Call Me Boss*, 197–99, 211.

326 *Eager for*: Arthur J. Rooney interview, February 25, 1981; *Bulletin Index*, June 9, 1938.

326 *Hillman, a Republican*: Elsie Hillman interview, June 29, 2002.

327 *Democratic Congressman*: Arthur J. Rooney interview, February 25, 1981.

327 *O'Neill's dilemma*: Arthur J. Rooney interview, February 25, 1981.

327 *Clark*: Timothy Rooney interview, December 8, 2001.

328 *Both Governor*: Pat O'Neill, *Pittsburgh Post-Gazette Sun-Telegraph*, April 26, 27, 1960; Mon. Charles Owens Rice interview, August 16, 2001.

328 *Art took*: *Pittsburgh Post-Gazette*, April 27, 28, 1960.

328 *"Art Rooney, as"*: *Pittsburgh Post-Gazette*, April 29, 1960.

328 *Art's frustration*: Farrell, *Tip O'Neill*, 80; Weber, *Don't Call Me Boss*, 357–67.

329 *Art, who supported*: Clippings file on Coyne in the Pennsylvania Room, Carnegie Library of Pittsburgh, especially *Pittsburgh Post-Gazette*, 1954; Ed Kiely interview, April 27, 2001.

329 *Lawrence stumped*: Dan Rooney interview, November 21, 2001; Ed Kiely interview, January 4, 2002; Weber, *Don't Call Me Boss*, 357–67; *Pittsburgh Post-Gazette*, November 26, 1963.

329 *He tried*: Dan Rooney interview, June, 2002; Myron Cope, *The Saturday Evening Post*, October 26, 1963, reprinted in Roberts and Welty, *Steelers Reader*, 78–83.

330 *During the 1960*: Jack Butler interview, June 17, 2002.

330 *"With the Steelers"*: Layne, *Always on Sunday*, 109.

330 *Art added*: Edward Linn, "The Sad End of Big Daddy Lipscomb," *Saturday Evening Post*, July 27, 1963, reprinted in Roberts and Welty, *Steelers Reader*, 84–95.

331 *The league did*: Pat Livingston, *Pittsburgh Press*, November 29, 1961.

331 *At the team's*: Layne, *Always on Sunday*, 141–42.

331 *Early the next*: Pittsburgh Press, December 11, 12, 1961; Layne, *Always on Sunday*, 31–33.

331 *Art knew*: Didinger, *Great Teams*, 124.

331 *The Steelers finished*: Pat Livingston, *Pittsburgh Press*, August 1963.

332 *During the off-season*: Undated tape of interview with Art Rooney from the 1980s, Pittsburgh Steelers archives.

332 *Pittsburgh played*: Bob Collins, *Indianapolis Star*, January 31, 1982, quoted in Roberts and Welty, *Steelers Reader*, 77.

333 *Art hated*: Dan Rooney interview, June 4, 2002; Ed Linn, "The Sad End of Big Daddy Lipscomb," *The Saturday Evening Post*, July 27, 1963, reprinted in Roberts and Welty, *Steelers Reader*, 84–95; *Pittsburgh Press*, March 10, 1963; George Puscas, *Football News*, September 13, 1988.

333 *"John Henry was"*: Herb Gluck, *Pro Football Guide*, June 1970; Dan Rooney interview, June 4, 2002; Hugh Carr interview, May 7, 2002.

333 *Evan Baker*: Evan Baker Jr. interview, October 2, 2001.

334 *Later, Art*: Tucker, *Steelers' Victory*, 20–21; Dan Rooney interview, April 17, 2001.

335 *While Allegheny*: Timothy Rooney interview, December 8, 2001; John Rooney interview, November 30, 2001.

335 *With Lawrence's approval*: Dan Rooney interview, November 21, 2001.

335 *Art schooled*: John Rooney interview, November 30, 2001.

336 *At camp*: Didinger, *Great Teams*, 135–36.

336 *Ed Brown*: Didinger, *Great Teams*, 136.

337 *So was the game*: *Pittsburgh Post-Gazette*, November 23, 25, 1963; Dan Rooney interview, October 4, 2005.

337 *When Pittsburgh*: Ron Cook, *Pittsburgh Post-Gazette*, September 14, 2001.

338 *After Mass*: John Wiebusch, "Winning Isn't the Only Thing," *Gameday*, National Issue XV, 1972, reprint 1984; William Wallace, *New York Times*, December 15, 1963.

338 *Ed Brown, who*: William Wallace, *New York Times*, December 16, 1963; Gordon White, *New York Times*, December 16, 1963; Didinger, *Great Teams*, 84.

338 *Years later*: Didinger, *Great Teams*, 135–36.

338 *The inimitable*: Myron Cope, "The Steelers: Pro Football's Gashouse Gang," *True*, September 1964, reprinted in Roberts and Welty, *Steelers Reader*, 96–100.

339 *Art never*: Andy Russell interview, October 24, 2005; Didinger, *Great Teams*, 85.

339 *The fifteen hundred men*: Pat Livingston, *Pittsburgh Press*, January 19, 20, 1964.

340 *By the time*: Most of the remarks at the Saints and Sinners Banquet,

January 19, 1964, Pittsburgh, were recorded. The tape is in the possession of the Pittsburgh Steelers.

341 *Other speakers*: Les Biederman, *Pittsburgh Press*, January 19, 1964.

344 *He admitted that*: Lewis F. Atchison, no date or newspaper, Pittsburgh Steelers archives.

344 *A band played*: Pat Livingston, *Pittsburgh Press*, January 19, 20, 1964; Chester Smith, *Pittsburgh Press*, January 21, 1964; Jack Sell, *Pittsburgh Post-Gazette*, January 20, 1964.

345 *Art owned*: Pat Lynch, *New York Journal American*, March 20, 1964.

345 *Art's network*: The Catholic Church's Corporal Works of Mercy are to feed the hungry, give drink to the thirsty, clothe the naked, shelter the homeless, visit the sick, visit the imprisoned, and bury the dead, according to Catholic Culture: Living the Catholic Life, http://www.catholiccul ture.org.

345 *Kiely checked*: Ed Kiely interview, April 27, 2001.

345 *Art called on*: Hugh Carr interview, May 7, 2002.

346 *Art usually*: Jim Boston interview, November 11, 2001.

346 *"One of the worst"*: Jamie Rooney interview, May 7, 2002.

346 *Art had one*: Charlie Powell, no date or newspaper, Pittsburgh Steelers archives.

16. Not the Same Old Steelers—Worse

348 *Toward the end*: Arthur Daley, "Sports of the Times," *New York Times*, November 22, 1964.

349 *Although Parker's*: Al Abrams, *Pittsburgh Post-Gazette*, no date, August September 1965, Pittsburgh Steelers archives.

349 *Art Jr. was also*: Arthur Rooney Jr. interview, November 9, 2005. That began to change after the addition of Art Jr. and Bill Nunn Jr., and the creation of a scouting combine called BLESTO, for the Bears-Lions-Eagles-Steelers Talent Organization. By pooling resources, the four clubs were able to evaluate more players and still save money.

349 *Art was apprehensive*: Arthur Rooney Jr. interview, November 9, 2005.

350 *Art grudgingly*: Ed Kiely interview, June 4, 2002.

350 *None of them*: Al Abrams, *Pittsburgh Post-Gazette*, November 14, 1966: Dan Rooney interview, October 4, 2002; *Pittsburgh Press*, August 25, 1988.

350 *To do anything*: Ed Kiely interview, June 4, 2002; John Wiebusch, "Winning Isn't the Only Thing," no date, 1972, *Gameday*, National Issue XV, 1972, reprint 1984.

351 *The difference*: Johnny Bunardzya, *The Mail*, October 22, 1957.

352 *By the early 1960s*: Pittsburgh Press, January 29, 1964; *Pittsburgh Post-Gazette*, January 20, 1964; Lester Biederman, *Pittsburgh Press*, November 23, 1966.

352 *But McClelland's*: Merson, "Corporate Responsibility," 714–21; Dan Rooney interview, October 5, 2005.

353 *Meanwhile, Art's protégé*: Gene Ward, *New York Daily News*, September 15, 1968; Jerry Bergman interview, May 15, 2002.

354 *When the league*: Melvin Durslag, *Los Angeles Herald-Examiner*, February 17, 1965.

354 *Network bidding*: Christian Science Monitor, December 9, 1994.

354 *After losing*: Rader, *In Its Own Image*, 90–94; Arthur Daley, "Sports of the Times," *New York Times*, November 8, 1964.

354 *After Pennsylvania*: New York Times, November 21, 1968, February 25, March 16, May 25, 1969; Dan Rooney interview, April 17, 2001; Hugh Brown, *Philadelphia Evening Bulletin*, no date, Pittsburgh Steelers archives.

355 *Shamrock was*: Snowden Carter, "Art Rooney's Shamrock Farm in Carroll County," *The Maryland Horse*, March 1966.

355 *Talk of*: Snowden Carter, "Art Rooney's Shamrock Farm in Carroll County," *The Maryland Horse*, March 1966.

355 *But, as with football*: Hugh Brown, *Philadelphia Evening Bulletin*, May 24, 1967; Snowden Carter, "Art Rooney's Shamrock Farm in Carroll County," *The Maryland Horse*, March 1966.

355 *Art was part*: Dave Anderson, *New York Times*, August 26, 1988; John Wiebusch, "Winning Isn't the Only Thing," *Gameday*, National Issue XV, 1972, reprint 1984.

356 *Art himself told*: Gerald Holland, "The Winning Ways of a Thirty-year Loser," *Sports Illustrated*, November 23, 1964; Vito Stellino, "Football's Supergrand-daddy" *Modern Maturity*, October–November 1979, 24.

356 *Art was behind*: Dan Lacker interview, October 5, 2001.

357 *"When the AFL"*: Michael Gee, New England Patriots gameday notes, August 26, 1988.

358 *Austin forbad*: Joe King, *World Journal Tribune*, September 13, 1966; Lou Prato, no date or paper, Pittsburgh Steelers archives; Pat Livingston, *Pittsburgh Press*, August 17, 25, 1966; Jack Sell, *Pittsburgh Post-Gazette*, August 17, 1966; Al Abrams, *Pittsburgh Post-Gazette*, August 30, 1968.

358 *Austin cleaned*: Roy McHugh, *Pittsburgh Press*, no date, summer of 1966, Pittsburgh Steelers archives.

359 *Art said*: AP, September 7, 1966, Pittsburgh Steelers archives.

359 *The NFL scheduled*: Gene Ward, *New York Daily News*, September 15, 1968.

359 *Austin deserved*: Andy Russell interview, October 24, 2005.

359 *After Pitt halfback*: Paul Martha interview, January 10, 2006.

360 *Rookie Rocky*: Rocky Bleier interview, November 23, 2005.

360 *Austin's dismal*: Roy McHugh, *Pittsburgh Press*, December 16, 1968; *Evening Bulletin*, December 17, 1968.

360 *Although the NFL*: Ric Roberts, *Pittsburgh Courier*, no date, Pittsburgh Steelers archives.

361 *Jack O'Malley*: Rev. Jack O'Malley interview, May 16, 2002.

362 *Few men had higher*: Bill Nunn Jr. interview, July 11, 2001.

362 *Nunn's arrival*: Bill Nunn Jr. interview, July 11, 2001; Dan Rooney interview, November 27, 2001.

363 *Nunn's hiring*: *The New Pittsburgh Courier*, March 16, 1968.

363 *Art lost*: Margaret Rooney Laughlin interview, May 22, 2002.

363 *In 1968, former*: *Pittsburgh Post-Gazette*, *Pittsburgh Press*, November 21, 22, 1966.

364 *McGregor could not*: David Condon, "In the Wake of the News," no date or paper, Pittsburgh Steelers archives; Gerald Eskenazi, *New York Times*, June 26, 1965; William Wallace, *New York Times*, February 9, 1966; *New York Times*, February 10, 1966; Jack McGregor interview, October 27, 2005.

365 *"Dad thinks"*: UPI, September 22, 1966, Pittsburgh Steelers archives; Sandy Grady, no date or paper, Pittsburgh Steelers archives; John Rooney interview, June 22, 2003.

365 *The Spartans*: Dan Rooney interview, October 4, 2005.

366 *Art felt*: *Pittsburgh Post-Gazette*, *Pittsburgh Press*, April 25, 26, 1968, Pittsburgh Steelers archives.

366 *Art put it*: Morton Moss, *Los Angeles Herald Examiner*, September 22, 1968.

367 *But nobody*: Rich Koster, *St. Louis Globe-Democrat*, October 4, 5, 1968; Francis Stann, *The Sunday Star*, October 26, 1968; Sam Blair, *Dallas Morning News*, December 5, 1968.

367 *Jets owner*: Larry Merchant, *New York Post*, December 12, 1966; Al Abrams, *Pittsburgh Post-Gazette*, December 8, 1968 and no date; Benny

Marshall, unidentified Cleveland paper, October 1968, Pittsburgh Steelers archives.

367 *Art protested*: Bob Roesler, *Times-Picayune*, December 11, 1968; Gene Ward, *New York News*, no date, 1968, Pittsburgh Steelers archives.

17. Changing History

368 *At the team*: Arthur Rooney Jr. interview, November 9, 2005.

369 *Paterno turned*: Dan Rooney interview, November 2, 2005.

369 *Chuck Noll had*: Jack Sell, *Pittsburgh Post-Gazette*, January 28, 1969; Dan Rooney interview, November 2, 2005.

370 *Art Jr. had been*: Arthur Rooney Jr. interview, November 9, 2005.

370 *Noll was adamant*: Arthur Rooney Jr. interview, November 9, 2005.

371 *Pittsburgh selected*: Pat Livingston, *Pittsburgh Press*, January 27, 28, 1969; Les Biederman, *Pittsburgh Press*, January 28, 1969; Danyluk, *Super '70s*, 8.

371 *Nobody counted*: Rocky Bleier interview, November 23, 2005; Bleier, *Fighting Back*, 142–44.

372 *Later that month*: Rocky Bleier interview, November 23, 2005; Bleier, *Fighting Back*, 94–111.

372 *Russell had never*: Andy Russell interview, Pittsburgh, October 24, 2005.

373 *Instead Noll*: Andy Russell interview, October 24, 2005; see also: Russell, *Steeler Odyssey*, 241–44.

373 *Noll disagreed*: Andy Russell interview, October 24, 2005; see also: Russell, *Steeler Odyssey*.

373 *At practice afterward*: Andy Russell interview, October 24, 2005.

374 *During training camp*: Black Construction Coalition files in the Pennsylvania Room, Carnegie Library, Pittsburgh; *Pittsburgh Post-Gazette*, August 28, 30, September 17, 28, 1969; *Pittsburgh Press*, August 24, 28, 30, 31, September 9, 1969; *Pittsburgh Courier*, December 5, 1970, December 18, 1971.

374 *During the crisis*: Nate Smith interview, December 5, 2005.

374 *"We'll do what"*: Dan Rooney interview, November 27, 2001; *New York Times*, August 28, 1969.

375 *That August*: Roy McHugh, *Pittsburgh Press*, August 12, 1969.

375 *Now only Halas*: J. D. Fogarty interview, April 16, 2002.

376 *They won their*: Roy McHugh, *Pittsburgh Press*, November 24, 1969; *New York Times*, December 14, 1969.

376   *In late October*: Rocky Bleier interview, November 23, 2005.

376   *In the visitors'*: Pat Livingston, *Pittsburgh Press*, October 27, 1969.

376   *The season's*: Roy McHugh, *Pittsburgh Press*, November 10, 1969.

376   *Though they kept losing*: Pat Livingston, *Pittsburgh Press*, December 1, 1969.

377   *But "Rooney U"*: Pat Livingston, *Pittsburgh Press*, December 8, 1969.

377   *Art had befriended*: Toperoff, *Lost Sundays*, 51.

377   *Greene fought*: *New York Times*, December 14, 1969; Dan Rooney interview, November 27, 2001.

378   *Greene's play*: Bob Roesler, *Times-Picayune*, January 9, 1975.

378   *"I could see"*: "The Troika," *Newark Star Ledger*, no date or byline, Pittsburgh Steelers archives; *USA Today*, August 28, 1988.

379   *A feisty reporter*: Pat Livingston interview, April 5, 2001; *Pittsburgh Press*, July 19, 30, 1970.

380   *Art told Art Jr.*: Rocky Bleier interview, November 23, 2005; Bleier, *Fighting Back*, 134–42.

380   *That Pittsburgh ended*: Terry Bradshaw interview, February 10, 2003; Peter King, *Sports Illustrated*, January 20, 1990.

380   *A college All-American*: Bradshaw, *Only A Game*, 40–42.

381   *Football wasn't*: Terry Bradshaw interview, February 10, 2003; Bradshaw, *Looking Deep*, reprinted in Roberts and Welky, *Steelers Reader*, 203.

381   *Bradshaw's black*: Bradshaw, *Looking Deep*, reprinted in Roberts and Welky, *Steelers Reader*, 201–2.

381   *Art took on*: Pat Livingston, *Pittsburgh Press*, January 27, 1970.

382   *"Sports is a history"*: Pat Livingston, *Pittsburgh Press*, August 30, 1970.

382   *To Art's relief*: John Steadman, 1971, no date and no paper, Pittsburgh Steelers archives.

282   *While Dan ran*: Bradshaw, *Man of Steel*, 46

383   *On the other*: Skip Myslenski, *Philadelphia Inquirer*, 13, 14, 1973.

383   *Art, an unlit*: Andy Russell interview, October 24, 2005.

383   *Art knew all*: Timothy V. Rooney interview, June 20, 2002: Toperoff, *Lost Sundays*, 51.

384   *Art bucked*: Arthur Rooney Jr. interview, November 9, 2005.

384   *"He loved"*: Rocky Bleier interview, November 23, 2005.

384   *Joe Greene often*: Timothy V. Rooney interview, June 20, 2002.

384   *You didn't have to be*: Steve DiNardo interview, February 19, 2006; David Fink, *Pittsburgh Post-Gazette*, August 26, 1988.

385   *The team began*: Pat Livingston, *Pittsburgh Press*, October 12, November 9, 1970.

385   *In the final game*: Dan Rooney interview, Pittsburgh, November 1, 2001; Andy Russell interview, Pittsburgh, October 24, 2005; Russell, *Steeler Odyssey*, 107–8; Jack Sell, *Pittsburgh Post-Gazette*, December 21, 1970.

386   *Pittsburgh finished*: Ted Colton, *Pittsburgh Press*, December 19, 1972.

386   *While Noll*: *New York Times*, October 1, 1970; Timothy Rooney interview, April 26, 2005; John Rooney interview, November 30, 2001.

386   *Tim was the*: Timothy Rooney interview, April 26, 2005.

387   *Art set*: Joe Gordon interview, April 19, 2002.

388   *But employees*: Joe Gordon interview, April 19, 2002.

388   *His generosity*: Ralph Berlin interview, October 2, 2001.

388   *At the end of 1969*: Joe Gordon interview, April 19, 2002.

389   *That June*: Andy Russell interview, October 24, 2005; *New York Times*, June 5, 6 1971.

389   *During the 1970*: Charley Feeney, *Pittsburgh Post-Gazette*, January 29, 1971.

389   *Things were different*: Art Rooney Jr. interview, July 19, 2002.

389   *After selecting*: Lewis Atchison, *The Sunday Star*, February 21, 1971.

390   *Art listened*: Charley Feeney, *Pittsburgh Post-Gazette*, January 29, 1971.

390   *Art was seventy*: Tony Petrella, *Palm Beach Post-Times*, March 27, 1971.

390   *In August 1971*: Rocky Bleier interview, November 23, 2005; Bleier, *Fighting Back*, 152.

391   *White learned*: Dwight White interview, July 5, 2002.

391   *The 1971 season*: Pat Livingston, *Pittsburgh Press*, September 20, December 6, 13, 1971.

18. 1972

392   *Timothy V. Rooney*: Timothy Vincent Rooney interview, June 20, 2002.

393   *And among*: Red Smith, *New York Times*, April 12, 1972.

393   *The Rooneys paid*: Louis Effrat, *New York Times*, November 2, 5, 1971, March 17, May 24, June 22, 1972; Timothy Rooney interview, April 27, 2005; John Rooney interview, November 30, 2001.

393   *"We're thinking"*: Phil Musick, *Pittsburgh Press*, July 12, 1972

393   *Veterans Andy Russell*: Andy Russell interview, October 24, 2005.

393 *Art hosted*: Pat Livingston, *Pittsburgh Press*, July 11, 1972; Holway, *Josh and Satch*, 69.

394 *At camp*: Pat Livingston, *Pittsburgh Press*, July 11, 1972.

394 *Bill Nunn*: Peter King, *Sports Illustrated*, January 20, 1990.

394 *As anticipated*: Ted Colton, *McKeesport Daily News*, July 7, 1972; Phil Musick, *Pittsburgh Press*, no date, July, 1972, Pittsburgh Steelers archives.

394 *"I heard"*: Phil Musick, *Pittsburgh Press*, no date, 1972, Pittsburgh Steelers archives.

394 *If Bleier*: Danyluk, *Super '70s*, 13.

395 *The Steelers were scheduled*: Joe Gordon interview, April 19, 2002.

396 *In the fourth*: Pat Livingston, *Pittsburgh Press*, September 7, 1972.

396 *With over 51,000*: Sam Bechtel, *Beaver County Times*, September 18, 1972; Phil Musick, *Pittsburgh Press*, September 18, 1972.

396 *One game, however*: Phil Musick, *Pittsburgh Press*, October 1, 1972.

397 *Art kidded*: Bradshaw, *Man of Steel*, 45.

398 *Rhode Island senator*: "Blackout of Sporting Events on TV," U.S. Senate Subcommittee on Communications, October 4, 1972.

398 *Back in Pittsburgh*: Sam Bechtel, *Beaver County Times*, October 2, 1972.

398 *But after*: Sam Bechtel, *Beaver County Times*, October 16, 1972.

398 *The defensive line*: Dwight White interview, July 5, 2002.

399 *After beating Cincinnati*: Dick Stilley, *Beaver County Times*, November 6, 1972.

399 *The horde*: Jim Barniak, *Philadelphia Inquirer*, November 13, 1972.

399 *The game witnessed*: Ciotola, "Spignesi," 271–89.

399 *"We've been"*: Jim Barniak, *The Philadelphia Inquirer*, November 13, 1972.

399 *The Steelers took*: Phil Musick, *Pittsburgh Press*, November 20, 1972.

400 *Pittsburgh defenders*: Dave Anderson, *New York Times*, November 27, 1972.

400 *To do so*: Phil Musick, *Pittsburgh Press*, December 1, 1972; Phil Musick, "Stand Up and Cheer," *Pittsburgh Press*, no date; Pat Livingston, "Icing the Cake," *Pittsburgh Press*, no date, Pittsburgh Steelers archives.

400 *Because the NFL*: Ciotola, "Spignesi," 276–80.

401 *So had Gerela's*: Ted Colton, *McKeesport Daily News*, March 1973; Ted Majzer interview, January 28, 2006.

401   *The game itself*: Pat Livingston, *Pittsburgh Press*, November 27, 1972.

401   *"We've put the evil"*: Ciotola, "Spignesi," 276–80.

401   *The ninth win*: Phil Musick, *Pittsburgh Press*, December 1, 1972; Phil Musick, "Stand Up and Cheer," *Pittsburgh Press*, no date; Pat Livingston, *Pittsburgh Press*, "Icing the Cake," no date; Joe Grata, *Pittsburgh Press*, no date, Pittsburgh Steelers archives.

401   *Art, who had*: *Pittsburgh Press*, December 4, 1972; Phil Musick, *Pittsburgh Press*, December 9, 1972.

402   *That evening*: Gene Ward, *Daily News*, December 25, 1972.

402   *Losing still stung*: Bob Oates, *Los Angeles Times*, December 8, 1972.

403   *Art seemed unfazed*: Pat Livingston, *Pittsburgh Press*, December 6, 1972; William Wallace *New York Times,* December 23, 1972; Jim Haughton, *Football News*, December 4, 1972.

403   *The Steelers headed*: Gary Mihoces, AP, December 14, 1972, Pittsburgh Steelers archives.

404   *That week, the Rooneys*: *New York Times*, December 16, 1972; John Rooney interview, November 30, 2001.

404   *"Cope jumps up"*: Jim Boston interview, November 11, 2001; Ed Bouchette, *Pittsburgh Post-Gazette*, May 21, 1998; Pat Livingston, *Pittsburgh Press*, December 1972; Roy Harris Jr., *Wall Street Journal*, December 30, 1972.

405   *At practice*: Pat Livingston, *Pittsburgh Press*, December 1972.

406   *The Steelers were bemused*: Phil Musick, *Pittsburgh Press*, December 17, 1972; Skip Myslenski, *Philadelphia Inquirer*, December 13, 14, 1973.

406   *Art sat with*: Pat Livingston, *Pittsburgh Post-Gazette*, December 17, 1972.

406   *The game was*: Jimmy Miller, *Pittsburgh Post-Gazette*, December 18, 1972.

406   *When Art entered*: Pat Livingston, *Pittsburgh Press*, December 18, 1972; Al Abrams, *Pittsburgh Post-Gazette*, December 18, 1972; Ciotola, "Spignesi," 280; Skip Myslenski, *Philadelphia Inquirer*, December 13, 14, 1973.

407   *After Art sat down*: Ted Colton, *McKeesport Daily News*, December 13, 1972.

407   *Despite frigid*: *Pittsburgh Press*, December 18, 1972.

408   *At noon the next*: Rudy Cernkovic, *Beaver County Times*, December 19, 1972; Gary Mihoces, AP, no date, Pittsburgh Steelers archives; Charley Feeney, *Pittsburgh Post-Gazette*, December 19, 20, 21, 22, 1972.

408   *Another old friend*: Al Abrams, *Pittsburgh Post-Gazette*, December 19, 1972.

408   *While Art was*: Pat Livingston, *Pittsburgh Press*, December 8, 1972.

410   *The Friday before*: Gene Ward, *Daily News*, December 25, 1972.

410   *The Kilkenny native*: Ted Colton, *McKeesport Daily News*, December 26, 1972; Rudy Cernkovic, *Pittsburgh Press*, December 5, 1974.

410   *On game day*: Roy McHugh, *Pittsburgh Press*, December 26, 1972.

411   *Sportswriter Gene Ward*: Gene Ward, *New York Daily News*, December 24, 1972.

412   *As sportswriters composed*: Arthur Daley, *New York Times*, December 26, 1972; AP, December 29, 1972, Pittsburgh Steelers archives.

412   *"I was supposed"*: Alan Robinson, AP, June 21, 2005, Pittsburgh Steelers archives.

413   *Art pieced together*: Sahadi, *Super Steelers*, 4; AP, December 29, 1972, Pittsburgh Steelers archives.

413   *Fans had swarmed*: William Wallace, *New York Times*, December 24, 1972.

414   *It took another*: Arthur Daley, *New York Times*, December 26, 1972.

414   *Franco Harris*: Sam Bechtel, *Beaver County Times*, December 26, 1972.

414   *For Jack Ham*: News clippings, no dates or bylines, Pittsburgh Steelers archives.

415   *Joe Greene*: Jim Barniak, *The Philadelphia Inquirer*, no date, Pittsburgh Steelers archives.

415   *In Oakland's*: UPI, December 26, 1972; Bob Oates, *Los Angeles Times*, December 27, 1972, Jerry Bergman interview, May 15, 2002.

415   *If anybody*: Russell, *Steeler Odyssey*, 233.

415   *As Myron*: Pittsburgh Steelers Web site: "Immaculate Reception Notes", Blount, *About Three Bricks Shy*, 48.

416   *The city was*: Red Smith, *New York Times*, December 25, 1972.

416   *The national press*: Roy McHugh, *Pittsburgh Press*, December 26, 1972.

416   *Dan Rooney was*: Phil Musick, *Pittsburgh Press*, December 28, 1972.

416   *Arthur Daley*: Arthur Daley, *New York Times*, December 26, 1972.

417   *Before the AFC*: Red Smith, *New York Times*, December 29, 1972.

417   *Pittsburgh's opponent*: Ron Reid, *Sports Illustrated*, January 8, 1973.

417   *Coming after*: Ron Reid, *Sports Illustrated*, January 8, 1973.

418   *New Year's Day*: Ruck, "Remembering Roberto."

418   *Roberto Clemente*: Pat Livingston, *Pittsburgh Press*, January 2, 1973.

19. Football's Promised Land

420 *Art had mellowed*: John Rooney interview, November 30, 2001; Pat Livingston, *Pittsburgh Press*, no date, Winter 1973, Pittsburgh Steelers archives.

421 *While the boys*: Ted Colton, *McKeesport Daily News*, no date; Bill Christine, "Playing Games," no date, Pittsburgh Steelers archives; Roy Blount, *Sports Illustrated*, July 16, 1973; Myron Cope, *Sports Illustrated*, August 20, 1973.

421 *His players*: Ted Colton, *McKeesport Daily News*, no date, March 1973, Pittsburgh Steelers archives.

421 *While Ham*: Ernie Holmes interview, February 3, 2006.

421 *But Holmes*: Ernie Holmes interview, February 3, 2006; Blount, *About Three Bricks Shy*, 48–50; Phil Musick, *Pittsburgh Press*, no date, March 1973, Pittsburgh Steelers archives.

422 *The rest of spring*: Tim Rooney interview, April 26, 2005.

423 *Art's sons*: *Palm Beach Times*, May 8, 1973.

423 *"The monkey's off"*: Ted Colton, *McKeesport Daily News*, July 1973; Jack Sell, *Pittsburgh Post-Gazette*, January 30, 1973.

423 *After four months*: AP, no date or byline.

423 *When a helicopter*: Blount, *About Three Bricks Shy*, 20; Al Abrams, *Pittsburgh Post-Gazette*, January 8, 1972.

423 *Art never*: Sam Bechtel, *Beaver County Times*, no date, preseason 1973, Pittsburgh Steelers archives.

424 *"I suppose"*: Bradshaw, *Man of Steel*, 45; Sam Bechtel, *Beaver County Times*, Summer 1973, Pittsburgh Steelers archives.

424 *By March*: Phil Musick, *Pittsburgh Press*, no date, Summer 1973, Pittsburgh Steelers archives.

424 *Art was*: Roy McHugh, *Pittsburgh Press*, no date, September 1973, Pittsburgh Steelers archives.

424 *Their angst*: Phil Musick, *Pittsburgh Press*, September 24, 1973.

425 *In game seven*: Phil Musick, *Pittsburgh Press*, November 4, 1972; Blount, *About Three Bricks Shy*, 178–81.

425 *Steeler quarterbacks*: Blount, *About Three Bricks Shy*, 162; Sam Bechtel, *Beaver County Times*, October 8, 1973.

426 *Art thought*: Timothy Rooney interview, April 27, 2005; Pat Livingston, *Pittsburgh Press*, December 24, 1974.

426 *A few years*: Tuffy Hacker interview, June 2, 2005.

426 *After becoming*: Timothy Rooney interview, April 26, 2005; Tuffy Hacker interview, June 2, 2005.

427 *Art showed*: Both the Raiders and the Steelers had become national stories after the Immaculate Reception. Gonzo journalist Hunter Thompson covered the Raiders—until they barred him from their premises—while Blount chronicled the Steelers.

427 *After hitting*: Blount, *About Three Bricks Shy*, 192–93.

427 *At Shenandoah*: Blount, *About Three Bricks Shy*, 199–200.

428 *Leaving after*: Blount, *About Three Bricks Shy*, 202.

428 *But injuries*: Phil Musick, *Pittsburgh Press*, November 13, 1973; Sam Bechtel, *Beaver County Times*, November 12, 1973.

429 *But Art was inordinately*: Sam Bechtel, *Beaver County Times*, no date, December 1973, Pittsburgh Steelers archives.

429 *The morning*: Gary Michoces, AP, no date, Pittsburgh Steelers archives.

429 *A fierce*: Pat Livingston, *Pittsburgh Press*, December 23, 1973.

429 *To make*: Gerald Eskenazi, *New York Times*, December 21, 1973; Steve Cady, *New York Times*, December 22, 1973.

429 *Art headed*: *New York Times*, January 6, 1974; Shirley Povich, *Washington Post*, August 26, 1988.

430 *Swann came*. Sam Bechtel, *Beaver County Times*, July 11, 1974.

430 *At the winter*: Jerry Bergman interview, May 15, 2002.

431 *The business*: Bill Christine, *Pittsburgh Post-Gazette*, May 17, 1974.

431 *A battle-scarred*: Pat Livingston, *Pittsburgh Press*, June 1, 1974; Ted Colton, *McKeesport Daily News*, June 6, 1974; *Pittsburgh Post-Gazette*, June 7, 1974.

431 *The WFL debuted*: Sam Bechtel, *Beaver County Times*, May 23, 1974.

431 *Terry Bradshaw*: *New York Times*, June 3, July 4, 1974; John Clayton, *Steel City Sports*, June 5, 1974.

431 *The WFL sought*: Dwight White interview, July 5, 2002.

432 *"Joe," White*: Dwight White interview, July 5, 2002.

432 *Joe Greene rejected*: Dan Rooney interview, April 30, 2002.

432 *Art was especially*: Dan Rooney interview, April 30, 2002.

433 *The players struck*: McCambridge, *America's Game*, 316–17.

433 *The College All-Star*: UPI, *Pittsburgh Press*, July 12, 1974.

433 *Art wanted*: Dave Condon, *McKeesport Daily News*, July 24, 1974; Ted Colton, no paper, July 18, 1974, Pittsburgh Steelers archives.

433 *Dan Rooney was*: Jeff Samuels, *Pittsburgh Press*, July 12, 1974.

434 *Though their players*: Bill Christine, *Pittsburgh Post-Gazette,* July 15, 1974; Sam Bechtel, *Beaver County Times*, July 19, 1974.

434 *Joe Greene agonized*: Phil Musick, *Pittsburgh Press*, July 23, 1974.

434 *Sportswriters were*: Peter King, *Sports Illustrated*, January 20, 1990.

435 *Tuffy adored*: Tuffy Hacker interview, June 2, 2005.

435 *The strike gave*: Ernie Holmes interview, February 3, 2006; Phil Musick, *Pittsburgh Press*, July 31, 1974; Sam Bechtel, *Beaver County Times*, July 31, 1974.

436 *After a federal*: James Harris had started an opener for Buffalo due to the regular quarterback's injury.

436 *"This is the championship"*: Chastain, *Steel Dynasty* is one of several books that looks at this season.

436 *"Terry hit bottom"*: Art Rooney Jr. interview, November 9, 2005; David Fink, *Pittsburgh Post-Gazette*, September 10, 1974; Phil Musick, *Pittsburgh Press*, September 12, 1974; Dave Ailes, *Tribune Review*, September 12, 1974.

437 *"Terry," Andy Russell*: Andy Russell interview, October 24, 2005.

437 *Russell wasn't*: Timothy V. Rooney interview, June 20, 2002; Art Rooney Jr. interview, November 9, 2005.

437 *Even with*: David Fink, *Pittsburgh Post-Gazette*, October 9, 1974.

438 *Injuries*: Bob Smizik, *Pittsburgh Press*, November 1, 1974.

438 *The defensive line*: Phil Musick, *Pittsburgh Press*, October 14, 1974; David Fink, *Pittsburgh Post-Gazette*, November 7, 1974.

438 *Meanwhile*: Sam Bechtel, *Beaver County Times*, December 4, 1974; Ted Colton, *McKeesport Daily News*, December 5, 1974.

439 *Pittsburgh faced*: Dave Ailes, *Tribune Review*, December 9, 1974; *Valley News Dispatch*, December 16, 1974; *Pittsburgh Post-Gazette*, December 23, 1974.

439 *The national press*: *New York Times*, December 27, 1974; Murray Chass, *New York Times*, December 31, 1974; Blount, *About Three Bricks Shy*, 286; David Fink, *Pittsburgh Post-Gazette*, December 12, 1974.

439 *The man who*: *New York Times*, December 30, 1974; Blount, *About Three Bricks Shy*, 286.

440 *Art hardly*: William Wallace, *New York Times*, December 30, 1974: Dave Anderson, *New York Times*, February 16, 1982; Blount, *About Three Bricks Shy*, 286.

440 *Wearing*: Dave Anderson, *New York Times*, December 30, 1974; Pete

Axthelm, *Newsweek*, January 13, 1975; Vito Stellino, *Pittsburgh Post-Gazette*, December 30, 1974.

441 *In Pittsburgh*: *Valley News Dispatch*, December 30, 1974; no byline, *Daily News*, December 30, 1974; Regis Stefanik, *Pittsburgh Post-Gazette*, December 30, 1974; *Pittsburgh Press*, December 30 1974.

441 *Myron Cope*: Dave Ailes, *Tribune Review*, December 30, 1974.

441 *Art heeded*: Pat Livingston, *Pittsburgh Press*, December 24, 1974; Milton Richman, UPI, December 30, 1974, Pittsburgh Steelers archives.

442 *Art invited*: *Pittsburgh Press*, January 13, 1975: Dwight White interview, July 5, 2002.

442 *On New Year's*: Al Abrams, *Pittsburgh Post-Gazette*, January 1, 1973.

442 *The press*: Chuck Heaton, "Plain Talk," no paper, January 10, 1975, Pittsburgh Steelers archives; Red Smith, *New York Times*, January 11, 1975; Phil Musick, *Pittsburgh Press*, January 12, 1975.

443 *Art's celebrity*: Dave Anderson, *New York Times*, January 5, 1975.

443 *In New Orleans*: Bob Addie, *Washington Post*, January 4, 1975; "The Repository," AP, January 10, 1975, Pittsburgh Steelers archives; Charles Feeney, *Pittsburgh Post-Gazette*, November 28, 1974.

443 *Pittsburghers had swamped*: "The Repository," AP, January 10, 1975, Pittsburgh Steelers archives.

444 *The day before*: Joe Nichols, *New York Times*, January 12, 1975; Tuffy Hacker interview, June 2, 2005.

444 *Art had flown*: Vito Stellino, *Pittsburgh Post-Gazette*, January 11, 1975; Pat Livingston, *Pittsburgh Press*, January 12, 1975.

444 *On the eve*: John Macartney interview, February 1, 2001.

445 *In the locker*: William Wallace, *New York Times*, January 10, 1975.

445 *The Steelers and the Vikings*: Al Abrams, *Pittsburgh Post-Gazette*, May 17, 1975.

445 *Art headed*: Sam Bechtel, *Beaver County Times*, January 13, 1975.

446 *Art watched*: Red Smith, *New York Times*, January 13, 1975; Frank Luksa, *Times Herald*, September 1, 1988.

446 *Art sat*: John Wiebusch, *Gameday*, National Issue XV, 1972, reprint 1984; Jerry Izenberg, *Newark Star-Ledger*, January 24, 2006.

446 *When the gun*: *New York Times*, January 13, 1975; Blount, *About Three Bricks Shy*, 262; Rocky Bleier interview, November 23, 2005.

447 *As captain*: Andy Russell interview, October 24, 2005; Ralph Berlin interview, October 2, 2001; Chastain, *Steel Dynasty*, 119.

447　*Art kept*: Chastain, *Steel Dynasty*, 119; Dwight White interview, July 5, 2002.

447　*So did*: Mike Rabun, *Beaver County Times*, January 13, 1975; Milton Richman, UPI, no date, Pittsburgh Steelers archives.

447　*A few tears*: Bob Osbourne, *News Dispatch,* January 13, 1975; Mike Rabun, *Beaver County Times*, January 13, 1975.

447　*Art stayed*: Dave Anderson, *New York Times*, January 13, 1975; Frank Luksa, *Times Herald*, September 1, 1988; Roy McHugh interview, April 12, 2002.

448　*His first day*: *News Dispatch*, January 13, 1975; Joe Nichols, *New York Times*, January 26, 1975.

448　*The season over*: Dwight White interview, July 5, 2002.

448　*Franco Harris*: Dave Anderson, *New York Times*, January 14, 1975.

20. Super *Redux*

450　*In March*: Sam Bechtel, *Beaver County Times*, April 21, 1975.

451　*At the Dapper*: Vince Leonard, *Pittsburgh Post-Gazette*, February 10, 1975; Phil Musick, *Pittsburgh Press*, February 10, 1975; Rich Emert, *Beaver County Times*, February 10, 1975; Sam Bechtel, *Beaver County Times*, April 3, 1975.

451　*That week*: *Pittsburgh Post-Gazette*, February 19, 1975; *Pittsburgh Press*, February 19, 20, 1975; *Daily News*, February 19, 1975, Pittsburgh Steelers archives.

452　*Art Jr.*: Sam Bechtel, *Beaver County Times*, January 28, 1974; Phil Musick, *Pittsburgh Press*, January 26, 1975; January 27, 1985 *Pittsburgh Press*.

452　*After paying*: Tuffy Hacker interview, June 2, 2005.

452　*Ireland reminded*: Dave Anderson, *New York Times*, May 13, 1975.

453　*Art was*: Dan Rooney interview, Pittsburgh, November 21, 2001; Mort Sharnik interview, August 31, 2001.

453　*Tim and June*: John Kelly, *Irish Echo*, April 26, 1975.

454　*He wrote*: *Signature*, September 1975; John Rooney interview, November 30, 2001.

455　*After an interview*: Dan Rooney interview, November 12, 2001, Pittsburgh; John Kelly, *Irish Echo*, April 26, 1975.

455　*"The best part"*: Barney Nagler, *Daily Racing Form*, June 17, 1975; Pohla Smith interview, June 22, 2004; Al Abrams, *Pittsburgh Post-Gazette*, April 30, 1975.

456 *The dais*: Fallon, *The Player*, 309; *Irish Independent*, April 30, 1975; Jack Kelly, *Irish Echo*, April 26, May 24, 1975.

456 *"Gosh"*: Dave Anderson, *New York Times*, May 13, 1975; Al Abrams, *Pittsburgh Post-Gazette*, May 17, 1975.

456 *Art was determined*: Joe Gordon interview, April 19, 2002.

457 *Art was feted*: *Pittsburgh Post-Gazette*, May 22, 1975; Pat Livingston, *Pittsburgh Press*, June 1, 1975; Roy McHugh, *Pittsburgh Press*, June 1, 1975; *Boston Herald*, August 26, 1988.

457 *When the hoopla*: Barney Nagler, *Daily Racing Form*, June 17, 1975.

458 *The stallion's*: Bill Tanton, January 10, 1975, no paper.

458 *Christopher R*: Bill Fidati, *Bulletin Sports*, August, 19, 1973; John Wiebusch, "Winning Isn't the Only Thing," *Gameday*, National Issue XV, 1972, reprint 1984.

459 *While Art*: Steve Cady, *New York Times*, December 20, 1975. The five brothers and John Macartney were its only stockholders; Art was the chairman of the board but owned no stock.

459 *And profit*: Donnie McGee interview, June 7, 2005; John Rooney interview, November 30, 2001; Jim Steele interview, May 26, 2005.

459 *Tim, John, and Pat*: John Macartney interview, February 1, 2001.

459 *Ruanaidh*: Timothy Rooney interview, April 27, 2005; Ralph Berlin interview, October 2, 2001.

459 *Art's authority*: Michael Strauss, *New York Times*, November 21, 1975; Mort Sharnik interview, August 31, 2001.

460 *At camp*: Dave Ailes, *Tribune-Review*, July 15, 1975.

460 *It was a*: Rudy Cernkovic, *Beaver County Times*, July 3, 1975.

461 *Mayor Richard*: Jim Boston interview, November 11, 2001.

461 *Art preferred*: Sam Bechtel, *Beaver County Times*, July 30, 1975; Vito Stellino, *Pittsburgh Post-Gazette*, August 4, 1975; Pat Livingston, *Pittsburgh Press*, August 13, 1975; Dave Anderson, *New York Times*, August 28, 1988.

461 *Terry Bradshaw*: Bradshaw, *Man of Steel*, 45.

462 *In September*: Ed Jensen, *Pittsburgh Post-Gazette*, September 4, 1975.

463 *Pat Livingston*: Pat Livingston, *Pittsburgh Press*, September 4, 1975.

463 *While Art*: Dave Ailes, *Tribune-Review*, September 16, 1975.

463 *A strike*: Phil Musick, *Pittsburgh Press*, September 23, 1975.

464 *Art had few*: Vito Stellino, *Pittsburgh Post-Gazette*, October 17, 1975.

464 *Terry Bradshaw was*: Mendelson, *Pittsburgh Steelers*, 90.

464 *"After Joe"*: Art Rooney Jr. interview, November 9, 2005; Dave Ander-

son, *New York Times*, February 16, 1982; Ralph Berlin interview, October 2, 2001; Mendelson, *Pittsburgh Steelers*, 90.

465 *Ironically*: *Time*, December 8, 1975.

465 *After Fathers*: Father Richard Reardon interview, August 31, 2001.

466 *During the week*: Ralph Berlin interview, October 2, 2001.

466 *The only cloud*: Murray Chass, *New York Times*, December 27, 1975; Charley Feeney, *Pittsburgh Post-Gazette*, December 26, 1975.

467 *Baltimore proved*: Michael Katz, *New York Times*, January 3, 1976; Vince Leonard, *Pittsburgh Post-Gazette*, August 26, 1988.

467 *Wind chill*: Dave Anderson, *New York Times*, February 16, 1982.

467 *When Lynn*: Murray Chass, *New York Times*, January 4, 1976.

467 *Art could*: AP, January 1976, Pittsburgh Steelers archives; Phil Musick, *Pittsburgh Press*, January 9, 1976.

467 *The Steelers*: Dave Anderson, *New York Times*, January 15, 1976.

468 *Pittsburgh had beaten*: William Wallace, *New York Times*, January 18, 1976; Dave Anderson, *New York Times*, January 18, 1976; Dan Jenkins, *Sports Illustrated*, January 26, 1976.

468 *Art watched*: Bob Pastin, *Times Picayune*, January 15, 1975; *New York Times*, January 19, 1976; UPI, January 19, 1976, Pittsburgh Steelers archives.

468 *Fans stormed*: *Pittsburgh Press*, January 19, 20, 1976; *Pittsburgh Post-Gazette*, January 19, 20, 1976; AP, January 20, 1976, Pittsburgh Steelers archives.

469 *Sportswriters again*: Rich Koster, *Pittsburgh Press*, January 18, 1976.

469 *At the Dapper*: Rich Emert, *Beaver County Times*, January 26, 1976; Al Abrams and David Fink, *Pittsburgh Post-Gazette*, January 26, 1976.

469 *Steeler employees*: *Pittsburgh Post-Gazette*, February 3, 4, 1976.

469 *Joe Greene*: Glenn Sheeley, *Pittsburgh Press*, March 14, 1976; Phil Musick, *Pittsburgh Press*, June 4, 1976.

470 *Art, however*: *New York Times*, February 17, 1976; Lucy Acton, "Tim Rooney Directs Shamrock's Growth," *Maryland Horse*, July 1989.

470 *By then*: Snowden Carter, "Shamrock's Christopher R Is Best Ever," *The Maryland Horse*, November 1974; Marty McGee, "In the Tradition of 'The Chief,'" *Thoroughbred Times*, March 24, 1989.

470 *Art purchased*: Jim Steele interview, May 26, 2005; Marty McGee, "In the Tradition of 'The Chief,' *Thoroughbred Times*, March 24, 1989.

471 *At the track*: Jim Steele interview, May 26, 2005.

471 *Few people*: Jim Steele interview, May 26, 2005.

472 *Art didn't*: Steve Cady, *New York Times*, September 5, 1975.

473 *In Pittsburgh*: Ed Kiely interview, January 4, 2002; Dan Rooney interview, November 21, 2001.

473 *Art often*: Deborah Weisburg, "An Irishman Named Rooney," *Pittsburgher*, October 1977, 48.

473 *After the Super*: Ed Kiely interview, January 4, 2002.

473 *"This business"*: Dan Rooney interview, May 10, 2006.

21. City of Champions

475 *The Steelers had*: Sam Bechtel, *Beaver County Times*, October 11, 1976; Glenn Sheeley, *Pittsburgh Press*, no date, October 1976, Pittsburgh Steelers archives.

475 *Relieved*: Russ Brown, *Pittsburgh Post-Gazette*, October 12, 1976; Glen Sheeley, *Pittsburgh Press*, July 12, October 27, 1976.

476 *Nobody*: Sam Bechtel, *Beaver County Times*, September 14, 1976.

476 *The loss*: Norm Vargo, *Daily News*, September 29, 1976.

476 *In the next*: Vito Stellino, *Pittsburgh Post-Gazette*, October 20, 1976; Sam Bechtel, *Beaver County Times*, October 23, 1976; Glenn Sheeley, *Pittsburgh Press*, October 27, 1976.

477 *On his nightly*: Norm Vargo, *Daily News*, November 11, 1976.

477 *Although George*: Sam Bechtel, *Beaver County Times*, December 8, 1976.

477 *Art prowled*: Al Abrams, *Pittsburgh Post-Gazette*, November 15, 1976; Norm Vargo, *Daily News*, December 7, 1976; Glenn Sheeley, *Pittsburgh Press*, December 9, 1976; Byron Smialek, *Observer-Reporter*, November 15, 1980.

478 *Pittsburgh advanced*: Glenn Sheeley, *Pittsburgh Press*, December 27, 1976; *Pittsburgh Post-Gazette*, December 27, 1976.

479 *The old days*: Glenn Sheeley, *Pittsburgh Press*, January 18, 1977.

479 *In February*: Norm Vargo, *Daily News*, February 24, 1977.

479 *Rozelle's confidence*: UPI, March 6, 1977, Pittsburgh Steelers archives.

479 *Dan was playing*: Vito Stellino, *Pittsburgh Post-Gazette*, March 31, 1977.

480 *Though many*: Jim O'Brien, *Pittsburgh Press*, March 12, 1980.

480 *In March*: Pat Livingston, *Pittsburgh Press*, March 8, 1977.

480 *Though football*: Glenn Sheeley, *Pittsburgh Press*, April 21, 1977; Vito Stellino, *Pittsburgh Post-Gazette*, January 2, 1978.

481 *Art was the biggest*: Norm Vargo, *Daily News*, July 23, 1977.

481   *Dan, meanwhile*: Ed Kiely interview, January 4, 2002.

482   *"Fats Holmes"*: Norm Vargo, *Daily News*, August 1, 1977; Timothy V. Rooney interview, June 20, 2002.

482   *As the regular*: Norm Vargo, *Daily News*, September 9, 1977.

482   *But as Blount*: Glenn Shelley, *Pittsburgh Press*, September 17, 1977; Vito Stellino, *Pittsburgh Post-Gazette*, September 17, 1977.

482   *At least Bradshaw*: Vito Stellino, *Pittsburgh Post-Gazette*, May 24, 1977; Phil Musick, *Pittsburgh Press*, September 19, 1977; David Fink, *Pittsburgh Post-Gazette*, July 20, 1977.

483   *Pittsburgh won*: Rich Emert, *Beaver County Times*, November 7, 1977.

483   *Pittsburgh's record*: AP, November 8, 1977, Pittsburgh Steelers archives; *The Derrick,* November 8, 1977; Norm Vargo, *Daily News*, November 8, 1977.

483   *The game was*: Vito Stellino, *Pittsburgh Post-Gazette*, May 4, 1978.

484   *During the off-season*: Gary Long, *Miami Herald*, April 7, 1978; Thomas Rogers, *New York Times*, May 14, 1978.

484   *Of the forty-seven*: Rich Emert, *Beaver County Times*, July 27, 1978; Vince Leonard, *Pittsburgh Post-Gazette*, August 31, 1978.

484   *Art, seventy-six*: Ralph Berlin interview, October 2, 2001.

484   *So were*: Glenn Sheeley, *Pittsburgh Press*, September 25, 1978; Rich Emert, *Beaver County Times*, November 2, 1978.

485   *Pittsburgh beat*: Norm Vargo, *Daily News*, December 30, 1978.

485   *Bradshaw had played*: Dave Condon, no date or paper, January 1979, Pittsburgh Steelers archives.

486   *Art also talked*: AP, January 6, 1979; Mike O'Hara, *Detroit News*, January 14, 1979; Steve Marantz, *Boston Globe*, January 14, 1979.

486   *Bradshaw threw*: William Wallace, *New York Times*, January 22, 1979.

487   *Comparisons*: Vito Stellino, *Pittsburgh Post-Gazette*, Super Bowl week 1979, Pittsburgh Steelers archives.

487   *Pittsburgh had signed*: Dave Ailes, *Tribune-Review*, no date, Pittsburgh Steelers archives.

487   *Giving out*: Vito Stellino, *Pittsburgh Post-Gazette*, February 9, 1979.

488   *Ill at ease*: Ed Kiely interview, April 27, 2001; Mort Sharnik interview, August 31, 2001.

489   *Cast as*: Donald G McNeil Jr., *New York Times*, May 21, 1978; Will Grimsley, AP, no date, Pittsburgh Steelers archives; Jim O'Brien, *Pitts-*

burgh Press, July 8, 1979; Alan Richman, *New York Times*, August 26, 1979.

490 *In the world*: Jim O'Brien, *Pittsburgh Press*, October 8, 1982; Andrew King, Presidential Address of the Kenneth Burke Society, Duquesne University, Pittsburgh, Pennsylvania, May 11, 1996.

490 *By the time*: Bob Gretz, *Tribune-Democrat*, October 16, 1979.

490 *Pittsburgh rebounded*: Bob Gretz, *Tribune-Democrat*, November 4, 1979.

491 *Pittsburgh basked*: Frank Deford, *Sports Illustrated*, December 10, 1979.

491 *Despite injuries*: Ron Fimrite, *Sports Illustrated*, December 24, 1979.

491 *Red Smith*: Red Smith, *New York Times*, January 2, 1980.

492 *The Steelers looked*: Gerald Eskenazi, *New York Times*, January 14, 20, 1980.

492 *As the Super*: Bob Gretz, *Tribune-Democrat*, January 26, 1980; Jim O'Brien, *Pittsburgh Press*, January 13, 1980.

493 *Art, still fretting*: AP, January 21, 1980, Pittsburgh Steelers archives.

493 *Although Pittsburgh*: AP, January 21, 1980, Pittsburgh Steelers archives; Norm Vargo, *Daily News*, January 29, 1980; Paul Zimmerman, *Sports Illustrated*, January 28, 1980.

494 *Art wasn't*: Dave Anderson, *New York Times*, January 22, 1980.

494 *Three Rivers*: John Clayton, *Pittsburgh Press*, April 20, 1980; Roy McHugh, *Pittsburgh Press*, April 23, 1980; Rocky Bleier interview, November 23, 2005.

22. The Fourth Quarter

495 *Art was at Mercy*: Dan Rooney interview, June 28, 2006: Jim O'Brien, *Pittsburgh Press*, November 19, 1982.

495 *Dan looked*: Jim O'Brien, *Pittsburgh Press*, December 3, 1980; *Standard Observer*, January 20, 1981.

496 *The real trouble*: Carrie Seidman, *New York Times*, August 10, 1980; Rich Emert, *Beaver County Times*, October 27, 1980; Dwight White interview, July 5, 2002; Arthur Rooney Jr. interview, November 9, 2005.

496 *"I read"*: Byron Smialek, *Observer-Reporter*, November 15, 1980.

497 *A funeral*: Dave Anderson, *New York Times*, January 18, 1981; *Pittsburgh Press*, January 10, 1981; Art's sister Kathleen had died in childhood, Tommy during the World War II, and John in 1950.

497 *Art tried to find*: Ralph Berlin interview, October 2, 2001.

497 *By spring*: *Pittsburgh Press*, April 30, 1981.

497   *In May*: *Pittsburgh Post-Gazette*, May 1, 1981; *Washington Star*, May 16, 1981.

498   *Invigorated*: Timothy Rooney interview, July 29, 2003.

499   *In County Kildare*: Jim O'Brien, *Pittsburgh Press*, March 18, 1981; bbc sport.com, June 2, 2001.

499   *By the time*: Dave Ailes, *Tribune-Review*, July 24, 1981; Jim O'Brien, *Pittsburgh Press*, August 26, 1981.

499   *Two years*: Pete Axthelm, *Inside Sports*, December 1981.

500   *I hope*: Pete Axthelm, *Inside Sports*, December 1981.

500   *Art visited*: Vito Stellino, *Pittsburgh Post-Gazette*, December 25, 1981.

500   *At the Super*: Joe Falls, *Detroit News*, January 23, 1982.

500   *In February*: Mike Haky, *Daily News*, February 11, 1982; Dave Ailes, *Tribune-Review*, February 11, 1982; Bill Pinella, *Palm Beach Evening Times*, March 18, 1982; Dave Anderson, *New York Times*, February 16, 1982; Art Rooney Jr. interview, November 9, 2005.

501   *In March*: Jim O'Brien, *Pittsburgh Press*, March 23, 1982.

501   *Like his father*: *Pittsburgh Steelers Weekly*, April 1981; *Pittsburgh Post-Gazette*, July 10, 17, 1981.

501   *Despite*: John Clayton, *Pittsburgh Press*, May 30, 1982; Phil Musick, *Pittsburgh Press*, June 28, 1982.

502   *Art knew*: Bill Pinella, *Palm Beach Evening Times*, March 18, 1982.

502   *That summer*: Lee Chotiner, *Pittsburgh Press*, August 10, 1982.

502   *As the gathering*: Jim O'Brien, *Pittsburgh Press*, August 29, 1982.

502   *While Dan*: John Clayton, *Pittsburgh Press*, September 22, 1982; Ron Cook, *Beaver County Times*, September 22, 1982.

503   *Art sympathized*: Ron Cook, *Beaver County Times*, September 22, 1982.

503   *The strike*: Norm Vargo, *Daily News*, September 23, 1982.

503   *Each week*: Norm Vargo, *Daily News*, September 23, 1982.

503   *"Ralph"*: Ralph Berlin interview, October 2, 2001.

503   *He confessed*: Jim O'Brien, *Pittsburgh Press*, October 10, 1982; Tom Rose, *Observer-Reporter*, October 8, 1982.

503   *With football*: Phil Axelrod, *Post-Gazette*, September 30, 1982.

504   *Admission*: Norm Vargo, *Daily News*, October 8, 1982.

504   *Art spent*: Jim O'Brien, *Pittsburgh Press*, October 10, 1982; Tom Rose, *Observer-Reporter*, October 8, 1982.

504   *At the banquet*: Vic Ketchman, *Standard-Observer*, October 11, 1982; Rick Starr, *Valley News Dispatch*, October 11, 1982.

504   *Finally Art*: Ron Cook, *Beaver County Times*, October 10, 1982; Rick Starr, *Valley News Dispatch*, October 11, 1982.

505   *The twenty-five hundred*: Norm Vargo, *Daily News*, October 11, 1982.

505   *"I remember"*: Bob Labriola, *Pittsburgh Post-Gazette*, August 24, 1986; Dan Donovan, *Pittsburgh Press*, November 1, 1982; Bob Labriola, *Pittsburgh Post-Gazette*, November 17, 1982.

506   *Within a few*: *Pittsburgh Post-Gazette*, August 27, 1988.

506   *Dan Rooney took*: Jim O'Brien, *Pittsburgh Press*, November 19, 1982.

506   *Art's joy*: Dan Rooney interview, June 28, 2006; Ron Cook, *Beaver County Times*, November 29, 1982.

506   *Art was stunned*: Dan Rooney interview, June 28, 2006.

507   *But he did*: Alvin Rosensweet, *Pittsburgh Post-Gazette*, December 2, 1982; John Rooney interview, November 28, 1982.

507   *Kass and Art*: John Rooney interview, November 30, 2001.

507   *There would be*: Margaret Laughlin interview, May 22, 2002.

508   *Art gravitated*: Dirt DiNardo interview, February 19, 2006; Ron Cook, *Pittsburgh Press*, August 26, 1988.

508   *The ground crew*: Dirt DiNardo interview, February 19, 2006; David Fink, *Pittsburgh Post-Gazette*, August 26, 1988.

508   *Art also befriended*: Chet Wade, *Pittsburgh Post-Gazette*, August 27, 1988.

509   *The 1982 strike-shortened*: John Clayton, *Pittsburgh Press*, January 17, 1983; Norm Vargo, *Daily News*, February 18, 1983.

509   *"It's class"*: Jim O'Brien, *Pittsburgh Press*, March 23, 27, 1983.

510   *"Rooney made"*: Jim O'Brien, *Pittsburgh Press*, March 23, 27, 1983.

510   *Pittsburgh picked*: Dave Anderson, *New York Times*, January 6, 1985.

511   *Señor Sack*: Norm Vargo, *Daily News*, April 27, 1983; Sam Blair, *Dallas Morning News*, November 23, 1983; Ron Cook, *Pittsburgh Press*, August 26, 1988.

511   *"It's a big loss"*: Pat Livingston, *Pittsburgh Press*, November 2, 1983; Gary Tuma, *Pittsburgh Post-Gazette*, November 2, 1983.

512   *Art spent*: *Pittsburgh Post-Gazette*, August 27, 1988.

513   *When Pirate manager*: Bob Smizik, *Pittsburgh Press*, May 3, 1984.

513   *At Churchill*: Evan Pattak, *Pittsburgh*, September 1984.

513   *Although comfortable*: John Macartney interview, February 1, 2001; *Pittsburgh Press*, January 27, 1985.

514   *Art gave up*: *Pittsburgh Post-Gazette*, May 30, 1983.

514 *Neither Franco*: Vic Ketchman, *Standard Observer*, November 29, 1983; Ron Cook, *Pittsburgh Press*, January 20, 1985.

514 *"I'm worried"*: *Pittsburgh Post-Gazette*, May 28, 1985; Lindsey Gruson, *New York Times*, September 16, 1985.

515 *"I know I"*: Evan Pattak, *Pittsburgh*, September 1984.

515 *Subsequent drafts*: Dwight White interview, July 5, 2002.

515 *Art Jr., fifty-one*: Gary Tuma, *Pittsburgh Post-Gazette*, January 7, 1987.

516 *But he was devastated*: Ed Bouchette, *Pittsburgh Post-Gazette*, January 9, 1987; Ron Cook, *Pittsburgh Press*, January 7, 1987.

516 *His father was staggered*: *Pittsburgh Press*, August 25, 1988.

516 *Art retreated*: John Rooney interview, November 30, 2001.

516 *His wisdom*: Jim Boston interview, November 11, 2001; William Coyne interview, July 12, 2006. Congressman Bill Coyne was reelected easily every term until he retired in 2002.

517 *Time is starting*: The letter is included in Rooney, *Ruanaidh*, appendix.

517 *His humility*: Ralph Berlin interview, October 2, 2001.

517 *The admiration*: Will McDonough, *Boston Globe*, August 28, 1988.

517 *Blessed with*: *Steeler News*, no date, Pittsburgh Steelers archives; Bob Kravitz, *Pittsburgh Press*, January 27, 1985; Ralph Berlin interview, October 2, 2001.

518 *In March*: Dan Rooney interview, May 10, 2006; Dave Anderson, *New York Times*, August 26, 1988.

518 *Art was not too concerned*: Dan Rooney interview, October 4, 2005.

519 *Art had had a stroke*: *Pittsburgh Press*, August 25, 1988; *Pittsburgh Post-Gazette*, August 27, 1988; Jack O'Malley interview, May 16, 2002; Gary Miles, *Philadelphia Inquirer*, August 26, 1988.

519 *Tributes poured*: Gerald Eskenazi, *New York Times*, August 26, 1988; Ed Bouchette, *Pittsburgh Post-Gazette*, August 26, 1988; Ron Cook, *Pittsburgh Press*, August 28, 1988; *News-Chronicle*, no date; UPI, August 28, 1988, Pittsburgh Steelers archives.

520 *"I go to see"*: Rich Koster, *Pittsburgh Press*, January 18, 1976; Vito Stellino, *Baltimore Sun*, August 28, 1988.

520 *On Friday*: *Pittsburgh Post-Gazette*, August 29, 1988.

521 *As Art's grandchildren*: Dan Rooney interview, November 21, 2001.

521 *When the Steelers*: *Akron Beacon Journal*, September 3, 1988.

521 *The Post-Gazette*: *Pittsburgh Post-Gazette's* editorial on August 26, 1988.

Bibliography

Manuscripts, Archives, and Other Unpublished Sources

Allegheny County, Pennsylvania, Recorder of Deeds

All Saints Roman Catholic Church, Ebbw Vale, Wales. Baptismal records.

Archives and Record Center, Diocese of Pittsburgh. Baptismal records for St. John the Evangelist Church on the Southside.

Barrett, James R., and David R. Roediger. "Irish Everywhere: The Irish and the 'Americanization' of the 'New Immigrants' in the United States, 1900–1930." Paper presented at Rewriting Irish Histories, the Neale/Commonwealth Fund Conference at University College London, April 6, 2002; Newberry Library Labor History Seminar, May 3, 2002.

Beaver County, Pennsylvania, Recorder of Deeds. Historic property maps.

Indiana University of Pennsylvania Archives. Gradebooks of Normal School Students in Preparatory Subjects, 1919–1920.

King, Andrew. Presidential Address of the Kenneth Burke Society. Presented at Duquesne University, Pittsburgh, Pennsylvania, May 11, 1996.

Lauinger Library Special Collections, Georgetown University Archives. *Ye Domesday Booke* (Georgetown University Yearbook), 1921.

McHugh, Roy. "When Pittsburgh Was a Fight Town." Unpublished manuscript.

Montreal Central Library Archives. *Mackay's Montreal Directory*, 1856/57–1867/68.

———. The Montreal Directory 1842/43–1855/56.

———. Historical maps of Montreal, St. Ann's Ward.

Pittsburgh Steelers Archives. *The Instano* vol. 9 (1920) and vol. 10 (1921). The Pennsylvania State Normal School, Indiana, Pennsylvania.

———. Minute Book of the Philadelphia Eagles.

———. Minutes of the Pittsburgh Pirates Football Club.

———. Pittsburgh Pirates Football Club Articles of Incorporation.

———. Saints and Sinners Banquet recorded remarks, January 19, 1964, Pittsburgh PA.

Pro Football Hall of Fame Archives. "NFLPA History, the Early Years: 1956–1967," NFLPA Public Relations Department, typescript.

———. "National Football League Players Association: History."

———. Minutes of NFL Owners Meetings, January 24, 1947; January 21, 22, 1951; January 29, 1954; January 2, January 31–February 3, 1957; March 11, 12, 29, 1957; December 2, 1957; and January 29, May 18, 1958.

Registrar's Office, Duquesne University. Transcript for Arthur J. Rooney, January 7, 1920.

Rooney, Arthur Jr. Unpublished journals.

Rooney, Jamie. Maggie Murray Rooney's personal scrapbooks. War letters from John Rooney, Silas Rooney, and Tommy Rooney.

South Wales Public Library, Tredegar. British census records for Ebbw Vale, 1871 and 1881.

Stromquist, Shelton. "Working Class Organization and Industrial Change in Pittsburgh, 1860–1890: Some Themes." Unpublished seminar paper, History Department, University of Pittsburgh, 1973.

U.S. Census Bureau. U.S. Census manuscript for years 1880, 1900, 1910, and 1920.

U.S. Department of Justice. Federal Bureau of Investigation Freedom of Information Act Release, Subject file: Arthur J. Rooney.

University of Pittsburgh. "Historic Pittsburgh Maps," http://digital.library.pitt.edu/maps/hopkins.html.

Published Works

Anderson, Dave, ed. *The Red Smith Reader*. New York: Random House, 1982.

Barrett, James R. "Why Paddy Drank: The Social Importance of Whiskey in Pre–Famine Ireland." *The Journal of Popular Culture* 11:1 (1978): 155–66.

Benswanger, William. "Professional Baseball in Pittsburgh." *Western Pennsylvania Historical Magazine* 30 (March–June 1947): 9–14.

Betts, Toney. *Across the Board*. New York: Citadel, 1956.

Biederman, Lester. "Art Rooney: The New Pittsburgh Phil." *Turf and Sport Digest*, October 1937.

Bishop, M. Shannon. "And They're Off: The Legality of Interstate Pari–Mutuel Wagering and Its Impact on the Thoroughbred Horse Industry." *Kentucky Law Journal* 89 (Spring 2000–2001): 711–41.

Bleier, Rocky, with Terry O'Neil. *Fighting Back*. New York: Stein and Day, 1975.

Boegner, Peggie Phipps, and Richard Gachot. *Halcyon Days: An American Family through Three Generations*. New York: Old Westury Garden and Harry N. Abrams, 1986.

Bonk, Daniel. "Ballpark Figures: The Story of Forbes Field," *Pittsburgh History* 76.2 (Summer 1993): 52–71.

Blount, Roy, Jr. *About Three Bricks Shy . . . And the Load Filled Up*. Pittsburgh: University of Pittsburgh Press, 2004.

Bradshaw, Terry, with David Diles. *Man of Steel*. Grand Rapids MI: Zondervan, 1979.

———, with David Fisher. *It's Only a Game*. New York: Pocket Books, 2001.

———, with Buddy Martin. *Looking Deep*. Chicago: Contemporary Books, 1989.

Brophy, John. *A Miner's Life*. Madison: University of Wisconsin Press, 1964.

Brynn, Soeren Stewart. "Some Sports in Pittsburgh during the National Period, 1775–1860, Part 2." *Western Pennsylvania Historical Magazine* 52 (January 1969): 57–79.

Canavan, Tony. *Frontier Town: An Illustrated History of Newry*. Belfast, Northern Ireland: Blackstaff, 1989.

Carter, Snowden. "Art Rooney's Shamrock Farm in Carroll County." *The Maryland Horse*, March 1966.

Caswell, Barrie, John Gaydon, and Mel Warrender. *Ebbw Vale 'The Works' 1790–2002*. Broomyard, Herefordshire: Record Printers, 2002.

Chafe, William. *The Unfinished Journey*. New York: Oxford University Press, 2003.

Chastain, Bill. *Steel Dynasty: The Team that Changed the NFL*. Chicago: Triumph, 2005.

Ciotola, Nicholas P. "Spignesi, Sinatra, and the Pittsburgh Steelers: Franco's Italian Army as an Expression of Ethnic Identity, 1972–1977." *Journal of Sport History* 27.2 (Summer 2000): 271–98.

Clary, Jack. *PB: The Paul Brown Story*. New York: Atheneum, 1979.

Commission on Social Services of the Pittsburgh Council of Churches. *Crime and Its Treatment in Pittsburgh and Allegheny County*. Pittsburgh, 1924.

Cooper, John Irwin. *Montreal: A Brief History*. Montreal: McGill–Queen's University Press, 1969.

Cope, Myron. *The Game that Was: The Early Days of Pro Football*. New York: World Publishing, 1970.

Coultersville Book Committee, *Golden Memories of Coultersville, Alpsville and Osceola*. North Versailles PA: Larry O'Toole, 1997.

Couvares, Francis G. *The Remaking of Pittsburgh: Class and Culture in an Industrializing City 1877–1919*. Albany: The State University of New York Press, 1984.

Danyluk, Tom. *The Super '70s: Memories from Pro Football's Greatest Era*. Chicago: Mad Uke, 2005.

Davis, James J. *The Iron Puddler: My Life in the Rolling Mills and What Came of It*. Indianapolis: Bobbs Merrill, 1922.

Davis, Jeff. *Papa Bear: The Life and Legacy of George Halas*. New York: McGraw Hill, 2005.

Demaris, Ovid. *The Director: An Oral Biography of J. Edgar Hoover*. New York: Harper's Magazine Press, 1975.

Devereux, Edward C., Jr. *Gambling and The Social Structure: A Sociological Study of Lotteries and Horse Racing in Contemporary America*. New York: Arno, 1980.

Didinger, Ray. *Great Teams Great Years: Pittsburgh Steelers*. New York: Macmillan, 1974.

Diffenbacher, J. F. *Directory of Pittsburgh and Allegheny Cities*, 1884.

Fair, James R. *Give Him to the Angels*. New York: Smith and Durrell, 1946.

Farrell, John A. *Tip O'Neill and the Democratic Century*. Boston: Little, Brown, 2001.

Filippelli, Ronald L. *Labor in the USA: A History*. New York: Alfred A. Knopf, 1984.

Fitch, John. *Steel Workers*. Pittsburgh: University of Pittsburgh Press, 1989.

Gale, W. K. V. "The Technology of Iron Manufacture in Britain in the Decade 1850–1860." In *The Sorby Centennial Symposium on the History of Metallurgy*, edited by Cyril Stanley Smith, 451–65. New York: Gordon Breach Science, 1963.

Geological Survey of Pennsylvania for 1886. *Annual Report*. Part I. Harrisburg: Pennsylvania Board of Commissioners, 1887.

Gray–Jones, Arthur. *A History of Ebbw Vale*. Risca, Monmouthshire: Starling Press, 1970.

Gray–Jones, Arthur. "Quaker Ironmasters in Monmouthshire 1796–1842." In *Monmouthshire Medly 3*, edited by Reginald Nichols, 53–95. Newport, Gwent: Starling Press, 1978.

Hack, Richard. *Puppetmaster: The Secret Life of J. Edgar Hoover*. Beverly Hills: New Millenium, 2004.

Howland, Joan S. "Let's Not 'Spit the Bit' In Defense of 'The Law of the Horse:' The Historical and Legal Development of American Thoroughbred Racing." *Marquette Sports Law Review* 14.2 (Spring 2004): 473–507.

Halas, George, with Gwen Morgan and Arthur Veysey. *Halas by Halas: The Autobiography of George Halas.* New York: McGraw–Hill, 1979.

Hayllar, Benjamin Jr. "The Accommodation: The History and Rhetoric of the Rackets–Political Alliance in Pittsburgh." PhD diss., University of Pittsburgh, 1977.

Hillenbrand, Laura. *Seabiscuit: An American Legend.* New York: Random House, 2003.

Holway, John. *Josh and Satch.* Westport CT: Meckler, 1969.

Hutchinson, Dennis J. *The Man Who Once Was Whizzer White: A Portrait of Justice Byron R. White.* New York: Free Press.

Jackson, Anne. *Early Stages.* Boston and Toronto: Little, Brown, 1979.

Kenny, Kevin. *The American Irish: A History.* Harlow, England: Pearson Education, 2000.

King, Rufus. Gambling and Organized Crime. Washington DC: Public Affairs Press, 1969.

Klein, Philip S., and Ari Hoogenboom. *A History of Pennsylvania.* University Park: Pennsylvania State University Press, 1980.

Kleinberg, S. J. *The Shadow of the Mills: Working–Class Families in Pittsburgh, 1870–1907.* Pittsburgh: University of Pittsburgh Press, 1989.

Kramer, Charles, ed. *Middle Atlantic League 25th Anniversary, 1925–1949.* 1949.

Kudlik, John. "You Couldn't Keep an Iron Man Down: Rowing in Nineteenth Century Pittsburgh," *Pittsburgh History* 73.2 (Summer 1990): 51–63.

Kowett, Don. *The Rich Who Own Sports.* New York: Random House: 1977.

Lardner, John. *It Beats Working.* Philadelphia and New York: B. Lippincott, 1947.

Layne, Bobby, with Bob Drum. *Always on Sunday.* Englewood Cliffs NJ: Prentice–Hall, 1962.

Lieb, Frederick. *The Pittsburgh Pirates.* New York: Van Rees, 1948.

Livingston, Bernard. *Their Turf: America's Horsey Set & Its Princely Dynasties.* New York: Arbor House, 1973.

Lomax, Michael E. "Conflict and Compromise: The Evolution of American Professional Football's Labour Relations," *Football Studies* 4.1 (2001): 5–39.

Marx, Karl. *The Eighteenth Brumaire of Louis Napoleon*. Chicago: C. H. Kerr, 1913.

McCambridge, Michael. *America's Game: The Epic Story of How Pro Football Captured a Nation*. New York: Random House, 2004.

Mendelson, Abby. *The Pittsburgh Steelers: The Official Team History*. Dallas: Taylor, 1996.

Merson, Sherie R. "Corporate Responsibility and Urban Revitalization: The Allegheny Conference on Community Development, 1943–1968." PhD diss., Carnegie Mellon University, 2000.

Mitchell, Joseph. "The Markee," *The New Yorker*, November 4, 1939.

Mosbrook, Joe. "Jazzed in Cleveland." WMV Web News Cleveland, January 13, 2005.

Musick, Phil. "A Football Man." In *A Game of Passion: The NFL Literary Companion*, edited by John Wiebusch and Brian Silverman, 316–24. Atlanta: Turner, 1994.

O'Brien, Jim. *The Chief: Art Rooney and the Pittsburgh Steelers*. Pittsburgh: Geyer, 2001.

"Parish of Newry, County Down, Memoir of J.R. Ward, October 1836." In *Ordinance Survey, Memoirs of Ireland Parishes of County Down I, 1834–6, South Down*, edited by Angelique Day and Patrick McWilliams. Belfast: The Institute of Irish Studies at the Queen's University of Belfast, 1990.

Pennsylvania House of Representatives. *Journal of the House of Representatives*. Harrisburg: Commonwealth of Pennsylvania, January 3, 1933.

Patton, Phil. *Razzle Dazzle: The Curious Marriage of Television and Football*. Garden City: Dial, 1984.

Pegram, Thomas R. *Battling Demon Rum: The Struggle for Dry America, 1800–1933*. Chicago: Ivan R. Dee, 1998.

Percy, John. *Metallurgy: The Art of Extracting Metals from Their Ores and Adapting Them to Various Purposes of Manufacture*. London: John Murray, 1864.

Peterson, Robert. *Pigskin: The Early Years of Pro Football*. New York: Oxford University Press, 1997.

Polk, R. L. *Pittsburgh City Directory*. Pittsburgh PA, 1885.

Rader, Benjamin G. *In Its Own Image: How Television Has Transformed Sports*. New York: Free Press, 1984.

Riess, Steven A. *Touching Base: Professional Baseball and American Culture in the Progressive Era*. Urbana and Chicago: University of Illinois Press, 1990.

Rishel, Joseph F. *"The Spirit that Gives Life," The History of Duquesne University, 1878–1996*. Pittsburgh: Duquesne University Press, 1997.

Roberts, Leslie. *Montreal: From Mission Colony to World City*. Toronto: Macmillan of Canada, 1969.

Roberts, Randy, and David Welty. *The Steelers Reader*. Pittsburgh: University of Pittsburgh Press, 2001.

Rooney, Art Jr., with Roy McHugh. *Ruanaidh: The Story of Art Rooney and His Clan*. Pittsburgh: Geyer Printing, 2008.

Rooney, Dan, David F. Halas, and Andrew E. Masich. *Dan Rooney: My 75 Years with the Pittsburgh Steelers and the NFL*. New York: Da Capo, 2007.

Ruck, Rob. "Art Rooney and the Pittsburgh Steelers." In *Pittsburgh Sports: Stories from the Steel City*, edited by Randy Roberts. Pittsburgh: University of Pittsburgh Press, 2000.

———. "Remembering Roberto," *Pittsburgh*, December 1992.

———. "Sandlot Seasons: Sport in Black Pittsburgh." PhD diss., University of Pittsburgh, 1983.

———. *Sandlot Seasons: Sport in Black Pittsburgh*. Champaign: University of Illinois Press, 1987.

Russell, Andy. *A Steeler Odyssey*. Champaign: Sports Publishing, 1998.

Sahadi, Lou. *Super Steelers*. New York: Times Books, 1980.

Smith, Thomas G. "Outside the Pale: The Exclusion of Blacks from the National Football League, 1934–1946." *Journal of Sport History* 15. 3 (Winter, 1988): 255–81.

Sperber, Murray. *Shake Down the Thunder: The Creation of Notre Dame Football*. New York: Henry Holt, 1993.

Stellino, Vito. "Football's Supergrand–daddy." *Modern Maturity*, October–November 1979.

Thorn, John, Peter Palmer, Michael Gershman, and David Pietrusza. *Total Baseball*. 6th ed. New York: Warner, 1999.

Toperoff, Sam. *Lost Sundays*. New York: Random House, 1989.

Tucker, Joe. *Steelers' Victory After Forty*. New York: Exposition Press, 1973.

Walsh, Victor Anthony. "Across 'The Big Wather': Irish Community Life in Pittsburgh and Allegheny City, 1850–1885." PhD diss., University of Pittsburgh, 1983.

U.S. House of Representatives, Antitrust Subcommittee of the Committee on the Judiciary. "Organized Professional Team Sports." Washington: USGPO, 1957.

Bibliography

U.S. Senate, Special Committee to Investigate Organized Crime in Interstate Commerce. Report #725, 82nd Congress. August 31, 1951.
U.S. Senate, Subcomittee on Communications. "Blackout of Sporting Events on TV." Washington, October 4, 1972.
Weber, Michael P. *Don't Call Me Boss: David L. Lawrence, Pittsburgh's Renaissance Mayor*. Pittsburgh: University of Pittsburgh Press, 1988.
Value of a Dollar, 1860–1999, The. Lakeville CT: Grey House, 1999.
Weisberg, Deborah. "An Irishman Named Rooney." *Pittsburgher*, October 1977.
Wiebusch, John. "Winning Isn't the Only Thing." *Gameday*, National Issue 15.6, 1972, reprint, 1984.

604

Index

412–14; after Super Bowl IX, 447, 448;
draft of, 380–81, 389, 421, 485–86, 515;
fan reactions to, 397, 398, 416, 461–62,
475; Frank Sinatra's inquiry about, 405;
and horses, 472, 511; on Louisiana ranch,
451; relationships with teammates, 395;
relationship with Art Rooney, 383–85, 392,
397, 420, 441, 447, 466, 480, 485, 491, 499;
retirement of, 497, 514; salary (1977), 480;
season (1970), 385, 386; season (1971), 391;
season (1972), 402–3, 406, 417, 418; season
(1973), 423–25, 428–29; season (1974),
436–40; season (1975), 460, 464, 466;
season (1977), 482–83; in *Sports Illustrated*,
491; as Sportsman of the Year, 469, 491; in
Super Bowl X, 467, 468, 469; in Super Bowl
XIV, 493; on World Football League, 431
Bray, Maurice "Mule," 110
Bregman, Bo, 550
Brickley, Wilmer, 530
Bridgeport CT, 459
Bridgeville Speedway, 73, 86, 89–91
Briery Hill, 3
British Buddy (horse), 226, 227, 260
Bronx NY, 131
Brooklyn Dodgers (baseball team), 235, 305
Brooklyn Dodgers (football team): Jock
Sutherland hired by, 173; vs. Pittsburgh
Pirates, 102, 103, 138, 146, 147, 165, 166;
vs. Pittsburgh Steelers, 180–81, 197, 206
Brooklyn NY, 351
Brotherhood of Railroad Trainmen, 80–81
Brown, Bonnell and Company, 5
Brown, Ed, 332, 336, 338–39
Brown, Jim, 289, 333, 336, 401, 489, 490, 514
Brown, John, 414
Brown, Larry, 417
Brown, Mose, 194, 201, 202, 211
Brown, Paul, 236, 276, 302, 307, 309, 315,
369, 383
Brown, Willie, 476
Brownsville (football team), 53
Bubanic, Bob, 401, 411
Buckley, Red, 36
Buffalo Bills, 305, 316, 357, 385, 398–99, 439,
463–64, 586
Buffalo NY, 145, 166, 281, 364, 549
Bull Dog (horse), 241
Bulletin Index, 168

Bundles (Northside cop), 540
Burcky, Claire, 141, 148, 181
Burley, Charley, 157–59, 161, 162, 200, 209
Burns A. A. (football team), 53
Burns, Bill, 355
Butkus, Dick, 349
Butler, Jack: on Art Rooney's generosity,
295–96; to Belmont Stakes, 395–96; on
Buddy Parker, 318; as coach, 315–16, 330;
on draft picks (1968), 370; vs. Philadelphia
Eagles (1958), 309; on roster (1954), 284;
on roster (1957), 301; season (1959), 315; at
Shamrock Farm, 260
Butler, Johnny, 218
Butler PA, 211
Butler, Pat "Happy," 295
buttermilk, 259–60
Byrne, Ray, 286, 287

Caballero II (horse), 123
Cairo IL, 249
California State Normal, 36
California Suns, 431–32
Calvary Episcopal Church, 250
Cambria County coal mines, 156
Cambridge Springs PA, 244
Camden NJ, 268
Campbell, Father Jim, 198, 203, 241, 251,
290, 296, 411, 431
Campbell, Fritz, 268
Camp O'Connell, 202
Canada, xxii, 1, 2, 33–34, 214, 453, 499, 524
Canadian Football League, 313, 316
Canonero II (horse), 389
Canton Bulldogs, xxiv, 50, 57
Canton OH, 95, 346–47, 489
Cantor, Eddie, 155
Capital Handicap at Laurel (1946), 226–27
Cardiac Hill, 307
Carey, Hugh, 456
Carnegie, Andrew, 12, 22, 118, 531
Carnegie (suburb), 11
Carnegie Mellon University, xi
Carnegie Steel plant, 6
Carnegie Tech, 36, 73, 91, 152, 178, 179
Carnera, Primo, 85, 99–100, 156, 268
Carney, Art, 494
Carney, Luke, 177
Car-Pitts, 217–19

Cisneros, Henry, 518

Clack, Jim, 417, 446

Clark Candy Factory, 21, 86

Clark, James, 327–28, 335

Clarksburg wv, 34

Clay, Cassius (Muhammad Ali), 345

Clement, Johnny, 240

Clemente, Roberto, xxiii, 396, 418, 486, 502

Cleveland Browns: and AFC, 378; Chuck Noll with, 369; entry into NFL, 278; integration of, 236, 280; Mickey McBride as owner, 226; vs. Pittsburgh Steelers, 279, 283, 305, 307, 312, 315, 336, 367, 376, 385, 399–401, 410, 424–25, 428, 475–76, 490, 496; rivalry with Steelers, 277, 378–79, 490; season (1948–49), 276–77; season (1972), 403, 406; in standings (1963), 337; Steelers' comparison to, 494; television contract of, 321; Terry Bradshaw's injury against, 475

Cleveland OH, 68, 134, 226, 334, 367, 369, 402

Cleveland Rams, 138, 139, 147, 151–52, 194, 203–4, 276

coal industry, xxiii, 1, 15–16, 50, 326

Coca-Cola commercial, 490, 497

Cochrane, Red, 194

Cockcroft, Don, 401

cockfighting, 3, 470

cocoa market, 334

Coco, Imogene, 75

College All-Star games, 106–7, 143, 145, 203, 233, 433, 460–61

Collins, Rip, 48, 49

Colonial Hotel, 17–18, 529

Colonial Steel Works, 17

Colorado Springs CO, 150

Columbus OH, 326

Committee in Favor of Sunday Sports, 102

commodities, 334

Commodore Hotel, 240

compensation, 432–33, 479

Conacher, Lionel, 364

Concannon, Bridget Rooney, 3, 6, 12–14, 525, 527, 528, 530

Concannon, Michael, 12–14, 71, 527, 530

Conemaugh Polish Alliance, 170

Conn, Billy: in army, 200; career of, xxiv; at Charles-Wolcott bout, 268; compared to Fritzie Zivic, 210; courtship and marriage,

190–93; fight with father-in-law, 201–2; on fishing trip, 171; friendship with Art Rooney, 298; vs. Fritzie Zivic, 158, 159, 162, 209; vs. Gus Lesnevich, 169; vs. Joe Louis, 178, 189–92, 194, 200–202, 229, 345; management of, 177; vs. Melio Bettina, 157, 158, 161, 210; in movie, 554; photograph of, 382; possible comeback of, 267; promise of, 153; Rooney-McGinley promotion of, 178; stories about, 383; at Super Bowl IX, 444; vs. Teddy Yarosz, 158, 160; during World War II, 209

Conn, David, 201–2

Conn, Maggie, 192, 193

Conn, Mary Louise Smith, 190–93, 201

Conn, Timmy, 345

Connellsville PA, 526

Connolly, Margaret, 523

Considine, Bob, 124, 125, 132–33, 135, 180, 207, 239, 456

Cooke, Terence Cardinal, 423

Coon, Eugene, 448

Cope, Myron: on AFC playoff (1972), 413, 415; after AFC championship game (1974), 441; on Blood McNally, 146–47; on Ed Brown, 338; feature on Steelers, 421; on Frank Sinatra, 404–5; on freedom strike, 433, 434; Howard Cosell on, 504; on sale of Steelers, xxv; in stadium cafeteria, 409

Coral Gables FL, 241–42

Corbett, James "Gentleman Jim," 269, 554

Corum, Bill, 119, 121, 123–24, 126, 176

Corus Steel, 523, 525. *See also* Ebbw Vale Iron and Steel Works

Cosell, Howard, 385, 478, 490, 504

Cotton Club, 99

Coultersville PA, 14, 16–17, 22

Count Stone (horse), 119

County Armagh, Ireland, 1

County Cork, Ireland, 248

County Down, Ireland, 1

County Galway, Ireland, 61

County Kildare, Ireland, 499

County Mayo, Ireland, 454

County Roscommon, Ireland, 15

Coyne, James J.: closing of club, 554; effect of New Deal on, 115; fraud charge, 93; and Gus Greenlee, 69; and Jim Rooney, 80; as mentor, xxv, 60–63, 93–94, 542; nephew of, 516; political career of, 59, 167–69, 214;

Holmes, Ernie (*continued*)
423, 425; season (1975), 465; in Super Bowl
IX, 446, 447; trade of, 484
Homa, Marty, 413
Home Beverage Company, 65
"Homer in the Gloaming," 144
Homer Laughlins, 85
Homestead (football team), 28
Homestead Grays: Art Rooney's memories of,
25; Cool Papa Bell with, 469; Cum Posey's
ownership of, xii, 51; Dan Rooney against,
77; financial support of, 234–35; social role
of, 47; success of, xxiii, 29, 40, 69–70; Vic
Harris with, 393; William Nunn with, 361.
See also Posey, Cumberland "Cum"
Homestead Steel Works, 12, 20, 503
Homewood (neighborhood), 18, 22, 361
Homewood Cemetery, 250
Honus Wagner Trophy, 74
Hoover, Herbert, 55
Hoover, J. Edgar, 174, 264, 282
Hoover, J. Edgar Handicap, 470
"Hooverville," 87
Hope A. C. (football squad), 30
Hope Harvey Football Club, xxiv, 30, 44,
52–53, 56–58, 72–73, 111–13, 214. *See also*
sandlots
Hope Number 1 Engine House, 30
Hornung, Paul, 381
horse racing: in advanced age, 473–74;
after Super Bowl IX, 448; after wedding,
82–84; Art Rooney on changes in, 512–13;
Art Rooney's reputation in, xxiv, 158,
168, 262–63, 343, 471, 492, 519, 549;
connections through, 389, 398; exposure to,
59, 68; as family business, 104, 264, 334–36,
354–55, 386–87, 393, 420; Fran Fogarty's
management of, 248; during freedom strike,
435; in Ireland, 454, 455; at McGinley's
bar, 156; postwar surge in, 225–27; as
priority, 138–39; reasons for betting on,
452; routine of, 260–64; season (1932),
89–90; season (1936), 116; season (1937),
117–35; season (1938), 140–41, 154; season
(1939), 155; season (1946), 222, 241–44;
season (1955), 288; strike in Hollywood,
488; Terry Bradshaw on, 397; time spent
on, 286; during training camp, 231; during
World War II, 214. *See also* bookmaking;

Christopher R (horse); gambling; harness
racing; Kentucky Derby; pari-mutuel betting;
Shamrock Farm
Hot Springs AR 89, 234
House of David (baseball team), 25
Houston Oilers, 385, 398, 402–3, 477, 485,
491–92
Houston TX, 316
Howard, Charles and Marcela, 118
Howard, Paul, 484
Howell, Jim Lee, 309
Hoya, 42
Hubka, Gene, 249
Hughes, Carl, 217, 266, 275, 297
Hungerford, Cy, 328
Hunter, Kent, 127
Hunt, H. L., 316
Hunt, Lamar, 316
Hurricane (nightspot), 310
Huston, John, 168, 169
Hutchinson, Dennis, 550

Ideal Park, 58
Immaculate Reception, xxi–xxii, xxiii, 410–17,
486, 585
Independent Brewing Company, 65
Indiana Evening Gazette, 41
Indiana State Normal School, 34–36, 39–42,
534, 535
Indiana PA, 494
Indiantown Gap PA, 194
injury protection, 304
Inland Steel Company, 185
International Boxing Club, 268, 364
International Hockey League, 90
Interstate Wire Act (1961), 264
Iona College, 455–56
Ireland: attachment to, 26; famine in, 2, 5; Fr.
Silas's travels to, 206; land ownership in,
523; Murray family history in, 15; Rooney
family history in, xxii, 1–2; thoroughbred
horse breeding in, 513; trips to, 452–57,
498–99
Ireland Fund, 456, 487–88
Irish: in boxing, 31, 36–37; on Northside,
xxiii, 26, 31; in positions of power, 45–48,
59, 327; role in Pittsburgh Renaissance,
325–29; in Wales, 4–5
Irish Catholics: on bootlegging, 67; empathy